Colonels in Blue —
Illinois, Iowa,
Minnesota and Wisconsin

ALSO BY ROGER D. HUNT

*Colonels in Blue—Indiana, Kentucky and Tennessee:
A Civil War Biographical Dictionary* (McFarland, 2014)

*Colonels in Blue—Michigan, Ohio and West Virginia:
A Civil War Biographical Dictionary* (McFarland, 2011)

Colonels in Blue— Illinois, Iowa, Minnesota and Wisconsin

A Civil War Biographical Dictionary

Roger D. Hunt

McFarland & Company, Inc., Publishers
Jefferson, North Carolina

LIBRARY OF CONGRESS CATALOGUING-IN-PUBLICATION DATA

Names: Hunt, Roger D., author.
Title: Colonels in blue : Illinois, Iowa, Minnesota and Wisconsin :
a Civil War biographical dictionary / Roger D. Hunt.
Description: Jefferson, North Carolina : McFarland & Company, Inc.,
Publishers, 2017. | Includes bibliographical references and index.
Identifiers: LCCN 2017002637 | ISBN 9780786498550
(softcover : acid free paper) ∞
Subjects: LCSH: United States—History—Civil War, 1861–1865—
Biography—Dictionaries. | Illinois—History—Civil War, 1861–1865—
Biography—Dictionaries. | Iowa—History—Civil War, 1861–1865—
Biography—Dictionaries. | Minnesota—History—Civil War, 1861–1865—
Biography—Dictionaries. | Wisconsin—History—Civil War, 1861–1865—
Biography—Dictionaries. | United States.
Army—Officers—History—Civil War, 1861–1865—Dictionaries.
Classification: LCC E467 .H8927 2017 | DDC 973.7/170922 [B] —dc23
LC record available at https://lccn.loc.gov/2017002637

BRITISH LIBRARY CATALOGUING DATA ARE AVAILABLE

**ISBN (print) 978-0-7864-9855-0
ISBN (ebook) 978-1-4766-2635-2**

© 2017 Roger D. Hunt. All rights reserved

*No part of this book may be reproduced or transmitted in any form
or by any means, electronic or mechanical, including photocopying
or recording, or by any information storage and retrieval system,
without permission in writing from the publisher.*

On the cover *top to bottom* Edmund Baldwin Gray (Craig T. Johnson Collection);
Noel Byron Howard (author collection); Carter Van Vleck
(photographed by E.S. Carter, Beardstown, IL; author collection);
flag background and eagle insignia © Shutterstock

Printed in the United States of America

*McFarland & Company, Inc., Publishers
Box 611, Jefferson, North Carolina 28640
www.mcfarlandpub.com*

In memory
of my parents

Donald R. Hunt
(1904–1988)

and

Annabelle I. Hunt
(1910–2000)

TABLE OF CONTENTS

Acknowledgments

ix

Introduction

1

Illinois
Regiments 3
Biographies 15

Iowa
Regiments 154
Biographies 158

Minnesota
Regiments 205
Biographies 206

Wisconsin
Regiments 217
Biographies 221

Bibliography

275

Index of Names

301

ACKNOWLEDGMENTS

Although I appreciate the contributions of all of the individuals in the following list, I want to mention a few individuals whose contributions to this volume have been especially noteworthy. Randy Beck, Allen Cebula, the late Steve Saathoff, and Ray Zielin have been generous in providing access to their outstanding collections of Illinois images. Roger Davis and Mark Warren have been generous in providing images from their outstanding Iowa collections. Wayne Jorgenson has been generous in providing images from his outstanding Minnesota collection. Craig Johnson and Marc and Beth Storch have been generous in providing images from their outstanding Wisconsin collections. Richard Baumgartner, Everitt Bowles, Rick Carlile, Henry Deeks, and Steve Meadow have always been helpful in providing elusive photographs and valuable information. Roberta Fairburn and Jan Perone have been especially helpful in supporting my research activities at the Abraham Lincoln Presidential Library. Randy Hackenburg, Dr. Richard Sommers and the late Mike Winey have provided ready access to the unparalleled photo archives of the U.S. Army Military History Institute during the past 35 years. Alan Aimone has been equally hospitable in providing access to the outstanding collections at the U.S. Military Academy Library.

Jill M. Abraham, National Archives, Washington, D.C.
Alan C. Aimone, U.S. Military Academy Library, West Point, NY
Andrew Baraniak, Wisconsin Veterans Museum, Madison, WI
Gil Barrett, New Bern, NC
Richard A. Baumgartner, Huntington, WV
Randy Beck, St. Charles, MO
Mary Bennett, State Historical Society of Iowa, Iowa City, IA
Hank Bereman, Aurora, IL
Bruce P. Bonfield, Naples, FL
Everitt Bowles, Woodstock, GA
Mike Brackin, Winterville, NC
Franklin Brandt, Stewardson, IL
Rick Brown, Leesburg, VA
Paul J. Brzozowski, Fairfield, CT
Sheryl Byrd, Boring, OR
David L. Callihan, Harrisburg, PA
Nancy Campbell, Woodlawn Cemetery, Elmira, NY
Richard F. Carlile, Dayton, OH
Evelynn Cassady, Martin County Historical Society, Inez, KY
Allen Cebula, Naperville, IL
Lois Chaddick, New York City, NY
Ronald S. Coddington, Arlington, VA
Frank Crawford, Caledonia, IL
Carol A. Crisp, Pope Co., IL
Robert Wayne Dalton, Jacksonville, IL
Andy Dann, Warne, NC
Roger Davis, Keokuk, IA
Henry Deeks, Ashburnham, MA
Joyce Doris, Decatur, IL
Craig Dunn, Kokomo, IN
Rachel E. Dworkin, Chemung County Historical Society, Elmira, NY
Jerry Everts, Lambertville, MI
Roberta Fairburn, Abraham Lincoln Presidential Library, Springfield, IL
Heather Fox, The Filson Historical Society, Louisville, KY
Perry M. Frohne, Oshkosh, WI
Randy Hackenburg, Boiling Springs, PA
Kevin Hampton, Wisconsin Veterans Museum, Madison, WI
Kathryn M. Harris, Abraham Lincoln Presidential Library, Springfield, IL
Thomas Harris, New York, NY
Jessica Herczeg-Konecny, Chicago History Museum, Chicago, IL

Acknowledgments

Janna Heuer, Urbana Free Library, Urbana, IL
Michael A. Hogle, Okemos, MI
Russell Horton, Wisconsin Veterans Museum, Madison, WI
Jennifer Huebscher, Minnesota Historical Society, St. Paul, MN
Linda Simison Jackson, Madison, WI
Dale Stilwagen Jacobi, Riverhead, NY
Craig T. Johnson, New Freedom, PA
Wayne Jorgenson, Eden Prairie, MN
Alan Jutzi, The Huntington Library, San Marino, CA
Frank D. Korun, Ijamsville, MD
Andy Kraushaar, Wisconsin Historical Society, Madison, WI
Carol Krogan, Vernon County Historical Society, Viroqua, WI
Laurie Langland, Dakota Wesleyan University, Mitchell, SD
Samuel Lattuca, Marion, IL
Mary Beth Linné, National Archives, Washington, D.C.
Robert F. MacAvoy, Clark, NJ
Lisa Marine, Wisconsin Historical Society, Madison, WI
Catherine Martin, Le Mesnil-le-Roi, France
Elizabeth Martin, Bowie, MD
Vann R. Martin, Kingston, TN
Michael J. McAfee, Newburgh, NY
Maryjo McAndrew, Knox College Library, Galesburg, IL
Edward McGuire, New York State Library, Albany, NY
Sarah T. McNeive, Topeka, KS
Steven J. Meadow, Midland, MI
Mike Medhurst, North Liberty, IA
Tom Molocea, North Lima, OH
Jim Mundie, Kenner, LA
Simone O. Munson, Wisconsin Historical Society, Madison, WI
Steve Nemeth, South Bend, IN
Olaf, Berkeley, CA
Annabelle O'Neill, Daytona Beach, FL
Terry Orr, St. Louis, MO
Stephen E. Osman, Minneapolis, MN
Ronn Palm, Kittanning, PA
Jan Perone, Abraham Lincoln Presidential Library, Springfield, IL
Louise Pfotenhauer, Neville Public Museum, Green Bay, WI
Nicholas P. Picerno, Bridgewater, VA
Becki Plunkett, State Historical Society of Iowa, Des Moines, IA
Jim Quinlan, Alexandria, VA
Jeffrey I. Richman, Brooklyn, NY
Stephen B. Rogers, Ithaca, NY
Paul Russinoff, Baltimore, MD
Steve Saathoff, Franklin Grove, IL
Charles Scott, State Historical Society of Iowa, Iowa City, IA
Alan J. Sessarego, Gettysburg, PA
John Sickles, Merrillville, IN
Sam Small, Gettysburg, PA
Wes Small, Gettysburg, PA
Dr. Richard J. Sommers, Carlisle, PA
Richard J. Spades, Black Rock, AR
Marc and Beth Storch, DeForest, WI
Larry M. Strayer, Dayton, OH
Karl E. Sundstrom, North Riverside, IL
Kisha Tandy, Indiana State Museum, Indianapolis, IN
David W. Taylor, Sylvania, OH
Richard K. Tibbals, Berwyn, IL
Ken C. Turner, Ellwood City, PA
Becky Wadian, Upper Iowa University, Fayette, IA
Mark Warren, Bloomfield, IA
Michael W. Waskul, Ypsilanti, MI
Frank Watters, Photo Antiquities Museum of Photographic History, Pittsburgh, PA
Mark Weldon, Fort Wayne, IN
Stacie Williams, University of Kentucky–Special Collections Research Center, Lexington, KY
Michael J. Winey, Mechanicsburg, PA
Richard A. Wolfe, Bridgeport, WV
Jennifer Woods, Silver Spring, MD
Buck Zaidel, Cromwell, CT
Ray Zielin, Orland Park, IL
Dave Zullo, Lake Monticello, VA

I am also indebted to the staffs of the following libraries for their capable assistance:

Abraham Lincoln Presidential Library & Museum, Springfield, IL
Allen County Public Library, Fort Wayne, IN
Aurora Historical Society, Aurora, IL
Chicago History Museum, Chicago, IL
Civil War Library & Museum, Philadelphia, PA
Colorado Historical Society, Denver, CO
Connecticut State Library, Hartford, CT
Danville Public Library, Danville, IL
Family History Library, Salt Lake City, UT
Filson Historical Society, Louisville, KY
The Huntington Library, San Marino, CA
Indiana Historical Society, Indianapolis, IN
Indiana State Library, Indianapolis, IN
Indiana State Museum, Indianapolis, IN
Kansas State Historical Society, Topeka, KS
Kentucky Historical Society, Frankfort, KY
Knox College Library, Galesburg, IL
Library of Congress, Washington, D.C.
Martin County Historical Society, Inez, KY
Mattoon Public Library, Mattoon, IL
Milwaukee Public Library, Milwaukee, WI
Minnesota Historical Society, St. Paul, MN
National Archives, Washington, D.C.
National Society Daughters of the American Revolution, Washington, D.C.
Neville Public Museum of Brown County, Green Bay, WI
New England Historic Genealogical Society, Boston, MA

Acknowledgments

New Jersey State Archives, Trenton, NJ
New York Genealogical and Biographical Society, New York, NY
The New-York Historical Society, New York, NY
New York State Library, Albany, NY
The Nyack Library, Nyack, NY
Oakland Public Library, Oakland, CA
Ohio Genealogical Society, Mansfield, OH
Ohio Historical Society, Columbus, OH
Rockford Public Library, Rockford, IL
Rutherford B. Hayes Presidential Center, Fremont, OH
San Diego Public Library, San Diego, CA
Schaffer Library, Union College, Schenectady, NY
Spokane Public Library, Spokane, WA
State Historical Society of Iowa, Des Moines, IA
State Historical Society of Iowa, Iowa City, IA
State Historical Society of Missouri, Columbia, MO
Tacoma Public Library, Tacoma, WA
Tennessee State Library and Archives, Nashville, TN
University of Kentucky Special Collections and Archives, Lexington, KY
Urbana Free Library, Urbana, IL
U.S. Army Military History Institute, Carlisle, PA
U.S. Military Academy Library, West Point, NY
Vernon County Historical Society, Viroqua, WI
Western Reserve Historical Society, Cleveland, OH
Wisconsin Historical Society, Madison, WI
Wisconsin Veterans Museum, Madison, WI

Introduction

At the beginning of the Civil War the Regular Army of the United States numbered only 1,098 officers and 15,304 enlisted men. Faced with this shortage of manpower in suppressing the escalating rebellion, President Abraham Lincoln issued a call for 75,000 militia for three months service on April 15, 1861, and then a call for 500,000 volunteers for three years service on July 22, 1861. These calls for troops and others issued later in the war specified that the various state governors would appoint the commanding officers of the regiments raised in their states.

Patriotic fervor throughout the Northern states resulted in spirited competition to complete the organization of regiments to meet the state quotas. In most cases the prospective commanders of these regiments were prominent citizens whose military background (if any) consisted of service in a local militia organization. In general the early war Union army colonels were known more for their patriotic enthusiasm than for their military competence. Many of them were more successful in convincing their fellow townsmen to enlist than they were in actually leading them into battle. Fortunately for the Union cause, the colonels who stayed in the service eventually acquired the necessary military skills or were replaced by subordinates who proved their capabilities on the field of battle.

This book is the sixth in a series of books containing photographs and biographical sketches of that diverse group of motivated citizens who attained the rank of colonel in the Union army, but failed to win promotion to brigadier general or brevet brigadier general. This volume presents the colonels who commanded regiments from Illinois, Iowa, Minnesota and Wisconsin. Preceding the photographs and biographical sketches for each state is a breakdown by regiment of all the colonels who commanded regiments from that state, with the name of each colonel being followed by the dates of his service. Included in this breakdown are the colonels who were promoted beyond the rank of colonel, with their final rank indicated in bold letters. Those indicated as attaining the rank of brigadier general are covered in the book *Generals in Blue*, by Ezra J. Warner, while those attaining the rank of brevet brigadier general are covered in the book *Brevet Brigadier Generals in Blue*, by Roger D. Hunt and Jack R. Brown.

Some explanatory notes are necessary concerning the content of the biographical sketches:

1. The date associated with each rank may be the date when the colonel was commissioned or appointed or the date when he was mustered at that rank. Generally, the date of muster was used whenever available. The reader should be aware that these dates were often adjusted or corrected by the War Department during and after the war, so that any hope of providing totally consistent dates is virtually impossible.

Introduction

2. When the word "Colonel" is italicized, this indicates that the colonel was commissioned as colonel but never mustered as such.

3. Images not identified as to source are from the author's collection.

4. The following abbreviations are used in the text:

AAG	Assistant Adjutant General
ACM	Assistant Commissary of Musters
ACP	Appointment, Commission, and Personal
ADC	Aide-de-Camp
AGO	Adjutant General's Office
AIG	Assistant Inspector General
aka	also known as
AQM	Assistant Quartermaster
Brig.	Brigadier
Bvt.	Brevet
Capt.	Captain
CB	Commission Branch
Co.	County or Company
Col.	Colonel
CSA	Confederate States Army
DOW	Died of Wounds
GAR	Grand Army of the Republic
Gen.	General
GSW	Gun Shot Wound
KIA	Killed in Action
Lt.	Lieutenant
MOLLUS	Military Order of the Loyal Legion of the United States
NHDVS	National Home for Disabled Volunteer Soldiers
RQM	Regimental Quartermaster
Twp.	Township
U.S.	United States
USA	United States Army
USAMHI	United States Army Military History Institute
USCT	United States Colored Troops
USMA	United States Military Academy
USV	United States Volunteers
Vol.	Volume
VRC	Veteran Reserve Corps
VS	Volunteer Service

Illinois

Regiments

1st Cavalry
Thomas A. Marshall | July 17, 1861 | Mustered out July 14, 1862

2nd Cavalry
Silas Noble | Aug. 12, 1861 | Mustered out Feb. 16, 1863
John J. Mudd | Feb. 16, 1863 | KIA May 3, 1864
Daniel B. Bush, Jr. | May 4, 1864 | Mustered out July 24, 1865
Benjamin F. Marsh, Jr. | Aug. 29, 1865 | Mustered out Nov. 22, 1865

3rd Cavalry
Eugene A. Carr | Aug. 16, 1861 | Promoted **Brig. Gen., USV,** March 7, 1862
Lafayette McCrillis | July 25, 1862 | Mustered out Sept. 5, 1864, **Bvt. Brig. Gen., USV**
Robert H. Carnahan | April 9, 1865 | Mustered out Oct. 10, 1865, **Bvt. Brig. Gen., USV**

4th Cavalry
Theophilus L. Dickey | Oct. 12, 1861 | Resigned Feb. 16, 1863
Martin R.M. Wallace | June 3, 1863 | Mustered out Nov. 3, 1864, **Bvt. Brig. Gen., USV**

5th Cavalry
John J. Updegraff | Sept. 9, 1861 | Dismissed Dec. 3, 1861
Hall Wilson | Dec. 30, 1861 | Resigned Jan. 19, 1863
John McConnell | May 27, 1864 | Mustered out Oct. 27, 1865, **Bvt. Brig. Gen., USV**

6th Cavalry
Thomas H. Cavanaugh | Jan. 9, 1862 | Resigned March 28, 1862
Benjamin H. Grierson | April 12, 1862 | Promoted **Brig. Gen., USV,** June 3, 1863
Matthew H. Starr | July 19, 1864 | DOW Oct. 2, 1864
John Lynch | April 2, 1865 | Mustered out Nov. 5, 1865

7th Cavalry
William P. Kellogg | Sept. 8, 1861 | Resigned June 1, 1862
Edward Prince | June 2, 1862 | Mustered out Oct. 15, 1864
John M. Graham | March 2, 1865 | Mustered out Nov. 4, 1865

8th Cavalry
John F. Farnsworth | Sept. 18, 1861 | Promoted **Brig. Gen., USV,** Nov. 29, 1862
William Gamble | Dec. 5, 1862 | Mustered out July 17, 1865, **Brig. Gen., USV**

9th Cavalry
Albert G. Brackett | Oct. 26, 1861 | Mustered out Oct. 26, 1864
Joseph W. Harper | March 20, 1865 | Mustered out Oct. 31, 1865

10th Cavalry
James A. Barret | Nov. 25, 1861 | Resigned May 15, 1862

Illinois Regiments

Dudley Wickersham	May 16, 1862	Resigned May 10, 1864
James Stuart	May 11, 1864	Mustered out Nov. 22, 1865

11th Cavalry

Robert G. Ingersoll	Dec. 20, 1861	Resigned June 30, 1863
Lucien H. Kerr	April 25, 1864	Mustered out Dec. 19, 1864
Otto Funke	May 21, 1865	Mustered out Sept. 30, 1865, **Bvt. Brig. Gen., USV**

12th Cavalry

Arno Voss	Feb. 1, 1862	Resigned Aug. 11, 1863
Hasbrouck Davis	Jan. 5, 1864	Resigned Aug. 1, 1865, **Bvt. Brig. Gen., USV**
Hamilton B. Dox	Oct. 13, 1865	Mustered out May 29, 1866, **Bvt. Brig. Gen., USV**

13th Cavalry

Joseph W. Bell	Dec. 31, 1861	Mustered out May 25, 1863, **Bvt. Brig. Gen., USV**
George R. Marvel	Feb. 12, 1864	Discharged April 11, 1864
Albert Erskine	June 1, 1864	Mustered out Jan. 9, 1865, **Bvt. Brig. Gen., USV**
George M. Alden	Aug. 8, 1865	Mustered out Aug. 31, 1865

14th Cavalry

Horace Capron	Feb. 6, 1863	Resigned Jan. 23, 1865, **Bvt. Brig. Gen., USV**
Francis M. Davidson	Feb. 17, 1865	Mustered out July 31, 1865

15th Cavalry

Warren Stewart	Dec. 25, 1862	DOW Jan. 23, 1863
George A. Bacon	Jan. 24, 1863	Mustered out Aug. 25, 1864

16th Cavalry

Christian Thielemann	June 11, 1863	Discharged Aug. 9, 1864
Robert W. Smith	Aug. 9, 1864	Mustered out Aug. 19, 1865, **Bvt. Brig. Gen., USV**

17th Cavalry

John L. Beveridge	Jan. 28, 1864	Mustered out Feb. 7, 1866, **Bvt. Brig. Gen., USV**

1st Light Artillery

Joseph D. Webster	Feb. 1, 1862	Promoted **Brig. Gen., USV,** Nov. 29, 1862
Ezra Taylor	Oct. 27, 1863	Resigned Aug. 20, 1864, **Bvt. Brig. Gen., USV**
Charles Houghtaling	Aug. 20, 1864	Mustered out June 14, 1865, **Bvt. Brig. Gen., USV**

2nd Light Artillery

Thomas S. Mather	Jan. 30, 1862	Mustered out Aug. 17, 1865, **Bvt. Brig. Gen., USV**

7th Infantry (3 months)

John Cook	April 25, 1861	Mustered out July 24, 1861

7th Infantry (3 years)

John Cook	July 25, 1861	Promoted **Brig. Gen., USV,** March 21, 1862
Andrew J. Babcock	March 22, 1862	Resigned Feb. 28, 1863
Richard Rowett	July 2, 1863	Mustered out July 9, 1865, **Bvt. Brig. Gen., USV**

8th Infantry (3 months)

Richard J. Oglesby	April 25, 1861	Mustered out July 24, 1861

8th Infantry (3 years)

Richard J. Oglesby	July 25, 1861	Promoted **Brig. Gen., USV,** April 1, 1862
Franklin L. Rhoads	April 1, 1862	Resigned Oct. 7, 1862
John P. Post	Oct. 7, 1862	Resigned Sept. 28, 1863
Josiah A. Sheetz	Nov. 25, 1864	Resigned Feb. 9, 1866, **Bvt. Brig. Gen., USV**
Lloyd Wheaton	March 8, 1866	Mustered out May 4, 1866

9th Infantry (3 months)

Eleazer A. Paine	April 26, 1861	Mustered out July 26, 1861

Illinois Regiments

9th Infantry (3 years)

Eleazer A. Paine	July 26, 1861	Promoted **Brig. Gen., USV,** Sept. 3, 1861
August Mersy	Sept. 5, 1861	Mustered out Aug. 20, 1864, **Bvt. Brig. Gen., USV**
Samuel T. Hughes	July 9, 1865	Mustered out July 9, 1865

10th Infantry (3 months)

Benjamin M. Prentiss	April 29, 1861	Promoted **Brig. Gen., USV,** May 17, 1861
James D. Morgan	May 20, 1861	Mustered out July 29, 1861

10th Infantry (3 years)

James D. Morgan	July 29, 1861	Promoted **Brig. Gen., USV,** July 17, 1862
John Tillson	July 17, 1862	Mustered out July 4, 1865, **Bvt. Brig. Gen., USV**

11th Infantry (3 months)

William H. L. Wallace	May 1, 1861	Mustered out July 30, 1861

11th Infantry (3 years)

William H. L. Wallace	July 30, 1861	Promoted **Brig. Gen., USV,** March 21, 1862
Thomas E. G. Ransom	April 8, 1862	Promoted **Brig. Gen., USV,** Nov. 29, 1862
Garrett V. Nevius	March 17, 1863	KIA May 22, 1863
James H. Coates	July 8, 1863	Mustered out July 14, 1865, **Bvt. Brig. Gen., USV**

12th Infantry (3 months)

John McArthur	May 3, 1861	Mustered out Aug, 1, 1861

12th Infantry (3 years)

John McArthur	Aug. 1, 1861	Promoted **Brig. Gen., USV,** March 21, 1862
Augustus L. Chetlain	April 27, 1862	Promoted **Brig. Gen., USV,** Dec. 18, 1863
Henry Van Sellar	July 10, 1865	Mustered out July 10, 1865

13th Infantry

John B. Wyman	May 24, 1861	KIA Dec. 28, 1862
Adam B. Gorgas	Dec. 28, 1862	Mustered out June 18, 1864

14th Infantry

John M. Palmer	May 25, 1861	Promoted **Brig. Gen., USV,** Dec. 20, 1861
Cyrus Hall	Feb. 1, 1862	Mustered out May 25, 1864
Cyrus Hall	March 13, 1865	Mustered out Sept. 16, 1865, **Bvt. Brig. Gen., USV**

15th Infantry

Thomas J. Turner	May 24, 1861	Resigned Nov. 2, 1862
George C. Rogers	Nov. 2, 1862	Mustered out Sept. 16, 1865, **Bvt. Brig. Gen., USV**

16th Infantry

Robert F. Smith	May 24, 1861	Mustered out May 24, 1864, **Bvt. Brig. Gen., USV**
Charles D. Kerr	July 3, 1865	Mustered out July 8, 1865

17th Infantry

Leonard F. Ross	May 25, 1861	Promoted **Brig. Gen., USV,** April 25, 1862
Addison S. Norton	Aug. 1, 1862	Resigned July 9, 1863

18th Infantry

Michael K. Lawler	June 30, 1861	Promoted **Brig. Gen., USV,** Nov. 29, 1862
Daniel H. Brush	May 25, 1863	Resigned Sept. 8, 1863, **Bvt. Brig. Gen., USV**
Jabez J. Anderson	March 20, 1865	Resigned May 4, 1865
Jules C. Webber	June 12, 1865	Mustered out Dec. 16, 1865, **Bvt. Brig. Gen., USV**

19th Infantry

John B. Turchin	June 22, 1861	Promoted **Brig. Gen., USV,** July 17, 1862
Joseph R. Scott	Aug. 7, 1862	DOW July 8, 1863

20th Infantry

Charles C. Marsh	June 13, 1861	Resigned April 22, 1863
Daniel Bradley	Jan. 5, 1864	Mustered out Feb. 13, 1865
Henry King	July 15, 1865	Mustered out July 16, 1865

21st Infantry

Ulysses S. Grant	June 17, 1861	Promoted **Brig. Gen., USV,** Aug. 7, 1861
John W. S. Alexander	Aug. 30, 1861	KIA Sept. 20, 1863
James E. Callaway	May 11, 1865	Resigned May 23, 1865
William H. Jamison	July 13, 1865	Mustered out Dec. 16, 1865

22nd Infantry

Henry Dougherty	June 11, 1861	Discharged May 7, 1863

23rd Infantry

James A. Mulligan	June 18, 1861	DOW July 26, 1864, **Bvt. Brig. Gen., USV**
Samuel A. Simison	May 11, 1865	Mustered out July 24, 1865

24th Infantry

Friedrich Hecker	July 8, 1861	Resigned Dec. 23, 1861
Geza Mihalotzy	Dec. 24, 1861	DOW March 11, 1864

25th Infantry

William N. Coler	Aug. 21, 1861	Resigned Aug. 20, 1862
Thomas D. Williams	Aug. 31, 1862	DOW Jan. 6, 1863
Caswell P. Ford	Jan. 7, 1863	Resigned April 14, 1863
Richard H. Nodine	May 26, 1863	Mustered out Sept. 5, 1864

26th Infantry

John M. Loomis	Aug. 29, 1861	Resigned April 30, 1864
Robert A. Gillmore	April 30, 1864	Mustered out Oct. 27, 1864
Ira J. Bloomfield	May 11, 1865	Mustered out July 20, 1865, **Bvt. Brig. Gen., USV**

27th Infantry

Napoleon B. Buford	Aug. 10, 1861	Promoted **Brig. Gen., USV,** April 15, 1862
Fazilo A. Harrington	April 16, 1862	DOW Jan. 1, 1863
Jonathan R. Miles	Jan. 1, 1863	Resigned April 28, 1864
William A. Schmitt	April 28, 1864	Mustered out Sept. 20, 1864, **Bvt. Brig. Gen., USV**

28th Infantry

Amory K. Johnson	Sept. 28, 1861	Resigned June 17, 1864
Richard Ritter	May 10, 1865	Resigned July 23, 1865
Hinman Rhodes	Sept. 15, 1865	Mustered out March 15, 1866

29th Infantry

James S. Rearden	Aug. 19, 1861	Resigned April 15, 1862
Mason Brayman	April 19, 1862	Promoted **Brig. Gen., USV,** Sept. 24, 1862
Charles M. Ferrell	Sept. 24, 1862	Resigned Aug. 11, 1863
Loren Kent	Nov. 14, 1863	Mustered out Nov. 12, 1865, **Bvt. Brig. Gen., USV**

30th Infantry

Philip B. Fouke	Aug. 28, 1861	Resigned April 22, 1862
Elias S. Dennis	May 1, 1862	Promoted **Brig. Gen., USV,** Nov. 29, 1862
Warren Shedd	June 13, 1863	Mustered out July 17, 1865, **Bvt. Brig. Gen., USV**

31st Infantry

John A. Logan	Sept. 18, 1861	Promoted **Brig. Gen., USV,** March 21, 1862
Lindorf Ozburn	April 6, 1862	Resigned Feb. 24, 1863
Edwin S. McCook	April 9, 1863	Resigned Sept. 26, 1864, **Bvt. Brig. Gen., USV**
Robert N. Pearson	April 3, 1865	Mustered out July 19, 1865, **Bvt. Brig. Gen., USV**

32nd Infantry

John Logan	Dec. 17, 1861	Mustered out Dec. 30, 1864
George H. English	Dec. 30, 1864	Mustered out Sept. 16, 1865

33rd Infantry

Charles E. Hovey	Aug. 15, 1861	Promoted **Brig. Gen., USV,** Sept. 5, 1862
Charles E. Lippincott	Sept. 17, 1862	Mustered out Sept. 10, 1865, **Bvt. Brig. Gen., USV**
Isaac H. Elliott	Sept. 30, 1865	Mustered out Nov. 24, 1865, **Bvt. Brig. Gen., USV**

34th Infantry

Edward N. Kirk	Sept. 7, 1861	Promoted **Brig. Gen., USV,** Nov. 29, 1862
Hiram W. Bristol	Dec. 19, 1862	Resigned March 8, 1863
Alexander P. Dysart	April 12, 1863	Resigned Aug. 7, 1863
Peter Ege	June 7, 1865	Mustered out July 12, 1865

35th Infantry

Gustavus A. Smith	Sept. 1, 1861	Promoted **Brig. Gen., USV,** Sept. 19, 1862
William P. Chandler	Sept. 22, 1863	Mustered out Sept. 27, 1864

36th Infantry

Nicholas Greusel	Aug. 20, 1861	Resigned Feb. 7, 1863
Silas Miller	March 2, 1863	DOW July 27, 1864
Benjamin F. Campbell	May 10, 1865	Mustered out Oct. 8, 1865

37th Infantry

Julius White	Sept. 18, 1861	Promoted **Brig. Gen., USV,** June 9, 1862
Myron S. Barnes	June 9, 1862	Dismissed Nov. 20, 1862
John C. Black	Dec. 31, 1862	Resigned Aug. 15, 1865, **Bvt. Brig. Gen., USV**
Ransom Kennicott	Aug. 28, 1865	Mustered out April 19, 1866
Judson J. Huntley	May 15, 1866	Mustered out May 15, 1866

38th Infantry

William P. Carlin	Aug. 15, 1861	Promoted **Brig. Gen., USV,** Nov. 29, 1862
Daniel H. Gilmer	March 11, 1863	KIA Sept. 20, 1863
Edward Colyer	May 16, 1865	Mustered out March 20, 1866

39th Infantry

Austin Light	Oct. 11, 1861	Dismissed Nov. 25, 1861
Thomas O. Osborn	Jan. 1, 1862	Promoted **Brig. Gen., USV,** May 1, 1865
Orrin L. Mann	June 6, 1865	Mustered out Dec. 6, 1865, **Bvt. Brig. Gen., USV**

40th Infantry

Stephen G. Hicks	Aug. 10, 1861	Mustered out Sept. 6, 1865

41st Infantry

Isaac C. Pugh	Aug. 5, 1861	Mustered out Aug. 20, 1864, **Bvt. Brig. Gen., USV**

42nd Infantry

William A. Webb	July 22, 1861	Died Dec. 24, 1861
George W. Roberts	Dec. 25, 1861	KIA Dec. 31, 1862
Nathan H. Walworth	Jan. 1, 1863	Resigned April 13, 1864
Edgar D. Swain	April 13, 1864	Mustered out Dec. 16, 1865

43rd Infantry

Julius Raith	Oct. 13, 1861	DOW April 11, 1862
Adolph Engelmann	April 12, 1862	Mustered out Dec. 16, 1864, **Bvt. Brig. Gen., USV**
Adolf Dengler	April 11, 1865	Mustered out Nov. 30, 1865

44th Infantry

Charles Knobelsdorff	Sept. 13, 1861	Dismissed Aug. 20, 1862
Wallace W. Barrett	Jan. 1, 1863	Mustered out Dec. 14, 1865, **Bvt. Brig. Gen., USV**

Illinois Regiments

45th Infantry

John E. Smith	July 23, 1861	Promoted **Brig. Gen., USV,** Nov. 29, 1862
Jasper A. Maltby	March 5, 1863	Promoted **Brig. Gen., USV,** Aug. 4, 1863
Robert P. Sealy	Aug. 4, 1863	Mustered out Jan. 10, 1865
John O. Duer	May 11, 1865	Mustered out July 12, 1865, **Bvt. Brig. Gen., USV**

46th Infantry

John A. Davis	Dec. 26, 1861	DOW Oct. 10, 1862
Benjamin Dornblaser	Oct. 25, 1862	Mustered out Jan. 20, 1866, **Bvt. Brig. Gen., USV**

47th Infantry

John Bryner	Sept. 4, 1861	Resigned Sept. 2, 1862
William A. Thrush	Sept. 2, 1862	KIA Oct. 3, 1862
John N. Cromwell	Nov. 22, 1862	KIA May 16, 1863
John D. McClure	May 17, 1863	Mustered out Oct. 11, 1864
David W. Magee	March 25, 1865	Mustered out Jan. 21, 1866, **Bvt. Brig. Gen., USV**

48th Infantry

Isham N. Haynie	Nov. 10, 1861	Promoted **Brig. Gen., USV,** Nov. 29, 1862
William W. Sanford	Nov. 21, 1862	Resigned Jan. 22, 1864
Lucien Greathouse	Feb. 26, 1864	KIA July 22, 1864
Ashley T. Galbraith	July 22, 1864	Discharged Jan. 25, 1865
Thomas L. B. Weems	June 1, 1865	Mustered out Aug. 15, 1865

49th Infantry

William R. Morrison	Dec. 29, 1861	Resigned Dec. 13, 1862
Phineas Pease	March 6, 1863	Mustered out Jan. 9, 1865, **Bvt. Brig. Gen., USV**
William P. Moore	May 11, 1865	Mustered out Sept. 9, 1865

50th Infantry

Moses M. Bane	Aug. 20, 1861	Resigned June 11, 1864
William Hanna	June 11, 1864	Mustered out July 13, 1865, **Bvt. Brig. Gen., USV**

51st Infantry

Gilbert W. Cumming	Sept. 20, 1861	Resigned Sept. 30, 1862, **Bvt. Brig. Gen., USV**
Luther P. Bradley	Oct. 15, 1862	Promoted **Brig. Gen., USV,** July 30, 1864
Charles W. Davis	May 11, 1865	Discharged June 30, 1865
James S. Boyd	Sept. 24, 1865	Mustered out Sept. 25, 1865

52nd Infantry

Isaac G. Wilson	Nov. 19, 1861	Resigned Dec. 6, 1861
Thomas W. Sweeny	Jan. 21, 1862	Promoted **Brig. Gen., USV,** Nov. 29, 1862
John S. Wilcox	May 4, 1863	Resigned Feb. 20, 1864, **Bvt. Brig. Gen., USV**
Edwin A. Bowen	Feb. 20, 1864	Mustered out Oct. 24, 1864
Jerome D. Davis	May 11, 1865	Mustered out July 6, 1865

53rd Infantry

William H. W. Cushman	Jan. 1, 1862	Resigned Sept. 3, 1862
Daniel F. Hitt	Nov. 11, 1862	Resigned Jan. 2, 1863
Seth C. Earl	Jan. 3, 1863	KIA July 12, 1863
John W. McClanahan	Oct. 18, 1864	Resigned June 21, 1865
Robert H. McFadden	July 14, 1865	Mustered out July 22, 1865

54th Infantry

Thomas W. Harris	Feb. 18, 1862	Resigned Dec. 10, 1862
Greenville M. Mitchell	Jan. 18, 1863	Mustered out Oct. 15, 1865, **Bvt. Brig. Gen., USV**

55th Infantry

David Stuart	Oct. 31, 1861	Promoted **Brig. Gen., USV,** Nov. 29, 1862
Oscar Malmborg	Dec. 19, 1862	Resigned Sept. 20, 1864

56th Infantry (Mechanic Fusileers)

James W. Wilson	July 26, 1861	Discharged Feb. 5, 1862

56th Infantry

Robert Kirkham	Dec. 16, 1861	Resigned June 26, 1862
William R. Brown	June 26, 1862	Resigned Aug. 31, 1862
Green B. Raum	Aug. 31, 1862	Promoted **Brig. Gen., USV**, Feb. 15, 1865
John P. Hall	March 29, 1865	Mustered out Aug. 12, 1865

57th Infantry

Silas D. Baldwin	Dec. 26, 1861	Dismissed March 26, 1863
Frederick J. Hurlbut	Oct. 15, 1864	Died April 27, 1865
Frederick A. Battey	July 1, 1865	Mustered out July 7, 1865

58th Infantry

William F. Lynch	Jan. 25, 1862	Mustered out Feb. 7, 1865, **Bvt. Brig. Gen., USV**
Robert W. Healy	Oct. 3, 1865	Mustered out April 1, 1866, **Bvt. Brig. Gen., USV**

59th Infantry (originally 9th MO Infantry)

John C. Kelton	Sept. 19, 1861	Resigned March 1, 1862, **Bvt. Brig. Gen., USV**
Philip S. Post	March 20, 1862	Mustered out Dec. 8, 1865, **Bvt. Brig. Gen., USV**

60th Infantry

Silas C. Toler	Feb. 17, 1862	Died March 2, 1863
William B. Anderson	April 4, 1863	Resigned Dec. 26, 1864, **Bvt. Brig. Gen., USV**
George W. Evans	May 11, 1865	Mustered out July 31, 1865

61st Infantry

Jacob Fry	March 26, 1862	Resigned May 14, 1863
Simon P. Ohr	May 14, 1864	Died Sept. 14, 1864
Daniel Grass	Sept. 15, 1864	Mustered out May 15, 1865
Jerome B. Nulton	July 11, 1865	Mustered out Sept. 8, 1865

62nd Infantry

James M. True	April 10, 1862	Mustered out May 1, 1865, **Bvt. Brig. Gen., USV**
Lewis C. True	July 11, 1865	Mustered out March 6, 1866

63rd Infantry

Francis Moro	April 10, 1862	Resigned Sept. 29, 1862
Joseph B. McCown	Sept. 29, 1862	Mustered out April 9, 1865
James Isaminger	July 12, 1865	Mustered out July 13, 1865

64th Infantry

John Morrill	March 1, 1864	Mustered out July 3, 1865, **Bvt. Brig. Gen., USV**

65th Infantry

Daniel Cameron	May 1, 1862	Resigned July 31, 1864, **Bvt. Brig. Gen., USV**
William S. Stewart	June 29, 1865	Mustered out July 13, 1865, **Bvt. Brig. Gen., USV**

66th Infantry (originally 14 MO Infantry)

Patrick E. Burke	June 24, 1862	DOW May 20, 1864
Andrew K. Campbell	May 20, 1864	Mustered out July 7, 1865

67th Infantry

Rosell M. Hough	June 13, 1862	Mustered out Oct. 6, 1862

68th Infantry

Elias Stuart	July 16, 1862	Mustered out Sept. 26, 1862

69th Infantry

Joseph H. Tucker	June 13, 1862	Mustered out Dec. 31, 1862

Illinois Regiments

70th Infantry
Owen T. Reeves   July 23, 1862   Mustered out Oct. 23, 1862

71st Infantry
Othniel Gilbert   July 26, 1862   Mustered out Oct. 29, 1862

72nd Infantry
Frederick A. Starring   Aug. 21, 1862   Mustered out Aug. 21, 1865, **Bvt. Brig. Gen., USV**

73rd Infantry
James F. Jaquess   Aug. 21, 1862   Mustered out June 12, 1865

74th Infantry
Jason Marsh   Sept. 4, 1862   Resigned Aug. 24, 1864
Thomas J. Bryan   May 10, 1865   Mustered out June 10, 1865

75th Infantry
George Ryon   Sept. 2, 1862   Resigned Dec. 20, 1862
John E. Bennett   April 23, 1863   Mustered out June 12, 1865, **Bvt. Brig. Gen., USV**

76th Infantry
Alonzo W. Mack   Aug. 22, 1862   Resigned Jan. 7, 1863
Samuel T. Busey   Jan. 7, 1863   Mustered out July 22, 1865, **Bvt. Brig. Gen., USV**

77th Infantry
Charles Ballance   Sept. 2, 1862   Mustered out Sept. 3, 1862
David P. Grier   Sept. 11, 1862   Mustered out July 10, 1865, **Bvt. Brig. Gen., USV**

78th Infantry
William H. Benneson   Sept. 1, 1862   Resigned Sept. 2, 1863
Carter Van Vleck   Feb. 17, 1864   DOW Aug. 23, 1864
Maris R. Vernon   May 10, 1865   Mustered out June 7, 1865

79th Infantry
Lyman Guinnip   Aug. 28, 1862   Resigned Oct. 17, 1862
Sheridan P. Read   Oct. 18, 1862   KIA Dec. 31, 1862
Allen Buckner   Jan. 1, 1863   Mustered out June 12, 1865

80th Infantry
Thomas G. Allen   Aug. 25, 1862   Resigned April 21, 1863
Andrew F. Rodgers   April 21, 1863   Resigned Nov. 25, 1864
Erastus N. Bates   May 10, 1865   Mustered out June 10, 1865, **Bvt. Brig. Gen., USV**

81st Infantry
James J. Dollins   Aug. 26, 1862   KIA May 22, 1863
Franklin Campbell   May 23, 1863   Resigned Aug. 20, 1864
Andrew W. Rogers   Aug. 20, 1864   Mustered out Aug. 5, 1865

82nd Infantry
Friedrich Hecker   Oct. 23, 1862   Resigned March 21, 1864
Edward S. Salomon   March 21, 1864   Mustered out June 9, 1865, **Bvt. Brig. Gen., USV**

83rd Infantry
Abner C. Harding   Aug. 21, 1862   Promoted **Brig. Gen., USV,** March 13, 1863
Arthur A. Smith   June 4, 1863   Mustered out June 26, 1865, **Bvt. Brig. Gen., USV**

84th Infantry
Louis H. Waters   Sept. 1, 1862   Mustered out June 8, 1865, **Bvt. Brig. Gen., USV**

85th Infantry
Robert S. Moore   Aug. 27, 1862   Resigned June 14, 1863
Caleb J. Dilworth   June 26, 1863   Mustered out June 5, 1865, **Bvt. Brig. Gen., USV**

86th Infantry

David D. Irons	Aug. 27, 1862	Died Aug. 11, 1863
Allen L. Fahnestock	May 10, 1865	Mustered out June 6, 1865

87th Infantry

John E. Whiting	Sept. 22, 1862	Resigned Oct. 8, 1863
John M. Crebs	Oct. 8, 1863	Mustered out June 16, 1865

88th Infantry

Francis T. Sherman	Sept. 4, 1862	Promoted **Brig. Gen., USV,** July 21, 1865

89th Infantry

John Christopher	Aug. 25, 1862	Commission revoked Jan. 7, 1863
Charles T. Hotchkiss	Feb. 24, 1863	Mustered out June 10, 1865, **Bvt. Brig. Gen., USV**

90th Infantry

Timothy J. O'Meara	Nov. 21, 1862	DOW Nov. 26, 1863
Owen Stuart	Nov. 25, 1863	Mustered out June 6, 1865

91st Infantry

Henry M. Day	Sept. 8, 1862	Mustered out July 12, 1865, **Bvt. Brig. Gen., USV**

92nd Infantry

Smith D. Atkins	Sept. 4, 1862	Mustered out June 21, 1865, **Bvt. Brig. Gen., USV**

93rd Infantry

Holden Putnam	Oct. 13, 1862	KIA Nov. 25, 1863
Nicholas C. Buswell	Nov. 25, 1863	Mustered out June 23, 1865

94th Infantry

William W. Orme	Aug. 20, 1862	Promoted **Brig. Gen., USV,** Nov. 29, 1862
John McNulta	June 21, 1863	Mustered out July 17, 1865, **Bvt. Brig. Gen., USV**

95th Infantry

Lawrence S. Church	Sept. 4, 1862	Resigned Jan. 24, 1863
Thomas W. Humphrey	April 3, 1863	KIA June 10, 1864, **Bvt. Brig. Gen., USV**
Leander Blanden	Sept. 1, 1864	Mustered out Aug. 17, 1865, **Bvt. Brig. Gen., USV**

96th Infantry

Thomas E. Champion	Sept. 6, 1862	Resigned June 7, 1865, **Bvt. Brig. Gen., USV**

97th Infantry

Friend S. Rutherford	Sept. 16, 1862	Resigned June 15, 1864
Lewis D. Martin	June 15, 1864	Resigned Oct. 11, 1864
Victor Vifquain	May 10, 1865	Mustered out July 29, 1865, **Bvt. Brig. Gen., USV**

98th Infantry

John J. Funkhouser	Sept. 3, 1862	Resigned July 5, 1864
Edward Kitchell	July 5, 1864	Mustered out June 27, 1865, **Bvt. Brig. Gen., USV**

99th Infantry

George W. K. Bailey	Aug. 23, 1862	Mustered out Dec. 16, 1864
Asa C. Matthews	Dec. 16, 1864	Mustered out July 31, 1865

100th Infantry

Frederick A. Bartleson	Aug. 30, 1862	KIA June 23, 1864
Charles M. Hammond	March 11, 1865	Mustered out June 12, 1865

101st Infantry

Charles H. Fox	Aug. 22, 1862	Resigned May 1, 1864
John B. Le Sage	May 1, 1864	Mustered out June 7, 1865

Illinois Regiments

102nd Infantry

William McMurtry	Sept. 2, 1862	Resigned Oct. 24, 1862
Franklin C. Smith	Feb. 28, 1863	Mustered out June 6, 1865, **Bvt. Brig. Gen., USV**

103rd Infantry

Amos C. Babcock	Oct. 2, 1862	Resigned Oct. 18, 1862
Willard A. Dickerman	Oct. 18, 1862	DOW May 30, 1864
George W. Wright	May 28, 1864	Mustered out June 21, 1865

104th Infantry

Absalom B. Moore	Aug. 27, 1862	Resigned Sept. 9, 1863
Douglas Hapeman	Sept. 9, 1863	Mustered out June 6, 1865

105th Infantry

Daniel Dustin	Sept. 2, 1862	Mustered out June 7, 1865, **Bvt. Brig. Gen., USV**

106th Infantry

Robert B. Latham	Sept. 18, 1862	Resigned April 28, 1864
Henry Yates, Jr.	April 28, 1864	Resigned Sept. 8, 1864, **Bvt. Brig. Gen., USV**
Charles H. Miller	July 15, 1865	Mustered out July 12, 1865

107th Infantry

Thomas Snell	Sept. 4, 1862	Resigned Dec. 13, 1862
Joseph J. Kelly	Feb. 7, 1863	Resigned Nov. 10, 1863
Francis H. Lowry	Nov. 10, 1863	DOW Jan. 1, 1865
Thomas J. Milholland	May 10, 1865	Mustered out June 21, 1865

108th Infantry

John B. Warner	Aug. 28, 1862	Dismissed March 13, 1863
Charles Turner	July 9, 1863	Mustered out Aug. 5, 1865, **Bvt. Brig. Gen., USV**

109th Infantry

Alexander J. Nimmo	Sept. 11, 1862	Discharged April 10, 1863

110th Infantry

Thomas S. Casey	Sept. 11, 1862	Mustered out May 8, 1863

111th Infantry

James S. Martin	Sept. 18, 1862	Mustered out June 7, 1865, **Bvt. Brig. Gen., USV**

112th Infantry

Thomas J. Henderson	Sept. 22, 1862	Mustered out June 20, 1865, **Bvt. Brig. Gen., USV**

113th Infantry

George B. Hoge	Oct. 1, 1862	Mustered out June 20, 1865, **Bvt. Brig. Gen., USV**

114th Infantry

James W. Judy	Sept. 18, 1862	Resigned Aug. 4, 1863
John F. King	Aug. 4, 1863	Resigned Dec. 7, 1864, **Bvt. Brig. Gen., USV**
Samuel N. Shoup	May 11, 1865	Mustered out Aug. 3, 1865, **Bvt. Brig. Gen., USV**

115th Infantry

Jesse H. Moore	Sept. 13, 1862	Mustered out June 11, 1865, **Bvt. Brig. Gen., USV**

116th Infantry

Nathan W. Tupper	Sept. 30, 1862	Died March 10, 1864
John E. Maddux	June 7, 1865	Mustered out June 7, 1865

117th Infantry

Risdon M. Moore	Sept. 19, 1862	Mustered out Aug. 5, 1865

118th Infantry

John G. Fonda	Dec. 15, 1862	Mustered out Oct. 1, 1865, **Bvt. Brig. Gen., USV**

119th Infantry

Thomas J. Kinney	Oct. 7, 1862	Mustered out Aug. 26, 1865, **Bvt. Brig. Gen., USV**

120th Infantry

George W. McKeaig	Oct. 29, 1862	Mustered out Sept. 10, 1865
Spencer B. Floyd	June 12, 1864	Commission canceled

121st Infantry

Did not complete organization

122nd Infantry

John I. Rinaker	Sept. 4, 1862	Mustered out July 15, 1865, **Bvt. Brig. Gen., USV**

123rd Infantry

James Monroe	Sept. 6, 1862	KIA Oct. 7, 1863
Jonathan Biggs	Oct. 7, 1863	Mustered out June 28, 1865, **Bvt. Brig. Gen., USV**

124th Infantry

Thomas J. Sloan	Sept. 22, 1862	Dismissed Dec. 19, 1863
John H. Howe	Dec. 19, 1863	Mustered out Aug. 15, 1865, **Bvt. Brig. Gen., USV**

125th Infantry

Oscar F. Harmon	Sept. 4, 1862	KIA June 27, 1864
James W. Langley	May 10, 1865	Mustered out June 9, 1865

126th Infantry

Jonathan Richmond	Sept. 4, 1862	Resigned March 3, 1864
Lucius W. Beal	May 11, 1865	Mustered out July 12, 1865

127th Infantry

John Van Arman	Sept. 6, 1862	Resigned Feb. 23, 1863
Hamilton N. Eldridge	March 1, 1863	Resigned July 29, 1863, **Bvt. Brig. Gen., USV**

128th Infantry

Robert M. Hundley	Dec. 18, 1862	Discharged April 4, 1863

129th Infantry

George P. Smith	Sept. 8, 1862	Resigned May 8, 1863
Henry Case	May 15, 1863	Mustered out June 8, 1865, **Bvt. Brig. Gen., USV**

130th Infantry

Nathaniel Niles	Oct. 25, 1862	Resigned Dec. 5, 1863, **Bvt. Brig. Gen., USV**
John B. Reid	Aug. 16, 1865	Mustered out Aug. 15, 1865

131st Infantry

George W. Neely	Nov. 13, 1862	Mustered out Sept. 16, 1863

132nd Infantry

Thomas J. Pickett	June 1, 1864	Mustered out Oct. 17, 1864

133rd Infantry

Thaddeus Phillips	May 31, 1864	Mustered out Sept. 24, 1864

134th Infantry

Waters W. McChesney	May 31, 1864	Mustered out Oct. 25, 1864

135th Infantry

John S. Wolfe	June 6, 1864	Mustered out Sept. 28, 1864

136th Infantry

Frederick A. Johns	June 1, 1864	Mustered out Oct. 22, 1864

137th Infantry

John Wood	June 5, 1864	Mustered out Sept. 24, 1864

Illinois Regiments

138th Infantry
John W. Goodwin   June 21, 1864   Mustered out Oct. 14, 1864

139th Infantry
Peter Davidson   June 1, 1864   Mustered out Oct. 28, 1864

140th Infantry
Lorenzo H. Whitney   June 18, 1864   Mustered out Oct. 29, 1864

141st Infantry
Stephen Bronson   June 21, 1864   Mustered out Oct. 10, 1864, **Bvt. Brig. Gen., USV**

142nd Infantry
Rollin V. Ankeny   June 18, 1864   Mustered out Oct. 26, 1864, **Bvt. Brig. Gen., USV**

143rd Infantry
Dudley C. Smith   June 11, 1864   Mustered out Sept. 26, 1864

144th Infantry
Cyrus Hall   Oct. 21, 1864   Resigned March 7, 1865, **Bvt. Brig. Gen., USV**
John H. Kuhn   March 13, 1865   Mustered out July 14, 1865

145th Infantry
George W. Lackey   June 9, 1864   Mustered out Sept. 23, 1864

146th Infantry
Henry H. Dean   Sept. 20, 1864   Mustered out July 8, 1865

147th Infantry
Hiram F. Sickles   Feb. 21, 1865   Mustered out Jan. 20, 1866, **Bvt. Brig. Gen., USV**

148th Infantry
Horace H. Willsie   Feb. 21, 1865   Mustered out Sept. 5, 1865

149th Infantry
William C. Kueffner   Feb. 15, 1865   Mustered out Jan. 27, 1866, **Bvt. Brig. Gen., USV**

150th Infantry
George U. Keener   Feb. 14, 1865   Resigned July 20, 1865
Charles F. Springer   Dec. 8, 1865   Mustered out Jan. 16, 1866

151st Infantry
French B. Woodall   Feb. 25, 1865   Mustered out Jan. 24, 1866

152nd Infantry
Ferdinand D. Stephenson   Feb. 18, 1865   Mustered out Sept. 11, 1865

153rd Infantry
Stephen Bronson   Feb. 27, 1865   Mustered out Sept. 21, 1865, **Bvt. Brig. Gen., USV**

154th Infantry
McLean F. Wood   Feb. 22, 1865   Died Aug. 6, 1865
Francis Swanwick   Aug. 11, 1865   Mustered out Sept. 18, 1865

155th Infantry
Gustavus A. Smith   Feb. 28, 1865   Mustered out Dec. 14, 1865, **Brig. Gen., USV**

156th Infantry
Alfred T. Smith   April 4, 1865   Mustered out Sept. 20, 1865

Biographies

George Marcus Alden

Captain, Co. G, 13 IL Cavalry, Jan. 20, 1864. Lieutenant Colonel, 13 IL Cavalry, April 11, 1865. *Colonel,* 13 IL Cavalry, Aug. 8, 1865. Honorably mustered out, Aug. 31, 1865.

Born: Nov. 4, 1828, Newberry District, SC
Died: July 12, 1905, Lancaster, TX
Other Wars: Enlisted as Private, Co. G, 5 U.S. Infantry, Sept. 8, 1849. Deserted May 31, 1851.
Occupation: Grocer for several years after which he was a commission merchant dealing in flour and grain
Miscellaneous: Resided Ashley, Washington Co., IL, to 1867; Cairo, Alexander Co., IL, 1867–91; and Lancaster, Dallas Co., TX
Buried: Edgewood Cemetery, Lancaster, TX (Lot 218)
References: Pension File and Military Service File, National Archives. William H. Perrin, editor. *History of Alexander, Union and Pulaski Counties, Illinois.* Chicago, IL, 1883. Obituary, *Dallas Morning News,* July 15, 1905.

John Washington Shields Alexander

Lieutenant Colonel, 21 IL Infantry, June 28, 1861. Colonel, 21 IL Infantry, Aug. 30, 1861. Shell wound right foot, Stone's River, TN, Dec. 31, 1862. Described

Above: John Washington Shields Alexander (R.P. Layton, Photographer, Rockford, IL; Roger D. Hunt Collection, USAMHI [RG98S-CWP207.4]).

Left, top: George Marcus Alden (Mansfield's City Gallery, Opp. entrance Planters' House, St. Louis, MO; USAMHI [RG98S-CWP32.5]). *Left, bottom:* George Marcus Alden, right, with his brother, Captain Andrew Jackson Alden, 13 IL Cavalry (USAMHI [RG98S-CWP191.18]).

as "the bravest of the brave" in brigade commander William P. Carlin's report of the battle of Stone's River. GSW Chickamauga, GA, Sept. 20, 1863. Battle honors: Fredericktown, Perryville, Stone's River, Tullahoma Campaign (Liberty Gap), Chickamauga.

Born: Dec. 10, 1822, Giles Co., TN
Died: Sept. 20, 1863, KIA Chickamauga, GA
Education: Graduated Wabash College, Crawfordsville, IN, 1845
Other Wars: Mexican War (2 Lieutenant, Co. H, 4 IL Infantry)
Occupation: Hardware merchant
Miscellaneous: Resided Paris, Edgar Co., IL
Buried: Edgar Cemetery, Paris, IL (Section E, Lot 700)
References: Julian K. Larke, editor. *Strong's Pictorial and Biographical Record of the Great Rebellion.* New York City, 1866. Pension File and Military Service File, National Archives. Anne Mims Wright. *A Record of the Descendants of Isaac Ross and Jean Brown.* Jackson, MS, 1911. *The War of the Rebellion: A Compilation of the Official Records of the Union and Confederate Armies.* (Vol. 20, Part 1, p. 282). Washington, D.C., 1887. *Portrait and Biographical Album of Vermilion and Edgar Counties, Illinois.* Chicago, IL, 1889.

Thomas G. Allen

Colonel, 80 IL Infantry, Aug. 25, 1862. GSW Perryville, KY, Oct. 8, 1862. Commanded 33 Brigade, 10 Division, 1 Army Corps, Army of the Ohio, Oct. 1862. Nominated Brig. Gen., USV, Jan. 19, 1863, to rank from Nov. 29, 1862. Nomination as Brig. Gen., USV, withdrawn, Feb. 12, 1863. Resigned April 21, 1863, since "my personal affairs and the professional business left unfinished, involving the interests of clients to a very considerable amount, demand my prompt attention." Battle honors: Perryville.

Born: May 22, 1827, Fallsington, Bucks Co., PA
Died: Nov. 28, 1922, Ferguson, MO
Occupation: Lawyer
Miscellaneous: Resided Philadelphia, PA, to 1857; Chester, Randolph Co., IL, 1857–68; St. Louis, MO, 1868–81; Ferguson, St. Louis Co., MO, 1881–93 and 1916–22; Haddonfield, Camden Co., NJ, 1893–95; and Apollo, Armstrong Co., PA, 1895–1916
Buried: Bellefontaine Cemetery, St. Louis, MO (Block 14, Lot 3181)
References: Pension File and Military Service File, National Archives. *Combined History of Randolph, Monroe and Perry Counties, Illinois.* Philadelphia, PA, 1883. Death Notice, *St. Louis Post-Dispatch,* Nov. 29, 1922.

Jabez Jarvis Anderson

Captain, Co. F, 18 IL Infantry, May 30, 1861. Captain, Co. C, 18 IL Infantry, May 24, 1864. Commanded Pontoniers, Department of Arkansas, Jan.–April 1865. Colonel, 18 IL Infantry, March 20, 1865. Resigned May 4, 1865, due to "expiration of the term of service for which I enlisted … it now being four years that I have served." Battle honors: Shiloh.

Born: April 9, 1822, White Co., TN
Died: April 20, 1869, Middleton, IL
Other Wars: Mexican War (2 Lieutenant, Co. A, 5 IL Infantry)
Occupation: Stock dealer and farmer
Offices/Honors: Postmaster, Hopkins Grove, Wayne Co., IL, 1858–59
Miscellaneous: Resided Middleton, Wayne Co., IL
Buried: Salem (aka Mateer-Davis) Cemetery, near Keenes, Wayne Co., IL
References: Obituary, *Wayne County Press,* April 30, 1869. Military Service File, National Archives. http://www.jackwhitesfrontporch.com/17971.html.

Amos Charles Babcock

Colonel, 103 IL Infantry, Oct. 2, 1862. Resigned Oct. 18, 1862, "domestic bereavement (the loss of a widowed mother) throwing upon him the care of a large estate of which he is the administrator."

Born: Jan. 20, 1828, Penn Yan, NY
Died: Feb. 25, 1899, Chicago, IL

Amos Charles Babcock (post-war) ("Col. Amos C. Babcock, Who Died Saturday," *Chicago Daily Tribune,* Feb. 27, 1899).

Occupation: Merchant, building contractor, land speculator, and politician
Offices/Honors: Illinois House of Representatives, 1854–56
Miscellaneous: Resided Canton, Fulton Co., IL; and Chicago, IL, after 1881. Formed the syndicate which built the Texas State Capitol.
Buried: Greenwood Cemetery, Canton, IL (Division B, Lot 575)
References: *In Memoriam: Amos C. Babcock, Born Jan. 20, 1828, Died Feb. 25, 1899.* N.p., 1899. Obituary, *Chicago Inter Ocean*, Feb. 26, 1899. Obituary, *Canton Daily Register*, Feb. 27, 1899. Obituary, *Chicago Daily Tribune*, Feb. 26, 1899. "Col. Amos C. Babcock, Who Died Saturday," *Chicago Daily Tribune*, Feb. 27, 1899. Newton Bateman, Paul Selby, and Jesse Heylin, editors. *Historical Encyclopedia of Illinois and History of Fulton County.* Chicago, IL, 1908. Military Service File, National Archives. "Resignation of Col. Babcock," *Peoria Transcript*, Oct. 20, 1862.

Andrew Jackson Babcock

Captain, Co. I, 7 IL Infantry (3 months), April 25, 1861. Lieutenant Colonel, 7 IL Infantry (3 years), July 25, 1861. Colonel, 7 IL Infantry, March 22, 1862. Commanded 3 Brigade, 2 Division, District of West Tennessee, Oct.–Nov. 1862. Resigned Feb. 28, 1863, due to "long and continued sickness of my family which demands my presence and attention." Battle honors: Fort Donelson, Corinth.
Born: July 12, 1830, Dorchester, MA
Died: Jan. 12, 1911, St. Paul, MN
Occupation: Coppersmith and plumber

Andrew Jackson Babcock (Abraham Lincoln Presidential Library & Museum).

Offices/Honors: U.S. Internal Revenue Gauger, 1878–85
Miscellaneous: Resided Springfield, Sangamon Co., IL
Buried: Oak Ridge Cemetery, Springfield, IL (Block 9, Lot 143)
References: *Portrait and Biographical Album of Sangamon County, Illinois.* Chicago, IL, 1891. Obituary, *Illinois State Journal*, Jan. 13, 1911. Stephen Babcock. *The Babcock Genealogy.* New York City, NY, 1903. Joseph Wallace. *Past and Present of the City of Springfield and Sangamon County, Illinois.* Chicago, IL, 1904. Pension File and Military Service File, National Archives. *Proceedings of the Reunion Held in 1910 by the Association of Survivors 7th Regiment Illinois Veteran Infantry Volunteers.* Springfield, IL, 1911. D. Leib Ambrose. *History of the 7th Regiment Illinois Volunteer Infantry.* Springfield, IL, 1868.

George Albert Bacon

1 Lieutenant, Adjutant, 30 IL Infantry, Aug. 28, 1861. Major, 30 IL Infantry, Nov. 25, 1861. Lieutenant Colonel, 30 IL Infantry, April 23, 1862. Resigned Oct. 8, 1862, since "in consequence of the death of my father, I am left with an important estate on my hands to settle which requires my immediate

Andrew Jackson Babcock (Armstead & White, Artists, Corinth, MS; Allen Cebula Collection).

George Albert Bacon (T.W. Bankes, Photographer, Over the Post Office, Helena, AR).

George Washington Kelly Bailey (USAMHI [RG98S-CWP16.110]).

personal attention to save me from large losses." Lieutenant Colonel, 15 IL Cavalry, Dec. 31, 1862. Colonel, 15 IL Cavalry, Jan. 24, 1863. Commanded 3 Brigade, Cavalry Division, Left Wing, 16 Army Corps, Department of the Tennessee, July 13–Aug. 20, 1863. Honorably mustered out, Aug. 25, 1864. Battle honors: Fort Donelson.

Born: March 6, 1832, Owego, NY
Died: March 6, 1905, Carlyle, IL
Occupation: Civil engineer and farmer before war. Farmer and U.S. Government clerk after war.
Offices/Honors: Postmaster, Carlyle, IL, 1866–68. Assistant Doorkeeper, U.S. House of Representatives, 1884–87.
Miscellaneous: Resided Carlyle, Clinton Co., IL; and Washington, D.C.
Buried: Carlyle City Cemetery, Carlyle, IL (Section F, Row 11, Grave 65)
References: Obituary, *Carlyle Union Banner*, March 10, 1905. Pension File and Military Service File, National Archives. Letters Received, Volunteer Service Branch, Adjutant General's Office, File I299(VS)1863, National Archives. Granville B. McDonald. *A History of the 30th Illinois Veteran Volunteer Regiment of Infantry*. Sparta, IL, 1916.

George Washington Kelly Bailey

Colonel, 99 IL Infantry, Aug. 23, 1862. GSW right leg, Vicksburg, MS, May 22, 1863. Commanded 1 Brigade, 1 Division, 13 Army Corps, Department of the Gulf, April–June 1864. Commanded Post of Donaldsonville, District of La Fourche, Defenses of New Orleans, Department of the Gulf, June 1864. Honorably mustered out, Dec. 16, 1864. Battle honors: Port Gibson, Vicksburg Campaign, Rio Grande Expedition (Fort Esperanza).

Born: Dec. 23, 1823, Pike Co., MO
Died: May 25, 1907, Eureka, KS
Occupation: Blacksmith, farmer and stock raiser
Miscellaneous: Resided Pittsfield, Pike Co., IL; Nokomis, Montgomery Co., IL; Lapland, Greenwood Co., KS, 1880–97; and Eureka, Greenwood Co., KS, after 1897
Buried: Greenwood Cemetery, Eureka, KS
References: Obituary, *Eureka Democratic Messenger*, May 30, 1907. Alfred T. Andreas. *Atlas Map of Pike County, Illinois*. Davenport, IA, 1872. Pension File and Military Service File, National Archives. Letters Received, Volunteer Service Branch, Adjutant General's Office, File B1737(VS)1863, National Archives.

Silas Delos Baldwin

Brigade Major, Cairo Expedition, April 19–May 3, 1861. Brigade Inspector, 1 Brigade, IL Volunteers, May 18, 1861. Lieutenant Colonel, 57 IL Infantry, Sept. 28, 1861. Colonel, 57 IL Infantry, Dec. 26, 1861. Commanded 3 Brigade, 2 Division, Army of West Tennessee, April 7–Oct. 3, 1862. Shell wound left hand, Corinth, MS, Oct. 3, 1862. Nominated Brig. Gen., USV, Jan. 19, 1863, to rank from

Silas Delos Baldwin (S.M. Fassett, Artist, 122 & 124 Clark Street, Chicago, IL; Ray Zielin Collection).

Nov. 29, 1862. Nomination as Brig. Gen., USV, withdrawn, Feb. 12, 1863. Dismissed March 26, 1863, upon charges of cowardice for leaving his command in the face of the enemy at Fort Donelson and also at Corinth. On May 31, 1863, President Lincoln removed the disability imposed by the dismissal, allowing Governor Yates to recommission him as colonel, June 11, 1863. Major Gen. Stephen A. Hurlbut, however, refused to permit his muster as colonel, citing the reduced strength of the regiment. Meanwhile, on June 30, 1863, Brig. Gen. Grenville M. Dodge, whom Baldwin described as "my personal enemy," appealed to Lincoln to revoke his order permitting "a man whose cowardice and incompetency is notorious throughout the command" to again enter the army. Finally, on Sept. 25, 1863 Secretary of War Stanton issued an order revoking the order of May 31, 1863, explaining that it was issued "under a misapprehension of facts." Battle honors: Fort Donelson, Shiloh, Corinth.

Born: Jan. 15, 1821, New Haven, CT

Died: June 23, 1894, Chicago, IL

Occupation: Boot and shoe merchant and hotel-keeper before war. Manufacturer and inventor of gas apparatus after war, holding various patents for improvements in gas burners.

Offices/Honors: Chicago Gas Inspector, 1879–87

Silas Delos Baldwin (U.S. Military Academy Library).

Silas Delos Baldwin (post-war) (William W. Cluett. *History of the 57th Regiment Illinois Volunteer Infantry.* Princeton, IL, 1886).

Miscellaneous: Resided Bridgeport, Fairfield Co., CT, to 1857; Milwaukee, WI, 1857–60; and Chicago, IL, after 1860

Buried: Graceland Cemetery, Chicago, IL (Section P, Lot 245)

References: Alfred T. Andreas. *History of Chicago from the Earliest Period to the Present Time.* Chicago, IL, 1885. Richard P. Dexter, "Colonel Silas D. Baldwin: Guilty or not Guilty? A Case of Command Influence?," *Journal of the Illinois State Historical Society,* Vol. 107, Nos. 3–4 (Fall/Winter 2014). William W. Cluett. *History of the 57th Regiment Illinois Volunteer Infantry.* Princeton, IL, 1886. Pension File and Military Service File, National Archives. Letters Received, Volunteer Service Branch, Adjutant General's Office, File B1489(VS)1863, National Archives. Court-martial Case Files, 1809–1894, File LL-0586, National Archives. John Y. Simon, editor. *The Papers of Ulysses S. Grant.* Volume 7: December 9, 1862–March 31, 1863. Carbondale, IL, 1979. Obituary, *Chicago Daily Tribune,* June 25, 1894. Charles C. Baldwin. *The Baldwin Genealogy from 1500 to 1881.* Cleveland, OH, 1881.

Charles Ballance

Colonel, 77 IL Infantry, Sept. 2, 1862. Honorably mustered out, Sept. 3, 1862.

Born: Nov. 10, 1800, Silver Springs, Madison Co., KY

Died: Aug. 10, 1872, Peoria, IL

Occupation: Lawyer and real estate speculator

Offices/Honors: Mayor of Peoria, IL, 1855

Miscellaneous: Resided Peoria, Peoria Co., IL

Buried: Springdale Cemetery, Peoria, IL (Vista Hill Division, Section 5, Lot 535)

References: *Portrait and Biographical Album of Peoria County, Illinois.* Chicago, IL, 1890. *The History of Peoria County, Illinois.* Chicago, IL, 1880. Alfred T. Andreas. *Atlas Map of Peoria County, Illinois.* Chicago, IL, 1873. James M. Rice. *Peoria City and County, Illinois.* Chicago, IL, 1912. *Biographical Encyclopedia of Illinois of the Nineteenth Century.* Philadelphia, PA, 1875. Obituary, *Peoria Transcript,* Aug. 12, 1872. Letters Received, Volunteer Service Branch, Adjutant General's Office, File B612(VS) 1862, National Archives. Military Service File, National Archives. William H. Bentley. *History of the 77th Illinois Volunteer Infantry.* Peoria, IL, 1883.

Moses Milton Bane

Colonel, 50 IL Infantry, Aug. 20, 1861. GSW right arm (amputated) and right side, Shiloh, TN, April 6, 1862. Commanded 3 Brigade, District of Corinth, 13 Army Corps, Army of the Tennessee, Oct. 24–Dec. 18, 1862. Commanded 3 Brigade, District of Corinth, 17 Army Corps, Army of the Tennessee, Dec. 18, 1862–Jan. 20, 1863. Commanded 3 Brigade, District of Corinth, 16 Army Corps, Army of the Tennessee, Jan. 20–March 18, 1863. Commanded 3 Brigade, 2 Division, 16 Army Corps, Army of the Tennessee, March 18–Aug. 25, 1863 and Sept. 25, 1863–Jan. 18, 1864 and March 20–June 11, 1864. Resigned June 11, 1864, due to "disability arising from wounds received in the service and chronic dysentery contracted in the line of my

Charles Ballance (post-war) (*Portrait and Biographical Album of Peoria County, Illinois.* Chicago, IL, 1890).

Moses Milton Bane (Armstead & White, Artists, Corinth, MS; Allen Cebula Collection).

Moses Milton Bane (G.W. Armstead, Artist, Corinth, MS; Ray Zielin Collection).

duty." Battle honors: Fort Donelson, Shiloh, Atlanta Campaign (Parker's Cross Roads).
Born: Nov. 30, 1827, Athens Co., OH
Died: March 29, 1897, Washington, D.C.
Education: Graduated Starling Medical College, Columbus, OH, 1848. Graduated Harvard University Law School, Cambridge, MA, 1871.
Occupation: Physician before war. Lawyer and state and federal office holder after war.
Offices/Honors: Illinois House of Representatives, 1856–60. U.S. Internal Revenue Assessor, 1866–69. Commissioner of Illinois State Penitentiary. Secretary of Utah Territory, 1876–77. Receiver of Public Moneys, U.S. General Land Office, Salt Lake City, UT, 1877–84. Chief of Contest Division, U.S. General Land Office, Washington, D.C., 1889–91.
Miscellaneous: Resided Payson, Adams Co., IL; Quincy, Adams Co., IL; Salt Lake City, UT; Spokane, Spokane Co., WA; and Washington, D.C.
Buried: Arlington National Cemetery, Arlington, VA (Section 1, Lot 181-WS)
References: David F. Wilcox, editor. *Quincy and Adams County History and Representative Men.* Chicago and New York, 1919. Obituary, *Quincy Daily Journal,* March 31, 1897. Bridget Quinlivan, "Once Upon a Time: Moses Bane: Doctor, Lawyer, Soldier.... Tax Guy?," *Quincy Herald-Whig,* Sept. 16, 2012. Patrick H. Redmond. *History of Quincy and Its Men of Mark.* Quincy, IL, 1869. Charles F. Hubert. *History of the 50th Regiment Illinois Volunteer Infantry in the War of the Union.* Kansas City, MO, 1894. James Grant Wilson. *Biographical Sketches of Illinois Officers Engaged in the War Against the Rebellion of 1861.* Chicago, IL, 1862. Pension File and Military Service File, National Archives. *Report of the Proceedings of the Society of the Army of the Tennessee at the Twenty-Ninth Meeting.* Cincinnati, OH, 1898. William H. Ward, editor. *Records of Members of the Grand Army of the Republic.* San Francisco, CA, 1886.

Myron S. Barnes

Lieutenant Colonel, 37 IL Infantry, Sept. 18, 1861. Commanded Post of Boonville, MO, Department of Missouri, Dec. 1861–Jan. 1862. Colonel, 37 IL Infantry, June 9, 1862. Charged with "Disobedience of Orders, Disrespect to Superior Officers, and Conduct prejudicial to good order and military discipline," for his overly vigorous challenge to the authority of a Missouri State Militia officer who arrested two officers from his regiment, he was dismissed Nov. 20, 1862. The disability resulting from his dismissal was removed by President Lincoln, April 18, 1864. He then helped organize the 140 IL Infantry, but did not enter service with the regiment. Battle honors: Pea Ridge.

Moses Milton Bane (2nd from left) with Officers of the 50 Illinois, including Lt. Col. Thomas W. Gaines (3rd from left) and Major William Hanna (4th from left) (Rick Brown Collection).

Myron S. Barnes (James Grant Wilson. *Biographical Sketches of Illinois Officers Engaged in the War Against the Rebellion of 1861*. Chicago, IL, 1862).

Born: March 4, 1824, Malone, NY
Died: Nov. 3, 1889, Galesburg, IL
Education: Attended Attica (NY) Academy and Alexander Seminary, NY
Other Wars: Mexican War (Private, Co. E, 2 IL Infantry)
Occupation: Newspaper editor and journalist
Miscellaneous: Resided Rock Island, Rock Island Co., IL, to 1866; Dubuque, Dubuque Co., IA, 1866–71; and Galesburg, Knox Co., IL, 1872–89
Buried: Hope Cemetery, Galesburg, IL (Lot 47)
References: *Portrait and Biographical Album of Knox County, Illinois*. Chicago, IL, 1886. Obituary, *Galesburg Republican-Register*, Nov. 9, 1889. *Portrait and Biographical Album of Rock Island County, Illinois*. Chicago, IL, 1885. James Grant Wilson. *Biographical Sketches of Illinois Officers Engaged in the War Against the Rebellion of 1861*. Chicago, IL, 1862. Pension File and Military Service File, National Archives. Letters Received, Volunteer Service Branch, Adjutant General's Office, File B131(VS)1863, National Archives. Charles C. Chapman. *History of Knox County, Illinois*. Chicago, IL, 1878. Michael A. Mullins. *The Fremont Rifles: A History of the 37th Illinois Veteran Volunteer Infantry*. Wilmington, NC, 1990. Michael E. Banasik, editor. *Duty, Honor and Country: The Civil War Experiences of Captain William P. Black, Thirty-Seventh Illinois Infantry*. Iowa City, IA, 2006. Philip J. Reyburn and Terry L. Wilson, editors. *"Jottings from Dixie": The Civil War Dispatches of Sergeant Major Stephen F. Fleharty, U.S.A.* Baton Rouge, LA, 1999.

James Allen Barret

Colonel, 10 IL Cavalry, Nov. 25, 1861. Resigned May 15, 1862, due to "bad health in connection with other good reasons that can't well be communicated in a brief note." According to Lieutenant Colonel James K. Mills, Post Commander at Springfield, MO, one of the reasons was "his displeasure at his regiment being diverted from its original destination—the Plains." Incorrectly identified by most historians as the Grand Commander of the Missouri temple of the subversive Order of American Knights, a position actually held in 1864 by his brother, Dr. Joseph A. Barret of St. Louis.
Born: March 4, 1818, Greensburg, KY
Died: Jan. 18, 1895, Warfield, KY
Other Wars: Mexican War (Captain, AQM, 4 IL Infantry)
Occupation: Farmer and land speculator before war. Farmer and coal mine and salt works operator after war.
Miscellaneous: Resided Springfield, Sangamon Co., IL, before war; and Louisa, Lawrence Co., KY; and Warfield, Martin Co., KY, after war
Buried: Warfield Cemetery, Warfield, KY
References: Martin County Historical and Genealogical Society. *Martin County, Kentucky, Veterans*. Morley, MO, 2011. Obituary, *Daily Illinois State Register*, Jan. 24, 1895. Pension File and Military Service File, National Archives. Letters Received, Volunteer Service Branch, Adjutant General's Office, File B340(VS)1862, National Archives. Curtis Mann, "Historian Tracks Fate of Faded Family That Helped Shape Area," *Historico: Sangamon County Historical Society Newsletter*, Dec. 2009–Jan. 2010. Merrow E. Sorley. *Lewis of Warner Hall: The History of a Family*. Columbia, MO, 1937. *The War of the Rebellion: A Compilation of the Official Records of the Union and Confederate Armies*. (Series 2, Vol. 7, pp. 340, 411, 417, 447, 933). Washington, D.C., 1899. Frank L. Klement. *The Copperheads in the Middle West*. Chicago, IL, 1960.

Frederick A. Bartleson

Captain, Co. B, 20 IL Infantry, June 13, 1861. Major, 20 IL Infantry, Feb. 15, 1862. GSW left arm (amputated), Shiloh, TN, April 6, 1862. Colonel, 100 IL Infantry, Aug. 30, 1862. Commanded 1 Brigade, 1 Division, 21 Army Corps, Army of the Cumberland, July 25–Aug. 3, 1863. Taken prisoner, Chickamauga, GA, Sept. 20, 1863. Confined Libby Prison, Richmond, VA. Paroled March 7, 1864. GSW right side, Kenesaw Mountain, GA, June 23, 1864. Battle honors: Shiloh, Stone's River, Chickamauga, Atlanta Campaign (Kenesaw Mountain).

Frederick A. Bartleson ("Specialite," Hoag & Quick's Art Palace, No. 100 4th Street, Opposite P.O., Cincinnati, Ohio; Steve Saathoff Collection).

Frederick A. Bartleson (Terry Orr Collection).

Born: Nov. 10, 1833, Cincinnati, OH
Died: June 23, 1864, KIA Kenesaw Mountain, GA
Education: Attended Allegheny College, Meadville, PA
Occupation: Lawyer
Offices/Honors: District Attorney, Will Co., IL, 1857–61
Miscellaneous: Resided Joliet, Will Co., IL
Buried: Oakwood Cemetery, Joliet, IL (Section 7)
References: George H. Woodruff. *Fifteen Years Ago: or The Patriotism of Will County*. Joliet, IL, 1876. James Barnet, editor. *The Martyrs and Heroes of Illinois in the Great Rebellion*. Second Edition. Chicago, IL, 1866. Margaret W. Peelle, editor. *Letters from Libby Prison*. New York City, NY, 1956. Kathy Johnson. *Colonel Frederick Bartleson*. Lockport, IL, 1983. Pension File and Military Service File, National Archives. William W. Stevens. *Past and Present of Will County, Illinois*. Chicago, IL, 1907. James Grant Wilson. *Biographical Sketches of Illinois Officers Engaged in the War Against the Rebellion of 1861*. Third Edition. Chicago, IL, 1863. http://www.colfab.org/BartlesonFrederickA.html.

Frederick Adolphus Battey

Captain, Co. F, 57 IL Infantry, Dec. 26, 1861. GSW left leg, Shiloh, TN, April 6, 1862. Taken prisoner, Dalton, GA, Oct. 13, 1864. Paroled Oct. 15, 1864. Major, 57 IL Infantry, Oct. 17, 1864. Lieutenant Colonel, 57 IL Infantry, June 6, 1865. *Colonel, 57 IL Infantry, July 1, 1865.* Honorably mustered out, July 7, 1865. Battle honors: Shiloh, Corinth, Atlanta Campaign, Savannah Campaign, Campaign of the Carolinas.
Born: Nov. 21, 1838, Foster, RI
Died: Aug. 22, 1932, Miami, FL
Other Wars: 1 Lieutenant, 40 U.S. Infantry (July 28, 1866; honorably discharged Oct. 16, 1870)
Occupation: Farmer before war. Lumber merchant, book publisher and U.S. Internal Revenue official after war.
Offices/Honors: Postmaster, Englewood, Cook Co., IL, 1892–93
Miscellaneous: Resided Wyanet and Mineral, Bureau Co., IL, before war; and Chicago, IL, and LaGrange, Cook Co., IL, after war
Buried: Mount Greenwood Cemetery, Chicago, IL (Section 14, Lot 247)
References: Herbert V. Battey, compiler. *Samson Battey of Rhode Island*. Council Bluffs, IA, 1932. Obituary, *Chicago Daily Tribune*, Aug. 23, 1932. Pension File and Military Service File, National Archives. William C. Shaw. *Illustrated Roster of the Department of Illinois Grand Army of the Republic*. Chicago, IL, 1914. Letters Received, Commission

Frederick Adolphus Battey (in Memorial Day Parade at La Grange, IL, 1919).

Branch, Adjutant General's Office, File B364(CB) 1870, National Archives. William W. Cluett. *History of the 57th Regiment Illinois Volunteer Infantry*. Princeton, IL, 1886. Guy V. Henry. *Military Record of Civilian Appointments in the United States Army*. New York City, NY, 1869. George B. Harrington. *Past and Present of Bureau County, Illinois*. Chicago, IL, 1906.

Lucius Wells Beal

1 Sergeant, Robert H. Graham's Cavalry Co., 14 MO Home Guard Infantry, Aug. 1, 1861. Taken prisoner and paroled, Lexington, MO, Sept. 20, 1861. Honorably mustered out, Oct. 16, 1861. Captain, Co. E, 126 IL Infantry, Sept. 4, 1862. Provost Marshal, Post of Devall's Bluff, AR, July–Oct. 1864. Lieutenant Colonel, 126 IL Infantry, Aug. 15, 1864. *Colonel*, 126 IL Infantry, May 11, 1865. Commanded 2 Brigade, 2 Division, 7 Army Corps, Department of Arkansas, June 18–July 12, 1865. Honorably mustered out, July 12, 1865. Battle honors: Operations on the White River, AR.

Born: Jan. 20, 1838, Rock Island Co., IL
Died: Dec. 25, 1903, Cherokee, IA
Education: Attended Lombard College, Galesburg, IL
Occupation: School teacher before war. Farmer after war.
Offices/Honors: Cherokee County (IA) Audi-

Lucius Wells Beal (post-war) (Edinger, 606 & 605 W. Walnut Street, Des Moines, IA; State Historical Society of Iowa, Des Moines).

tor, 1886–96. Iowa House of Representatives, 1898–1900.
Miscellaneous: Resided Port Byron, Rock Island Co., IL, to 1882; and Cherokee, Cherokee Co., IA, after 1882
Buried: Oak Hill Cemetery, Cherokee, IA (Block 7, Lot 3)
References: *Biographical History of Cherokee County, Iowa*. Chicago, IL, 1889. Pension File and Military Service File, National Archives. Obituary, *Cherokee Times-Herald*, Dec. 28, 1903. Letters Received, Volunteer Service Branch, Adjutant General's Office, File B2241(VS)1864, National Archives.

William H. Benneson

Colonel, 78 IL Infantry, Sept. 1, 1862. Commanded Detached Brigade, 10 Division, Army of the Ohio, Oct. 1862. Resigned Sept. 2, 1863, on account of physical disability due to "a predisposition to diarrhea, great nervous derangement, and a generally debilitated condition of the system." Brig. Gen. Charles C. Gilbert forwarded the resignation with the comment, "This officer is and always has been a detriment to the service, is always sick or in arrest." Battle honors: Morgan's Second Kentucky Raid.

Born: Dec. 31, 1818, Newark, DE
Died: Jan. 27, 1899, Quincy, IL
Education: Graduated Delaware College, Newark, DE, 1840
Occupation: Lawyer

William H. Benneson (post-war) (*Portrait and Biographical Record of Adams County, Illinois.* Chicago, IL, 1892).

Offices/Honors: Postmaster, Quincy, IL, 1867–69
Miscellaneous: Resided Quincy, Adams Co., IL
Buried: Woodland Cemetery, Quincy, IL (Block 11, Lot 92)
References: *Portrait and Biographical Record of Adams County, Illinois.* Chicago, IL, 1892. Obituary, *Quincy Daily Journal,* Jan. 28, 1899. Steve Raymond. *In the Very Thickest of the Fight: The Civil War Service of the 78th Illinois Volunteer Infantry Regiment.* Guilford, CT, 2012. Pension File and Military Service File, National Archives. William H. Collins and Cicero F. Perry. *Past and Present of the City of Quincy and Adams County, Illinois.* Chicago, IL, 1905. David F. Wilcox, editor. *Quincy and Adams County History and Representative Men.* Chicago and New York, 1919. Carter Van Vleck. *Emerging Leader: The Letters of Carter Van Vleck to His Wife, Patty, 1862–1864.* Transcribed and edited by Teresa K. Lehr and Philip L. Gerber. Bloomington, IN, 2012.

Edwin Anson Bowen

Captain, Co. B, 52 IL Infantry, Oct. 8, 1861. Major, 52 IL Infantry, May 11, 1862. Lieutenant Colonel, 52 IL Infantry, March 11, 1863. Provost Marshal, Post of LaGrange, TN, Army of the Tennessee, Sept. 18–Oct. 31, 1863. *Colonel,* 52 IL Infantry, Feb. 20, 1864. Honorably mustered out, Oct. 24, 1864. Battle honors: Shiloh, Atlanta Campaign (Atlanta), Allatoona.
Born: Nov. 11, 1831, near Fitzwilliam, NH
Died: Jan. 8, 1900, Jacksonville, FL

Edwin Anson Bowen (Ray Zielin Collection).

Education: Attended Judson College, Mount Palatine, IL
Occupation: Merchant and Colorado mine operator before war. Banker after war.
Miscellaneous: Resided LaMoille, Bureau Co., IL; and Clear Creek Co., CO, before war; and Mendota, La Salle Co., IL, after war
Buried: Greenfield Cemetery, LaMoille, IL
References: *History of La Salle County, Illinois.* Chicago, IL, 1886. *Memorials of Deceased Companions of the Commandery of the State of Illinois MOLLUS, from May 8, 1879, to July 1, 1901.* Chicago, IL, 1901. Obituary Circular, Whole No. 358, Illinois MOLLUS. Obituary, *LaMoille Gazette,* Jan. 19, 1900. Pension File and Military Service File, National Archives. Letters Received, Volunteer Service Branch, Adjutant General's Office, File B1806(VS) 1862, National Archives. *Historical Memoranda of the 52nd Regiment Illinois Infantry Volunteers, from Its Organization, Nov. 19th, 1861, to Its Muster Out, on the 6th Day of July 1865.* Elgin, IL, 1868.

James S. Boyd

2 Lieutenant, Co. D, 51 IL Infantry, Jan. 20, 1862. 1 Lieutenant, Co. D, 51 IL Infantry, July 9, 1862. Captain, Co. B, 51 IL Infantry, Oct. 1, 1862. GSW left thigh, Stone's River, TN, Dec. 31, 1862. Assistant Provost Marshal, Nashville, TN, June 1863–April 1864 and June1864–Feb. 1865. Acting ADC, Staff of Colonel Joseph Conrad, 3 Brigade, 2 Divi-

James S. Boyd (Taylor & Seavey, Photographers for the Army of the Tennessee; Dale R. Niesen Collection).

Albert Gallatin Brackett (Massachusetts MOLLUS Collection, USAMHI [Vol. 72, p. 3560L]).

Albert Gallatin Brackett (USAMHI [RG98S-CWP7.119]).

sion, 4 Army Corps, Army of the Cumberland, April 1865. Major, 51 IL Infantry, July 13, 1865. Lieutenant Colonel, 51 IL Infantry, July 31, 1865. *Colonel, 51 IL Infantry, Sept. 24, 1865.* Honorably mustered out, Sept. 25, 1865. Battle honors: Stone's River.

Born: 1835, Isle of Jersey, Great Britain
Died: Sept. 15, 1870, Eureka, KS
Occupation: Bookkeeper
Miscellaneous: Resided Chicago, IL, to Feb. 1870; and Eureka, Greenwood Co., KS, after Feb. 1870
Buried: Rosehill Cemetery, Chicago, IL (Section C, Lot 259)
References: *Society of the Army of the Cumberland. Fourth Reunion, Cleveland, OH, 1870.* Cincinnati, OH, 1870. Pension File and Military Service File, National Archives.

Albert Gallatin Brackett

Captain, 2 U.S. Cavalry, March 3, 1855. Captain, 5 U.S. Cavalry, Aug. 3, 1861. Colonel, 9 IL Cavalry, Oct. 26, 1861. GSW breast, Stewart's Plantation, Jackson Co., AR, June 27, 1862. Bvt. Major, USA, June 28, 1862, for gallant and meritorious services in the campaign in Arkansas. Major, 1 U.S. Cavalry, July 17, 1862. Chief of Cavalry, Staff of Major Gen. Samuel R. Curtis, Department of the Missouri, Nov. 1862–June 1863. ACM, Staff of Major Gen. John M. Schofield, Department of the Missouri, July–Dec. 1863. Commanded 2 Brigade, Cavalry Division, 16 Army Corps, Army of the Tennessee, Jan. 5–Feb. 7, 1864. Mustering and Disbursing Officer,

Albert Gallatin Brackett (Bradley & Rulofson, San Francisco, CA; Roger D. Hunt Collection, USAMHI [RG98S-CWP80.101]).

St. Louis, MO, Feb.–April 1864. Special Inspector of Cavalry, Army of the Cumberland, July 1864–Feb. 1865. Bvt. Lieutenant Colonel, USA, Sept. 1, 1864, for gallant and meritorious services during the Atlanta Campaign. Honorably mustered out of volunteer service, Oct. 26, 1864. Bvt. Colonel, USA, March 13, 1865, for gallant and meritorious services during the war. Battle honors: Stewart's Plantation, Atlanta Campaign.

Born: Feb. 14, 1829, Cherry Valley, NY
Died: June 25, 1896, Washington, D.C.
Education: Graduated Castleton (VT) Medical College, 1849
Other Wars: Mexican War (1 Lieutenant, Co. I, 4 IN Infantry)
Occupation: Physician before accepting Regular Army commission in 1855. Regular Army (Colonel, 3 U.S. Cavalry, March 20, 1879; retired Feb. 18, 1891).
Miscellaneous: Resided Logansport, Cass Co., IN; and Rock Island, Rock Island Co., IL, before war; and Washington, D.C., after retirement. Author of *General Lane's Brigade in Central Mexico* (1854) and *The History of the United States Cavalry* (1865).
Buried: Arlington National Cemetery, Arlington, VA (Section 2, Lot 1052)
References: Herbert I. Brackett. *Brackett Genealogy: Descendants of Anthony Brackett of Portsmouth and Captain Richard Brackett of Braintree.* Portland, ME, 1907. George F. Price. *Across the Continent with the Fifth Cavalry.* New York City, 1883. Edward A. Davenport, editor. *History of the Ninth Regiment Illinois Cavalry Volunteers.* Chicago, IL, 1888. William H. Ward, editor. *Records of Members of the Grand Army of the Republic.* San Francisco, CA, 1886. James Grant Wilson. *Biographical Sketches of Illinois Officers Engaged in the War Against the Rebellion of 1861.* Chicago, IL, 1862. Obituary, *Washington Evening Star,* June 25, 1896. *Historic Rock Island County.* Rock Island, IL, 1908. Constance Wynn Altshuler. *Cavalry Yellow & Infantry Blue: Army Officers in Arizona Between 1851 and 1886.* Tucson, AZ, 1991. James Grant Wilson and John Fiske, editors. *Appletons' Cyclopedia of American Biography.* New York City, 1888. Pension File and Military Service File, National Archives.

Daniel Bradley

1 Lieutenant, Co. A, 20 IL Infantry, June 13, 1861. 1 Lieutenant, Adjutant, 20 IL Infantry, Aug. 9, 1861. Captain, Co. A, 20 IL Infantry, Nov. 1, 1861. Acting ADC, Staff of Colonel Charles C. Marsh, 1 Brigade, 3 Division, 17 Army Corps, Army of the Tennessee, Dec. 1862–Jan. 1863. Major, 20 IL Infantry, April 3, 1863. Lieutenant Colonel, 20 IL Infantry, June 17, 1863. *Colonel,* 20 IL Infantry, Jan. 5, 1864. Acting AIG, Staff of Brig. Gen. Mortimer D. Leggett, 3 Division, 17 Army Corps, Army of the Tennessee, Aug. 1864. Honorably mustered out, Feb. 13, 1865. Battle honors: Vicksburg Campaign, Meridian Expedition, Atlanta Campaign.

Born: Oct. 1, 1835, Roxbury, MA
Died: June 3, 1878, Champaign, IL
Occupation: Merchant, lawyer, and farmer
Miscellaneous: Resided Champaign, Champaign Co., IL

Daniel Bradley (Abraham Lincoln Presidential Library & Museum).

Buried: Mount Hope Cemetery, Urbana, IL (Burt and Beardsley Addition, Block 2, Lot 9)
References: *History of Champaign County, Illinois.* Philadelphia, PA, 1878. Obituary, *Champaign County Gazette,* June 5, 1878. Robert H. Behrens. *From Salt Fork to Chickamauga: Champaign County Soldiers in the Civil War.* Urbana, IL, 1988. Pension File and Military Service File, National Archives. Obituary, *Chicago Daily Tribune,* June 4, 1878. Letters Received, Volunteer Service Branch, Adjutant General's Office, File B385(VS)1865, National Archives. George H. Woodruff. *Fifteen Years Ago: or The Patriotism of Will County.* Joliet, IL, 1876.

Hiram Warren Bristol

Captain, Co. B, 34 IL Infantry, Sept. 1, 1861. Major, 34 IL Infantry, April 8, 1862. Lieutenant Colonel, 34 IL Infantry, April 24, 1862. *Colonel,* 34 IL Infantry, Dec. 19, 1862. Resigned March 8, 1863, "on account of ill health which for the last four months has unfitted me for duty and which threatens me with confinement for months to come." His illness was described by his attending physician as "chronic diarrhea attended with ulceration of the bowels." Battle honors: Shiloh, Stone's River.
Born: Nov. 3, 1836, Ravenna, OH
Died: June 21, 1868, Sandusky, OH
Education: Attended Allegheny College, Meadville, PA
Occupation: Lawyer and merchant
Miscellaneous: Resided Ravenna, Portage Co., OH; Morrison, Whiteside Co., IL; and Fremont, Sandusky Co., OH
Buried: Oakwood Cemetery, Fremont, OH (Section 3, Lot 2)
References: William Sumner Dodge. *History of the Old Second Division, Army of the Cumberland.* Chicago, IL, 1864. Charles B. Whittlesey. *Genealogy of the Whittlesey-Whittelsey Family.* Second Edition. New York and London, 1941. Obituary, *Fremont Journal,* June 26, 1868. Pension File and Military Service File, National Archives. Edwin W. Payne. *History of the 34th Regiment of Illinois Volunteer Infantry.* Clinton, IA, 1902. Thomas M. Eddy. *The Patriotism of Illinois.* Chicago, IL, 1865.

William Robert Brown

1 Lieutenant, RQM, 29 IL Infantry, Aug. 11, 1861. Lieutenant Colonel, 56 IL Infantry, Nov. 7, 1861. Colonel, 56 IL Infantry, June 26, 1862. After receiving an adverse report from a Board of Examination, he resigned Aug. 31, 1862, "in consequence of the dangerous illness of my wife and now only remaining daughter, having to mourn the loss of four beautiful and interesting children since I have been in the service."
Born: Jan. 19, 1832, Louisville, KY

William Robert Brown (post-war) (Scholten Portraits, 1312 & 1314 Olive Street, St. Louis, MO; Abraham Lincoln Presidential Library & Museum).

Died: Jan. 20, 1905, East St. Louis, IL
Occupation: Merchant before war. Banker and insurance agent after war.
Offices/Honors: Illinois House of Representatives, 1870–72
Miscellaneous: Resided Metropolis, Massac Co., IL; Cairo, Alexander Co., IL; and East St. Louis, St. Clair Co., IL, after 1901
Buried: Masonic Cemetery, Metropolis, IL (Old Section, Lot 200)
References: *The United States Biographical Dictionary and Portrait Gallery of Eminent and Self-Made Men.* Illinois Volume. Chicago, Cincinnati, and New York, 1876. *The Biographical Review of Johnson, Massac, Pope, and Hardin Counties, Illinois.* Chicago, IL, 1893. Oliver J. Page. *History of Massac County, Illinois.* Metropolis, IL, 1900. Obituary, *St. Louis Globe-Democrat,* Jan. 21, 1905. Pension File and Military Service File, National Archives.

Thomas James Bryan

Private, Co. D, 11 IL Infantry (3 months), April 24, 1861. Honorably mustered out, July 30, 1861. Sergeant, Co. H, 74 IL Infantry, Sept. 4, 1862. Captain, Co. H, 74 IL Infantry, Sept. 8, 1862. GSW hip, Stone's River, TN, Dec. 31, 1862. Lieutenant Colonel, 74 IL Infantry, Aug. 25, 1864. *Colonel,* 74 IL Infantry, May 10, 1865. Honorably mustered out, June 10, 1865. Battle honors: Stone's River, Missionary Ridge, Atlanta Campaign.
Born: April 21, 1838, Burritt Twp., Winnebago Co., IL

Thomas James Bryan (courtesy Mike Medhurst).

Died: Jan. 14, 1924, Lemon Grove, CA
Occupation: Farmer, live stock raiser, lumber merchant, and citrus fruit grower
Miscellaneous: Resided Durand, Winnebago Co., IL; Dunlap, Harrison Co., IA, 1866–81; Miles City, Custer Co., MT, 1881–95; and Lemon Grove, San Diego Co., CA, after 1895
Buried: Mount Hope Cemetery, San Diego, CA (Division 6, Section 4, Lot 1)
References: Helen Fitzgerald Sanders. *A History of Montana.* Chicago and New York, 1913. Michael A. Leeson. *History of Montana, 1739–1885.* Chicago, IL, 1885. Obituary, *San Diego Union,* Jan. 15, 1924. Pension File and Military Service File, National Archives. *Society of the 74th Illinois Volunteer Infantry: Reunion Proceedings and History of the Regiment.* Rockford, IL, 1903.

John Bryner

Colonel, 47 IL Infantry, Sept. 4, 1861. Commanded 1 Brigade, 5 Division, Army of the Mississippi, March 4–April 24, 1862. Suffering from "attacks of diarrhea and derangement of the liver," he resigned Sept. 2, 1862, since "the Southern climate and extreme heat has debilitated me to such a degree that I have been unable to attend to the requirements of my office for forty days." 1 Lieutenant, RQM, 139 IL Infantry, May 18, 1864. Honorably

John Bryner (Richard F. Carlile Collection).

mustered out, Oct. 28, 1864. Battle honors: New Madrid, Island No. 10.
Born: Oct. 6, 1820, Juniata Co., PA
Died: March 19, 1865, Springfield, IL
Occupation: Leather goods merchant and stoneware manufacturer
Offices/Honors: Sheriff of Peoria County, IL, 1858–60
Miscellaneous: Resided Peoria, Peoria Co., IL
Buried: Springdale Cemetery, Peoria, IL (Mount Repose Division, Section 1, Lot 475)
References: *Portrait and Biographical Album of Peoria County, Illinois.* Chicago, IL, 1890. *The History of Peoria County, Illinois.* Chicago, IL, 1880. Pension File and Military Service File, National Archives. Letters Received, Volunteer Service Branch, Adjutant General's Office, File B51(VS) 1862, National Archives. Byron Cloyd Bryner. *Bugle Echoes: The Story of Illinois 47th.* Springfield, IL, 1905. Death notice, *Illinois State Journal,* March 21, 1865.

Allen Buckner

1 Lieutenant, Co. H, 25 IL Infantry, July 20, 1861. Resigned June 13, 1862, "in consequence of the affliction of my wife, owing to the death of my son by drowning." Major, 79 IL Infantry, Aug. 28, 1862. Colonel, 79 IL Infantry, Jan. 1, 1863. Commanded 2 Brigade, 2 Division, 20 Army Corps, Army of the Cumberland, Oct. 1863. GSW right side, Rocky Face Ridge, GA, May 9, 1864. Honorably mustered out, June 12, 1865. Battle honors: Pea Ridge, Stone's River, Tullahoma Campaign (Liberty Gap), Chick-

Allen Buckner (Abraham Lincoln Presidential Library & Museum).

amauga, Missionary Ridge, Atlanta Campaign (Rocky Face Ridge), Franklin, Nashville.

Born: Oct. 8, 1830, York Twp., Clark Co., IL
Died: Nov. 9, 1900, West Union, IA
Occupation: Methodist clergyman
Offices/Honors: Chaplain, Kansas State Senate, 1881–89. Superintendent, Institution for Education of the Blind, Wyandotte, KS, 1890–91.
Miscellaneous: Resided Grandview, Edgar Co., IL; Arcola, Douglas Co., IL, and Chatham, Sangamon Co., IL, to 1871. Moved to Kansas in 1871, where he served pastorates in many cities, including Eureka, Greenwood Co., KS; Emporia, Lyon Co., KS; McPherson, McPherson Co., KS; Baldwin City, Douglas Co., KS; Humboldt, Allen Co., KS; Kansas City, Wyandotte Co., KS; and Wellsville, Franklin Co., KS.
Buried: Oakwood Cemetery, Baldwin City, KS
References: *Wyandotte County and Kansas City, Kansas, Historical and Biographical.* Chicago, IL, 1890. Allen Buckner Papers (SC 1855), Abraham Lincoln Presidential Library, Springfield, IL. Obituary, *Baldwin Ledger*, Nov. 16, 1900. William Sumner Dodge. *History of the Old Second Division, Army of the Cumberland.* Chicago, IL, 1864. Pension File and Military Service File, National Archives. Letters Received, Volunteer Service Branch, Adjutant General's Office, File B2207(VS)1864, National Archives. Thomas M. Eddy. *The Patriotism of Illinois.* Chicago, IL, 1865.

Patrick Emmet Burke

1 Lieutenant, 13 U.S. Infantry, May 14, 1861. Captain, Co. K, 1 MO Infantry (3 months), May 18, 1861. Captain, Co. K, 1 MO Infantry (3 years), June 11, 1861. Unit designation changed to Battery K, 1 MO Light Artillery, Sept. 1, 1861. Captain, 14 U.S. Infantry, Oct. 24, 1861. Colonel, Western Sharpshooters, 14 MO Infantry, June 24, 1862. Commanded Post of Corinth, MS, Oct. 1862. Designation of regiment changed to 66 IL Infantry, Nov. 20, 1862. Commanded Camp Davies, District of Corinth, Nov. 1862–Oct. 1863. Commanded 2 Brigade, 2 Division, Left Wing, 16 Army Corps, Army of the Tennessee, April 22–May 16, 1864. GSW left leg (amputated), Rome Crossroads, GA, May 16, 1864. Bvt. Major, USA, May 14, 1864, for gallant and meritorious services in the battle of Resaca, GA. Battle honors: Wilson's Creek, Corinth, Atlanta Campaign (Resaca, Rome Crossroads).

Born: 1830?, County Tipperary, Ireland
Died: May 20, 1864, DOW Resaca, GA

Patrick Emmet Burke (Armstead & White, Artists, Corinth, MS; Steve Saathoff Collection).

Patrick Emmet Burke (Ray Zielin Collection).

Patrick Emmet Burke (N. Brown, Photographer, S.E. Corner Fourth & Pine Streets, Opposite Planters' House, St. Louis, MO; courtesy Steve Meadow).

Education: Graduated St. Mary's of the Barrens Seminary, Perryville, MO, 1848
Occupation: Lawyer
Offices/Honors: Missouri House of Representatives, 1856–58
Miscellaneous: Resided St. Louis, MO
Buried: Calvary Cemetery, St. Louis, MO (Section 7, Lot 80)
References: Obituary, *Daily Missouri Republican*, June 7, 1864. Pension File and Military Service File, National Archives. Letters Received, Adjutant General's Office, File B356(AGO)1861, National Archives. Lorenzo A. Barker. *Military History (Michigan Boys) Company D, 66th Illinois, Birge's Western Sharpshooters in the Civil War, 1861–1865.* Huntington, WV, 1994.

Daniel Brown Bush, Jr.

Major, 2 IL Cavalry, Dec. 10, 1861. Lieutenant Colonel, 2 IL Cavalry, Feb. 16, 1863. Chief of Cavalry, 13 Army Corps, Army of the Tennessee, July 1863. Colonel, 2 IL Cavalry, May 4, 1864. On July 30, 1864, twenty-two officers of the regiment forwarded a petition to Department Headquarters requesting that Colonel Bush be mustered out since he is "not competent from want of energy, courage, and ability requisite for a cavalry officer, that we cannot serve in the regiment under him with any certainty that the former good reputation of our

Daniel Brown Bush, Jr. (A.J. Fox, Photographer, St. Louis, MO; Abraham Lincoln Presidential Library & Museum).

regiment will be maintained." The petition further commends Lt. Col. Benjamin F. Marsh as "true and tried and one who never shrinks from danger." Influential friends in Illinois, such as Secretary of State Ozias M. Hatch, however, rushed to Bush's defense, citing Lt. Col. Marsh's "overweening ambition" and his "insubordinate attacks" on previous superior officers. Commanded 2 Brigade, Cavalry Division, District of Baton Rouge and Port Hudson, Department of the Gulf, Aug. 1864. Provost Marshal General, Staff of Brig. Gen. John W. Davidson, Cavalry Forces, Military Division of West Mississippi, Nov.–Dec. 1864. Honorably mustered out, July 24, 1865. Battle honors: Operations on the Mississippi Central Railroad (Holly Springs), Vicksburg Campaign.

Born: Nov. 4, 1827, Pittsfield, MA
Died: July 16, 1913, Portland, OR
Other Wars: Mexican War (Private, Co. A, 1 IL Infantry)
Occupation: Newspaper editor and insurance agent
Miscellaneous: Resided Pittsfield, Pike Co., IL, to 1873; San Diego, CA, 1873–78; Portland, Multnomah Co., OR, 1878–1913
Buried: Lone Fir Cemetery, Portland, OR (Block 8, Lot 204)
References: Pension File and Military Service File, National Archives. "Late Colonel Bush First Editor to Support Lincoln," *Portland Sunday Oregonian*, July 27, 1913. Obituary Circular, Whole No. 235, Oregon MOLLUS. Obituary, *Oregon Daily Journal*, July 16, 1913. Letters Received, Volunteer Service Branch, Adjutant General's Office, File B1347(VS)1863, National Archives. Samuel H. Fletcher. *The History of Company A, 2nd Illinois Cavalry*. Chicago, IL, 1912. *Proceedings of the Reunion Held in 1906 by the Association of Survivors 2nd Regiment Illinois Veteran Cavalry Volunteers at Springfield, Illinois*. Pana, IL, 1907.

Nicholas Colby Buswell

Lieutenant Colonel, 93 IL Infantry, Oct. 13, 1862. *Colonel*, 93 IL Infantry, Nov. 25, 1863. Commanded 1 Brigade, 1 Division, 15 Army Corps, Army of the Tennessee, June 15–23, 1865. Honorably mustered out, June 23, 1865. Battle honors: Vicksburg Campaign, Missionary Ridge, Dalton, Atlanta Campaign, Savannah Campaign, Campaign of the Carolinas.

Born: Dec. 5, 1831, Peacham, Caledonia Co., VT
Died: April 10, 1913, Neponset, IL
Occupation: Hotelkeeper and livery stable keeper before war. Livery stable keeper and dealer/importer of horses after war.
Offices/Honors: Sheriff of Bureau Co., IL, 1866–68

Nicholas Colby Buswell (Harvey M. Trimble. *History of the 93rd Regiment Illinois Volunteer Infantry*. Chicago, IL, 1898).

Miscellaneous: Resided Neponset, Bureau Co., IL; and Princeton, Bureau Co., IL
Buried: Floral Hill Cemetery, Neponset, IL
References: H. C. Bradsby, editor. *History of Bureau County, Illinois*. Chicago, IL, 1885. Obituary, *Bureau County Republican*, April 17, 1913. *Soldiers' and Patriots' Biographical Album*. Chicago, IL, 1892. Harvey M. Trimble, editor. *History of the 93rd Regiment Illinois Volunteer Infantry*. Chicago, IL, 1898. Military Service File, National Archives. Letters Received, Volunteer Service Branch, Adjutant General's Office, File B2172(VS)1863, National Archives.

James Edmund Callaway

Captain, Co. D, 21 IL Infantry, June 14, 1861. Major, 21 IL Infantry, Sept. 19, 1862. In temporary command of 81 IN Infantry, Chickamauga, GA, Sept. 19–20, 1863. Judge Advocate, Staff of Major Gen. James B. Steedman, District of the Etowah, Department of the Cumberland, Nov. 4, 1864–Feb. 2, 1865. Lieutenant Colonel, 21 IL Infantry, Dec. 8, 1864. *Colonel*, 21 IL Infantry, May 11, 1865. Resigned May 23, 1865, since "the war has virtually ended, ... it is my duty and my choice to immediately return to the practice of my profession and to the protection of those who are depending on me

James Edmund Callaway (J.H. Concannon, Photographer and Ambrotype Artist, Tuscola, IL).

James Edmund Callaway (J.H. Concannon, Photographer and Ambrotype Artist, Tuscola, IL; Allen Cebula Collection).

for support." Battle honors: Chickamauga, Atlanta Campaign.

Born: July 7, 1835, Trigg Co., KY
Died: Aug. 21, 1905, Virginia City, MT
Education: Attended Eureka (IL) College
Occupation: Lawyer
Offices/Honors: Illinois House of Representatives, 1868–70. Secretary of Montana Territory, 1871–77. Montana Territory House of Representatives (Speaker), 1885.
Miscellaneous: Resided Tuscola, Douglas Co., IL, to 1871; and Virginia City, Madison Co., MT, after 1871
Buried: Virginia City Cemetery, Virginia City, MT
References: Helen Fitzgerald Sanders. *A History of Montana.* Chicago and New York, 1913. *Progressive Men of the State of Montana.* Chicago, IL, 1902. Obituary, *Virginia City Madisonian,* Aug. 24, 1905. Michael A. Leeson. *History of Montana, 1739–1885.* Chicago, IL, 1885. Charles F. Ritter and Jon L. Wakelyn. *American Legislative Leaders, 1850–1910.* Westport, CT, 1989. Pension File and Military Service File, National Archives. Letters Received, Volunteer Service Branch, Adjutant General's Office, File C689(VS)1864, National Archives. Jessie W. Hart. *The Callaway Family of Virginia and Some Kentucky Descendants.* Los Angeles, CA, 1928.

Andrew K. Campbell

Captain, Co. E, Western Sharpshooters, 14 MO Infantry, Sept. 16, 1861. Designation of regiment changed to 66 IL Infantry, Nov. 20, 1862. Major, 66 IL Infantry, Jan. 21, 1863. Lieutenant Colonel, 66 IL Infantry, Jan. 11, 1864. Colonel, 66 IL Infantry, May 20, 1864. GSW through left side of neck, passing over the spine, and exiting through the right shoulder blade, Atlanta, GA, July 22, 1864. Honorably mustered out, July 7, 1865. Battle honors: Atlanta Campaign (Atlanta), Savannah Campaign, Campaign of the Carolinas.

Born: April 1827, Monroe Co., VA (now WV)
Died: May 12, 1867, Paris, IL
Other Wars: Mexican War (Private, Co. B, 12 U.S. Infantry)
Occupation: Tailor before war. Grocer after war.
Miscellaneous: Resided Paris, Edgar Co., IL
Buried: Edgar Cemetery, Paris, IL (Section L, Lot 518)

Andrew K. Campbell (Richard F. Carlile Collection).

Andrew K. Campbell (Armstead & White, Artists, Corinth, MS; Richard F. Carlile Collection).

References: Pension File and Military Service File, National Archives. Lorenzo A. Barker. *Military History (Michigan Boys) Company D, 66th Illinois, Birge's Western Sharpshooters in the Civil War, 1861–1865.* Huntington, WV, 1994.

Benjamin Franklin Campbell

Sergeant, Co. C, 7 IL Infantry (3 months), April 25, 1861. Honorably mustered out, July 25, 1861. 2 Lieutenant, Co. B, 36 IL Infantry, Sept. 3, 1861. Captain, Co. B, 36 IL Infantry, Sept. 18, 1862. Acting ADC, Staff of Major Gen. Gordon Granger, 5 Division, Army of the Mississippi, Sept. 1862. GSW right thigh and taken prisoner, Stone's River, TN, Dec. 31, 1862. Confined Libby Prison, Richmond, VA. Paroled April 12, 1863. GSW right breast and taken prisoner, Chickamauga, GA, Sept. 20, 1863. Confined Richmond, VA; Macon, GA; and Columbia, SC. Paroled Dec. 10, 1864. Lieutenant Colonel, 36 IL Infantry, Dec. 31, 1864. *Colonel,* 36 IL Infantry, May 10, 1865. Honorably mustered out, Oct. 8, 1865. Bvt. Colonel, USV, March 13, 1865, for gallant and meritorious services during the war. Battle honors: Stone's River, Chickamauga.

Born: Oct. 30, 1838, Machias, ME
Died: June 27, 1898, Sioux Falls, SD
Occupation: Hardware merchant
Offices/Honors: Register of U.S. Land Office, Vermillion and Sioux Falls, SD, 1869–81
Miscellaneous: Resided Aurora, Kane Co., IL; and Sioux Falls, Minnehaha Co., SD, after 1874
Buried: Mount Pleasant Cemetery, Sioux Falls, SD (Block 14, Lot 7)
References: Obituary, *Sioux Falls Daily Argus-Leader,* June 27, 1898. Dana R. Bailey. *History of Minnehaha County, South Dakota.* Sioux Falls, SD, 1899. Pension File and Military Service File, National Archives. Letters Received, Volunteer Service

Benjamin Franklin Campbell (D.C. Pratt, Photographic Artist, Broadway, Aurora, IL; USAMHI [RG98S-CWP85.54]).

Benjamin Franklin Campbell (seated left, on the Staff of Brig. Gen. Emerson Opdycke, with, left to right, Capt. Edward P. Bates, 125 OH; Lt. Col. John Russell, 44 IL; Lt. Col. Thomas J. Bryan, 74 IL; Opdycke; Major Wilson Burroughs, 73 IL; Lt. Col. George W. Smith, 88 IL; Surgeon William P. Peirce, 88 IL; and Major Arthur MacArthur, 24 WI) (Massachusetts MOLLUS Collection, USAMHI [Vol. 29, p. 1437]).

Branch, Adjutant General's Office, File C573(VS) 1863, National Archives. Lyman G. Bennett and William M. Haigh. *History of the 36th Regiment Illinois Volunteers During the War of the Rebellion.* Aurora, IL, 1876.

Franklin Campbell

Lieutenant Colonel, 81 IL Infantry, Aug. 26, 1862. Colonel, 81 IL Infantry, May 23, 1863. Commanded 3 Brigade, 3 Division, 17 Army Corps, Army of the Tennessee, July 20–Sept. 8, 1863. Resigned Aug. 20, 1864, due to a "double inguinal hernia of such a character as to wholly unfit him for any physical active duty." Battle honors: Raymond, Champion's Hill, Vicksburg Campaign, Brice's Cross Roads.

Born: Jan. 17, 1815, Middleburg, VT
Died: Aug. 11, 1889, Kirwin, KS
Occupation: Coal mine operator before war. Boarding house keeper and merchant after war.
Offices/Honors: Register of U.S. Land Office, Kirwin, KS, 1876–78
Miscellaneous: Resided Sparta, Randolph Co., IL; and DuQuoin, Perry Co., IL, before war; Manhattan, Riley Co., KS, 1865–71; Smith Center, Smith Co., KS, 1871–76; and Kirwin, Phillips Co., KS, 1876–89
Buried: Kirwin Cemetery, Kirwin, KS
References: Obituary, *Kirwin Chief*, Aug. 15, 1889. Pension File and Military Service File, National Archives. Edmund Newsome. *Experience in the War of the Great Rebellion, by a Soldier of the 81st Regiment Illinois Volunteer Infantry, from August 1862 to August 1865.* Second Edition. Carbondale, IL, 1880.

Thomas Sloo Casey

Colonel, 110 IL Infantry, Sept. 11, 1862. Honorably mustered out, May 8, 1863, as a supernumerary officer upon consolidation of regiment into a battalion of four companies. Battle honors: Stone's River.

Born: April 6, 1832, Mount Vernon, IL
Died: March 1, 1891, Springfield, IL
Education: Graduated McKendree College, Lebanon, IL, 1851
Occupation: Lawyer and judge
Offices/Honors: Illinois House of Representatives, 1870–72. Illinois Senate, 1872–76. Judge of Appellate Court, 1879–85.
Miscellaneous: Resided Mount Vernon, Jefferson Co., IL, to 1885; and Springfield, Sangamon Co., IL, 1885–91
Buried: Calvary Cemetery, Springfield, IL (Block 12, Lot 81)
References: John M. Palmer, editor. *The Bench and Bar of Illinois: Historical and Reminiscent.* Chicago, IL, 1899. William H. Perrin, editor. *History of Jefferson County, Illinois.* Chicago, IL, 1883. Obituary, *Illinois State Journal*, March 2, 1891. Newton

Thomas Sloo Casey (post-war) (John M. Palmer, editor. *The Bench and Bar of Illinois: Historical and Reminiscent.* Chicago, IL, 1899).

Bateman and Paul Selby, editors. *Historical Encyclopedia of Illinois and History of Sangamon County.* Chicago, IL, 1912. Joseph Guandolo, editor. *Centennial McKendree College, With St. Clair County History.* Lebanon, IL, 1928. *Biographical Encyclopedia of Illinois of the Nineteenth Century.* Philadelphia, PA, 1875. *The United States Biographical Dictionary and Portrait Gallery of Eminent and Self-Made Men.* Illinois Volume. Chicago and New York, 1883. Pension File and Military Service File, National Archives.

Thomas Horne Cavanaugh

Colonel, 6 IL Cavalry, Jan. 9, 1862. Having failed in his efforts to organize a brigade under his command, he resigned March 28, 1862, due to "business matters of vital importance, to myself and the future of my family, requiring my personal attention."

Born: Sept. 24, 1809, Hunterdon Co., NJ
Died: Feb. 10, 1892, Quincy, IL
Education: Attended Jefferson Medical College, Philadelphia, PA
Occupation: A physician by profession, he also found employment as a newspaper publisher, a steamboat captain, and a wholesale druggist in the 1840's and 1850's
Miscellaneous: Resided St. Louis, MO; Springfield, Sangamon Co., IL; Jacksonville, Morgan Co., IL; Chicago, IL; Louisville, Jefferson Co., KY; and Illinois Soldiers' and Sailors' Home, Quincy, Adams Co., IL
Buried: Sunset Cemetery, Quincy, IL (Division 13, Row 18)

References: *The United States Biographical Dictionary.* Kansas Volume. Chicago and Kansas City, 1879. Pension File and Military Service File, National Archives. Patricia B. Burnette. *James F. Jaquess; Scholar, Soldier and Private Agent for President Lincoln.* Jefferson, NC, 2013. John Y. Simon, editor. *The Papers of Ulysses S. Grant.* Volume 4: January 8–March 31, 1862. Carbondale, IL, 1972.

William Palmer Chandler

Lieutenant Colonel, 35 IL Infantry, July 3, 1861. Taken prisoner, Pea Ridge, AR, March 7, 1862. Exchanged March 21, 1862. Commanded 3 Brigade, 1 Division, 20 Army Corps, Army of the Cumberland, March 1863. *Colonel*, 35 IL Infantry, Sept. 22, 1863. Honorably mustered out, Sept. 27, 1864. Battle honors: Pea Ridge, Perryville, Stone's River, Tullahoma Campaign, Chickamauga, Missionary Ridge, Atlanta Campaign.

Born: Nov. 27, 1820, Boscawen, NH
Died: June 13, 1898, Danville, IL
Occupation: Civil engineer and coal mine operator
Offices/Honors: Illinois House of Representatives, 1870–72. Surveyor General of Idaho Territory, 1878–85
Miscellaneous: Resided Danville, Vermilion Co., IL; and Boise, Idaho Territory
Buried: Spring Hill Cemetery, Danville, IL (Block 8, Lot 87)

William Palmer Chandler (W. Boyce, Danville, IL; Abraham Lincoln Presidential Library & Museum).

References: George Chandler. *The Chandler Family. The Descendants of William and Annis Chandler Who Settled in Roxbury, Mass., 1637.* Worcester, MA, 1883. Obituary, *Danville Evening Commercial,* June 14, 1898. *Society of the Army of the Cumberland. Thirty-First Reunion, Washington, D.C., Oct. 14, 15, 16, 1903.* Cincinnati, OH, 1904. Pension File and Military Service File, National Archives. Letters Received, Volunteer Service Branch, Adjutant General's Office, File I358(VS)1863, National Archives. "William P. Chandler," *The Kimball Family News,* Vol. 1, No. 1 (January 1898). Donald G. Richter. *Vermilion County and the Civil War.... We are Coming, Father Abraham, Three Hundred Thousand More!* Danville, IL, 2011. Ebenezer Mack Treman and Murray E. Poole. *History of the Treman, Tremaine, Truman Family in America; With the Related Families of Mack, Dey, Board and Ayers.* Ithaca, NY, 1901.

John Christopher

Private, Co. F, 19 PA Infantry (3 months), April 27, 1861. Honorably discharged, July 1, 1861, to accept appointment as 1 Lieutenant, 16 U.S. Infantry (dated May 14, 1861). Assigned to duty in Sept. 1861 as Mustering and Disbursing officer at Chicago, IL, with additional duties as Acting Commissary of Subsistence at Camp Douglas Military Prison. Captain, 16 U.S. Infantry, Feb. 21, 1862. Appointed Colonel, 89 IL Infantry, Aug. 25, 1862, with permission of the War Department to join the regiment as soon as relieved from his duties in Chicago. In apparent retaliation for his wasteful handling of Government funds at Camp Douglas, as charged by William Hoffman, Commissary General of Prisoners, his muster as colonel was revoked, Jan. 7, 1863, and he was ordered to join his Regular Army command without delay. Taken prisoner, Chickamauga, GA, Sept. 19, 1863. Confined Libby Prison, Richmond, VA; Danville, VA; Macon, GA; Charleston, SC; and Columbia, SC. Paroled Dec. 17, 1864. Bvt. Major, USA, Sept. 20, 1863, for gallant and meritorious services at the battle of Chickamauga, GA. Bvt. Lieutenant Colonel, USA, March 13, 1865, for gallant and meritorious services during the war. Battle honors: Chickamauga.

Born: 1834?, Philadelphia, PA
Died: May 4, 1874, Yorkville, SC (committed suicide by gunshot)
Other Wars: Private, Co. H, 10 U.S. Infantry, 1858–60
Occupation: Accountant before war. Regular Army (Captain, 18 U.S. Infantry, April 26, 1869).
Miscellaneous: Resided Philadelphia, PA
Buried: Laurel Hill Cemetery, Philadelphia, PA (Section W, Lot 295)
References: Letters Received, Appointment, Commission, and Personal Branch, Adjutant General's Office, File 1791(ACP)1874, National Archives. Letters Received, Volunteer Service Branch, Adjutant General's Office, Files H975(VS)1862 and K376(VS)1862, National Archives. Pension File and Military Service File, National Archives. Obituary, *Philadelphia Public Ledger,* May 6, 1874. Obituary, *Philadelphia Inquirer,* May 6, 1874. Philip J. Reyburn. *Clear the Track: A History of the 89th Illinois Volunteer Infantry, The Railroad Regiment.* Bloomington, IN, 2012.

Lawrence Smith Church

Colonel, 95 IL Infantry, Sept. 4, 1862. Resigned Jan. 24, 1863, "on account of protracted illness of a permanent character and the debility occasioned thereby." A regimental surgeon described his illness as "severe neuralgia of the right side of the head and chest, chronic inflammation of the stomach..., and severe piles of a very painful character."

Born: March 8, 1820, Nunda, NY
Died: July 21, 1870, Woodstock, IL
Occupation: Lawyer
Offices/Honors: Illinois House of Representatives, 1856–62
Miscellaneous: Resided Woodstock, McHenry Co., IL
Buried: Oakland Cemetery, Woodstock, IL
References: Obituary, *Woodstock Sentinel,* July 28, 1870. *History of McHenry County, Illinois.* Chicago, IL, 1885. Newton Bateman and Paul Selby,

Lawrence Smith Church (USAMHI [RG98S-CWP151.20).

editors. *Historical Encyclopedia of Illinois.* Chicago and New York, 1900. John M. Palmer, editor. *The Bench and Bar of Illinois: Historical and Reminiscent.* Chicago, IL, 1899. Obituary, *Chicago Tribune,* July 22, 1870. Wales W. Wood. *A History of the 95th Regiment Illinois Infantry Volunteers.* Belvidere, IL, 1993. Military Service File, National Archives.

William Nichols Coler

Colonel, 25 IL Infantry, Aug. 21, 1861. Commanded 1 Brigade, 1 Division, Army of the Southwest, March 1862. Commanded 1 Brigade, 4 Division, Army of the Mississippi, June–Aug. 1862. Resigned Aug. 20, 1862, since "one misfortune, rapidly followed by others, has not only quite ruined me pecuniarily, but is in a fair way in my absence to compromise my honor and destroy my good name among my fellow men." Battle honors: Pea Ridge.

Born: March 12, 1827, Mount Vernon, OH
Died: Aug. 16, 1911, Interlaken, Switzerland
Other Wars: Mexican War (Sergeant, Co. B, 2 OH Infantry)
Occupation: Lawyer, bond broker, and banker
Offices/Honors: Illinois House of Representatives, 1862 (seat successfully contested by John S. Busey)
Miscellaneous: Resided Urbana and Champaign, Champaign Co., IL, to 1872; and Brooklyn and New York City, NY, after 1872. Author of *A Practical Treatise on the Law of Municipal Bonds* (1873).
Buried: Green-Wood Cemetery, Brooklyn, NY (Section 140, Lots 25616/25619)

William Nichols Coler (Mansfield's City Gallery, Opp. entrance Planters' House, St. Louis, MO).

William Nichols Coler (post-war) (*Sketches of Men of Mark.* New York City, NY, 1871).

References: Newton Bateman, Paul Selby, and Joseph O. Cunningham, editors. *Historical Encyclopedia of Illinois and History of Champaign County.* Chicago, IL, 1905. Milton W. Mathews and Lewis A. McLean. *Early History and Pioneers of Champaign County.* Urbana, IL, 1886. *Sketches of Men of Mark.* New York City, NY, 1871. Mrs. Sarah J. Williams. *The Coler Family History and Genealogy.* Warrensburg, MO, 1900. Obituary, *Brooklyn Daily Eagle,* Aug. 17, 1911. Robert H. Behrens. *From Salt Fork to Chickamauga: Champaign County Soldiers in the Civil War.* Urbana, IL, 1988. Military Service File, National Archives. Obituary, *New York Times,* Aug. 18, 1911.

Edward Colyer

2 Lieutenant, Co. I, 38 IL Infantry, Sept. 2, 1861. 1 Lieutenant, Co. I, 38 IL Infantry, June 27, 1863. Slightly wounded right side of head by close passage of a cannon ball, Chickamauga, GA, Sept. 20, 1863. Lieutenant Colonel, 38 IL Infantry, Jan. 30, 1865. *Colonel,* 38 IL Infantry, May 16, 1865. Commanded Post of Victoria, TX, Dec. 1865–Feb. 1866. Honorably mustered out, March 20, 1866. Battle honors: Chickamauga, Atlanta Campaign.

Born: Nov. 22, 1831, Albion, IL
Died: Nov. 6, 1913, Howard, KS
Occupation: Farmer, druggist, and miller
Miscellaneous: Resided Albion, Edwards Co., IL, to 1866; Carthage, Jasper Co., MO, 1866–69; and Union Center and Howard, Elk Co., KS, after 1869
Buried: Grace Lawn Cemetery, Howard, KS

Edward Colyer (Abraham Lincoln Presidential Library & Museum).

References: Obituary, *Howard Courant,* Nov. 13, 1913. Alfred T. Andreas. *History of the State of Kansas.* Chicago, IL, 1883. Pension File and Military Service File, National Archives.

John Montgomery Crebs

Lieutenant Colonel, 87 IL Infantry, Oct. 3, 1862. *Colonel,* 87 IL Infantry, Oct. 8, 1863. Commanded 3 Brigade, Cavalry Division, Department of the Gulf, April 8–Aug. 24, 1864. Commanded Cavalry Brigade, 19 Army Corps, Department of the Gulf, Military Division of West Mississippi, Aug. 24–Oct. 1864. Honorably mustered out, June 16, 1865. Battle honors: Jackson, Red River Campaign (Sabine Crossroads, Monett's Ferry).

Born: April 9, 1830, Middleburg, Loudoun Co., VA

Died: June 25, 1890, Carmi, IL

Occupation: Lawyer

Offices/Honors: U.S. House of Representatives, 1869–73

Miscellaneous: Resided Carmi, White Co., IL

Buried: Maple Ridge Cemetery, Carmi, IL

References: Obituary, *Carmi Courier,* June 26, 1890. *Biographical Encyclopedia of Illinois of the Nineteenth Century.* Philadelphia, PA, 1875. *History of White County, Illinois.* Chicago, IL, 1883. Harriet B. Vaught, editor. *Letters Written by Dr. Daniel Berry to Marry Berry Crebs Berry During the Civil War.* Carmi, IL, 1976. James L. Harrison, compiler. *Biographical Directory of the American Congress, 1774–1949.* Washington, D.C., 1950. Military Service File, National Archives. Thomas M. Eddy. *The Patriotism of Illinois.* Chicago, IL, 1865.

John Montgomery Crebs (post-war) (Brady-Handy Photograph Collection, Library of Congress [LC-DIG-cwpbh-00130]).

John Nelson Cromwell

Captain, Co. A, 47 IL Infantry, Aug. 16, 1861. Major, 47 IL Infantry, May 14, 1862. Taken prisoner, Iuka, MS, Sept. 19, 1862. Paroled Sept. 26, 1862. Colonel, 47 IL Infantry, Nov. 22, 1862. Returned to regiment, March 5, 1863. GSW heart, Jackson, MS, May 16, 1863, while fleeing from a squadron of Confederate cavalry which intercepted him behind the lines on a mission of mercy to regimental wounded. Battle honors: Farmington, Iuka, Jackson.

Born: March 23, 1830, Plainfield, NJ

Died: May 16, 1863, KIA Jackson, MS

Occupation: Silver plater and bell hanger, in partnership with Colonel Abraham H. Ryan (3 AR Cavalry)

Miscellaneous: Resided Peoria, Peoria Co., IL

Buried: Evergreen Cemetery, Plainfield, NJ

References: John Nelson Cromwell Papers (SC 357), Abraham Lincoln Presidential Library, Springfield, IL. Pension File and Military Service File, National Archives. "The Murder of Col. Cromwell of the 47th Illinois Vols.," *Peoria Transcript,* June 11, 1863. Byron Cloyd Bryner. *Bugle Echoes: The Story of Illinois 47th.* Springfield, IL, 1905.

John Nelson Cromwell (Cole's Photographic Gallery, 5 N. Adams Street, Peoria, IL; Roger D. Hunt Collection, USAMHI [RG98S-CWP80.28]).

William Hercules Washburn Cushman

Colonel, 53 IL Infantry, Jan. 1, 1862. "Being reduced by the fatigues and exposures of the march and camp life ... to that state that I could not, in my opinion, do justice to the Government and also to my command," he resigned Sept. 3, 1862.

Born: May 13, 1813, Freetown, MA
Died: Oct. 29, 1878, Ottawa, IL
Education: Attended Norwich (VT) Military Academy
Occupation: Merchant, banker, and capitalist
Offices/Honors: Illinois House of Representatives, 1842–46
Miscellaneous: Resided Ottawa, La Salle Co., IL; and Chicago, IL
Buried: Ottawa Avenue Cemetery, Ottawa, IL (Old Cemetery, Section 6, Lot 1)
References: *Biographical Encyclopedia of Illinois of the Nineteenth Century*. Philadelphia, PA, 1875. *History of La Salle County, Illinois*. Chicago, IL, 1886. Wayne C. Temple, "Lincoln and W. H. W. Cushman," *Lincoln Herald*, Vol. 68, No. 2 (Summer 1966). Obituary, *Ottawa Free Trader*, Nov. 2, 1878. Newton Bateman and Paul Selby, editors. *Historical Encyclopedia of Illinois*. Chicago, IL, 1900. Urias J. Hoffman. *History of La Salle County, Illinois*. Chicago, IL, 1906. James Grant Wilson. *Biographical Sketches of Illinois Officers Engaged in the War Against the Rebellion of 1861*. Chicago, IL, 1862. Henry W. Cushman. *A Historical and Biographical Genealogy of the Cushmans: The Descendants of Robert Cush-*

John Nelson Cromwell (J.B. Gardner, Photographer, 305 6th Ave., S.W. Cor. 19th Street, New York).

William Hercules Washburn Cushman (James Grant Wilson. *Biographical Sketches of Illinois Officers Engaged in the War Against the Rebellion of 1861*. Chicago, IL, 1862).

Francis Marion Davidson

Captain, Co. A, 60 IL Infantry, Feb. 17, 1862. Suffering from "an obstinate chronic diarrhea in conjunction with a naturally feeble constitution," he resigned July 3, 1862, since "my health will not permit me to do full justice to my command." Major, 14 IL Cavalry, Jan. 7, 1863. Commanded 2 Brigade, 2 Division, Cavalry Corps, Department of the Ohio, March 1864. Taken prisoner, Athens, GA, Aug. 3, 1864. Confined Macon, GA, and Charleston, SC. Paroled Sept. 28, 1864. Colonel, 14 IL Cavalry, Feb. 17, 1865. Commanded 2 Brigade, 6 Division, Cavalry Corps, Military Division of the Mississippi, June 1865. Honorably mustered out, July 31, 1865. Battle honors: East Tennessee Campaign (Dandridge), Atlanta Campaign (Stoneman's Raid).

Born: 1832, Jonesboro, IL
Died: Feb. 3, 1869, Anna, IL
Occupation: Merchant and commercial traveler
Miscellaneous: Resided Anna, Union Co., IL; and Jonesboro, Union Co., IL. Brother-in-law of Colonel Silas C. Toler (60 IL Infantry).
Buried: Jonesboro Cemetery, Jonesboro, IL
References: Darrel Dexter, compiler. *Union County, Illinois, Soldiers*. Carterville, IL, 1997. Washington L. Sanford, compiler. *History of 14th Illinois Cavalry and the Brigades to Which It Belonged*. Chicago, IL, 1898. Pension File and Military Service File, National Archives. Letters Received, Volunteer Service Branch, Adjutant General's Office, File 1611 (VS) 1862, National Archives.

Peter Davidson

Captain, Battery A, 2 IL Light Artillery, Aug. 17, 1861. Commanded Artillery Brigade, 2 Division, District of Eastern Arkansas, Department of the Missouri, Dec. 1862. Chief of Artillery, District of Eastern Arkansas, 13 Army Corps, Department of the Tennessee, Feb.–May 1863. Major, 2 IL Light Artillery, April 12, 1863. Colonel, 139 IL Infantry, June 1, 1864. Honorably mustered out, Oct. 28, 1864. Battle honors: Pea Ridge, Vicksburg Campaign.

Born: Feb. 17, 1827, Schenectady, NY
Died: March 18, 1869, Titusville, PA (killed by explosion of fulminating powder)
Occupation: Lawyer before war. Oil speculator after war.
Miscellaneous: Resided Peoria, Peoria Co., IL; and Titusville, Crawford Co., PA
Buried: Reformed Presbyterian Church Cemetery, Duanesburg, NY
References: Obituary, *Peoria Transcript*, March 23, 1869. Obituary, *Petroleum Centre Daily Record*, March 19, 1869. *The History of Peoria County, Illinois*. Chicago, IL, 1880. Military Service File, Na-

Willliam Hercules Washburn Cushman (Abraham Lincoln Presidential Library & Museum).

William Hercules Washburn Cushman (postwar) (*Biographical Encyclopedia of Illinois of the Nineteenth Century*. Philadelphia, PA, 1875).

man, the Puritan, from the Year 1617 to 1855. Boston, MA, 1855. Military Service File, National Archives.

tional Archives. Letters Received, Volunteer Service Branch, Adjutant General's Office, File K450(VS) 1863, National Archives.

Charles Wilder Davis

I Lieutenant, Adjutant, 51 IL Infantry, Oct. 15, 1861. Acting AAG, 2 Brigade, 4 Division, Army of the Mississippi, March 1862. Major, 51 IL Infantry, Oct. 1, 1862. GSW right forearm, Stone's River, TN, Dec. 31, 1862. Lieutenant Colonel, 51 IL Infantry, Oct. 7, 1863. GSW right thigh, Missionary Ridge, TN, Nov. 25, 1863. Inspector of Prisons, Department of the Missouri, Oct.–Nov. 1864. Acting Provost Marshal General, Department of the Missouri, Dec. 11–26, 1864. Assistant Provost Marshal General, Department of the Missouri, Dec. 26, 1864–June 30, 1865. Received the surrender of Brig. Gen. M. Jeff Thompson, CSA, and his Army of Northern Arkansas, May 11, 1865. *Colonel,* 51 IL Infantry, May 11, 1865. Honorably discharged on account of physical disability, June 30, 1865. Battle honors: Island No. 10, Stone's River, Chickamauga, Missionary Ridge.

Born: Oct. 11, 1833, Concord, MA
Died: Dec. 15, 1898, Chicago, IL
Occupation: Clerk and manager of book publishing house
Miscellaneous: Resided Chicago, IL; and Springfield, Sangamon Co., IL
Buried: Graceland Cemetery, Chicago, IL (Section N, Lot 168)
References: *In Memoriam, Charles Wilder Davis, Born October 11, 1833, Died December 15, 1898.* Chicago, IL, 1899. *Memorials of Deceased Companions of the Commandery of the State of Illinois MOLLUS, from May 8, 1879, to July 1, 1901.* Chicago, IL, 1901. William H. Powell, editor. *Officers of the Army and Navy (Volunteer) Who Served in the Civil War.* Philadelphia, PA, 1893. Obituary Circular, Whole No. 331, Illinois MOLLUS. Obituary, *Chicago Daily Tribune,* Dec. 16, 1898. Pension File and Military Service File, National Archives. Letters Received, Volunteer Service Branch, Adjutant General's Office, File M2834(VS)1864, National Archives. Alfred T. Andreas. *History of Chicago from the Earliest Period to the Present Time.* Chicago, IL, 1885.

Jerome Dean Davis

Corporal, Co. I, 52 IL Infantry, Oct. 25, 1861. Sergeant, Co. I, 52 IL Infantry, March 19, 1862. GSW left thigh, Shiloh, TN, April 6, 1862. 2 Lieutenant, Co. I, 52 IL Infantry, Oct. 6, 1862. Acting AIG, 1 Brigade, 2 Division, 16 Army Corps, Army of the Tennessee, June 2–Oct. 23, 1863. 1 Lieutenant, Co. I, 52 IL Infantry, Feb. 3, 1864. ACM, 2 Division, 16 Army Corps, Army of the Tennessee, June–Sept.

Charles Wilder Davis (Massachusetts MOLLUS Collection, USAMHI [Vol. 118, p. 6088]).

Jerome Dean Davis (Armstead & White, Artists, Corinth, MS; courtesy Henry Deeks).

Jerome Dean Davis (post-war) (J. Merle Davis. *Davis Soldier Missionary*. Boston, MA, 1916).

1864. ACM, 4 Division, 15 Army Corps, Army of the Tennessee, Sept.–Oct. 1864. Lieutenant Colonel, 52 IL Infantry, Dec. 17, 1864. *Colonel,* 52 IL Infantry, May 11, 1865. Honorably mustered out, July 6, 1865. Battle honors: Shiloh, Atlanta Campaign, Savannah Campaign, Campaign of the Carolinas.

Born: Jan. 17, 1838, Groton, NY

Died: Nov. 4, 1910, Oberlin, OH

Education: Attended Lawrence College, Appleton, WI. Graduated Beloit (WI) College, 1866. Graduated Chicago (IL) Theological Seminary, 1869.

Occupation: Congregational clergyman and missionary to Japan

Offices/Honors: One of the founders of Doshisha University, Kyoto, Japan

Miscellaneous: Resided Dundee, Kane Co., IL, to 1862; Beloit, Rock Co., WI, 1865–66; Chicago, IL, 1866–69; Cheyenne, Laramie Co., WY, 1869–71; Kobe, Japan, 1871–75; Kyoto, Japan, 1875–1908

Buried: Originally interred Westwood Cemetery, Oberlin, OH (Section E, Lot 136). Reinterred Kyoto, Japan, before 1953.

References: *Dictionary of American Biography.* J. Merle Davis. *Davis: Soldier, Missionary. A Biography of Rev. Jerome D. Davis.* Boston and Chicago, 1916.

Obituary Circular, Whole No. 1012, California MOLLUS. Obituary, *Oberlin News,* Nov. 9, 1910. Pension File and Military Service File, National Archives. *Historical Memoranda of the 52nd Regiment Illinois Infantry Volunteers, from Its Organization, Nov. 19th, 1861, to Its Muster Out, on the 6th Day of July, 1865.* Elgin, IL, 1868.

John A. Davis

Colonel, 46 IL Infantry, Dec. 26, 1861. GSW right breast, Shiloh, TN, April 7, 1862. Shell wound, Hatchie Bridge, TN, Oct. 5, 1862. Battle honors: Fort Donelson, Shiloh, Hatchie Bridge.

Born: Oct. 25, 1823, Meadville, PA

Died: Oct. 10, 1862, DOW Bolivar, TN

Occupation: Farmer

Offices/Honors: Illinois House of Representatives, 1856–60

Miscellaneous: Resided Davis, Stephenson Co., IL

Buried: Davis Cemetery, Davis, IL

References: Thomas B. Jones. *Complete History of the 46th Regiment Illinois Volunteer Infantry.* Freeport, IL, 1907. Amy Davis Winship. *My Life Story.* Boston, MA, 1920. James Grant Wilson. *Biographical Sketches of Illinois Officers Engaged in the War Against the Rebellion of 1861.* Chicago, IL, 1862. Newton Bateman and Paul Selby, editors. *Historical Encyclopedia of Illinois.* Chicago and New York, 1900. Pension File and Military Service File, National Archives. Obituary, *Freeport Bulletin,* Oct. 16, 1862. Thomas M. Eddy. *The Patriotism of Illinois.* Chicago, IL, 1865.

John A. Davis (Thomas B. Jones. *Complete History of the 46th Regiment Illinois Volunteer Infantry.* Freeport, IL, 1907).

Henry Hobart Dean

1 Sergeant, Co. D, 11 IL Infantry (3 months), April 30, 1861. 1 Lieutenant, Co. D, 11 IL Infantry (3 years), July 30, 1861. 1 Lieutenant, Adjutant, 11 IL Infantry, May 7, 1863. Honorably mustered out, July 31, 1864. Captain, Co. B, 146 IL Infantry, Sept. 17, 1864. Colonel, 146 IL Infantry, Sept. 20, 1864. Commanded Post of Quincy (IL), District of Illinois, Northern Department, Oct. 1864–Feb. 1865. Commanded Post of Springfield (IL), District of Illinois, Northern Department, April 1865. Honorably mustered out, July 8, 1865. Battle honors: Fort Donelson, Shiloh, Vicksburg Campaign, Meridian Expedition.

Born: May 2, 1837, Mount Morris, NY
Died: Nov. 16, 1899, Lincoln, NE
Occupation: Hardware merchant, commercial traveler, and in later years engaged in pump and water supply business
Miscellaneous: Resided Rockford, Winnebago Co., IL, to 1871; Mendota, La Salle Co., IL, 1871–73; Chicago, IL, 1873–76; St. Joseph, Buchanan Co., MO, 1876–82; and Lincoln, Lancaster Co., NE, 1882–99
Buried: Wyuka Cemetery, Lincoln, NE (Section 11, Lot 2440)

Henry Hobart Dean (Barnes, Nevius & Co., Photographers, Rockford, IL; Frank D. Korun Collection).

References: Pension File and Military Service File, National Archives. Obituary, *Nebraska State Journal*, Nov. 17, 1899. Jim Huffstodt. *Hard Dying Men: The Story of General W. H. L. Wallace, General T. E. G. Ransom, and Their "Old Eleventh" Illinois In-

Henry Hobart Dean (George W. Barnes, Photographer, Rockford, IL; Frank D. Korun Collection).

Henry Hobart Dean (George W. Barnes, Photographer, Rockford, IL; Randy Beck Collection).

fantry in the American Civil War (1861–1865). Bowie, MD, 1991.

Adolf Dengler

Captain, Co. G, 3 MO Infantry (3 months), April 28, 1861. Honorably mustered out, Sept. 4, 1861. Major, 43 IL Infantry, Oct. 14, 1861. Lieutenant Colonel, 43 IL Infantry, April 12, 1862. Commanded 1 Brigade, 1 Division, 7 Army Corps, Department of Arkansas, Feb. 18–March 22, 1865 and June 24–Aug. 22, 1865. Colonel, 43 IL Infantry, April 11, 1865. Honorably mustered out, Nov. 30, 1865. Battle honors: Shiloh, Forrest's Expedition into West Tennessee (Jackson), Vicksburg Campaign, Camden Expedition (Jenkins' Ferry).

Born: June 13, 1825, Freiburg, Baden, Germany
Died: Feb. 16, 1885, New York City, NY
Other Wars: Participated in the defense of Freiburg during the German Revolution of 1848
Occupation: Hat maker, truss maker, and municipal office clerk
Miscellaneous: Resided Belleville, St. Clair Co., IL, before war; and New York City, NY, after war
Buried: Green-Wood Cemetery, Brooklyn, NY (Section 153, Lot 20563)

Adolf Dengler (photograph by T.L. Rivers, S.E. Cor. Fourth & Chesnut Sts., St. Louis, MO; Abraham Lincoln Presidential Library & Museum).

References: Obituary, *New York Tribune,* Feb. 18, 1885. Letters Received, Volunteer Service Branch, Adjutant General's Office, File V180(VS) 1865, National Archives. Military Service File, National Archives. Obituary, *Boston Evening Transcript,* Feb. 18, 1885. Adolf E. Zucker, editor. *The Forty-Eighters: Political Refugees of the German Revolution of 1848.* New York City, NY, 1950. Wilhelm Kaufmann. *The Germans in the American Civil War.* Translated by Steven Rowan and edited by Don Heinrich Tolzmann with Werner D. Mueller and Robert E. Ward. Carlisle, PA, 1999.

Willard Arms Dickerman

1 Lieutenant, RQM, 7 Illinois Cavalry, Oct. 25, 1861. Honorably mustered out, May 26, 1862. 1 Lieutenant, RQM, 103 IL Infantry, Aug. 25, 1862. Colonel, 103 IL Infantry, Oct. 18, 1862. Commanded 1 Brigade, Detachment 15 Army Corps, Army of the Tennessee, Feb. 1864. Commanded 2 Brigade, 4 Division, 15 Army Corps, Army of the Tennessee, March 12–April 15, 1864. GSW left side of bowels, Dallas, GA, May 28, 1864. Battle honors: Vicksburg Campaign, Jackson Campaign, Chattanooga-Ringgold Campaign, Dalton, Atlanta Campaign (Resaca, Dallas).

Born: Jan. 1, 1823, Boston, MA

Adolf Dengler.

Willard Arms Dickerman (J. A. Scholten, 273 South 4th Street, Corner of Convent, St. Louis, MO; Randy Beck Collection).

Died: May 30, 1864, DOW near Dallas, GA
Occupation: Dry goods merchant
Offices/Honors: Postmaster, Liverpool, IL, 1861–62
Miscellaneous: Resided Liverpool, Fulton Co., IL
Buried: Greenwood Cemetery, Canton, IL (Division A, Lot 313)
References: Edward D. and George S. Dickerman. *Dickerman Genealogy: Descendants of Thomas Dickerman, An Early Settler of Dorchester, Massachusetts.* New Haven, CT, 1922. *Reminiscences of the Civil War from Diaries of Members of the 103rd Illinois Volunteer Infantry.* Chicago, IL, 1904. Pension File and Military Service File, National Archives. Obituary, *Fulton County Ledger,* June 7, 1864.

Theophilus Lyle Dickey

Colonel, 4 IL Cavalry, Oct. 12, 1861. Chief of Cavalry, Staff of Major Gen. Ulysses S. Grant, Department of the Tennessee, June 11, 1862–Feb. 16, 1863. Commanded Cavalry Division, 13 Army Corps, Army of the Tennessee, Nov. 26–Dec. 18, 1862. Commanded Cavalry Division, 16 Army Corps, Army of the Tennessee, Dec. 18, 1862–Feb. 16, 1863. Resigned Feb. 16, 1863, since "an experience of eighteen months in active service has taught me that I am too old a man for a cavalry officer," and

Theophilus Lyle Dickey (courtesy Steve Meadow).

Theophilus Lyle Dickey (post-war) (Brady's National Photographic Portrait Galleries, 627 Pennsylvania Avenue, Washington, DC).

also since "private business and domestic cares demand my attention." Although his resignation was accepted to date Feb. 16, 1863, he did not learn of its acceptance until he returned from a leave of absence, April 17, 1863. Battle honors: Fort Donelson, Shiloh, Corinth.

Born: Oct. 2, 1811, Paris, Bourbon Co., KY
Died: July 22, 1885, Atlantic City, NJ
Education: Attended Ohio University, Athens, OH. Graduated Miami University, Oxford, OH, 1831.
Other Wars: Mexican War (Captain, 1 IL Infantry)
Occupation: Lawyer and judge
Offices/Honors: Circuit Court Judge, 1848–52. Assistant U.S. Attorney General, 1868–69. Associate Justice, Illinois Supreme Court, 1875–85.
Miscellaneous: Resided Ottawa, La Salle Co., IL; and Chicago, IL. Father-in-law of Brig. Gen. William H. L. Wallace.
Buried: Wallace-Dickey Cemetery, near Ottawa, IL
References: *Dictionary of American Biography.* Urias J. Hoffman. *History of La Salle County, Illinois.* Chicago, IL, 1906. *Biographical Encyclopedia of Illinois of the Nineteenth Century.* Philadelphia, PA, 1875. *The United States Biographical Dictionary and Portrait Gallery of Eminent and Self-Made Men.* Illinois Volume. Chicago and New York, 1883. James Grant Wilson. *Biographical Sketches of Illinois Officers Engaged in the War Against the Rebellion of 1861.* Chicago, IL, 1862. Obituary, *Chicago Daily Tribune,* July 23, 1885. Phineas O. Avery. *History of the 4th Illinois Cavalry Regiment.* Humboldt, NE, 1903. *The Bench and Bar of Chicago: Biographical Sketches.* Chicago, IL, 1883. Letters Received, Volunteer Service Branch, Adjutant General's Office, File D91(VS)1863, National Archives. Military Service File, National Archives. John Y. Simon, editor. *The Papers of Ulysses S. Grant.* Volume 7: December 9, 1862–March 31, 1863. Carbondale, IL, 1979.

James Jackson Dollins

Captain, Co. C, 15 IL Cavalry, Aug. 27, 1861. Senior ADC, Staff of Brig. Gen. John A. Logan, 1 Brigade, 1 Division, Army of West Tennessee, April–July 1862. Colonel, 81 IL Infantry, Aug. 26, 1862. GSW head, Vicksburg, MS, May 22, 1863. Battle honors: Belmont, Fort Henry, Fort Donelson, Corinth, Port Gibson, Raymond, Vicksburg Campaign.
Born: May 9, 1832, Benton Twp., Franklin Co., IL
Died: May 22, 1863, KIA Vicksburg, MS
Occupation: Farmer
Offices/Honors: Franklin County (IL) Court Clerk, 1857–61
Miscellaneous: Resided Benton, Franklin Co., IL
Buried: Veterans Memorial (Old Benton) Cemetery, Benton, IL
References: Edmund Newsome. *Experience in the War of the Great Rebellion, by a Soldier of the 81st*

James Jackson Dollins (*Illinois at Vicksburg.* Chicago, IL, 1907).

James Jackson Dollins (Abraham Lincoln Presidential Library & Museum).

Regiment Illinois Volunteer Infantry, from August 1862 to August 1865. Second Edition. Carbondale, IL, 1880. Pension File and Military Service File, National Archives. *Illinois at Vicksburg.* Chicago, IL, 1907. Miles C. Williams. *The Descendants of Richard Dollins of Albemarle County, VA.* Logan, UT, 1973. *History of Gallatin, Saline, Hamilton, Franklin and Williamson Counties, Illinois.* Chicago, IL, 1887.

Henry Dougherty

Colonel, 22 IL Infantry, June 11, 1861. GSW, Charleston, MO, Aug. 20, 1861. GSW right arm, left shoulder, and left leg (amputated), Belmont, MO, Nov. 7, 1861. Taken prisoner, Belmont, MO, Nov. 7, 1861. Paroled Dec. 6, 1861. Commanded Post of Paducah, KY, Dec. 13, 1862–April 10, 1863. Honorably discharged May 7, 1863, "on account of wounds, having been absent from his command in the field since Nov. 7, 1861, and the regiment being without field officers." Battle honors: Charleston, Belmont.

Born: Aug. 15, 1827, Wilmington, NC
Died: April 7, 1868, Carlyle, IL
Other Wars: Mexican War (Private, Troop G, 1 U.S. Dragoons)
Occupation: Farmer and house carpenter
Miscellaneous: Resided Carlyle, Clinton Co., IL
Buried: Carlyle City Cemetery, Carlyle, IL (Section F, Row 14, Grave 98)
References: Obituary, *Carlyle Banner,* April 9, 1868. "Colonel Dougherty of the Twenty-Second Illinois Regiment," *Harper's Weekly,* Vol. 5, No. 256

Henry Dougherty ("Colonel Dougherty of the Twenty-Second Illinois Regiment," *Harper's Weekly,* Vol. 5, No. 256 [Nov. 23, 1861]).

(Nov. 23, 1861). Pension File and Military Service File, National Archives. Letters Received, Volunteer Service Branch, Adjutant General's Office, File D315(VS)1863, National Archives. James Grant Wilson. *Biographical Sketches of Illinois Officers Engaged in the War Against the Rebellion of 1861.* Chicago, IL, 1862. Nathaniel C. Hughes, Jr. *The Battle of Belmont: Grant Strikes South.* Chapel Hill, NC, 1991. John Y. Simon, editor. *The Papers of Ulysses S. Grant.* Volume 8: April 1–July 6, 1863. Carbondale, IL, 1979. Thomas M. Eddy. *The Patriotism of Illinois.* Chicago, IL, 1865.

Alexander P. Dysart

Captain, Co. C, 34 IL Infantry, Sept. 7, 1861. Major, 34 IL Infantry, April 24, 1862. Colonel, 34 IL Infantry, Apr. 12, 1863. Resigned Aug. 7, 1863, since "my wife has been in delicate health for the past eighteen months and her health has been much more reduced by sickness amongst my children, so much so as to require my immediate presence." Battle honors: Stone's River, Tullahoma Campaign.

Born: Feb. 3, 1826, Huntingdon Co., PA
Died: Feb. 21, 1895, Chicago, IL
Occupation: Farmer and municipal official
Offices/Honors: Postmaster, Nachusa, IL, 1855–61. Illinois House of Representatives, 1878–82.
Miscellaneous: Resided Nachusa, Lee Co., IL
Buried: Emmert Cemetery, Nachusa, IL
References: *Portrait and Biographical Record of Lee County, Illinois.* Chicago, IL, 1892. Obituary, *Dixon Evening Telegraph,* Feb. 21, 1895. Edwin W. Payne. *History of the 34th Regiment of Illinois Volun-*

Henry Dougherty.

Alexander P. Dysart (T.M. Schleier's Cartes de Visite Photograph Gallery, Corner Cherry and Union Streets, Nashville, TN; Steve Saathoff Collection).

teer Infantry. Clinton, IA, 1902. William Sumner Dodge. *History of the Old Second Division, Army of the Cumberland*. Chicago, IL, 1864. Pension File and Military Service File, National Archives. Thomas M. Eddy. *The Patriotism of Illinois*. Chicago, IL, 1865.

Seth Clark Earl

Captain, Co. F, 53 IL Infantry, Jan. 1, 1862. Major, 53 IL Infantry, May 23, 1862. Lieutenant Colonel, 53 IL Infantry, Nov. 11, 1862. Colonel, 53 IL Infantry, Jan. 3, 1863. GSW right thigh and head, Jackson, MS, July 12, 1863. Battle honors: Hatchie Bridge, Jackson Campaign.

Born: April 15, 1809, Nantucket, MA
Died: July 12, 1863, KIA Jackson, MS
Occupation: Merchant dealing in paints and paper
Miscellaneous: Resided Ottawa, La Salle Co., IL
Buried: Vicksburg National Cemetery, Vicksburg, MS (Section O, Grave 4291). Cenotaph Yantic Cemetery, Norwich, CT (Section 124, Lot 44).
References: *History of La Salle County, Illinois*. Chicago, IL, 1886. Pension File and Military Service File, National Archives. Elijah B. Huntington. *A Genealogical Memoir of the Lo-Lathrop Family in This Country*. Ridgefield, CT, 1884.

Seth Clark Earl (S. Alschuler, Photographer, Ottawa, IL; Steve Saathoff Collection).

Peter Ege

1 Lieutenant, Co. A, 34 IL Infantry, Aug. 25, 1861. Captain, Co. A, 34 IL Infantry, Dec. 7, 1862. GSW abdomen, Rome, GA, May 17, 1864. Major,

Peter Ege (Wisconsin Historical Society, WHi-119514).

Peter Ege (William W. Davis. *History of Whiteside County, Illinois, From Its Earliest Settlement to 1908.* Chicago, IL, 1908).

34 IL Infantry, Sept. 13, 1864. Lieutenant Colonel, 34 IL Infantry, Nov. 7, 1864. GSW right hand, Savannah, GA, Dec. 13, 1864. Colonel, 34 IL Infantry, June 7, 1865. Commanded 2 Brigade, 2 Division, 14 Army Corps, Army of the Cumberland, June 20–July 12, 1865. Honorably mustered out, July 12, 1865. Battle honors: Atlanta Campaign (Rome, Kenesaw Mountain), Savannah Campaign, Campaign of the Carolinas.
Born: Nov. 10, 1835, Pine Grove, Cumberland Co., PA
Died: March 11, 1920, Albany, IL
Occupation: Civil engineer before war. Lawyer and lumber merchant after war.
Miscellaneous: Resided Albany, Whiteside Co., IL. Brother of Lt. Col. Joseph A. Ege (187 PA Infantry).
Buried: Oakridge-Lusk Memorial Cemetery, Albany, IL
References: William W. Davis. *History of Whiteside County, Illinois, from Its Earliest Settlement to 1908.* Chicago, IL, 1908. Obituary, *Albany Review,* March 19, 1920. Pension File and Military Service File, National Archives. Thompson P. Ege. *History and Genealogy of the Ege Family in the United States, 1738–1911.* Harrisburg, PA, 1911. Edwin W. Payne. *History of the 34th Regiment of Illinois Volunteer Infantry.* Clinton, IA, 1902.

George Harrison English

Captain, Co. D, 32 IL Infantry, Sept. 6, 1861. GSW forehead, Shiloh, TN, April 6, 1862. Major,

George Harrison English (post-war) (*The Illinois College Alumni Fund Association: Book of Memorial Memberships.* **Centennial Edition, 1829–1929.** Jacksonville, IL, 1929).

32 IL Infantry, April 12, 1862. Lieutenant Colonel, 32 IL Infantry, Aug. 15, 1863. Provost Marshal, Post of Natchez (MS), Oct. 1863–Jan. 1864. *Colonel,* 32 IL Infantry, Dec. 30, 1864. Honorably mustered out, Sept. 16, 1865. Battle honors: Shiloh, Hatchie Bridge, Meridian Expedition, Atlanta Campaign.
Born: Jan. 21, 1836, near Newark, OH
Died: April 11, 1919, Kansas City, MO
Education: Graduated Illinois College, Jacksonville, IL, 1857
Occupation: Lawyer
Miscellaneous: Resided Greenfield, Greene Co., IL, to 1866; Leavenworth, Leavenworth Co., KS, 1866–74; Wichita, Sedgwick Co., KS, 1874–78; and Kansas City, MO, after 1878
Buried: Elmwood Cemetery, Kansas City, MO (Block C, Lot 115)
References: *The United States Biographical Dictionary and Portrait Gallery of Eminent and Self-Made Men.* Missouri Volume. New York, Chicago, St. Louis, and Kansas City, 1878. Pension File and Military Service File, National Archives. Letters Received, Volunteer Service Branch, Adjutant General's Office, File E371(VS)1865, National Archives. *Catalogue of Phi Alpha Society, Illinois College, 1845–*

1890. Jacksonville, IL, 1890. *The Illinois College Alumni Fund Association: Book of Memorial Memberships.* Centennial Edition, 1829–1929. Jacksonville, IL, 1929. George Creel and John Slavens, compilers. *Men Who Are Making Kansas City: A Biographical Directory.* Kansas City, MO, 1902.

George W. Evans

Captain, Co. E, 60 IL Infantry, Feb. 17, 1862. Major, 60 IL Infantry, March 8, 1863. Lieutenant Colonel, 60 IL Infantry, May 22, 1863. *Colonel,* 60 IL Infantry, May 11, 1865. Commanded 1 Brigade, 2 Division, 14 Army Corps, Army of the Cumberland, June 1865. Honorably mustered out, July 31, 1865. Battle honors: Dalton, Savannah Campaign, Campaign of the Carolinas (Bentonville).
Born: Dec. 20, 1832, Preston Co., WV
Died: Nov. 14, 1900, Mount Vernon, IL
Occupation: Farmer and banker
Miscellaneous: Resided Mount Vernon, Jefferson Co., IL. Brother-in-law of Bvt. Brig. Gen. William B. Anderson.

George W. Evans (T.M. Schleier, Artist, Nashville, TN; Roger D. Hunt Collection, USAMHI [RG98S-CWP160.19]).

Buried: Oakwood Cemetery, Mount Vernon, IL (Lot 115)
References: William H. Perrin, editor. *History of Jefferson County, Illinois.* Chicago, IL, 1883. Obituary, *Wayne County Press,* Nov. 22, 1900. Obituary, *Sumner (IL) Press,* Nov. 22, 1900. Military Service File, National Archives.

Allen Lewis Fahnestock

Captain, Co. I, 86 IL Infantry, Aug. 27, 1862. Major, 86 IL Infantry, Oct. 13, 1863. Lieutenant Colonel, 86 IL Infantry, March 26, 1864. *Colonel,* 86 IL Infantry, May 10, 1865. Honorably mustered out, June 6, 1865. Battle honors: Chickamauga, Dalton, Atlanta Campaign (Resaca, Kenesaw Mountain, Peach Tree Creek), Savannah Campaign, Campaign of the Carolinas (Bentonville).
Born: Feb. 9, 1828, Abbottstown, PA
Died: June 12, 1920, Glasford, IL
Occupation: Barrel manufacturer before war. Merchant (groceries, dry goods, and general merchandise) after war.
Offices/Honors: Peoria County Treasurer, 1865–67. Postmaster, Glasford, IL, 1869–74.
Miscellaneous: Resided Lancaster, Peoria Co., IL; and Glasford, Peoria Co., IL

George W. Evans (T.M. Schleier's Cartes de Visite Photograph Gallery, Corner Square & Deaderick Street, Nashville, TN; courtesy Henry Deeks).

Allen Lewis Fahnestock (Metropolitan Photograph Gallery, 53 College Street, Nashville, TN, J.H. Van Stavoren, Proprietor; Richard F. Carlile Collection).

Buried: Lancaster Cemetery, Glasford, IL
References: H. Minot Pitman. *Fahnestock Genealogy: Descendants of Johann Diedrich Fahnestock.* Concord, NH, 1945. Obituary, *Peoria Journal-Transcript,* June 13, 1920. Newton Bateman, Paul Selby, and David McCulloch, editors. *Historical Encyclopedia of Illinois and History of Peoria County.* Chicago and Peoria, IL, 1902. James M. Rice. *Peoria City and County, Illinois.* Chicago, IL, 1912. John R. Kinnear. *History of the 86th Regiment Illinois Volunteer Infantry, During Its Term of Service.* Chicago, IL, 1866. George W. Warvelle, editor. *A Compendium of Freemasonry in Illinois.* Chicago, IL, 1897. Military Service File, National Archives.

Charles M. Ferrell

Captain, Co. A, 29 IL Infantry, Aug. 19, 1861. Lieutenant Colonel, 29 IL Infantry, March 15, 1862. Colonel, 29 IL Infantry, Sept. 24, 1862. Taken prisoner and paroled, Holly Springs, MS, Dec. 20, 1862. Resigned Aug. 11, 1863, since "my wife … has been for several years past an invalid and her health long impaired is now such as to cause just fears on my part that she cannot long survive." Battle honors: Shiloh, Operations on the Mississippi Central Railroad (Holly Springs).
Born: Nov. 30, 1819, Marshall Co., TN
Died: July 9, 1901, Madison, WI
Occupation: Wharf master before war. Merchant and produce dealer after war.
Offices/Honors: Postmaster, Elizabethtown, IL, 1865–71. Illinois Senate, 1872–74.
Miscellaneous: Resided Elizabethtown, Hardin Co., IL, to 1890; and Evansville, Vanderburgh Co., IN, and Madison, Dane Co., WI, in later years
Buried: Price Cemetery, Elizabethtown, IL
References: Ed Ferrell. *Biographies and Genealogical Abstracts from Hardin County, Illinois, Newspapers, 1872–1938.* Bowie, MD, 1999. Obituary, *Wisconsin State Journal,* July 9, 1901. Pension File and Military Service File, National Archives.

Spencer Beebe Floyd

Major, 120 IL Infantry, Oct. 29, 1862. Lieutenant Colonel, 120 IL Infantry, April 29, 1864. *Colonel,* 120 IL Infantry, June 12, 1864. Commission as colonel canceled. Honorably mustered out, Sept. 10, 1865. Battle honors: Brice's Cross Roads.
Born: May 18, 1815, Bedford Co., TN
Died: Aug. 15, 1881, Blue Hill, Mitchell Co., KS
Occupation: Farmer

Left: **Allen Lewis Fahnestock (J. Thurlow, Photographer, Next Door to Second National Bank, Cor. Main & Washington Streets, Peoria, IL; Abraham Lincoln Presidential Library & Museum).**

Spencer Beebe Floyd (J.H. Jennings, Eldorado, IL; courtesy Elizabeth Martin).

Offices/Honors: Sheriff of Pope Co., IL, 1860–61 and 1869–71. Probate Judge, Mitchell Co., KS, 1872–76.

Miscellaneous: Resided Golconda, Pope Co., IL, to 1871; and Beloit, Mitchell Co., KS, after 1871

Buried: Rose Valley Cemetery, Hayes Twp., Mitchell Co., KS

References: Obituary, *Beloit Courier*, Aug. 25, 1881. Pension File and Military Service File, National Archives.

Caswell Pierce Ford

1 Lieutenant, RQM, 25 IL Infantry, Aug. 7, 1861. Acting ADC, Staff of Colonel William E. Woodruff, 3 Brigade, 1 Division, Right Wing, 14 Army Corps, Army of the Cumberland, Dec. 1862. Colonel, 25 IL Infantry, Jan. 7, 1863. Anticipating a summons to appear before a Board of Examination, he resigned April 14, 1863, "having been recently promoted to the position of Colonel ... over Lt. Col. J. S. McClelland and Major R. H. Nodine ..., who are disposed to question my right of promotion as well as my ability to perform the duties of my present position and who use their every effort to render my position as disagreeable as may be ... and having no desire for self-aggrandizement." Battle honors: Stone's River.

Born: March 3, 1827, Fayette Co., KY
Died: Dec. 29, 1911, Oswego, KS
Occupation: Saddler and harness maker before war. Coal merchant and railroad construction engineer after war.

Caswell Pierce Ford (post-war) (*History of DeWitt County, Illinois*. Philadelphia, PA, 1882).

Offices/Honors: Doorkeeper, Illinois House of Representatives, 1860–62. Postmaster, Clinton, IL, 1867–71.

Miscellaneous: Resided Clinton, DeWitt Co., IL, to 1884; Pittsburg, Crawford Co., KS, 1884–1907; Oswego, Labette Co., KS, 1907–11

Buried: Oswego Cemetery, Oswego, KS (Block 6, Lot 99)

References: *History of DeWitt County, Illinois*. Philadelphia, PA, 1882. Obituary, *Oswego Independent*, Jan. 5, 1912. Pension File and Military Service File, National Archives. Robert H. Behrens. *From Salt Fork to Chickamauga: Champaign County Soldiers in the Civil War*. Urbana, IL, 1988.

Philip Bond Fouke

Colonel, 30 IL Infantry, Aug. 28, 1861. Commanded Post of Fort Donelson, TN, March–April 1862. Resigned April 22, 1862, since "justice requires that I should hold my seat as a member of Congress." Battle honors: Belmont, Fort Donelson.

Born: Jan. 23, 1819, Kaskaskia, IL
Died: Oct. 3, 1876, Washington, D.C.
Occupation: Lawyer
Offices/Honors: Illinois House of Representatives, 1851–52. U.S. House of Representatives, 1859–63.

Miscellaneous: Resided Belleville, St. Clair Co., IL; New Orleans, LA; and Washington, D.C.

Buried: Congressional Cemetery, Washington, D.C. (Range 75, Site 350)

References: Newton Bateman, Paul Selby, A.S. Wilderman, and A.A. Wilderman, editors. *Historical*

Philip Bond Fouke (U.S. House of Representatives) (Frederick Hill Meserve. Historical Portraits, A Part of the Collection of Americana of Frederick Hill Meserve, New York City, 1913–1915; courtesy New York State Library).

Philip Bond Fouke (Massachusetts MOLLUS Collection, USAMHI [Vol. 72, p. 3580]).

Encyclopedia of Illinois and History of St. Clair County. Chicago, IL, 1907. James L. Harrison, compiler. *Biographical Directory of the American Congress, 1774–1949.* Washington, DC, 1950. Pension File and Military Service File, National Archives. Obituary, *Washington National Republican*, Oct. 4, 1876. Nathaniel C. Hughes, Jr. *The Battle of Belmont: Grant Strikes South.* Chapel Hill, NC, 1991. Granville B. McDonald. *A History of the 30th Illinois Veteran Volunteer Regiment of Infantry.* Sparta, IL, 1916.

Charles H. Fox

Colonel, 101 IL Infantry, Aug. 22, 1862. Taken prisoner and paroled, Holly Springs, MS, Dec. 20, 1862. Commanded 1 Brigade, 6 Division, 16 Army Corps, Army of the Tennessee, Aug. 22–Sept. 3, 1863. Commanded 1 Brigade, 3 Division, 11 Army Corps, Army of the Cumberland, Feb. 15–March 13, 1864. Awaiting trial on charges of conduct prejudicial to good order and military discipline preferred by Lieutenant Colonel John B. Le Sage (101 IL Infantry), he resigned May 1, 1864, citing "physical debility" due to chronic inflammation of the kidneys. Battle honors: Operations on the Mississippi Central Railroad (Holly Springs), Chattanooga-Ringgold Campaign.

Born: May 22, 1823, Providence, RI
Died: Aug. 3, 1886, Minneapolis, MN
Occupation: Lawyer
Miscellaneous: Resided Jacksonville, Morgan Co., IL; and New Orleans, LA, 1864–70

Charles H. Fox (post-war) (Abraham Lincoln Presidential Library & Museum).

Buried: Diamond Grove Cemetery, Jacksonville, IL (Section D, Lot 172)

References: Obituary, *Jacksonville Daily Courier*, Aug. 5, 1886. Pension File and Military Service File, National Archives. Letters Received, Volunteer Service Branch, Adjutant General's Office, File F533(VS)1864, National Archives. *History of Morgan County, Illinois: Its Past and Present*. Chicago, IL, 1878.

Jacob Fry

Lieutenant Colonel, 61 IL Infantry, Feb. 5, 1862. Colonel, 61 IL Infantry, March 26, 1862. Commanded 4 Brigade, 2 Division, District of Jackson, Department of the Tennessee, Aug.–Oct. 1862. Commanded Post of Trenton, TN, Nov.–Dec. 1862. Taken prisoner and paroled, Trenton, TN, Dec. 20, 1862. Resigned May 14, 1863, due to "cataract of the right eye, palsy of the nerves of sensation of the left leg, and a general lack of physical energy arising from advanced age." Battle honors: Shiloh, Forrest's Expedition into West Tennessee (Trenton).

Born: Sept. 20, 1799, Fayette Co., KY

Died: Jan. 27, 1881, Kane, IL

Other Wars: Black Hawk War (Colonel, 2 Regiment, 3 Brigade, Illinois Mounted Militia)

Occupation: Merchant and farmer

Offices/Honors: Sheriff, Greene Co., IL, 1828–38. California Senate, 1852. U.S. Collector of Customs, Chicago, IL, 1857–58.

Miscellaneous: Resided Kane, Greene Co., IL; Ottawa, La Salle Co., IL; and Placer Co., CA, 1850–53. Father of Brig. Gen. James B. Fry.

Buried: Oak Ridge Cemetery, Springfield, IL (Block 7, Lot 36)

References: *The United States Biographical Dictionary and Portrait Gallery of Eminent and Self-Made Men*. Illinois Volume. Chicago, Cincinnati, and New York, 1876. *History of Greene and Jersey Counties, Illinois*. Springfield, IL, 1885. Edward Miner. *Past and Present of Greene County, Illinois*. Chicago, IL, 1905. Obituary, *Illinois State Journal*, Jan. 29, 1881. Newton Bateman and Paul Selby, editors. *Historical Encyclopedia of Illinois and History of Sangamon County*. Chicago, IL, 1912. Pension File and Military Service File, National Archives. Drew D. Dukett. *Glimpses of Glory: The Regimental History of the 61st Illinois Volunteers*. Bowie, MD, 1999. Letters Received, Volunteer Service Branch, Adjutant General's Office, File F37(VS)1863, National Archives. Leander Stillwell. *The Story of a Common Soldier of Army Life in the Civil War, 1861–1865*. Second Edition. Erie, KS, 1920.

John Jackson Funkhouser

Captain, Co. A, 26 IL Infantry, Aug. 2, 1861. Resigned Nov. 24, 1861, since "my father has recently died and by his death a large unsettled estate has fallen upon my hands and will of necessity require

Jacob Fry (Library of Congress [LC-DIG-cwpb-04710]).

John Jackson Funkhouser (post-war) (Lawson S. Kilborn. *Dedication of the Wilder Brigade Monument on Chickamauga Battlefield*. Marshall, IL, 1900).

my special supervision." Colonel, 98 IL Infantry, Sept. 3, 1862. GSW left thigh, Chickamauga, GA, Sept. 20, 1863. Commanded Post of Columbia, TN, District of Nashville, Department of the Cumberland, April–June 1864. Resigned July 5, 1864, since "I have been physically unable to perform active duty in the saddle, and I am led to believe the disability will become permanent." Battle honors: Stone's River, Tullahoma Campaign (Hoover's Gap), Chickamauga.

Born: March 18, 1835, Summit Twp., Effingham Co., IL

Died: Oct. 13, 1894, East Chicago, IN

Occupation: Livestock farmer and merchant before war. Merchant and railroad land agent after war.

Offices/Honors: Postmaster, Effingham, IL, 1859–60

Miscellaneous: Resided Effingham, Effingham Co., IL; Ottumwa, Wapello Co., IA; Indianapolis, IN; and East Chicago, Lake Co., IN, 1887–94

Buried: Oakridge Cemetery, Effingham, IL (Old Section, Lot 38)

References: Hilda Engbring Feldhake, editor. *Effingham County Illinois—Past and Present.* Effingham, IL, 1968. William H. Perrin, editor. *History of Effingham County, Illinois.* Chicago, IL, 1883. Obituary, *Effingham Democrat,* Oct. 19, 1894. Pension File and Military Service File, National Archives. Lawson S. Kilborn. *Dedication of the Wilder Brigade Monument on Chickamauga Battlefield.* Marshall, IL, 1900. Richard A. Baumgartner. *Blue Lightning: Wilder's Mounted Infantry Brigade in the Battle of Chickamauga.* Huntington, WV, 1997. Glenn W. Sunderland. *Lightning at Hoover's Gap: Wilder's Brigade in the Civil War.* New York City, 1969.

Ashley T. Galbraith

Captain, Co. I, 48 IL Infantry, Sept. 15, 1861. Major, 48 IL Infantry, Oct. 1, 1863. Lieutenant Colonel, 48 IL Infantry, Feb. 26, 1864. GSW right ankle, Chattahoochee River, GA, July 10, 1864. Colonel, 48 IL Infantry, July 22, 1864. Honorably discharged, Jan. 25, 1865, on account of physical disability. Battle honors: Jackson Campaign, Atlanta Campaign (Chattahoochee River).

Born: 1828?, IL

Died: Jan. 14, 1899, Flora, IL

Occupation: Farmer and railway mail agent

Offices/Honors: Illinois House of Representatives, 1870–72. Postmaster, Flora, IL, 1884–89.

Miscellaneous: Resided Johnsonville, Wayne Co., IL; and Flora, Clay Co., IL, 1880–99

Buried: Johnsonville Cemetery, Johnsonville, IL (West Side, Row 1, grave markers for wife and children only)

References: Pension File and Military Service File, National Archives. Obituary, *Wayne County*

Ashley T. Galbraith (courtesy Everitt Bowles).

Press, Jan. 19, 1899. Letters Received, Volunteer Service Branch, Adjutant General's Office, File G80(VS)1865, National Archives. *History of Wayne and Clay Counties, Illinois.* Chicago, IL, 1884.

Othniel Gilbert

Private, Co. C, 12 IL Infantry (3 months), May 2, 1861. Honorably mustered out, Aug. 1, 1861. Colonel, 71 IL Infantry, July 26, 1862. Honorably mustered out, Oct. 29, 1862.

Born: Aug. 29, 1813, Rushville, NY

Died: Feb. 24, 1872, Danville, IL

Other Wars: Black Hawk War (Private, Captain Bailey's Co., Colonel Moore's Regiment, Mounted Volunteers, Illinois Militia)

Occupation: Reformer (1850 U.S. Census)

Offices/Honors: Postmaster, Danville, IL, 1849–50

Miscellaneous: Resided Danville, Vermilion Co., IL

Buried: Spring Hill Cemetery, Danville, IL (Block 8, Lot 58, unmarked)

References: Obituary, *Danville Times,* March 2, 1872. Donald G. Richter. *Vermilion County and the Civil War.... We are Coming, Father Abraham, Three Hundred Thousand More!* Danville, IL, 2011. Hiram W. Beckwith. *History of Vermilion County, Together With Historic Notes on the Northwest.* Chicago, IL, 1879. Military Service File, National Archives.

Donna P. Phillips. *Gilbert Gallery: Family Quest.* Vol. 1 (Jan. 1986). Spokane, WA, 1986.

Robert Addison Gillmore

Major, 26 IL Infantry, Aug. 29, 1861. Lieutenant Colonel, 26 IL Infantry, Oct. 8, 1862. GSW left thigh, Missionary Ridge, TN, Nov. 25, 1863. *Colonel,* 26 IL Infantry, April 30, 1864. Honorably mustered out, Oct. 27, 1864. Battle honors: Farmington, Iuka, Corinth, Jackson Campaign, Missionary Ridge, Atlanta Campaign (Atlanta, Ezra Church).
Born: April 18, 1833, New Hartford, NY
Died: Aug. 9, 1867, Chicago, IL (drowned in Lake Michigan)
Occupation: Railway ticket agent
Offices/Honors: Postmaster, Chicago, IL, 1866–67
Miscellaneous: Resided Chicago, IL
Buried: Oakwoods Cemetery, Chicago, IL (Section C, Division 1, Lot 14)
References: Charles Ulysses Gordon. *Chicago Postmasters from Jonathan Nash Bailey to Ernest J. Kruetgen, 1831 to 1945.* Chicago, IL, 1953. Thomas M. Eddy. *The Patriotism of Illinois.* Chicago, IL, 1865. Obituary, *Chicago Tribune,* Aug. 11, 1867. Pension File and Military Service File, National Archives. Letters Received, Volunteer Service Branch, Adjutant General's Office, File W141(VS) 1864, National Archives. "Portraits of Chicago's Postmasters in a Giant Frame," *Chicago Sunday Times-Herald,* July 30, 1899.

Daniel Harvie Gilmer

Captain, Co. H, 10 IL Infantry (3 months), April 29, 1861. Honorably mustered out, July 29, 1861.

Major, 38 IL Infantry, Aug. 15, 1861. Lieutenant Colonel, 38 IL Infantry, Oct. 25, 1862. Colonel, 38 IL Infantry, March 11, 1863. GSW lower abdomen, Chickamauga, GA, Sept. 20, 1863. Battle honors: Fredericktown, Perryville, Stone's River, Tullahoma Campaign (Liberty Gap), Chickamauga.
Born: Sept. 10, 1814, Christian Co., KY
Died: Sept. 20, 1863, KIA Chickamauga, GA
Occupation: Lawyer
Miscellaneous: Resided Pittsfield, Pike Co., IL
Buried: Oakwood Cemetery, Pittsfield, IL
References: *History of Pike County, Illinois.* Chicago, IL, 1880. John G. Speed. *The Gilmers in America.* New York City, NY, 1897. LeRoy H. Fischer, "Lincoln's 1858 Visit to Pittsfield, Illinois," *Journal of the Illinois State Historical Society,* Vol. 61, No. 3 (Autumn 1968). Pension File and Military Service File, National Archives.

John W. Goodwin

1 Lieutenant, Co. B, 20 IL Infantry, April 22, 1861. Major, 20 IL Infantry, June 13, 1861. Having expressed dissatisfaction with "the government of the Regt (20th Ills. Vol. Colonel C. C. Marsh)," he resigned Dec. 17, 1861, anticipating "an appointment in the Second Regt. Ill. Artillery," which he failed to receive. Colonel, 138 IL Infantry, June 21, 1864. Commanded Post of Fort Leavenworth, Department of Kansas, July–Sept. 1864. Honorably mustered out, Oct. 14, 1864. Battle honors: Fredericktown.
Born: Sept. 3, 1829, Morristown, St. Lawrence Co., NY
Died: Nov. 14, 1888, Santa Paula, CA
Other Wars: Mexican War (Private, Co. M, 2 U.S. Artillery)
Occupation: Lawyer and merchant
Offices/Honors: Postmaster, Ventura, CA, 1870–80
Miscellaneous: Resided Joliet, Will Co., IL, before war; and Ventura, Ventura Co., CA, after war
Buried: Santa Paula Cemetery, Santa Paula, CA (Block 23, Plot 3, Lot 1, unmarked)
References: Obituary, *Ventura Daily Free Press,* Nov. 15, 1888. George H. Woodruff. *Fifteen Years Ago: or The Patriotism of Will County.* Joliet, IL, 1876. Military Service File, National Archives. "Regimental Election," *Joliet Signal,* May 21, 1861. "An Item That Will Interest the Old Members of Twentieth Illinois Regiment," *Clinton (IL) Public,* Nov. 2, 1883.

Adam Bassler Gorgas

Major, 13 IL Infantry, May 24, 1861. Lieutenant Colonel, 13 IL Infantry, June 27, 1861. Colonel, 13

Left: Daniel Harvie Gilmer (Allen Cebula Collection).

IL Infantry, Dec. 28, 1862. Honorably mustered out, June 18, 1864. Battle honors: Chickasaw Bluffs, Vicksburg Campaign, Cane Creek, Atlanta Campaign (Madison Station).
Born: Jan. 4, 1828, Myerstown, Lebanon Co., PA
Died: Sept. 1, 1895, Crookston, Polk Co., MN
Education: Attended Myerstown Academy, Myerstown, PA
Occupation: Conveyancer, bookkeeper, and real estate agent
Miscellaneous: Resided Stillwater, Washington Co., MN; and Dixon, Lee Co., IL, before war; and Germantown, Philadelphia Co., PA; Minersville, Schuylkill Co., PA; and Crookston, Polk Co., MN, after war
Buried: St. John's Lutheran Cemetery, Pine Grove, Schuylkill Co., PA
References: *Military History and Reminiscences of the 13th Regiment of Illinois Volunteer Infantry in the Civil War in the United States, 1861–1865.* Chicago, IL, 1892. Pension File and Military Service File, National Archives. Letters Received, Volunteer Service Branch, Adjutant General's Office, File O251(VS)1864, National Archives.

John M. Graham

Captain, Co. E, 7 IL Cavalry, Sept. 8, 1861. Major, 7 IL Cavalry, March 15, 1863. GSW right arm, Nashville, TN, Dec. 16, 1864. Colonel, 7 IL Cavalry, March 2, 1865. Honorably mustered out, Nov. 4, 1865. Battle honors: Grierson's Raid, Chalmers' Raid, Nashville.
Born: 1826?, IL
Died: Nov. 1, 1888, Gainesville, FL
Occupation: Physician, merchant, and real estate agent
Offices/Honors: Postmaster, Cairo, IL, 1866–70
Miscellaneous: Resided Phillipstown, White Co., IL; Cairo, Alexander Co., IL; and Gainesville, Alachua Co., FL
Buried: Evergreen Cemetery, Gainesville, FL (Section 20)
References: Pension File and Military Service File, National Archives. Letters Received, Volunteer Service Branch, Adjutant General's Office, File G644(VS)1865, National Archives.

Daniel Grass

Captain, Co. I, 8 IL Infantry (3 months), April 25, 1861. Honorably mustered out, July 24, 1861. 1 Lieutenant, Co. H, 61 IL Infantry, March 7, 1862. Captain, Co. H, 61 IL Infantry, Dec. 2, 1862. Major, 61 IL Infantry, May 14, 1863. Lieutenant Colonel, 61 IL Infantry, Sept. 14, 1864. Taken prisoner, Murfreesboro, TN, Dec. 15, 1864. Paroled Jan. 6, 1865. *Colonel*, 61 IL Infantry, Sept. 15, 1864. Hon-

Daniel Grass (post-war) (Leander Stillwell. *The Story of a Common Soldier of Army Life in the Civil War, 1861–1865.* **Second Edition. Erie, KS, 1920).**

orably mustered out, May 15, 1865. Battle honors: Murfreesboro.
Born: Sept. 21, 1824, Rockport, Spencer Co., IN
Died: Dec. 21, 1894, Coffeyville, KS (struck by railroad engine)
Education: Attended Indiana Asbury (now DePauw) University, Greencastle, IN
Occupation: Lawyer
Offices/Honors: Kansas Senate, 1876–80
Miscellaneous: Resided Lawrenceville, Lawrence Co., IL, to 1870; and Independence and Cherryvale, Montgomery Co., KS, after 1870
Buried: Mount Hope Cemetery, Independence, KS
References: *The United States Biographical Dictionary.* Kansas Volume. Chicago and Kansas City, 1879. Obituary, *Independence Star and Kansan*, Dec. 21, 1894. L. Wallace Duncan, compiler. *History of Montgomery County, Kansas.* Iola, KS, 1903. Pension File and Military Service File, National Archives. Letters Received, Volunteer Service Branch, Adjutant General's Office, File G885(VS)1865, National Archives. Thomas M. Eddy. *The Patriotism of Illinois.* Chicago, IL, 1865. Leander Stillwell. *The Story of a Common Soldier of Army Life in the Civil War,*

1861–1865. Second Edition. Erie, KS, 1920. Drew D. Dukett. *Glimpses of Glory: The Regimental History of the 61st Illinois Volunteers*. Bowie, MD, 1999.

Lucien Greathouse

Private, Co. H, 8 IL Infantry (3 months), April 25, 1861. Honorably mustered out, July 25, 1861. Captain, Co. C, 48 IL Infantry, Sept. 6, 1861. Major, 48 IL Infantry, Oct. 9, 1862. Lieutenant Colonel, 48 IL Infantry, Nov. 21, 1862. Colonel, 48 IL Infantry, Feb. 26, 1864. GSW right breast, Atlanta, GA, July 22, 1864. Battle honors: Shiloh, Vicksburg Campaign, Jackson Campaign, Atlanta Campaign (Kenesaw Mountain, Atlanta).

Born: June 7, 1842, Carlinville, IL
Died: July 22, 1864, KIA Atlanta, GA
Education: Attended McKendree College, Lebanon, IL. Graduated Indiana University, Bloomington, IN, 1858.
Occupation: Law student
Miscellaneous: Resided Vandalia, Fayette Co., IL. General John A. Logan described him as "the bravest man in the Army of the Tennessee." General William T. Sherman added, "His example was worth a thousand men."
Buried: Old State Cemetery, Vandalia, IL

References: James Barnet, editor. *The Martyrs and Heroes of Illinois in the Great Rebellion*. Second Edition. Chicago, IL, 1866. Thomas M. Eddy. *The Patriotism of Illinois*. Chicago, IL, 1865. Obituary, Illinois State Register, Aug. 28, 1864. Paul and Chester Farthing, editors. *Philo History: Chronicles and Biographies of the Philosophian Literary Society of McKendree College*. Lebanon, IL, 1911. *History of Fayette County, Illinois*. Philadelphia, PA, 1878. Theophilus A. Wylie. *Indiana University, Its History from 1820 to 1890*. Indianapolis, 1890. Military Service File, National Archives. http://www.greathouse.us/library/biographies/greathouse-lucien.htm.

Nicholas Greusel

Captain, Co. C, 7 IL Infantry (3 months), April 18, 1861. Major, 7 IL Infantry, April 25, 1861. Lieutenant Colonel, 7 IL Infantry (3 years), July 24, 1861. Colonel, 36 IL Infantry, Sept. 23, 1861. Commanded 2 Brigade, 1 Division, Army of the Southwest, Feb.–March 1862. Commanded 2 Brigade, 5 Division, Army of the Mississippi, Aug.–Sept. 1862. Commanded 37 Brigade, 11 Division, 3 Army Corps, Army of the Ohio, Sept.–Nov. 1862. Commanded 1 Brigade, 3 Division, Right Wing, 14 Army Corps, Army of the Cumberland, Dec. 31, 1862–Jan. 9, 1863. Commanded 1 Brigade, 3 Division, 20 Army Corps, Army of the Cumberland, Jan. 9–Feb. 7, 1863. Resigned Feb. 7, 1863, due to disability from "inflammatory rheumatism of both knee joints." Battle honors: Pea Ridge, Perryville, Stone's River.

Lucien Greathouse (courtesy Henry Deeks).

Nicholas Greusel (Abraham Lincoln Presidential Library & Museum).

Nicholas Greusel (Lyman G. Bennett and William M. Haigh. *History of the 36th Regiment Illinois Volunteers during the War of the Rebellion.* Aurora, IL, 1876).

Born: July 4, 1817, Blieskastel, Bavaria
Died: April 25, 1896, Aurora, IL
Other Wars: Mexican War (Captain, Co. D, 1 MI Infantry)
Occupation: Lumber yard worker and railroad conductor before war. Railroad roadmaster and expressman after war.
Miscellaneous: Resided Detroit, MI; Aurora, Kane Co., IL; and Mount Pleasant, Henry Co., IA, 1866–93
Buried: Spring Lake Cemetery, Aurora, IL (Section N-West, Lot 20)
References: *Portrait and Biographical Album of Henry County, Iowa.* Chicago, IL, 1888. Obituary, *Aurora Beacon,* April 25, 1896. James Grant Wilson. *Biographical Sketches of Illinois Officers Engaged in the War Against the Rebellion of 1861.* Chicago, IL, 1862. Thomas M. Eddy. *The Patriotism of Illinois.* Chicago, IL, 1865. Biography, *Detroit Sunday News-Tribune,* Nov. 3, 1895. *Memorials of Deceased Companions of the Commandery of the State of Illinois MOLLUS, from May 8, 1879, to July 1, 1901.* Chicago, IL, 1901. Obituary Circular, Whole No. 274, Illinois MOLLUS. Pension File and Military Service File, National Archives. Lyman G. Bennett and William M. Haigh. *History of the 36th Regiment Illinois Volunteers during the War of the Rebellion.* Aurora, IL, 1876. Letters Received, Volunteer Service Branch, Adjutant General's Office, File G603(VS) 1862 and G219(VS)1870, National Archives. Letters Received, Commission Branch, Adjutant General's Office, File G416(CB)1863, National Archives.

Lyman Guinnip

Colonel, 79 IL Infantry, Aug. 28, 1862. Under arrest on "very grave charges," he resigned Oct. 17, 1862. While urging the acceptance of the resignation without delay, Brig. Gen. Joshua W. Sill listed several of the charges, including "appropriating plate and liquors at a house where he was quartered in Louisville, ... making speeches to his men calculated to produce insubordination and disrespect to their superior officers, and ... flagrant breaches of duty on the march, disobeying orders in the most audacious manner." Imprisoned later by Louisville civil authorities for "aiding a slave to escape," he was eventually released upon forfeiture of bail, with President Lincoln taking an interest in the case, remarking in a letter (March 17, 1863) to his friend Joshua Speed, "He (Guinnip) was not of bad character at home, and I scarcely think he is guilty of any real crime."

Born: Aug. 21, 1828, Greenwood, Steuben Co., NY
Died: Aug. 4, 1892, Chicago, IL (killed in elevator accident)
Other Wars: Mexican War (Private, Co. K, 1 IL Infantry)
Occupation: Agricultural implement dealer, inventor (an improved horse collar and a butter-making process), and butter manufacturer
Miscellaneous: Resided Danville, Vermilion Co., IL, to 1877; and Chicago, IL, after 1877
Buried: Spring Hill Cemetery, Danville, IL (Block 2, Lot 58, unmarked)
References: Obituary, *Chicago Inter Ocean,* Aug. 5, 1892. Pension File and Military Service File, National Archives. Obituary, *Danville Daily Commercial,* Aug. 5, 1892. Letters Received, Volunteer Service Branch, Adjutant General's Office, File P1122(VS)1862, National Archives. "He Scotched the Vipers: Sketch of the Career of Colonel Lyman Guinnip in Dealing with Copperheads," *Chicago Inter Ocean,* Sept. 25, 1888. "Lyman Guinnip," *Louisville Daily Democrat,* Nov. 12, 1862. Donald G. Richter. *Vermilion County and the Civil War.... We are Coming, Father Abraham, Three Hundred Thousand More!* Danville, IL, 2011. Roy P. Basler, editor. *The Collected Works of Abraham Lincoln.* New Brunswick, NJ, 1953.

John P. Hall

Captain, Co. F, 56 IL Infantry, Nov. 16, 1861. Major, 56 IL Infantry, Nov. 1, 1862. Lieutenant Colonel, 56 IL Infantry, April 26, 1863. GSW left leg, Vicksburg, MS, May 22, 1863. *Colonel,* 56 IL Infantry, March 29, 1865. Honorably mustered out,

John P. Hall (Pension File, National Archives).

Aug. 12, 1865. Battle honors: Corinth, Vicksburg, Atlanta Campaign, Operations in North Georgia and North Alabama, Campaign of the Carolinas.

Born: Oct. 16, 1830, Union Co., KY
Died: May 8, 1874, Paducah, KY
Occupation: Carpenter before war. U.S. Pension agent and U.S. Internal Revenue official after war.
Offices/Honors: U.S. Internal Revenue Collector, 1st District of Kentucky, 1869–74
Miscellaneous: Resided Morganfield, Union Co., KY, to 1870; and Paducah, McCracken Co., KY, 1870–74.

Buried: Mount Kenton Cemetery, Paducah, KY (Section 4A)
References: *Report of the Proceedings of the Society of the Army of the Tennessee at the Eighth Annual Meeting.* Cincinnati, OH, 1877. Pension File and Military Service File, National Archives. Obituary, *Hickman Courier*, May 16, 1874.

Charles Morrel Hammond

Major, 100 IL Infantry, Aug. 30, 1862. GSW right leg, Stone's River, TN, Dec. 31, 1862. GSW knee, Tunnel Hill, GA, May 10, 1864. Lieutenant Colonel, 100 IL Infantry, July 21, 1864. *Colonel,* 100 IL Infantry, March 11, 1865. Honorably mustered out, June 12, 1865. Battle honors: Stone's River, Chickamauga, Missionary Ridge, Atlanta Campaign (Tunnel Hill, Kenesaw Mountain), Franklin, Nashville.

Born: Sept. 16, 1824, Swanzey, NH
Died: Aug. 25, 1903, NHDVS, Los Angeles, CA
Occupation: Tinsmith and livery keeper before war. Real estate agent and lawyer after war.
Offices/Honors: U.S. Internal Revenue Collector, 6th District of Illinois, 1867–71
Miscellaneous: Resided Wilmington, Will Co., IL; Joliet, Will Co., IL (1870); Chicago, IL (1880); and Salt Lake City, Salt Lake Co., UT
Buried: Los Angeles National Cemetery, Los Angeles, CA (Section 9, Row D, Site 7)
References: Frederick S. Hammond. *History and Genealogies of the Hammond Families in America.* Oneida, NY, 1902. George H. Woodruff. *Fifteen Years Ago: or The Patriotism of Will County.* Joliet,

Charles Morrel Hammond (Taylor & Seavey, Army of the Tennessee; Terry Orr Collection).

IL, 1876. Pension File and Military Service File, National Archives.

Douglas Hapeman

2 Lieutenant, Co. H, 11 IL Infantry (3 months), April 30, 1861. 2 Lieutenant, Co. H, 11 IL Infantry (3 years), July 30, 1861. Lieutenant Colonel, 104 IL Infantry, Oct. 3, 1862. Taken prisoner, Hartsville, TN, Dec. 7, 1862. Confined at Atlanta, GA, and Libby Prison, Richmond, VA. Paroled April 23, 1863. Colonel, 104 IL Infantry, Sept. 9, 1863. Commanded 1 Brigade, 1 Division, 14 Army Corps, Army of the Cumberland, Sept. 20–Nov. 5, 1864. Honorably mustered out, June 6, 1865. Bvt. Colonel, USV, March 13, 1865, for meritorious services. Battle honors: Shiloh, Hartsville, Chickamauga, Missionary Ridge, Atlanta Campaign (Peach Tree Creek), Savannah Campaign.

Born: Jan. 15, 1839, Ephratah, Fulton Co., NY
Died: June 3, 1905, Ottawa, IL
Occupation: Printer before war. Newspaper publisher and bookseller after war.
Offices/Honors: Medal of Honor, Peach Tree Creek, GA, July 20, 1864. "With conspicuous coolness and bravery rallied his men under a severe attack, reformed the broken ranks, and repulsed the attack."
Miscellaneous: Resided Ottawa, La Salle Co., IL
Buried: Ottawa Avenue Cemetery, Ottawa, IL (Bushnell Addition, Section A, Lot 76)

References: William W. Calkins. *The History of the 104th Regiment of Illinois Volunteer Infantry. War of the Great Rebellion, 1862–1865*. Chicago, IL, 1895. Urias J. Hoffman. *History of La Salle County, Illinois*. Chicago, IL, 1906. *Biographical and Genealogical Record of La Salle County, Illinois*. Chicago, IL, 1900. *History of La Salle County, Illinois*. Chicago, IL, 1886. Steven J. Adolphson, "'Our Little Colonel': Douglas Hapeman," *Lincoln Herald*, Vol. 75, No. 1 (Spring 1973). *Memorials of Deceased Companions of the Commandery of the State of Illinois MOLLUS, from July 1, 1901, to Dec. 31, 1911*. Chicago, IL, 1912. *Soldiers' and Patriots' Biographical Album*. Chicago, IL, 1892. *Society of the Army of the Cumberland. Thirty-Third Reunion, Chattanooga, TN, Sept. 18, 19, 20, 1905*. Cincinnati, OH, 1906. Obituary, *Ottawa Republican-Times*, June 3, 1905. Pension File and Military Service File, National Archives. Letters Received, Volunteer Service Branch, Adjutant General's Office, File H1018(VS)1865, National Archives.

Oscar Fitzalan Harmon

Colonel, 125 IL Infantry, Sept. 4, 1862. Commanded 3 Brigade, 2 Division, 14 Army Corps, Army of the Cumberland, Dec. 16, 1863–Feb. 15, 1864 and June 27, 1864. GSW heart, Kenesaw Mountain, GA, June 27, 1864. Battle honors: Perryville, Stone's River, Chickamauga, Missionary Ridge, Atlanta Campaign (Kenesaw Mountain).

Douglas Hapeman (Massachusetts MOLLUS Collection, USAMHI [Vol. 112, p. 5763L]).

Oscar Fitzalan Harmon (U.S. Military Academy Library).

Oscar Fitzalan Harmon (Terry Orr Collection).

Born: May 31, 1827, Wheatland, Monroe Co., NY

Died: June 27, 1864, KIA Kenesaw Mountain, GA

Education: Attended Williston Seminary, Easthampton, MA

Occupation: Lawyer

Offices/Honors: Illinois House of Representatives, 1858–60

Miscellaneous: Resided Danville, Vermilion Co., IL

Buried: Spring Hill Cemetery, Danville, IL (Block 1, Lot 1)

References: Lucy Harmon McPherson. *Life and Letters of Oscar Fitzalan Harmon*. Trenton, NJ, 1914. David L. Thomas, "Danville's Forgotten Hero of the Civil War," *The Heritage of Vermilion County*, Vol. 22, No. 3 (Summer 1986). Hiram W. Beckwith. *History of Vermilion County, Illinois, Together with Historic Notes on the Northwest*. Chicago, IL, 1879. Lottie E. Jones. *History of Vermilion County, Illinois*. Chicago, IL, 1911. Robert H. Behrens. *From Salt Fork to Chickamauga: Champaign County Soldiers in the Civil War*. Urbana, IL, 1988. Obituary, *Chicago Daily Tribune*, July 30, 1864. James Barnet, editor. *The Martyrs and Heroes of Illinois in the Great Rebellion*. Second Edition. Chicago, IL, 1866. Thomas M. Eddy. *The Patriotism of Illinois*. Chicago, IL, 1865. Robert M. Rogers. *The 125th Regiment Illinois Volunteer Infantry. Attention Batallion!* Champaign, IL, 1882. Donald G. Richter. *Vermilion County and the Civil War.... We are Coming, Father Abraham, Three Hundred Thousand More!* Danville, IL, 2011. Anne Mims Wright. *A Record of the Descendants of Isaac Ross and Jean Brown*. Jackson, MS, 1911. Pension File and Military Service File, National Archives.

Joseph Wilson Harper

2 Lieutenant, Co. B, 15 IL Infantry, May 24, 1861. Not commissioned and returned home, June 14, 1861. 2 Lieutenant, Co. I, 9 IL Cavalry, Oct. 23, 1861. 1 Lieutenant, Co. I, 9 IL Cavalry, Nov. 17, 1861. Captain, Co. I, 9 IL Cavalry, Oct. 29, 1862. Lieutenant Colonel, 9 IL Cavalry, Dec. 4, 1864. GSW right forearm, Nashville, TN, Dec. 15, 1864. Colonel, 9 IL Cavalry, March 20, 1865. Commanded 2 Brigade, 1 Cavalry Division, Department of Alabama, July–Aug. 1865. Commanded Post of Tuscaloosa, AL, Sept.–Oct. 1865. Honorably mustered out, Oct. 31, 1865. Battle honors: Campbellsville, Nashville.

Born: July 13, 1839, Huron Co., OH

Died: Jan. 20, 1924, Hamilton, MO

Occupation: Merchant before war. Farmer, cattle raiser and coal company executive after war.

Offices/Honors: Sheriff of Caldwell Co., MO,

Joseph Wilson Harper (Webster & Bro., Louisville, KY).

1873–75. Missouri House of Representatives, 1881–83.

Miscellaneous: Resided Belvidere, Boone Co., IL; and Hamilton, Caldwell Co., MO, after 1868

Buried: Highland Cemetery, Hamilton, MO (Section 3)

References: Carrie P. Johnston and W. H. S. McGlumphy. *History of Clinton and Caldwell Counties, Missouri.* Topeka, KS, 1923. *History of Caldwell and Livingston Counties, Missouri.* St. Louis, MO, 1886. Obituary, *Hamilton Advocate-Hamiltonian,* Jan. 24, 1924. Pension File and Military Service File, National Archives. Edward A. Davenport, editor. *History of the 9th Regiment Illinois Cavalry Volunteers.* Chicago, IL, 1888.

Fazilo A. Harrington

Lieutenant Colonel, 27 IL Infantry, Aug. 10, 1861. Colonel, 27 IL Infantry, April 16, 1862. Commanded 1 Brigade, 1 Division, Army of the Mississippi, July–Aug. 1862. GSW face and thigh, Stone's River, TN, Dec. 31, 1862. Battle honors: Belmont, Island No. 10, Stone's River.

Born: Nov. 22, 1831, Medina, NY

Died: Jan. 1, 1863, DOW Murfreesboro, TN

Education: Attended U.S. Military Academy, West Point, NY (Class of 1854)

Occupation: Civil engineer

Miscellaneous: Resided Erie, Whiteside Co., IL

Buried: City Cemetery, South Bend, IN (Section 1 East, Block 9, Lot 33, unmarked)

References: Obituary, *St. Joseph Valley Register,* Feb. 5, 1863. Obituary, *St. Joseph County Forum,* Feb. 7, 1863. Obituary, *Orleans Republican,* Jan. 7, 1863. Henry L. Abbot. *United States Military Academy: Half Century of a West Point Class, 1850 to 1854.* Boston, MA, 1904. Pension File and Military Service File, National Archives. Cullum File, U.S. Military Academy Library. U.S. Military Academy Cadet Application Papers, 1805–1866, National Archives. Timothy E. Howard. *A History of St. Joseph County, Indiana.* Chicago and New York, 1907. Charles Bent, editor. *History of Whiteside County, Illinois, from Its First Settlement to the Present Time.* Morrison, IL, 1877. Robert J. Kerner, editor, "The Diary of Edward W. Crippin, Private 27th Illinois Volunteers, War of the Rebellion, August 7, 1861 to September 19, 1863," *Transactions of the Illinois State Historical Society for the Year 1909.* Springfield, IL, 1910.

Thomas Woolen Harris

Colonel, 54 IL Infantry, Feb. 18, 1862. Suffering from rheumatism and diarrhea and diagnosed by brigade commander, Isaac F. Quinby, as never being "able to do duty with his regiment in the field," he resigned Dec. 10, 1862. Battle honors: Meriwether's Ferry.

Born: June 28, 1822, Newport, KY

Died: April 29, 1901, Paris, IL

Occupation: Commission merchant and capitalist before war. Dry goods merchant, hotelkeeper, and railroad superintendent after war.

Offices/Honors: Illinois House of Representatives, 1860–62

Miscellaneous: Resided Shelbyville, Shelby Co., IL; Indianapolis, IN (1880); and Paris, Edgar Co., IL

Buried: Edgar Cemetery, Paris, IL (Section E, Lot 898)

References: James Grant Wilson. *Biographical Sketches of Illinois Officers Engaged in the War Against the Rebellion of 1861.* Chicago, IL, 1862. Obituary, *Paris Daily Beacon,* April 30, 1901. Pension File and Military Service File, National Archives.

Fazilo A. Harrington (T. M. Schleier's Cartes de Visite Photograph Gallery, Corner Square and Deaderick Street, Nashville, TN; Massachusetts MOLLUS Collection, USAMHI [Vol. 83, p. 4186L]).

Thomas Woolen Harris (Abraham Lincoln Presidential Library & Museum).

Friedrich Karl Franz Hecker

Private, Co. K, 3 MO Infantry (3 months), May 19, 1861. Honorably discharged, June 6, 1861. Colonel, 24 IL Infantry, July 8, 1861. In a long letter to Major Gen. Fremont lamenting the lack of discipline and harmony within his regiment due to the incompetency and bad example of his company officers, he resigned to date Dec. 23, 1861, since "it is under the present circumstances impossible for me to lead the regiment into battle." Colonel, 82 IL Infantry, Oct. 23, 1862. GSW left thigh, Chancellorsville, VA, May 2, 1863. Commanded 1 Brigade, 3 Division, 11 Army Corps, Army of the Potomac, Sept. 19–25, 1863. Commanded 1 Brigade, 3 Division, 11 Army Corps, Army of the Cumberland, Sept. 25–Oct. 19, 1863. Commanded 3 Brigade, 3 Division, 11 Army Corps, Army of the Cumberland, Oct. 19, 1863–Feb. 15, 1864. Resigned March 21, 1864, since "my affairs at home have come to such a state that my presence there is absolutely necessary" and "wounds in this war ... render it impossible for me to fulfill the duties of my position in such a way as I wish to see them done." Battle honors: Chancellorsville, Wauhatchie, Chattanooga-Ringgold Campaign.

Friedrich Karl Franz Hecker.

Born: Sept. 28, 1811, Eichtersheim, Baden, Germany

Died: March 24, 1881, Summerfield, IL

Education: Attended University of Munich. Graduated University of Heidelberg, 1834.

Other Wars: A leader in the fight for a German Republic, he came to America after his small revolutionary army was defeated at Kandern, April 20, 1848

Occupation: German revolutionist, farmer and social activist

Miscellaneous: Resided Lebanon and Summerfield, St. Clair Co., IL

Buried: Summerfield Cemetery, Summerfield, IL (North Section)

References: Sabine Freitag. *Friedrich Hecker: Two Lives for Liberty.* Translated from the German and edited by Steven Rowan. St. Louis, MO, 2006. *Dictionary of American Biography. The United States Biographical Dictionary and Portrait Gallery of Eminent and Self-Made Men.* Illinois Volume. Chicago, Cincinnati, and New York, 1876. Obituary, *St. Louis Globe-Democrat,* March 25, 1881. Newton Bateman, Paul Selby, A.S. Wilderman, and A.A. Wilderman, editors. *Historical Encyclopedia of Illinois and History of St. Clair County.* Chicago, IL, 1907. Pension File and Military Service File, National Archives. Ray Burhop. *The Twenty-Fourth Illinois Infantry Regiment: 1861–1864.* Lexington, KY, 2013. William L. Burton. *Melting Pot Soldiers: The Union's Ethnic Regiments.* Ames, IA, 1988. Letters Received, Volunteer

Service Branch, Adjutant General's Office, File W493(VS)1867, National Archives. Thomas M. Eddy. *The Patriotism of Illinois*. Chicago, IL, 1865.

Stephen G. Hicks

Colonel, 40 IL Infantry, Aug. 10, 1861. Commanded 1 Brigade, 5 Division, Army of West Tennessee, March 1–20, 1862. GSW left shoulder, Shiloh, TN, April 6, 1862. Discharged for disability, Oct. 13, 1862. Discharge revoked and restored to his command, Dec. 13, 1862. Commanded 2 Brigade, 1 Division, 16 Army Corps, Army of the Tennessee, March–July 28, 1863. Commanded 2 Brigade, 4 Division, 15 Army Corps, Army of the Tennessee, July 28–Oct. 1863. Commanded Post of Paducah, KY, Oct. 25, 1863–Jan. 23, 1865. Commanded Post of Columbus, KY, Jan. 23–June 15, 1865. Commanded District of Western Kentucky, June 15–Aug. 4, 1865. Honorably mustered out, Sept. 6, 1865. Battle honors: Shiloh, Vicksburg Campaign, Jackson Campaign, Forrest's Expedition into West Tennessee and Kentucky (Paducah).

Born: Feb. 22, 1807, Jackson Co., GA
Died: Dec. 14, 1869, Salem, IL
Other Wars: Black Hawk War (Sergeant, Captain Bowman's Company, Spy Battalion, 1 Brigade, IL Mounted Volunteers). Mexican War (Captain, Co. H, 3 IL Infantry, and Lieutenant Colonel, 6 IL Infantry).
Occupation: Lawyer
Offices/Honors: Illinois House of Representatives, 1840–46
Miscellaneous: Resided Mount Vernon, Jefferson Co., IL; and Salem, Marion Co., IL
Buried: East Lawn Cemetery, Salem, IL
References: William H. Perrin, editor. *History of Jefferson County, Illinois*. Chicago, IL, 1883. Newton Bateman and Paul Selby, editors. *Historical Encyclopedia of Illinois*. Chicago and New York, 1900. Pension File and Military Service File, National Archives. Ephraim J. Hart. *History of the Fortieth Illinois Infantry (Volunteers)*. Cincinnati, OH, 1864. J.H.G. Brinkerhoff. *Brinkerhoff's History of Marion County, Illinois*. Indianapolis, IN, 1909. John M. Palmer, editor. *The Bench and Bar of Illinois: Historical and Reminiscent*. Chicago, IL, 1899. Letters Received, Volunteer Service Branch, Adjutant General's Office, File S1249(VS)1862, National Archives. Thomas M. Eddy. *The Patriotism of Illinois*. Chicago, IL, 1865. *Illinois at Vicksburg*. Chicago, IL, 1907.

Daniel Fletcher Hitt

Lieutenant Colonel, 53 IL Infantry, Nov. 11, 1861. Colonel, 53 IL Infantry, Nov. 11, 1862. Suffering from back and spine injuries incurred in a fall from

Stephen G. Hicks (USAMHI [RG98S-CWP 12.7]).

Daniel Fletcher Hitt (S. Alschuler, Photographer, Ottawa, IL; Abraham Lincoln Presidential Library & Museum).

Daniel Fletcher Hitt (post-war) (George W. Warvelle, editor. *A Compendium of Freemasonry in Illinois.* **Chicago, IL, 1897).**

his horse, he resigned Jan. 2, 1863, due to "utter prostration of the physical powers necessary to a discharge the duties of my office."

Born: June 13, 1810, Bourbon Co., KY
Died: May 11, 1899, Ottawa, IL
Education: Attended Miami University, Oxford, OH
Other Wars: Black Hawk War
Occupation: Civil engineer, surveyor and farmer
Offices/Honors: Postmaster, Utica, La Salle Co., IL, 1834–36
Miscellaneous: Resided Ottawa, La Salle Co., IL
Buried: Ottawa Avenue Cemetery, Ottawa, IL (Old Cemetery, Section 7, Lot 14)
References: Obituary, *Ottawa Republican-Times,* May 18, 1899. *History of La Salle County, Illinois.* Chicago, IL, 1886. *Biographical Encyclopedia of Illinois of the Nineteenth Century.* Philadelphia, PA, 1875. *Soldiers' and Patriots' Biographical Album.* Chicago, IL, 1892. Michael C. O'Byrne. *History of La Salle County, Illinois.* Chicago and New York, 1924. Newton Bateman and Paul Selby, editors. *Historical Encyclopedia of Illinois.* Chicago and New York, 1900. Pension File and Military Service File, National Archives. George W. Warvelle, editor. *A Compendium of Freemasonry in Illinois.* Chicago, IL, 1897. Letters Received, Volunteer Service Branch, Adjutant General's Office, File H1223(VS)1862, National Archives. Barbara Jeanne Grim Littlefield. *Descendants of Herman (Harmon) Hitt and Mary Weaver.* Decorah, IA, 1999.

Rosell Marion Hough

Brigade Quartermaster, Cairo Expedition, April 19–May 3, 1861. Major, 9 IL Cavalry, Sept. 10, 1861. Acting ADC, Staff of Major Gen. David Hunter, Department of Kansas and Department of the South, Sept. 1861–April 1862. GSW left hip, near Warrensburg, MO, Nov. 18, 1861. Resigned April 23, 1862, since "our business is of that magnitude that it requires my undivided attention for the next three months." Colonel, 67 IL Infantry, June 13, 1862. Honorably mustered out, Oct. 6, 1862. Battle honors: Warrensburg, Fort Pulaski.

Born: Feb. 17, 1819, Gouverneur, St. Lawrence Co., NY
Died: March 8, 1892, Chicago, IL
Occupation: Meat packing executive and farmer
Offices/Honors: Postmaster, Roselle, IL, 1873–76
Miscellaneous: Resided Bloomingdale, Du Page Co., IL, to 1877; Girard, Crawford Co., KS, 1877–79; Roselle, Du Page Co., IL, 1879–82; Lincoln, Logan Co., IL, 1882–87; and Chicago, IL, 1887–92
Buried: Old Union Cemetery, Lincoln, IL (Section A, Block 18, Lot 15)
References: Obituary, *Chicago Daily Tribune,* March 9, 1892. Obituary, *Lincoln Daily Courier,* March 9, 1892. Pension File and Military Service File, National Archives. James Grant Wilson. *Biographical Sketches of Illinois Officers Engaged in the War Against the Rebellion of 1861.* Chicago, IL, 1862.

Rosell Marion Hough (Crater's Union Photographic Gallery, 55 Clark Street, Chicago, IL; Chicago History Museum [ICHi-67610])

Rosell Marion Hough (James Grant Wilson. *Biographical Sketches of Illinois Officers Engaged in the War Against the Rebellion of 1861*. Chicago, IL, 1862).

Alfred T. Andreas. *History of Chicago from the Earliest Period to the Present Time*. Chicago, IL, 1885. Edward A. Davenport, editor. *History of the Ninth Regiment Illinois Cavalry Volunteers*. Chicago, IL, 1888.

Samuel T. Hughes

Private, Co. I, 9 IL Infantry (3 months), May 27, 1861. Honorably mustered out, July 26, 1861. 2 Lieutenant, Co. I, 9 IL Infantry (3 years), Aug. 19, 1861. 1 Lieutenant, Co. I, 9 IL Infantry, Aug. 16, 1862. Taken prisoner, Corinth, MS, Oct. 3, 1862. Paroled Oct. 18, 1862. GSW abdomen, Mud Creek, MS, June 20, 1863. Captain, Co. I, 9 IL Infantry, Nov. 17, 1863. Lieutenant Colonel, 9 IL Infantry, Sept. 1, 1864. *Colonel*, 9 IL Infantry, July 9, 1865. Honorably mustered out, July 9, 1865. Battle honors: Corinth, Operations in Northeastern Mississippi (Mud Creek), Atlanta Campaign, Savannah Campaign, Campaign of the Carolinas.

Born: 1838, IL
Died: Oct. 6, 1873, near Edwardsville, Madison Co., IL
Occupation: Farmer
Miscellaneous: Resided Upper Alton, Madison Co., IL; and Venice, Madison Co., IL
Buried: Wanda Cemetery, South Roxana, Madison Co., IL (Section 1, Lot 67)
References: Obituary, *Alton Weekly Telegraph*, Oct. 10, 1873. W.T. Norton, editor. *Centennial History of Madison County, Illinois, and Its People, 1812–*

Samuel T. Hughes (Armstead & White, Artists, Corinth, MS; Abraham Lincoln Presidential Library & Museum).

1912. Chicago and New York, 1912. Pension File and Military Service File, National Archives. Letters Received, Volunteer Service Branch, Adjutant General's Office, File H2401(VS)1864, National Archives. *History of Madison County, Illinois*. Edwardsville, IL, 1882. Marion Morrison. *A History of the Ninth Regiment Illinois Volunteer Infantry, With the Regimental Roster*. Carbondale, IL, 1997.

Robert M. Hundley

Colonel, 128 IL Infantry, Dec. 18, 1862. "The 128 IL Infantry having, in its short period of service of less than five months, been reduced from an aggregate of 860 to 161—principally by desertions—and there having been an utter want of discipline in it," he, with most of the regimental officers, was discharged, April 4, 1863. Identified as a member of the subversive Sons of Liberty in late 1864.

Born: June 12, 1820, TN
Died: May 2, 1881, Marion, IL
Other Wars: Mexican War (2 Lieutenant, Co. B, 5 IL Infantry)
Occupation: Physician and banker
Miscellaneous: Resided Marion, Williamson Co., IL
Buried: Rose Hill Cemetery, Marion, IL (SW Section)
References: Milo Erwin. *The History of Williamson County, Illinois. From the Earliest Times, Down to the Present*. Marion, IL, 1876. http://www.mihp.org/2012/12/hundley-robert-m/. Obituary, *Marion Egyptian Press*, May 5, 1881. Obituary, *Marion Monitor*, May 5, 1881. Military Service File, National

Robert M. Hundley (post-war) (Marion Illinois History Preservation, www.mihp.org, courtesy Samuel Lattuca).

Archives. *Report of the Adjutant General of the State of Illinois. Containing Reports for the Years 1861–66.* Revised by Brig. Gen. J. N. Reece. (Vol. 6, p. 532). Springfield, IL, 1900. *The War of the Rebellion: A Compilation of the Official Records of the Union and Confederate Armies.* (Vol. 45, Part 1, p. 1083). Washington, D.C., 1894.

Judson John (aka John Judson) Huntley

1 Lieutenant, Co. C, 37 IL Infantry, Aug. 1, 1861. GSW thigh, Pea Ridge, AR, March 7, 1862. Captain, Co. C, 37 IL Infantry, Nov. 20, 1862. Acting ADC, Staff of Brig. Gen. Michael K. Lawler, Department of the Gulf, July 1864–Sept. 1865. Major, 37 IL Infantry, Oct. 4, 1865. Acting AIG, Staff of Major Gen. Joseph A. Mower, Eastern District of Texas, Oct.–Nov. 1865. Lieutenant Colonel, 37 IL Infantry, May 2, 1866. *Colonel,* 37 IL Infantry, May 15, 1866. Honorably mustered out, May 15, 1866. Battle honors: Pea Ridge.
Born: 1837, Addison Co., VT
Died: Sept. 3, 1868, Baton Rouge, LA
Occupation: Lawyer
Miscellaneous: Resided Antioch Twp., Lake Co., IL; Waukegan, Lake Co., IL; and Baton Rouge, LA, after war
Buried: Magnolia Cemetery, Baton Rouge, LA (possibly Section 3, Lot 90, with his widow, Henrietta, who died Jan. 28, 1905)
References: Virgil W. Huntley. *John Huntley of Boston and Roxbury, MA, and Lyme, CT, 1647–1996.* Raleigh, NC, 1996. Pension File and Military Service File, National Archives. Michael A. Mullins. *The Fremont Rifles: A History of the 37th Illinois Veteran Volunteer Infantry.* Wilmington, NC, 1990. Death notice, *Baton Rouge Daily Advocate,* Sept. 4, 1868.

Frederick Judson Hurlbut

Lieutenant Colonel, 57 IL Infantry, Dec. 26, 1861. Commanded 3 Brigade, 2 Division, 16 Army Corps, Army of the Tennessee, Aug. 25–Sept. 25, 1863. Commanded 3 Brigade, 4 Division, 15 Army Corps, Army of the Tennessee, Oct. 6, 1864–April 22, 1865. Colonel, 57 IL Infantry, Oct. 15, 1864. Battle honors: Corinth, Operations in North Georgia and North Alabama, Savannah Campaign, Campaign of the Carolinas (Bentonville).
Born: Dec. 30, 1828, Oswegatchie, NY
Died: April 27, 1865, Chicago, IL (drowned in Chicago River)
Occupation: Commission merchant
Miscellaneous: Resided Chicago, IL
Buried: Graceland Cemetery, Chicago, IL (Section D, Lot 160)
References: Obituary, *Chicago Daily Tribune,*

Frederick Judson Hurlbut (Armstead & White, Artists, Corinth, MS; USAMHI [RG98S-CWP 49.6]).

May 9, 1865. Henry H. Hurlbut. *The Hurlbut Genealogy, or Record of the Descendants of Thomas Hurlbut.* Albany, NY, 1888. Military Service File, National Archives. Letters Received, Volunteer Service Branch, Adjutant General's Office, File B2119(VS) 1862, National Archives. Alfred T. Andreas. *History of Chicago from the Earliest Period to the Present Time.* Chicago, IL, 1885. William W. Cluett. *History of the 57th Regiment Illinois Volunteer Infantry.* Princeton, IL, 1886.

Robert Green Ingersoll

Colonel, 11 IL Cavalry, Dec. 20, 1861. Chief of Cavalry, Staff of Brig. Gen. Jeremiah C. Sullivan, District of Jackson, Army of the Tennessee, Dec. 1862. Taken prisoner, Lexington, TN, Dec. 18, 1862. Paroled Dec. 19, 1862. The regiment having been reduced to "not half the maximum number," he resigned June 30, 1863, since "My affairs are in such condition at home that my presence is absolutely necessary, and by remaining in the service in my present position, I should do the Government little good, and myself harm." Battle honors: Shiloh, Corinth, Forrest's Expedition into West Tennessee (Lexington).

Born: Aug. 11, 1833, Dresden, NY

Robert Green Ingersoll (post-war) (Brady-Handy Photograph Collection, Library of Congress [LC-DIG-cwpbh-04126]).

Died: July 21, 1899, Dobbs Ferry, NY
Occupation: Lawyer, orator and lecturer
Offices/Honors: Attorney General of Illinois, 1867–69
Miscellaneous: Resided Peoria, Peoria Co., IL, to 1879; Washington, D.C., 1879–85; and Dobbs Ferry, Westchester Co., NY, 1885–99. Best known in his lifetime as "the Great Agnostic."
Buried: Arlington National Cemetery, Arlington, VA (Section 3, Lot 1620)
References: *Dictionary of American Biography.* Edward Garstin Smith. *The Life and Reminiscences of Robert G. Ingersoll.* New York City, 1904. Cameron Rogers. *Colonel Bob Ingersoll: A Biographical Narrative of the Great American Orator and Agnostic.* Garden City, NY, 1927. Susan Jacoby. *The Great Agnostic: Robert Ingersoll and American Freethought.* New Haven, CT, 2013. Obituary, *Chicago Daily Tribune,* July 22, 1899. *Biographical Encyclopedia of Illinois of the Nineteenth Century.* Philadelphia, PA, 1875. *The History of Peoria County, Illinois.* Chicago, IL, 1880. Lillian D. Avery. *A Genealogy of the Ingersoll Family in America, 1629–1925.* New York City, 1926. Pension File and Military Service File, National Archives. Mark R. Dawson. *Ho! for the War! The Eleventh Illinois Cavalry: A Regimental History.* N.p., 2010.

Robert Green Ingersoll (Abraham Lincoln Presidential Library & Museum).

David D. Irons

Colonel, 86 IL Infantry, Aug. 27, 1862. Battle honors: Perryville.

Born: July 28, 1816, NY

Died: Aug. 11, 1863, Nashville, TN (typhoid fever)

Occupation: Clerk and insurance agent

Offices/Honors: Sheriff of Peoria Co., IL, 1854–56

Miscellaneous: Resided Peoria, Peoria Co., IL

Buried: Springdale Cemetery, Peoria, IL (Mount Prospect Division, Section 1, Lot 341)

References: Pension File and Military Service File, National Archives. Obituary, *Peoria Transcript*, Aug. 13, 1863. Funeral account, *Peoria Transcript*, Aug. 17, 1863. Col. David D. Irons (1816–1863)- Find A Grave Memorial. John R. Kinnear. *History of the 86th Regiment Illinois Volunteer Infantry, During Its Term of Service*. Chicago, IL, 1866. *The History of Peoria County, Illinois*. Chicago, IL, 1880. James M. Rice. *Peoria City and County, Illinois*. Chicago, IL, 1912.

David D. Irons (Cole's Photographic Gallery, No. 5 North Adams Street, Peoria, IL; Roger D. Hunt Collection, USAMHI [RG98S-CWP64.17]).

James Isaminger

Captain, Co. B, 27 MO Mounted Infantry, July 24, 1861. Honorably mustered out, Jan. 27, 1862. 1 Lieutenant, Co. D, 63 IL Infantry, April 10, 1862. Captain, Co. D, 63 IL Infantry, Dec. 31, 1862. Lieutenant Colonel, 63 IL Infantry, Aug. 12, 1863. Commanded 1 Brigade, 7 Division, 17 Army Corps, Army of the Tennessee, Aug. 21–Sept. 14, 1863. Taken prisoner, Big Black Creek, near Cheraw, SC, March 3, 1865. Confined Libby Prison, Richmond, VA. Paroled April 2, 1865. *Colonel*, 63 IL Infantry, July 12, 1865. Honorably mustered out, July 13, 1865. Battle honors: Atlanta Campaign, Savannah Campaign, Campaign of the Carolinas (Big Black Creek).

Born: March 28, 1826, PA

Died: Oct. 10, 1895, Black Rock, AR

Occupation: Farmer, machinist and iron works superintendent

Offices/Honors: Missouri House of Representatives, 1866. Postmaster, Pocahontas, AR, 1882–83.

Miscellaneous: Resided Jefferson Twp., Johnson Co., MO (1860); Pana, Christian Co., IL (1863); Taberville, St. Clair Co., MO (1870); Pocahontas, Randolph Co., AR (1880); and Black Rock, Lawrence Co., AR

James Isaminger (Photographic Studio, Southwest Cor. Third & Main Sts., Entrance on Third Street, Louisville, KY, Alcan & Gorbutt, Portrait Painters).

Buried: Oak Forest Cemetery, Black Rock, AR (Section 3, Block 4, Lot 3)

References: Pension File and Military Service File, National Archives. "The Old 63rd Illinois Infantry," *Decatur Weekly Republican*, Aug. 29, 1889. "The Osage Iron Works Co.," *Sedalia Daily Democrat*, June 14, 1873. *History of Johnson County, Missouri*. Kansas City, MO, 1881. Letters Received, Volunteer Service Branch, Adjutant General's Office, File I652(VS)1863, National Archives. Dean C. Cherrington and Henrietta C. Evans. *The Cherrington Family History and Genealogy*. Scotch Plains, NJ, 1999.

William H. Jamison

1 Lieutenant, Co. C, 21 IL Infantry, June 14, 1861. Captain, Co. C, 21 IL Infantry, March 15, 1862. Major, 21 IL Infantry, Dec. 8, 1864. Lieutenant Colonel, 21 IL Infantry, June 2, 1865. *Colonel*, 21 IL Infantry, July 13, 1865. Honorably mustered out, Dec. 16, 1865. Battle honors: Chickamauga, Atlanta Campaign, Franklin, Nashville.

Born: Oct. 6, 1831, Salem, NY
Died: May 1, 1878, Monticello, IL
Occupation: Blacksmith
Miscellaneous: Resided Monticello, Piatt Co., IL; and Humboldt, Allen Co., KS
Buried: Monticello Township Cemetery, Monticello, IL (Block 165)
References: Charles McIntosh, editor. *Past and Present of Piatt County, Illinois*. Chicago, IL, 1903.

William H. Jamison (Butler & Smetters, Artists, North Side Capitol Square, Over S.B. Fisher's Store, Springfield, IL; Allen Cebula Collection).

Obituary, *Piatt County Herald*, May 8, 1878. Pension File and Military Service File, National Archives.

James Frazier Jaquess

Chaplain, 6 IL Cavalry, Jan. 9, 1862. Colonel, 73 IL Infantry, Aug. 21, 1862. Commanded 1 Brigade, 2 Division, 4 Army Corps, Army of the Cumberland, March 4–April 6, 1864. Persuading himself that he might be an instrument in bringing the war to a peaceful conclusion, he organized, with James R. Gilmore, an unofficial peace mission into Confederate territory. Meeting with Jefferson Davis on July 17, 1864, he determined that the South would only settle for independence or annihilation, thereby benefiting the re-election of President Lincoln by demonstrating that the negotiated settlement advocated by the Peace Democrats was impossible. Honorably mustered out, June 12, 1865. Battle honors: Perryville, Chickamauga, Missionary Ridge.

Born: Nov. 18, 1819, Posey Co., IN
Died: June 17, 1898, St. Paul, MN
Education: Graduated Indiana Asbury (now De Pauw) University, Greencastle, IN, 1845
Occupation: Methodist clergyman, educator, cotton planter and business agent
Offices/Honors: President, Illinois Female Col-

William H. Jamison (courtesy Everitt Bowles).

Clayton, Tunica Co., MS; traveling in U.S. and England, 1870–84; London, England, 1884–94; and St. Paul, MN, after war.

Buried: Oakland Cemetery, St. Paul, MN (Section 43, Lot 16)

References: Patricia B. Burnette. *James F. Jaquess; Scholar, Soldier and Private Agent for President Lincoln.* Jefferson, NC, 2013. *Dictionary of American Biography.* William H. Newlin. *A History of the 73rd Regiment of Illinois Infantry Volunteers.* Springfield, IL, 1890. Pension File and Military Service File, National Archives. Henry A. Castle. *Minnesota, Its Story and Biography.* Chicago and New York, 1915. James R. Gilmore. *Personal Recollections of Abraham Lincoln and the Civil War.* Boston, MA, 1898. Henry A. Castle, "A Perilous Trip to Richmond," *The National Tribune,* March 5, 1903. Lester L. Swift, "Tribulations of the Rev. Col. Jaquess and the Preacher Regiment: A New Lincoln Note Discovered," *Lincoln Herald,* Vol. 69, No. 4 (Winter 1967). Thomas M. Eddy. *The Patriotism of Illinois.* Chicago, IL, 1865. Letters Received, Volunteer Service Branch, Adjutant General's Office, File 1673(VS)1862, National Archives. Obituary, *St. Paul Pioneer Press,* June 18, 1898.

James Frazier Jaquess (Roger D. Hunt Collection, USAMHI [RG98S-CWP80.32]).

Frederick A. Johns

Captain, Co. G, 98 IL Infantry, Sept. 3, 1862. Suffering from "'fistula in ano' of twelve months standing," he resigned Dec. 20, 1863. Colonel, 136 IL Infantry, June 1, 1864. Honorably mustered out, Oct. 22, 1864. Captain, Co. E, 154 IL Infantry, Feb. 22, 1865. Honorably mustered out, Sept. 18, 1865.

Born: Feb. 28, 1830, Manchester, England
Died: May 15, 1915, Chicago, IL
Occupation: Blacksmith, auctioneer and constable
Miscellaneous: Resided Olney, Richland Co., IL; Freeport, Stephenson Co., IL; Edgewood, Effingham Co., IL; and Chicago, IL, after 1890
Buried: Haven Hill Cemetery, Olney, IL (Section B, unmarked)
References: Pension File and Military Service File, National Archives. Obituary, *Olney Advocate,* May 20, 1915. Death notice, *Chicago Daily Tribune,* May 16, 1915.

Amory Kinney Johnson

Lieutenant Colonel, 14 IL Infantry, May 25, 1861. Colonel, 28 IL Infantry, Sept. 28, 1861. Commanded 3 Brigade, 4 Division, Right Wing, 13 Army Corps, Army of the Tennessee, Nov. 2–Dec. 18, 1862. Commanded 3 Brigade, 4 Division, 17 Army Corps, Army of the Tennessee, Dec. 18, 1862–Jan. 20, 1863. Commanded 3 Brigade, 4 Division, 16 Army Corps, Army of the Tennessee, Jan. 20–Feb. 3, 1863, April 5–May 5, 1863, and June 9–July 5,

James Frazier Jaquess (Roger D. Hunt Collection, USAMHI [RG98S-CWP80.31]).

lege, Jacksonville, IL, 1849–55. President, Methodist College, Quincy, IL, 1856–61.

Miscellaneous: Resided Jacksonville, Morgan Co., IL; and Quincy, Adams Co., IL, before war.

Top, left: **Amory Kinney Johnson** (Edwin L. Hobart. *Semi-History of a Boy-Veteran of the Twenty-Eighth Regiment Illinois Infantry Volunteers, in a Black Regiment.* Denver, CO, 1905). *Top, right:* **Amory Kinney Johnson** (seated right, with Governor Richard Yates) (Abraham Lincoln Presidential Library & Museum). *Below:* **Amory Kinney Johnson** (standing left, as commander of the Post of Natchez, with other officers of the post, including 1 Lieutenant James M. Gale, standing right, and 1 Lieutenant Albert J. Moses, Adjutant Thomas A. Ralston, and Captain James R. Walker, seated left-to-right) (Edwin L. Hobart. *Semi-History of a Boy-Veteran of the Twenty-Eighth Regiment Illinois Infantry Volunteers, in a Black Regiment.* Denver, CO, 1905).

1863. Acting ADC, Staff of Major Gen. William T. Sherman, 15 Army Corps, Army of the Tennessee, Feb.–March 1863. Commanded 3 Brigade, 4 Division, 13 Army Corps, Army of the Tennessee, July 28–Aug. 7, 1863. Commanded 3 Brigade, 4 Division, 17 Army Corps, Army of the Tennessee, Aug. 7–Aug. 26, 1863. Commanded Post of Natchez, MS, Nov. 1863–March 1864. His "immediate and unconditional" resignation, written on Executive Mansion stationery and delivered personally to President Lincoln, was accepted to date, June 17, 1864, with Lincoln's endorsement, "From personal knowledge I have no doubt that this resignation is tendered in good faith, without anything wrong, and therefore direct that it be accepted." Battle honors: Fort Henry, Shiloh, Corinth, Hatchie Bridge, Vicksburg Campaign.

Born: Dec. 18, 1829, Mount Pleasant, Martin Co., IN

Died: May 2, 1876, New Orleans, LA (accidentally drowned after fall from the Gretna ferryboat)

Other Wars: Mexican War (Private, Co. F, 4 IL Infantry)

Occupation: Farmer before war. U.S. Internal Revenue official and tax collector after war.

Offices/Honors: Sheriff of Menard Co., IL, 1860–62. U.S. Internal Revenue Gauger, 1873–74. State Tax Collector, Jefferson Parish, LA, 1875–76.

Miscellaneous: Resided Petersburg, Menard Co., IL; and Gretna, Jefferson Parish, LA

Buried: Metairie Cemetery, New Orleans, LA (possibly with his widow, Anna, who died March 1, 1917)

References: Obituary, *Le Meschacebe* (English edition), Edgard, LA, May 13, 1876. Obituary, *Cincinnati Commercial*, May 22, 1876. Obituary, *New Orleans Daily Picayune*, May 19, 1876. Pension File and Military Service File, National Archives. Letters Received, Volunteer Service Branch, Adjutant General's Office, File J407(VS)1864, National Archives. Research files of Andy Dann, Warne, NC. Edwin L. Hobart. *Semi-History of a Boy-Veteran of the Twenty-Eighth Regiment Illinois Infantry Volunteers, in a Black Regiment*. Denver, CO, 1905. *The History of Menard and Mason Counties, Illinois.* Chicago, IL, 1879. *Illinois at Vicksburg.* Chicago, IL, 1907.

James William Judy

Colonel, 114 IL Infantry, Sept. 18, 1862. Commanded 3 Brigade, 8 Division, 16 Army Corps, Army of the Tennessee, Feb. 12–April 3, 1863. Complaining that "my pay has been stopped without any just cause," he resigned Aug. 4, 1863, "unwilling to remain longer in the service and be thus imposed upon in not receiving my just dues." The March 27, 1863, order stopping his pay was revoked, May 9, 1864, upon determination of the validity of accounts he had submitted for subsistence of his men before muster into service. Battle honors: Vicksburg Campaign.

James William Judy (Abraham Lincoln Presidential Library & Museum).

Born: May 8, 1822, Winchester, KY

Died: Sept. 16, 1916, Tallula, IL

Occupation: Farmer and live stock auctioneer. Described as "the most prominent live stock auctioneer in the United States."

Offices/Honors: Member of the Illinois State Board of Agriculture, 1874–96, serving as President, 1894–96. Trustee, University of Illinois, 1895–97.

Miscellaneous: Resided Tallula, Menard Co., IL

Buried: Greenwood Cemetery, Tallula, IL

References: *The History of Menard and Mason Counties, Illinois.* Chicago, IL, 1879. Obituary, *Illinois State Journal*, Sept. 17, 1916. Obituary, *Petersburg Observer*, Sept. 22, 1916. Newton Bateman and Paul Selby, editors. *Historical Encyclopedia of Illinois.* Chicago and New York, 1900. Pension File and Military Service File, National Archives. Letters Received, Volunteer Service Branch, Adjutant General's Office, File J225(VS)1863, National Archives. Franklin W. Scott, editor. *The Semi-Centennial Alumni Record of the University of Illinois.* Chicago, IL, 1918. Marion P. Carlock. *History and Genealogy of the Judy-Judah-Tschudy-Tschudin-Tschudi-Schudi Family.* Los Angeles, CA, 1954. John L. Satterlee. *The Journal & the 114th, 1861 to 1865.* Springfield, IL, 1979.

George U. Keener

Captain, Co. C, 26 IL Infantry, Aug. 23, 1861. Resigned April 1, 1862, "having been offered the position of lieutenant colonel in the regiment of Missouri State Troops commanded by Col. Lipscomb," a position he failed to accept. Colonel, 150 IL Infantry, Feb. 14, 1865. Commanded Post of Bridgeport, AL, March 1865. Commanded 2 Brigade, 2 Separate Division, Army of the Cumberland, June 1865. While visiting his family on a leave of absence, he tendered his resignation, July 20, 1865, in order to care for his sick wife. The resignation was, however, suppressed or lost, resulting in his dismissal from the service, to date Nov. 20, 1865, for absence without leave. By an order dated Dec. 27, 1865, the order dismissing him was revoked and his resignation finally accepted to date July 20, 1865.

Born: Oct. 2, 1826, Dandridge, Jefferson Co., TN
Died: Oct. 4, 1889, Allenton, MO (died of injuries from being gored by a bull)
Other Wars: Mexican War (Private, Co. D, 1 U.S. Dragoons)
Occupation: Physician before war. Physician and Methodist clergyman after war.
Miscellaneous: Resided Mount Vernon, Jefferson Co., IL (1860); St. Louis, MO; Sniabar Twp., Jackson Co., MO (1880); Richmond, Ray Co., MO; and Allenton, St. Louis Co., MO
Buried: Allen Cemetery, near Allenton, MO (unmarked)
References: Pension File and Military Service File, National Archives. Letters Received, Volunteer Service Branch, Adjutant General's Office, File S2621(VS)1865, National Archives. Obituary, *St. Louis Globe-Democrat*, Oct. 6, 1889.

William Pitt Kellogg

Colonel, 7 IL Cavalry, Sept. 8, 1861. Commanded 1 Brigade, Cavalry Division, Army of the Mississippi, April 24–June 1, 1862. Resigned June 1, 1862, since "I have been quite sick for some time past and see no immediate prospect of regaining my health." Battle honors: New Madrid, Island No. 10.

Born: Dec. 8, 1831, Orwell, VT
Died: Aug. 10, 1918, Washington, D.C.
Education: Attended Norwich (VT) University
Occupation: Lawyer
Offices/Honors: Chief Justice, Nebraska Territory, 1861–62. Collector of Customs, New Orleans, LA, 1865–68. U.S. Senate, 1868–72, 1877–83. Governor of Louisiana, 1873–77. U.S. House of Representatives, 1883–85.
Miscellaneous: Resided Canton, Fulton Co., IL, before war; and New Orleans, LA; and Washington, D.C., after war

William Pitt Kellogg (U.S. Senate, 1869) (Brady-Handy Photograph Collection, Library of Congress [LC-DIG-cwpbh-00475]).

Buried: Arlington National Cemetery, Arlington, VA (Section 3, Lot 2538)
References: *Dictionary of American Biography*. William A. Ellis, editor. *History of Norwich University, 1819–1911, Her History, Her Graduates, Her Roll of Honor*. Montpelier, VT, 1911. Joseph G. Dawson, III, editor. *The Louisiana Governors: From Iberville to Edwards*. Baton Rouge, LA, 1990. John M. Palmer, editor. *The Bench and Bar of Illinois: Historical and Reminiscent*. Chicago, IL, 1899. William H. Powell, editor. *Officers of the Army and Navy (Volunteer) Who Served in the Civil War*. Philadelphia, PA, 1893. Obituary, *Washington Post*, Aug. 11, 1918. James L. Harrison, compiler. *Biographical Directory of the American Congress, 1774–1949*. Washington, D.C., 1950. Pension File and Military Service File, National Archives. Timothy Hopkins. *The Kelloggs in the Old World and the New*. San Francisco, CA, 1903. James Grant Wilson. *Biographical Sketches of Illinois Officers Engaged in the War Against the Rebellion of 1861*. Chicago, IL, 1862.

Joseph James Kelly

Major, 107 IL Infantry, Sept. 4, 1862. Colonel, 107 IL Infantry, Feb. 7, 1863. Resigned Nov. 10, 1863, since "the interests of my family, as well as that of my business relations, imperatively demand my personal attention." Battle honors: Morgan's Ohio Raid, East Tennessee Campaign, Knoxville Campaign (Campbell's Station).

Joseph James Kelly (Ray Zielin Collection).

Joseph James Kelly (USAMHI [RG98S-CWP 167.2]).

Miscellaneous: Resided Clinton, DeWitt Co., IL, to 1881; Lincoln, Lancaster Co., NE, 1881–1900; Los Angeles, CA, 1900–03. Brother of Bvt. Brig. Gen. John H. Kelly (114 OH Infantry).

Buried: Evergreen Cemetery, Los Angeles, CA (Section H, Lot 4936)

References: Obituary, *Los Angeles Times*, Jan. 21, 1903. Obituary Circular, Whole No. 206, Nebraska MOLLUS. Pension File and Military Service File, National Archives. *History of DeWitt County, Illinois*. Chicago, IL, 1910. "Milestones in *The Clinton Public* for the Year 1881," *DeWitt County Genealogical Quarterly*, Vol. 18, No. 1 (Spring 1992).

Ransom Kennicott

Captain, Co. I, 37 IL Infantry, Sept. 9, 1861. GSW arm, Prairie Grove, AR, Dec. 7, 1862. Major, 37 IL Infantry, March 8, 1864. Lieutenant Colonel, 37 IL Infantry, Sept. 10, 1864. Commanded Post of Sabine City, TX, July 1865. Commanded Post of Beaumont, TX, Aug. 1865. *Colonel*, 37 IL Infantry, Aug. 28, 1865. Honorably mustered out, April 19, 1866. Battle honors: Pea Ridge, Prairie Grove, Mobile Campaign (Fort Blakeley).

Born: Feb. 16, 1838, Half Day, Lake Co., IL
Died: Dec. 23, 1910, Chicago, IL

Joseph James Kelly (courtesy Karl E. Sundstrom).

Born: Sept. 16, 1827, near Zanesville, OH
Died: Jan. 20, 1903, Los Angeles, CA
Occupation: Lawyer and banker
Offices/Honors: Circuit Court Clerk, 1860–68. National Bank Examiner, 1877–81.

Ransom Kennicott (Randy Beck Collection).

Ransom Kennicott (Randy Beck Collection).

Occupation: Farmer and dentist before war. Regular Army (1 Lieutenant, 37 U.S. Infantry, lost left arm, Nov. 3, 1866, due to accidental GSW, retired Nov. 5, 1868). U.S. Internal Revenue Gauger, 1873–1909.

Miscellaneous: Resided Wheeling, Cook Co., IL, before war; and Hyde Park, Cook Co., IL; and Chicago, IL, after war. A member of the pre-war United States Zouave Cadets of Chicago.

Buried: Mount Hope Cemetery, Chicago, IL (Section 15, Lot 120)

References: Pension File and Military Service File, National Archives. Obituary, *Chicago Daily Tribune*, Dec. 24, 1910. Wyllys C. Ransom. *Historical Outline of the Ransom Family of America and Genealogical Record of the Colchester, Conn., Branch.* Ann Arbor, MI, 1903. Letters Received, Commission Branch, Adjutant General's Office, File K200(CB)1866, National Archives. Michael A. Mullins. *The Fremont Rifles: A History of the 37th Illinois Veteran Volunteer Infantry.* Wilmington, NC, 1990. Michael E. Banasik, editor. *Duty, Honor and Country: The Civil War Experiences of Captain William P. Black, Thirty-Seventh Illinois Infantry.* Iowa City, IA, 2006.

Charles Deal Kerr

Private, Co. D, 16 IL Infantry, May 24, 1861. 1 Lieutenant, Adjutant, 16 IL Infantry, Oct. 1, 1861. Acting AAG, 2 Brigade, 1 Division, Army of the Mississippi, May–July 1862. Acting AIG, 2 Brigade, 1 Division, Army of the Mississippi, Nov. 18–Dec. 13, 1862. Acting AAG, 1 Brigade, 4 Division, 14 Army Corps, Army of the Cumberland, Dec. 13, 1862–June 1863. Acting AAG, 1 Brigade, 2 Division, Reserve Corps, Department of the Cumberland, June–Oct. 1863. Acting ADC, Staff of Brig. Gen. Jefferson C. Davis, 2 Division, 14 Army Corps,

Charles Deal Kerr (A.C. Townsend, Photographer, Springfield, IL; Lincoln Financial Foundation Collection [LFA-0286], courtesy of the Indiana State Museum and Allen County Public Library).

Charles Deal Kerr (post-war) (J. Hill, Photographer, Washington Avenue, Bet. St. Germain & Lake Streets, St. Cloud, MN).

Army of the Cumberland, Nov.–Dec. 1863. Acting AAG, Staff of Brig. Gen. Julius White, Draft Rendezvous, Springfield, IL, Feb.–Oct. 1864. Honorably mustered out, April 5, 1865. Lieutenant Colonel, 16 IL Infantry, May 19, 1865. *Colonel, 16 IL Infantry,* July 3, 1865. Honorably mustered out, July 8, 1865. Battle honors: Savannah Campaign, Campaign of the Carolinas.

Born: Sept. 9, 1835, Philadelphia, PA
Died: Dec. 25, 1896, San Antonio, TX
Education: Graduated Illinois College, Jacksonville, IL, 1857
Occupation: Lawyer and judge
Offices/Honors: District Court Judge, 1888–96
Miscellaneous: Resided Jacksonville, Morgan Co., IL; and Carthage, Hancock Co., IL, before war; St. Cloud, Stearns Co., MN, 1865–73; and St. Paul, MN, 1873–96
Buried: Oakland Cemetery, St. Paul, MN (Block 51, Lot 76)
References: Christopher C. Andrews, editor. *History of St. Paul, Minnesota.* Syracuse, NY, 1890. *Biographical Dictionary and Portrait Gallery of Representative Men of Chicago, Minnesota Cities and the World's Columbian Exposition.* Chicago and New York, 1892. Obituary Circular, Whole No. 175, Minnesota MOLLUS. Obituary, *St. Paul Pioneer Press,* Dec. 27, 1896. Hiram F. Stevens. *History of the Bench and Bar of Minnesota.* Minneapolis and St. Paul, 1904. Pension File and Military Service File, National Archives. Letters Received, Volunteer Service Branch, Adjutant General's Office, File K14(VS) 1863, National Archives. Gertrude B. Gove. *A History of St. Cloud in the Civil War, 1858–1865.* St. Cloud, MN, 1976.

Lucien H. Kerr

Battalion Adjutant, 11 IL Cavalry, Dec. 20, 1861. Major, 11 IL Cavalry, July 4, 1862. Commanded Cavalry, District of Jackson (TN), Sept. 1862. Taken prisoner, Lexington, TN, Dec. 18, 1862. Paroled Dec. 20, 1862. Lieutenant Colonel, 11 IL Cavalry, Sept. 15, 1863. Commanded Cavalry Brigade, 17 Army Corps, Army of the Tennessee, Feb. 1864. Colonel, 11 IL Cavalry, April 25, 1864. Commanded Cavalry Forces, District of Vicksburg, Department of the Tennessee, July 1864 and Sept. 1864. Honorably mustered out, Dec. 19, 1864. Battle honors: Forrest's Expedition into West Tennessee (Lexington), Meridian Expedition.

Born: May 4, 1831, London, OH
Died: Oct. 31, 1873, Peoria, IL
Occupation: Lawyer
Offices/Honors: Illinois Senate, 1870–72
Miscellaneous: Resided Elmwood, Peoria Co., IL; and Peoria, Peoria Co., IL
Buried: Springdale Cemetery, Peoria, IL (Prospect Hill Division, Section 3, Lot 811)
References: Newton Bateman, Paul Selby, and

Lucien H. Kerr (D.P. Barr, Army Photographer, Palace of Art, Vicksburg, MS; Abraham Lincoln Presidential Library & Museum).

David McCulloch, editors. *Historical Encyclopedia of Illinois and History of Peoria County.* Chicago and Peoria, 1902. Obituary, *Peoria Daily Transcript*, Nov. 1, 1873. Mark R. Dawson. *Ho! for the War! The Eleventh Illinois Cavalry: A Regimental History.* N.p., 2010. Military Service File, National Archives.

Henry King

2 Lieutenant, Co. B, 20 IL Infantry, June 13, 1861. 1 Lieutenant, Co. B, 20 IL Infantry, March 25, 1862. GSW head, Vicksburg, MS, May 22, 1863. Captain, Co. B, 20 IL Infantry, Dec. 26, 1863. GSW Atlanta, GA, July 22, 1864. Lieutenant Colonel, 20 IL Infantry, June 2, 1865. *Colonel*, 20 IL Infantry, July 15, 1865. Honorably mustered out, July 16, 1865. Battle honors: Fort Donelson, Shiloh, Vicksburg Campaign, Atlanta Campaign, Savannah Campaign, Campaign of the Carolinas.

Born: 1836?, Hamilton, Ontario, Canada
Died: Sept. 1872, Annapolis, MO
Occupation: Shoemaker
Miscellaneous: Resided Joliet, Will Co., IL; and Annapolis, Iron Co., MO
Buried: Horton Cemetery, Annapolis, MO (location of cemetery unknown)
References: Death Notice, *Iron County Register*, Sept. 28, 1872. George H. Woodruff. *Fifteen Years Ago: or The Patriotism of Will County.* Joliet, IL, 1876. Military Service File, National Archives. Card Records of Headstones Provided for Deceased Union Civil War Veterans, 1879–1903.

Robert Kirkham

Colonel, 56 IL Infantry, Dec. 16, 1861. Suffering from chronic diarrhea and partial paralysis of the left side, he resigned June 26, 1862.

Born: 1817?, KY
Died: March 22, 1893, Carbondale, IL
Occupation: Grocer and dry goods merchant before war. Farmer, livery stable operator and grocer after war.
Miscellaneous: Resided Shawneetown, Gallatin Co., IL, to 1866; Carbondale, Jackson Co., IL, 1866–76; Murphysboro, Jackson Co., IL, 1876–77; and Anna, Union Co., IL, 1877–93.
Buried: Oakland Cemetery, Carbondale, IL (Block 23, Lot 21)
References: *History of Jackson County, Illinois.* Philadelphia, PA, 1878. John W. D. Wright. *A History of Early Carbondale, Illinois, 1852–1905.* Carbondale, IL, 1977. Pension File and Military Service File, National Archives.

Charles Knobelsdorff

Took an active part in the formation of 24 IL Infantry and served as its Lieutenant Colonel (without commission), May 1–July 1, 1861. Colonel, 44 IL Infantry, Sept. 13, 1861. Found guilty by a court martial of "oppressing three of the commissioned officers of his regiment, by depriving them, for a long time, of their commands, in spite of orders of his superiors requiring him to restore said officers to duty," he was sentenced, April 21, 1862, to be reprimanded, a sentence described by the reviewing officer as "a remarkably mild sentence for his misconduct." Commanded 2 Brigade, 2 Division, Army of the Mississippi, May 1862. Commanded 2 Brigade, 5 Division, Army of the Mississippi, Aug. 1862. Charged by Brig. Gen. Gordon Granger with "Disobedience of Orders and Conduct Unbecoming an Officer and a Gentleman" for refusing to obey an order to prefer charges for theft of sheep against several men of his regiment, he was dismissed Aug. 20, 1862. In approving the dismissal, Major Gen. William S. Rosecrans commented, "I am satisfied that he is a selfish, mischief-making man and untruthful—without the true spirit of a soldier, whose influence would be dangerous to discipline and demoralizing to the troops." Knobelsdorff appealed his dismissal directly to President Lincoln, backed by a letter from Governor Richard Yates, who characterized the charges against Knobelsdorff as "of a very trifling nature." Lacking the authority to reverse the findings of the court martial, Lincoln did, however, direct that an order be issued (Dec. 31, 1863) removing the disability to re-enter service. Meanwhile, Knobelsdorff organized 2 IL Volunteer Militia for the emergency defense of Chicago (with commission as colonel dated Aug. 2, 1863). Battle honors: Pea Ridge.

Born: Oct. 31, 1827, Prussia
Died: April 26, 1892, Kansas City, MO
Education: Attended military school in Culm, Prussia
Other Wars: Officer in the Schleswig-Holstein army during the revolutions of 1848–51 (GSW right arm, Missunde, Schleswig-Holstein, Sept. 12, 1850)
Occupation: Land agent and notary public before war. Pension claim agent, notary public, railroad ticket agent and real estate agent after war.
Miscellaneous: Resided Milwaukee, WI, 1854–59; St. Louis, MO, 1859–60; Chicago, IL, 1860–78; and Kansas City, MO, 1878–92. Brother-in-law of Colonel Joseph Vandor (7 WI Infantry).
Buried: Graceland Cemetery, Chicago, IL (Section I, Lot 317)
References: James Grant Wilson. *Biographical Sketches of Illinois Officers Engaged in the War Against the Rebellion of 1861.* Chicago, IL, 1862. Pension File and Military Service File, National Archives. Letters Received, Volunteer Service Branch, Adjutant General's Office, File K367(VS)1862, National Archives. Court-martial Case Files, 1809–1894, File II-855, National Archives. Thomas P. Lowry. *Tar-

nished Eagles: The Courts-Martial of Fifty Union Colonels and Lieutenant Colonels. Mechanicsburg, PA, 1997. John Y. Simon, editor. *The Papers of Ulysses S. Grant.* Volume 6: September 1, 1862–December 8, 1862. Carbondale, IL, 1977. Joseph G. Rosengarten. *The German Soldier in the Wars of the United States.* Second edition, revised and enlarged. Philadelphia, PA, 1890. William L. Burton. *Melting Pot Soldiers: The Union's Ethnic Regiments.* Ames, IA, 1988. Alfred T. Andreas. *History of Chicago from the Earliest Period to the Present Time.* Chicago, IL, 1885. Obituary, *Kansas City Star,* April 28, 1892. Ryan P. Semmes, "From Pea Ridge to the Potomac: Lemon G. Hine and the 44th Illinois Regiment, 1861–1862," *Journal of the Illinois State Historical Society,* Vol. 104, No. 1–2 (Spring-Summer 2011).

John Henry Kuhn

Captain, Co. K, 9 IL Infantry (3 months), April 25, 1861. Honorably mustered out, July 26, 1861. Captain, Co. A, 9 IL Infantry (3 years), July 28, 1861. Major, 9 IL Infantry, Sept. 5, 1861. Provost Marshal, Post of Paducah (KY), Oct. 1861–Feb. 1862. GSW left thigh, Corinth, MS, Oct. 3, 1862. Honorably mustered out, Aug. 20, 1864. Lieutenant Colonel, 144 IL Infantry, Sept. 26, 1864. Colonel, 144 IL Infantry, March 13, 1865. Commanded Post of Alton (IL) and Alton Military Prison, March–July 1865. Honorably mustered out, July 14, 1865. Battle honors: Corinth, Atlanta Campaign.

Born: May 26, 1833, St. Gallen, Switzerland
Died: Oct. 20, 1865, Alton, IL (asphyxiated by gases while cleaning brewery vats)
Occupation: Laborer for several years after arriving in America in 1849. Engaged in lumber business and as an interpreter in a banking house before war. Brewer after war.
Miscellaneous: Resided Alton, Madison Co., IL.
Buried: Alton Cemetery, Alton, IL (Old Yard Section, Lot 121)
References: Obituary, *Alton Telegraph,* Oct. 27, 1865. Marion Morrison. *A History of the Ninth Regiment Illinois Volunteer Infantry, With the Regimental Roster.* Carbondale, IL, 1997. Pension File and Military Service File, National Archives. Letters Received, Volunteer Service Branch, Adjutant General's Office, File K115(VS) 1869, National Archives. W.T. Norton, editor. *Centennial History of Madison County, Illinois, and Its People, 1812–1912.* Chicago and New York, 1912.

George W. Lackey

Captain, Co. A, 1 Battalion, IL State Militia, May 26, 1862. Honorably mustered out, June 10, 1862. Major, 68 IL Infantry, June 20, 1862. Honorably mustered out, Sept. 26, 1862. Colonel, 145 IL Infantry, June 9, 1864. Reprimanded by Major Gen.

George W. Lackey (Photographed by Scibird & Rex, Cor. Center & Jefferson Sts., Bloomington, IL).

William S. Rosecrans, Sept. 12, 1864, for neglect of duty in not being aware of the "disgracefully filthy condition" of four companies of his regiment guarding Alton (IL) Military Prison. Honorably mustered out, Sept. 23, 1864.

Born: March 29, 1842, Cambridge City, IN
Died: March 7, 1886, Chicago, IL
Occupation: Druggist and dealer in tobacco and cigars
Miscellaneous: Resided Bloomington, McLean Co., IL, to 1872; and Chicago, IL, 1872–86. Active in the post-war Illinois National Guard, serving as Captain of the Lackey Zouaves, 1875–86.
Buried: East Batavia Cemetery, Batavia, IL (Section 10, Lot 151)
References: Obituary, *Chicago Inter Ocean,* March 8, 1886. Pension File and Military Service File, National Archives. Obituary, *Chicago Daily Tribune,* March 8, 1886. *The War of the Rebellion: A Compilation of the Official Records of the Union and Confederate Armies.* (Vol. 41, Part 3, pp. 165–166). Washington, D.C., 1893. *The History of McLean County, Illinois.* Chicago, IL, 1879.

James Weston Langley

Lieutenant Colonel, 125 IL Infantry, Sept. 4, 1862. Provost Marshal, 14 Army Corps, Army of the Cumberland, April–May 1864. GSW Chattahoo-

James Weston Langley.

James Weston Langley (post-war) (Robert M. Rogers. *The 125th Regiment Illinois Volunteer Infantry. Attention Batallion!* Champaign, IL, 1882).

chee River, GA, July 7, 1864. Commanded 3 Brigade, 2 Division, 14 Army Corps, Army of the Cumberland, Sept. 1, 1864–Jan. 10, 1865 and March 19–June 9, 1865. *Colonel,* 125 IL Infantry, May 10, 1865. Honorably mustered out, June 9, 1865. Bvt. Colonel, USV, March 13, 1865, for meritorious services. Battle honors: Perryville, Chickamauga, Missionary Ridge, Atlanta Campaign (Resaca, Kenesaw Mountain, Peach Tree Creek, Atlanta, Jonesborough), Operations in North Georgia and North Alabama, Savannah Campaign, Campaign of the Carolinas (Averasborough, Bentonville).

Born: Jan. 17, 1836, Summit Twp., Erie Co., PA
Died: April 22, 1915, Seattle, WA
Occupation: Lawyer and judge
Offices/Honors: Illinois Senate, 1870–72. Judge of Champaign County Court, 1877–90. Judge of King County Superior Court, 1892–96.
Miscellaneous: Resided Champaign, Champaign Co., IL, to 1890; and Seattle, King Co., WA, after 1890. Brother-in-law of Colonel John S. Wolfe (135 IL Infantry).
Buried: Lake View Cemetery, Seattle, WA (Lot 1220)
References: Obituary, *Seattle Post-Intelligencer,* April 23, 1915. *The United States Biographical Dictionary and Portrait Gallery of Eminent and Self-Made Men.* Illinois Volume. Chicago and New York, 1883. Robert H. Behrens. *From Salt Fork to Chickamauga: Champaign County Soldiers in the Civil War.* Urbana, IL, 1988. Pension File and Military Service File, National Archives. Obituary Circular, Whole No. 239, Washington MOLLUS. Robert M. Rogers. *The 125th Regiment Illinois Volunteer Infantry. Attention Batallion!* Champaign, IL, 1882. David W. Godwin. *A Biographical History of Western Star Lodge No. 240 A.F. & A.M.* Champaign, IL, 1998.

Robert Briggs Latham

Colonel, 106 IL Infantry, Sept. 18, 1862. Commanded 3 Brigade, 2 Division, Army of Arkansas, Department of the Missouri, Jan. 1864. Resigned April 28, 1864, due to "physical disability caused by sickness contracted in the service in a southern climate, having had an attack last summer while in the vicinity of Vicksburg which rendered me unable for duty for more than two months and another very severe attack at Little Rock, AR, this winter." President Lincoln endorsed his resignation, "I personally and intimately know Robert B. Latham, the writer of the within, and have no doubt of the correctness of all he says. Let his resignation be accepted at once."

Born: June 21, 1818, Union Co., KY
Died: April 16, 1895, Daytona, FL
Occupation: Farmer, real estate dealer, and railroad developer
Offices/Honors: Sheriff, Logan Co., IL, 1850–52. Illinois House of Representatives, 1860–62.
Miscellaneous: Resided Mount Pulaski, Logan Co., IL; and Lincoln, Logan Co., IL. Founder of the city of Lincoln, IL, named after his friend, Abraham Lincoln.
Buried: Old Union Cemetery, Lincoln, IL (Section A, Block 15, Lot 1)
References: Newton Bateman and Paul Selby. *Biographical and Memorial Edition of the Historical*

Robert Briggs Latham (Roger D. Hunt Collection, USAMHI [RG98S-CWP58.31]).

Encyclopedia of Illinois. Chicago, IL, 1915. *The United States Biographical Dictionary and Portrait Gallery of Eminent and Self-Made Men.* Illinois Volume. Chicago, Cincinnati, and New York, 1876. *History of Logan County, Illinois.* Chicago, IL, 1886. *History of Logan County, Illinois: Its Past and Present.* Chicago, IL, 1878. Pension File and Military Service File, National Archives. Obituary, *Illinois State Register,* April 20, 1895. Dolorus Briggs Mansfield. *History of the Briggs-Bridge Family: Since Its Settlement in America (Virginia) in 1752.* Edmonds, WA, 1960.

John B. Le Sage

Captain, Co. A, 101 IL Infantry, Sept. 2, 1862. Major, 101 IL Infantry, April 9, 1863. Lieutenant Colonel, 101 IL Infantry, Jan. 3, 1864. *Colonel,* 101 IL Infantry, May 1, 1864. Honorably mustered out, June 7, 1865. Bvt. Colonel, USV, March 13, 1865, for distinguished gallantry and meritorious services during the war. Battle honors: Atlanta Campaign (Resaca, New Hope Church, Peach Tree Creek), Savannah Campaign, Campaign of the Carolinas.

Born: Dec. 29, 1824, near Montreal, Canada
Died: Sept. 26, 1903, Clayton, IL
Other Wars: Mexican War (Private, Co. H, 1 U.S. Infantry, and Private, Co. K, 6 U.S. Infantry)
Occupation: Steamboat captain before war. Hotelkeeper after war.

John B. Le Sage (T.L. Rivers Gallery, Corner 4th & Olive Streets, St. Louis, MO; Abraham Lincoln Presidential Library & Museum).

Miscellaneous: Resided Meredosia, Morgan Co., IL, to 1865; and Clayton, Adams Co., IL, after 1865
Buried: South Side Cemetery, Clayton, IL (Section A, Row 13)
References: *Portrait and Biographical Record of Adams County, Illinois.* Chicago, IL, 1892. Obituary, *Quincy Daily Journal,* Sept. 28, 1903. *The History of Adams County, Illinois.* Chicago, IL, 1879. Pension File and Military Service File, National Archives. Letters Received, Volunteer Service Branch, Adjutant General's Office, File M2211(VS)1865, National Archives.

Austin Light

Colonel, 39 IL Infantry, Oct. 11, 1861. Dismissed Nov. 25, 1861, upon discovery of his dishonorable pre-war military record.

Born: June 28, 1822, Chautauqua Co., NY
Died: Nov. 5, 1893, Chicago, IL
Other Wars: Corporal, Battery B, 4 U.S. Artillery, 1840–45. Mexican War (Permanent Garrison, Carlisle Barracks, PA). Enlisted as Private, Co. D, 1 U.S. Cavalry, March 30, 1857. Promoted to Corporal. Deserted Nov. 23, 1857. Apprehended Aug. 28, 1860. Dishonorably discharged, Sept. 10, 1860.

Occupation: Regular Army enlisted man before war. Shipping clerk and packer after war.
Miscellaneous: Resided Roxbury, Dane Co., WI; and Chicago, IL
Buried: Rosehill Cemetery, Chicago, IL (Section J, Lot 95)
References: Pension File and Military Service File, National Archives. William H. Ranstead, "The Case of Col. Austin Light," *Chicago Daily Tribune*, Dec. 7, 1861. Court-martial Case Files, 1809–1894, File II-250, National Archives. Death Notice, *Chicago Daily Tribune*, Nov. 7, 1893. Charles M. Clark. *The History of the 39th Regiment Illinois Volunteer Veteran Infantry (Yates Phalanx) in the War of the Rebellion, 1861–1865*. Chicago, IL, 1889. George H. Woodruff. *Fifteen Years Ago: or The Patriotism of Will County*. Joliet, IL, 1876. Alfred T. Andreas. *History of Chicago from the Earliest Period to the Present Time*. Chicago, IL, 1885. Letters Received, Volunteer Service Branch, Adjutant General's Office, File L925(VS)1864, National Archives.

John Logan

Colonel, 32 IL Infantry, Dec. 17, 1861. GSW left shoulder, Shiloh, TN, April 6, 1862. Nominated Brig. Gen., USV, Jan. 19, 1863, to rank from Nov. 29, 1862. Nomination as Brig. Gen., USV, withdrawn, Feb. 12, 1863. Commanded 2 Brigade, 4 Division, 17 Army Corps, Army of the Tennessee, July

John Logan (Abraham Lincoln Presidential Library & Museum).

John Logan (James Grant Wilson. *Biographical Sketches of Illinois Officers Engaged in the War Against the Rebellion of 1861*. Chicago, IL, 1862).

John Logan (post-war) (*The United States Biographical Dictionary and Portrait Gallery of Eminent and Self-Made Men*. Illinois Volume. Chicago and New York, 1883).

19–Oct. 1, 1864. Honorably mustered out, Dec. 30, 1864. Battle honors: Shiloh, Hatchie Bridge, Vicksburg Campaign, Jackson Campaign, Atlanta Campaign.
Born: Dec. 30, 1809, North Bend, Hamilton Co., OH

Died: Aug. 24, 1885, Carlinville, IL
Other Wars: Black Hawk War (Captain Jenkins' Company, Illinois Volunteer Militia)
Occupation: Physician
Offices/Honors: U.S. Marshal, Southern District of Illinois, 1866–70
Miscellaneous: Resided Chesterfield, Macoupin Co., IL; and Carlinville, Macoupin Co., IL
Buried: City Cemetery, Carlinville, IL
References: Tom Emery. *The Other John Logan: Col. John Logan and the 32nd Illinois.* Carlinville, IL, 1998. Obituary, *Carlinville Democrat,* Aug. 27, 1885. *The United States Biographical Dictionary and Portrait Gallery of Eminent and Self-Made Men.* Illinois Volume. Chicago and New York, 1883. James Grant Wilson. *Biographical Sketches of Illinois Officers Engaged in the War Against the Rebellion of 1861.* Chicago, IL, 1862. *History of Macoupin County, Illinois.* Philadelphia, PA, 1879. Charles A. Walker, editor. *History of Macoupin County, Illinois: Biographical and Pictorial.* Chicago, IL, 1911. Newton Bateman and Paul Selby, editors. *Historical Encyclopedia of Illinois.* Chicago and New York, 1900. Pension File and Military Service File, National Archives. Letters Received, Volunteer Service Branch, Adjutant General's Office, File L149(VS)1865, National Archives.

John Mason Loomis

Colonel, 26 IL Infantry, Aug. 29, 1861. Commanded 2 Brigade, 5 Division, Army of the Missis-

John Mason Loomis (post-war) (Massachusetts MOLLUS Collection, USAMHI [Vol. 54, p. 2659]).

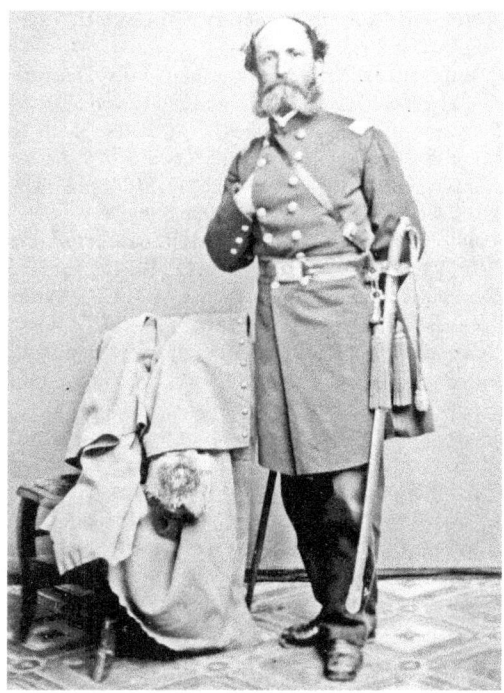

John Mason Loomis (Washington Gallery, Odd Fellows Hall, Vicksburg, MS; Library of Congress [LC-DIG-cwpb-04713]).

sippi, March 4–April 24, 1862. Commanded 2 Brigade, 2 Division, Army of the Mississippi, May 8–9, 1862 and Sept. 1862. Commanded 2 Brigade, 8 Division, Left Wing, 13 Army Corps, Army of the Tennessee, Nov. 1–Dec. 16, 1862. Commanded Post of Oxford, MS, Dec. 1862. Commanded 1 Brigade, 1 Division, 16 Army Corps, Army of the Tennessee, March 22–July 28, 1863. Commanded 1 Brigade, 4 Division, 15 Army Corps, Army of the Tennessee, July 28–Aug. 7, 1863; Sept. 8, 1863–Jan. 15, 1864; and March 12–April 30, 1864. Resigned April 30, 1864, since "the implied incompetency and disgrace which attends the continual promotion over me mortifies the pride and self-respect a soldier is bound to maintain." Battle honors: Island No. 10, Farmington, Vicksburg Campaign, Jackson Campaign, Missionary Ridge.
Born: Jan. 5, 1825, Windsor, CT
Died: Aug. 2, 1900, Chicago, IL
Education: Attended Connecticut Literary Institute, Suffield, CT
Occupation: Lumber commission merchant and philanthropist
Miscellaneous: Resided Chicago, IL. In 1874 he and his four siblings founded the Loomis Institute (now Loomis Chaffee School), Windsor, CT, which received an endowment of $1,250,000 upon the death of his widow in 1910.

Buried: Rosehill Cemetery, Chicago, IL (Section O, Lot 202)
References: Arba N. Waterman, editor. *Historical Review of Chicago and Cook County and Selected Biography.* Chicago and New York, 1908. Elisha S. Loomis. *Descendants of Joseph Loomis in America and His Antecedents in the Old World.* Berea, OH, 1909. *Memorials of Deceased Companions of the Commandery of the State of Illinois MOLLUS, from May 8, 1879 to July 1, 1901.* Chicago, IL, 1901. Obituary Circular, Whole No. 378, Illinois MOLLUS. Obituary, *Chicago Daily Tribune,* Aug. 3, 1900. *National Cyclopedia of American Biography.* James Grant Wilson. *Biographical Sketches of Illinois Officers Engaged in the War Against the Rebellion of 1861.* Chicago, IL, 1862. *Report of the Proceedings of the Society of the Army of the Tennessee at the Thirty-Second Meeting.* Cincinnati, OH, 1901. Alfred T. Andreas. *History of Chicago from the Earliest Period to the Present Time.* Chicago, IL, 1885. Military Service File, National Archives. Thomas M. Eddy. *The Patriotism of Illinois.* Chicago, IL, 1865. *Illinois at Vicksburg.* Chicago, IL, 1907.

Francis Hubert Lowry

Captain, Co. E, 107 IL Infantry, Aug. 11, 1862. Lieutenant Colonel, 107 IL Infantry, Feb. 7, 1863. *Colonel,* 107 IL Infantry, Nov. 10, 1863. GSW head, Franklin, TN, Nov. 30, 1864. Battle honors: Knoxville Campaign (Campbell's Station), Atlanta Campaign, Franklin.
Born: June 21, 1837, DeWitt County, IL
Died: Jan. 1, 1865, DOW Franklin, TN

Occupation: Farmer
Offices/Honors: Sheriff of Piatt Co., IL, 1861
Miscellaneous: Resided Monticello, Piatt Co., IL
Buried: Monticello Township Cemetery, Monticello, IL (Block 104)
References: Emma C. Piatt. *History of Piatt County Together With a Brief History of Illinois from the Discovery of the Upper Mississippi to the Present Time.* Chicago, IL, 1883. Pension File and Military Service File, National Archives. Shirley D. Harris. *The Chenoweth Family in America: Some Descendants of John Chenoweth, Born ca 1682.* Tucson, AZ, 1994.

John Lynch

Captain, Co. D, 8 IL Infantry (3 months), April 25, 1861. Resigned May 25, 1861. 1 Lieutenant, Co. E, 6 IL Cavalry, Nov. 19, 1861. Captain, Co. E, 6 IL Cavalry, Feb. 13, 1862. Major, 6 IL Cavalry, March 2, 1864. Lieutenant Colonel, 6 IL Cavalry, July 1, 1864. Colonel, 6 IL Cavalry, April 2, 1865. Commanded 2 Brigade, 5 Division, Cavalry Corps, Military Division of the Mississippi, April 1865. Commanded Sub-District of Montgomery, AL, Sept. 1865. Honorably mustered out, Nov. 5, 1865. Battle honors: Operations on the Mississippi Central Railroad, Grierson's Raid, Meridian Expedition, Nashville.
Born: Nov. 8, 1831, Olney, IL
Died: Aug. 28, 1906, Olney, IL
Occupation: Farmer
Miscellaneous: Resided Olney, Richland Co., IL
Buried: Haven Hill Cemetery, Olney, IL (Section C)

Francis Hubert Lowry (Chicago History Museum [ICHi-68786]).

John Lynch (Frank Crawford Collection).

References: Pension File and Military Service File, National Archives. John M. Palmer, editor. *The Bench and Bar of Illinois: Historical and Reminiscent.* Chicago, IL, 1899. Obituary, *Olney Times,* Aug. 30, 1906. *Biographical and Reminiscent History of Richland, Clay and Marion Counties, Illinois.* Indianapolis, IN, 1909. *Memorials of Deceased Companions of the Commandery of the State of Illinois MOLLUS, from July 1, 1901, to Dec. 31, 1911.* Chicago, IL, 1912.

Alonzo W. Mack

Colonel, 76 IL Infantry, Aug. 22, 1862. In a telegraph message to President Lincoln, he resigned Jan. 7, 1863, "to hold my place as State Senator." Lincoln endorsed the message, "Let this resignation be accepted and Col. Mack notified thereof by telegraph."
Born: Oct. 20, 1822, Moretown, VT
Died: Jan. 4, 1871, Chicago, IL
Occupation: Physician, lawyer and newspaper publisher
Offices/Honors: Illinois House of Representatives, 1858–60. Illinois Senate, 1860–68.
Miscellaneous: Resided Kalamazoo, Kalamazoo Co., MI; Kankakee, Kankakee Co., IL; and Chicago, IL
Buried: Limestone Cemetery, Limestone Twp., Kankakee Co., IL
References: Obituary and editorial, *Chicago Daily Tribune,* Jan. 5, 1871. Obituary, *Kankakee Gazette,* Jan. 12, 1871. Obituary, *New York Times,* Jan. 7, 1871. Tom M. George, "Mechem or Mack: How a One-Word Correction in the *Collected Works of Abraham Lincoln* Reveals the Truth About an 1856 Political Event," *Journal of the Abraham Lincoln Association,* Vol. 33, Issue 2 (Summer 2012). Pension File and Military Service File, National Archives. Newton Bateman, Paul Selby, William F. Kenaga, and George R. Letourneau, editors. *Historical Encyclopedia of Illinois and History of Kankakee County.* Chicago, IL, 1906. *Atlas of Kankakee County, Illinois.* Chicago, IL, 1883.

John Edward Maddux

Captain, Co. K, 116 IL Infantry, Sept. 30, 1862. GSW right leg, Vicksburg, MS, May 22, 1863. Provost Marshal, Staff of Brig. Gen. Morgan L. Smith, 2 Division, 15 Army Corps, Army of the Tennessee, June–July 1864. Lieutenant Colonel, 116 IL Infantry, June 16, 1864. Bayonet wound left temple, Atlanta, GA, July 22, 1864. Taken prisoner near Atlanta, GA, July 22, 1864. Confined Charleston, SC. Paroled Sept. 28, 1864. Based primarily on allegations of failing eyesight, he was discharged Feb. 8, 1865, upon adverse report of a Board of Examination. "Under the special circumstances, and the recommendation of his Brigade, Division, Corps and

John Edward Maddux (Ray Zielin Collection).

Army Commanders, and by direction of the President," the order discharging him was revoked, and he was restored to his command, June 2, 1865. Colonel, 116 IL Infantry, June 7, 1865. Honorably mustered out, June 7, 1865. Battle honors: Vicksburg Campaign, Atlanta Campaign (Kenesaw Mountain, Atlanta), Savannah Campaign (Fort McAllister), Campaign of the Carolinas.
Born: 1828?, Pickaway Co., OH
Died: Jan. 8, 1898, Wichita, KS
Occupation: Grocer, dry goods merchant, and livestock dealer before war. Cattle trader and real estate dealer after war.
Miscellaneous: Resided Lovington, Moultrie Co., IL, 1850–59; Decatur, Macon Co., IL, 1859–65; Des Moines, Polk Co., IA, 1865–67; Palmyra, Marion Co., MO, 1867–69; Glenwood, Schuyler Co., MO, 1869–70; Kirksville, Adair Co., MO, 1870–72; and Wichita, Sedgwick Co., KS, 1872–98
Buried: Highland Cemetery, Wichita, KS (Block 2, Lot 15)
References: Pension File and Military Service File, National Archives. Letters Received, Volunteer Service Branch, Adjutant General's Office, File M338(VS)1865, National Archives. Death Notice, *Wichita Daily Beacon,* Jan. 8, 1898. "Letter from J.E. Maddux," *Decatur Daily Republican,* Sept. 17, 1889. Larry M. Strayer and Richard A. Baumgartner, editors. *Echoes of Battle: The Atlanta Campaign.* Huntington, WV, 1991.

Oscar Malmborg

Lieutenant Colonel, 55 IL Infantry, Oct. 31, 1861. Commanded 2 Brigade, 5 Division, Army of the Tennessee, April 6, 1862. Colonel, 55 IL Infantry, Dec. 19, 1862. GSW near right eye, Vicksburg, MS, May 19, 1863. Shell wound near left eye, Vicksburg, MS, May 22, 1863. Commanded 2 Brigade, 2 Division, 15 Army Corps, Army of the Tennessee, Aug. 6–Sept. 10, 1863. Chief Engineer, Staff of Major Gen. James B. McPherson, 17 Army Corps, Army of the Tennessee, April 26–July 18, 1864. Resigned Sept. 20, 1864, since "my health has become so impaired by fatigue and exposure in the discharge of the double duties as regimental commander and engineer that I deem it my duty to my country no longer to hold my commission in so reduced a command." Colonel, 2 U.S. Veteran Volunteer Infantry, Jan. 1, 1865. Honorably discharged, May 30, 1865, on account of physical disability. Battle honors: Shiloh, Chickasaw Bayou, Arkansas Post, Vicksburg Campaign, Atlanta Campaign.

Born: Feb. 29, 1820, Kraklingbo, Gotland, Sweden

Died: April 29, 1880, Visby, Sweden

Education: Attended Karlberg Military Academy, Stockholm, Sweden

Occupation: Immigration agent for the Illinois Central Railroad before war. Accountant and U.S. Treasury Department clerk after war.

Above: Oscar Malmborg (S.M. Fassett, Artist, 122 & 124 Clark Street, Chicago, IL; courtesy Karl E. Sundstrom). *Below:* Oscar Malmborg (USAMHI [RG98S-CWP7.129]).

Oscar Malmborg (Abraham Lincoln Presidential Library & Museum).

Miscellaneous: Resided Chicago, IL; Washington, D.C.; and Visby, Gotland, Sweden, after 1874

Buried: Eastern Cemetery (Ostra Kyrkogarden), Visby, Sweden

References: Ernst W. Olson, editor. *History of the Swedes of Illinois.* Chicago, IL, 1908. Obituary, *Chicago Inter Ocean,* May 28, 1880. Pension File and Military Service File, National Archives. Letters Received, Volunteer Service Branch, Adjutant General's Office, File M392(VS)1868, National Archives. Otto Eisenschiml, "The 55th Illinois at Shiloh," *Journal of the Illinois State Historical Society,* Vol. 56, No. 2 (Summer 1963). *The Story of the Fifty-Fifth Regiment Illinois Volunteer Infantry in the Civil War, 1861–1865.* Huntington, WV, 1993. Nels Hokanson. *Swedish Immigrants in Lincoln's Time.* New York and London, 1942. Thomas M. Eddy. *The Patriotism of Illinois.* Chicago, IL, 1865.

Benjamin Franklin Marsh, Jr.

2 Lieutenant, Co. D, 16 IL Infantry, May 24, 1861. Resigned Aug. 8, 1861. Captain, Co. G, 2 IL Cavalry,

Benjamin Franklin Marsh, Jr. (Wayne Jorgenson Collection).

Aug. 12, 1861. GSW neck, Holly Springs, MS, Dec. 20, 1862. Major, 2 IL Cavalry, Jan. 1, 1863. Lieutenant Colonel, 2 IL Cavalry, May 4, 1864. Commanded 3 Brigade, Cavalry Division, Department of the Gulf, Sept. 1864. *Colonel,* 2 IL Cavalry, Aug. 29, 1865. Commanded 1 Brigade, 1 Cavalry Division, Military Division of the Gulf, Sept. 1865. Honorably mustered out, Nov. 22, 1865. Battle honors: Operations on the Mississippi Central Railroad (Holly Springs), Vicksburg Campaign, Jackson Campaign, Red River Campaign.

Born: Nov. 19, 1835, Wythe Twp., Hancock Co., IL

Died: June 2, 1905, Warsaw, IL

Education: Attended Jubilee College, near Peoria, IL

Occupation: Lawyer and farmer

Offices/Honors: U.S. House of Representatives, 1877–83, 1893–1901, and 1903–05

Miscellaneous: Resided Warsaw, Hancock Co., IL

Buried: Oakland Cemetery, Warsaw, IL (Block 3, Lot 62)

References: *Biographical Review of Hancock County, Illinois.* Chicago, IL, 1907. Obituary, *Warsaw Bulletin,* June 9, 1905. Samuel H. Fletcher. *The History of Company A, 2nd Illinois Cavalry.* Chicago, IL, 1912. *Proceedings of the Reunion Held in 1906 by the Association of Survivors 2nd Regiment Illinois Veteran Cavalry Volunteers at Springfield, Illinois.* Pana, IL, 1907. *Address of Col. W. Bowen Moore, Late Adjutant of the 2nd Regiment Illinois Cavalry, Delivered*

Benjamin Franklin Marsh, Jr. (Washburn, Photographer, 113 Canal Street, New Orleans, LA; Wayne Jorgenson Collection).

Before the Reunion of the Survivors of the Regiment, at Urbana, Champaign Co., Illinois, Oct. 15, 1879. N.p., 1879. Dwight W. Marsh. *Marsh Genealogy: Giving Several Thousand Descendants of John Marsh of Hartford, CT, 1636–1895.* Amherst, MA, 1895. Military Service File, National Archives. James L. Harrison, compiler. *Biographical Directory of the American Congress, 1774–1949.* Washington, D.C., 1950.

Charles Carroll Marsh

Colonel, 20 IL Infantry, June 13, 1861. Commanded Post of Cape Girardeau (MO), Western Department, Aug. 1861. Commanded 2 Brigade, 1 Division, Army of the Tennessee, March 29–May 3, 1862. Commanded 3 Brigade, 1 Division, Reserve Corps, Army of the Tennessee, June 1862. Commanded 3 Brigade, 1 Division, District of Jackson, Army of the Tennessee, July–Aug. 1862. Commanded 3 Brigade, District of Jackson, Army of the Tennessee, Sept.–Oct. 1862. Commanded 1 Brigade, 3 Division, Right Wing, 13 Army Corps, Army of the Tennessee, Nov.–Dec. 1862. Commanded 1 Brigade, 3 Division, 17 Army Corps, Army of the Tennessee, Dec. 1862–Jan. 1863 and March–April 1863. Nominated Brig. Gen., USV, Jan. 19, 1863, to rank from Nov. 29, 1862. Nomination as Brig. Gen., USV, withdrawn, Feb. 12, 1863. He tendered his resignation, Jan. 21, 1863, since "I am submitted to the mortification of having the Government select from those who have been my subordinates, and whom it is not immodest in me

Charles Carroll Marsh (courtesy Photo Antiquities Museum of Photographic History, Pittsburgh, PA).

Charles Carroll Marsh.

to assert my military inferiors and who have done vastly less service than myself, for promotion over my head." Major Gen. Grant recommended acceptance of the resignation with the comment, "Seeing so many promoted over him and feeling as he does on the subject, I do not believe the service would be benefitted by retaining him." Grant prefaced his recommendation with the remark, "Colonel Marsh has been one of the best brigade commanders in this department and has done most excellent service on the battlefield and in camp and has frequently been recommended for promotion." General-in-Chief Henry W. Halleck, however, disapproved the resignation with the comment, "The reasons given equally apply to many other officers." When Marsh again tendered his resignation, April 13, 1863, he gave as the reason, "Loss of interest in the service," explaining further, "I do not believe it is in human nature, I know it is not in mine, to submit to such continued mortifications and maintain that zeal and energy for the service which an officer in my position should." His resignation was finally accepted to date April 22, 1863. Battle honors: Fredericktown, Fort Donelson, Shiloh, Operations on the Mississippi Central Railroad.

Born: Sept. 17, 1829, Oswego, NY
Died: Oct. 2, 1904, Oakland, CA
Occupation: Lawyer
Miscellaneous: Resided Chicago, IL; Oswego, Oswego Co., NY; and Oakland, Alameda Co., CA, after 1873
Buried: Mountain View Cemetery, Oakland, CA (Plot 23, Lot 57, unmarked)
References: Obituary, *Oakland Tribune*, Oct. 3, 1904. Obituary, *San Francisco Chronicle*, Oct. 3,

1904. James Grant Wilson. *Biographical Sketches of Illinois Officers Engaged in the War Against the Rebellion of 1861*. Chicago, IL, 1862. Pension File and Military Service File, National Archives. Letters Received, Volunteer Service Branch, Adjutant General's Office, File M336(VS)1862, National Archives. John Y. Simon, editor. *The Papers of Ulysses S. Grant*. Volume 7: December 9, 1862–March 31, 1863. Carbondale, IL, 1979. George H. Woodruff. *Fifteen Years Ago: or The Patriotism of Will County*. Joliet, IL, 1876.

Jason Marsh

Colonel, 74 IL Infantry, Sept. 4, 1862. GSW left shoulder, Missionary Ridge, TN, Nov. 25, 1863. "Under medical treatment for the past two months in consequence of being worn out and exhausted by the previous severe service of this campaign," he resigned Aug. 24, 1864, since "I am now past 56 years old and realizing that my power of endurance is materially diminished, I cannot doubt that further continuance in service would shorten my life." Battle honors: Stone's River, Missionary Ridge, Atlanta Campaign.

Born: March 4, 1807, Woodstock, VT
Died: March 13, 1881, Chicago, IL
Occupation: Lawyer and farmer
Offices/Honors: Circuit Court Clerk, 1846–47. Rockford City Clerk, 1866–76.
Miscellaneous: Resided Rockford, Winnebago Co., IL; and Durand, Winnebago Co., IL, after 1876
Buried: Cedar Bluff Cemetery, Rockford, IL
References: Obituary, *Rockford Daily Gazette*, March 14, 1881. Charles A. Church. *History of Rockford and Winnebago County, Illinois, from the First Settlement in 1834 to the Civil War*. Rockford, IL, 1900. Obituary, *Rockford Daily Register*, March 14, 1881. Newton Bateman, Paul Selby, and Charles A. Church, editors. *Historical Encyclopedia of Illinois and History of Winnebago County*. Chicago, IL, 1916. *History of Winnebago County, Illinois, Its Past and Present*. Chicago, IL, 1877. Obituary, *Chicago Inter Ocean*, March 15, 1881. Thomas M. Eddy. *The Patriotism of Illinois*. Chicago, IL, 1865. *Society of the 74th Illinois Volunteer Infantry: Reunion Proceedings and History of the Regiment*. Rockford, IL, 1903. Pension File and Military Service File, National Archives. Letters Received, Volunteer Service Branch, Adjutant General's Office, File M815(VS) 1869, National Archives.

Thomas Alexander Marshall

Colonel, 1 IL Cavalry, July 17, 1861. Taken prisoner, Lexington, MO, Sept. 20, 1861. Exchanged

Jason Marsh (George W. Barnes, Photographer, Rockford, IL).

Thomas Alexander Marshall (Klauber, Photographer and Art Dealer, 332 4th Avenue, Louisville, KY; The Filson Historical Society [PC13. 0218]).

Sept. 21, 1861. Under arrest, Feb. 5, 1862, and facing court martial on various charges of misconduct, including "gross and unqualified cowardice" at Lexington, he escaped trial when several of the charges were withdrawn, March 27, 1862, as being "destitute of foundation." Due to the discharge of the enlisted men taken prisoner at Lexington and widespread dissatisfaction in the reorganized regiment, the regiment was disbanded and the field and staff officers (including Marshall) mustered out, July 14, 1862, "their services no longer required." Battle honors: Lexington.

Born: Nov. 4, 1817, Frankfort, KY
Died: Nov. 11, 1873, Charleston, IL
Education: Attended Kenyon College, Gambier, OH. Graduated Transylvania University, Lexington, KY, 1837.
Occupation: Lawyer, banker, and farmer
Offices/Honors: Illinois Senate, 1858–62 (President pro tem, 1860–62)
Miscellaneous: Resided Charleston, Coles Co., IL
Buried: Mound Cemetery, Charleston, IL (1st Addition, Block 1, Lot 13)
References: *The History of Coles County, Illinois.* Chicago, IL, 1879. Pension File and Military Service File, National Archives. William M. Paxton. *The Marshall Family.* Cincinnati, OH, 1885. Newton Bateman, Paul Selby, and Charles Edward Wilson, editors. *Historical Encyclopedia of Illinois and History of Coles County.* Chicago, IL, 1906. Obituary, *Illinois State Journal,* Nov. 15, 1873. Obituary, *New York Times,* Nov. 16, 1873. Sarah S. Young. *Genealogical Narrative of the Hart Family in the United States.* Memphis, TN, 1882. "Col. Thomas A. Marshall— Response to the Charges Against Him," *Illinois State Register,* Oct. 4, 1861. "First Illinois Cavalry Disbanded," *Illinois State Register,* July 10, 1862. Marshall Family Papers, 1815–1897, A\M367, Filson Historical Society, Louisville, KY.

Lewis Drake Martin

Lieutenant Colonel, 97 IL Infantry, Sept. 16, 1862. *Colonel,* 97 IL Infantry, June 15, 1864. Resigned Oct. 11, 1864, "debilitated and emaciated from chronic bronchitis affecting both lungs." Battle honors: Chickasaw Bluffs, Arkansas Post, Port Gibson, Vicksburg Campaign, Jackson Campaign.

Born: Nov. 16, 1824, Jersey, OH
Died: July 12, 1868, Jersey, OH
Education: Attended Marietta (OH) College
Occupation: Physician
Miscellaneous: Resided St. Louis, MO (1850); Shelbyville, Shelby Co., IL (1860); and Jersey, Licking Co., OH
Buried: Presbyterian Cemetery, Jersey, OH
References: Pension File and Military Service

Lewis Drake Martin (Moses & Piffet, Successors to E. Jacobs, 93 Camp Street, New Orleans, LA; courtesy Catherine Martin).

File, National Archives. *Combined History of Shelby and Moultrie Counties, Illinois.* Philadelphia, PA, 1881. Correspondence with Catherine Martin, Le Mesnil-le-Roi, France.

George Rogers Marvel

Farrier, Co. C, 15 IL Cavalry, Aug. 27, 1861. Honorably discharged, April 10, 1863, for disability due to deafness in both ears, being "unable to hear ordinary conversation or words of command." Colonel, 13 IL Cavalry, Feb. 12, 1864. Honorably discharged, April 11, 1864, having been found "incompetent and unfit for his position" by a Board of Examination.

Born: March 8, 1815, Gibson Co., IN
Died: Feb. 16, 1889, Locust Grove, IL
Occupation: Farmer
Miscellaneous: Resided Locust Grove, Cave Twp., Franklin Co., IL
Buried: Liberty Methodist Churchyard, near Thompsonville, IL
References: *History of Gallatin, Saline, Hamilton, Franklin, and Williamson Counties, Illinois.* Chicago, IL, 1887. Pension File and Military Service File, National Archives. Letters Received, Volunteer Service Branch, Adjutant General's Office, File M1041(VS) 1864, National Archives. Carla Pulliam. *Obits and Tidbits, Franklin County, Illinois, 1885–1899.* West Frankfort, IL, 1996. http://marvel.hoosierroots.com/getperson.php?pid=117.

Asa Carrington Matthews

Captain, Co. C, 99 IL Infantry, Aug. 23, 1862. Provost Marshal, Staff of Brig. Gen. William P. Benton, 1 Division, 13 Army Corps, Department of the Gulf, July–Sept. 1863. Major, 99 IL Infantry, Dec. 7, 1863. Acting AIG, Staff of Brig. Gen. William P. Benton, 1 Division, 13 Army Corps, Department of the Gulf, Jan.–Feb. 1864. Acting AIG, U.S. Forces, Pass Cavallo, TX, Feb.8–March 13, 1864. Acting AIG, Staff of Major Gen. Napoleon J.T. Dana, 1 Division, 13 Army Corps, Department of the Gulf, March–April 1864. Lieutenant Colonel, 99 IL Infantry, May 22, 1864. *Colonel,* 99 IL Infantry, Dec. 16, 1864. Bvt. Colonel, USV, March 13, 1865, for gallant and meritorious services during the war. Acting as Commissioner of the U.S. Government, he accepted the surrender of CSA Generals Douglas H. Cooper and Stand Watie and negotiated treaties with the Choctaw, Chicksasaw, Cherokee, and other tribes to end hostilities in the Indian Territory, June–July 1865. Honorably mustered out, July 31, 1865. Battle honors: Vicksburg Campaign, Mobile Campaign.

Born: March 22, 1833, Perry Twp., Pike Co., IL
Died: June 14, 1908, Pittsfield, IL
Education: Attended McKendree College, Lebanon, IL. Graduated Illinois College, Jacksonville, IL, 1855.

Asa Carrington Matthews (Abraham Lincoln Presidential Library & Museum).

Occupation: Lawyer
Offices/Honors: Collector of U.S. Internal Revenue, 1869–75. Illinois House of Representatives, 1876–80 and 1888–89 (Speaker 1889). First Comptroller, U.S. Treasury Department, 1889–93.
Miscellaneous: Resided Newburg Twp., Pike Co., IL; and Pittsfield, Pike Co., IL
Buried: Pittsfield West Cemetery, Pittsfield, IL
References: Melville D. Massie. *Past and Present of Pike County, Illinois.* Chicago, IL, 1906. Obituary, *Pike County Democrat,* June 17, 1908. *Portrait and Biographical Album of Pike and Calhoun Counties, Illinois.* Chicago, IL, 1891. *The United States Biographical Dictionary and Portrait Gallery of Eminent and Self-Made Men.* Illinois Volume. Chicago, Cincinnati, and New York, 1876. Pension File and Military Service File, National Archives. John M. Palmer, editor. *The Bench and Bar of Illinois: Historical and Reminiscent.* Chicago, IL, 1899. *The Illinois College Alumni Fund Association: Book of Memorial Memberships.* Centennial Edition, 1829–1929. Jacksonville, IL, 1929. Charles F. Ritter and Jon L. Wakelyn. *American Legislative Leaders, 1850–1910.* Westport, CT, 1989. William H. Powell, editor. *Officers of the Army and Navy (Volunteer) Who Served in the Civil War.* Philadelphia, PA, 1893. Letters Received, Volunteer Service Branch, Adjutant General's Office, File M1610(VS)1864, National Archives.

Waters W. McChesney

Colonel, 10 NY Infantry, May 2, 1861. Submitted resignation, June 15, 1861, based on Surgeon's Certificate stating that he was "incapable of performing the duties of a soldier because of valvular disease of the heart." The regimental historian, however, attributed his resignation to "the discovery that he did not possess the confidence of the officers of his regiment." For reasons unknown, official acceptance of his resignation did not occur until Nov. 17, 1868, when he was discharged to date Sept. 1, 1861. Volunteer ADC, Staff of Colonel Charles A. Heckman, 1 Brigade, 2 Division, Department of North Carolina, Dec. 1862. Colonel, 134 IL Infantry, May 31, 1864. Commanded Post of Mayfield, KY, Aug.–Sept. 1864. Although arrested Sept. 17, 1864, for alleged "disgraceful extortion and oppression" of the citizens of Mayfield, he was never charged, and he was finally honorably mustered out, Feb. 21, 1865, to date Oct. 25, 1864. Battle honors: Expedition from New Bern to Goldsborough, NC (Kinston, White Hall).

Born: Oct. 30, 1838, Troy, NY
Died: April 19, 1865, Chicago, IL
Occupation: Clerk and bookkeeper
Miscellaneous: Resided Chicago, IL. A member of the pre-war United States Zouave Cadets of Chicago.

Above: Waters W. McChesney (Brady's National Photographic Portrait Gallery, Broadway & Tenth Street, New York; Massachusetts MOLLUS Collection, USAMHI [Vol. 66, p. 3264]). *Below:* Waters W. McChesney (Brady's National Photographic Portrait Gallery, Broadway & Tenth Street, New York; Richard F. Carlile Collection).

Buried: Oakwood Cemetery, Troy, NY (Section D-1, Lot 69)

References: Pension File and Military Service File, National Archives. Paul W. Prindle and Katherine E. Schultz. *The McChesney Family of Rensselaer County, NY.* Annville, PA, 1969. Charles W. Cowtan. *Services of the 10th New York Volunteers (National Zouaves) in the War of the Rebellion.* New York City, NY, 1882. Letters Received, Volunteer Service Branch, Adjutant General's Office, File M155(VS) 1862, National Archives. Lewis Collins and Richard H. Collins. *Collins' Historical Sketches of Kentucky: History of Kentucky.* Frankfort, KY, 1966. Death notice, *Chicago Daily Tribune*, April 20, 1865.

John W. McClanahan

2 Lieutenant, Co. B, 11 IL Infantry (3 months), April 30, 1861. Honorably mustered out, July 30, 1861. Captain, Co. H, 53 IL Infantry, Nov. 2, 1861. Major, 53 IL Infantry, Nov. 12, 1862. Lieutenant Colonel, 53 IL Infantry, Jan. 3, 1863. Shell wound right hip, Jackson, MS, July 12, 1863. Colonel, 53 IL Infantry, Oct. 18, 1864. Resigned June 21, 1865, since "It has been over four years since I entered the service, and my business is such that it becomes absolutely necessary that I should quit the service."

John W. McClanahan (J.S. Porter, Photographer and Dealer in Photographic Albums and Oval Frames, Ottawa, IL; Abraham Lincoln Presidential Library & Museum).

Battle honors: Hatchie Bridge, Jackson Campaign, Atlanta Campaign (Atlanta), Savannah Campaign, Campaign of the Carolinas.
Born: Sept. 22, 1840, Carlisle, IN
Died: May 21, 1901, Sparland, IL
Occupation: Druggist before war. Hotelkeeper and U.S. Internal Revenue official after war.
Miscellaneous: Resided Lacon, Marshall Co., IL; and Sparland, Marshall Co., IL
Buried: Sparland Cemetery, Sparland, IL
References: Pension File and Military Service File, National Archives. Obituary, *Peoria Herald-Transcript,* May 23, 1901. Letters Received, Volunteer Service Branch, Adjutant General's Office, File M480(VS)1870, National Archives.

John Dickson McClure

Captain, Co. C, 47 IL Infantry, Sept. 1, 1861. Major, 47 IL Infantry, Nov. 27, 1862. Chief of Staff, Staff of Brig. Gen. James M. Tuttle, 3 Division, 15 Army Corps, Army of the Tennessee, May–June 1863. Colonel, 47 IL Infantry, May 17, 1863. GSW right breast, Vicksburg, MS, June 20, 1863. Commanded 2 Brigade, 1 Division, 16 Army Corps, Army of the Tennessee, July 14–Aug. 17, 1864. Honorably mustered out, Oct. 11, 1864. Battle honors: Vicksburg Campaign, Meridian Expedition, Red River Campaign (Pleasant Hill), Lake Chicot, Tupelo.
Born: Nov. 4, 1835, Franklin Co., PA

John Dickson McClure (Richard F. Carlile Collection).

Died: March 2, 1911, Peoria, IL
Occupation: Lumber and grain dealer before war. Real estate and loan agent after war.
Offices/Honors: Clerk of Peoria County Court, 1865–82
Miscellaneous: Resided Elmwood, Peoria Co., IL; and Peoria, Peoria Co., IL
Buried: Springdale Cemetery, Peoria, IL (Prospect Hill Division, Section 1, Lot 7)
References: Newton Bateman, Paul Selby, and David McCulloch, editors. *Historical Encyclopedia of Illinois and History of Peoria County.* Chicago and Peoria, 1902. James M. Rice. *Peoria City and County, Illinois.* Chicago, IL, 1912. *Soldiers' and Patriots' Biographical Album.* Chicago, IL, 1892. Obituary, *Peoria Herald-Transcript,* March 3, 1911. Pension File and Military Service File, National Archives. *Memorials of Deceased Companions of the Commandery of the State of Illinois MOLLUS, from July 1, 1901, to Dec. 31, 1911.* Chicago, IL, 1912. *The History of Peoria County, Illinois.* Chicago, IL, 1880. Byron Cloyd Bryner. *Bugle Echoes: The Story of Illinois 47th.* Springfield, IL, 1905. Robert J. Burdette. *The Drums of the 47th.* Indianapolis, IN, 1914. Obituary Circular, Whole No. 677, Illinois MOLLUS.

Joseph B. McCown

Lieutenant Colonel, 63 IL Infantry, April 10, 1862. Colonel, 63 IL Infantry, Sept. 29, 1862. Commanded 1 Brigade, 3 Division, 15 Army Corps, Army of the Tennessee, March 12–April 2, 1864 and Sept. 1, 1864–Jan. 26, 1865. Honorably mustered out, April 9, 1865. Battle honors: Vicksburg Campaign,

John Dickson McClure (Thurlow, Photographer, Next door above Howell & Co.'s Bank, Main Street, Peoria, IL; Roger D. Hunt Collection, USAMHI [RG98S-CWP80.29]).

Joseph B. McCown (Frank Crawford Collection).

Missionary Ridge, Atlanta Campaign, Savannah Campaign, Campaign of the Carolinas.
  Born: 1819 (or 1824)?, Nelson Co., KY
  Died: Nov. 21, 1869, Camargo, IL
  Other Wars: Mexican War (Sergeant, Co. H, 4 IL Infantry)
  Occupation: Dry goods merchant
  Miscellaneous: Resided District 19, Edgar Co., IL; and Camargo, Douglas Co., IL
  Buried: Vermilion Grove Cemetery, near Georgetown, Vermilion Co., IL
  References: John Gresham. *Historical and Biographical Record of Douglas County, Illinois.* Logansport, IN, 1900. *County of Douglas, Illinois: Historical and Biographical.* Chicago, IL, 1884. Pension File and Military Service File, National Archives. Letters Received, Volunteer Service Branch, Adjutant General's Office, File M2535(VS)1863, National Archives.

Robert Hugh McFadden

2 Lieutenant, Co. B, 7 IL Infantry (3 months), April 25, 1861. Honorably mustered out, July 25, 1861. 1 Lieutenant, Co. D, 41 IL Infantry, July 30, 1861. Captain, Co. D, 41 IL Infantry, Feb. 15, 1862. Major, 41 IL Infantry, Sept. 30, 1863. Commanded 2 Brigade, 4 Division, 17 Army Corps, Army of the Tennessee, Oct. 1–Nov. 6, 1864. Lieutenant Colonel, 53 IL Infantry, Jan. 1, 1865. Colonel, 53 IL Infantry, July 14, 1865. Honorably mustered out, July 22, 1865. Battle honors: Fort Donelson, Shiloh, Atlanta Campaign, Savannah Campaign.

Robert Hugh McFadden (Vann R. Martin Collection).

  Born: Sept. 13, 1833, Zanesville, OH
  Died: Jan. 31, 1914, Mattoon, IL
  Occupation: Cabinet maker, pension claim agent, and justice of the peace
  Miscellaneous: Resided Mattoon, Coles Co., IL
  Buried: Dodge Grove Cemetery, Mattoon, IL (Section 2, Lot 96)
  References: Obituary, *Mattoon Daily Journal-Gazette,* Feb. 2, 1914. *Portrait and Biographical Album of Coles County, Illinois.* Chicago, IL, 1887. *The United States Biographical Dictionary and Portrait Gallery of Eminent and Self-Made Men.* Illinois Volume. Chicago and New York, 1883. Pension File and Military Service File, National Archives. Letters Received, Volunteer Service Branch, Adjutant General's Office, File M2584(VS)1863, National Archives. *The History of Coles County, Illinois.* Chicago, IL, 1879.

George Williamson McKeaig

Colonel, 120 IL Infantry, Oct. 29, 1862. GSW right breast and right arm, Ripley, MS, June 11, 1864. Taken prisoner, Ripley, MS, June 11, 1864. Paroled July 7, 1864. Exchanged Jan. 2, 1865. Commanded 1 Infantry Brigade, District of West Tennessee, Department of the Tennessee, July–Sept. 1865. Honorably mustered out, Sept. 10, 1865. Battle honors: Vicksburg Campaign, Ripley.
  Born: May 20, 1824, Jefferson Co., KY
  Died: April 23, 1897, Cairo, IL

Education: Attended Hanover (IN) College. Attended Indiana University, Bloomington, IN.
Other Wars: Mexican War (Sergeant, Co. E, 1 KY Infantry)
Occupation: Lawyer, hotelkeeper, and real estate agent
Offices/Honors: Postmaster, Shawneetown, IL, 1853–58. Postmaster, Cairo, IL, 1870–83.
Miscellaneous: Resided Shawneetown, Gallatin Co., IL, before war; and Cairo, Alexander Co., IL, after war
Buried: Beech Grove Cemetery, Mounds, IL
References: *Biographical Encyclopedia of Illinois of the Nineteenth Century.* Philadelphia, PA, 1875. Obituary, *Cairo Weekly Citizen,* April 29, 1897. Pension File and Military Service File, National Archives.

William McMurtry

Colonel, 102 IL Infantry, Sept. 2, 1862. Resigned Feb. 22, 1863, "in consequence of long-continued disease of the liver, lungs and the organs of digestion," to date Oct. 24, 1862, when he left the regiment on recruiting service.
Born: Feb. 20, 1801, Mercer Co., KY
Died: April 10, 1875, Henderson, IL
Other Wars: Black Hawk War (Captain, McMurtry's Co., Odd Battalion, Mounted Rangers, Illinois Volunteers)
Occupation: Farmer
Offices/Honors: Illinois House of Representatives, 1836–38. Illinois Senate, 1842–46. Lieutenant Governor of Illinois, 1849–53.
Miscellaneous: Resided Henderson, Knox Co., IL
Buried: Rice-Blue Cemetery, near Henderson, IL
References: *Portrait and Biographical Album of Knox County, Illinois.* Chicago, IL, 1886. Newton Bateman, Paul Selby, W. Selden Gale, and George C. Gale, editors. *Historical Encyclopedia of Illinois and Knox County.* Chicago and New York, 1899. Military Service File, National Archives. Letters Received, Volunteer Service Branch, Adjutant General's Office, File I42(VS)1866, National Archives. Philip J. Reyburn and Terry L. Wilson, editors. *"Jottings from Dixie": The Civil War Dispatches of Sergeant Major Stephen F. Fleharty, U.S.A.* Baton Rouge, LA, 1999. Charles C. Chapman. *History of Knox County, Illinois.* Chicago, IL, 1878. Albert J. Perry. *History of Knox County, Illinois: Its Cities, Towns and People.* Chicago, IL, 1912. Stephen F. Fleharty. *Our Regiment: A History of the 102nd Illinois Infantry Volunteers.* Chicago, IL, 1865.

Geza Mihalotzy

Captain, Lincoln Riflemen, Cairo Expedition, April 19–May 3, 1861. Lieutenant Colonel, 24 IL Infantry, July 8, 1861. Colonel, 24 IL Infantry,

William McMurtry (Albert J. Perry. *History of Knox County, Illinois: Its Cities, Towns and People.* Chicago, IL, 1912).

Geza Mihalotzy (Webster & Bro., Louisville, KY).

Dec. 24, 1861. Although he was found guilty, Aug. 13, 1862, of "Disobedience of Orders" for allowing peaceable citizens to be molested during the Union occupation of Athens, AL, his court-martial sentence was remitted since he "exhibited a commendable zeal and determination to suppress the bad conduct of his troops when it was brought to his notice." GSW right hand, Chickamauga, GA, Sept. 19, 1863. GSW right arm and right side, Buzzard Roost, near Dalton, GA, Feb. 25, 1864. Battle honors: Stone's River, Tullahoma Campaign, Chickamauga, Buzzard Roost.

Born: April 21, 1825, Nagyvarad, Hungary
Died: March 11, 1864, DOW Chattanooga, TN
Education: Attended Austrian Military Academy, Wiener Neustadt, Austria
Other Wars: Hungarian War of Independence, 1848–49
Occupation: Druggist
Miscellaneous: Resided Chicago, IL
Buried: Chattanooga National Cemetery, Chattanooga, TN (Section A, Site 439)
References: Istvan Kornel Vida. *Hungarian Emigres in the American Civil War.* Jefferson, NC, 2012. Edmund Vasvary. *Lincoln's Hungarian Heroes: The Participation of Hungarians in the Civil War, 1861–1865.* Washington, D.C., 1939. Ray Burhop. *The Twenty-Fourth Illinois Infantry Regiment, 1861–1864.* Lexington, KY, 2003. Eugene Pivany. *Hungarians in the American Civil War.* Cleveland, OH, 1913. Thomas P. Lowry. *Tarnished Eagles: The Courts-Martial of Fifty Union Colonels and Lieutenant Colonels.* Mechanicsburg, PA, 1997. Court-martial Case Files, 1809–1894, File KK-0194, National Archives. Pension File and Military Service File, National Archives. William L. Burton. *Melting Pot Soldiers: The Union's Ethnic Regiments.* Ames, IA, 1988. Alfred T. Andreas. *History of Chicago from the Earliest Period to the Present Time.* Chicago, IL, 1885. Obituary, *Chicago Daily Tribune*, March 15, 1864.

Jonathan Rice Miles

Captain, Co. F, 27 IL Infantry, Aug. 10, 1861. Major, 27 IL Infantry, Dec. 18, 1861. Lieutenant Colonel, 27 IL Infantry, April 16, 1862. Colonel, 27 IL Infantry, Jan. 1, 1863. Commanded 3 Brigade, 3 Division, 20 Army Corps, Army of the Cumberland, Feb. 1863. Resigned April 28, 1864, since "my wife's health has been gradually declining during my absence and is now so delicate that I think it a duty I owe to her to come home." Battle honors: Belmont, Chickamauga, Missionary Ridge.

Born: Nov. 17, 1817, near Russellville, Logan Co., KY
Died: April 1, 1903, Miles Station, IL
Occupation: Farmer

Jonathan Rice Miles (courtesy Henry Deeks).

Jonathan Rice Miles (*History of Macoupin County, Illinois.* Philadelphia, PA, 1879).

Miscellaneous: Resided Miles Station, Macoupin Co., IL
Buried: Miles Station Cemetery, Miles Station, IL
References: *Portrait and Biographical Record of Macoupin County, Illinois.* Chicago, IL, 1891. *History*

of Macoupin County, Illinois. Philadelphia, PA, 1879. Pension File and Military Service File, National Archives. Letters Received, Volunteer Service Branch, Adjutant General's Office, File M2026(VS) 1862, National Archives. Obituary, *Alton Evening Telegraph*, April 2, 1903. William A. Schmitt. *History of the Twenty-Seventh Illinois Volunteers, With a Roster of the Surviving Members.* Winchester, IL, 1892.

Thomas J. Milholland

2 Lieutenant, Co. A, 107 IL Infantry, Aug. 22, 1862. Captain, Co. A, 107 IL Infantry, Feb. 7, 1863. Major, 107 IL Infantry, Sept. 26, 1864. Acting AIG, 2 Division, 23 Army Corps, Army of the Ohio, Oct. 1, 1864–Jan. 13, 1865. Lieutenant Colonel, 107 IL Infantry, Jan. 2, 1865. *Colonel,* 107 IL Infantry, May 10, 1865. Honorably mustered out, June 21, 1865. Battle honors: Knoxville Campaign (Campbell's Station), Atlanta Campaign, Franklin, Nashville, Campaign of the Carolinas.
Born: Feb. 2, 1835, OH
Died: Nov. 29, 1883, Edwardsville, IL
Occupation: Lawyer before war. Grocer after war.
Miscellaneous: Resided Okeana, Butler Co., OH (1860); Wapella, DeWitt Co., IL; Paola, Miami Co., KS (1870); and Wellington, Sumner Co., KS
Buried: Wellington Pioneer Cemetery, Wellington, KS. Cenotaph in Prairie Lawn Cemetery, Wellington, KS (GAR Section).
References: Military Service File, National Archives. Letters Received, Volunteer Service Branch, Adjutant General's Office, File 7901(VS) 1884, National Archives. U.S. Census (1860 and 1870). Obituary, *Clinton Public,* Dec. 7, 1883. http://www.findagrave.com.

Charles Henry Miller

2 Lieutenant, Co. H, 38 IL Infantry, Aug. 15, 1861. Declined to be mustered and left regiment, Dec. 20, 1861, due to disagreement with Colonel William P. Carlin. 1 Lieutenant, Adjutant, 106 IL Infantry, Sept. 18, 1862. Acting AAG, 2 Brigade, 2 Division, 7 Army Corps, Department of Arkansas, July 20–Sept. 3, 1864. Lieutenant Colonel, 106 IL Infantry, May 30, 1865. *Colonel,* 106 IL Infantry, July 15, 1865. Honorably mustered out, July 12, 1865. Battle honors: Fredericktown, Jackson (TN).
Born: Feb. 2, 1832, Newark, Nottinghamshire, England
Died: Dec. 31, 1925, Columbus, OH
Occupation: School teacher and lumber merchant before war. Manufacturer and real estate agent after war.
Miscellaneous: Resided Lincoln, Logan Co., IL, to 1874; Tiffin, Seneca Co., OH, 1874–81; and Columbus, Franklin Co., OH, after 1881

Charles Henry Miller.

Buried: Greenlawn Cemetery, Columbus, OH (Section 50, Lot 54)
References: *A Centennial Biographical History of the City of Columbus and Franklin County, Ohio.* Chicago, IL, 1901. Pension File and Military Service File, National Archives. Obituary, *Ohio State Journal,* Jan. 1, 1926. Circular, Whole No. 863, Ohio MOLLUS. Obituary Circular, Whole No. 1304, Ohio MOLLUS. Letters Received, Commission Branch, Adjutant General's Office, File M627(CB) 1865, National Archives.

Silas Miller

2 Lieutenant, Co. C, 7 IL Infantry (3 months), April 18, 1861. 1 Lieutenant, Co. C, 7 IL Infantry, April 25, 1861. Honorably mustered out, July 25, 1861. Captain, Co. B, 36 IL Infantry, Sept. 3, 1861. Major, 36 IL Infantry, Nov. 25, 1862. GSW left thigh, Stone's River, TN, Dec. 31, 1862. Taken prisoner, Stone's River, TN, Dec. 31, 1862. Confined Atlanta, GA, and Libby Prison, Richmond, VA. Paroled May 5, 1863. Colonel, 36 IL Infantry, March 2, 1863. Commanded 1 Brigade, 3 Division, 20 Army Corps, Army of the Cumberland, Sept. 19–28, 1863. GSW right shoulder, Kenesaw Mountain, GA, June 27, 1864. Battle honors: Pea Ridge, Perryville, Stone's River, Tullahoma Campaign, Chickamauga, Missionary Ridge, Atlanta Campaign (Kenesaw Mountain).
Born: April 15, 1839, Tompkins Co., NY
Died: July 27, 1864, DOW Nashville, TN
Education: Attended Clark Seminary, Aurora,

Silas Miller (D. C. Pratt, Photographic Artist, Broadway, Aurora, IL; Roger D. Hunt Collection, USAMHI [RG98S-CWP64.3]).

Silas Miller (standing, with Captain Irving Parkhurst, left, and Captain Abel Longworth, right) (courtesy Tom Molocea).

IL; and Washington County Seminary, Fort Edward, NY

Occupation: Law student and newspaper office employee

Miscellaneous: Resided Aurora, Kane Co., IL

Buried: Spring Lake Cemetery, Aurora, IL (Section K-West, Lot 1)

References: James Barnet, editor. *The Martyrs and Heroes of Illinois in the Great Rebellion.* Second Edition. Chicago, IL, 1866. Obituary, *Aurora Beacon*, Aug. 4, 1864. Lyman G. Bennett and William M. Haigh. *History of the 36th Regiment Illinois Volunteers during the War of the Rebellion.* Aurora, IL, 1876. Military Service File, National Archives.

James Monroe

Captain, Co. B, 7 IL Infantry (3 months), April 25, 1861. Honorably mustered out, July 25, 1861. Captain, Co. B, 7 IL Infantry (3 years), July 25, 1861. Major, 7 IL Infantry, March 22, 1862. Resigned Sept. 3, 1862, to accept promotion. Colonel, 123 IL Infantry, Sept. 6, 1862. GSW heart, Farmington, TN, Oct. 7, 1863. Battle honors: Fort Donelson, Shiloh, Perryville, Stone's River, Tullahoma Campaign, Chickamauga, Wheeler and Roddey's Raid on Rosecrans' Communication (Farmington).

Born: Jan. 4, 1832, Greensburg, KY

Silas Miller (courtesy Tom Molocea).

James Monroe (Abraham Lincoln Presidential Library & Museum).

Died: Oct. 7, 1863, KIA Farmington, TN
Occupation: Dry goods merchant
Offices/Honors: Mayor of Mattoon, IL, 1861
Miscellaneous: Resided Mattoon, Coles Co., IL
Buried: Dodge Grove Cemetery, Mattoon, IL (Section 4, Lot 162)
References: Alexander Summers. *Gone to Glory at Farmington: A Profile of Col. James Monroe of Mattoon, Hero of Two Regiments in the Civil War.* Mattoon, IL, 1963. *Portrait and Biographical Album of Coles County, Illinois.* Chicago, IL, 1887. Pension File and Military Service File, National Archives. Paul M. Angle, editor. *Three Years in the Army of the Cumberland: The Letters and Diary of Major James A. Connolly.* Bloomington, IN, 1959. Richard A. Baumgartner. *Blue Lightning: Wilder's Mounted Infantry Brigade in the Battle of Chickamauga.* Huntington, WV, 1997. Jean Johnston. *Mattoon: A Pictorial History.* St. Louis, MO, 1988. Glenn W. Sunderland. *Lightning at Hoover's Gap: Wilder's Brigade in the Civil War.* New York City, 1969.

Absalom B. Moore

Colonel, 104 IL Infantry, Aug. 27, 1862. Commanded 39 Brigade, 12 Division, Army of the Ohio, Oct. 15–Nov. 6, 1862 and Dec. 2–7, 1862. Taken prisoner, Hartsville, TN, Dec. 7, 1862. Confined Atlanta, GA, and Libby Prison, Richmond, VA. Paroled Feb. 9, 1863. Accused of neglect of duty for not properly preparing for the enemy's attack on Hartsville and recommended for dismissal, he escaped dismissal through an administrative error but had to "endure the odium of failure," with the regimental historian observing, "It was his misfortune to hold a command for which he was unfitted by reason of inexperience, the want of confidence on the part of many of his officers, and the absence of those military instincts which soldiers recognize and trust in." Commanded 1 Brigade, 2 Division, 14 Army Corps, Army of the Cumberland, Aug. 1863. Resigned Sept. 9, 1863, since "I am growing rapidly deaf, and I must do something to prevent the further advance of my disease.... I have become so afflicted that I am unable to distinguish the direction of sound, and it is with great difficulty that I can hear conversation at all." Battle honors: Hartsville, Tullahoma Campaign.

Born: Jan. 8, 1828, NJ
Died: June 7, 1879, Chicago, IL
Occupation: Railroad purchasing agent before war. Manufacturer and U.S. Internal Revenue official after war.
Offices/Honors: Circuit Court Clerk, La Salle Co., IL, 1861–64. County Clerk, La Salle Co., IL, 1865–69.
Miscellaneous: Resided Ottawa, La Salle Co., IL, to 1873; and Chicago, IL
Buried: Ottawa Avenue Cemetery, Ottawa, IL (Ford Addition, Section 12, Lot 32)
References: William W. Calkins. *The History of the 104th Regiment of Illinois Volunteer Infantry. War of the Great Rebellion, 1862–1865.* Chicago, IL, 1895. Obituary, *Ottawa Republican,* June 12, 1879. Obituary, *Ottawa Free Trader,* June 14, 1879. Pension File and Military Service File, National Archives. Letters Received, Volunteer Service Branch, Adjutant General's Office, File A735(VS)1863, National Archives. Obituary, *Chicago Daily Tribune,* June 10, 1879. Thomas M. Eddy. *The Patriotism of Illinois.* Chicago, IL, 1865. *History of La Salle County, Illinois.* Chicago, IL, 1886.

Risdon Marshall Moore

Colonel, 117 IL Infantry, Sept. 19, 1862. Commanded 3 Brigade, 3 Division, 16 Army Corps, Army of the Tennessee, Feb. 28–May 21, 1864. Commanded 3 Brigade, 2 Division, 16 Army Corps, Military Division of West Mississippi, Feb. 18–March 5, 1865. Honorably mustered out, Aug. 5, 1865. Battle honors: Meridian Expedition, Red River Campaign (Pleasant Hill), Tupelo, Mobile Campaign (Fort Blakely).

Born: Feb. 16, 1827, near Cahokia, IL
Died: Jan. 26, 1909, San Antonio, TX
Education: Graduated McKendree College, Lebanon, IL, 1850
Occupation: Professor of Mathematics and Astronomy, McKendree College, Lebanon, IL, before

Risdon Marshall Moore (H.A. Balch's Star Photograph Gallery, Nos. 219 and 221 Main Street, Memphis, TN; Abraham Lincoln Presidential Library & Museum).

war. Coal mine operator and Special Agent, U.S. Treasury Department after war.

Miscellaneous: Resided Lebanon, St. Clair Co., IL, to 1866; Selma, Dallas Co., AL, 1866–75; Mobile, Mobile Co., AL, 1875–77; San Antonio, Bexar Co., TX, 1877–1909

Buried: San Antonio National Cemetery, San Antonio, TX (Section A, Grave 44)

References: Joseph Guandolo, editor. *Centennial McKendree College, With St. Clair County History.* Lebanon, IL, 1928. Edwin G. Gerling. *The One Hundred Seventeenth Illinois Infantry Volunteers (The McKendree Regiment) 1862–1865.* Highland, IL, 1992. Obituary Circular, Whole No. 348, Missouri MOLLUS. "Col. Risdon M. Moore," *Journal of the Illinois State Historical Society,* Vol. 2, No. 1 (April 1909). Pension File and Military Service File, National Archives. Letters Received, Volunteer Service Branch, Adjutant General's Office, File M2631(VS) 1865, National Archives. Obituary, *San Antonio Daily Express,* Jan. 27, 1909. Paul and Chester Farthing, editors. *Philo History: Chronicles and Biographies of the Philosophian Literary Society of McKendree College.* Lebanon, IL, 1911.

Robert Steele Moore

Captain, Co. E, 27 IL Infantry, Aug. 16, 1861. GSW right shoulder, Farmington, MS, May 9, 1862.

Robert Steele Moore (Henry J. Aten. *History of the Eighty-Fifth Regiment Illinois Volunteer Infantry.* Hiawatha, KS, 1901).

Colonel, 85 IL Infantry, Aug. 27, 1862. Resigned June 14, 1863, due to "partial hemiplegia, the muscles of the right hip and thigh being partially paralyzed and much atrophied with loss of sensation and motion." Battle honors: Belmont, Farmington, Perryville, Stone's River.

Born: March 19, 1827, Green Co., KY

Died: May 23, 1906, Denver, CO

Other Wars: Mexican War (Private, Co. F, 4 IL Infantry)

Occupation: Grain commission merchant before war. Contractor and hot springs proprietor after war.

Offices/Honors: Postmaster, Waunita, CO, 1887–91. Postmaster, Littleton, CO, 1895.

Miscellaneous: Resided Havana, Mason Co., IL, to 1879; Waunita Hot Springs, Gunnison Co., CO; Littleton, Arapahoe Co., CO; and Denver, Arapahoe Co., CO

Buried: Riverside Cemetery, Denver, CO (Block 27, Lot 54)

References: Obituary, *Rocky Mountain News,* May 24, 1906. Henry J. Aten. *History of the Eighty-Fifth Regiment Illinois Volunteer Infantry.* Hiawatha, KS, 1901. Joseph Cochrane. *Centennial History of Mason County.* Springfield, IL, 1876. Pension File and Military Service File, National Archives.

William Pinckard Moore

Captain, Co. B, 49 IL Infantry, Dec. 31, 1861. Taken prisoner, Henderson's Station, TN, Nov. 25, 1862. Paroled Feb. 26, 1863. Acting AIG, Staff of Colonel James I. Gilbert, Gilbert's Brigade, District of Memphis, 16 Army Corps, Army of the Tennessee, Jan. 1864. GSW right shoulder, Pleasant Hill, LA, April 9, 1864. Major, 49 IL Infantry, April 20, 1864. Lieutenant Colonel, 49 IL Infantry, July 1, 1864. *Colonel,* 49 IL Infantry, May 11, 1865. Honorably mustered out, Sept. 9, 1865. Battle honors: Henderson's Station, Red River Campaign (Pleasant Hill), Nashville.

Born: July 8, 1833, Waterloo, IL
Died: March 9, 1903, Tulsa, OK
Occupation: Merchant before war. Cattle drover and hotel proprietor after war.
Miscellaneous: Resided Waterloo, Monroe Co., IL; Chetopa, Labette Co., KS; Independence, Montgomery Co., KS; Butler, Bates Co., MO; and Tulsa, Tulsa Co., OK, after 1872
Buried: Oaklawn Cemetery, Tulsa, OK (Section 2, Row 26)
References: N. Dale Talkington and Deone K. Pearcy. *Tributes of Blue: Obituaries of Civil War Union Soldiers and Sailors Buried in Oklahoma.* Tehachapi, CA, 1996. Obituary, *Tulsa Democrat,* March 13, 1903. Pension File and Military Service File, National Archives. http://civilwar.illinoisgenweb.org/photos/moorewmpcolonel.html.

William Pinckard Moore (Roger D. Hunt Collection, USAMHI [RG98S-CWP207.5]).

William Pinckard Moore.

Francis Moro

Colonel, 63 IL Infantry, April 10, 1862. On Aug. 2, 1862, he addressed a letter to President Lincoln complaining, "I have become utterly disgusted with the course pursued by my superiors" in their overly protective attitude toward the slaves and other property of the rebel citizens of Jackson, TN. "Let the families of rebels be driven without our lines, let rebel soldiers be made to feel the care of their own families and property, and I assure you that they are half whipped, but as long as the Union army protects the wives, children and property of traitors, they fight us with courage and great hopes of success. We may kill a rebel and it is taken very coolly by them, but if we take a Negro it produces great excitement in their midst…. I ask of you as a favor that you transfer my regiment to some other command … where I can take a prisoner or use contraband help and be free from orders to deliver slaves to traitors." Failing to get a response to his letter, he resigned Sept. 29, 1862, since "I cannot longer conscientiously continue in command of the regiment. My family and property are threatened by traitors

Francis Moro (James Grant Wilson. *Biographical Sketches of Illinois Officers Engaged in the War Against the Rebellion of 1861.* Chicago, IL, 1862).

at home to such an extent as to demand my presence for their protection."

Born: Sept. 5, 1824, New York City, NY

Died: Sept. 11, 1904, Warsaw, IN

Education: Attended Cincinnati (OH) Eclectic Medical Institute

Other Wars: Claimed two years service in Mexican War, "went out as private and passed through the different positions to that of major." However, National Archives has no record of any such service.

Occupation: Physician and Baptist clergyman

Miscellaneous: Resided Mount Carmel, Wabash Co., IL, 1856–61; Olney, Richland Co., IL, 1861–63; Middletown, Vigo Co., IN, 1863–66; Franklin, Johnson Co., IN, 1866–67; Vevay, Switzerland Co., IN, 1867–69; Columbus, Bartholomew Co., IN, 1869–71; and Warsaw, Kosciusko Co., IN, after 1871

Buried: Oakwood Cemetery, Warsaw, IN (Block 23, Lot 80)

References: Obituary, *Warsaw Daily Times*, Sept. 12, 1904. James Grant Wilson. *Biographical Sketches of Illinois Officers Engaged in the War Against the Rebellion of 1861.* Chicago, IL, 1862. Pension File and Military Service File, National Archives. Letters Received, Volunteer Service Branch, Adjutant General's Office, Files M757(VS)1862 and M1517(VS)1862, National Archives. Kingman Brothers, compilers. *Combination Atlas Map of Kosciusko County, IN.* Chicago, IL, 1879.

William Ralls Morrison

Colonel, 49 IL Infantry, Dec. 29, 1861. Commanded 3 Brigade, 1 Division, Army of the Tennessee, Feb. 15, 1862. GSW right hip, Fort Donelson, TN, Feb. 15, 1862. Commanded Post of Bethel, TN, Dec. 1862. Resigned Dec. 13, 1862, since "my fellow citizens of the 12th Congressional District of Illinois have confided to me the duty of representing them in the next Congress of the United States, and that I may be more competent to discharge that duty my attention should at once be given to matters pertaining thereto." General Grant reluctantly forwarded the resignation with the observation, "He is one of our best officers." Battle honors: Fort Donelson.

Born: Sept. 14, 1825, Prairie du Long, near Waterloo, IL

Died: Sept. 29, 1909, Waterloo, IL

Education: Attended McKendree College, Lebanon, IL

Other Wars: Mexican War (Private, Co. I, 2 IL Infantry)

Occupation: Lawyer

Offices/Honors: Illinois House of Representatives, 1854–60 (Speaker 1859–60), 1870–72. U.S. House of Representatives, 1863–65, 1873–87. Interstate Commerce Commission, 1887–97.

Miscellaneous: Resided Waterloo, Monroe Co., IL

Buried: Waterloo Cemetery, Waterloo, IL

References: *Portrait and Biographical Record of Randolph, Jackson, Perry, and Monroe Counties, Illi-*

William Ralls Morrison.

William Ralls Morrison (post-war) (Brady's National Photographic Portrait Gallery, No. 352 Pennsylvania Ave., Washington, DC; courtesy Olaf).

nois. Chicago, IL, 1894. Obituary, *Waterloo Republican*, Oct. 6, 1909. Obituary, *Washington National Tribune*, Oct. 7, 1909. James L. Harrison, compiler. *Biographical Directory of the American Congress, 1774–1949*. Washington, D.C., 1950. Joseph Guandolo, editor. *Centennial McKendree College, With St. Clair County History*. Lebanon, IL, 1928. Charles F. Ritter and Jon L. Wakelyn. *American Legislative Leaders, 1850–1910*. Westport, CT, 1989. John M. Palmer, editor. *The Bench and Bar of Illinois: Historical and Reminiscent*. Chicago, IL, 1899. Military Service File, National Archives. Letters Received, Volunteer Service Branch, Adjutant General's Office, File M2174(VS) 1862, National Archives. *Biographical Encyclopedia of Illinois of the Nineteenth Century*. Philadelphia, PA, 1875.

John January Mudd

Major, 2 IL Cavalry, Sept. 23, 1861. GSW lumbar region, Fort Donelson, TN, Feb. 16, 1862, at the hands of a traitorous citizen. Acting ADC, Staff of Major Gen. John A. McClernand, District of Jackson, Army of the Tennessee, June–Aug. 1862. Lieutenant Colonel, 2 IL Cavalry, Dec. 31, 1862. Colo-

Right, top: John January Mudd (Roger D. Hunt Collection, USAMHI [RG98S-CWP107.81]). *Middle:* John January Mudd (Carte de Visite by J. Carbutt, Photographic Artist, 131 Lake St., Chicago, IL; Wayne Jorgenson Collection). *Bottom:* John January Mudd (*Proceedings of the Reunion Held in 1906 by the Association of Survivors 2nd Regiment Illinois Veteran Cavalry Volunteers at Springfield, Illinois*. Pana, IL, 1907).

nel, 2 IL Cavalry, Feb. 16, 1863. Sentenced by court martial to be reprimanded for "Disobedience of Orders" during an expedition to Greenville, MS, Feb. 23, 1863, he escaped punishment when Major Gen. McClernand disapproved the sentence since "his general good character as an officer, soldier, and gentleman, which is abundantly established by the evidence, entitles him to acquittal." Chief of Cavalry, Staff of Major Gen. John A. McClernand, 13 Army Corps, Army of the Tennessee, April–June 1863. GSW face and neck, near Vicksburg, MS, June 15, 1863. Commanded Cavalry Brigade, 13 Army Corps, Department of the Gulf, Aug. 14–Sept. 14, 1863. Commanded 2 Brigade, Cavalry Division, Department of the Gulf, Sept. 14–Nov. 3, 1863. GSW head, Dunn's Bayou, LA, May 3, 1864. Battle honors: Fort Donelson, Operations on the Mississippi Central Railroad (Holly Springs), Port Gibson, Champion's Hill, Big Black River Bridge, Vicksburg Campaign, Operations in the Teche Country (Bayou Bourbeau), Red River Campaign.

Born: Jan. 9, 1820, St. Charles Co., MO
Died: May 3, 1864, KIA Dunn's Bayou, near Cheneyville, LA (during capture of U.S. Steamer, City Belle)
Occupation: Commission merchant
Offices/Honors: Postmaster, Florence, Pike Co., IL, 1846–49
Miscellaneous: Resided Pittsfield, Pike Co., IL; St. Louis, MO; and Chicago, IL
Buried: Oakwood Cemetery, Pittsfield, IL
References: Samuel H. Fletcher. *The History of Company A, Second Illinois Cavalry.* Chicago, IL, 1912. *Proceedings of the Reunion Held in 1906 by the Association of Survivors 2nd Regiment Illinois Veteran Cavalry Volunteers at Springfield, Illinois.* Pana, IL, 1907. Newton Bateman and Paul Selby, editors. *Historical Encyclopedia of Illinois.* Chicago and New York, 1900. James Barnet, editor. *The Martyrs and Heroes of Illinois in the Great Rebellion.* Second Edition. Chicago, IL, 1866. Obituary, *Pike County Democrat,* June 4, 1864. Thomas M. Eddy. *The Patriotism of Illinois.* Chicago, IL, 1865. Pension File and Military Service File, National Archives. Letters Received, Commission Branch, Adjutant General's Office, File M1563(CB)1864, National Archives. Court-martial Case Files, 1809–1894, File LL-0378, National Archives.

George Washington Neely

Colonel, 131 IL Infantry, Nov. 13, 1862. Commanded Detached Brigade, District of Northeast Louisiana, Army of the Tennessee, May–Aug. 1863. Honorably mustered out, Sept. 16, 1863, upon consolidation of regiment with 29 IL Infantry. Battle honors: Arkansas Post, Vicksburg Campaign.

Born: Feb. 17, 1830, Caldwell Co., KY

George Washington Neely (Relief Portrait, Vicksburg National Military Park).

Died: May 15, 1867, Newburgh, IN
Occupation: Lawyer and pension claim agent
Miscellaneous: Resided New Liberty, Pope Co., IL; and Metropolis, Massac Co., IL
Buried: Lewis-Neely Cemetery, near Hamletsburg, Pope Co., IL (unmarked)
References: *Pope County, Illinois: History and Families, 1816–1989.* Paducah, KY, 1989. Obituary, *Metropolis Promulgator,* May 23, 1867. Paul E. Fellows, editor. *Massac County Memories, Volume 1, 1849–67.* Metropolis, IL, 1992. Military Service File, National Archives. Carol A. Crisp, compiler. *Pope County, Illinois, Cemeteries: Results of a Graveyard Obsession.* Vol. 3. N.p., 2010. *Illinois at Vicksburg.* Chicago, IL, 1907.

Garrett Voorhees Nevius

Captain, Co. D, 11 IL Infantry (3 months), April 30, 1861. Honorably mustered out, July 30, 1861. Major, 11 IL Infantry (3 years), July 30, 1861. Lieutenant Colonel, 11 IL Infantry, March 21, 1862. GSW hand, Shiloh, TN, April 6, 1862. Colonel, 11 IL Infantry, March 17, 1863. GSW head, Vicksburg, MS, May 22, 1863. Battle honors: Fort Donelson, Shiloh, Vicksburg Campaign.

Born: July 8, 1838, Lodi, Seneca Co., NY
Died: May 22, 1863, KIA Vicksburg, MS
Occupation: Merchant and photographer

Above: Garrett Voorhees Nevius (Barnes, Nevius & Co., Photographers, Rockford, IL; Frank D. Korun Collection). *Below:* Garrett Voorhees Nevius (Barnes, Nevius & Co., Photographers, Rockford, IL).

Miscellaneous: Resided Rockford, Winnebago Co., IL

Buried: Lake View Cemetery, Interlaken, NY (Lot 181)

References: James T. Huffstodt, "One Who Didn't Come Back: The Story of Colonel Garrett Nevius," *Lincoln Herald*, Vol. 82, No. 1 (Spring 1980). Harvey M. Parker. *Proceedings of the First Reunion of the 11th Regiment Illinois Volunteer Infantry.* Ottawa, IL, 1875. Jim Huffstodt. *Hard Dying Men: The Story of General W. H. L. Wallace, General T. E. G. Ransom, and Their "Old Eleventh" Illinois Infantry in the American Civil War (1861–1865).* Bowie, MD, 1991. A. Van Doren Honeyman. *Joannes Nevius and His Descendants, 1627–1900.* Plainfield, NJ, 1900. Charles A. Church. *Past and Present of the City of Rockford and Winnebago County, Illinois.* Chicago, IL, 1905. Charles A. Church. *History of Rockford and Winnebago County, Illinois, from the First Settlement in 1834 to the Civil War.* Rockford, IL, 1900. Thomas M. Eddy. *The Patriotism of Illinois.* Chicago, IL, 1865. Military Service File, National Archives.

Alexander Jackson Nimmo

Colonel, 109 IL Infantry, Sept. 11, 1862. By order of the Secretary of War, he was discharged, April 10, 1863, with other officers of the regiment, "having been reported as utterly incompetent to perform the duties of their respective commissions, and evincing no disposition to improve themselves."

Born: Sept. 30, 1822, Union Co., IL

Died: July 21, 1902, Jonesboro, IL

Other Wars: Mexican War (Sergeant, Co. F, 2 IL Infantry)

Occupation: Saddler, farmer, county office holder, and police magistrate

Offices/Honors: Sheriff of Union Co., IL, 1850–62 and 1874–78. Union County Clerk, 1862–64 and 1870–74.

Miscellaneous: Resided Jonesboro, Union Co., IL

Buried: Jonesboro Cemetery, Jonesboro, IL

References: William H. Perrin, editor. *History of Alexander, Union, and Pulaski Counties, Illinois.* Chicago, IL, 1883. Obituary, *Jonesboro Gazette*, July 26, 1902. George E. Parks, "One Story of the 109th Illinois Volunteer Infantry Regiment," *Journal of the Illinois State Historical Society*, Vol. 56, No. 2 (Summer 1963). Pension File and Military Service File, National Archives. Darrel Dexter. *A House Divided: Union County, Illinois, 1818–1865.* Anna, IL, 1994. Letters Received, Volunteer Service Branch, Adjutant General's Office, File T99(VS)1863, National Archives. Darrel Dexter, compiler. *Union County, Illinois, Soldiers.* Carterville, IL, 1997.

Silas Noble

Colonel, 2 IL Cavalry, Aug. 12, 1861. Commanded Post of Paducah (KY), District of Columbus (KY), Department of the Tennessee, March–May 1862 and Nov.–Dec. 1862. Chief of Cavalry, Staff of Brig. Gen. Isaac F. Quinby, District of the Mississippi, Department of the Tennessee, June–Sept. 1862. On Dec. 29, 1862, fifteen officers of his regiment addressed a petition to General Grant requesting that Colonel Noble "be dismissed the service for incapacity, inefficiency and indolence which is so notorious with yourself ... that we deem it superfluous to give particulars." Grant forwarded the petition to General-in-Chief Halleck "with the urgent recommendation that Col. Noble be mustered out of service. Although a very clever old gentleman, he is entirely unfit for any military position whatever." He was finally mustered out for "inefficiency," Feb. 16, 1863. Battle honors: Fort Donelson.

Born: Feb. 19, 1808, Great Barrington, MA
Died: Feb. 3, 1867, Dixon, IL
Occupation: Lawyer and banker
Offices/Honors: Illinois Senate, 1846–48
Miscellaneous: Resided Dixon, Lee Co., IL. Uncle of Colonel Henry T. Noble (Quartermaster Department).
Buried: Oakwood Cemetery, Dixon, IL (Lot 127)
References: Samuel H. Fletcher. *The History of Company A, Second Illinois Cavalry.* Chicago, IL, 1912. *Proceedings of the Reunion Held in 1906 by the Association of Survivors 2nd Regiment Illinois Veteran Cavalry Volunteers at Springfield, Illinois.* Pana, IL, 1907. Lucius M. Boltwood, compiler. *History and Genealogy of the Family of Thomas Noble of Westfield, Massachusetts.* Hartford, CT, 1878. Military Service File, National Archives. Letters Received, Volunteer Service Branch, Adjutant General's Office, File N756(VS)1862, National Archives. John Y. Simon, editor. *The Papers of Ulysses S. Grant.* Volume 7: December 9, 1862–March 31, 1863. Carbondale, IL, 1979. Newton Bateman, Paul Selby, and A.C. Bardwell, editors. *Historical Encyclopedia of Illinois and History of Lee County.* Chicago, IL, 1904. "Col. Silas Noble, Cavalry Officer," *Dixon Evening Telegraph,* Centennial Edition, May 1, 1951.

Richard Howard Nodine

Major, 25 IL Infantry, Aug. 21, 1861. Engineer Officer, Staff of Major Gen. Alexander McD. McCook, Right Wing, 14 Army Corps, Army of the Cumberland, Dec. 27, 1862–Jan. 8, 1863. Colonel, 25 IL Infantry, May 26, 1863. Chief of Army Police, Department of the Cumberland, Aug. 29–Nov. 8, 1863. Commanded 1 Brigade, 3 Division, 4 Army

Richard Howard Nodine (Abraham Lincoln Presidential Library & Museum).

Corps, Army of the Cumberland, Jan. 8–March 11, 1864, and June 21–22, 1864. Honorably mustered out, Sept. 5, 1864. Battle honors: Pea Ridge, Stone's River, Missionary Ridge, Atlanta Campaign (Kenesaw Mountain).

Born: Feb. 4, 1825, Westchester Co., NY
Died: June 26, 1872, Champaign, IL
Other Wars: Artificer, U.S. Engineers, 1847–52
Occupation: Railroad land agent and U.S. Internal Revenue assessor
Miscellaneous: Resided Champaign, Champaign Co., IL; and Burlington, Des Moines Co., IA
Buried: Mount Hope Cemetery, Urbana, IL (Original Plat, Block 8, Lot 46)
References: Pension File and Military Service File, National Archives. Robert H. Behrens. *From Salt Fork to Chickamauga: Champaign County Soldiers in the Civil War.* Urbana, IL, 1988. David W. Godwin. *A Biographical History of Western Star Lodge No. 240 A.F. & A.M.* Champaign, IL, 1998. John Y. Simon, editor. *The Papers of Ulysses S. Grant.* Volume 19: July 1, 1868–October 31, 1869. Carbondale, IL, 1995.

Addison S. Norton

Captain, Co. A, 17 IL Infantry, May 25, 1861. Major, Additional ADC, USV, May 14, 1862. Acting AAG, Staff of Major Gen. John A. McClernand, Re-

Addison S. Norton (Thurlow, Next Door Above Howell & Co.'s Bank, Main Street, Peoria, IL; Abraham Lincoln Presidential Library & Museum).

serve Corps, Army of the Tennessee, May–June 1862. Acting AAG, Staff of Major Gen. John A. McClernand, District of Jackson, Army of the Tennessee, June–July 1862. Colonel, 17 IL Infantry, Aug. 1, 1862. Provost Marshal, District of Jackson, Army of the Tennessee, Aug. 1862. Commanded Post of LaGrange, TN, Nov.–Dec. 1862. Provost Marshal, Staff of Major Gen. John A. McClernand, 13 Army Corps, Army of the Tennessee, Feb.–April 1863. Resigned as Colonel, July 9, 1863, "on account of edema of left leg, the sequel of a fracture of the tibia received, May 4, 1862, and also of an indolent ulcer of great toe of left foot which renders him unable to wear a boot or shoe on that foot." Commanded General Rendezvous of Recruits, Illinois Volunteers, Springfield, IL, Sept. 1863–Feb. 1864. Provost Marshal, 5 Congressional District of Illinois, Jan. 26–March 8, 1865. Provost Marshal, 10 Congressional District of Illinois, May 6–Oct. 15, 1865. Resigned as Major, Additional ADC, Oct. 15, 1865. Bvt. Lieutenant Colonel, USV, June 22, 1865, for meritorious and faithful services in the recruitment of the armies of the United States.

Born: 1821?, NY
Died: Dec. 16, 1874, Salina, KS
Other Wars: Claimed service as private in Regular Army during Seminole War (ending 1842), but there is no record of such service at National Archives
Occupation: House and sign painter before war. Real estate agent after war.
Miscellaneous: Resided New Hartford, Oneida Co., NY (1850), Peoria, Peoria Co., IL, to 1867; and Salina, Saline Co., KS
Buried: Gypsum Hill Cemetery, Salina, KS (Block A, Lot 60)
References: Obituary, *Saline County Journal*, Dec. 17, 1874. Pension File and Military Service File, National Archives. Letters Received, Commission Branch, Adjutant General's Office, File N130(CB)1865, National Archives. John Y. Simon, editor. *The Papers of Ulysses S. Grant.* Volume 7: December 9, 1862–March 31, 1863. Carbondale, IL, 1979. *The History of Peoria County, Illinois.* Chicago, IL, 1880. Robert W. Campbell. "Brief History of the 17th Regiment Illinois Volunteer Infantry, 1861–1864," *Transactions of the Illinois State Historical Society for the Year 1914.* Springfield, IL, 1915.

Jerome Bonaparte Nulton

Captain, Co. G, 61 IL Infantry, Feb. 5, 1862. Major, 61 IL Infantry, Sept. 14, 1864. Colonel, 61 IL Infantry, July 11, 1865. Honorably mustered out, Sept. 8, 1865. Battle honors: Little Rock, Murfreesboro.

Jerome Bonaparte Nulton (Randy Beck Collection).

Born: Feb. 1, 1835, Washington Co., OH
Died: Aug. 7, 1905, Carrollton, IL
Occupation: Farmer before war. Grain merchant, mining superintendent, and lawyer after war.
Offices/Honors: Illinois House of Representatives, 1872–74
Miscellaneous: Resided Carrollton, Greene Co., IL; and Kansas, Colorado, and New Mexico, 1875–85
Buried: Carrollton Cemetery, Carrollton, IL (Section 2)
References: Obituary, *Carrollton Gazette*, Aug. 11, 1905. *History of Greene and Jersey Counties, Illinois.* Springfield, IL, 1885. Pension File and Military Service File, National Archives. *History of Greene County, Illinois: Its Past and Present.* Chicago, IL, 1879. Drew D. Dukett. *Glimpses of Glory: The Regimental History of the 61st Illinois Volunteers.* Bowie, MD, 1999. Leander Stillwell. *The Story of a Common Soldier of Army Life in the Civil War, 1861–1865.* Second Edition. Erie, KS, 1920. Edward Miner. *Past and Present of Greene County, Illinois.* Chicago, IL, 1905.

Simon P. Ohr

Captain, Co. A, 61 IL Infantry, Feb. 5, 1862. Major, 61 IL Infantry, March 7, 1862. Lieutenant Colonel, 61 IL Infantry, May 14, 1863. *Colonel*, 61 IL Infantry, May 14, 1864. Battle honors: Forrest's Expedition into West Tennessee (Jackson), Vicksburg Campaign, Arkansas Expedition.
Born: July 17, 1832, Frederick Co., MD
Died: Sept. 14, 1864, Springfield, IL (chronic bronchitis)
Occupation: Newspaper editor
Offices/Honors: Postmaster, Carrollton, IL, 1861
Miscellaneous: Resided Indianapolis, Marion Co., IN; Carrollton, Greene Co., IL; and Springfield, Sangamon Co., IL. Unsuccessful applicant for U.S. Military Academy appointment.
Buried: Oak Ridge Cemetery, Springfield, IL (Block 8, Lot 84)
References: Pension File and Military Service File, National Archives. Drew D. Dukett. *Glimpses of Glory: The Regimental History of the 61st Illinois Volunteers.* Bowie, MD, 1999. *History of Greene and Jersey Counties, Illinois.* Springfield, IL, 1885. Letters Received, Volunteer Service Branch, Adjutant General's Office, Files O19(VS)1863 and P2547(VS)1864, National Archives. Leander Stillwell. *The Story of a Common Soldier of Army Life in the Civil War, 1861–1865.* Second Edition. Erie, KS, 1920. Obituary, *Illinois State Journal*, Sept. 15, 1864. U.S. Military Academy Cadet Application Papers, 1805–1866, National Archives.

Timothy J. O'Meara

1 Lieutenant, Adjutant, 42 NY Infantry, May 3, 1861. Captain, Co. E, 42 NY Infantry, June 28, 1861.

Simon P. Ohr (Treadwell & Peaslee, 16 East Washington Street, Indianapolis, IN; Leander Stillwell. *The Story of a Common Soldier of Army Life in the Civil War, 1861–1865.* Second Edition. Erie, KS, 1920).

Timothy J. O'Meara (Abraham Lincoln Presidential Library & Museum).

Timothy J. O'Meara.

Taken prisoner, Ball's Bluff, VA, Oct. 21, 1861. Confined Tuscaloosa, AL, and Salisbury, NC. Exchanged Sept. 21, 1862. Honorably discharged, Oct. 9, 1862, to accept promotion. Colonel, 90 IL Infantry, Nov. 21, 1862. GSW left side, Missionary Ridge, TN, Nov. 25, 1863. Battle honors: Ball's Bluff, Operations on the Mississippi Central Railroad (Holly Springs), Vicksburg Campaign, Jackson Campaign, Missionary Ridge.

Born: Aug. 15, 1836, County Tipperary, Ireland
Died: Nov. 26, 1863, DOW Chattanooga, TN
Other Wars: Enlisted as Private, Co. A, U.S. Mounted Rifles, May 21, 1855. Promoted to Sergeant, he deserted July 25, 1859, to accept a commission in Benito Juarez's Constitutionalist Mexican Army.
Occupation: Carpenter before entering U.S. Army
Miscellaneous: Resided New York City, NY
Buried: Calvary Cemetery, Long Island City, NY (Section 4, Range 7, Plot U)
References: William J. O'Meara. *Colonel Timothy O'Meara "An Unknown Hero of the War."* Brooklyn, NY, 1914. John G. Coyle, "An Unknown Hero of the Great Civil War," *The Journal of the American Irish Historical Society*, Vol. 15, No. 3 (Oct. 1916). James B. Swan. *Chicago's Irish Legion: The 90th Illinois Volunteers in the Civil War.* Carbondale, IL, 2009. Pension File and Military Service File, National Archives. George H. Woodruff. *Fifteen Years Ago: or the Patriotism of Will County.* Joliet, IL, 1876. Obituary, *New York Times*, Dec. 20, 1863. Obituary, *Irish American*, Dec. 19, 1863. William L. Burton. *Melting Pot Soldiers: The Union's Ethnic Regiments.* Ames, IA, 1988. Register of Enlistments in the United States Army, 1798–1914, National Archives.

Lindorf Ozburn

1 Lieutenant, RQM, 31 IL Infantry, Sept. 8, 1861. Colonel, 31 IL Infantry, April 6, 1862. Commanded 2 Brigade, District of Jackson, Army of the Tennessee, Sept.–Nov. 1862. Resigned Feb. 24, 1863, due to oblique inguinal hernia which "renders me unfit for field service longer." Battle honors: Belmont, Corinth.

Born: May 21, 1823, Jackson Co., IL
Died: April 28, 1864, Carbondale, IL (killed by four-pound scale weight wielded by William Weaver, a disgruntled recruit of Co. K, 31 IL Infantry)
Other Wars: Mexican War (1 Sergeant, Co. H, 5 IL Infantry)

Lindorf Ozburn (Massachusetts MOLLUS Collection, USAMHI [Vol. 112, p. 5766]).

Lindorf Ozburn (seated right, with officers of the 31 IL Infantry, including Major John D. Rees, seated left, and 1 Lt. Thomas M. Logan and Lt. Col. Edwin S. McCook, standing left to right) (Ronn Palm Collection).

Occupation: Lumber merchant and flour miller
Offices/Honors: Postmaster, Murphysboro, IL, 1858–59
Miscellaneous: Resided Murphysboro, Jackson Co., IL
Buried: City Cemetery, Murphysboro, IL (Block 9, Lot 9)
References: Barbara Burr, "Letters from Two Wars," *Journal of the Illinois State Historical Society*, Vol. 30, No. 1 (April 1937). James Grant Wilson. *Biographical Sketches of Illinois Officers Engaged in the War Against the Rebellion of 1861*. Chicago, IL, 1862. "Grandfather of Ozburn Slain in Carbondale," *Carbondale Daily Free Press*, July 5, 1930. P. Michael Jones, Robert R. Morefield, and Clifton Swafford, compilers. *Murphysboro Illinois 150 Years: A Pictorial History, 1843–1993*. Murphysboro, IL, 1994. Pension File and Military Service File, National Archives. George Washington Smith. *A History of Southern Illinois*. Chicago and New York, 1912. William S. Morris. *History 31st Illinois Volunteers, Organized by John A. Logan*. Evansville, IN, 1902.

Thaddeus Phillips

Captain, Co. C, 32 IL Infantry, Oct. 22, 1861. GSW leg, Pittsburg Landing, TN, March 1, 1862. Suffering from a severe attack of typhoid fever, he resigned Nov. 4, 1862, since "I do not feel that my health will admit of my remaining in the position longer without further injury to myself and prejudice to the service." Colonel, 133 IL Infantry, May 31, 1864. Honorably mustered out, Sept. 24, 1864. Battle honors: Pittsburg Landing.
Born: Dec. 18, 1820, Charles City Co., VA
Died: Sept. 9, 1892, Seattle, WA
Occupation: House painter
Miscellaneous: Resided Carlinville, Macoupin Co., IL; and Seattle, King Co., WA, after 1888
Buried: Lake View Cemetery, Seattle, WA (Lot 667)
References: Pension File and Military Service File, National Archives. Obituary, *Seattle Post-Intelligencer*, Sept. 11, 1892. Obituary, *Carlinville Democrat*, Sept. 15, 1892. Myron J. Smith, Jr. *Civil War Biographies from the Western Waters*. Jefferson, NC, 2015. http://www.findagrave.com.

Thomas Johnson Pickett

Lieutenant Colonel, 69 IL Infantry, June 13, 1862. Honorably mustered out, Sept. 22, 1862. Colonel, 132 IL Infantry, June 1, 1864. Honorably mustered out, Oct. 17, 1864.
Born: March 17, 1821, Louisville, KY
Died: Dec. 24, 1891, Ashland, NE
Occupation: Newspaper editor
Offices/Honors: Illinois Senate, 1860–62. Postmaster, Paducah, KY, 1865–67 and 1869–72.
Miscellaneous: Resided Peoria, Peoria Co., IL, to 1858; Moline, Rock Island Co., IL, 1858–65; Paducah, McCracken Co., KY, 1865–79; and Lincoln, Lancaster Co., NE, after 1880

Thomas Johnson Pickett (Randy Beck Collection).

Buried: Ashland Cemetery, Ashland, NE
References: Charles L. Wilson, "Representative Men: Colonel Thomas Johnson Pickett, of Nebraska, the Man Who First Proposed the Nomination of Abraham Lincoln." *The Midland Monthly*, Vol. 5, No. 6 (June 1896). Thomas J. Pickett, "Reminiscences of Abraham Lincoln," Introduction by Ernest E. East, *Lincoln Herald*, Vol. 45, No. 4 (Dec. 1943). Newton Bateman, Paul Selby, and David McCulloch, editors. *Historical Encyclopedia of Illinois and History of Peoria County*. Chicago and Peoria, IL, 1902. *The United States Biographical Dictionary and Portrait Gallery of Eminent and Self-Made Men.* Illinois Volume. Chicago, Cincinnati, and New York, 1876. Obituary, *Daily Nebraska State Journal*, Dec. 26, 1891. Pension File and Military Service File, National Archives.

John Pratt Post

Major, 8 IL Infantry (3 months), April 25, 1861. Major, 8 IL Infantry (3 years), July 25, 1861. Taken prisoner, Fort Donelson, TN, Feb. 15, 1862. Confined Memphis, TN; Tuscaloosa, AL; Montgomery, AL; and Madison, GA. Lieutenant Colonel, 8 IL Infantry, May 16, 1862. Colonel, 8 IL Infantry, Oct. 7, 1862. Paroled Oct. 12, 1862. Charged with "Misbehavior before the Enemy, Cowardice, and Absence without Leave" for leaving his regiment at the battle of Port Gibson, May 1, 1863, and remaining absent until July 5, 1863, he was found guilty by a court-martial and dismissed Sept. 28, 1863. Major Gen. Richard J. Oglesby appealed his case to President Lincoln with the observation, "He is an unfortunate man at best, never meant wrong but does not always know how to do right." On Nov. 7, 1863, Lincoln replied with the comment, "The application does not seem to be sustained by sufficient showing to justify action at present." His dismissal was, nevertheless, revoked, April 23, 1864, upon acceptance of his resignation to date, Sept. 28, 1863. 1 Lieutenant, RQM, 154 IL Infantry, Feb. 22, 1865. Honorably mustered out, Sept. 18, 1865. Battle honors: Fort Donelson, Port Gibson.
Born: March 30, 1819, Geneva, NY
Died: Feb. 24, 1903, Denver, CO
Other Wars: Mexican War (2 Lieutenant, Co. C, 4 IL Infantry)
Occupation: Clerk and justice of the peace before war. Salesman, janitor, and justice of the peace after war.
Offices/Honors: Postmaster, Decatur, IL, 1853–58. Mayor, Decatur, IL, 1856–57.
Miscellaneous: Resided Decatur, Macon Co., IL, to 1871; Central City, Gilpin Co., CO, 1871–72; and Georgetown, Clear Creek Co., CO, 1872–1903
Buried: Alvarado Cemetery, Georgetown, CO
References: *History of Clear Creek and Boulder Valleys, Colorado.* Chicago, IL, 1880. Obituary, *Decatur Daily Herald*, March 4, 1903, and March 15, 1903. Pension File and Military Service File, National Archives. Court-martial Case Files, 1809–1894, File NN-345, National Archives. Letters Received, Volunteer Service Branch, Adjutant General's Office, File P1985(VS)1863, National Archives. Obituary, *Rocky Mountain News*, Feb. 25, 1903. William E. Nelson, editor. *City of Decatur and Macon County, Illinois: A Record of Settlement, Organization, Progress and Achievement.* Chicago, IL, 1910. "First Mayor Was Soldier," *Decatur Daily Review*, Feb. 23, 1957.

Edward Prince

Lieutenant Colonel, 7 IL Cavalry, Sept. 8, 1861. GSW right leg, Bird's Point, MO, Jan. 10, 1862. Colonel, 7 IL Cavalry, June 2, 1862. Honorably mustered out, Oct. 15, 1864. Battle honors: Iuka, Operations on the Mississippi Central Railroad (Coffeeville), Grierson's Raid, Port Hudson, Forrest's Attack on Memphis.
Born: Dec. 8, 1832, West Bloomfield, Ontario Co., NY
Died: Dec. 5, 1908, Chicago, IL
Education: Graduated Illinois College, Jacksonville, IL, 1852
Occupation: Lawyer and civil engineer
Miscellaneous: Resided Quincy, Adams Co., IL
Buried: Woodland Cemetery, Quincy, IL (Block 15, Lot 93)

Edward Prince (Randy Beck Collection).

Edward Prince (Richard W. Surby. *Grierson Raids, and Hatch's Sixty-Four Days March, with Biographical Sketches, Also the Life and Adventures of Chickasaw, the Scout.* Chicago, IL, 1865).

References: *Portrait and Biographical Record of Adams County, Illinois.* Chicago, IL, 1892. Obituary, *Quincy Daily Journal*, Dec. 7, 1908. Richard W. Surby. *Grierson Raids, and Hatch's Sixty-Four Days March, with Biographical Sketches, Also the Life and Adventures of Chickasaw, the Scout.* Chicago, IL, 1865. Newton Bateman and Paul Selby. *Biographical and Memorial Edition of the Historical Encyclopedia of Illinois.* Chicago, IL, 1915. *History of Adams County, Illinois.* Chicago, IL, 1879. *The Illinois College Alumni Fund Association: Book of Memorial Memberships.* Centennial Edition, 1829–1929. Jacksonville, IL, 1929. Pension File and Military Service File, National Archives. Letters Received, Volunteer Service Branch, Adjutant General's Office, File P249(VS)1862, National Archives.

Holden Putnam

Colonel, 93 IL Infantry, Oct. 13, 1862. Commanded 3 Brigade, 7 Division, 17 Army Corps, Army of the Tennessee, May 22–June 2, 1863. GSW head, Missionary Ridge, TN, Nov. 25, 1863. Battle honors: Champion's Hill, Vicksburg Campaign, Missionary Ridge.

Born: Feb. 12, 1821, Middlesex, Washington Co., VT

Died: Nov. 25, 1863, KIA Missionary Ridge, TN

Occupation: In early life a harness maker, he later became a banker

Miscellaneous: Resided Freeport, Stephenson Co., IL

Buried: City Cemetery, Freeport, IL (NW ¼, Range 13, Lot 1)

Above: Holden Putnam (Fassett's Gallery, Nos. 122 & 124 Clark Street, Chicago, IL). *Below:* Holden Putnam (Fassett's Gallery, Nos. 122 & 124 Clark Street, Chicago, IL; courtesy Steve Meadow).

References: John W. Huelskamp, "Never Forsake the Colors! Colonel Holden Putnam and the 93rd Illinois Volunteer Infantry," *Civil War Regiments: A Journal of the American Civil War*, Vol. 3, No. 3 (1993). John W. Huelskamp, "We are Coming, Father Abraham.... Colonel Putnam Answers Lincoln's Call," *The Gun Report*, Vol. 39, No. 3 (August 1993). Obituary, *Freeport Bulletin*, Dec. 3, 1863. Harvey M. Trimble, editor. *History of the 93rd Regiment Illinois Volunteer Infantry.* Chicago, IL, 1898. Pension File and Military Service File, National Archives. *The History of Stephenson County, Illinois.* Chicago, IL, 1880. *Illinois at Vicksburg.* Chicago, IL, 1907. Vermont Vital Records Through 1870.

Julius Raith

Colonel, 43 IL Infantry, Oct. 13, 1861. Commanded 3 Brigade, 1 Division, Army of the Tennessee, April 6, 1862. GSW right leg (amputated), Shiloh, TN, April 6, 1862. Battle honors: Shiloh.

Born: March 29, 1819, Goppingen, Germany
Died: April 11, 1862, DOW Pittsburg Landing, TN
Other Wars: Mexican War (Captain, Co. H, 2 IL Infantry)

Occupation: Millwright
Miscellaneous: Resided Belleville and Shiloh, St. Clair Co., IL
Buried: Shiloh Valley Cemetery, Shiloh, IL (Block 12, Lot 17)
References: James Grant Wilson. *Biographical Sketches of Illinois Officers Engaged in the War Against the Rebellion of 1861.* Chicago, IL, 1862. Thomas M. Eddy. *The Patriotism of Illinois.* Chicago, IL, 1865. Pension File and Military Service File, National Archives. "Funeral of Col. Raith," *Daily Missouri Republican*, April 28, 1862. Newton Bateman, Paul Selby, A.S. Wilderman, and A.A. Wilderman, editors. *Historical Encyclopedia of Illinois and History of St. Clair County.* Chicago, IL, 1907.

Sheridan Pitt Read

Lieutenant Colonel, 79 IL Infantry, Aug. 21, 1862. *Colonel*, 79 IL Infantry, Oct. 18, 1862. GSW head, Stone's River, TN, Dec. 31, 1862. Battle honors: Stone's River.

Born: 1829, Champaign Co., OH
Died: Dec. 31, 1862, KIA Stone's River, TN
Education: Attended Ohio University, Athens, OH. Graduated Indiana University, Bloomington, IN, 1850.
Occupation: Lawyer
Offices/Honors: Edgar County (IL) School Commissioner, 1857–59

Julius Raith (Massachusetts MOLLUS Collection, USAMHI [Vol. 118, p. 6088]).

Sheridan Pitt Read (Chicago History Museum [ICHi-68787]).

Miscellaneous: Resided Terre Haute, Vigo Co., IN; and Paris, Edgar Co., IL. Uncle of Bvt. Brig. Gen. Theodore Read (Half-brother of Theodore's father, Daniel Read). Brother-in-law of Colonel Dudley C. Smith (143 IL Infantry).
Buried: Edgar Cemetery, Paris, IL (Section L, Lot 350)
References: William Sumner Dodge. *History of the Old Second Division, Army of the Cumberland.* Chicago, IL, 1864. Thomas M. Eddy. *The Patriotism of Illinois.* Chicago, IL, 1865. Jacob W. Reed. *History of the Reed Family in Europe and America.* Boston, MA, 1861. Pension File and Military Service File, National Archives. *The History of Edgar County, Illinois.* Chicago, IL, 1879. Theophilus A. Wylie. *Indiana University, Its History from 1820 to 1890.* Indianapolis, 1890.

James Siddall Rearden

Colonel, 29 IL Infantry, Aug. 19, 1861. Commanded 3 Brigade, 1 Division, Army of the Tennessee, April 1–6, 1862. Resigned April 15, 1862, "for reasons best known to myself, and which I do not desire to disclose, being of domestic and pecuniary character." Major Gen. Ulysses S. Grant finally forwarded the resignation on May 2, 1862, with the endorsement, "This resignation was withheld not wishing to have Col. Rearden resign. He was sick, however, and absented himself from his regiment on the 6th and 7th instant, and is now absent without leave." Battle honors: Fort Donelson.
Born: Oct. 17, 1827, Carmi, White Co., IL
Died: June 11, 1909, Cairo, IL
Other Wars: Mexican War (2 Lieutenant, Co. G, 3 IL Infantry)
Occupation: Store clerk and merchant before war. Lumber merchant and insurance agent after war.
Offices/Honors: Served 25 years as Chief of Police and City Comptroller, Cairo, IL.
Miscellaneous: Resided Shawneetown, Gallatin Co., IL, to 1865; and Cairo, Alexander Co., IL, after 1865
Buried: Beech Grove Cemetery, Mounds, Pulaski Co., IL (unmarked)
References: Obituary, *Cairo Evening Citizen*, June 12, 1909. Pension File and Military Service File, National Archives. Anne Healy Field, "Descendants of Elmira Peirce and William Rearden of White County, Illinois," www.annefield.net/elmira_peirce_rearden_desc_04.pdf.

Owen Thornton Reeves

Captain, Co. H, 70 IL Infantry, July 4, 1862. Colonel, 70 IL Infantry, July 23, 1862. Honorably mustered out, Oct. 23, 1862.

Owen Thornton Reeves (post-war) (*Transactions of the McLean County Historical Society, Volume 1, War Record of McLean County with Other Papers.* Bloomington, IL, 1899).

Born: Dec. 18, 1829, Ross Co., OH
Died: March 2, 1912, Bloomington, IL
Education: Graduated Ohio Wesleyan University, Delaware, OH, 1850
Occupation: Lawyer and judge
Offices/Honors: Circuit Court Judge, 1877–91
Miscellaneous: Resided Bloomington, McLean Co., IL
Buried: Evergreen Memorial Cemetery, Bloomington, IL (Section G, Lot 894)
References: *Portrait and Biographical Album of McLean County, Illinois.* Chicago, IL, 1887. John Moses, editor. *Biographical Dictionary and Portrait Gallery of the Representative Men of the United States.* Illinois Volume. Chicago, IL, 1896. Obituary, *Bloomington Pantagraph*, March 4, 1912. John M. Palmer, editor. *The Bench and Bar of Illinois: Historical and Reminiscent.* Chicago, IL, 1899. *The History of McLean County, Illinois.* Chicago, IL, 1879. Pension File, National Archives. *The United States Biographical Dictionary and Portrait Gallery of Eminent and Self-Made Men.* Illinois Volume. Chicago and New York, 1883. Newton Bateman, Paul Selby, Ezra M. Prince, and John H. Burnham, editors. *Historical Encyclopedia of Illinois and History of McLean*

County. Chicago, IL, 1908. *Transactions of the McLean County Historical Society, Volume 1, War Record of McLean County with Other Papers*. Bloomington, IL, 1899.

John Barclay Reid

Major, 130 IL Infantry, Sept. 18, 1862. Shell wound, Vicksburg, MS, May 22, 1863. GSW left shoulder, Sabine Cross Roads, LA, April 8, 1864. Taken prisoner, Sabine Cross Roads, LA, April 8, 1864. Confined Tyler, TX. Paroled June 16, 1864. Lieutenant Colonel, 130 IL Infantry, July 22, 1864. Lieutenant Colonel, 77 IL Infantry, Jan. 26, 1865, upon consolidation of 77 and 130 IL Infantry. *Colonel*, 130 IL Infantry, Aug. 16, 1865, upon muster out of 77 IL Infantry and reorganization of 130 IL Infantry. Honorably mustered out, Aug. 15, 1865. Battle honors: Vicksburg Campaign, Operations in the Teche Country, Red River Campaign (Sabine Cross Roads), Mobile Campaign (Spanish Fort).

Born: Aug. 8, 1830, County Donegal, Ireland
Died: Dec. 25, 1907, Greenville, IL
Occupation: Shoemaker and flour mill operator

John Barclay Reid (Abraham Lincoln Presidential Library & Museum).

Offices/Honors: Postmaster, Greenville, IL, 1856–61 and 1886–90. Clerk of Circuit Court, 1861–68.

Miscellaneous: Resided Greenville, Bond Co., IL

Buried: Montrose Cemetery, Greenville, IL (Lot 204)

References: Franklin Thomas Reid. *History and Reminiscences of Col. John B. Reid and Family*. Springfield, IL, 1903. *The United States Biographical Dictionary and Portrait Gallery of Eminent and Self-Made Men*. Illinois Volume. Chicago, Cincinnati, and New York, 1876. Obituary, *Greenville Advocate*, Dec. 26, 1907. William H. Perrin, editor. *History of Bond and Montgomery Counties, Illinois*. Chicago, IL, 1882. Pension File and Military Service File, National Archives. Letters Received, Volunteer Service Branch, Adjutant General's Office, Files R835(VS) 1864 and R250(VS)1865, National Archives. Obituary Circular, Whole No. 608, Illinois MOLLUS. John B. Reid. *Civil War Letters of John B. Reid*. Greenville, IL, 1991. *Memorials of Deceased Companions of the Commandery of the State of Illinois MOLLUS, from July 1, 1901, to Dec. 31, 1911*. Chicago, IL, 1912.

John Barclay Reid (W.D. McPherson, Photographer, No. 132 Canal Street, New Orleans, LA; USAMHI [RG98S-CWP69.3]).

Franklin Lawrence Rhoads

Captain, Co. F, 8 IL Infantry (3 months), April 25, 1861. Lieutenant Colonel, 8 IL Infantry, May 3, 1861. Lieutenant Colonel, 8 IL Infantry (3 years), July 25, 1861. Colonel, 8 IL Infantry, April 1, 1862. Commanded 4 Brigade, District of Jackson, Army of the Tennessee, Sept. 1862. Charged with "Disrespect toward a Superior Officer" for verbally attacking Brig. Gen. Michael K. Lawler on the drill field after being ordered to report to a junior officer, Colonel Mason Brayman, he was found guilty by a court martial, Sept. 22, 1862, and sentenced to a thirty-day suspension from command. Upon reviewing the case Major Gen. Ulysses S. Grant released him from arrest and ordered him back to duty with the comment, "The suspension of an officer from his command without forfeiture of pay is no punishment adequate to the offence of which the accused is found guilty." Resigned Oct. 7, 1862, since "the notoriety and disgrace of a General Court Martial, coupled with a reprimand, has placed me in a false position in this command, as well as to my friends at home." Battle honors: Fort Donelson.

Born: Oct. 20, 1824, New Berlin, PA
Died: Jan. 5, 1879, Shawneetown, IL
Other Wars: Mexican War (Private, Co. G, 4 IL Infantry)
Occupation: Steamboat captain before war. Real estate agent and farmer after war.
Miscellaneous: Resided Pekin, Tazewell Co., IL, before war; and Shawneetown, Gallatin Co., IL, after war
Buried: Westwood Cemetery, Shawneetown, IL
References: *The United States Biographical Dictionary and Portrait Gallery of Eminent and Self-Made Men.* Illinois Volume. Chicago, Cincinnati, and New York, 1876. Newton Bateman, Paul Selby, and Ben C. Allensworth, editors. *Historical Encyclopedia of Illinois and History of Tazewell County.* Chicago, IL, 1905. Pension File and Military Service File, National Archives. Court-martial Case Files, 1809–1894, File KK-233, National Archives. Thomas P. Lowry. *Tarnished Eagles: The Courts-Martial of Fifty Union Colonels and Lieutenant Colonels.* Mechanicsburg, PA, 1997. Obituary, *Shawnee Herald*, Jan. 24, 1879.

Hinman Rhodes

Captain, Co. H, 28 IL Infantry, Aug. 24, 1861. Major, 28 IL Infantry, Dec. 2, 1862. Sentenced by court martial, Oct. 31, 1864, to be reprimanded and suspended from rank and pay for an altercation with fellow officers and citizens of Natchez, MS, he was honorably mustered out, Nov. 25, 1864, upon consolidation of the regiment into a battalion of four companies. Major, 28 IL Infantry, Dec. 23, 1864. Lieutenant Colonel, 28 IL Infantry, May 10, 1865. Colonel, 28 IL Infantry, Sept. 15, 1865. Commanded Separate Brigade, District of the Rio Grande, Department of Texas, Dec. 14, 1865–March 15, 1866. Honorably mustered out, March 15, 1866. Battle honors: Shiloh, Corinth, Vicksburg Campaign, Jackson Campaign, Mobile Campaign.

Franklin Lawrence Rhoads (Abraham Lincoln Presidential Library & Museum).

Hinman Rhodes (courtesy Henry Deeks).

Hinman Rhodes.

Born: June 14, 1827, Sussex Co., DE
Died: Dec. 30, 1907, Pasadena, CA
Education: Attended Jones' Commercial College, St. Louis, MO
Other Wars: Mexican War (Private, Capt. Dunlap's Independent Company, IL Mounted Volunteers)
Occupation: California gold miner before war. Lumber merchant, real estate agent and sewing machine agent after war.
Offices/Honors: Nebraska House of Representatives, 1869–73
Miscellaneous: Resided Vermont, Fulton Co., IL, 1861–66; Tecumseh, Johnson Co., NE, 1866–71; Beatrice, Gage Co., NE, 1871–73; Cherokee, Crawford Co., KS, 1873–80; Columbus, Cherokee Co., KS, 1880–82; Engle, Socorro Co., NM; Las Cruces, Dona Ana Co., NM; and Pasadena, CA, 1896–1907. Father of novelist Eugene Manlove Rhodes.
Buried: Mountain View Cemetery, Altadena, CA (Section A, Row 2, Lot 9)
References: A.C. Edmunds. *Pen Sketches of Nebraskans*. Lincoln, NE, 1871. Pension File and Military Service File, National Archives. Letters Received, Volunteer Service Branch, Adjutant General's Office, File G1349(VS)1865, National Archives. Court-martial Case Files, 1809–1894, File LL-2819, National Archives. Edwin L. Hobart. *Semi-History of a Boy-Veteran of the Twenty-Eighth Regiment Illinois Infantry Volunteers, in a Black Regiment.* Denver, CO, 1905. Obituary, *Los Angeles Herald*, Jan. 1, 1908. William A. Keleher. *The Fabulous Frontier: Twelve New Mexico Items*. Santa Fe, NM, 1945.

Jonathan Richmond

Colonel, 126 IL Infantry, Sept. 4, 1862. Commanded 3 Brigade, District of Jackson, 16 Army Corps, Army of the Tennessee, Dec. 18, 1862–March 18, 1863. Commanded Post of La Grange, TN, Dec. 1862–Jan. 1863. Commanded Post of Humboldt, TN, Jan.–Feb. 1863. Commanded 2 Brigade, 3 Division, 16 Army Corps, Army of the Tennessee, May 4–28, 1863. Commanded 2 Brigade, Kimball's Provisional Division, 16 Army Corps, Army of the Tennessee, May 28–Aug. 10, 1863. Commanded Post of Devall's Bluff, AR, Oct. 1863–Feb. 1864. Resigned March 3, 1864, "on account of continued ill health" caused by lithiasis of the urinary organs. Battle honors: Vicksburg Campaign.
Born: March 25, 1823, Butler Co., OH
Died: Aug. 5, 1893, Mattoon, IL
Other Wars: Mexican War (1 Lieutenant, Adjutant, 1 OH Infantry)
Occupation: Dry goods merchant before war. Hardware merchant, flour mill operator and bank president after war.
Offices/Honors: U.S. Collector of Internal Revenue, 1869–76

Jonathan Richmond (Walter Kilner's Photograph Gallery, Mattoon, IL; Roger D. Hunt Collection, USAMHI [RG98S-CWP81.50]).

Jonathan Richmond (Relief Portrait, Vicksburg National Military Park).

Miscellaneous: Resided Hamilton, Butler Co., OH, to 1860; and Mattoon, Coles Co., IL, after 1860

Buried: Dodge Grove Cemetery, Mattoon, IL (Section 2, Lot 10)

References: Obituary, *Mattoon Weekly Gazette*, Aug. 11, 1893. Pension File and Military Service File, National Archives. Newton Bateman, Paul Selby, and Charles E. Wilson, editors. *Historical Encyclopedia of Illinois and History of Coles County.* Chicago, IL, 1906. *The History of Coles County, Illinois.* Chicago, IL, 1879. Letters Received, Volunteer Service Branch, Adjutant General's Office, File R916(VS)1863, National Archives. *Illinois at Vicksburg.* Chicago, IL, 1907.

Richard Ritter

Captain, Co. A, 28 IL Infantry, Aug. 2, 1861. Lieutenant Colonel, 28 IL Infantry, April 21, 1862. GSW right foot, Hatchie Bridge, TN, Oct. 5, 1862. Colonel, 28 IL Infantry, May 10, 1865. Commanded 1 Brigade, 3 Division, 13 Army Corps, Military Division of West Mississippi, June 3–July 20, 1865. Resigned July 23, 1865. Battle honors: Shiloh, Hatchie Bridge, Mobile Campaign (Spanish Fort).

Born: Feb. 4, 1832, near Petersburg, IL
Died: July 3, 1902, Sedalia, MO

Occupation: Merchant and lawyer before war. Lumber merchant after war.

Offices/Honors: Mason Co. (IL) School Commissioner, 1854–57. Circuit Court Clerk, 1856–60.

Miscellaneous: Resided Havana, Mason Co., IL, to 1866; and Sedalia, Pettis Co., MO, after 1866

Buried: Crown Hill Cemetery, Sedalia, MO (Section 30, Lot 4)

References: *The History of Pettis County, Missouri.* N.p., 1882. Obituary, *Sedalia Daily Capital*, July 5, 1902. Pension File and Military Service File, National Archives. *The History of Menard and Mason Counties, Illinois.* Chicago, IL, 1879. Edwin L. Hobart. *Semi-History of a Boy-Veteran of the Twenty-Eighth Regiment Illinois Infantry Volunteers, in a Black Regiment.* Denver, CO, 1905.

George Williamson Roberts

Major, 42 IL Infantry, July 22, 1861. Lieutenant Colonel, 42 IL Infantry, Sept. 17, 1861. While stationed at Smithton, MO, in Dec. 1861, he was acquitted by court martial of charges based on citizen complaints which were proven to be "false, slanderous and malicious." Colonel, 42 IL Infantry, Dec. 25, 1861. Nominated as Bvt. Brig. Gen., USV,

George Williamson Roberts (J. Carbutt, Photograph Artist, 131 Lake Street, Chicago, IL; Ray Zielin Collection).

George Williamson Roberts (Van Stavoren, Photographer, No. 53 College Street, Between Union Street & Square, Nashville, TN; Richard F. Carlile Collection).

April 28, 1862, for gallant service at Island No. 10. Nomination withdrawn, July 14, 1862. Commanded 1 Brigade, 1 Division, Army of the Mississippi, Aug.–Oct. 1862. Commanded 1 Brigade, 13 Division, Army of the Ohio, Oct.–Nov. 1862. Commanded 3 Brigade, 3 Division, Right Wing, 14 Army Corps, Army of the Cumberland, Nov. 5–Dec. 31, 1862. GSW Stone's River, TN, Dec. 31, 1862. Battle honors: Island No. 10, Farmington, Siege of Corinth, Stone's River.

Born: Oct. 2, 1833, East Goshen Twp., Chester County, PA

Died: Dec. 31, 1862, KIA Stone's River, TN

Education: Attended Haverford (PA) College. Graduated Yale University, New Haven, CT, 1857.

Occupation: Lawyer

Miscellaneous: Resided West Chester, Chester Co., PA; and Chicago, IL, after 1860

Buried: Oaklands Cemetery, West Chester, PA (Section F)

References: James Barnet, editor. *The Martyrs and Heroes of Illinois in the Great Rebellion.* Second Edition. Chicago, IL, 1866. Curtis H. Hannum, compiler. *Genealogy of the Hannum Family Descended from John and Margery Hannum.* West Chester, PA, 1911. John Fitch. *Annals of the Army of the Cumberland.* Philadelphia, PA, 1864. Thomas M. Eddy. *The Patriotism of Illinois.* Chicago, IL, 1865. James Grant Wilson. *Biographical Sketches of Illinois Officers Engaged in the War Against the Rebellion of 1861.* Chicago, IL, 1862. J. Smith Futhey and Gilbert Cope. *History of Chester County, Pennsylvania, With Genealogical and Biographical Sketches.* Philadelphia, PA, 1881. Court-martial Case Files, 1809–1894, File KK-121, National Archives. Thomas P. Lowry. *Tarnished Eagles: The Courts-Martial of Fifty Union Colonels and Lieutenant Colonels.* Mechanicsburg, PA, 1997. Douglas R. Harper. *"If Thee Must Fight," A Civil War History of Chester County, Pennsylvania.* West Chester, PA, 1990. Military Service File, National Archives. *Biographical Catalog of the Matriculates of Haverford College, 1833–1922.* Philadelphia, PA, 1922.

Andrew Fuller Rodgers

Lieutenant Colonel, 80 IL Infantry, Aug. 25, 1862. Shell wound head, Perryville, KY, Oct. 8, 1862. Colonel, 80 IL Infantry, April 21, 1863. Taken prisoner, Rome, GA, May 3, 1863. Confined Libby Prison, Richmond, VA; Macon, GA; Savannah, GA; and Charleston, SC. Paroled Aug. 3, 1864. Denied the command of a new regiment (144 IL Infantry) for which he recruited 800 men, he resigned Nov. 25, 1864, since "I have family affairs of such a nature that it is impossible for me to return to the field." Battle honors: Perryville, Streight's Raid.

Andrew Fuller Rodgers (Massachusetts MOLLUS Collection, USAMHI [Vol. 118, p. 6087L]).

Andrew Watts Rogers (Walter B. Palmer. *The History of the Phi Delta Theta Fraternity.* Menasha, WI, 1906).

Born: Oct. 13, 1827, near Fayette, Howard Co., MO
Died: Jan. 20, 1922, Upper Alton, IL
Education: Attended Shurtleff College, Alton, IL
Other Wars: Mexican War (Private, Co. E, 2 IL Infantry)
Occupation: Farmer and insurance agent
Offices/Honors: Illinois House of Representatives, 1870-72
Miscellaneous: Resided Wood River, Madison Co., IL; and Upper Alton, Madison Co., IL
Buried: Oakwood Cemetery, Upper Alton, IL (Section 102, Block 523, Lot 1)
References: *Portrait and Biographical Record of Madison County, Illinois.* Chicago, IL, 1894. W.T. Norton, editor. *Centennial History of Madison County, Illinois, and Its People, 1812-1912.* Chicago and New York, 1912. Obituary, *Alton Evening Telegraph*, Jan. 20, 1922. William W. Greene. *Semi-Centennial History of the Alpha Zeta Society of Shurtleff College.* Alton, IL, 1898. Pension File and Military Service File, National Archives. Letters Received, Volunteer Service Branch, Adjutant General's Office, File M2282(VS)1864, National Archives.

Andrew Watts Rogers

Major, 81 IL Infantry, Aug. 26, 1862. Lieutenant Colonel, 81 IL Infantry, May 23, 1863. *Colonel,* 81 IL Infantry, Aug. 20, 1864. Honorably mustered out, Aug. 5, 1865. Battle honors: Red River Campaign, Brice's Cross Roads, Price's Missouri Expedition, Nashville, Mobile Campaign (Spanish Fort).
Born: March 12, 1825, near Greenfield, Highland Co., OH
Died: Feb. 26, 1901, Warrensburg, MO
Education: Graduated Miami University, Oxford, OH, 1851
Occupation: Lawyer
Offices/Honors: Missouri House of Representatives, 1883-85
Miscellaneous: Resided Bloomington, McLean Co., IL, 1853-58; Carbondale, Jackson Co., IL, 1858-65; and Warrensburg, Johnson Co., MO, after 1865. One of the founders of the Phi Delta Theta fraternity. Brother-in-law of Colonel Stanley Matthews (51 Ohio Infantry).
Buried: Sunset Hill Cemetery, Warrensburg, MO
References: Walter B. Palmer. *The History of the Phi Delta Theta Fraternity.* Menasha, WI, 1906. *Portrait and Biographical Record of Johnson and Pettis Counties, Missouri.* Chicago, IL, 1895. Pension File and Military Service File, National Archives. Edmund Newsome. *Experience in the War of the Great Rebellion, by a Soldier of the 81st Regiment Illinois Volunteer Infantry, from August 1862 to August 1865.* Second Edition. Carbondale, IL, 1880.

Friend Smith Rutherford

Captain, Commissary of Subsistence, USV, June 30, 1862. Resigned Sept. 2, 1862. Colonel, 97 IL Infantry, Sept. 16, 1862. Suffering from a severe case of "camp dysentery," he took leave of absence, July 5, 1863, and returned to his home in Alton, IL. Failing to get his leave properly extended, he was dismissed, Oct. 16, 1863, for "absence without leave." Upon appeal to President Lincoln, his dismissal was revoked, Nov. 11, 1863, and he was restored to his command. Unable to completely recover his health, he resigned June 15, 1864, "on account of physical disability." Nominated as Brig. Gen., USV, June 18, 1864. Nomination confirmed by U.S. Senate, June 27, 1864. Battle honors: Chickasaw Bluffs, Arkansas Post, Port Gibson, Champion's Hill, Vicksburg Campaign.
Born: Sept. 25, 1820, Schenectady, NY
Died: June 20, 1864, Alton, IL (chronic diarrhea)
Occupation: Lawyer
Miscellaneous: Resided Edwardsville, Madison Co., IL; and Alton, Madison Co., IL, after 1857. Brother of Bvt. Brig. Gen. George V. Rutherford and Bvt. Brig. Gen. Reuben C. Rutherford.
Buried: Alton Cemetery, Alton, IL (Old Yard Section, Lot 28)
References: James Grant Wilson and John Fiske, editors. *Appletons' Cyclopedia of American Biography.*

Friend Smith Rutherford (Massachusetts MOLLUS Collection, USAMHI [Vol. 69, p. 3417L]).

New York City, 1888. Obituary, *Alton Telegraph*, June 24 and July 1, 1864. *The Union Army*. Vol. 8. Madison, WI, 1908. Newton Bateman and Paul Selby, editors. *Historical Encyclopedia of Illinois and History of Sangamon County*. Chicago, IL, 1912. Obituary, *Illinois State Journal*, June 22, 1864. Pension File and Military Service File, National Archives. Letters Received, Volunteer Service Branch, Adjutant General's Office, File R990(VS) 1863, National Archives. W.T. Norton, editor. *Centennial History of Madison County, Illinois, and Its People, 1812–1912*. Chicago and New York, 1912. *History of Madison County, Illinois*. Edwardsville, IL, 1882. Letters Received, Commission Branch, Adjutant General's Office, Files R376(CB) 1863 and R430(CB) 1864, National Archives. Letters Received, Adjutant General's Office, Files R580 (AGO) 1862 and R628(AGO) 1862, National Archives.

George Ryon

Colonel, 75 IL Infantry, Sept. 2, 1862. Resigned Dec. 20, 1862, on account of "chronic inflammation of the stomach, which entirely unfits me for performing the duties of my position." Battle honors: Perryville.

Born: June 5, 1827, Elkland, Tioga Co., PA
Died: June 27, 1897, Amboy, IL
Education: Attended Rush Medical College, Chicago, IL
Occupation: Physician and lawyer before war. Physician and banker after war.
Offices/Honors: Illinois House of Representatives, 1860–62 and 1866–68
Miscellaneous: Resided Paw Paw, Lee Co., IL, to 1869; Amboy, Lee Co., IL, 1869–73; Streator, La Salle Co., IL, 1873–76; Chicago, IL, 1876–79; and Amboy, Lee Co., IL, after 1879
Buried: Prairie Repose Cemetery, Amboy, IL
References: *Portrait and Biographical Record of Lee County, Illinois*. Chicago, IL, 1892. Obituary, *Dixon Telegraph*, June 28, 1897. Obituary, *Amboy News*, July 1, 1897. Pension File and Military Service File, National Archives. *The United States Biographical Dictionary and Portrait Gallery of Eminent and Self-Made Men*. Illinois Volume. Chicago and New York, 1883. Thomas M. Eddy. *The Patriotism of Illinois*. Chicago, IL, 1865. Fred S. South. *It Never Recoiled: A History of the 75th Illinois Volunteer Infantry*. Prophetstown, IL, 2003. William Sumner Dodge. *A Waif of the War; or, The History of the 75th Illinois Infantry, Embracing the Entire Campaigns of the Army of the Cumberland*. Chicago, IL, 1866. Frank E. Stevens. *History of Lee County, Illinois*. Chicago, IL, 1914.

William Wilson Sanford

Major, 48 IL Infantry, Aug. 18, 1861. Lieutenant Colonel, 48 IL Infantry, Feb. 16, 1862. GSW left forearm, Shiloh, TN, April 6, 1862. Colonel, 48 IL Infantry, Nov. 21, 1862. Commanded Post of Bethel (TN), District of Jackson, 16 Army Corps, Army of the Tennessee, Jan.–March 1863. Commanded 4 Brigade, 1 Division, 16 Army Corps, Army of the Tennessee, March 22–July 28, 1863. Commanded 4 Brigade, 4 Division, 15 Army Corps, Army of the Tennessee, July 28–Aug. 27, 1863. Suffering from chronic rheumatism, he resigned Jan. 22, 1864, "on account of failing health and my inability to stand the exposure and fatigue of active service in the field with my regiment any longer." Battle honors: Fort Donelson, Shiloh, Vicksburg Campaign, Jackson Campaign

Born: 1835?, Baltimore, MD
Died: Feb. 5, 1882, St. Louis, MO
Occupation: Purser on a merchant ship and tobacconist before war. Crockery merchant, real estate agent and financial agent after war.
Miscellaneous: Resided St. Louis, MO
Buried: Green-Wood Cemetery, Brooklyn, NY (Section 119, Lot 699)
References: Pension File and Military Service File, National Archives. *Report of the Proceedings of*

William Wilson Sanford (Relief Portrait, Vicksburg National Military Park).

the Society of the Army of the Tennessee at the Twenty-Second Meeting. Cincinnati, OH, 1893. *Illinois at Vicksburg.* Chicago, IL, 1907.

Joseph R. Scott

Served on the staff of Brig. Gen. Richard K. Swift during the Cairo Expedition of April–May 1861. Lieutenant Colonel, 19 IL Infantry, June 17, 1861. Failing to receive recognition for the role the regiment played in the occupation of Huntsville, AL, in April 1862, he resigned July 22, 1862, since "I feel the stigma unjustly cast upon the regiment," after it was "sent to the rear (Tennessee), while in the face of the enemy," to guard railroads. Colonel, 19 IL Infantry, Aug. 7, 1862, upon the promotion of Colonel John B. Turchin to brigadier general. GSW left thigh and groin, Stone's River, TN, Jan. 2, 1863. Battle honors: Hartsville, Stone's River.

Born: Feb. 2, 1838, Brantford, Ontario, Canada
Died: July 8, 1863, DOW Chicago, IL
Occupation: Clerk in a dry goods store
Miscellaneous: Resided Chicago, IL. In 1856 formed a military organization called the National Guard Cadets, which, under the guidance of Colonel Elmer Ellsworth, was reorganized as the United States Zouave Cadets of Chicago in 1859.
Buried: Graceland Cemetery, Chicago, IL (Section A, Lot 26)

Joseph R. Scott (J. Henry Haynie, editor. *The Nineteenth Illinois: A Memoir of a Regiment of Volunteer Infantry Famous in the Civil War of Fifty Years Ago for Its Drill, Bravery, and Distinguished Services.* Chicago, IL, 1912).

Joseph R. Scott (James Barnet, editor. *The Martyrs and Heroes of Illinois in the Great Rebellion.* Second Edition. Chicago, IL, 1866).

References: James Barnet, editor. *The Martyrs and Heroes of Illinois in the Great Rebellion.* Second Edition. Chicago, IL, 1866. Obituary, *Chicago Daily Tribune,* July 9, 1863. Thomas M. Eddy. *The Patriotism of Illinois.* Chicago, IL, 1865. J. Henry Haynie, editor. *The Nineteenth Illinois: A Memoir of a Regiment of Volunteer Infantry Famous in the Civil War of Fifty Years Ago for Its Drill, Bravery, and Distinguished Services.* Chicago, IL, 1912. Alfred T. Andreas. *History of Chicago from the Earliest Period to the Present Time.* Chicago, IL, 1885. Pension File and Military Service File, National Archives.

Robert P. Sealy

1 Lieutenant, Co. G, 45 IL Infantry, Sept. 17, 1861. Captain, Co. G, 45 IL Infantry, Nov. 11, 1861. Lieutenant Colonel, 45 IL Infantry, June 29, 1863. *Colonel,* 45 IL Infantry, Aug. 4, 1863. Honorably mustered out, Jan. 10, 1865. Battle honors: Shiloh, Vicksburg Campaign, Atlanta Campaign.
Born: Jan. 13, 1835, Somersetshire, England
Died: March 13, 1888, Council Bluffs, IA
Occupation: Painter
Miscellaneous: Resided Rockford, Winnebago Co., IL, to 1865; Helena, MT, 1865–68; and Council Bluffs, Pottawattamie Co., IA, 1868–88
Buried: Fairview Cemetery, Council Bluffs, IA (Section A, Lot 237)
References: Obituary, *Council Bluffs Daily Nonpareil,* March 15, 1888. Pension File and Military Service File, National Archives. John M. Adair. *Historical Sketch of the 45th Illinois Regiment.* Lanark, IL, 1869.

Robert P. Sealy (George W. Barnes, Photographer, Rockford, IL; Randy Beck Collection).

Samuel Andrew Simison

Captain, Co. D, 23 IL Infantry, June 15, 1861. Taken prisoner, Lexington, MO, Sept. 20, 1861.

Samuel Andrew Simison (C.L. Lochman, Artist, Main Street, Opposite Marion Hall, Carlisle, PA; courtesy Linda Simison Jackson).

Paroled Sept. 26, 1861. Exchanged Nov. 15, 1861. Lieutenant Colonel, 23 IL Infantry, Sept. 28, 1864. *Colonel,* 23 IL Infantry, May 11, 1865. Commanded 1 Brigade, Independent Division, 24 Army Corps, Department of Virginia, June–July 1865. Honorably mustered out, July 24, 1865. Battle honors: Lexington, Shenandoah Valley Campaign (Winchester).
Born: Jan. 3, 1830, Carlisle, PA
Died: Dec. 18, 1897, Breckenridge, CO
Occupation: Carpenter and miner
Miscellaneous: Resided Earlville, La Salle Co., IL; and Kokomo, Summit Co., CO, after 1872. Received a patent in 1867 for an improved ticket-holder for railroad tickets.
Buried: Valley Brook Cemetery, Breckenridge, CO
References: Ralph Tallmadge Briggs. *Our Family Heritage and History, Comprising McColgin Clan and Some Allied Families.* Las Vegas, NV, 1986. Obituary, *Summit County Journal,* Dec. 25, 1897. Pension File and Military Service File, National Archives. Obituary, *Salt Lake Herald,* Dec. 21, 1897. Obituary, *Salt Lake Tribune,* Dec. 19, 1897. Alfred T. Andreas. *History of Chicago from the Earliest Period to the Present Time.* Chicago, IL, 1885. Letters Received, Commission Branch, Adjutant General's Office, File S1569(CB)1866, National Archives.

Thomas J. Sloan

Colonel, 124 IL Infantry, Sept. 22, 1862. Commanded 1 Brigade, 3 Division, 17 Army Corps,

Army of the Tennessee, March 1863. His dictatorial control of the regiment resulted in the enmity of Lt. Col. John H. Howe and charges of "Conduct unbecoming an officer and a gentleman, Gross neglect of duty and disobedience of orders, and Conduct prejudicial to good order and military discipline." Court-martialed on these charges, he was dismissed Dec. 19, 1863. He appealed his dismissal to President Lincoln, who referred the case to Judge Advocate General Joseph Holt. Upon Holt's observation that "the sentence inflicted a punishment which … was somewhat disproportionate to the degree of culpability naturally and properly attaching to the actual facts. … extremely doubtful cause for his expulsion from the service of his country," Lincoln on March 7, 1864, removed the disability resulting from his dismissal, potentially allowing him to be re-commissioned as colonel. Battle honors: Port Gibson, Vicksburg Campaign.

Born: 1825?, Philadelphia, PA

Died: June 9, 1877, Portland, OR

Education: Attended Lafayette College, Easton, PA. Graduated Washington (PA) College, 1849.

Occupation: Physician and educator. President and proprietor of Sloan's Commercial College, Chicago, IL, before war.

Miscellaneous: Resided Chicago, IL; and Portland, Multnomah Co., OR, after 1868

Buried: Lone Fir Cemetery, Portland, OR (Block 1, Lot 39)

References: Obituary, *Portland Morning Oregonian*, June 11, 1877. Letters Received, Volunteer Service Branch, Adjutant General's Office, File S519(VS)1864, National Archives. Military Service File, National Archives. Court-martial Case Files, 1809–1894, File NN-0956, National Archives. Richard L. Howard. *History of the 124th Regiment Illinois Infantry Volunteers, Otherwise Known as the "Hundred and Two Dozen," from August 1862 to August 1865.* Springfield, IL, 1880. Selden J. Coffin. *Record of the Men of Lafayette: Brief Biographical Sketches of the Alumni of Lafayette College.* Easton, PA, 1879.

Alfred Theophilus Smith

1 Lieutenant, 8 U.S. Infantry, May 14, 1861. Assistant Professor of Mathematics, USMA, Sept. 1862–March 1865. Captain, 8 U.S. Infantry, Sept. 19, 1863. Colonel, 156 IL Infantry, April 4, 1865. Commanded Post of Chattanooga, TN, June 1865. Commanded 3 Brigade, 2 Separate Division, District of the Etowah, Department of the Cumberland, June–Aug. 1865. Acting AIG, Staff of Major Gen. John E. Smith, District of West Tennessee, Aug.–Sept. 1865. Honorably mustered out, Sept. 20, 1865. Bvt. Captain, USA, July 1, 1862, for gallant and meritorious services during the Peninsular Campaign. Bvt. Major and Bvt. Lieutenant Colonel, USA,

Thomas J. Sloan (Barr & Young, Army Photographers, Fort Pickering, Memphis, TN).

Alfred Theophilus Smith (post-war) (Ulysses G. McAlexander. *History of the Thirteenth Regiment United States Infantry.* Fort McDowell, CA, 1905).

March 13, 1865, for gallant and meritorious services during the war. Battle honors: Virginia Peninsular Campaign.

Born: May 29, 1838, St. Louis, MO
Died: May 23, 1905, Buffalo, NY
Education: Graduated U.S. Military Academy, West Point, NY, 1860
Other Wars: Spanish American War (Colonel, 13 U.S. Infantry)
Occupation: Regular Army (Colonel, 13 U.S. Infantry, retired June 16, 1899). Promoted to Brig. Gen., USA, on the retired list, April 23, 1904.
Miscellaneous: Resided Buffalo, Erie Co., NY. Son of Major Gen. John E. Smith.
Buried: Cremated Forest Lawn Cemetery, Buffalo, NY. Cenotaph in Greenwood Cemetery, Galena, IL (Division 2, Lot 23).
References: Constance W. Altshuler. *Cavalry Yellow & Infantry Blue.* Tucson, AZ, 1991. Obituary, *Buffalo Morning Express,* May 24, 1905. George W. Cullum. *Biographical Register of the Officers and Graduates of the U.S. Military Academy.* 3rd Edition. Boston, MA, 1891. *Memorials of Deceased Companions of the Commandery of the State of Illinois MOLLUS, from July 1, 1901, to Dec. 31, 1911.* Chicago, IL, 1912. Obituary Circular, Whole No. 532, Illinois MOLLUS. Pension File and Military Service File, National Archives. Letters Received, Appointment, Commission and Personal Branch, Adjutant General's Office, File 1161(ACP)1879, National Archives. Ulysses G. McAlexander. *History of the Thirteenth Regiment United States Infantry.* Fort McDowell, CA, 1905.

Dudley Chase Smith

1 Lieutenant, Co. B, 14 IL Infantry, May 25, 1861. Captain, Co. B, 14 IL Infantry, Sept. 21, 1861. GSW right thigh, Shiloh, TN, April 6, 1862. Upon the death of his brother-in-law and business partner, he resigned May 8, 1863, in order to continue the business, since "two widowed sisters and their families, with three other sisters and the child of a deceased sister, are all dependent upon me for protection, there being neither brother nor brother-in-law in the family besides myself." Colonel, 143 IL Infantry, June 11, 1864. Honorably mustered out, Sept. 26, 1864. Battle honors: Shiloh, Hatchie Bridge.

Born: Dec. 9, 1833, Shelbyville, IL
Died: May 22, 1920, Normal, IL
Education: Attended Jubilee College, near Peoria, IL
Occupation: Dry goods merchant
Miscellaneous: Resided Shelbyville, Shelby Co., IL; and Normal, McLean Co., IL, after 1871. Brother-in-law of Colonel Sheridan P. Read (79 IL Infantry). Married a daughter of the late Brig. Gen. William W. Orme in 1885.

Buried: Evergreen Memorial Cemetery, Bloomington, IL (Section B, Lot 12)
References: George D. Chafee, "Dudley Chase Smith, 1833–1920," *Journal of the Illinois State Historical Society,* Vol. 13, No. 2 (July 1920). Jacob L. Hasbrouck. *History of McLean County, Illinois.* Topeka and Indianapolis, 1924. *Combined History of Shelby and Moultrie Counties, Illinois.* Philadelphia, PA, 1881. Obituary, *Bloomington Daily Pantagraph,* May 24, 1920. Pension File and Military Service File, National Archives.

George Price Smith

Captain, Volunteer ADC, Staff of Brig. Gen. Thomas A. Morris (three months) and Brig. Gen. William S. Rosecrans (two Months), 1861. Major, 69 IL Infantry, June 14, 1862. Colonel, 129 IL Infantry, Sept. 8, 1862. Commanded Post of Mitchellsville (TN), District of Western Kentucky, Dec. 1862. "Laboring under extreme debility after two attacks of fever and a severe attack of erysipelas of the face and head, now followed by chronic diarrhea," he resigned May 8, 1863.

Born: Aug. 14, 1828, Wooster, OH
Died: Aug. 23, 1889, near Knoxville, Jefferson Co., OH
Education: Attended Cincinnati (OH) Eclectic Medical Institute
Occupation: Physician and newspaper editor before war. Lawyer, newspaper editor, and U.S. Pension Bureau examiner after war.
Offices/Honors: Kansas House of Representatives, 1872. Kansas Attorney General, 1884–85.
Miscellaneous: Resided Wheeling, Ohio Co., WV, to 1856; Mazon, Grundy Co., IL, 1856–59; Danville, Vermilion Co., IL, 1859–61; Dwight, Livingston Co., IL, 1861–65; Jacksonville, Morgan Co., IL, 1865–69; Humboldt, Allen Co., KS, 1869–85; Pittsburgh, PA, 1885–89
Buried: Island Creek Presbyterian Churchyard, near Knoxville, Jefferson Co., OH
References: *History of the Upper Ohio Valley.* Madison, WI, 1891. *The United States Biographical Dictionary.* Kansas Volume. Chicago and Kansas City, 1879. L. Wallace Duncan and Charles F. Scott, editors. *History of Allen and Woodson Counties, Kansas.* Iola, KS, 1901. Obituary, *Steubenville Daily Herald,* Aug. 26, 1889. Obituary, *Humboldt Union,* Aug. 31, 1889. Pension File and Military Service File, National Archives. D. O. Kellogg, editor. *A Young Scholar's Letters: Being a Memoir of Byron Caldwell Smith.* New York and London, 1897. Charles M. Eames, compiler. *Historic Morgan and Classic Jacksonville.* Jacksonville, IL, 1885.

Thomas Snell

Colonel, 107 IL Infantry, Sept. 4, 1862. Arrested

Thomas Snell (post-war) (*History of DeWitt County, Illinois.* Philadelphia, PA, 1882).

Nov. 10, 1862, for allowing his men, without provisions for thirty hours, to forage from the citizens of Elizabethtown, KY, thereby violating the established policy of respectful treatment of civilians. Jailed without charges being preferred, he was finally released upon the intercession of influential friends from Illinois. Perhaps as an aftermath of this incident, he was mustered out, Dec. 13, 1862, "on account of inefficiency, neglect of duty, and absence without leave," by order of the Secretary of War. The order mustering him out was revoked and his resignation accepted to date, Dec. 13, 1862, upon receipt by Secretary Stanton of the following communication from President Lincoln, "Thomas Snell has been summarily dismissed the service as Colonel of the 107th Illinois Volunteers. I have known him personally more than twenty years, and while I do not expect he possesses large military capacity, he is too true a patriot to be dealt with recklessly. Without, therefore, entering a contest with those whose action has led to his removal, I have concluded to say, 'Let him be restored, and his resignation, herewith tendered, be accepted.'"

Born: Dec. 26, 1818, Cincinnati, OH
Died: June 19, 1907, Bloomington, IL
Occupation: Merchant and railroad contractor before war. Banker and capitalist after war.
Miscellaneous: Resided Clinton, DeWitt Co., IL. His will, leaving an estate of $2,000,000 primarily to an adopted daughter, was challenged by his only surviving son and not settled until Feb. 1910.
Buried: Woodlawn Cemetery, Clinton, IL (Section H, Lot 97)

References: *Portrait and Biographical Album of DeWitt and Piatt Counties, Illinois.* Chicago, IL, 1891. *The Biographical Record of DeWitt County, Illinois.* Chicago, IL, 1901. *History of DeWitt County, Illinois.* Philadelphia, PA, 1882. Obituary, *Clinton Register,* June 21, 1907. Military Service File, National Archives. Letters Received, Volunteer Service Branch, Adjutant General's Office, File F561 (VS) 1862, National Archives. "The Case of Col. Thomas Snell," *Chicago Daily Tribune.* Dec. 13, 1862. "Breaks Col. Snell's Will: Illinois Supreme Court Decides Aged Millionaire Was of Unsound Mind," *New York Times,* Feb. 17, 1910.

Charles Franklin Springer

1 Lieutenant, Co. K, 140 IL Infantry, June 18, 1864. Honorably mustered out, Oct. 29, 1864. Lieutenant Colonel, 150 IL Infantry, Feb. 14, 1865. Colonel, 150 IL Infantry, Dec. 8, 1865. Honorably mustered out, Jan. 16, 1866.

Born: Aug. 10, 1834, Sullivan Co., IN
Died: Nov. 15, 1870, Edwardsville, IL
Education: Graduated Indiana Asbury (now DePauw) University, Greencastle, IN, 1858
Occupation: Lawyer
Miscellaneous: Resided Edwardsville, Madison Co., IL
Buried: Riverside Cemetery, Anamosa, IA
References: *Memorials, Addresses, and Poems, on the Life and Character of Hon. Chas. F. Springer of*

Charles Franklin Springer.

Illinois. Davenport, IA, 1877. *The History of Jones County, Iowa.* Chicago, IL, 1879. Obituary, *Anamosa Eureka,* Nov. 24, 1870. *History of Madison County, Illinois.* Edwardsville, IL, 1882. W.T. Norton, editor. *Centennial History of Madison County, Illinois, and Its People, 1812–1912.* Chicago and New York, 1912. "Re-Interment of Col. Chas. F. Springer," *Anamosa Eureka,* May 6, 1875. Obituary, *Edwardsville Intelligencer,* Nov. 17, 1870. Charles A. Martin, editor. *DePauw University: Alumnal Register of Officers, Faculties and Graduates, 1837–1900.* Greencastle, IN, 1901. Pension File and Military Service File, National Archives.

Matthew Henry Starr

2 Lieutenant, Co. L, 6 IL Cavalry, May 7, 1862. 1 Lieutenant, Co. L, 6 IL Cavalry, July 30, 1862. Captain, Co. L, 6 IL Cavalry, Oct. 24, 1862. Major, 6 IL Cavalry, Oct. 25, 1862. Acting AIG, Staff of Brig. Gen. Benjamin H. Grierson, Cavalry Division, 16 Army Corps, Army of the Tennessee, Aug. 4, 1863–April 4, 1864. Lieutenant Colonel, 6 IL Cavalry, Jan. 25, 1864. Colonel, 6 IL Cavalry, July 19, 1864. GSW left thigh, Memphis, TN, Aug. 21, 1864. Battle honors: Grierson's Raid, Meridian Expedition (Okolona), Expedition to Oxford, MS (Hurricane Creek), Forrest's Attack on Memphis.

Born: Oct. 3, 1839, Jacksonville, IL
Died: Oct. 2, 1864, DOW Jacksonville, IL

Matthew Henry Starr (Lyle Family Photographic Collection, PA62M49, Special Collections, University of Kentucky).

Occupation: Lawyer
Miscellaneous: Resided Platte City, Platte Co., MO; and Jacksonville, Morgan Co., IL
Buried: Jacksonville East Cemetery, Jacksonville, IL (New Part, Section 6, Lot 318)
References: Cecil Tendick, "Forrest Cavalry Raids Memphis: Col. Starr a Victim of Raid," *Jacksonville Journal Courier,* Aug. 23, 1964. "Mourn Death of Col. Starr," *Jacksonville Journal Courier,* Oct. 11, 1964. Obituary, *Illinois State Journal,* Oct. 7, 1864. Obituary, *Illinois State Register,* Oct. 6, 1864. Obituary, *Jacksonville Sentinel,* Oct. 7, 1864. Pension File and Military Service File, National Archives. Letters Received, Volunteer Service Branch, Adjutant General's Office, File I399(VS)1864, National Archives.

Ferdinand D. Stephenson

1 Lieutenant, Co. B, 48 IL Infantry, Sept. 30, 1861. GSW left arm, Fort Donelson, TN, Feb. 15, 1862. Captain, Co. B, 48 IL Infantry, Nov. 21, 1862. GSW neck, Dallas, GA, June 1, 1864. Resigned Nov. 19, 1864, upon "expiration of term of service." Colonel, 152 IL Infantry, Feb. 18, 1865. Honorably mustered out, Sept. 11, 1865. Battle honors: Fort Donelson, Atlanta Campaign (Dallas).

Born: Feb. 8, 1840, Athens Co., OH

Matthew Henry Starr (G.A.M. Campbell, Photographer, Jacksonville, IL; Roger D. Hunt Collection, USAMHI [RG98S-CWP107.16]).

Died: Sept. 15, 1906, Herndon, VA
Education: Graduated Columbian College, Washington, D.C., 1872
Occupation: Pension claim agent and insurance agent to 1869. Lawyer and U.S. Pension Bureau clerk after 1869.
Miscellaneous: Resided Louisville and Flora, Clay Co., IL, to 1869; Washington, D.C.; and Herndon, Fairfax Co., VA
Buried: Arlington National Cemetery, Arlington, VA (Section 3, Lot 1666)
References: Obituary, *Washington Evening Star*, Sept. 15, 1906. Pension File and Military Service File, National Archives. Letters Received, Volunteer Service Branch, Adjutant General's Office, File 162(VS)1865, National Archives. Obituary, *Washington National Tribune*, Sept. 20, 1906. Obituary Circular, Whole No. 469, District of Columbia MOLLUS.

Warren Stewart

Captain, Co. A, 15 IL Cavalry, Aug. 10, 1861. Major, 15 IL Cavalry, Feb. 1, 1862. Acting ADC, Staff of Major Gen. John A. McClernand, 1 Division, Army of the Tennessee, Feb.–July 1862. GSW head, Shiloh, TN, April 6, 1862. *Colonel*, 15 IL Cavalry, Dec. 25, 1862. Chief of Cavalry, Staff of Major Gen. John A. McClernand, Army of the Mississippi, Jan. 1863. GSW body, near New Carthage, LA,

Above: Ferdinand D. Stephenson (Abraham Lincoln Presidential Library & Museum). *Below:* Ferdinand D. Stephenson (post-war) (C.M. Bell, Artist, 459, 461, 463 & 465 Pennsylvania Avenue, Washington, DC).

Warren Stewart (City Gallery, South Side Public Square, Springfield, IL; Chicago History Museum [ICHi-68730]).

Warren Stewart (James Grant Wilson. *Biographical Sketches of Illinois Officers Engaged in the War Against the Rebellion of 1861*. Third Edition. Chicago, IL, 1863).

Jan. 23, 1863. Battle honors: Fredericktown, Fort Henry, Fort Donelson, Shiloh, Corinth, Arkansas Post.
Born: Feb. 11, 1813, Campbell, Steuben Co., NY
Died: Jan. 23, 1863, DOW near New Carthage, LA
Occupation: Provision merchant and farmer
Offices/Honors: Postmaster, Clear Creek Landing, IL, 1848–61
Miscellaneous: Resided Clear Creek Landing, Alexander Co., IL. General McClernand reported his death to Governor Richard Yates in a lengthy letter describing his valuable services and praising him as "a hero and a patriot, a man cool and wise in counsel, and devoid of all consciousness of personal danger in battle."
Buried: Hope Cemetery, Campbell, Steuben Co., NY
References: James Grant Wilson. *Biographical Sketches of Illinois Officers Engaged in the War Against the Rebellion of 1861*. Third Edition. Chicago, IL, 1863. Obituary, *Illinois State Journal*, Feb. 2, 1863. "Statement Concerning the Remains of Col. Stewart," *Illinois State Journal*, Feb. 10, 1863. Obituary, *Daily Alta California*, Feb. 10, 1863. Obituary, *Chicago Daily Tribune*, Feb. 4, 1863. "The Death of Col. Stewart Below Vicksburgh," *New York Times*, Feb. 8, 1863. *The War of the Rebellion: A Compilation of the Official Records of the Union and Confederate Armies*. (Vol. 24, Part 3, pp. 13–14). Washington, D.C., 1889. Military Service File, National Archives.

Elias Stuart

Captain, Co. C, 40 IL Infantry, July 25, 1861. Resigned May 15, 1862, on account of chronic rheumatism. Colonel, 68 IL Infantry, July 16, 1862. Honorably mustered out, Sept. 26, 1862.
Born: Dec. 4, 1827, White Co., IL
Died: March 2, 1910, Dallas, TX
Education: Attended Rush Medical College, Chicago, IL
Occupation: Physician
Offices/Honors: Mayor, Atlanta, IL, 1873–74
Miscellaneous: Resided Atlanta, Logan Co., IL, to 1876; Dallas, TX, 1876–78; Ennis, Ellis Co., TX, 1878–1907; Winfield, Cowley Co., KS, 1907–10
Buried: Edgewood Cemetery, Lancaster, TX (Lot 403)
References: Philip Lindsley and Luther B. Hill, editors. *A History of Greater Dallas and Vicinity*. Chicago, IL, 1909. Pension File and Military Service File, National Archives. Obituary, *Dallas Morning News*, March 3, 1910. Ephraim J. Hart. *History of the Fortieth Illinois Infantry (Volunteers)*. Cincinnati, OH, 1864.

James Stuart

1 Lieutenant, Adjutant, 10 IL Cavalry, Nov. 25, 1861. Captain, Co. H, 10 IL Cavalry, April 7, 1862. Lieutenant Colonel, 10 IL Cavalry, May 15, 1862. Commanded Post of Bloomfield (MO), Army of the Frontier, May 1863. Colonel, 10 IL Cavalry, May 11, 1864. Commanded Post of Huntersville (AR), Department of Arkansas, June–July 1864. Commanded 2 Provisional Brigade, Cavalry Division, 7 Army Corps, Department of Arkansas, Aug. 1864. Commanded 1 Brigade, Cavalry Division, 7 Army Corps, Department of Arkansas, April 1865. Commanded 2 Brigade, 1 Cavalry Division, Military Division of the Southwest, June 1865. Commanded 2 Brigade, 1 Cavalry Division, Military Division of the Gulf, July–Aug. 1865. Honorably mustered out, Nov. 22, 1865. Battle honors: Prairie Grove, Advance upon Little Rock (Bayou Fourche), Camden Expedition.
Born: 1828?
Died: Date and place of death unknown
Occupation: Engaged in the cattle trade in Texas after war. Later associated with the U.S. Quartermaster's Department in Galveston, TX, he was arrested in Kansas City, MO, May 12, 1871, charged with embezzling $8,000 in government funds. Subsequent whereabouts unknown.
Miscellaneous: Resided Springfield, Sangamon Co., IL; and Indianola, Calhoun Co., TX
Buried: Place of burial unknown
References: Military Service File, National Archives. "Col. James Stuart," *Illinois State Register*,

May 13, 16 and 17, 1871. Letters Received, Volunteer Service Branch, Adjutant General's Office, File S159(VS)1868, National Archives.

Owen Stuart

Major, 90 IL Infantry, Sept. 23, 1862. Lieutenant Colonel, 90 IL Infantry, March 7, 1863. Dismissed June 12, 1863, for presenting "a claim against the government for subsisting recruits, which has been ascertained to be in all respects false and fraudulent, though sworn to." His dismissal was revoked, July 25, 1863, following an appeal to President Lincoln and an investigation by Judge Advocate General Joseph Holt, who determined that "he never had any claim against the United States for subsisting recruits … and that all the papers connected with the claim are forgeries and were fabricated without his knowledge." GSW abdomen, Missionary Ridge, TN, Nov. 25, 1863. Erroneously reported as dying from his wound, he was nursed back to health by his wife, who had gone to Chattanooga to bring his body home. *Colonel,* 90 IL Infantry, Nov. 25, 1863. Honorably mustered out, June 6, 1865. Battle honors: Missionary Ridge, Atlanta Campaign (Resaca, Atlanta), Savannah Campaign, Campaign of the Carolinas.

Born: Dec. 26, 1827, Armagh, County Armagh, Ireland

Died: Feb. 6, 1914, Riverside, CA

Occupation: Printer before war. U.S. Internal Revenue officer after war, serving as assessor, 1867–72, and gauger, 1872–1906.

Miscellaneous: Resided Chicago, Jefferson, and Park Ridge, Cook Co., IL, to 1906; and Riverside, Riverside Co., CA, 1906–14. Brother-in-law of Bvt. Brig. Gen. Daniel Cameron.

Buried: Olivewood Cemetery, Riverside, CA (Section L, Division 2, Lot 5)

References: John R. Brumgardt, "A Scottish Printer at 'Johnston's Heels': The Civil War Letters of Colonel Owen Stuart (90th Illinois)," Owen Stuart Papers (SC 2405), Abraham Lincoln Presidential Library, Springfield, IL. Pension File and Military Service File, National Archives. Letters Received, Volunteer Service Branch, Adjutant General's Office, File I558(VS)1863, National Archives. James B. Swan. *Chicago's Irish Legion: The 90th Illinois Volunteers in the Civil War.* Carbondale, IL, 2009. "Death of Lieut. Col. Stuart," *Chicago Daily Tribune,* Dec. 4, 1863. George H. Woodruff. *Fifteen Years Ago: or the Patriotism of Will County.* Joliet, IL, 1876. "The Irish Ninetieth," *Chicago Inter Ocean,* Nov. 26, 1890. Sally Coplen Hogan, editor. *General Reub Williams' Memories of Civil War Times.* Westminster, MD, 2006. Death Notice, *Riverside Daily Press,* Feb. 6, 1914.

Edgar Denman Swain

Captain, Co. I, 42 IL Infantry, Aug. 15, 1861. Lieutenant Colonel, 42 IL Infantry, Oct. 30, 1863. *Colonel,* 42 IL Infantry, April 13, 1864. GSW left knee, New Hope Church, GA, June 3, 1864. Bvt. Colonel, USV, March 13, 1865, for gallant and meritorious services. Commanded 2 Brigade, 2 Division, 4 Army Corps, Army of the Cumberland, July 12–Aug. 1, 1865. Commanded Post of Port Lavaca (TX), Department of Texas, Aug. 1865. Honorably mustered out, Dec. 16, 1865. Battle honors: Missionary Ridge, Atlanta Campaign (New Hope Church), Nashville.

Born: Aug. 14, 1836, Westford, VT

Died: April 28, 1904, Batavia, IL

Occupation: Dentist

Offices/Honors: President, Illinois State Dental Society, 1875. Colonel, Illinois National Guard, 1877–81. Senior Vice Commander-in-Chief, GAR, 1880. Dean of Northwestern University Dental School, 1891–97.

Miscellaneous: Resided Oshkosh, Winnebago Co., WI, 1857–59; Batavia, Kane Co., IL 1859–61; and Chicago, IL, after 1865

Edgar Denman Swain.

Above: Edgar Denman Swain (C.C. Giers' Photograph Gallery, Corner Square & Deadrick Street, Nashville, TN; Ray Zielin Collection). *Below:* Edgar Denman Swain (USAMHI [RG98S-CWP37.49]).

Buried: West Batavia Cemetery, Batavia, IL
References: *Memorials of Deceased Companions of the Commandery of the State of Illinois MOLLUS, from July 1, 1901, to Dec. 31, 1911.* Chicago, IL, 1912. Obituary Circular, Whole No. 484, Illinois MOLLUS. *Album of Genealogy and Biography Cook County, Illinois.* Chicago, IL, 1897. Alfred T. Andreas. *History of Chicago from the Earliest Period to the Present Time.* Chicago, IL, 1885. *A Biographical History with Portraits of Prominent Men of the Great West.* Chicago, IL, 1894. *The United States Biographical Dictionary and Portrait Gallery of Eminent and Self-Made Men.* Illinois Volume. Chicago, Cincinnati, and New York, 1876. "Dr. Edgar Denman Swain," *The Dental Cosmos,* Vol. 46, No. 6 (June 1904). William H. Ward, editor. *Records of Members of the Grand Army of the Republic.* San Francisco, CA, 1886. Pension File and Military Service File, National Archives.

Francis Swanwick

Captain, Co. H, 22 IL Infantry, June 11, 1861. Major, 22 IL Infantry, Jan. 17, 1862. Lieutenant Colonel, 22 IL Infantry, Aug. 4, 1862. GSW left arm, Stone's River, TN, Dec. 31, 1862. Taken prisoner, Stone's River, TN, Dec. 31, 1862. Confined Atlanta, GA, and Libby Prison, Richmond, VA. Paroled May 5, 1863. Honorably mustered out, July 7, 1864. Major, 154 IL Infantry, Feb. 22, 1865. Lieutenant Colonel, 154 IL Infantry, June 12, 1865. *Colonel,* 154 IL Infantry, Aug. 11, 1865. Honorably mustered out, Sept. 18, 1865. Battle honors: Stone's River, Tullahoma Campaign, Chickamauga, Missionary Ridge, Atlanta Campaign (Resaca).

Born: April 22, 1809, Chester, Cheshire, England

Francis Swanwick (Randy Beck Collection).

Francis Swanwick (USAMHI [RG98S-CWP 6.3]).

Died: March 4, 1883, near Oswego, KS

Other Wars: Black Hawk War (Sergeant, Captain Gordon's Spy Company, IL Mounted Militia)

Occupation: Miller and plank road superintendent before war. Miller and farmer after war.

Miscellaneous: Resided Chester, Randolph Co., IL, before war; and Oswego, Labette Co., KS, after war. Married the daughter of Shadrach Bond, the first governor of Illinois.

Buried: Oswego Cemetery, Oswego, KS (Block 3, Lot 2)

References: Thomas M. Eddy. *The Patriotism of Illinois*. Chicago, IL, 1865. Pension File and Military Service File, National Archives. *Combined History of Randolph, Monroe and Perry Counties, Illinois*. Philadelphia, PA, 1883. Letters Received, Commission Branch, Adjutant General's Office, File S2319(CB)1865, National Archives. Death notice, *Labette County Democrat*, March 9, 1883.

Christian Thielemann

Captain, Co. M, 1 IL Cavalry (later Co. A, 16 IL Cavalry), July 2, 1861. Major, Thielemann's Independent Battalion IL Cavalry, Nov. 1, 1861. Colonel, 16 IL Cavalry, June 11, 1863. Commanded Post of

Christian Thielemann (A. Hesler, Artist, 113 Lake Street, Chicago, IL; Richard K. Tibbals Collection, USAMHI [RG98S-CWP40.72]).

Camp Butler (IL), District of Illinois, Department of the Ohio, June–Sept. 1863. Commanded Post of Tazewell (TN), Left Wing Forces in East Tennessee, Department of the Ohio, Dec. 1863–Jan. 1864. Disabled by severe neuralgia of the left leg in April 1864, upon returning to his regiment in August, he suffered a fracture of his left thigh, Aug. 6, 1864, near Atlanta, resulting in his honorable discharge, effective Aug. 9, 1864, "on account of physical disability." Upon learning of his discharge, he protested the "gross injustice," blaming the action upon the "improper motives" of Lieutenant Colonel Robert W. Smith, "of my regiment, a man without any military knowledge, not fit to command a corporal's guard." Battle honors: Shiloh, Atlanta Campaign.

Born: Oct. 9, 1809, Hessen Kassel, Germany

Died: Oct. 23, 1875, Chicago, IL

Occupation: Theatre manager and proprietor

Offices/Honors: U.S. Internal Revenue gauger, 1870–73

Miscellaneous: Resided Cincinnati, OH, before war; and Chicago, IL, after war

Buried: Graceland Cemetery, Chicago, IL (Section R, Lot 49, unmarked)

References: Pension File and Military Service File, National Archives. Letters Received, Volunteer Service Branch, Adjutant General's Office, File O985(VS)1864. "Sponsor of the German Theater in Cincinnati Dies: Colonel Christian Thielemann," *Der Deutsche Pionier,* Vol. 7, No. 8 (Oct. 1875). Clifford Neal Smith. *Early Nineteenth-Century German Settlers in Ohio, Kentucky, and Other States.* McNeal, AZ, 1988.

William Augustus Thrush

Captain, Co. C, 47 IL Infantry, Aug. 18, 1861. Major, 47 IL Infantry, Aug. 25, 1861. Lieutenant Colonel, 47 IL Infantry, May 9, 1862. Colonel, 47 IL Infantry, Sept. 2, 1862. GSW heart, Corinth, MS, Oct. 3, 1862. Battle honors: Iuka, Corinth.
 Born: April 1831, Shippensburg, PA
 Died: Oct. 3, 1862, KIA Corinth, MS
 Occupation: For several years a druggist, he was later a produce and commission merchant
 Miscellaneous: Resided Peoria, Peoria Co., IL
 Buried: Springdale Cemetery, Peoria, IL (Mount Auburn Division, Section 4, Lot 295)
 References: James Grant Wilson. *Biographical Sketches of Illinois Officers Engaged in the War Against the Rebellion of 1861.* Third Edition. Chicago, IL, 1863. Byron Cloyd Bryner. *Bugle Echoes: The Story of Illinois 47th.* Springfield, IL, 1905. Pension File and Military Service File, National Archives. Obituary, *Peoria Transcript,* Oct. 17, 1862. "Obsequies of Col. W.A. Thrush," *Peoria Transcript,* Oct. 20, 1862. *The History of Peoria County, Illinois.* Chicago, IL, 1880.

William Augustus Thrush (Cole's Photographic Gallery, 5 N. Adams Street, Peoria, IL; Richard F. Carlile Collection).

Silas Cox Toler

Colonel, 60 IL Infantry, Feb. 17, 1862. Battle honors: Stone's River.
 Born: July 16, 1831, Union Co., IL
 Died: March 2, 1863, Harrisburg, PA (chronic hepatitis)
 Occupation: Physician
 Offices/Honors: Postmaster, Jonesboro, IL, 1856–58
 Miscellaneous: Resided Jonesboro, Union Co., IL. Brother-in-law of Colonel Francis M. Davidson (14 IL Cavalry).
 Buried: Jonesboro Cemetery, Jonesboro, IL
 References: Darrel Dexter, compiler. *Union County, Illinois, Soldiers.* Carterville, IL, 1997. Obituary, *Jonesboro Weekly Gazette,* March 7 and 14, 1863. "Colonel Silas C. Toler," *Jonesboro Weekly Gazette,* April 11, 1863. Alice Craft, compiler. *Tolar, Toler, Toller, Towler: A One Name Study.* Cambridge, England, 1996. Pension File and Military Service File, National Archives. William H. Perrin, editor. *History of Alexander, Union, and Pulaski Counties, Illinois.* Chicago, IL, 1883.

Silas Cox Toler (USAMHI [RG98S-CWP121.81]).

Lewis Corbin True

Sergeant, Co. E, 38 IL Infantry, Aug. 21, 1861. 1 Lieutenant, Adjutant, 62 IL Infantry, April 10, 1862.

Captain, Co. D, 62 IL Infantry, July 1, 1862. Acting AIG, 3 Brigade, 3 Division, 16 Army Corps, Army of the Tennessee, June–Aug. 1863. Major, 62 IL Infantry, Aug. 17, 1863. Lieutenant Colonel, 62 IL Infantry, Feb. 3, 1865. Commanded 2 Brigade, 2 Division, 7 Army Corps, Department of Arkansas, April 30–May 7, 1865, and July 26–Aug. 1, 1865. *Colonel*, 62 IL Infantry, July 11, 1865. Commanded District of South Kansas, Department of Arkansas, Aug.–Oct. 1865. Honorably mustered out, March 6, 1866.

Born: April 4, 1842, Coles Co., IL
Died: Feb. 5, 1918, Kansas City, KS
Education: Attended Illinois College, Jacksonville, IL
Occupation: Farmer before war. Cattle trader and lawyer after war.
Miscellaneous: Resided Mattoon, Coles Co., IL, to 1868; Ottawa, Franklin Co., KS; Chetopa, Labette Co., KS; Oswego, Labette Co., KS; and Kansas City, Wyandotte Co., KS, after 1882. Nephew of Bvt. Brig. Gen. James M. True.
Buried: Oak Hill Cemetery, Chetopa, KS (Block 21, Lot 5)
References: Perl W. Morgan, editor. *History of Wyandotte County, Kansas, and Its People.* Chicago, IL, 1911. William E. Connelley. *A Standard History of Kansas and Kansans.* Chicago and New York, 1918. *The United States Biographical Dictionary.* Kansas Volume. Chicago and Kansas City, 1879. Obituary, *Kansas City Star*, Feb. 6, 1918. Obituary, *Chetopa Advance*, Feb. 7, 1918. Pension File and Military Service File, National Archives. Letters Received, Volunteer Service Branch, Adjutant General's Office, File B9(VS)1867, National Archives.

Above: Lewis Corbin True (Abraham Lincoln Presidential Library & Museum). *Below:* Lewis Corbin True.

Joseph H. Tucker

Acting AAG, Staff of Illinois Governor Richard Yates, Feb. 14–April 2, 1862. Colonel, 69 IL Infantry, June 13, 1862. Commanded Camp Douglas Military Prison, Chicago, IL, June 19–Dec. 31, 1862. Retained in service after muster out of 69 IL Infantry, Oct. 6, 1862, since "there was at that time much business connected with the prisoners of war unsettled and also several regiments and batteries of Illinois volunteers then being organized for the field at this camp and no officer here to relieve me." Honorably mustered out, Dec. 31, 1862.

Born: 1819?, NY
Died: Oct. 22, 1894, New York City, NY
Occupation: Banker, commission merchant and stock broker
Offices/Honors: Mayor of Cumberland, MD, 1856–57. Board of Directors, Chicago Board of Trade, 1859–60.
Miscellaneous: Resided Cumberland, Allegany Co., MD, to 1858; Chicago, IL, 1858–64; and New

York City, NY, after 1864. Commanded pre-war 60 IL State Militia.
Buried: Graceland Cemetery, Chicago, IL (Section D, Lot 384)
References: Obituary, *New York Tribune*, Oct. 25, 1894. Obituary, *New York Times*, Oct. 25, 1894. Obituary, *Chicago Daily Tribune*, Oct. 25, 1894. George Levy. *To Die in Chicago: Confederate Prisoners at Camp Douglas, 1862–65*. Gretna, LA, 1999. Alfred T. Andreas. *History of Chicago from the Earliest Period to the Present Time*. Chicago, IL, 1885. Letters Received, Volunteer Service Branch, Adjutant General's Office, File I284(VS)1862, National Archives. Military Service File, National Archives. John Thomas Scharf. *History of Western Maryland, Being a History of Frederick, Montgomery, Carroll, Washington, Allegany, and Garrett Counties from the Earliest Period to the Present Day*. Philadelphia, PA, 1882.

Nathan Willis Tupper

Colonel, 116 IL Infantry, Sept. 30, 1862. Commanded 1 Brigade, 2 Division, 15 Army Corps, Army of the Tennessee, Sept. 10–Oct. 19, 1863 and Nov. 24, 1863–Jan. 1, 1864. Battle honors: Chickasaw Bluffs, Vicksburg Campaign, Missionary Ridge.
Born: July 8, 1830, Parishville, NY
Died: March 10, 1864, Decatur, IL (remittent fever)
Education: Attended St. Lawrence Academy, Potsdam, NY
Occupation: Lawyer
Miscellaneous: Resided Decatur, Macon Co., IL
Buried: Greenwood Cemetery, Decatur, IL (Block 1, Lot 132)
References: *Past and Present of the City of Decatur and Macon County, Illinois*. Chicago, IL, 1903. Eleanor Tupper. *Tupper Genealogy, 1578–1971*. Beverly, MA, 1972. *History of Macon County, Illinois*. Philadelphia, PA, 1880. Obituary, *Illinois State Journal*, March 11, 1864. Carl Zillier, editor. *History of Sheboygan County, Wisconsin, Past and Present*. Chicago, IL, 1912. Pension File and Military Service File, National Archives.

Thomas Johnston Turner

Colonel, 15 IL Infantry, May 24, 1861. Commanded 1 Division, District of Central Missouri, Department of the Missouri, Nov. 1861–Jan. 1862. Commanded 1 Brigade, 4 Division, District of West Tennessee, Feb. 1862. "Incapable of discharging the duties of his office because of organic disease of the liver," he resigned Nov. 2, 1862.
Born: April 5, 1815, Trumbull Co., OH
Died: April 3, 1874, Hot Springs, AR
Occupation: Lawyer and journalist
Offices/Honors: U.S. House of Representatives, 1847–49. Illinois House of Representatives, 1854–56 (Speaker 1855) and 1870–72.

Nathan Willis Tupper (*Past and Present of the City of Decatur and Macon County, Illinois*. Chicago, IL, 1903).

Thomas Johnston Turner (Roger D. Hunt Collection, USAMHI [RG98S-CWP160.14]).

Miscellaneous: Resided Freeport, Stephenson Co., IL, to 1871; and Chicago, IL, 1871–74

Buried: City Cemetery, Freeport, IL (SW ¼, Range 2, Lot 14)

References: *Portrait and Biographical Album of Stephenson County, Illinois.* Chicago, IL, 1888. Obituary, *Freeport Bulletin,* April 9, 1874. James Grant Wilson. *Biographical Sketches of Illinois Officers Engaged in the War Against the Rebellion of 1861.* Third Edition. Chicago, IL, 1863. John M. Palmer, editor. *The Bench and Bar of Illinois: Historical and Reminiscent.* Chicago, IL, 1899. *In the Foot-Prints of the Pioneers of Stephenson County, Illinois: A Genealogical Record.* Freeport, IL, 1900. *Biographical Encyclopedia of Illinois of the Nineteenth Century.* Philadelphia, PA, 1875. Addison L. Fulwider. *History of Stephenson County, Illinois: A Record of Its Settlement, Organization and Three-Quarters of a Century of Progress.* Chicago, IL, 1910. Pension File and Military Service File, National Archives. Lucius W. Barber. *Army Memoirs of Lucius W. Barber, Co. D, 15th Illinois Volunteer Infantry.* Chicago, IL, 1894.

Thomas Johnston Turner (post-war) (*Biographical Encyclopedia of Illinois of the Nineteenth Century.* Philadelphia, PA, 1875).

John Jacob Updegraff

Colonel, 5 IL Cavalry, Sept. 9, 1861. Arraigned before a State of Illinois court martial on a charge of "Conduct unbecoming an officer and a gentleman," preferred by Lieutenant Colonel Benjamin L. Wiley and Major Thomas A. Apperson, he was dismissed Dec. 3, 1861, after a lengthy and irregular trial in which he was found guilty of only one of eleven specifications, that of "at various times openly and notoriously visiting houses of prostitution at Springfield, to public disgrace of the regiment and the service generally."

Born: March 20, 1817, Rockville, Dauphin Co., PA

Died: Sept. 1882, Flint, MI (according to his widow, Anna, in her pension application, as mother of Joseph M. Updegraff)

Education: Attended the Medical Department of Pennsylvania College, Philadelphia, PA

Occupation: Physician specializing in eye and ear surgery

Miscellaneous: Resided Danville, Montour Co., PA (1850); Selinsgrove, Snyder Co., PA (1853); Elmira, Chemung Co., NY (1860); Mattoon, Coles Co., IL (1861); Pittston, Luzerne Co., PA (1863); Reading, Berks Co., PA (1868); Wilkes-Barre, Luzerne Co., PA (1870); Scranton, Lackawanna Co., PA (1876); and Elmira, Chemung Co., NY (1880). Described in an obituary of his son, Dr. Thaddeus S. Updegraff, as "a distinguished surgeon of eccentric habits and great mechanical genius, but unfortunately a slave to the opium habit." Received a patent in 1853 for an Improvement in Heating Stoves. In 1868 invented the "Berks County Perpetual Motion Machine," which he exhibited throughout Pennsylvania.

Buried: Woodlawn Cemetery, Elmira, NY (Section C, Lot 43, unmarked)

References: June (Shaull) Lutz. *History of the Op Den Graef/Updegraff Family.* Grand Rapids, MI, 1988. Pension File of Joseph M. Updegraff, National Archives. Letters Received, Volunteer Service Branch, Adjutant General's Office, File U4(VS) 1863, National Archives. "The Case of Col. Updegraff," *Illinois State Journal,* Oct. 25 and Dec. 5, 1861. Catherine M. Berger. *Op den Graeff, Updegraff, Updegrove: Indices and Pedigrees of Known Descendants of Herman Op den Graeff.* Sacramento, CA, 1991. George E. Blackham, "Memoir of Thad S. Up de Graff, M.D., F.R.M.S.," *Proceedings of the American Society of Microscopists,* Vol. 7, Eighth Annual Meeting (1885). Rhonda M. Kohl. *The Prairie Boys Go To War: The Fifth Illinois Cavalry, 1861–1865.* Carbondale, IL, 2013. "Important Invention," *Harrisburg Telegraph,* Aug. 25, 1868. "Dr. Updegraff's Idea: A Perpetual Motion Machine That Ran for Eight Years," *Philadelphia Inquirer,* July 17, 1876.

John Van Arman

Colonel, 127 IL Infantry, Sept. 6, 1862. Suffering from frequent attacks of pneumonia, he resigned Feb. 23, 1863, since "there is now a degree of subacute inflammation existing in the upper portion of the lung, which would under unfavorable circumstances result in more complete disease of the lung."

Born: March 3, 1820, Plattsburgh, NY

Died: April 6, 1890, San Diego, CA
Other Wars: Mexican War (Captain, Co. I, 1 Michigan Infantry)
Occupation: Lawyer. Described by one of his peers as "one of the most noted criminal lawyers of the country."
Miscellaneous: Resided Marshall, Calhoun Co., MI, to 1858; Chicago, IL, 1858–85; and San Diego, CA, after 1885
Buried: Mount Hope Cemetery, San Diego, CA (Division 3, Section 9, Lot 14 1/2)
References: *The United States Biographical Dictionary and Portrait Gallery of Eminent and Self-Made Men.* Illinois Volume. Chicago and New York, 1883. *The Bench and Bar of Chicago: Biographical Sketches.* Chicago, IL, 1883. Franc B. Wilkie. *Sketches and Notices of the Chicago Bar.* Chicago, IL, 1871. John M. Palmer, editor. *The Bench and Bar of Illinois: Historical and Reminiscent.* Chicago, IL, 1899. Obituary, *Chicago Daily Tribune,* April 7, 1890. Obituary, *San Diego Union,* April 7, 1890. Obituary, *Chicago Inter Ocean,* April 8, 1890. Pension File and Military Service File, National Archives.

John Van Arman (post-war) (*The United States Biographical Dictionary and Portrait Gallery of Eminent and Self-Made Men.* Illinois Volume. Chicago and New York, 1883).

Henry Van Sellar

1 Sergeant, Co. E, 12 IL Infantry (3 months), May 2, 1861. 2 Lieutenant, Co. E, 12 IL Infantry (3 years), Aug. 1, 1861. Captain, Co. E, 12 IL Infantry, Oct. 18, 1861. Provost Marshal, Corinth, MS, Jan.–April 1863. Lieutenant Colonel, 12 IL Infantry, Feb. 20, 1864. Commanded 2 Brigade, 4 Division, 15 Army Corps, Army of the Tennessee, Oct. 1864. *Colonel,* 12 IL Infantry, July 10, 1865. Honorably

Henry Van Sellar.

mustered out, July 10, 1865. Battle honors: Shiloh, Corinth, Atlanta Campaign (Atlanta), Savannah Campaign, Campaign of the Carolinas.
Born: Dec. 11, 1839, Delaware Co., OH
Died: April 27, 1915, Paris, IL
Education: Attended Ohio Wesleyan University, Delaware, OH. Attended Dennison University, Granville, OH.
Occupation: Lawyer and judge
Offices/Honors: Illinois Senate, 1884–86. Circuit Court Judge, 1897–1903.
Miscellaneous: Resided Paris, Edgar Co., IL
Buried: Edgar Cemetery, Paris, IL (Section K, Lot 1356)
References: *Memorials of Deceased Companions of the Commandery of the State of Illinois MOLLUS, from Jan. 1, 1912 to Dec. 31, 1922.* Chicago, IL, 1923. Obituary Circular, Whole No. 763, Illinois MOLLUS. Obituary, *Paris Daily Beacon,* April 27, 1915. D. Alexander Brown, "A Civil War Love Story," *Civil War Times Illustrated,* Vol. 5, No. 9 (Jan. 1967). Newton Bateman, Paul Selby, and Henry Van Sellar, editors. *Historical Encyclopedia of Illinois and History of Edgar County.* Chicago, IL, 1905. Frederic B. Crossley. *Courts and Lawyers of Illinois.* Chicago, IL, 1916. Pension File and Military Service File, National Archives. Letters Received, Volunteer Service Branch, Adjutant General's Office, File 12378(VS) 1887, National Archives.

Carter Van Vleck

Lieutenant Colonel, 78 IL Infantry, Sept. 1, 1862. GSW left forearm, Chickamauga, GA, Sept. 20, 1863. Colonel, 78 IL Infantry, Feb. 17, 1864. Commanded 2 Brigade, 2 Division, 14 Army Corps, Army of the Cumberland, Feb. 1864. GSW head, near Atlanta, GA, Aug. 11, 1864. Battle honors: Tullahoma Campaign, Chickamauga, Chattanooga-Ringgold Campaign, Dalton, Atlanta Campaign (Kenesaw Mountain).

Above: Carter Van Vleck (Photographed by E.S. Carter, Beardstown, IL). *Below:* Carter Van Vleck (Hawkins & Philpot, Photographers, S.E. Cor. Public Square, Macomb, IL).

Born: June 11, 1830, Fenner Twp., Madison Co., NY
Died: Aug. 23, 1864, DOW near Atlanta, GA
Education: Attended Hamilton (NY) Academy
Occupation: Lawyer
Miscellaneous: Resided Macomb, McDonough Co., IL
Buried: Oakwood Cemetery, Macomb, IL (Block 3, Lot 176)
References: Carter Van Vleck. *Emerging Leader: The Letters of Carter Van Vleck to His Wife, Patty, 1862–1864.* Transcribed and Edited by Teresa K. Lehr and Philip L. Gerber. Bloomington, IN, 2012. Pension File and Military Service File, National Archives. Jane Van Vleck. *Ancestry and Descendants of Tielman Van Vleeck of New Amsterdam.* New York City, NY, 1955. Steve Raymond. *In the Very Thickest of the Fight: The Civil War Service of the 78th Illinois Volunteer Infantry Regiment.* Guilford, CT, 2012. *History of McDonough County, Illinois.* Springfield, IL, 1885.

Maris Ralph Vernon

Captain, Co. K, 78 IL Infantry, Sept. 1, 1862. Lieutenant Colonel, 78 IL Infantry, Feb. 17, 1864. Colonel, 78 IL Infantry, May 10, 1865. Honorably mustered out, June 7, 1865. Battle honors: Atlanta Campaign (Kenesaw Mountain, Jonesborough), Savannah Campaign, Campaign of the Carolinas (Bentonville).

Born: Nov. 10, 1833, Unionville, Chester Co., PA
Died: Dec. 10, 1916, Oakland, CA
Occupation: Lawyer, real estate agent, journalist and mine operator
Miscellaneous: Resided Quincy, Adams Co., IL (1862); St. Louis, MO (1872–75); San Francisco, CA (1876–81); Los Angeles, CA (1884–1900); El Dorado, El Dorado Co., CA; and Oakland, CA (1910–16)
Buried: Mountain View Cemetery, Oakland, CA (Plot 45, Grave 155, unmarked)
References: Pension File and Military Service File, National Archives. Obituary Circular, Whole No. 1240, California MOLLUS. Obituary, *Oakland Tribune,* Dec. 12, 1916. Steve Raymond. *In the Very Thickest of the Fight: The Civil War Service of the 78th Illinois Volunteer Infantry Regiment.* Guilford, CT, 2012. Carter Van Vleck. *Emerging Leader: The Letters of Carter Van Vleck to His Wife, Patty, 1862–1864.* Transcribed and Edited by Teresa K. Lehr and Philip L. Gerber. Bloomington, IN, 2012.

Arno Voss

Colonel, 12 IL Cavalry, Feb. 1, 1862. Commanded 2 Brigade, 3 Division, Cavalry Corps, Army of the Potomac, March–April 1863. Described by Major Gen. Alfred Pleasanton as "not competent to command either a regiment or brigade of cavalry in the field," he was relieved from the command of his regiment, Aug. 9, 1863, whereupon he resigned, Aug. 11, 1863. Battle honors: Maryland Campaign (Harper's Ferry).

Born: April 15, 1816, Rahden, Westphalia, Germany
Died: March 23, 1888, Chicago, IL
Occupation: Lawyer
Offices/Honors: Chicago City Attorney, 1852–53. Illinois House of Representatives, 1876–78.
Miscellaneous: Resided Chicago, IL; and Monee, Will Co., IL (1870)
Buried: Waldheim Cemetery, Forest Park, IL (Section D, Lot 881)
References: Obituary, *Chicago Daily Tribune*, March 24, 1888. Pension File and Military Service File, National Archives. Alfred T. Andreas. *History of Chicago from the Earliest Period to the Present Time.* Chicago, IL, 1885. *The Bench and Bar of Chicago: Biographical Sketches.* Chicago, IL, 1883. Newton Bateman, Paul Selby, Harvey B. Hurd, and Robert D. Sheppard, editors. *Historical Encyclopedia of Illinois and History of Evanston.* Chicago, IL, 1906. Allan L. Tischler. *The History of the Harpers Ferry Cavalry Expedition, September 14 & 15, 1862.* Winchester, VA, 1993.

Nathan Halbert Walworth

Captain, Co. C, 42 IL Infantry, July 22, 1861. Major, 42 IL Infantry, Dec. 25, 1861. Lieutenant Colonel, 42 IL Infantry, Sept. 27, 1862. Colonel, 42 IL Infantry, Jan. 1, 1863. Commanded 3 Brigade, 3 Division, 20 Army Corps, Army of the Cumberland, April 1863 and Sept. 19–Oct. 9, 1863. Commanded Demi-brigade, 3 Brigade, 2 Division, 4 Army Corps, Army of the Cumberland, Nov. 1863–Jan. 1864. Resigned April 13, 1864, since "my regiment has been reduced to less than half of the maximum and is not entitled to an officer of my rank." Battle honors: Stone's River, Tullahoma Campaign, Chickamauga, Missionary Ridge.

Born: Feb. 14, 1832, Westernville, Oneida Co., NY
Died: Oct. 29, 1892, Evanston, IL
Education: Attended Cazenovia (NY) Seminary
Occupation: Lumber merchant
Offices/Honors: Postmaster, Oneida, IL, 1857–61
Miscellaneous: Resided Oneida, Knox Co., IL, to 1868; Chicago, IL, 1868–90; and Evanston, Cook Co., IL, 1890–92
Buried: Rosehill Cemetery, Chicago, IL (Section 102, Lot 24)
References: Newton Bateman, Paul Selby, Harvey B. Hurd, and Robert D. Sheppard, editors. *Historical Encyclopedia of Illinois and History of Evanston.* Chicago, IL, 1906. *Memorials of Deceased Companions of the Commandery of the State of Illinois MOLLUS, from May 8, 1879 to July 1, 1901.* Chicago, IL, 1901. Obituary Circular, Whole No. 182, Illinois MOLLUS. *Society of the Army of the Cumberland. Twenty-Fourth Reunion, Cleveland, OH, 1893.* Cincinnati, OH, 1894. Reginald W. Walworth. *Walworth-Walsworth Genealogy, 1689–1962.* Centreville, MD, 1962. Clarence A. Walworth. *The Walworths of America.* Albany, NY, 1897. Pension File and Military Service File, National Archives. Letters Received, Volunteer Service Branch, Adjutant General's Office, File W864(VS)1864, National Archives. Obituary, *Chicago Daily Tribune*, Oct. 30, 1892. Obituary, *Chicago Inter Ocean*, Oct. 31, 1892.

John Baptist Warner

Colonel, 108 IL Infantry, Aug. 28, 1862. Dismissed March 13, 1863, for "making false musters, in allowing men of one company to be borrowed to swell the ranks of another about to muster in the service." Battle honors: Chickasaw Bluffs, Arkansas Post.

Born: Oct. 11, 1826, near Somerset, Perry Co., OH
Died: Dec. 28, 1920, Peoria, IL
Occupation: Clothing merchant before war. Liquor merchant and municipal official after war.
Offices/Honors: Mayor, Peoria, IL, 1874–76, 1878–82, 1884–86, 1888–90, 1892, 1897–99. Postmaster, Peoria, IL, 1885–86.

Nathan Halbert Walworth (post-war) (Massachusetts MOLLUS Collection, USAMHI [Vol. 69, p. 3448]).

Miscellaneous: Resided Peoria, Peoria Co., IL
Buried: Springdale Cemetery, Peoria, IL (Vista Hill Division, Section 2, Lot 1669)
References: *Portrait and Biographical Album of Peoria County, Illinois.* Chicago, IL, 1890. *The History of Peoria County, Illinois.* Chicago, IL, 1880. Jerry W. Pitstick, "A Presentation Colt M1851 Navy," *Man at Arms,* Vol. 20, No. 3 (June 1998). Obituary, *Peoria Transcript,* Dec. 29, 1920. *The United States Biographical Dictionary and Portrait Gallery of Eminent and Self-Made Men.* Illinois Volume. Chicago and New York, 1883. Military Service File, National Archives. Letters Received, Volunteer Service Branch, Adjutant General's Office, File W1168(VS) 1863, National Archives. James M. Rice. *Peoria City and County, Illinois.* Chicago, IL, 1912.

John Baptist Warner (post-war) (*The History of Peoria County, Illinois.* Chicago, IL, 1880).

William Appleton Webb

Captain, 16 U.S. Infantry, May 14, 1861. Colonel, 42 IL Infantry, July 22, 1861.
Born: 1831?, Dover, ME
Died: Dec. 24, 1861, Smithton, MO (typhoid fever)
Education: Graduated U.S. Military Academy, West Point, NY, 1853
Occupation: Regular Army (Captain, died 1861)
Miscellaneous: Resided Governor's Island, NY (1860)
Buried: Graceland Cemetery, Chicago, IL (Section I, Lot A, marker illegible)
References: George W. Cullum. *Biographical Register of the Officers and Graduates of the U.S. Military Academy.* 3rd Edition. Boston, MA, 1891. Obituary, *Chicago Daily Tribune,* Dec. 27, 1861. "The Funeral of Col. W.A. Webb," *Chicago Daily Tribune,* Dec. 29, 1861. Military Service File, National Archives. U.S. Military Academy Cadet Application Papers, 1805–1866, National Archives.

William Appleton Webb (Wallis Brothers, Premium Photograph Gallery, 117 Lake Street, Chicago, IL).

Thomas Leroy Braxton Weems

1 Sergeant, Co. I, 48 IL Infantry, Sept. 15, 1861. 2 Lieutenant, Co. I, 48 IL Infantry, April 7, 1862. 1 Lieutenant, Co. I, 48 IL Infantry, Nov. 11, 1862. Captain, Co. I, 48 IL Infantry, Oct. 1, 1863. GSW leg, near Atlanta, GA, July 28, 1864. Lieutenant Colonel, 48 IL Infantry, Jan. 25, 1865. GSW face, Duck Branch, SC, Feb. 2, 1865. Colonel, 48 IL Infantry, June 1, 1865. Honorably mustered out, Aug. 15, 1865. Battle honors: Shiloh, Atlanta Campaign, Campaign of the Carolinas.
Born: Sept. 13, 1836, Marion Co., IL
Died: May 7, 1909, Wasco, CA
Occupation: Farmer
Miscellaneous: Resided Johnsonville, Wayne

Co., IL; Hanford, Kings Co., CA; and Wasco, Kern Co., CA, 1908–09

Buried: Hanford Cemetery, Hanford, CA (Old Section, Lot 434)

References: *History of Wayne and Clay Counties, Illinois.* Chicago, IL, 1884. Pension File and Military Service File, National Archives.

Thomas Leroy Braxton Weems.

Above: **Loyd Wheaton** (Allen Cebula Collection). *Below:* **Loyd Wheaton** (post-war) (*Companions of the Military Order of the Loyal Legion of the United States.* **New York City, NY, 1901**).

Loyd Wheaton

1 Sergeant, Co. E, 8 IL Infantry (3 months), April 20, 1861. 1 Lieutenant, Co. E, 8 IL Infantry (3 years), July 25, 1861. Acting AAG, Staff of Brig. Gen. Eleazer A. Paine, 2 Brigade, District of Cairo, Jan.–Feb. 1862. Captain, Co. E, 8 IL Infantry, March 25, 1862. GSW right shoulder, Shiloh, TN, April 6, 1862. Acting AAG, Staff of Major Gen. John A. Logan, 3 Division, 17 Army Corps, Army of the Tennessee, Jan.–April 1863. Acting AIG, Staff of Major Gen. John A. Logan, 3 Division, 17 Army Corps, Army of the Tennessee, April–July 1863 and Sept.–Oct. 1863. Major, 8 IL Infantry, Aug. 28, 1863. Senior ADC, Acting Judge Advocate, and Provost Marshal, Staff of Major Gen. John A. Logan, 15 Army Corps, Army of the Tennessee, Nov. 1863–April 1864. Lieutenant Colonel, 8 IL Infantry, Nov. 25, 1864. Commanded Post of Marshall, TX, June 1865. Acting AIG, District of Western Louisiana, Department of Louisiana, Aug.–Sept. 1865. *Colonel,* 8 IL Infantry, March 8, 1866. Honorably mustered out, May 4, 1866. Bvt. Colonel, USV, March 26, 1865, for faithful and meritorious services during the campaign against the city of Mobile and its defenses. Bvt. Major, USA, March 2, 1867, for gallant and meritorious services in the siege of Vicksburg, MS. Bvt. Lieutenant Colonel, USA, March 2, 1867, for gallant and meritorious services in the assault

on Fort Blakely, AL. Battle honors: Shiloh, Port Gibson, Vicksburg Campaign, Mobile Campaign (Fort Blakely).

Born: July 15, 1838, Pennfield, Calhoun Co., MI
Died: Sept. 17, 1918, Chicago, IL
Other Wars: Spanish American War (Brig. Gen., USV). Philippine-American War (Bvt. Major Gen., USV, June 19, 1899, for gallantry in action against insurgent forces near Imus, Philippine Islands.
Occupation: Civil engineer before war. Regular Army (Captain 34 U.S. Infantry, July 28, 1866; Major Gen., March 30, 1901; retired July 15, 1902)
Offices/Honors: Medal of Honor, Fort Blakely, AL, April 9, 1865. "Led the right wing of his regiment, and, springing through an embrasure, was the first to enter the enemy's works, against a strong fire of artillery and infantry."
Miscellaneous: Resided Peoria, Peoria Co., IL, before war; and Chicago, IL, after retirement
Buried: Greenwood Cemetery, Rockford, IL (Section 11, Lot 4)
References: William H. Powell and Edward Shippen, editors. *Officers of the Army and Navy (Regular) Who Served in the Civil War.* Philadelphia, PA, 1892. *Who Was Who in America.* Vol. 1, 1897–1942. Chicago, IL, 1942. Obituary, *Chicago Daily Tribune,* Sept. 18, 1918. Obituary, *Rockford Register-Gazette,* Sept. 18, 1918. Obituary Circular, Whole No. 447, Kansas MOLLUS. W.F. Beyer and O.F. Keydel, editors. *Deeds of Valor.* Detroit, MI, 1906. Thomas M. Eddy. *The Patriotism of Illinois.* Chicago, IL, 1865. James Grant Wilson, editor. *Appletons' Cyclopedia of American Biography.* Vol. 7. New York City, 1900. Military Service File, National Archives. Letters Received, Appointment, Commission and Personal Branch, Adjutant General's Office, File 105(ACP) 1878, National Archives. *Companions of the Military Order of the Loyal Legion of the United States.* New York City, NY, 1901.

John E. Whiting

Colonel, 87 IL Infantry, Sept. 22, 1862. Resigned Oct. 8, 1863, due to "chronic diarrhea contracted while in service." Battle honors: Vicksburg Campaign.

Born: April 23, 1821, Vanderburgh Co., IN
Died: Oct. 25, 1866, Carmi, IL
Occupation: Lawyer
Offices/Honors: Illinois House of Representatives, 1856–58
Miscellaneous: Resided Carmi, White Co., IL
Buried: Old Cemetery, Carmi, IL (Lot 291)
References: *History of White County, Illinois.* Chicago, IL, 1883. Pension File and Military Service File, National Archives. Harriet B. Vaught, editor. *Letters Written by Dr. Daniel Berry to Marry Berry Crebs Berry During the Civil War.* Carmi, IL, 1976. Letters Received, Volunteer Service Branch, Adjutant General's Office, File W1141(VS)1863, National Archives. Claire A. Williams. *The Silent Park: The Old Cemetery of Carmi, Illinois, 1817–1966.* Carmi, IL, 1985.

Lorenzo Harper Whitney

Sergeant, Co. F, 13 IL Infantry, May 24, 1861. Captain, Co. B, 8 IL Cavalry, Aug. 27, 1861. GSW right groin, Gaines' Mill, VA, June 27, 1862. Resigned July 15, 1862, since "my friends in northern Illinois are anxious that I should return and organize a regiment for the service of the Government." Colonel, 140 IL Infantry, June 18, 1864. Honorably mustered out, Oct. 29, 1864. Battle honors: Virginia Peninsular Campaign (Gaines' Mill).

Born: Sept. 12, 1834, Berlin, Erie Co., OH
Died: Feb. 16, 1912, Ocean Springs, MS
Education: Attended Rock River Seminary, Mount Morris, IL. Attended Indiana Asbury (now DePauw) University, Greencastle, IN.
Occupation: Lawyer and author. His projected general history of the Civil War, *The History of the War for the Preservation of the Federal Union* (1863), comprised only one volume covering the pre-war years and six months of 1861. He also authored several religious works: *The Life and Teachings of Zoroaster, The Great Persian* (1905) and *A Question of Miracles: Parallels in the Lives of Buddha and Jesus* (1908).

Lorenzo Harper Whitney (post-war) (Loren Harper Whitney. *A Question of Miracles: Parallels in the Lives of Buddha and Jesus.* **Chicago, IL, 1908).**

Miscellaneous: Resided Kingston, DeKalb Co., IL (1850); Albia, Monroe Co., IA (1860); Chicago, IL; Topeka, Shawnee Co., KS, 1875–79; and River Forest, Cook Co., IL

Buried: Forest Home Cemetery, Forest Park, IL (Section 3, Lot 65)

References: *Biographical Dictionary and Portrait Gallery of Representative Men of Chicago and the World's Columbian Exposition.* Chicago and New York, 1892. Frederick Clifton Pierce. *Whitney: The Descendants of John Whitney, Who Came from London, England, to Watertown, Massachusetts, in 1635.* Chicago, IL, 1895. *The United States Biographical Dictionary.* Kansas Volume. Chicago and Kansas City, 1879. *Who Was Who in America.* Vol. 1, 1897–1942. Chicago, IL, 1942. *The Bench and Bar of Chicago: Biographical Sketches.* Chicago, IL, 1883. Obituary, *Chicago Daily Tribune*, Feb. 18, 1912. Pension File and Military Service File, National Archives. Letters Received, Volunteer Service Branch, Adjutant General's Office, File W68(VS) 1862, National Archives. Loren Harper Whitney. *A Question of Miracles: Parallels in the Lives of Buddha and Jesus.* Chicago, IL, 1908.

Dudley Wickersham

Lieutenant Colonel, 10 IL Cavalry, Nov. 25, 1861. Colonel, 10 IL Cavalry, May 16, 1862. Commanded 1 Brigade, 3 Division, Army of the Frontier, Department of the Missouri, Dec. 1862. Commanded Post of Fayetteville, AR, Department of the Missouri, Dec. 1862. Commanded 2 Division, Army of the Frontier, Department of the Missouri, March–April 1863. Commanded Cavalry Brigade, 2 Division, Army of the Frontier, Department of the Missouri, June 1863. Suffering from hemorrhoids, he resigned, May 10, 1864, since "the horse back exercise attendant on field duty constantly aggravates the disease." *Colonel,* U.S. Veteran Volunteers, Feb. 14, 1865. Major, 3 U.S. Veteran Volunteers, July 1, 1865. Honorably mustered out, April 30, 1866. Battle honors: Prairie Grove, Advance upon Little Rock (Bayou Meto).

Born: Nov. 21, 1819, Woodford Co., KY

Died: Aug. 8, 1898, Springfield, IL

Other Wars: Mexican War (Sergeant, Co. A, 4 IL Infantry)

Occupation: Dry goods merchant and grocer

Offices/Honors: Assessor of U.S. Internal Revenue for several years after war

Miscellaneous: Resided Springfield, Sangamon Co., IL

Buried: Oak Ridge Cemetery, Springfield, IL (Block 10, Lot 243)

References: Obituary, *Illinois State Journal*, Aug. 9, 1898. *History of Sangamon County, Illinois.* Chicago, IL, 1881. Obituary, *Illinois State Register*,

Dudley Wickersham (C.S. German, Photographer, National Gallery, Springfield, IL; Abraham Lincoln Presidential Library & Museum).

Aug. 9, 1898. *The United States Biographical Dictionary and Portrait Gallery of Eminent and Self-Made Men.* Illinois Volume. Chicago, Cincinnati, and New York, 1876. Newton Bateman and Paul Selby, editors. *Historical Encyclopedia of Illinois and History of Sangamon County.* Chicago, IL, 1912. Thomas M. Eddy. *The Patriotism of Illinois.* Chicago, IL, 1865. Pension File and Military Service File, National Archives. Letters Received, Volunteer Service Branch, Adjutant General's Office, File O787(VS) 1865, National Archives.

Thomas Dean Williams

Captain, Co. G, 25 IL Infantry, Aug. 8, 1861. Colonel, 25 IL Infantry, Aug. 31, 1862. GSW right breast, Stone's River, TN, Dec. 31, 1862. Battle honors: Stone's River.

Born: March 8, 1826, Ormskirk, Lancashire, England

Died: Jan. 6, 1863, DOW Murfreesboro, TN

Other Wars: Mexican War (Rocket and Howitzer Battery)

Occupation: Sergeant, U.S. Engineer Corps, 1848–55; and railroad station agent

Miscellaneous: Resided Chebanse, Iroquois Co., IL

Buried: Oakwood Cemetery, Troy, NY (Section H-3, Lot 79)

References: Hiram W. Beckwith. *History of Iroquois County, Together With Historic Notes on the Northwest.* Chicago, IL, 1880. James W. Kern. *Past and Present of Iroquois County, Illinois.* Chicago, IL, 1907. Obituary, *Troy Daily Whig,* Jan. 22, 1863. Pension File and Military Service File, National Archives. Robert H. Behrens. *From Salt Fork to Chickamauga: Champaign County Soldiers in the Civil War.* Urbana, IL, 1988.

Thomas Dean Williams (Chicago History Museum [ICHi-68791]).

Above: Horace Hudson Willsie (Z.P. McMillen, Photographer, No. 25 Main Street, Galesburg, IL). *Below:* Horace Hudson Willsie (post-war) (Special Collections and Archives, Knox College Library, Galesburg, Illinois).

Horace Hudson Willsie

Captain, Co. D, 102 IL Infantry, Sept. 2, 1862. Resigned April 9, 1863, "for the reason of ill health," due to chronic disease of the kidneys and bladder. Lieutenant Colonel, 139 IL Infantry, June 7, 1864. Honorably mustered out, Oct. 28, 1864. Colonel, 148 IL Infantry, Feb. 21, 1865. Honorably mustered out, Sept. 5, 1865.

Born: Jan. 27, 1827, Hemmingford, Quebec, Canada

Died: June 17, 1906, Galesburg, IL

Occupation: Dry goods clerk, livery stable keeper and deputy sheriff before war. City marshal and livery stable keeper after war.

Miscellaneous: Resided Galesburg, Knox Co., IL

Buried: Hope Cemetery, Galesburg, IL (Lot 533)

References: *Portrait and Biographical Album of Knox County, Illinois.* Chicago, IL, 1886. Obituary, *Galesburg Republican-Register,* June 18, 1906. *Soldiers' and Patriots' Biographical Album.* Chicago, IL, 1892. Charles C. Chapman. *History of Knox County, Illinois.* Chicago, IL, 1878. Albert J. Perry. *History of Knox County, Illinois: Its Cities, Towns and People.* Chicago, IL, 1912. "Rich Hanson's Civil War Stories: Colonel Horace H. Willsie," http://monmouthrl-hcw.blogspot.com/2013/08/colonel-horace-h-willsie_31.html. Pension File and Military Service File, National Archives. John E. Morris, compiler. *The Felt Genealogy, A Record of the Descendants of George Felt of Casco Bay.* Hartford, CT, 1893. Philip J. Reyburn and Terry L. Wilson, editors. *"Jottings from Dixie": The Civil War Dispatches of Sergeant Major Stephen F. Fleharty, U.S.A.* Baton Rouge, LA, 1999.

Hall Wilson

Major, 27 IL Infantry, Aug. 10, 1861. Colonel, 5 IL Cavalry, Dec. 30, 1861. Commanded 2 Brigade, 4 Division, Army of the Southwest, Department of the Missouri, Sept.–Oct. 1862. Resigned Jan. 19, 1863, due to "physical incapacity for active service, on account of chronic diarrhea and hemorrhoids of seven months duration." Battle honors: Belmont.

Born: Jan. 17, 1832, Stamfordham, Northumberland, England

Died: March 21, 1869, Springfield, IL

Occupation: Clerk in the office of the Illinois State Auditor, serving as chief clerk, 1865–69

Miscellaneous: Resided Fairfield, Wayne Co., IL; and Springfield, Sangamon Co., IL

Buried: Oak Ridge Cemetery, Springfield, IL (Block 8, Lot 188)

References: Obituary, *Illinois State Journal,* March 22, 1869. Obituary, *Illinois State Register,* March 22, 1869. Obituary, *Peoria Transcript,* March 23, 1869. Rhonda M. Kohl. *The Prairie Boys Go To War: The Fifth Illinois Cavalry, 1861–1865.* Carbondale, IL, 2013. Pension File and Military Service File, National Archives. Letters Received, Volunteer Service Branch, Adjutant General's Office, File I227(VS)1862, National Archives. Rhonda M. Kohl, "On Grant's Front Line: The Fifth Illinois Cavalry in Mississippi," *Illinois Historical Journal,* Vol. 91, No. 1 (Spring, 1998).

Isaac Grant Wilson

Colonel, 52 IL Infantry, Nov. 19, 1861. Resigned Dec. 6, 1861, due to "chronic laryngitis and general debility consequent upon the same."

Born: April 26, 1816, Middlebury, Wyoming Co., NY

Isaac Grant Wilson (post-war) (*Commemorative Biographical and Historical Record of Kane County, Illinois.* Chicago, IL, 1888).

Died: June 8, 1891, Geneva, IL

Education: Graduated Brown University, Providence, RI, 1838. Attended Harvard University Law School, Cambridge, MA.

Occupation: Lawyer and judge

Offices/Honors: Circuit Court Judge, 1851–67 and 1879–91

Miscellaneous: Resided Geneva, Kane Co., IL; and Chicago, IL, 1867–71

Buried: West Side Cemetery, Geneva, IL

References: *Commemorative Biographical and Historical Record of Kane County, Illinois.* Chicago, IL, 1888. *The Bench and Bar of Chicago: Biographical Sketches.* Chicago, IL, 1883. Obituary, *Chicago Daily Tribune,* June 9, 1891. *Biographical Encyclopedia of Illinois of the Nineteenth Century.* Philadelphia, PA, 1875. *The United States Biographical Dictionary and Portrait Gallery of Eminent and Self-Made Men.* Illinois Volume. Chicago and New York, 1883. Newton Bateman, Paul Selby and John S. Wilcox, editors. *Historical Encyclopedia of Illinois and History of Kane County.* Chicago, IL, 1904. Obituary, *Chicago Inter Ocean,* June 10, 1891. Military Service File, National Archives.

James W. Wilson

Colonel, 56 IL Infantry (Mechanic Fusileers), July 26, 1861. The members of the regiment were enlisted from Illinois and surrounding states upon fraudulent promises that they would receive more than the usual compensation and were to perform only a special kind of service, as skilled laborers, mechanics, and carpenters. Upon learning of the deception and fraud practiced in their enlistment, they became dissatisfied and refused to be mustered in as infantry. In consequence of its demoralized condition, the regiment was mustered into and out of service on the same day, Feb. 5, 1862. Colonel Wilson, however, refused to accept muster in and muster out, claiming that termination of his services as colonel required a specific order from the War Department. He, then, began a persistent campaign for an honorable discharge and payment for his services as colonel. Acting Paymaster General Timothy P. Andrews, in a report dated Dec. 30, 1862, described one encounter with Wilson, "There is a large stout old man (60 years of age or upwards) hovering about the city, claiming to be a colonel of a volunteer regiment of engineers in Illinois or other western state.... He claimed his pay as such colonel of me in fall of last year. Failing in that, he claimed to be, also, an officer of the Army, and to be Lieutenant James M. Wilson of the Topographical Engineers and forged Lieutenant W's name in my office and presence. I had him immediately arrested and placed his case in the hands of the U.S. Attorney. When I left St. Louis, he was still in jail untried. How he has got off of this absolute forgery, or out of jail, is to me a mystery." Wilson's repeated applications to the War Department, as late as April 9, 1866, were always rejected with the statement, "As the claimant was never in the service, he has no just or legal claim for a discharge therefrom, or pay, now attempted to be secured, by asking that his resignation be accepted."

Born: 1804?, MA? or New Brunswick, Canada?
Died: Oct. 13, 1866, Chicago, IL
Other Wars: Claimed service in Florida War (1838–43)
Occupation: Butcher (1850). No occupation (1860).
Miscellaneous: Buffalo, NY (1850); and Chicago, IL
Buried: Graceland Cemetery, Chicago, IL (Section N, Lot 95)
References: Letters Received, Volunteer Service Branch, Adjutant General's Office, Files G80(VS) 1861, W178(VS)1861, and P1206(VS)1862, National Archives. Interment Records, Graceland Cemetery, Chicago, IL. "The Trouble in Col. Wilson's Mechanic Fusileer Regiment," *Chicago Daily Tribune*, Dec. 18, 1861. "The Last of the Mechanic Fusileers," *Chicago Daily Tribune*, Feb. 6, 1862. C. Knight Aldrich, editor. *Quest for a Star: The Civil War Letters and Diaries of Colonel Francis T. Sherman of the 88th Illinois.* Knoxville, TN, 1999. Regular Army Enlistment Papers, 1798–1912, National Archives. Letters Received by the Secretary of War, Irregular Series, 1861–1866, File W153, Book 1, 1861, National Archives.

John Simms Wolfe

Captain, Co. A, 20 IL Infantry, April 22, 1861. Resigned Oct. 27, 1861, citing his unwillingness "longer to endure the privations and hardships of the service, in addition to reasons which I desire not to mention." In later correspondence he revealed these reasons as "unjust practices against me by my superiors," including Colonel C. Carroll Marsh, "whose negligence of duty and incompetency renders him totally unfit to hold command of this regiment." Commissioner, Board of Enrollment, 7 District of Illinois, May 7–June 15, 1863. Colonel, 135 IL Infantry, June 6, 1864. Commanded Post of Jefferson City (MO), District of Central Missouri, Department of the Missouri, July–Sept. 1864. Honorably mustered out, Sept. 28, 1864.

Born: Sept. 21, 1833, Acadia, Morgan Co., IL
Died: June 23, 1904, Champaign, IL
Occupation: Lawyer
Miscellaneous: Resided Carlinville, Macoupin Co., IL, to 1860; Chicago, IL, 1864–67; and Champaign, Champaign Co., IL

James W. Wilson.

John Simms Wolfe (Troxell & Brother, Photographers, S.W. cor. of 4th and Locust Streets, St. Louis, MO).

Buried: Mount Hope Cemetery, Urbana, IL (East Lawn, Block 5, Lot 154)
References: Newton Bateman and Paul Selby, editors. *Biographical and Memorial Edition of the Historical Encyclopedia of Illinois.* Chicago, IL, 1915. Newton Bateman, Paul Selby, and Joseph O. Cunningham, editors. *Historical Encyclopedia of Illinois and History of Champaign County.* Chicago, IL, 1905. Obituary, *Champaign Daily Gazette,* June 24, 1904. *Portrait and Biographical Album of Champaign County, Illinois.* Chicago, IL, 1887. *Biographical Encyclopedia of Illinois of the Nineteenth Century.* Philadelphia, PA, 1875. Pension File and Military Service File, National Archives. Letters Received, Volunteer Service Branch, Adjutant General's Office, File W797(VS)1862, National Archives.

John Wood

Quartermaster General of Illinois, 1861–65. Served during the Virginia Peninsular Campaign as a volunteer with the 8 IL Cavalry. Colonel, 137 IL Infantry, June 5, 1864. Commanded 3 Brigade, District of Memphis, Department of the Tennessee, Aug.–Sept. 1864. Honorably mustered out, Sept. 24, 1864. Battle honors: Virginia Peninsular Campaign, Forrest's Attack on Memphis.
Born: Dec. 20, 1798, Moravia, NY
Died: June 4, 1880, Quincy, IL
Occupation: Farmer and municipal officeholder
Offices/Honors: Illinois Senate, 1850–54. Lieutenant Governor of Illinois, 1857–60. Governor of Illinois, 1860–61.
Miscellaneous: Resided Quincy, Adams Co., IL.

John Wood (post-war) (Abner Hard. *History of the Eighth Cavalry Regiment, Illinois Volunteers, During the Great Rebellion.* Aurora, IL, 1868).

First settler of the city of Quincy. Delegate to the Washington Peace Convention, 1861. Father-in-law of Bvt. Brig. Gen. John Tillson.
Buried: Woodland Cemetery, Quincy, IL (Block 6, Lot 33)
References: William H. Collins and Cicero F. Perry. *Past and Present of the City of Quincy and Adams County, Illinois.* Chicago, IL, 1905. David F. Wilcox, supervising editor. *Quincy and Adams County History and Representative Men.* Chicago and New York, 1919. *History of Adams County, Illinois.* Chicago, IL, 1879. Obituary, *Quincy Daily Herald,* June 5, 1880. *Biographical Encyclopedia of Illinois of the Nineteenth Century.* Philadelphia, PA, 1875. Military Service File, National Archives. Abner Hard. *History of the Eighth Cavalry Regiment, Illinois Volunteers, During the Great Rebellion.* Aurora, IL, 1868.

McLean F. Wood

Captain, Co. G, 10 IL Infantry (3 months), April 29, 1861. Honorably mustered out, July 29, 1861. Captain, Co. A, 10 IL Infantry (3 years), Aug. 9, 1861. Lieutenant Colonel, 10 IL Infantry, June 23, 1862. Honorably mustered out, Jan. 12, 1865. Colonel, 154 IL Infantry, Feb. 22, 1865. Commanded Post of Nashville (TN), District of Middle Tennessee, Department of the Cumberland, July–Aug. 1865. Battle honors: Savannah Campaign.
Born: 1826?, Jacksonville, IL
Died: Aug. 6, 1865, Nashville, TN (typhoid and spotted fever)

McLean F. Wood.

Other Wars: Mexican War (Private, Co. F, 4 IL Infantry)
Occupation: Saddler and jailer
Miscellaneous: Resided Jacksonville, Morgan Co., IL
Buried: Jacksonville East Cemetery, Jacksonville, IL (New Part, Section 4, Lot 302, unmarked)
References: Obituary, *Illinois State Journal*, Aug. 10, 1865. "Funeral of Col. M. F. Wood," *Illinois State Journal*, Aug. 16, 1865. Pension File and Military Service File, National Archives. Obituary, *Nashville Daily Union*, Aug. 8, 1865. Obituary, *Jacksonville Journal*, Aug. 10, 1865. Letters Received, Volunteer Service Branch, Adjutant General's Office, File 2856(VS)1879, National Archives. Ephraim A. Wilson. *Memoirs of the War.* Cleveland, OH, 1893.

French Battelle Woodall

1 Lieutenant, Co. K, 16 IL Infantry, May 24, 1861. Honorably mustered out, June 12, 1864. Captain, Co. C, 151 IL Infantry, Feb. 21, 1865. Colonel, 151 IL Infantry, Feb. 25, 1865. Accepted the surrender of the Confederate forces under Brig. Gen. William T. Wofford at Kingston, GA, May 12, 1865. Honorably mustered out, Jan. 24, 1866. Battle honors: Wilson's Raid.

Above: French Battelle Woodall (Mrs. W.A. Reed, Artist, 81½ Hamshire Street, Quincy, IL; courtesy Jennifer Woods). *Below:* French Battelle Woodall (courtesy Jennifer Woods).

Born: 1840?, Philadelphia, PA
Died: June 11, 1869, New York City, NY (body found in the East River, presumably a victim of murder)
Education: Attended Collegiate and Commercial Institute, New Haven, CT
Occupation: Clerk, employed by Adams Ex-

press Co. (1867) and Asbury Life Insurance Co. (1869). Declined commission as 2 Lieutenant, 17 U.S. Infantry, Jan. 30, 1867.

Miscellaneous: Resided Bushnell, McDonough Co., IL (1860); Quincy, Adams Co., IL (1861); Cincinnati, OH (1867); and Astoria, Long Island, NY

Buried: Arlington National Cemetery, Arlington, VA (Section 1, Lot 696)

References: Obituary, *Quincy Daily Whig,* June 17, 1869. Obituary, *New York Daily Tribune,* June 12, 1869. Obituary, *New York Times,* June 12, 1869. Obituary, *New York Herald,* June 12, 1869. Pension File and Military Service File, National Archives. Letters Received, Commission Branch, Adjutant General's Office, Files W1121(CB)1865 and W77(CB)1867, National Archives. House of Representatives, 50th Congress, 1st Session, Report No. 3485, Sept. 19, 1888. *History of McDonough County, Illinois.* Springfield, IL, 1885.

French Battelle Woodall (with a souvenir of the surrender of CSA General William T. Wofford) (Richard K. Tibbals Collection, USAMHI [RG98S-CWP62.70]).

George Washington Wright

Sergeant, Co. C, 17 IL Infantry, May 25, 1861. Captain, Co. C, 17 IL Infantry, Dec. 24, 1861. Suffering from "sub-acute inflammation of the lungs," he resigned April 18, 1862, since "I am now and have been for the last two months entirely unable to perform the duties of my office." Captain, Co. H, 103 IL Infantry, Aug. 22, 1862. Major, 103 IL Infantry, Sept. 9, 1862. Lieutenant Colonel, 103 IL Infantry, Oct. 18, 1862. Acting AIG, Staff of Brig. Gen. William Harrow, 4 Division, 15 Army Corps, Army of the Tennessee, Feb.–June 1864. *Colonel,* 103 IL Infantry, May 28, 1864. GSW left leg, Kenesaw Mountain, GA, June 27, 1864. Acting AIG, Staff of Major Gen. John A. Logan, 15 Army Corps, Army of the Tennessee, Sept. 12–17, 1864. Honorably mustered out, June 21, 1865. Battle honors: Fort Donelson, Jackson Campaign, Atlanta Campaign (Resaca, Kenesaw Mountain), Campaign of the Carolinas (Bentonville).

Born: Aug. 12, 1832, Lewistown, IL

Died: June 17, 1878, Shenandoah, IA (committed suicide by pistol shot)

Education: Attended Keokuk (IA) Medical College. Graduated Bellevue Hospital Medical College, New York City, NY, 1868.

Occupation: Physician

Miscellaneous: Resided Fairview, Fulton Co., IL (1860); Canton, Fulton Co., IL, 1865–78; and Shenandoah, Page Co., IA (1878)

Buried: Rose Hill Cemetery, Shenandoah, IA (Original Section, Block 23, Lot 1)

References: *Biographical Encyclopedia of Illinois of the Nineteenth Century.* Philadelphia, PA, 1875. Obituary, *Fulton County Ledger,* June 28, 1878. *Reminiscences of the Civil War from Diaries of Members of the 103rd Illinois Volunteer Infantry.* Chicago, IL,

George Washington Wright (Armstead & White, Artists, Corinth, MS; Ray Zielin Collection).

1904. Pension File and Military Service File, National Archives. Letters Received, Volunteer Service Branch, Adjutant General's Office, File W1875(VS) 1865, National Archives. William M. Anderson, "The Fulton County War at Home and in the Field," *Illinois Historical Journal*, Vol. 85, No. 1 (Spring, 1992).

John Baker Wyman

Colonel, 13 IL Infantry, May 24, 1861. Commanded Post of Rolla (MO), Western Department and Department of the Missouri, July 1861–Feb. 1862. Acting Brig. Gen., 1 Brigade, 1 Division, Western Department, Oct.–Nov. 1861. Commanded 1 Brigade, 2 Division, Army of the Southwest, May–Sept. 1862. Commanded 2 Division, Army of the Southwest, Oct. 1862. GSW left side, Chickasaw Bayou, MS, Dec. 28, 1862. Battle honors: Chickasaw Bayou.

Born: July 12, 1817, Shrewsbury, MA
Died: Dec. 28, 1862, KIA Chickasaw Bayou, MS
Occupation: Railroad superintendent and miller
Miscellaneous: Resided New Haven, CT (1850); Chicago, IL, 1851–56; and Amboy, Lee Co., IL, 1856–62
Buried: Rosehill Cemetery, Chicago, IL (Section E, Lot 48)
References: Clair V. Mann. *An Account of the Life and Career of Col. John B. Wyman, Intrepid Leader of*

Above: John Baker Wyman (S. M. Fassett, Artist, 122 & 124 Clark Street, Chicago, IL; Roger D. Hunt Collection, USAMHI [RG98S-CWP58.21]). *Below:* John Baker Wyman (Library of Congress [LC-DIG-cwpb-07243]).

John Baker Wyman (R.K. Fossett's Sky Light Gallery, Over the Post Office, Helena, AR; Roger D. Hunt Collection, USAMHI [RG98S-CWP 80.24]).

the *Thirteenth Regiment of Illinois Volunteer Infantry*. Rolla, MO, 1962. James Barnet, editor. *The Martyrs and Heroes of Illinois in the Great Rebellion*. Second Edition. Chicago, IL, 1866. James Grant Wilson. *Biographical Sketches of Illinois Officers Engaged in the War Against the Rebellion of 1861*. Chicago, IL, 1862. Thomas M. Eddy. *The Patriotism of Illinois*. Chicago, IL, 1865. *Military History and Reminiscences of the 13th Regiment of Illinois Volunteer Infantry in the Civil War in the United States, 1861–1865*. Chicago, IL, 1892. "The Late General J.B. Wyman," *Chicago Daily Tribune*, Feb. 4, 1864. Newton Bateman and Paul Selby, editors. *Historical Encyclopedia of Illinois*. Chicago and New York, 1900. Pension File and Military Service File, National Archives.

IOWA

Regiments

1st Cavalry

Fitz Henry Warren	June 13, 1861	Promoted **Brig. Gen., USV,** July 16, 1862
James O. Gower	Aug. 26, 1862	Resigned Aug. 20, 1863
Daniel Anderson	Aug. 21, 1863	Resigned May 28, 1864
William Thompson	June 20, 1864	Mustered out Feb. 15, 1866, **Bvt. Brig. Gen., USV**

2nd Cavalry

Washington L. Elliott	Sept. 14, 1861	Promoted **Brig. Gen., USV,** June 11, 1862
Edward Hatch	June 13, 1862	Promoted **Brig. Gen., USV,** April 27, 1864
Datus E. Coon	May 5, 1864	Mustered out Sept. 19, 1865, **Bvt. Brig. Gen., USV**

3rd Cavalry

Cyrus Bussey	Sept. 5, 1861	Promoted **Brig. Gen., USV,** April 10, 1864
Henry C. Caldwell	May 1, 1864	Resigned June 25, 1864
John W. Noble	June 27, 1864	Mustered out Aug. 9, 1865, **Bvt. Brig. Gen., USV**

4th Cavalry

Asbury B. Porter	Dec. 5, 1861	Resigned March 19, 1863
Edward F. Winslow	July 4, 1863	Mustered out Aug. 10, 1865, **Bvt. Brig. Gen., USV**

5th Cavalry

William W. Lowe	Jan. 1, 1862	Mustered out Jan. 24, 1865, **Bvt. Brig. Gen., USV**
J. Morris Young	Jan. 25, 1865	Mustered out Aug. 11, 1865

6th Cavalry

David S. Wilson	Jan. 9, 1863	Resigned June 21, 1864
Samuel M. Pollock	July 1, 1864	Mustered out Oct. 17, 1865, **Bvt. Brig. Gen., USV**

7th Cavalry

Samuel W. Summers	July 25, 1863	Mustered out Jan. 31, 1865
Herman H. Heath	May 29, 1865	Mustered out July 1, 1866, **Bvt. Brig. Gen., USV**

8th Cavalry

Joseph B. Dorr	Aug. 27, 1863	Died May 28, 1865
Horatio G. Barner	June 15, 1865	Mustered out Aug. 13, 1865

9th Cavalry

Matthew M. Trumbull	Nov. 19, 1863	Mustered out Feb. 28, 1866, **Bvt. Brig. Gen., USV**

1st Infantry

John F. Bates	May 14, 1861	Mustered out Aug. 21, 1861

2nd Infantry

Samuel R. Curtis	May 31, 1861	Promoted **Brig. Gen., USV,** July 17, 1861

James M. Tuttle	Sept. 6, 1861	Promoted **Brig. Gen., USV,** June 9, 1862
James Baker	June 22, 1862	DOW Oct. 7, 1862
Noah W. Mills	Oct. 8, 1862	DOW Oct. 12, 1862
James B. Weaver	Nov. 10, 1862	Mustered out May 27, 1864, **Bvt. Brig. Gen., USV**
Noel B. Howard	Dec. 17, 1864	Mustered out July 12, 1865

3rd Infantry

Nelson G. Williams	June 26, 1861	Resigned Nov. 27, 1862, **Brig. Gen., USV**
Aaron Brown	Nov. 27, 1862	Resigned July 13, 1864

4th Infantry

Grenville M. Dodge	July 6, 1861	Promoted **Brig. Gen., USV,** March 21, 1862
James A. Williamson	July 21, 1862	Promoted **Brig. Gen., USV,** Jan. 13, 1865
Samuel D. Nichols	May 12, 1865	Mustered out July 24, 1865

5th Infantry

William H. Worthington	July 15, 1861	Died May 22, 1862
Charles L. Matthies	May 23, 1862	Promoted **Brig. Gen., USV,** Nov. 29, 1862
Jabez Banbury	May 12, 1863	Mustered out Sept. 28, 1864

6th Infantry

John A. McDowell	July 17, 1861	Resigned March 12, 1863
John M. Corse	March 29, 1863	Promoted **Brig. Gen., USV,** Aug. 11, 1863
William H. Clune	June 18, 1865	Mustered out July 21, 1865

7th Infantry

Jacob G. Lauman	July 11, 1861	Promoted **Brig. Gen., USV,** March 21, 1862
Elliott W. Rice	April 7, 1862	Promoted **Brig. Gen., USV,** June 20, 1864
James C. Parrott	June 13, 1865	Mustered out July 12, 1865, **Bvt. Brig. Gen., USV**

8th Infantry

Frederick Steele	Sept. 23, 1861	Promoted **Brig. Gen., USV,** Jan. 29, 1862
James L. Geddes	Feb. 7, 1862	Resigned June 30, 1865, **Bvt. Brig. Gen., USV**
William Stubbs	July 1, 1865	Mustered out Nov. 14, 1865

9th Infantry

William Vandever	Sept. 24, 1861	Promoted **Brig. Gen., USV,** Nov. 29, 1862
David Carskaddon	June 4, 1863	Mustered out Jan. 14, 1865

10th Infantry

Nicholas Perczel	Sept. 29, 1861	Resigned Nov. 1, 1862
William E. Small	Nov. 2, 1862	Discharged Aug. 19, 1863
Paris P. Henderson	Aug. 20, 1863	Mustered out Dec. 19, 1864
William H. Silsby	Aug. 7, 1865	Mustered out Aug. 15, 1865

11th Infantry

Abraham M. Hare	Nov. 1, 1861	Resigned Aug. 31, 1862
William Hall	Sept. 1, 1862	Resigned Aug. 1, 1864
John C. Abercrombie	Aug. 7, 1864	Mustered out Nov. 5, 1864
Benjamin Beach	July 29, 1865	Mustered out July 15, 1865

12th Infantry

Joseph J. Woods	Nov. 25, 1861	Mustered out Nov. 22, 1864
John H. Stibbs	Feb. 11, 1865	Mustered out Jan. 20, 1866, **Bvt. Brig. Gen., USV**

13th Infantry

Marcellus M. Crocker	Dec. 30, 1861	Promoted **Brig. Gen., USV,** Nov. 29, 1862
John Shane	April 18, 1863	Mustered out Nov. 9, 1864
James Wilson	Jan. 19, 1865	Mustered out July 21, 1865, **Bvt. Brig. Gen., USV**

14th Infantry

William T. Shaw	Nov. 16, 1861	Discharged Nov. 16, 1864

15th Infantry

Hugh T. Reid	Feb. 22, 1862	Promoted **Brig. Gen., USV,** March 13, 1863
William W. Belknap	June 3, 1863	Promoted **Brig. Gen., USV,** July 30, 1864
John M. Hedrick	March 22, 1865	Discharged Aug. 11, 1866, **Bvt. Brig. Gen., USV**

16th Infantry

Alexander Chambers	March 15, 1862	Promoted **Brig. Gen., USV,** Aug. 11, 1863
Josiah T. Herbert	July 1, 1865	Mustered out July 19, 1865

17th Infantry

John W. Rankin	April 7, 1862	Resigned Sept. 3, 1862
David B. Hillis	Sept. 4, 1862	Resigned May 30, 1863, **Bvt. Brig. Gen., USV**
Clark R. Wever	June 3, 1863	Resigned June 3, 1865, **Bvt. Brig. Gen., USV**
Sampson M. Archer	June 12, 1865	Mustered out July 25, 1865

18th Infantry

John Edwards	Aug. 8, 1862	Promoted **Brig. Gen., USV,** Sept. 26, 1864
Hugh J. Campbell	Dec. 1, 1864	Mustered out July 20, 1865

19th Infantry

Benjamin Crabb	Aug. 21, 1862	Resigned March 16, 1863
John Bruce	July 3, 1865	Mustered out July 10, 1865, **Bvt. Brig. Gen., USV**

20th Infantry

William McE. Dye	Aug. 25, 1862	Mustered out July 8, 1865, **Bvt. Brig. Gen., USV**

21st Infantry

Samuel Merrill	Aug. 22, 1862	Resigned June 21, 1864

22nd Infantry

William M. Stone	Sept. 9, 1862	Resigned Aug. 13, 1863, **Bvt. Brig. Gen., USV**
Harvey Graham	May 5, 1864	Mustered out July 25, 1865, **Bvt. Brig. Gen., USV**

23rd Infantry

William Dewey	Sept. 19, 1862	Died Nov. 30, 1862
William H. Kinsman	Dec. 1, 1862	DOW May 18, 1863
Samuel L. Glasgow	May 19, 1863	Mustered out July 26, 1865, **Bvt. Brig. Gen., USV**

24th Infantry

Eber C. Byam	Sept. 17, 1862	Resigned June 30, 1863
John Q. Wilds	June 18, 1864	DOW Nov. 18, 1864
Ed Wright	Nov. 18, 1864	Mustered out July 17, 1865, **Bvt. Brig. Gen., USV**

25th Infantry

George A. Stone	Sept. 27, 1862	Mustered out June 6, 1865, **Bvt. Brig. Gen., USV**

26th Infantry

Milo Smith	Aug. 31, 1862	Resigned Jan. 28, 1865
John Lubbers	June 19, 1865	Mustered out June 6, 1865

27th Infantry

James I. Gilbert	Oct. 3, 1862	Promoted **Brig. Gen., USV,** Feb. 9, 1865
Jed Lake	June 26, 1865	Mustered out Aug. 8, 1865

28th Infantry

William E. Miller	Oct. 10, 1862	Resigned March 13, 1863
John Connell	March 14, 1863	Resigned March 17, 1865
Bartholomew W. Wilson	June 15, 1865	Mustered out July 31, 1865

29th Infantry

Thomas H. Benton, Jr.	Dec. 1, 1862	Mustered out Aug. 10, 1865, **Bvt. Brig. Gen., USV**

30th Infantry

Charles H. Abbott	Sept. 23, 1862	KIA May 22, 1863
William M.G. Torrence	May 29, 1863	KIA Oct. 21, 1863

31st Infantry

William Smyth	Oct. 13, 1862	Resigned Dec. 15, 1864
Jeremiah W. Jenkins	May 11, 1865	Mustered out June 27, 1865

32nd Infantry

John Scott	Aug. 22, 1862	Resigned May 27, 1864, **Bvt. Brig. Gen., USV**
Gustavus A. Eberhart	May 28, 1864	Mustered out Aug. 24, 1865

33rd Infantry

Samuel A. Rice	Oct. 1, 1862	Promoted **Brig. Gen., USV,** Aug. 4, 1863
Cyrus H. Mackey	April 22, 1864	Mustered out July 17, 1865

34th Infantry

George W. Clark	Oct. 15, 1862	Mustered out Aug. 15, 1865, **Bvt. Brig. Gen., USV**

35th Infantry

Sylvester G. Hill	Sept. 18, 1862	KIA Dec. 15, 1864, **Bvt. Brig. Gen., USV**

36th Infantry

Charles W. Kittredge	Oct. 4, 1862	Mustered out Aug. 24, 1865

37th Infantry

George W. Kincaid	Dec. 15, 1862	Mustered out May 24, 1865

38th Infantry

William Brush	Sept. 12, 1862	Revoked Oct. 26, 1862
D. Henry Hughes	Oct. 27, 1862	Died Aug. 7, 1863

39th Infantry

Henry J.B. Cummings	Nov. 24, 1862	Mustered out Dec. 22, 1864
Joseph M. Griffiths	May 12, 1865	Mustered out June 5, 1865

40th Infantry

John A. Garrett	Sept. 17, 1862	Mustered out Aug. 2, 1865

41st Infantry

Regiment not entitled to a colonel since it never attained full strength

42nd Infantry

Did not complete organization

43rd Infantry

Did not complete organization

44th Infantry

Stephen H. Henderson	June 1, 1864	Mustered out Sept. 15, 1864

45th Infantry

Alvah H. Bereman	May 25, 1864	Mustered out Sept. 16, 1864

46th Infantry

David B. Henderson	June 10, 1864	Mustered out Sept. 23, 1864

47th Infantry

James P. Sanford	June 4, 1864	Mustered out Sept. 28, 1864

48th Infantry

Regiment not entitled to a colonel since it never attained full strength

Biographies

Charles Henry Abbott

Colonel, 30 IA Infantry, Sept. 23, 1862. GSW passing through chin and neck, Vicksburg, MS, May 22, 1863. Battle honors: Chickasaw Bluffs, Vicksburg Campaign.
Born: Jan. 25, 1819, Concord, NH
Died: May 22, 1863, KIA Vicksburg, MS
Education: Attended Kimball Union Academy, Meriden, NH
Occupation: Banker and land agent
Miscellaneous: Resided Oakland Twp., Louisa Co., IA; Chicago, IL (1860); and Muscatine, Muscatine Co., IA.
Buried: Greenwood Cemetery, Muscatine, IA (Ogilvie Addition, Block 11, Lot 34)
References: Addison A. Stuart. *Iowa Colonels and Regiments.* Des Moines, IA, 1865. Pension File and Military Service File, National Archives. Benjamin F. Gue. *History of Iowa from the Earliest Times to the Beginning of the Twentieth Century.* New York City, NY, 1903. *General Catalogue of Kimball Union Academy, Meriden, NH, 1813–1930.* Hanover, NH, 1930. Irving B. Richman, editor. *History of Muscatine County, Iowa, from the Earliest Settlements to the Present Time.* Chicago, IL, 1911. James A. Fowler and Miles M. Miller. *History of the 30th Iowa Infantry Volunteers.* Mediapolis, IA, 1908.

John Cree Abercrombie

1 Lieutenant, Co. E, 1 IA Infantry, May 9, 1861. Honorably mustered out, Aug. 21, 1861. Major, 11 IA Infantry, Oct. 18, 1861. GSW head, Shiloh, TN, April 6, 1862. Lieutenant Colonel, 11 IA Infantry, Sept. 1, 1862. Shell wound right hip, Atlanta, GA, July 22, 1864. *Colonel*, 11 IA Infantry, Aug. 7, 1864. Commanded 3 Brigade, 4 Division, 17 Army Corps, Army of the Tennessee, Sept. 21–Oct. 23, 1864. Honorably mustered out, Nov. 5, 1864. Battle honors: Wilson's Creek, Shiloh, Corinth, Vicksburg Campaign, Atlanta Campaign (Atlanta).
Born: Oct. 30, 1823, Landisburg, Perry Co., PA
Died: Jan. 25, 1890, Burlington, IA
Other Wars: Mexican War (1 Sergeant, Co. K, 15 U.S. Infantry)
Occupation: Dentist before war. Commission merchant and agent for steamboat line after war.
Offices/Honors: Surveyor of the Port of Burlington, IA, 1866–79

Charles Henry Abbott (State Historical Society of Iowa, Des Moines).

John Cree Abercrombie (State Historical Society of Iowa, Des Moines).

Miscellaneous: Resided Burlington, Des Moines Co., IA

Buried: Aspen Grove Cemetery, Burlington, IA (Block 126, Lot 4)

References: *Portrait and Biographical Album of Des Moines County, Iowa.* Chicago, IL, 1888. *Biographical Review of Des Moines County, Iowa.* Chicago, IL, 1905. Obituary, *Burlington Daily Hawk-Eye,* Jan. 26, 1890. Obituary, *Davenport Morning Tribune,* Jan. 28, 1890. J. Campbell, "Regarding the History of the Dental Profession in the West and South," *Missouri Dental Journal,* Vol. 7, No. 9 (Sept. 1875). Pension File and Military Service File, National Archives.

Daniel Anderson

Captain, Co. H, 1 IA Cavalry, Aug. 3, 1861. Major, 1 IA Cavalry, July 11, 1862. Lieutenant Colonel, 1 IA Cavalry, Feb. 13, 1863. Colonel, 1 IA Cavalry, Aug. 21, 1863. Commanded 3 Brigade, 1 Cavalry Division, Army of Arkansas, Department of the Missouri, Dec. 5, 1863–Jan. 6, 1864. Commanded 3 Brigade, 1 Cavalry Division, 7 Army Corps, Department of Arkansas, Jan. 6–May 11, 1864. Commanded Post of Little Rock (AR), Department of Arkansas, April–May 1864. Resigned May 28, 1864, due to "partial paralysis of right arm and leg, the sequitur of rheumatism from which he has suffered many years and which is greatly aggravated by exposure or fatigue." Battle honors: Advance upon Little Rock (Bayou Meto), Camden Expedition.

Born: April 5, 1821, Monroe Co., IN
Died: Feb. 4, 1901, Albia, IA
Occupation: Lawyer
Offices/Honors: Iowa Senate, 1854–61. Register in Bankruptcy, 1867–79.
Miscellaneous: Resided Albia, Monroe Co., IA
Buried: Oak View Cemetery, Albia, IA
References: *A Memorial and Biographical Record of Iowa.* Chicago, IL, 1896. Obituary, *Albia Republican,* Feb. 7, 1901. Obituary, *Monroe County News and Albia Democrat,* Feb. 8, 1901. "Daniel Anderson," *Annals of Iowa,* 3rd Series, Vol. 5, No. 1 (April 1901). Edward H. Stiles. *Recollections and Sketches of Notable Lawyers and Public Men of Early Iowa.* Des Moines, IA, 1916. Addison A. Stuart. *Iowa Colonels and Regiments.* Des Moines, IA, 1865. Benjamin F. Gue. *History of Iowa from the Earliest Times to the Beginning of the Twentieth Century.* New York City, NY, 1903. Pension File and Military Service File, National Archives. *History of Monroe County, Iowa.* Chicago, IL, 1878. Frank Hickenlooper. *An Illustrated History of Monroe County, Iowa.* Kansas City, MO, 1896. Charles H. Lothrop. *A History of the First Regiment Iowa Cavalry Veteran Volunteers.* Lyons, IA, 1890.

Sampson Mathew Archer

2 Lieutenant, Co. A, 2 IA Infantry, May 27, 1861. Resigned Oct. 8, 1861. Captain, Co. C, 17 IA Infantry, March 25, 1862. GSW right thigh, Iuka, MS, Sept. 19, 1862. Major, 17 IA Infantry, Jan. 23, 1863. Lieutenant Colonel, 17 IA Infantry, June 3, 1863. Taken prisoner, Missionary Ridge, TN,

Daniel Anderson (post-war) (State Historical Society of Iowa, Des Moines).

Sampson Mathew Archer (State Historical Society of Iowa, Des Moines).

Nov. 25, 1863. Confined Richmond, VA. Paroled March 7, 1864. Picket officer, Staff of Brig. Gen. John E. Smith, 3 Division, 15 Army Corps, Army of the Tennessee, Dec. 1864–March 1865. *Colonel,* 17 IA Infantry, June 12, 1865. Honorably mustered out, July 25, 1865. Battle honors: Iuka, Missionary Ridge, Atlanta Campaign, Operations in North Georgia and North Alabama (Tilton), Campaign of the Carolinas.

Born: July 25, 1825, Nicholas Co., KY
Died: March 5, 1877, Keokuk, IA
Occupation: Wagon maker and plow manufacturer before war. Trader and steamboat agent after war.
Miscellaneous: Resided Keokuk, Lee Co., IA
Buried: Oakland Cemetery, Keokuk, IA (Block 17, Lot 16)
References: Pension File and Military Service File, National Archives. Obituary, *Keokuk Daily Gate City*, March 6–7, 1877.

James Baker (State Historical Society of Iowa, Des Moines).

Sampson Mathew Archer (State Historical Society of Iowa, Des Moines).

James Baker

Captain, Co. G, 2 IA Infantry, May 27, 1861. Lieutenant Colonel, 2 IA Infantry, Nov. 2, 1861. Commanded 1 Brigade, 2 Division, Army of the Tennessee, April 1862. Colonel, 2 IA Infantry, June 22, 1862. GSW abdomen, Corinth, MS, Oct. 3, 1862. Battle honors: Fort Donelson, Shiloh, Corinth.

Born: Dec. 25, 1823, Gallatin Co., KY
Died: Oct. 7, 1862, DOW Corinth, MS
Education: Attended Cincinnati (OH) Law School
Occupation: Lawyer
Miscellaneous: Resided Bloomfield, Davis Co., IA
Buried: Bloomfield IOOF Cemetery, Bloomfield, IA
References: Addison A. Stuart. *Iowa Colonels and Regiments.* Des Moines, IA, 1865. Edward H. Stiles. *Recollections and Sketches of Notable Lawyers and Public Men of Early Iowa.* Des Moines, IA, 1916. Benjamin F. Gue. *History of Iowa from the Earliest Times to the Beginning of the Twentieth Century.* New York City, NY, 1903. Pension File and Military Service File, National Archives. *History of Davis County, Iowa.* Des Moines, IA, 1882.

Jabez Banbury

1 Lieutenant, Co. D, 5 IA Infantry, July 15, 1861. Captain, Co. D, 5 IA Infantry, Feb. 26, 1862. Major, 5 IA Infantry, Sept. 1, 1862. Colonel, 5 IA Infantry,

May 12, 1863. Commanded 3 Brigade, 2 Division, 17 Army Corps, Army of the Tennessee, Nov. 25–Dec. 20, 1863. Commanded 3 Brigade, 3 Division, 15 Army Corps, Army of the Tennessee, Dec. 20, 1863–March 14, 1864, and June 1–July 25, 1864. Honorably mustered out Sept. 28, 1864. Battle honors: Corinth (temporarily commanded 17 IA Infantry), Vicksburg Campaign, Missionary Ridge, Atlanta Campaign.

Born: March 4, 1830, County Cornwall, England
Died: Dec. 9, 1900, Pasadena, CA
Occupation: Cabinet maker and grocer before war. Fruit grower, lumber merchant and real estate agent after war.
Offices/Honors: Auditor, Marshall Co., IA, 1869–73. California Assembly, 1885–86. Treasurer, Los Angeles Co., CA, 1888–92.
Miscellaneous: Resided Marshalltown, Marshall Co., IA, to 1873; and Pasadena, Los Angeles Co., CA, 1873–1900
Buried: Mountain View Cemetery, Altadena, CA (Section K, Lot 83)
References: James M. Guinn. *Historical and Biographical Record of Los Angeles and Vicinity.* Chicago, IL, 1901. Sarah Noble Ives. *Altadena.* Pasadena, CA, 1938. Addison A. Stuart. *Iowa Colonels and Regiments.* Des Moines, IA, 1865. Pension File and Military Service File, National Archives. Letters Received, Volunteer Service Branch, Adjutant General's Office, File B2399 (VS) 1865, National Archives. Obituary, *Los Angeles Herald,* Dec. 10, 1900. Obituary, *Pasadena Evening Star,* Dec. 10, 1900. Benjamin F. Gue. *History of Iowa from the Earliest Times to the Beginning of the Twentieth Century.* New York City, NY, 1903. "Jabez Banbury," *Annals of Iowa,* 3rd Series, Vol. 4, No. 8 (January 1901). *The History of Marshall County, Iowa.* Chicago, IL, 1878.

Horatio Gates Barner

1 Lieutenant, RQM, 13 IA Infantry, Nov. 1, 1861. Resigned April 1, 1862, since "my health is such as to render me wholly incompetent to discharge the duties of the office." Lieutenant Colonel, 8 IA Cavalry, Sept. 30, 1863. Colonel, 8 IA Cavalry, June 15, 1865. Honorably mustered out Aug. 13, 1865. Battle honors: Atlanta Campaign.

Born: June 25, 1821, Fayette Co., IN
Died: Jan. 30, 1879, Manhattan, KS
Occupation: Lawyer
Offices/Honors: Iowa House of Representatives, 1856–58
Miscellaneous: Resided Sidney, Fremont Co., IA; and Davenport, Scott Co., IA, before war; St. Louis, MO; Kansas City, MO; and Manhattan, Riley Co., KS, after war
Buried: Sunset Cemetery, Manhattan, KS (Section 2, Lot 97)
References: Pension File and Military Service File, National Archives. Obituary, *Manhattan Nationalist,* Feb. 7, 1879. Obituary, *Topeka Daily Commonwealth,* Feb. 2, 1879.

Jabez Banbury (State Historical Society of Iowa, Des Moines).

Horatio Gates Barner (State Historical Society of Iowa, Des Moines).

John Francis Bates

Colonel, 1 IA Infantry, May 14, 1861. Honorably mustered out, Aug. 21, 1861. Battle honors: Dug Springs.

Born: Jan. 3, 1831, Utica, NY
Died: Sept. 4, 1892, Washington, D.C.
Occupation: Insurance agent and district court clerk before war. Insurance and real estate agent and lawyer after war.
Offices/Honors: Superintendent of Free Delivery System, U.S. Post Office, 1886–91
Miscellaneous: Resided Dubuque, Dubuque Co., IA; and Washington, D.C., 1886–91
Buried: Arlington National Cemetery, Arlington, VA (Section 1, Lot 35-A)
References: Addison A. Stuart. *Iowa Colonels and Regiments*. Des Moines, IA, 1865. Pension File, National Archives. Obituary, *Dubuque Daily Times*, Sept. 7, 1892. Benjamin F. Gue. *History of Iowa from the Earliest Times to the Beginning of the Twentieth Century*. New York City, NY, 1903. Obituary, *Washington Evening Star*, Sept. 5, 1892. Eugene F. Ware. *The Lyon Campaign in Missouri, Being a History of the First Iowa Infantry*. Topeka, KS, 1907. William Garrett Piston, "The 1st Iowa Volunteers: Honor and Community in a Ninety-Day Regiment," *Civil War History*, Vol. 44, No. 1 (March 1998).

John Francis Bates (post-war) (State Historical Society of Iowa, Des Moines).

John Francis Bates (State Historical Society of Iowa, Iowa City).

Benjamin Beach

1 Lieutenant, Co. A, 1 IA Infantry, May 14, 1861. Honorably mustered out, Aug. 21, 1861. Captain, Co. H, 11 IA Infantry, Oct. 18, 1861. Lieutenant Colonel, 11 IA Infantry, Nov. 6, 1864. Commanded 3 Brigade, 4 Division, 17 Army Corps, Army of the Tennessee, May 30–June 17, 1865. *Colonel*, 11 IA Infantry, July 29, 1865. Honorably mustered out, July 15, 1865. Battle honors: Shiloh, Corinth, Atlanta Campaign, Savannah Campaign, Campaign of the Carolinas.

Born: Jan. 20, 1827, Hamilton, OH
Died: May 16, 1913, Muscatine, IA
Other Wars: Mexican War (Private, Co. I, 1 OH Infantry)
Occupation: Tinsmith before war. Hardware merchant and grocer after war.
Offices/Honors: Postmaster, Muscatine, IA, 1878–86
Miscellaneous: Resided Muscatine, Muscatine Co., IA
Buried: Greenwood Cemetery, Muscatine, IA (Fletcher 2nd Addition, Block 11, Lot 29)
References: *History of Muscatine County, Iowa, from the Earliest Settlements to the Present Time*. Chicago, IL, 1911. Obituary, *Muscatine Journal*, May 17, 1913. *The United States Biographical Dictionary and Portrait Gallery of Eminent and Self-Made Men*. Iowa Volume. Chicago and New York, 1878. *The History of Muscatine County, Iowa*. Chicago, IL, 1879.

Benjamin Beach (post-war) (State Historical Society of Iowa, Des Moines).

Obituary, *Muscatine News-Tribune,* May 17, 1913. "Benjamin Beach," *Annals of Iowa,* 3rd Series, Vol. 11, No. 2–3 (July–Oct. 1913). Pension File and Military Service File, National Archives. Lurton D. Ingersoll. *Iowa and the Rebellion.* Philadelphia, PA, 1866.

Alvah Hamilton Bereman

Captain, 18 U.S. Infantry, May 14, 1861. Accidental GSW left leg, Nashville, TN, March 7, 1862. Unfit for duty and unable to rejoin his command due to his wound, he resigned July 22, 1862. Colonel, 45 IA Infantry, May 25, 1864. Commanded 3 Brigade, District of Memphis, District of West Tennessee, Department of the Tennessee, June 22–July 16, 1864. Commanded Post of Moscow (TN), Department of the Tennessee, Aug. 1864. Honorably mustered out Sept. 16, 1864.

Born: April 13, 1829, Mercer Co., KY
Died: Feb. 6, 1887, Pomona, Los Angeles Co., CA
Education: Graduated Knox College, Galesburg, IL, 1853
Offices/Honors: Iowa House of Representatives, 1860–61, 1864
Occupation: Lawyer and newspaper editor
Miscellaneous: Resided Mount Pleasant, Henry Co., IA, to 1866; St. Louis, MO, 1866–83; Denver, Arapahoe Co., CO, 1884–86. One of six brothers who served in Iowa regiments.
Buried: Pomona Cemetery, Pomona, CA (Lot 38)
References: Pension File and Military Service File, National Archives. Edward H. Stiles. *Recollec-*

Alvah Hamilton Bereman (post-war) (State Historical Society of Iowa, Des Moines).

tions and Sketches of Notable Lawyers and Public Men of Early Iowa. Des Moines, IA, 1916. Obituary, *Chicago Inter Ocean,* Feb. 12, 1887. *The History of Henry County, Iowa.* Chicago, IL, 1879. Letters Received, Commission Branch, Adjutant General's Office, File B868(CB) 1863, National Archives.

Aaron Brown

2 Lieutenant, Co. F, 3 IA Infantry, May 20, 1861. GSW hand, Blue Mills Landing, MO, Sept. 17, 1861. Captain, Co. F, 3 IA Infantry, April 9, 1862. Major, 3 IA Infantry, Oct. 15, 1862. Colonel, 3 IA Infantry, Nov. 27, 1862. Commanded 1 Brigade, 4 Division, 16 Army Corps, Army of the Tennessee, Jan. 1863. GSW right thigh, Jackson, MS, July 12, 1863. Resigned July 13, 1864, since "I am not able to perform active field service in consequence of wounds." Battle honors: Blue Mills Landing, Vicksburg Campaign, Jackson.

Born: June 7, 1822, Marion Co., MS
Died: July 2, 1904, Mitchellville, IA
Occupation: Farmer and physician
Offices/Honors: Iowa Senate, 1856–60. Iowa House of Representatives, 1868–72.
Miscellaneous: Resided Fayette, Fayette Co., IA; and Mitchellville, Polk Co., IA
Buried: Grandview Cemetery, Fayette, IA (Section E, Lot 226)
References: *Portrait and Biographical Album of Fayette County, Iowa.* Chicago, IL, 1891. Obituary,

Aaron Brown (with Lt. Col. James Tullis, right, and Major George W. Crosley, left) (State Historical Society of Iowa, Des Moines).

Iowa Postal Card (Fayette, IA), July 7, 1904. "Aaron Brown," *Annals of Iowa*, 3rd Series, Vol. 6, No. 8 (Jan. 1905). *Past and Present of Fayette County, Iowa*. Indianapolis, IN, 1910. Addison A. Stuart. *Iowa Colonels and Regiments*. Des Moines, IA, 1865. Pension File and Military Service File, National Archives. Letters Received, Volunteer Service Branch, Adjutant General's Office, File I299(VS) 1862, National Archives. Benjamin F. Gue. *History of Iowa from the Earliest Times to the Beginning of the Twentieth Century*. New York City, NY, 1903. Seymour D. Thompson. *Recollections with the Third Iowa Regiment*. Cincinnati, OH, 1864.

William Brush

Colonel, 38 Iowa Infantry, Sept. 12, 1862. Commission revoked, Oct. 26, 1862, due to incompetence.

Born: Feb. 19, 1827, New Fairfield, CT
Died: April 29, 1895, Englewood, Cook Co., IL
Education: Graduated Yale University, New Haven, CT, 1850
Occupation: Methodist clergyman and college president
Offices/Honors: President, Upper Iowa University, Fayette, IA, 1860–69. President, Dakota Wesleyan University, Mitchell, SD, 1885–91. U.S. Consul, Messina, Italy, 1891–92.
Miscellaneous: Resided Westfield, Fayette Co., IA (1860); Charles City, Floyd Co., IA (1870); and Mitchell, Davison Co., SD
Buried: Grandview Cemetery, Fayette, IA (Section A, Lot 116)
References: Stuart C. Brush, compiler. *The Descendants of Thomas and Richard Brush of Hunt-*

William Brush (post-war) (Upper Iowa University Archives).

ington, Long Island. Baltimore, MD, 1982. *Obituary Record of Graduates of Yale University Deceased from June 1890 to June 1900*. New Haven, CT, 1900. Obituary, *Cedar Rapids Evening Gazette*, May 3, 1895. *Biographical Record of the Class of 1850 of Yale College*. New Haven, CT, 1877. Obituary, *Waterloo Daily Courier*, May 3, 1895. David Wildman. *Iowa's Martyr Regiment: The Story of the Thirty-eighth Iowa Infantry*. Iowa City, IA, 2010.

Eber Cole Byam

Colonel, 24 IA Infantry, Sept. 17, 1862. "Suffering from chronic dysentery and debility incident to the exposure and fatigue of recent marches and severe field service," he resigned June 30, 1863. Battle honors: Port Gibson, Champion's Hill, Vicksburg Campaign.

Born: Sept. 14, 1822, Ontario, Canada
Died: July 24, 1887, Rochester, NY
Occupation: A tinsmith by trade, he became a Methodist clergyman in 1856 after a brief career as a lawyer. Land agent, inventor, and manufacturer of hardware specialities (curtain fixtures) after war.
Offices/Honors: Register, U.S. General Land Office, Fort Dodge, IA, 1871–75
Miscellaneous: Resided Fayette, Fayette Co., IA; Marion, Linn Co., IA, to 1869; Fort Dodge, Webster Co., IA, 1869–75; Elkhart, Elkhart Co., IN; and Rochester, Monroe Co., NY. Father of Commodore Perry Byam (1852–1922), Drummer, Co. D, 24 IA Infantry, one of the youngest Boys in Blue.
Buried: Mount Hope Cemetery, Rochester, NY (Section L, Lot 33)
References: Obituary, *Rochester Democrat and Chronicle*, July 25, 1887. Edwin C. Byam. *Descendants of George Byam (?-1680)*. Suffield, CT, 1975. Obituary, *Cedar Rapids Evening Gazette*, Aug. 6, 1887. *Past and Present of Fayette County, Iowa*. Indianapolis, IN, 1910. Pension File and Military Service File, National Archives. Letters Received, Volunteer Service Branch, Adjutant General's Office, File I249(VS)1863, National Archives. Thaddeus L. Smith, "The Twenty-Fourth Iowa Volunteers," *Annals of Iowa*, 3rd Series, Vol. 1, No. 1–3 (April–Oct. 1893). Benjamin F. Gue. *History of Iowa from the Earliest Times to the Beginning of the Twentieth Century*. New York City, NY, 1903. Addison A. Stuart. *Iowa Colonels and Regiments*. Des Moines, IA, 1865. Jay S. Hoar. *Callow Brave and True: A Gospel of Civil War Youth*. Gettysburg, PA, 1999.

Henry Clay Caldwell

Major, 3 IA Cavalry, Sept. 2, 1861. Lieutenant Colonel, 3 IA Cavalry, Sept. 5, 1862. Commanded Reserve Brigade, 1 Cavalry Division, Department of the Missouri, July 6–Aug. 10, 1863. Chief of Staff, Staff of Brig. Gen. John W. Davidson, 1 Cavalry Division, Department of the Missouri, Aug.–Oct. 1863. Commanded 1 Brigade, 1 Cavalry Division, Army of Arkansas, Department of the Missouri, Nov. 1863. Colonel, 3 IA Cavalry, May 1, 1864. Resigned June 25, 1864, "to enable me to accept and discharge the duties of the office of United States District Judge for the District of Arkansas." Battle honors: Kirksville, Hartville, Advance upon Little Rock, Pine Bluff.

Born: Sept. 4, 1832, Marshall Co., WV
Died: Feb. 15, 1915, Los Angeles, CA

Eber Cole Byam (post-war) (State Historical Society of Iowa, Des Moines).

Henry Clay Caldwell.

Occupation: Lawyer and judge

Offices/Honors: Iowa House of Representatives, 1860–61. Judge, U.S. District Court, Western District of Arkansas, 1864–71. Judge U.S. District Court, Eastern District of Arkansas, 1871–90. Judge, U.S. Circuit Court, Eighth Circuit, 1890–1891. Judge, U.S. Court of Appeals, Eighth Circuit, 1891–1903.

Miscellaneous: Resided Keosauqua, Van Buren Co., IA, before war; Little Rock, Pulaski Co., AR, to 1906; and Los Angeles, CA, 1906–15

Buried: Oakland Cemetery, Little Rock, AR (Lily Street, Lot 594)

References: John Hallum. *Biographical and Pictorial History of Arkansas.* Albany, NY, 1887. Edward H. Stiles. *Recollections and Sketches of Notable Lawyers and Public Men of Early Iowa.* Des Moines, IA, 1916. *Dictionary of American Biography.* Addison A. Stuart. *Iowa Colonels and Regiments.* Des Moines, IA, 1865. *National Cyclopedia of American Biography.* Benjamin F. Gue. *History of Iowa from the Earliest Times to the Beginning of the Twentieth Century.* New York City, NY, 1903. Obituary circular, Whole No. 1175, California MOLLUS. Pension File and Military Service File, National Archives. Letters Received, Volunteer Service Branch, Adjutant General's Office, File C818(VS)1866, National Archives.

Hugh James Campbell

1 Sergeant, Co. A, 1 IA Infantry, May 7, 1861. GSW left leg, Wilson's Creek, MO, Aug. 10, 1861. Honorably mustered out, Aug. 20, 1861. Major, 18 IA Infantry, Aug. 2, 1862. Judge Advocate and Provost Marshal General, Staff of Brig. Gen. James Totten, 2 Division, Army of the Frontier, Department of the Missouri, Nov. 1862. Lieutenant Colonel, 18 IA Infantry, July 17, 1863. Commanded Post of Springfield (MO), District of Southwestern Missouri, Department of the Missouri, July–Aug. 1863. Commanded Post of Clarksville (AR), District of the Frontier, Department of Arkansas, July 1864. Colonel, 18 IA Infantry, Dec. 1, 1864. Honorably mustered out, July 20, 1865. Battle honors: Wilson's Creek.

Born: Dec. 31, 1831, Uniontown, PA
Died: April 19, 1898, Yankton, SD
Education: Graduated Ohio University, Athens, OH, 1851
Occupation: School teacher before war. Lawyer and Louisiana carpetbagger after war.
Offices/Honors: Louisiana Senate, 1868–70. Major Gen., Louisiana State Militia, 1870–72 and 1875. U.S. Attorney, Dakota Territory, 1877–85.
Miscellaneous: Resided Muscatine, Muscatine Co., IA, before war; New Orleans, LA, 1865–77; and Yankton, Yankton Co., SD, after 1877
Buried: Yankton Cemetery, Yankton, SD
References: Obituary, *Sioux Falls Daily Argus-Leader*, April 19, 1898. *Sketch of Gen. Hugh J. Campbell.* N.p., N.d. Pension File and Military Service File, National Archives. Doane Robinson. *Doane Robinson's Encyclopedia of South Dakota.* Pierre, SD, 1925. *Annual Catalogue of the Ohio University, 1875.* Athens, OH, 1876. George W. Kingsbury. *History of Dakota Territory.* Chicago, IL, 1915. "Major General Hugh J. Campbell," *Louisiana Democrat (Alexandria, LA),* May 11, 1870. "Scandalous Conduct of a Radical State Senator," *Ouachita Telegraph (Monroe, LA),* Oct. 2, 1869.

David Carskaddon

Captain, Co. K, 9 IA Infantry, Sept. 24, 1861. Colonel, 9 IA Infantry, June 4, 1863. Commanded 2 Brigade, 1 Division, 15 Army Corps, Army of the Tennessee, Dec. 11, 1863–Jan. 29, 1864 and April 20–May 5, 1864. GSW forehead, Ezra Church, GA, July 28, 1864. Honorably mustered out Jan. 14, 1865. Battle honors: Pea Ridge, Chickasaw Bayou, Arkansas Post, Vicksburg Campaign, Lookout Mountain, Missionary Ridge, Ringgold, Atlanta Campaign (Resaca, Dallas, Ezra Church).

Born: July 8, 1825, Hamilton, OH
Died: Aug. 14, 1894, Lake City, IA
Occupation: Proprietor of livery stable before war. Farmer and furniture merchant after war.
Offices/Honors: Sheriff, Linn Co., IA, 1877–79
Miscellaneous: Resided Marion, Linn Co., IA, to 1880; and Lake City, Calhoun Co., IA, 1880–94
Buried: Oak Shade Cemetery, Marion, IA
References: David E. McLain. *Descendants of James and Lettice Carskaddon of Chillisquaque Town-*

Hugh James Campbell (post-war) (*Sketch of Gen. Hugh J. Campbell.* N.p., N.d).

David Carskaddon (State Historical Society of Iowa, Des Moines).

ship, Northumberland County, Pennsylvania. Moorhead, MN, 1970. Obituary, *Marion Register,* Aug. 22, 1894. *The History of Linn County, Iowa.* Chicago, IL, 1878. Addison A. Stuart. *Iowa Colonels and Regiments.* Des Moines, IA, 1865. Pension File and Military Service File, National Archives. Letters Received, Volunteer Service Branch, Adjutant General's Office, File G1866(VS)1864, National Archives.

William Henry Clune

Quartermaster Sergeant, 6 IA Infantry, July 19, 1861. 1 Lieutenant, Co. B, 6 IA Infantry, Sept. 6, 1861. 1 Lieutenant, Co. H, 6 IA Infantry, Nov. 7, 1861. Captain, Co. I, 6 IA Infantry, Oct. 26, 1862. Acting AIG, Staff of Brig. Gen. William Sooy Smith, 1 Division, 16 Army Corps, Army of the Tennessee, June–July 1863. Acting AIG, Staff of Brig. Gen. Hugh Ewing and Brig. Gen. John M. Corse, 4 Division, 15 Army Corps, Army of the Tennessee, July–Dec. 1863. Major, 6 IA Infantry, July 29, 1864. Contused stomach wound, Griswoldville, GA, Nov. 22, 1864. Lieutenant Colonel, 6 IA Infantry, Dec. 30, 1864. *Colonel,* 6 IA Infantry, June 18, 1865. Honorably mustered out, July 21, 1865. Battle honors: Shiloh, Jackson Campaign, Missionary Ridge, Atlanta Campaign (Dallas, Kenesaw Mountain,

William Henry Clune (State Historical Society of Iowa, Des Moines).

Ezra Church), Savannah Campaign (Griswoldville), Campaign of the Carolinas.
  Born: 1833?, Orwell/New Haven, VT?
  Died: Aug. 28, 1867, Galveston, TX
  Occupation: Lawyer
  Offices/Honors: Iowa House of Representatives, 1858–60
  Miscellaneous: Resided Burlington, Des Moines Co., IA; and Galveston, Galveston Co., TX, 1866–67
  Buried: New City Cemetery, Galveston, TX (unmarked)
  References: Pension File and Military Service File, National Archives. Edward H. Stiles. *Recollections and Sketches of Notable Lawyers and Public Men of Early Iowa.* Des Moines, IA, 1916. Letters Received, Volunteer Service Branch, Adjutant General's Office, Files C1555(VS)1865 and W1875(VS) 1865, National Archives. Death Notice, *Galveston Daily News,* Aug. 29, 1867. Henry H. Wright. *A History of the Sixth Iowa Infantry.* Iowa City, IA, 1923. *The History of Des Moines County, Iowa.* Chicago, IL, 1879.

John Connell

Lieutenant Colonel, 28 IA Infantry, Oct. 10, 1862. Colonel, 28 IA Infantry, March 14, 1863. GSW left arm (amputated), Sabine Cross Roads, LA, April 8, 1864. Taken prisoner, Sabine Cross Roads, LA, April 8, 1864. Confined Shreveport, LA. Paroled June 16, 1864. Resigned March 17, 1865, since "the stump (of his arm) is excessively painful and renders him incapable of active exercise, save at the expense of great suffering, also rendering him unfit for active duty." Battle honors: Port Gibson, Champion's Hill, Vicksburg Campaign, Jackson Campaign, Red River Campaign (Sabine Cross Roads).

Born: March 16, 1823, Paisley, Scotland
Died: June 10, 1891, Toledo, IA
Occupation: Farmer and merchant
Offices/Honors: Iowa House of Representatives, 1854–56. U.S. Internal Revenue Assessor, 1865–1873. U.S. Internal Revenue Collector, 4th District of Iowa, 1873–83.
Miscellaneous: Resided Buckingham, Tama Co., IA; and Toledo, Tama Co., IA
Buried: Woodlawn Cemetery, Toledo, IA
References: *History of Tama County, Iowa.* Springfield, IL, 1883. Obituary, *Toledo Chronicle,* June 18, 1891. Addison A. Stuart. *Iowa Colonels and Regiments.* Des Moines, IA, 1865. *Report of the Proceedings of the Society of the Army of the Tennessee at the Twenty-Third Meeting.* Cincinnati, OH, 1893. Pension File and Military Service File, National Archives. Letters Received, Volunteer Service Branch, Adjutant General's Office, Files C1925(VS) 1864 and C824(VS) 1865, National Archives. Benjamin F. Gue. *History of Iowa from the Earliest Times to the Beginning of the Twentieth Century.* New York City, NY, 1903. Janette Stevenson Murray. *They Came to North Tama: Old Buckingham Tranquillity Folk.* Traer, IA, 1953.

Benjamin Crabb

Captain, Co. H, 7 IA Infantry, July 24, 1861. Taken prisoner, Belmont, MO, Nov. 7, 1861. Confined Memphis, TN, Mobile, AL, and Montgomery, AL. Exchanged July 7, 1862. Resigned Aug. 13, 1862, to accept promotion. Colonel, 19 IA Infantry, Aug. 21, 1862. Commanded Post of Springfield (MO), District of Southwestern Missouri, Department of the Missouri, Dec. 1862–March 1863. Suffering with chronic rheumatism, he resigned March 16, 1863, "being at this time unable to perform the duties of my office in the field without endangering (permanently) my health." Battle honors: Belmont, Marmaduke's Expedition into Missouri (Springfield).

Born: Oct. 29, 1821, Amity, Madison Co., OH
Died: Sept. 4, 1906, McCool Junction, NE
Occupation: Flour mill operator and hotel proprietor
Miscellaneous: Resided Washington, Washington Co., IA; York, York Co., NE; and McCool Junction, York Co., NE
Buried: Greenwood Cemetery, York, NE (Division H, Lot 28)
References: Pension File and Military Service File, National Archives. Addison A. Stuart. *Iowa Colonels and Regiments.* Des Moines, IA, 1865. Obituary, *Nebraska State Journal,* Sept. 6, 1906. Letters Received, Volunteer Service Branch, Adjutant General's Office, File C631(VS) 1862, National Ar-

John Connell (State Historical Society of Iowa, Des Moines).

Benjamin Crabb (State Historical Society of Iowa, Des Moines).

chives. Gerald E. Sherard, compiler. *Civil War Veterans York County, Nebraska.* Knoxville, TN, 1985. T. E. Sedgwick, editor. *York County, Nebraska, and Its People.* Chicago, IL, 1921. J. Irvine Dungan. *History of the Nineteenth Regiment Iowa Volunteer Infantry.* Davenport, IA, 1865. Kathy Fisher. *In the Beginning There Was Land: A History of Washington County, Iowa.* Washington, IA, 1978.

Henry Johnson Brodhead Cummings

Captain, Co. F, 4 IA Infantry, July 20, 1861. Discharged Sept. 4, 1862, "to enable him to accept the command of a new regiment of volunteers." Colonel, 39 IA Infantry, Nov. 24, 1862. Commanded Post of Corinth (MS), District of Corinth, Department of the Tennessee, June–Sept. 1863. Commanded Post of Athens (AL), Department of the Tennessee, April 1864. Commanded 3 Brigade, 2 Division, 16 Army Corps, Army of the Tennessee, Aug. 2–15, 1864. Honorably mustered out, Dec. 22, 1864. Battle honors: Forrest's Expedition into West Tennessee (Parker's Cross Roads), Atlanta Campaign.

Henry Johnson Brodhead Cummings (L. H. Morse, Photographer, Davenport, IA; State Historical Society of Iowa, Des Moines).

Left, top: Benjamin Crabb (Dudley & Co., Photographers, Washington, IA; USAMHI [RG98S-CWP193.4]). *Bottom:* Benjamin Crabb (Rick Brown Collection).

Born: May 21, 1831, Newton, NJ
Died: April 16, 1909, Winterset, IA
Occupation: Lawyer and newspaper editor
Offices/Honors: U.S. House of Representatives, 1877–79
Miscellaneous: Resided Winterset, Madison Co., IA
Buried: Winterset Cemetery, Winterset, IA
References: *A Memorial and Biographical Record of Iowa.* Chicago, IL, 1896. *The United States Biographical Dictionary and Portrait Gallery of Eminent and Self-Made Men.* Iowa Volume. Chicago and New York, 1878. Addison A. Stuart. *Iowa Colonels and Regiments.* Des Moines, IA, 1865. Obituary, *Winterset Madisonian,* April 22, 1909. Herman A. Mueller, editor. *History of Madison County, Iowa, and Its People.* Chicago, IL, 1915. James L. Harrison, compiler. *Biographical Directory of the American Congress, 1774–1949.* Washington, D.C., 1950. Pension File and Military Service File, National Archives. Letters Received, Volunteer Service Branch, Adjutant General's Office, File I204(VS) 1862, National Archives. "Henry J.B. Cummings," *Annals of Iowa,* 3rd Series, Vol. 9, No. 1 (April 1909). Benjamin F. Gue. *History of Iowa from the Earliest Times to the Beginning of the Twentieth Century.* New York City, NY, 1903.

William Dewey (State Historical Society of Iowa, Des Moines).

Education: Attended U.S. Military Academy, West Point, NY (Class of 1833)
Occupation: Physician
Offices/Honors: Iowa House of Representatives, 1854–56
Miscellaneous: Resided Sidney, Fremont Co., IA
Buried: Woodland Cemetery, Des Moines, IA (Block 6, Lot 114)
References: Addison A. Stuart. *Iowa Colonels and Regiments.* Des Moines, IA, 1865. Benjamin F. Gue. *History of Iowa from the Earliest Times to the Beginning of the Twentieth Century.* New York City, NY, 1903. Obituary, *Iowa State Register,* Dec. 17, 1862. Pension File and Military Service File, National Archives. *History of Fremont County, Iowa.* Des Moines, IA, 1881. http://ozarkscivilwar.org/photographs/dewey-william/.

Henry Johnson Brodhead Cummings (Mark Warren Collection).

William Dewey

Lieutenant Colonel, 15 IA Infantry, Nov. 6, 1861. Colonel, 23 IA Infantry, Sept. 19, 1862. Battle honors: Shiloh, Pitman's Ferry.
Born: March 26, 1811, Sheffield, MA
Died: Nov. 30, 1862, Camp Patterson, MO (erysipelas)

Joseph Bartlett Dorr

1 Lieutenant, RQM, 12 IA Infantry, Nov. 5, 1861. Taken prisoner, Shiloh, TN, April 6, 1862. Confined Montgomery, AL. Escaped May 24, 1862. Honorably mustered out, May 28, 1863, to accept promotion. Colonel, 8 IA Cavalry, Aug. 27, 1863. Commanded 1 Brigade, 1 Division, Cavalry Corps, Army of the Cumberland, April 12–July 20, 1864, and July 30, 1864. GSW right side, Lovejoy's Station,

GA, July 29, 1864. Taken prisoner, Newnan, GA, July 30, 1864. Confined Charleston, SC. Paroled Sept. 28, 1864. Battle honors: Fort Donelson, Shiloh, Atlanta Campaign (Lovejoy's Station, Newnan), Franklin, Nashville, Wilson's Raid.

Born: Aug. 6, 1825, Hamburg, Erie Co., NY
Died: May 28, 1865, Macon, GA (congestive chills)
Occupation: Newspaper editor and publisher
Miscellaneous: Resided Dubuque, Dubuque Co., IA
Buried: Linwood Cemetery, Dubuque, IA (Section 1-E, Lot 4465)
References: Homer Mead. *The 8th Iowa Cavalry in the Civil War.* Carthage, IL, 1927. Addison A. Stuart. *Iowa Colonels and Regiments.* Des Moines, IA, 1865. Obituary, *Dubuque Democratic Herald,* June 3, 1865. Obituary, *Davenport Daily Gazette,* June 6, 1865. Edward H. Stiles. *Recollections and Sketches of Notable Lawyers and Public Men of Early Iowa.* Des Moines, IA, 1916. Pension File and Military Service File, National Archives. Letters Received, Volunteer Service Branch, Adjutant General's Office, File A211(VS)1863, National Archives. David W. Reed. *Campaigns and Battles of the Twelfth Regiment Iowa Veteran Volunteer Infantry.* Evanston, IL, 1903. Franklin T. Oldt and Patrick J. Quigley, editors. *History of Dubuque County, Iowa.* Chicago, IL, 1911. Ted Genoways and Hugh H. Genoways, editors. *A Perfect Picture of Hell: Eyewitness Accounts by Civil War Prisoners from the 12th Iowa.* Iowa City, IA, 2001. David Evans. *Sherman's Horsemen: Union Cavalry Operations in the Atlanta Campaign.* Bloomington, IN, 1996.

Gustavus Adolphus Eberhart

2 Lieutenant, Co. I, 3 IA Infantry, June 10, 1861. Resigned May 1, 1862, since "my health for two months past has been so poor that I have not been able for duty." Major, 32 IA Infantry, Sept. 19, 1862. Commanded Post of Cape Girardeau (MO), District of St. Louis, Department of the Missouri, Dec. 1862–Feb. 1863. Lieutenant Colonel, 32 IA Infantry, May 22, 1864. *Colonel,* 32 IA Infantry, May 28, 1864. Honorably mustered out, Aug. 24, 1865. Battle honors: Advance upon Little Rock (Bayou Meto), Red River Campaign (Yellow Bayou), Lake Chicot, Nashville, Mobile Campaign (Fort Blakely).

Born: Nov. 27, 1836, Carmichaels, PA
Died: June 30, 1916, Pasadena, CA
Occupation: Civil engineer and bridge builder
Offices/Honors: District Court Clerk, Black Hawk Co., IA, 1867–72
Miscellaneous: Resided Waterloo, Black Hawk Co., IA, to 1886; Des Moines, Polk Co., IA, 1886–1910; and Pasadena, Los Angeles Co., CA, 1910–16

Joseph Bartlett Dorr (T. M. Schleier, Photographer, Nashville, TN; Richard F. Carlile Collection).

Gustavus Adolphus Eberhart (post-war) (State Historical Society of Iowa, Des Moines).

Buried: Woodland Cemetery, Des Moines, IA (Block 22, Lot 117)

References: Obituary Circular, Whole No. 444, Iowa MOLLUS. Pension File and Military Service File, National Archives. Uriah Eberhart. *History of the Eberharts in Germany and the United States.* Chicago, IL, 1891. Letters Received, Volunteer Service Branch, Adjutant General's Office, File E520 (VS)1863, National Archives. Obituary, *Waterloo Evening Courier and Reporter,* July 1, 1916. Isaiah Van Metre, editor. *History of Black Hawk County, Iowa, and Representative Citizens.* Chicago, IL, 1904. John Scott. *Story of the Thirty Second Iowa Infantry Volunteers.* Nevada, IA, 1896. Myron J. Smith, Jr. *Civil War Biographies from the Western Waters.* Jefferson, NC, 2015.

John Alexander Garrett

Captain, Co. I, 10 IA Infantry, Sept. 7, 1861. Lieutenant Colonel, 22 IA Infantry, Aug. 2, 1862. Colonel, 40 IA Infantry, Sept. 17, 1862. Commanded Fort Halleck, District of Columbus (KY), 16 Army Corps, Department of the Tennessee, Feb. 1863. Commanded 2 Brigade, 1 Division, 7 Army Corps, Department of Arkansas, and Post of Little Rock, Nov. 10, 1864–Feb. 6, 1865. Commanded 1 Brigade, 1 Division, 7 Army Corps, Department of Arkansas, Feb. 6–18, 1865. Commanded 1 Brigade, 3 Division, 7 Army Corps, Department of Arkansas, May 7–June 27, 1865. Commanded District of South Kansas, Department of Kansas, June 28–Aug. 1, 1865. Honorably mustered out, Aug. 2, 1865. Battle honors: Vicksburg Campaign, Camden Expedition (Okolona, Prairie D'Ane, Jenkins' Ferry).

John Alexander Garrett (Addison A. Stuart. *Iowa Colonels and Regiments.* Des Moines, IA, 1865).

John Alexander Garrett (Mark Warren Collection).

Born: Nov. 15, 1824, Carlisle, Sullivan Co., IN
Died: Jan. 23, 1877, Newton, IA
Education: Attended Hanover (IN) College. Attended Indiana University, Bloomington, IN.
Other Wars: Mexican War (Private, Co. G, 4 IN Infantry)
Occupation: Dry goods merchant
Miscellaneous: Resided Carlisle, Sullivan Co., IN, to 1857; and Newton, Jasper Co., IA
Buried: Newton Union Cemetery, Newton, IA (Block 4, Lot 28)
References: A.K. Campbell, "Col. John A. Garrett," *Annals of Iowa,* 1st Series, Vol. 9, No. 1 (January 1871). Charles R. Tuttle and Daniel S. Durrie. *An Illustrated History of the State of Iowa.* Chicago, IL, 1876. Addison A. Stuart. *Iowa Colonels and Regiments.* Des Moines, IA, 1865. Benjamin F. Gue. *History of Iowa from the Earliest Times to the Beginning of the Twentieth Century.* New York City, NY, 1903. Pension File and Military Service File, National Archives. Letters Received, Volunteer Service Branch, Adjutant General's Office, File G988(VS) 1863, National Archives.

James Otis Gower

Captain, Co. F, 1 IA Cavalry, Aug. 1, 1861. Major, 1 IA Cavalry, Sept. 1, 1861. Commanded Post of Clinton (MO), Department of the Missouri, May–

Above: **James Otis Gower (pre-war) (State Historical Society of Iowa, Iowa City).** *Below:* **James Otis Gower (State Historical Society of Iowa, Des Moines).**

July 1862. Lieutenant Colonel, 1 IA Cavalry, July 16, 1862. Colonel, 1 IA Cavalry, Aug. 26, 1862. Commanded 1 Brigade, 3 Division, Army of the Frontier, Department of the Missouri, Dec. 1862–Jan. 1863 and May 1863. Commanded 3 Division, Army of the Frontier, Department of the Missouri, Jan.–Feb. 1863. "Unfit for military duty in consequence of chronic diarrhea and acute anasarca," he resigned Aug. 20, 1863. Battle honors: Prairie Grove.

Born: May 30, 1834, Abbot, ME
Died: Sept. 12, 1865, Iowa City, IA
Education: Attended Knox College, Galesburg, IL. Graduated Kentucky Military Institute, Frankfort, KY, 1855.
Occupation: Banker and produce merchant
Miscellaneous: Resided Iowa City, Johnson Co., IA
Buried: Oakland Cemetery, Iowa City, IA (Outlot 3)
References: Addison A. Stuart. *Iowa Colonels and Regiments.* Des Moines, IA, 1865. Benjamin F. Gue. *History of Iowa from the Earliest Times to the Beginning of the Twentieth Century.* New York City, NY, 1903. James D. Stephens. *Reflections: A Portrait-Biography of the Kentucky Military Institute (1845–1971).* Georgetown, KY, 1991. Obituary, *Davenport Daily Gazette*, Sept. 18, 1865. Charles H. Lothrop. *A History of the First Regiment Iowa Cavalry Veteran Volunteers.* Lyons, IA, 1890. George E. Fisher, editor. *Catalogue of the Delta Kappa Epsilon Fraternity: Biographical and Statistical.* New York City, NY, 1890. Military Service File, National Archives.

Joseph Murray Griffiths

Major, 39 IA Infantry, Nov. 24, 1862. Shell wound head, Parker's Cross Roads, TN, Dec. 31, 1862. Lieutenant Colonel, 39 IA Infantry, Dec. 17,

Joseph Murray Griffiths (J.R. Laughlin's Photograph Rooms, N.W. Corner of Twelfth and Market Streets, Philadelphia, PA; Mark Warren Collection).

1864. *Colonel*, 39 IA Infantry, May 12, 1865. Honorably mustered out, June 5, 1865. Battle honors: Forrest's Expedition into West Tennessee (Parker's Cross Roads), Atlanta Campaign, Allatoona, Savannah Campaign, Campaign of the Carolinas.

Born: March 9, 1823, Philadelphia, PA
Died: June 22, 1921, Des Moines, IA
Occupation: Merchant, grain dealer, and, after 1882, clerk in the money order department of the Des Moines post office
Offices/Honors: U.S. Customs Examiner, 1875–79
Miscellaneous: Resided Des Moines, Polk Co., IA; and New Orleans, LA, 1875–79
Buried: Woodland Cemetery, Des Moines, IA (Block 1, Lot 40)
References: *Portrait and Biographical Album of Polk County, Iowa*. Chicago, IL, 1890. Obituary, *Des Moines News*, June 22, 1921. Pension File and Military Service File, National Archives. Johnson Brigham. *Des Moines Together with the History of Polk County, Iowa*. Chicago, IL, 1911.

William Hall

Lieutenant Colonel, 11 IA Infantry, Oct. 11, 1861. GSW left ankle, Shiloh, TN, April 6, 1862. Colonel, 11 IA Infantry, Sept. 1, 1862. Commanded 3 Brigade, 6 Division, 17 Army Corps, Army of the Tennessee, April 30–June 6, 1863, and July 30–Aug. 23, 1863. Commanded 6 Division, 17 Army Corps, Army of the Tennessee, Aug. 23–Sept. 3, 1863. Commanded 3 Brigade, 1 Division, 17 Army Corps, Army of the Tennessee, Sept. 14–Oct. 10, 1863. Commanded 3 Brigade, 4 Division, 17 Army Corps, Army of the Tennessee, May 27–July 20, 1864 and July 21–31, 1864. Commanded 4 Division, 17 Army Corps, Army of the Tennessee, July 20–21, 1864. "Col. Wm. W. Belknap, 15 Iowa, junior colonel of my late command having been appointed Brigadier General and assigned to the command, in front of the enemy," he resigned Aug. 1, 1864, adding the bitter comment, "I can but know that my services are not deemed of any value to a Government which I have ever been anxious to serve to the best of my ability." Battle honors: Shiloh, Corinth, Vicksburg Campaign, Meridian Expedition, Atlanta Campaign (Kenesaw Mountain, Atlanta).

Born: Jan. 25, 1832, Montreal, Canada
Died: Dec. 20, 1865, Davenport, IA
Education: Attended Oberlin (OH) College. Attended Kentucky Military Institute, Frankfort, KY. Graduated Harvard Law School, Cambridge, MA, 1854.
Occupation: Lawyer
Miscellaneous: Resided Davenport, Scott Co., IA
Buried: Oakdale Cemetery, Davenport, IA (Section 2, Lot 97, marker illegible)
References: Addison A. Stuart. *Iowa Colonels and Regiments*. Des Moines, IA, 1865. Obituary, *Davenport Daily Gazette*, Dec. 21, 1865. Pension File and Military Service File, National Archives. Frederick Lloyd, "War Memories," *Iowa Historical Record*, Vol. 5, No. 1 (Jan. 1889). Alexander G. Downing. *Downing's Civil War Diary*. Edited by Olynthus B. Clark. Des Moines, IA, 1916. Obituary, *Burlington Daily Hawk-Eye*, Dec. 23, 1865.

Abraham M. Hare

Colonel, 11 IA Infantry, Nov. 1, 1861. Commanded 1 Brigade, 1 Division, Army of the Tennessee, March 15–April 6, 1862. GSW right hand and forearm, Shiloh, TN, April 6, 1862. Commanded 3 Brigade, 6 Division, Army of the Tennessee, June 1862. Suffering from "a painful stump of a finger and a cicatrix of the palm of his right hand," he resigned Aug. 31, 1862, since "my wound has become worse, making another amputation necessary, and further, I am also ... laboring under a severe attack of dysentery, rendering me entirely unfit for service." Battle honors: Shiloh.

Born: Nov. 13, 1811, near Columbus, OH
Died: Feb. 7, 1903, Muscatine, IA
Occupation: Farmer, after early employment as a hatter

William Hall (State Historical Society of Iowa, Des Moines).

Miscellaneous: Resided Muscatine, Muscatine Co., IA; and Wilton, Muscatine Co., IA
Buried: Greenwood Cemetery, Muscatine, IA (Ogilvie Addition, Block 1, Lot 16)
References: Linda Alstrom Hare. *Seven Hares in the Civil War.* Atlanta, KS, 2005. *Portrait and Biographical Album of Muscatine County, Iowa.* Chicago, IL, 1889. Obituary, *Muscatine Journal,* Feb. 9, 1903. *The History of Muscatine County, Iowa.* Chicago, IL, 1879. *Proceedings Crocker's Iowa Brigade at the Eleventh Biennial Reunion and Twelfth Biennial Reunion.* Cedar Rapids, IA, 1905. *Proceedings Crocker's Iowa Brigade at the Thirteenth Biennial Reunion and Fourteenth Biennial Reunion.* Mount Vernon, IA, 1910. Addison A. Stuart. *Iowa Colonels and Regiments.* Des Moines, IA, 1865. Pension File and Military Service File, National Archives. Letters Received, Volunteer Service Branch, Adjutant General's Office, File I221(VS)1862, National Archives. William W. Belknap. *History of the Fifteenth Regiment Iowa Veteran Volunteer Infantry, from October 1861 to August 1865.* Keokuk, IA, 1887. Alexander G. Downing. *Downing's Civil War Diary.* Edited by Olynthus B. Clark. Des Moines, IA, 1916.

David Bremner Henderson

1 Lieutenant, Co. C, 12 IA Infantry, Oct. 24, 1861. GSW throat, Fort Donelson, TN, Feb. 15, 1862. GSW left foot (amputated), Corinth, MS, Oct. 4, 1862. Discharged on account of disability from wounds, Feb. 16, 1863. Commissioner, Board of Enrollment, 3rd District of Iowa, April 30, 1863–June 10, 1864, and Oct. 10, 1864–May 5, 1865. Colonel, 46 IA Infantry, June 10, 1864. Commanded Post of Collierville (TN), District of West Ten-

Above: Abraham M. Hare (State Historical Society of Iowa, Des Moines). *Below:* Abraham M. Hare (William W. Belknap. *History of the Fifteenth Regiment Iowa Veteran Volunteer Infantry, from October 1861 to August 1865.* Keokuk, IA, 1887).

David Bremner Henderson.

nessee, Department of the Tennessee, July 1864. Honorably mustered out, Sept. 23, 1864. Battle honors: Fort Donelson, Corinth.
Born: March 14, 1840, Old Deer, Aberdeenshire, Scotland

Above: **David Bremner Henderson (A.P. White, Photographer, West Union, IA).** *Below:* **David Bremner Henderson (post-war) (State Historical Society of Iowa, Des Moines).**

Died: Feb. 25, 1906, Dubuque, IA
Education: Attended Upper Iowa University, Fayette, IA
Occupation: Lawyer
Offices/Honors: U.S. Collector of Internal Revenue, 1865–69. U.S. House of Representatives, 1883–1903. Speaker, U.S. House of Representatives, 1899–1903.
Miscellaneous: Resided Clermont, Fayette Co., IA, before war; and Dubuque, Dubuque Co., IA, after war
Buried: Linwood Cemetery, Dubuque, IA (Section 3-A, Lot 41)
References: *Dictionary of American Biography.* Willard L. Hoing, "David B. Henderson: Speaker of the House," *Iowa Journal of History,* Vol. 55, No. 1 (Jan. 1957). Edward H. Stiles. *Recollections and Sketches of Notable Lawyers and Public Men of Early Iowa.* Des Moines, IA, 1916. Obituary, *Des Moines Daily News,* Feb. 26, 1906. Obituary Circular, Whole No. 292, Iowa MOLLUS. James L. Harrison, compiler. *Biographical Directory of the American Congress, 1774–1949.* Washington, D.C., 1950. Benjamin F. Gue. *History of Iowa from the Earliest Times to the Beginning of the Twentieth Century.* New York City, NY, 1903. *The History of Dubuque County, Iowa.* Chicago, IL, 1880. Pension File and Military Service File, National Archives. Letters Received, Volunteer Service Branch, Adjutant General's Office, File H1145(VS)1862, National Archives. Charles B. Clark and Roger B. Bowen. *University Recruits; Company C, 12th Iowa Infantry Regiment, U.S.A., 1861–1866.* Elverson, PA, 1991. David W. Reed. *Campaigns and Battles of the Twelfth Regiment Iowa Veteran Volunteer Infantry.* Evanston, IL, 1903.

Paris Perrin Henderson

Captain, Co. G, 10 IA Infantry, Sept. 7, 1861. Lieutenant Colonel, 10 IA Infantry, Jan. 27, 1863. *Colonel,* 10 IA Infantry, Aug. 20, 1863. Commanded Post of Kingston (GA), 15 Army Corps, Department of the Tennessee, Sept.–Oct. 1864. Honorably mustered out, Dec. 19, 1864. Battle honors: Missionary Ridge, Atlanta Campaign, Savannah Campaign.
Born: Jan. 3, 1825, Liberty, Union Co., IN
Died: Jan. 4, 1908, Indianola, IA
Occupation: Farmer before war. Lawyer, real estate agent, and bookkeeper after war.
Offices/Honors: Sheriff, Warren County, IA, 1849–51. Warren County Judge, 1851–59. Iowa Senate, 1860–61. Warren County Treasurer, 1865–73. Later served twelve years as Mayor of Indianola, IA.
Miscellaneous: Resided Indianola, Warren Co., IA
Buried: IOOF Cemetery, Indianola, IA
References: W. C. Martin. *History of Warren*

County, Iowa, from Its Earliest Settlement until 1908. Chicago, IL, 1908. *A Memorial and Biographical Record of Iowa.* Chicago, IL, 1896. *The History of Warren County, Iowa.* Des Moines, IA, 1879. Addison A. Stuart. *Iowa Colonels and Regiments.* Des Moines, IA, 1865. Pension File and Military Service File, National Archives. Obituary, *Indianola Herald,* Jan. 9, 1908. Obituary, *Cedar Rapids Evening Gazette,* Jan. 9, 1908. Benjamin F. Gue. *History of Iowa from the Earliest Times to the Beginning of the Twentieth Century.* New York City, NY, 1903.

Stephen Howard Henderson

Captain, Co. A, 24 IA Infantry, Sept. 17, 1862. Suffering from chronic diarrhea, he resigned Aug. 22, 1863. Colonel, 44 IA Infantry, June 1, 1864. Commanded Post of LaGrange (TN), District of West Tennessee, Department of the Tennessee, Aug. 1864. Honorably mustered out, Sept. 15, 1864. Battle honors: Champion's Hill, Vicksburg Campaign.

Born: March 4, 1829, Brownsville, TN
Died: April 15, 1899, Lincoln, NE
Occupation: Surveyor, lawyer, and Methodist clergyman after 1858
Miscellaneous: Resided Toulon, Stark Co., IL; Mitchell, Mitchell Co., IA; Clarksville, Butler Co., IA (1860); and Sabula, Jackson Co., IA, before war; and LeClaire, Scott Co., IA; Cedar Rapids, Linn Co., IA; Anamosa, Jones Co., IA; Marshalltown, Marshall Co., IA; Belle Plaine, Benton Co., IA (1870); Mount Vernon, Linn Co., IA; and Decorah, Winneshiek Co., IA, to 1877; and Lincoln, Lancaster Co., NE; Falls City, Richardson Co., NE (1880); Hastings, Adams Co., NE; Crete, Saline Co., NE; Stockville, Frontier Co., NE; and York, York Co., NE, after 1877. Brother of Bvt. Brig. Gen. Thomas J. Henderson (112 IL Infantry).
Buried: Greenwood Cemetery, York, NE (Division B, Lot 89)
References: Alfred T. Andreas. *History of the State of Nebraska.* Chicago, IL, 1882. Pension File

Above and below: **Both photographs, Paris Perrin Henderson (State Historical Society of Iowa, Des Moines).**

Stephen Howard Henderson (State Historical Society of Iowa, Des Moines).

and Military Service File, National Archives. Obituary, *Nebraska State Journal*, April 16, 1899. Thaddeus L. Smith, "The Twenty-Fourth Iowa Volunteers," *Annals of Iowa*, 3rd Series, Vol. 1, No. 1–3 (April–Oct. 1893). Michael A. Leeson. *Documents and Biography Pertaining to the Settlement and Progress of Stark County, Illinois.* Chicago, IL, 1887.

Josiah Thompson Herbert

Private, Co. C, 16 IA Infantry, Dec. 11, 1861. Quartermaster Sergeant, 16 IA Infantry, March 24, 1862. 1 Lieutenant, Adjutant, 16 IA Infantry, Nov. 14, 1862. Taken prisoner, Atlanta, GA, July 22, 1864. Confined Andersonville, GA. Paroled Sept. 28, 1864. Acting ADC and Provost Marshal, Staff of Brig. Gen. Giles A. Smith, 4 Division, 17 Army Corps, Army of the Tennessee, Feb. 10–July 3, 1865. Major, 16 IA Infantry, May 21, 1865. Lieutenant Colonel, 16 IA Infantry, June 27, 1865. *Colonel*, 16 IA Infantry, July 1, 1865. Honorably mustered out, July 19, 1865. Battle honors: Shiloh, Iuka, Atlanta Campaign (Atlanta), Campaign of the Carolinas.

Born: July 14, 1837, St. Clair Twp., Columbiana Co., OH

Died: March 30, 1875, St. Louis, MO

Occupation: Farmer and school teacher before war. Engaged in oil drilling business and as traveling pottery salesman after war.

Miscellaneous: Resided LeGrand, Marshall Co., IA; and East Liverpool, Columbiana Co., OH

Buried: Riverview Cemetery, East Liverpool, OH (Section 2, Lot 336)

References: Pension File and Military Service File, National Archives. *Report of the Proceedings of the Society of the Army of the Tennessee at the Ninth Annual Meeting.* Cincinnati, OH, 1877. Letters Received, Volunteer Service Branch, Adjutant General's Office, File H1650(VS)1863, National Archives.

Noel Byron Howard

1 Lieutenant, Co. I, 2 IA Infantry, May 28, 1861. Captain, Co. I, 2 IA Infantry, April 1, 1862. GSW hip, Corinth, MS, Oct. 4, 1862. Major, 2 IA Infantry, Nov. 15, 1862. Judge Advocate, Staff of Brig. Gen. Grenville M. Dodge, District of Corinth (2 Division) and Left Wing, 16 Army Corps, Army of the Tennessee, Jan. 1863–Jan. 1864. Lieutenant Colonel, 2 IA Infantry, May 2, 1864. GSW groin, Atlanta, GA, July 22, 1864. Colonel, 2 IA Infantry, Dec. 17, 1864. Commanded 1 Brigade, 4 Division, 15 Army Corps, Army of the Tennessee, March 1865. Honorably mustered out, July 12, 1865. Battle honors: Fort Donelson, Corinth, Atlanta Campaign (Dallas, Atlanta), Savannah Campaign, Campaign of the Carolinas.

Born: Sept. 11, 1837, Fairfax, VT

Died: Feb. 21, 1871, Chattanooga, TN

Education: Attended Norwich (VT) University

Occupation: School teacher

Offices/Honors: Clerk of Courts, Clinton Co., IA, 1867–70

Josiah Thompson Herbert (State Historical Society of Iowa, Des Moines).

Noel Byron Howard.

Above: Noel Byron Howard (Roger Davis Collection). *Below:* Noel Byron Howard (W.P. Egbert, Photographic Artist, Davenport, IA; Roger Davis Collection).

Miscellaneous: Resided Lyons, Clinton Co., IA; and Palatka, Putnam Co., FL, 1870–1871. Unsuccessful applicant for U.S. Military Academy appointment.

Noel Byron Howard (State Historical Society of Iowa, Des Moines).

Buried: Oakland Cemetery, Clinton, IA (Block 19, Lot 8)

References: William A. Ellis, editor. *History of Norwich University, 1819–1911.* Montpelier, VT, 1911. Addison A. Stuart. *Iowa Colonels and Regiments.* Des Moines, IA, 1865. Obituary, *Davenport Daily Gazette,* Feb. 27, 1871. Obituary, *Clinton Age,* March 3, 1871. Pension File and Military Service File, National Archives. Benjamin F. Gue. *History of Iowa from the Earliest Times to the Beginning of the Twentieth Century.* New York City, NY, 1903. John T. Bell. *Tramps and Triumphs of the Second Iowa Infantry, Briefly Sketched.* Des Moines, IA, 1961. *The History of Clinton County, Iowa.* Chicago, IL, 1879. U.S. Military Academy Cadet Application Papers, 1805–1866, File No. 141, 1853.

Daniel Henry Hughes

Colonel, 38 IA Infantry, Oct. 27, 1862. Commanded Post of New Madrid (MO), District of St. Louis, Department of the Missouri, Jan.–May 1863. Battle honors: Vicksburg Campaign.

Born: Sept. 11, 1830, Jefferson Co., NY
Died: Aug. 7, 1863, Port Hudson, LA (malarial poisoning/diarrhea)
Education: Graduated New York State Normal School, Albany, NY, 1849

Occupation: Lawyer and county judge
Miscellaneous: Resided Decorah, Winneshiek Co., IA
Buried: Phelps Cemetery, Decorah, IA
References: Charles H. Sparks. *History of Winneshiek County, with Biographical Sketches of Its Eminent Men.* Decorah, IA, 1877. W. E. Alexander. *History of Winneshiek and Allamakee Counties, Iowa.* Sioux City, IA, 1882. Edwin C. Bailey. *Past and Present of Winneshiek County, Iowa.* Chicago, IL, 1913. Addison A. Stuart. *Iowa Colonels and Regiments.* Des Moines, IA, 1865. David Wildman. *Iowa's Martyr Regiment: The Story of the Thirty-eighth Iowa Infantry.* Iowa City, IA, 2010. Pension File and Military Service File, National Archives. *An Historical Sketch of the State Normal College at Albany, N.Y., and a History of Its Graduates for Fifty Years.* Albany, NY, 1894.

Daniel Henry Hughes (State Historical Society of Iowa, Des Moines).

Jeremiah Williams Jenkins

Lieutenant Colonel, 31 IA Infantry, Sept. 16, 1862. GSW left leg, Vicksburg, MS, May 22, 1863. Commanded 2 Brigade, 1 Division, 15 Army Corps, Army of the Tennessee, Jan. 29–March 8, 1864 and April 1864. Shell wound right shoulder, Resaca, GA, May 13, 1864. *Colonel,* 31 IA Infantry, May 11, 1865. Honorably mustered out, June 27, 1865. Battle honors: Vicksburg Campaign, Lookout Mountain, Missionary Ridge, Ringgold, Atlanta Campaign (Resaca), Savannah Campaign, Campaign of the Carolinas (Columbia, Bentonville).
Born: Jan. 28, 1825, Warren Co., NY

Jeremiah Williams Jenkins (Campbell & Ecker, Photographers, 407 Main Street, Louisville, KY).

Died: June 24, 1903, Kansas City, MO
Education: Graduated New York State Normal School, Albany, NY, 1846
Occupation: Lawyer
Offices/Honors: Iowa Senate, 1856–60
Miscellaneous: Resided Maquoketa, Jackson Co., IA, before war; and Kansas City, MO, after war
Buried: Elmwood Cemetery, Kansas City, MO (Block D, Lot 356)
References: Harvey Reid, "Col. J. W. Jenkins, a Soldier and Pioneer," *Annals of Jackson County, Iowa.* No. 2. Maquoketa, IA, 1906. James W. Ellis. *History of Jackson County, Iowa.* Chicago, IL, 1910. Theodore S. Case, editor. *History of Kansas City, Missouri.* Syracuse, NY, 1888. Obituary, *Kansas City Star,* June 24, 1903. Obituary, *Cedar Rapids Republican,* June 28, 1903. "J.W. Jenkins," *Annals of Iowa,* 3rd Series, Vol. 6, No. 3 (Oct. 1903). Pension File and Military Service File, National Archives. Letters Received, Volunteer Service Branch, Adjutant General's Office, File J765(VS)1864, National Archives. *An Historical Sketch of the State Normal College at Albany, N.Y., and a History of Its Graduates for Fifty Years.* Albany, NY, 1894.

George Washington Kincaid

Colonel, 37 IA Infantry, Dec. 15, 1862. Commanded Post of Franklin (MO), District of St. Louis, Department of the Missouri, May–June 1863. Commanded Post of Alton (IL), Department of the Missouri, July–Aug. 1863. Commanded Alton (IL) Military Prison, Aug. 1863–Jan. 1864. Commanded 2 Brigade, District of Memphis,

Above: George Washington Kincaid (State Historical Society of Iowa, Des Moines). *Below:* George Washington Kincaid (State Historical Society of Iowa, Iowa City).

George Washington Kincaid (post-war) (State Historical Society of Iowa, Iowa City).

Occupation: Farmer

Miscellaneous: Resided Muscatine, Muscatine Co., IA

Buried: Greenwood Cemetery, Muscatine, IA (Bloomington Addition, Block 21, Lot 10)

References: *The United States Biographical Dictionary and Portrait Gallery of Eminent and Self-Made Men.* Iowa Volume. Chicago and New York, 1878. *Portrait and Biographical Album of Muscatine County, Iowa.* Chicago, IL, 1889. *The History of Muscatine County, Iowa.* Chicago, IL, 1879. Irving B. Richman, editor. *History of Muscatine County, Iowa, from the Earliest Settlements to the Present Time.* Chicago, IL, 1911. Benton McAdams, "Greybeards in Blue," *Civil War Times Illustrated,* Vol. 36, No. 7 (Feb. 1998). Pension File and Military Service File, National Archives. Harriet Stevens, editor. *The Graybeards: The Letters of Major Lyman Allen, of the 37th Regiment Iowa Volunteer Infantry.* Iowa City, IA, 1998. Letters Received, Volunteer Service Branch, Adjutant General's Office, File M2421(VS)1864, National Archives. Addison A. Stuart. *Iowa Colonels and Regiments.* Des Moines, IA, 1865.

Department of the Tennessee, June 22–Aug. 27, 1864. Honorably mustered out, May 24, 1865.

Born: April 24, 1812, West Union, Adams Co., OH

Died: Oct. 19, 1876, Muscatine, IA

William Henry Kinsman

2 Lieutenant, Co. B, 4 IA Infantry, Aug. 8, 1861. Captain, Co. B, 4 IA Infantry, Oct. 10, 1861. Captain, AAG, USV, Aug. 27, 1862. Resigned Sept. 17, 1862. Lieutenant Colonel, 23 IA Infantry, Sept. 19, 1862.

Above: William Henry Kinsman (A.J. Fox, Artist, Cor. Fourth and Olive Streets, St. Louis, MO; Roger D. Hunt Collection, USAMHI [RG98S-CWP58.43]). *Below:* William Henry Kinsman (A.J. Fox, Artist, Cor. Fourth and Olive Streets, St. Louis, MO; courtesy Steve Meadow).

William Henry Kinsman (State Historical Society of Iowa, Des Moines).

Colonel, 23 IA Infantry, Dec. 1, 1862. By sentence of court martial, April 1, 1863, upon a charge of "Positive and willful disobedience of the lawful commands of his superior officer," Brig. Gen. John W. Davidson, he was suspended from command for thirty days, to date from March 19, 1863. GSW abdomen and chest, Big Black River Bridge, MS, May 17, 1863. Battle honors: Pea Ridge, Pitman's Ferry, Big Black River Bridge.

Born: July 11, 1832, Cornwallis, Kings Co., Nova Scotia

Died: May 18, 1863, DOW Big Black River Bridge, MS

Education: Attended Claverack (NY) Academy

Occupation: Lawyer

Miscellaneous: Resided Council Bluffs, Pottawattamie Co., IA

Buried: Fairview Cemetery, Council Bluffs, IA (Section L)

References: Grenville M. Dodge, "Colonel William H. Kinsman," *Annals of Iowa*, 3rd Series, Vol. 5, No. 4 (Jan. 1902). Addison A. Stuart. *Iowa Colonels and Regiments.* Des Moines, IA, 1865. Dick Barton, "Charge at Big Black River," *America's Civil War*, Vol. 12, No. 4 (Sept. 1999). Military Service File, National Archives. Court-martial Case Files, 1809–1894, File LL-426, National Archives. *History of Pottawattamie County, Iowa.* Chicago, IL, 1883.

Bobby Roberts and Carl Moneyhon. *Portraits of Conflict: A Photographic History of Mississippi in the Civil War.* Fayetteville, AR, 1993. Benjamin F. Gue. *History of Iowa from the Earliest Times to the Beginning of the Twentieth Century.* New York City, NY, 1903. Lucy W. Stickney. *The Kinsman Family: Genealogical Record of the Descendants of Robert Kinsman of Ipswich, Mass.* Boston, MA, 1876.

Charles Woodman Kittredge

Captain, Co. F, 7 IA Infantry, July 24, 1861. GSW right groin, Belmont, MO, Nov. 7, 1861. Taken prisoner and paroled, Belmont, MO, Nov. 7, 1861. "Unable to perform the duties of an officer of the line," he resigned June 11, 1862. Colonel, 36 IA Infantry, Oct. 4, 1862. Commanded 1 Brigade, 13 Division, 13 Army Corps, District of Eastern Arkansas, Army of the Tennessee, Jan. 22–Feb. 8, 1863. Commanded 1 Brigade, 3 Division, Arkansas Expedition, 16 Army Corps, Department of the Tennessee, Aug. 4–Sept. 7, 1863. Commanded Post of Little Rock (AR), District of Little Rock, Department of Arkansas, June–July 1864. Although acquitted by court martial, March 8, 1865, on a charge of "Drunkenness on duty" preferred by disgruntled

Charles Woodman Kittredge.

Charles Woodman Kittredge (seated third from left, with Surgeon Colin G. Strong, Lt. Col. Francis M. Drake, and Major Augustus H. Hamilton, seated left to right; and Adjutant Stephen K. Mahon, Chaplain Michael H. Hare, and RQM Stevens W. Merrill, standing left to right) (Roger Davis Collection).

Lt. Col. Francis M. Drake in the aftermath of criticism following the regiment's disaster at Marks' Mills (AR), he was dismissed from the service when Major Gen. Joseph J. Reynolds, commanding the Department of Arkansas, disapproved the findings of the court martial. Judge Advocate General Joseph Holt approved the action of General Reynolds with the statement, "In the face of the evidence to Col. Kittredge's habitual intemperance during the last year, and his consequent unfitness to command, it is difficult to understand by what process of thought the Court arrived at their conclusions." The dismissal was, however, revoked June 4, 1865, and he was restored to his command, to date March 30, 1865, upon appeal to President Andrew Johnson. Honorably mustered out Aug. 24, 1865. Battle honors: Belmont, Shiloh, Helena, Advance upon Little Rock, Camden Expedition (Elkin's Ferry).

Born: Jan. 16, 1826, Portland, ME
Died: Sept. 29, 1897, Garden City, KS
Education: Attended Lyndon (VT) Academy
Occupation: Grocer before war. Wagon manufacturer and rancher after war.
Miscellaneous: Resided Ottumwa, Wapello Co., IA, before war; Chariton, Lucas Co., IA (1870); Florissant, El Paso Co., CO; and Cripple Creek, Teller Co., CO
Offices/Honors: Colorado House of Representatives, 1876–78
Buried: Evergreen Cemetery, Colorado Springs, CO (Block 25, Lot 14)
References: Addison A. Stuart. *Iowa Colonels and Regiments.* Des Moines, IA, 1865. Pension File and Military Service File, National Archives. Letters Received, Volunteer Service Branch, Adjutant General's Office, File I197(VS) 1862, National Archives. Court-martial Case Files, 1809–1894, File NN-3523, National Archives. Mabel T. Kittredge. *The Kittredge Family in America.* Rutland, VT, 1936. Benjamin F. Gue. *History of Iowa from the Earliest Times to the Beginning of the Twentieth Century.* New York City, NY, 1903. Henry I. Smith. *History of the Seventh Iowa Veteran Volunteer Infantry During the Civil War.* Mason City, IA, 1903.

Jed Lake

Lieutenant Colonel, 27 IA Infantry, Sept. 4, 1862. Commanded Post of LaGrange (TN), Left Wing, 16 Army Corps, Department of the Tennessee, June 1863. Convicted by court martial, Jan. 18, 1864, of "Grossly insubordinate conduct" toward his commanding officer, Colonel James I. Gilbert, he was sentenced to be severely reprimanded in the presence of officers of his regiment and suspended from rank and pay for three months. He was suspended from rank and pay for an additional two months, by court-martial verdict, March 31, 1865, upon additional charges preferred by Colonel Gilbert. Colonel, 27 IA Infantry, June 26, 1865. Honorably mustered out, Aug. 8, 1865. Battle honors: Advance upon Little Rock, Nashville, Mobile Campaign (Fort Blakely).

Born: Nov. 18, 1830, Virgil, Cortland Co., NY

Charles Woodman Kittredge (Mark Warren Collection).

Jed Lake (courtesy Mike Brackin).

Jed Lake (post-war) (State Historical Society of Iowa, Des Moines).

Died: June 7, 1914, Independence, IA
Education: Attended New York Central College, McGrawville, NY
Occupation: Lawyer
Offices/Honors: Iowa House of Representatives, 1862
Miscellaneous: Resided Independence, Buchanan Co., IA
Buried: Oakwood Cemetery, Independence, IA
References: Harry Church Chappell and Katharyn Joella Chappell. *History of Buchanan County, Iowa, and Its People.* Chicago, IL, 1914. Obituary, *Independence Bulletin-Journal,* June 11, 1914. *History of Buchanan County, Iowa.* Cleveland, OH, 1881. *A Memorial and Biographical Record of Iowa.* Chicago, IL, 1896. Pension File and Military Service File, National Archives. Letters Received, Adjutant General's Office, File G439(AGO)1865, National Archives. Letters Received, Volunteer Service Branch, Adjutant General's Office, File L538(VS)1865, National Archives. Court-martial Case Files, 1809–1894, Files LL-1724 and OO-549, National Archives. Benjamin F. Gue. *Biographies and Portraits of the Progressive Men of Iowa: Leaders in Business, Politics and the Professions.* Des Moines, IA, 1899. *The United States Biographical Dictionary and Portrait Gallery of Eminent and Self-Made Men.* Iowa Volume. Chicago and New York, 1878. Benjamin F. Gue. *History of Iowa from the Earliest Times to the Beginning of the Twentieth Century.* New York City, NY, 1903. "Jed Lake," *Annals of Iowa,* 3rd Series, Vol. 11, No. 6 (July 1914).

John Lubbers

Captain, Co. E, 26 IA Infantry, Sept. 30, 1862. Major, 26 IA Infantry, March 1, 1864. GSW right

Above: John Lubbers (State Historical Society of Iowa, Des Moines). *Below:* John Lubbers (Patrick B. Wolfe, editor. *Wolfe's History of Clinton County, Iowa.* Indianapolis, IN, 1911).

shoulder, Kenesaw Mountain, GA, June 15, 1864. Lieutenant Colonel, 26 IA Infantry, May 4, 1865. *Colonel,* 26 IA Infantry, June 19, 1865. Honorably mustered out, June 6, 1865. Battle honors: Atlanta Campaign (Kenesaw Mountain), Savannah Campaign, Campaign of the Carolinas.

Born: Dec. 22, 1825, Bremen, Germany
Died: Nov. 5, 1886, Lyons, IA (committed suicide by pistol shot)
Occupation: Farmer and hotelkeeper
Miscellaneous: Resided Lyons, Clinton Co., IA
Buried: Oakland Cemetery, Clinton, IA (Block 9, Lot 6, unmarked)
References: Patrick B. Wolfe, editor. *Wolfe's History of Clinton County, Iowa.* Indianapolis, IN, 1911. Obituary, *Clinton Age,* Nov. 12, 1886. Pension File and Military Service File, National Archives. *The Biographical Record of Clinton County, Iowa.* Chicago, IL, 1901.

Cyrus H. Mackey

Lieutenant Colonel, 33 IA Infantry, Aug. 13, 1862. Colonel, 33 IA Infantry, April 22, 1864. GSW right arm, Jenkins' Ferry, AR, April 30, 1864. Commanded 1 Brigade, 1 Division, 7 Army Corps, Department of Arkansas, Nov. 28, 1864–Jan. 7, 1865. Honorably mustered out, July 17, 1865. Battle honors: Helena, Advance upon Little Rock, Camden Expedition (Jenkins' Ferry), Mobile Campaign.

Born: Aug. 22, 1837, Lewiston, IL

Cyrus H. Mackey (post-war) (State Historical Society of Iowa, Des Moines).

Died: July 17, 1909, Sigourney, IA
Occupation: Lawyer
Offices/Honors: Iowa House of Representatives, 1880–82
Miscellaneous: Resided Sigourney, Keokuk Co., IA
Buried: Pleasant Grove Cemetery, Sigourney, IA
References: Edward H. Stiles. *Recollections and Sketches of Notable Lawyers and Public Men of Early Iowa.* Des Moines, IA, 1916. Obituary, *Keokuk County News,* July 22, 1909. Obituary, *Oskaloosa Daily Herald,* July 19, 1909. *The History of Keokuk County, Iowa.* Des Moines, IA, 1880. Addison A. Stuart. *Iowa Colonels and Regiments.* Des Moines, IA, 1865. Pension File and Military Service File, National Archives. Andrew F. Sperry. *History of the 33d Iowa Infantry Volunteer Regiment, 1863–6.* Edited by Gregory J.W. Urwin and Cathy Kunzinger Urwin. Fayetteville, AR, 1999. Benjamin F. Gue. *History of Iowa from the Earliest Times to the Beginning of the Twentieth Century.* New York City, NY, 1903. Letters Received, Volunteer Service Branch, Adjutant General's Office, File M3187(VS)1864, National Archives.

John Adair McDowell

Colonel, 6 IA Infantry, July 17, 1861. Commanded 1 Brigade, 5 Division, Army of the Tennessee, March 16–May 12, 1862. Commanded 2 Brigade, 5 Division, Army of the Tennessee, May 12–July 21, 1862. Commanded 2 Brigade, 5 Division, District of Memphis, Army of the Tennessee, July 21–Oct. 26, 1862. Commanded 2 Brigade, 1

Cyrus H. Mackey (B. Kihlholz, Photographic Artist, 29 North Fourth Street, St. Louis, MO; USAMHI [RG98S-CWP28.12]).

Above: John Adair McDowell (Addison A. Stuart. *Iowa Colonels and Regiments.* Des Moines, IA, 1865). *Below:* John Adair McDowell (post-war) (Massachusetts MOLLUS Collection, USAMHI [Vol. 56, p. 2779]).

Division, Right Wing, 13 Army Corps, Army of the Tennessee, Nov. 12–Dec. 18, 1862. Commanded 1 Brigade, 1 Division, 17 Army Corps, Army of the Tennessee, Dec. 18, 1862–Jan. 19, 1863. Commanded 1 Division, 16 Army Corps, Army of the Tennessee, Jan. 20–Feb. 19, 1863. Commanded 2 Brigade, 1 Division, 16 Army Corps, Army of the Tennessee, Feb. 1863. Suffering from hemorrhoids and chronic rheumatism which "have lately become so aggravated by the exposures incident to the camp life as to render him entirely unable to ride upon horseback or perform the duties which devolve upon him," he resigned March 12, 1863. Battle honors: Shiloh.

Born: July 22, 1825, Columbus, OH
Died: July 4, 1887, Huntsville, AL
Education: Graduated Kenyon College, Gambier, OH, 1846
Occupation: Civil engineer
Offices/Honors: Postmaster, Keokuk, IA, 1866–67. Mayor of Keokuk, IA, 1868. Superintendent of U.S. Public Buildings, Chicago, IL, 1878–80.
Miscellaneous: Resided Keokuk, Lee County, IA; and Chicago, IL, after 1873. Brother of Major Gen. Irvin McDowell.
Buried: Maple Hill Cemetery, Huntsville, AL (Block 11, Row 4)
References: Addison A. Stuart. *Iowa Colonels and Regiments.* Des Moines, IA, 1865. Alfred T. Andreas. *History of Chicago from the Earliest Period to the Present Time.* Chicago, IL, 1885. Obituary, *Chicago Daily Tribune,* July 5, 1887. Sophie Selden Rogers, Elizabeth Selden Lane, and Edwin Van Deusen Selden. *Selden Ancestry: A Family History Giving the Ancestors and Descendants of George Shattuck Selden and His Wife Elizabeth Wright Clark.* Oil City, PA, 1931. Calvin D. Cowles, compiler. *The Genealogy of the Cowles Families in America.* New Haven, CT, 1929. Military Service File, National Archives. Henry H. Wright. *A History of the Sixth Iowa Infantry.* Iowa City, IA, 1923. Obituary, *Keokuk Daily Gate City,* July 5, 1887. *The History of Lee County, Iowa.* Chicago, IL, 1879.

Samuel Merrill

Colonel, 21 IA Infantry, Aug. 22, 1862. Commanded 1 Brigade, 2 Division, Army of Southeast Missouri, Department of the Missouri, Jan. and March 1863. GSW both thighs, Big Black River Bridge, MS, May 17, 1863. Honorably discharged on account of physical disability from wounds, Sept. 25, 1863. Restored to his command, Dec. 21, 1863, and rejoined the regiment for duty, Feb. 11, 1864. Commanded 2 Brigade, 1 Division, 13 Army Corps, Department of the Gulf, Feb. 11–March 10, 1864. Resigned June 21, 1864, since "my regiment is now reduced to about 500 soldiers ... and a wound through both thighs a year since renders it still difficult to ride my horse with comfort." Battle honors: Hartville, Port Gibson, Big Black River Bridge.

Born: Aug. 7, 1822, Turner, ME
Died: Aug. 31, 1899, Pasadena, CA
Occupation: Banker and merchant
Offices/Honors: New Hampshire legislature, 1854–55. Iowa House of Representatives, 1860–61. Governor of Iowa, 1868–72.

Samuel Merrill (Bruce P. Bonfield Collection).

Miscellaneous: Resided Tamworth, Carroll Co., NH, to 1856; McGregor, Clayton Co., IA, 1856–68; Des Moines, Polk Co., IA, 1868–89; and Pasadena, Los Angeles Co., CA, after 1889
Buried: Woodland Cemetery, Des Moines, IA (Block 14, Lot 50)
References: *National Cyclopedia of American Biography.* William H. Fleming, "Governor Samuel Merrill," *Annals of Iowa*, 3rd Series, Vol. 5, No.5 (April 1902). *The United States Biographical Dictionary and Portrait Gallery of Eminent and Self-Made Men.* Iowa Volume. Chicago and New York, 1878. Charles R. Tuttle and Daniel S. Durrie. *An Illustrated History of the State of Iowa.* Chicago, IL, 1876. Addison A. Stuart. *Iowa Colonels and Regiments.* Des Moines, IA, 1865. "Samuel Merrill," *Annals of Iowa*, 3rd Series, Vol. 4, No. 3 (Oct. 1899). Obituary, *Los Angeles Herald*, Sept. 1, 1899. Obituary, *Cedar Rapids Evening Gazette*, Sept. 1, 1899. Pension File and Military Service File, National Archives. Letters Received, Volunteer Service Branch, Adjutant General's Office, File I701(VS) 1863, National Archives. George Crooke, compiler. *The Twenty-first Regiment of Iowa Volunteer Infantry: A Narrative of Its Experience in Active Service.* Milwaukee, WI, 1891. Benjamin F. Gue. *History of Iowa from the Earliest Times to the Beginning of the Twentieth Century.* New York City, NY, 1903.

William Edward Miller

Colonel, 28 IA Infantry, Oct. 10, 1862. Resigned March 13, 1863, since "I am entirely disabled to perform military duty by reason of piles and dyspepsia."
Born: Oct. 18, 1823, near Mount Pleasant, PA
Died: Nov. 9, 1896, Des Moines, IA
Occupation: Lawyer and judge
Offices/Honors: District Court Judge, 1859–62. Circuit Court Judge, 1869–70. Iowa Supreme Court, 1870–75 (Chief Justice, 1874–75).
Miscellaneous: Resided Iowa City, Johnson Co., IA; and Des Moines, Polk Co., IA, after 1873
Buried: Woodland Cemetery, Des Moines, IA (Block 17, Lot 95)
References: *Portrait and Biographical Album of Polk County, Iowa.* Chicago, IL, 1890. "Chief Justice Miller," *Annals of Iowa*, 1st Series, Vol. 12, No. 4 (Oct. 1874). *The History of Polk County, Iowa.* Des Moines, IA, 1880. Obituary, *Daily Iowa Capital*, Nov. 10, 1896. Obituary, *Des Moines Daily News*, Nov. 10, 1896. Edward H. Stiles. *Recollections and Sketches of Notable Lawyers and Public Men of Early Iowa.* Des Moines, IA, 1916. *The United States Biographical Dictionary and Portrait Gallery of Eminent and Self-Made Men.* Iowa Volume. Chicago and New York, 1878. Charles R. Tuttle and Daniel S. Durrie. *An Illustrated History of the State of Iowa.* Chicago, IL, 1876. Addison A. Stuart. *Iowa Colonels and Regiments.* Des Moines, IA, 1865. Pension File and Military Service File, National Archives. Benjamin F. Gue. *History of Iowa from the Earliest Times to the*

William Edward Miller (post-war) ("Chief Justice Miller," *Annals of Iowa*, **1st Series, Vol. 12, No. 4 (Oct. 1874)).**

Beginning of the Twentieth Century. New York City, NY, 1903.

Noah Webster Mills

2 Lieutenant, Co. D, 2 IA Infantry, May 27, 1861. Captain, Co. D, 2 IA Infantry, June 1, 1861. Major, 2 IA Infantry, June 22, 1862. Lieutenant Colonel, 2 IA Infantry, July 25, 1862. GSW foot, Corinth, MS, Oct. 4, 1862. *Colonel,* 2 IA Infantry, Oct. 8, 1862. Battle honors: Fort Donelson, Shiloh, Corinth.
   Born: June 21, 1834, Montgomery Co., IN
   Died: Oct. 12, 1862, DOW Corinth, MS
   Education: Attended Wabash College, Crawfordsville, IN
   Occupation: Lawyer and printer
   Miscellaneous: Resided Des Moines, Polk Co., IA. Son-in-law of Brig. Gen. Pleasant A. Hackleman (KIA Corinth).
   Buried: Woodland Cemetery, Des Moines, IA (Block 9, Lot 16)
   References: Addison A. Stuart. *Iowa Colonels and Regiments.* Des Moines, IA, 1865. Frank Moody Mills. *Something About the Mills Family and Its Collateral Branches with Autobiographical Reminiscences.* Sioux Falls, SD, 1911. "Memoir of Col. N.W. Mills," *Annals of Iowa,* 1st Series, Vol. 8, No. 3 (July 1870). *Portrait and Biographical Album of Polk County, Iowa.* Chicago, IL, 1890. Obituary, *Iowa State Register,* Oct. 15, 1862. Leonard Brown. *American Patriotism; or, Memoirs of "Common Men."* Des Moines, IA, 1869. Frank Moody Mills. *Early Days in a College Town and Wabash College in Early Days and Now.* Sioux Falls, SD, 1924. Pension File and Military Service File, National Archives. Benjamin F. Gue. *History of Iowa from the Earliest Times to the Beginning of the Twentieth Century.* New York City, NY, 1903. John T. Bell. *Tramps and Triumphs of the Second Iowa Infantry, Briefly Sketched.* Des Moines, IA, 1961.

Noah Webster Mills ("Memoir of Col. N.W. Mills," *Annals of Iowa,* 1st Series, Vol. 8, No. 3 [July 1870]).

Noah Webster Mills (William Schreck, Photographist, Union Block, Court Avenue, Des Moines, IA; Mark Warren Collection)

Samuel D. Nichols

1 Lieutenant, Co. C, 4 IA Infantry, July 20, 1861. Captain, Co. C, 4 IA Infantry, Jan. 1, 1862. Major, 4 IA Infantry, Oct. 19, 1863. Lieutenant Colonel, 4 IA Infantry, April 5, 1864. GSW right thigh, Atlanta, GA, July 22, 1864. Acting AIG, Staff of Major Gen. Peter J. Osterhaus, 15 Army Corps, Army of the Tennessee, Oct. 1864. Acting AIG, Staff of Major Gen. John A. Logan, 15 Army Corps, Army of the Tennessee, March–May 1865. *Colonel,* 4 IA Infantry, May 12, 1865. Honorably mustered out, July 24, 1865. Battle honors: Lookout Mountain, Missionary Ridge, Ringgold, Atlanta Campaign (Resaca, Dallas, Atlanta), Savannah Campaign, Campaign of the Carolinas (Columbia, Bentonville).
   Born: Feb. 8, 1835, near New Brunswick, NJ
   Died: Aug. 6, 1911, Los Angeles, CA
   Occupation: Lawyer
   Offices/Honors: Iowa Senate, 1876–84

Above: **Samuel D. Nichols (Photographed by Schreck & Barnett, Union Block, Court Avenue, Des Moines, IA).** *Below:* **Samuel D. Nichols (post-war) (State Historical Society of Iowa, Des Moines).**

Miscellaneous: Resided Panora, Guthrie Co., IA; and Los Angeles, CA, after 1908
Buried: Hollywood Memorial Park Cemetery, Hollywood, CA (Section 6, Lot 329)
References: *History of Guthrie and Adair Counties, Iowa.* Springfield, IL, 1884. Obituary, *Los Angeles Times*, Aug. 7, 1911. Pension File and Military Service File, National Archives. Letters Received, Volunteer Service Branch, Adjutant General's Office, File B1453(VS)1862, National Archives.

Nicholas Perczel

Colonel, 10 IA Infantry, Sept. 29, 1861. Commanded 2 Brigade, 2 Division, Army of the Mississippi, March 4–April 26, 1862. Commanded 2 Brigade, 3 Division, Army of the Mississippi, April 26–June 20, 1862. "Suffering from great general debility caused by chronic diarrhea and hemorrhoids, the result of exposure in camp and field, which disqualifies him for the duties of his office," he resigned Nov. 1, 1862. Battle honors: New Madrid, Island No. 10, Siege of Corinth, Iuka.
Born: Dec. 15, 1812, Bonyhad, Tolna County, Hungary
Died: March 14, 1904, Baja, Hungary
Other Wars: Hungarian War of Independence, 1848–49 (Colonel in Revolutionary Army)
Occupation: School teacher and merchant before war. Wine merchant in New York City after war.
Miscellaneous: Resided Davenport, Scott Co.,

Nicholas Perczel (Michael W. Waskul Collection).

IA; and England, before war. Returned to Hungary after 1870.

Buried: Roman Catholic Szent Rokus Cemetery, Baja, Hungary

References: Istvan Kornel Vida. *Hungarian Emigres in the American Civil War.* Jefferson, NC, 2012. Edmund Vasvary. *Lincoln's Hungarian Heroes: The Participation of Hungarians in the Civil War, 1861–1865.* Washington, D.C., 1939. Addison A. Stuart. *Iowa Colonels and Regiments.* Des Moines, IA, 1865. Eugene Pivany. *Hungarians in the American Civil War.* Cleveland, OH, 1913. Alma Gaul, "Walls CAN Talk: Home's Builder Fled Hungary, Became Civil War General," *Quad-City Times,* Nov. 3, 2013. Military Service File, National Archives. Stephen Beszedits, "The Life and Times of Nicholas Perczel," http://www.sk-szeged.hu/statikus_html/vasvary/newsletter/06jun/perczel.html.

Asbury Bateman Porter

Major, 1 IA Infantry, May 14, 1861. Honorably mustered out, Aug. 21, 1861. Colonel, 4 IA Cavalry, Dec. 5, 1861. Commanded 2 Brigade, 2 Division, Army of Southwest Missouri, May–June 1862. On Feb. 26, 1863, a communication, dated Jan. 15, 1863, and signed by 25 officers of the regiment, was addressed to the Secretary of War, asking for Porter's dismissal, accompanied by a list of eight charges, including intemperate habits and inefficiency. Recognizing Porter's absence from his command and wishing to avoid a court martial on the charges, the War Department chose to dismiss him by charging him with "Absence Without Authority," to be effective March 8, 1863. Meanwhile, Porter, suffering from "granular ophthalmia," submitted his resignation, March 5, 1863, citing "continued ill health for the past four months." His resignation was accepted March 19, 1863. Although Porter immediately asked for revocation of his dismissal, providing evidence that his absence from his regiment was authorized, the War Department refused to take action. However, a later review of his case, requested by his daughter, resulted in the determination, April 25, 1895, that acceptance of his resignation, March 19, 1863, nullified his dismissal, which was not announced until April 3, 1863. Battle honors: Wilson's Creek.

Born: June 20, 1808, Bourbon Co., KY
Died: July 30, 1885, Mount Pleasant, IA
Occupation: Merchant
Offices/Honors: Iowa Territory House of Representatives, 1838 and 1840–41
Miscellaneous: Resided Mount Pleasant, Henry Co., IA
Buried: Forest Home Cemetery, Mount Pleasant, IA (Section 17, Lot 47)
References: *The History of Henry County, Iowa.* Chicago, IL, 1879. Pension File and Military Service File, National Archives. Letters Received, Volunteer Service Branch, Adjutant General's Office, File P503(VS)1863, National Archives. Edward H. Stiles. *Recollections and Sketches of Notable Lawyers and Public Men of Early Iowa.* Des Moines, IA, 1916. Addison A. Stuart. *Iowa Colonels and Regiments.* Des Moines, IA, 1865. Benjamin F. Gue. *History of Iowa from the Earliest Times to the Beginning of the Twentieth Century.* New York City, NY, 1903. Eugene F. Ware. *The Lyon Campaign in Missouri: Being a History of the First Iowa Infantry.* Topeka, KS, 1907. William Forse Scott. *The Story of a Cavalry Regiment: The Career of the Fourth Iowa Veteran Volunteers.* New York and London, 1893.

John Walker Rankin

Captain, AQM, USV, Aug. 3, 1861. Resigned April 1, 1862. Colonel, 17 IA Infantry, April 7, 1862. His law partner, Samuel F. Miller, having been appointed to the U.S. Supreme Court, he resigned effective Sept. 3, 1862, to handle the workload of "the largest law business in Iowa." Major Gen. William S. Rosecrans forwarded his resignation, Sept. 27, 1862, with the notation, "His behavior upon the battle field at Iuka is reported to have been anything but creditable." Battle honors: Iuka.

Born: June 11, 1823, Warren, OH
Died: July 10, 1869, Keokuk, IA
Education: Graduated Washington (PA) College, 1841

Asbury Bateman Porter (post-war) (*The History of Henry County, Iowa.* **Chicago, IL, 1879**).

Occupation: Lawyer and judge
Offices/Honors: District Court Judge, 1857. Iowa Senate, 1858–60.
Miscellaneous: Resided Keokuk, Lee Co., IA
Buried: Oakland Cemetery, Keokuk, IA (Block 8, Lot 31)
References: *The History of Lee County, Iowa.* Chicago, IL, 1879. Addison A. Stuart. *Iowa Colonels and Regiments.* Des Moines, IA, 1865. Obituary, *Burlington Daily Hawk-Eye,* July 13, 1869. Edward H. Stiles. *Recollections and Sketches of Notable Lawyers and Public Men of Early Iowa.* Des Moines, IA, 1916. George Frazee. *Our Judges: Brief Sketches of the Judges Who Have Occupied the Bench in the First Judicial District of Iowa.* Burlington, IA, 1895. Nelson C. Roberts and S.W. Moorhead, editors. *Story of Lee County, Iowa.* Chicago, IL, 1914. *Biographical and Historical Catalogue of Washington and Jefferson College.* Cincinnati, OH, 1889. Pension File and Military Service File, National Archives. "Col. J.W. Rankin," *Iowa State Register,* Oct. 22, 1862. Letters Received, Volunteer Service Branch, Adjutant General's Office, File R148(VS)1862, National Archives. Benjamin F. Gue. *History of Iowa from the Earliest Times to the Beginning of the Twentieth Century.* New York City, NY, 1903.

James Pomeroy Sanford (post-war) (P. Datesman, Photographer, Marshalltown, IA; Roger D. Hunt Collection, USAMHI [RG98S-CWP207.16]).

John Walker Rankin (Massachusetts MOLLUS Collection, USAMHI [Vol. 130, p. 6660]).

James Pomeroy Sanford

1 Lieutenant, Co. H, 2 IA Cavalry, Sept. 4, 1861. Captain, Co. H, 2 IA Cavalry, Sept. 28, 1861. "Suffering horribly from gravel, so much so he cannot mount his horse," he resigned May 3, 1862. Colonel, 47 IA Infantry, June 4, 1864. Major Gen. Napoleon J.T. Dana, in his Aug. 15, 1864 inspection report of the Post of Helena, AR, made the following derogatory remark concerning Sanford and his regiment: "The colonel, although reported not to be alarmingly ill, has taken advantage of a slight sickness to abandon a regiment of cowards, one-third of whom are sick and some dying daily, to go North on a week's leave with the consciousness that it would be impossible for him to be back at its expiration." Honorably mustered out Sept. 28, 1864. Battle honors: Siege of Corinth.

Born: Nov. 11, 1832, Ovid, Seneca Co., NY
Died: June 1, 1896, Wheaton, IL
Education: Attended State University of Iowa, Iowa City, IA
Occupation: Universalist clergyman, lecturer, and world traveler
Miscellaneous: Resided Marshalltown, Marshall Co., IA; and Wheaton, DuPage Co., IL after 1891. On his grave marker is the sentiment, "In many lands I've roamed but no place like home."

Buried: St. Michael's Cemetery, Wheaton, IL (New Ground, Block 16, Lot 41)
References: *Portrait and Biographical Record of DuPage and Cook Counties, Illinois.* Chicago, IL, 1894. Obituary, *Wheaton Illinoisan,* June 5, 1896. Obituary, *Chicago Daily Tribune,* June 2, 1896. Obituary, *Daily Iowa Capital,* June 2, 1896. Obituary, *Cedar Rapids Evening Gazette,* June 4, 1896. *The History of Marshall County, Iowa.* Chicago, IL, 1878. *Soldiers' and Patriots' Biographical Album.* Chicago, IL, 1892. Mrs. Nettie Sanford. *History of Marshall County, Iowa.* Clinton, IA, 1867. Benjamin F. Gue. *History of Iowa from the Earliest Times to the Beginning of the Twentieth Century.* New York City, NY, 1903. Pension File and Military Service File, National Archives. *The War of the Rebellion: A Compilation of the Official Records of the Union and Confederate Armies.* (Vol. 41, Part 2, p. 716). Washington, D.C., 1893.

John Shane

Captain, Co. G, 13 IA Infantry, Oct. 28, 1861. Major, 13 IA Infantry, Oct. 30, 1861. GSW left shoulder, Shiloh, TN, April 6, 1862. Lieutenant Colonel, 13 IA Infantry, April 17, 1862. Colonel, 13 IA Infantry, April 18, 1863. Commanded 3 Brigade, 4 Division, 17 Army Corps, Army of the Tennessee, July 21, 1864. Honorably mustered out, Nov. 9, 1864. Battle honors: Shiloh, Corinth, Vicksburg Campaign, Meridian Expedition, Atlanta Campaign (Bald Hill, Atlanta).
Born: May 26, 1822, Bacon Ridge, Jefferson Co., OH
Died: Sept. 18, 1899, Vinton, IA
Education: Graduated Franklin College, New Athens, OH, 1845
Occupation: Lawyer and judge
Offices/Honors: Iowa Senate, 1872–76. District Court Judge, 1876–82.
Miscellaneous: Resided Vinton, Benton Co., IA
Buried: Evergreen Cemetery, Vinton, IA
References: John D. Nichols, "A Splendid Example: A Sketch of Judge Shane by an Old Time Contemporary," *Proceedings Crocker's Iowa Brigade at the Tenth Biennial Reunion.* Cedar Rapids, IA, 1902. Addison A. Stuart. *Iowa Colonels and Regiments.* Des Moines, IA, 1865. Benjamin F. Gue. *History of Iowa from the Earliest Times to the Beginning of the Twentieth Century.* New York City, NY, 1903. Obituary, *Daily Iowa Capital,* Sept. 18, 1899. "John Shane," *Annals of Iowa,* 3rd Series, Vol. 4, No. 3 (Oct. 1899). *Franklin College Register: Biographical and Historical.* Wheeling, WV, 1908. William W. Belknap. *History of the Fifteenth Regiment Iowa Veteran Volunteer Infantry, from October 1861 to August 1865.* Keokuk, IA, 1887. Pension File and Military Service File, National Archives. *The History of Benton County, Iowa.* Chicago, IL, 1878.

William Tuckerman Shaw

Colonel, 14 IA Infantry, Nov. 16, 1861. Taken prisoner, Shiloh, TN, April 6, 1862. Confined Madison, GA, and Richmond, VA. Paroled Oct. 12, 1862. Commanded Post of Columbus (KY), District of Columbus, 16 Army Corps, Army of the Tennessee, Dec. 1863. Commanded 2 Brigade, 3 Division, 16 Army Corps, Army of the Tennessee, Jan. 24–June 11, 1864. Commanded 3 Division, Right Wing, 16 Army Corps, Army of the Tennessee, July 31–Oct. 29, 1864. In Sept. 1864 Brig. Gen. William Dwight, 1 Division, 19 Army Corps, preferred charges against Shaw, alleging misbehavior before the enemy at the battle of Pleasant Hill, April 9, 1864, and violation of army regulations for sending a letter (subsequently published in an Iowa newspaper) containing "false, malicious and defamatory statements regarding officers and military operations." Despite the apparent truthfulness of Shaw's critical statements, the War Department issued an order, Oct. 4, 1864, dishonorably dismissing him "for violation of Army Regulations, and General Orders from the War Department, in regard to publications over his own signature in relation to the operations of the Armies of the United States." Claiming to be

John Shane (State Historical Society of Iowa, Des Moines).

unaware of any charges against him and referring to Major Gen. Andrew J. Smith's order of Oct. 29, 1864, relieving him from command and praising him as "an energetic, thorough and competent officer," Shaw appealed his dismissal to President Lincoln, who referred the matter to Judge Advocate General Joseph Holt. Although Holt recommended taking no action in the matter, the War Department finally issued an order, Dec. 23, 1865, revoking Shaw's dismissal and honorably discharging him to date, Nov. 16, 1864, based on his "efficiency and promptitude as a soldier," as shown by General Smith's order. Battle honors: Fort Donelson, Shiloh, Meridian Expedition, Red River Campaign (Pleasant Hill, Yellow Bayou).

Born: Sept. 22, 1822, Steuben, ME
Died: April 29, 1909, Anamosa, IA
Education: Attended Maine Wesleyan Seminary, Readfield, ME
Other Wars: Mexican War (Sergeant, Co. C, 2 KY Infantry)
Occupation: Banker, real estate dealer, and railroad builder
Offices/Honors: Iowa House of Representatives, 1876–78
Miscellaneous: Resided Anamosa, Jones Co., IA. He was a first cousin of the father of Colonel Robert Gould Shaw (54 MA Infantry).
Buried: Riverside Cemetery, Anamosa, IA
References: *In Memoriam: William Tuckerman Shaw, 1822–1909.* Anamosa, IA, 1910. Robert M.

William Tuckerman Shaw (Massachusetts MOLLUS Collection, USAMHI [Vol. 130, p. 6660]).

Corbit, editor. *History of Jones County, Iowa, Past and Present.* Chicago, IL, 1910. *The History of Jones County, Iowa.* Chicago, IL, 1879. Addison A. Stuart. *Iowa Colonels and Regiments.* Des Moines, IA, 1865. Benjamin F. Gue. *Biographies and Portraits of the Progressive Men of Iowa: Leaders in Business, Politics and the Professions.* Des Moines, IA, 1899. *The United States Biographical Dictionary and Portrait Gallery of Eminent and Self-Made Men.* Iowa Volume. Chicago and New York, 1878. Obituary, *Anamosa Eureka,* May 6, 1909. Obituary Circular, Whole No. 339, Iowa MOLLUS. Obituary, *Cedar Rapids Evening Gazette,* May 1, 1909. Obituary, *Monticello Express,* May 6, 1909. *Portrait and Biographical Record of Dubuque, Jones and Clayton Counties, Iowa.* Chicago, IL, 1894. *National Cyclopedia of American Biography.* Pension File and Military Service File, National Archives. Letters Received, Volunteer Service Branch, Adjutant General's Office, File S2289(VS)1864, National Archives. Lurton D. Ingersoll. *Iowa and the Rebellion.* Philadelphia, PA, 1866. William T. Shaw, "The Battle of Pleasant Hill," *Annals of Iowa,* 3rd Series, Vol. 3, Nos. 5–6 (April–July 1898). Benjamin F. Gue. *History of Iowa from the Earliest Times to the Beginning of the Twentieth Century.* New York City, NY, 1903.

William Hayes Silsby

1 Lieutenant, Co. I, 10 IA Infantry, Sept. 7, 1861. Captain, Co. A, 10 IA Infantry, Jan. 26, 1862. Acting

William Tuckerman Shaw (*In Memoriam: William Tuckerman Shaw, 1822–1909.* Anamosa, IA, 1910).

AIG, Staff of Brig. Gen. Charles L. Matthies, 3 Brigade, 3 Division, 15 Army Corps, Army of the Tennessee, April–May 1864. Lieutenant Colonel, 10 IA Infantry, Jan. 4, 1865. Shell wound, head and chest, Cox's Bridge, NC, March 20, 1865. *Colonel, 10 IA Infantry,* Aug. 7, 1865. Honorably mustered out, Aug. 15, 1865. Battle honors: Champion's Hill, Vicksburg Campaign, Savannah Campaign, Campaign of the Carolinas (Cox's Bridge).

Born: Aug. 31, 1822, Union Co., PA
Died: May 8, 1901, Salem, OR
Occupation: Farmer, justice of the peace, and postmaster before war. Furniture dealer and farmer after war.
Offices/Honors: Postmaster, Newton, IA, 1856 and 1857–61
Miscellaneous: Resided Newton, Jasper Co., IA; and Ashland, Jackson Co., OR, after 1893
Buried: Ashland Cemetery, Ashland, OR (Section 1, Lot 1)
References: *The History of Jasper County, Iowa.* Chicago, IL, 1878. Pension File and Military Service File, National Archives. Thomas W. Herringshaw, editor. *Herringshaw's Encyclopedia of American Biography of the Nineteenth Century.* Chicago, IL, 1906. Obituary, *Medford Mail,* May 17, 1901.

William Edward Small

Lieutenant Colonel, 10 IA Infantry, Sept. 10, 1861. Colonel, 10 IA Infantry, Nov. 2, 1862. Honorably discharged, Aug. 19, 1863, on account of physical disability due to "spasmodic affection of the muscular coating of the bowels." Battle honors: Siege of Corinth.

Born: Sept. 3, 1822, Portland, ME
Died: Feb. 12, 1907, Marshalltown, IA

Above: William Hayes Silsby (Peplow & Balch, Artists, Star Gallery, 221 Main Street, Memphis, TN; State Historical Society of Iowa, Des Moines). *Below:* William Hayes Silsby (State Historical Society of Iowa, Des Moines).

William Edward Small (State Historical Society of Iowa, Iowa City).

Occupation: Lumber merchant before war. Grain merchant after war.
Miscellaneous: Resided Iowa City, Johnson Co., IA, to 1864; Sabula, Jackson Co., IA, 1864–71; Brooklyn, Poweshiek Co., IA, 1871–1901; Marshalltown, Marshall Co., IA, 1901–07
Buried: Brooklyn Memorial Cemetery, Brooklyn, IA (Block 4, Lot 6)
References: Benjamin F. Gue. *Biographies and Portraits of the Progressive Men of Iowa: Leaders in Business, Politics and the Professions.* Des Moines, IA, 1899. Addison A. Stuart. *Iowa Colonels and Regiments.* Des Moines, IA, 1865. Obituary, *Marshalltown Evening Times-Republican,* Feb. 12, 1907. Obituary, *Annals of Jackson County, Iowa.* No. 5 (May 1907–Aug. 1908). Maquoketa, IA, 1908. Obituary, *Iowa City Daily Press,* Feb. 14, 1907. Obituary, *Cedar Rapids Daily Republican,* Feb. 14, 1907. Pension File and Military Service File, National Archives. Letters Received, Volunteer Service Branch, Adjutant General's Office, File H1041(VS) 1863, National Archives.

William Edward Small (post-war) (State Historical Society of Iowa, Des Moines).

Milo Smith

Colonel, 26 IA Infantry, Aug. 31, 1862. GSW right leg, Arkansas Post, AR, Jan. 11, 1863. Shell wound right shoulder, Walnut Hills, MS, May 19, 1863. Commanded 3 Brigade, 1 Division, 15 Army Corps, Army of the Tennessee, July 1863. Commanded 1 Brigade, 1 Division, 15 Army Corps, Army of the Tennessee, Dec. 14, 1863–Feb. 6, 1864; July 15–Aug. 19, 1864; and Aug. 23, 1864–Jan. 21, 1865. Resigned Jan. 28, 1865, since "my services are no longer needed by the Government. My regiment has three field officers and has less than 150 privates for duty." Battle honors: Arkansas Post, Vicksburg Campaign (Walnut Hills), Jackson Campaign, Lookout Mountain, Ringgold, Atlanta Campaign (Resaca, Dallas, Atlanta, Jonesborough), Savannah Campaign.
Born: Jan. 25, 1819, Shoreham, VT
Died: Feb. 28, 1904, Clinton, IA
Occupation: Civil engineer and railroad contractor before war. Civil engineer, banker, and dealer in agricultural implements after war.
Offices/Honors: Superintendent, Iowa Soldiers' Home, Marshalltown, IA, 1887–92
Miscellaneous: Resided Clinton, Clinton Co., IA; and Marshalltown, Marshall Co., IA, 1887–92. His third wife was the widow of Colonel James Baker (2 IA Infantry).
Buried: Springdale Cemetery, Clinton, IA (Section 10, Lot 1)
References: *The Biographical Record of Clinton County, Iowa.* Chicago, IL, 1901. *The United States Biographical Dictionary and Portrait Gallery of Eminent and Self-Made Men.* Iowa Volume. Chicago and New York, 1878. Obituary, *Cedar Rapids Evening Gazette,* March 1, 1904. "Milo Smith," *Annals of Iowa,* 3rd Series, Vol. 6, No. 5 (April 1904). Addison A. Stuart. *Iowa Colonels and Regiments.* Des Moines, IA, 1865. Pension File and Military Service File, National Archives. Letters Received, Volunteer Service Branch, Adjutant General's Office, File S1561(VS)1863, National Archives. Benjamin F. Gue. *History of Iowa from the Earliest Times to the Beginning of the Twentieth Century.* New York City, NY, 1903.

Milo Smith (courtesy Mike Brackin).

William Smyth

Colonel, 31 IA Infantry, Oct. 13, 1862. Suffering since Aug. 1863 from "an abscess under the pectoral muscle of the right side," he was discharged, Feb. 1, 1864, on account of physical disability, and for absence without leave, having failed to forward the required medical certificates. Upon producing evidence that he had provided the medical certificates, he was restored to his command, March 22, 1864. Commanded 3 Brigade, 1 Division, 15 Army Corps, Army of the Tennessee, Sept. 25–Oct. 31, 1864. Resigned Dec. 15, 1864, since "my regiment has only 490 officers and men and still has a Lt. Col. and Major," and also since "I am the only surviving parent of five children … who stand greatly in need of my more immediate personal care and attention." Battle honors: Arkansas Post, Vicksburg Campaign, Atlanta Campaign (Resaca, Dallas).

Born: Jan. 3, 1824, Eden, County Tyrone, Ireland

Died: Sept. 30, 1870, Marion, IA

Education: Attended State University of Iowa, Iowa City, IA

Occupation: Lawyer and judge

Offices/Honors: District Court Judge, 1853–57. U.S. House of Representatives: 1869–70.

Miscellaneous: Resided Marion, Linn Co., IA

William Smyth (Photographed by Jennings, 66 4th Street, Louisville, KY; Roger Davis Collection).

William Smyth (post-war) (The National Archives [B-3322]).

Buried: Oak Shade Cemetery, Marion, IA

References: Obituary, *Marion Weekly Register*, Oct. 6, 1870 and Oct. 20, 1870. *The History of Linn County, Iowa*. Chicago, IL, 1878. Obituary, *Davenport Daily Gazette*, Oct. 3, 1870. Luther A. Brewer and Barthinius L. Wick. *History of Linn County, Iowa, from Its Earliest Settlement to the Present Time*. Cedar Rapids, IA, 1911. Addison A. Stuart. *Iowa Colonels and Regiments*. Des Moines, IA, 1865. Edward H. Stiles. *Recollections and Sketches of Notable Lawyers and Public Men of Early Iowa*. Des Moines, IA, 1916. James L. Harrison, compiler. *Biographical Directory of the American Congress, 1774–1949*. Washington, D.C., 1950. Military Service File, National Archives. Letters Received, Volunteer Service Branch, Adjutant General's Office, Files I557(VS)1864 and I633(VS)1864, National Archives. Benjamin F. Gue. *History of Iowa from the Earliest Times to the Beginning of the Twentieth Century*. New York City, NY, 1903.

William Stubbs

Captain, Co. G, 8 IA Infantry, Sept. 20, 1861. Taken prisoner, Shiloh, TN, April 6, 1862. Confined Madison, GA, and Richmond, VA. Paroled Oct. 12, 1862. Major, 8 IA Infantry, July 28, 1863. *Colonel,* 8 IA Infantry, July 1, 1865. Commanded Post of Tuskegee (AL), District of Montgomery, Department of Alabama, Sept.–Oct. 1865. Honorably mustered out, Nov. 14, 1865. Battle honors: Shiloh,

William Stubbs (State Historical Society of Iowa, Des Moines).

Samuel William Summers (State Historical Society of Iowa, Des Moines).

Jackson Campaign, Forrest's Attack on Memphis, Mobile Campaign (Spanish Fort).
Born: 1831?, London, England
Died: Dec. 31, 1901, Chicago, IL
Other Wars: Mexican War (Private, Co. F, 4 U.S. Infantry)
Occupation: Express company messenger and postal clerk
Miscellaneous: Resided Iowa County, IA; and Chicago, IL
Buried: Graceland Cemetery, Chicago, IL (Section I, Lot 188)
References: Pension File and Military Service File, National Archives. Obituary, *Chicago Daily Tribune*, Jan. 1, 1902. *The History of Iowa County, Iowa*. Des Moines, IA, 1881. Frazar Kirkland. *The Pictorial Book of Anecdotes and Incidents of the War of the Rebellion*. Hartford, CT, 1867.

Samuel William Summers

Colonel, 7 IA Cavalry, July 25, 1863. Commanded Post of Omaha (NE), District of Nebraska, Department of the Missouri, Sept.–Dec. 1863. Commanded Post of Omaha (NE), District of Nebraska, Department of Kansas, Jan.–April 1864 and June–July 1864. Commanded District of Nebraska, Department of Kansas, Feb. 1864. Commanded Post of Fort Kearny, District of Nebraska, Department of Kansas, July–Aug. 1864. Commanded Post of Fort Cottonwood, Eastern Sub-District of Nebraska, Department of Kansas, Sept. 1864–Jan. 1865. Honorably mustered out, Jan. 31, 1865. Battle honors: Operations Against Indians in Nebraska Territory.
Born: March 8, 1820, Fairfax Co., VA
Died: April 10, 1890, Ottumwa, IA (killed in carriage accident)
Occupation: Lawyer
Miscellaneous: Resided Ottumwa, Wapello Co., IA
Buried: Ottumwa Cemetery, Ottumwa, IA (Block J, Lot 387)
References: Edward H. Stiles. *Recollections and Sketches of Notable Lawyers and Public Men of Early Iowa*. Des Moines, IA, 1916. *The History of Wapello County, Iowa*. Chicago, IL, 1878. Pension File and Military Service File, National Archives. Addison A. Stuart. *Iowa Colonels and Regiments*. Des Moines, IA, 1865. Dean Knudsen, "Southern-born Union Colonel," *Civil War Times Illustrated*, Vol. 33, No. 2 (May/June 1994). Obituary, *Davenport Daily Republican*, April 12, 1890. Obituary, *Cedar Rapids Evening Gazette*, April 11, 1890. Eugene F. Ware. *The Indian War of 1864*. New York City, NY, 1960. Benjamin F. Gue. *History of Iowa from the Earliest Times to the Beginning of the Twentieth Century*. New York City, NY, 1903.

William M. Gray Torrence

Captain, Co. A, 1 IA Cavalry, July 30, 1861. Major, 1 IA Cavalry, Oct. 31, 1861. Commanded Post of Sedalia (MO), Department of the Missouri, Jan. 1862. Commanded Warrensburg (MO), District of Central Missouri, Department of the Missouri, April 1862. Resigned May 3, 1862, since "I am fully satisfied my present circumstances, both moral and financial, forbid the continuation of the service in the state of Missouri, my present field of labor." Lieutenant Colonel, 30 IA Infantry, Sept. 23, 1862. Colonel, 30 IA Infantry, May 29, 1863. GSW head and chest, Cherokee Station, AL, Oct. 21, 1863. Battle honors: Arkansas Post, Vicksburg Campaign, Operations on the Memphis and Charleston Railroad (Cherokee Station).

Born: Sept. 1, 1824, Westmoreland Co., PA
Died: Oct. 21, 1863, KIA Cherokee Station, AL
Other Wars: Mexican War (1 Lieutenant, Co. G, 1 KY Cavalry)
Occupation: School teacher
Miscellaneous: Resided Keokuk, Lee Co., IA
Buried: Oakland Cemetery, Keokuk, IA (Block 7, Lot 27)
References: Addison A. Stuart. *Iowa Colonels and Regiments*. Des Moines, IA, 1865. Robert M. Torrence. *Torrence and Allied Families*. Philadelphia, PA, 1938. Pension File and Military Service File, National Archives. Sylvester E. Parker, "The Death of Colonel Torrence," *Washington National Tribune*, April 10, 1884. Obituary, *Burlington Weekly Hawk-Eye*, Oct. 31, 1863. Benjamin F. Gue. *History of Iowa from the Earliest Times to the Beginning of the Twentieth Century*. New York City, NY, 1903. James A. Fowler and Miles M. Miller. *History of the 30th Iowa Infantry Volunteers*. Mediapolis, IA, 1908. Charles H. Lothrop. *A History of the First Regiment Iowa Cavalry Veteran Volunteers*. Lyons, IA, 1890.

John Quincy Wilds

Captain, Co. A, 13 IA Infantry, Oct. 18, 1861. Suffering from acute bronchitis, he resigned April 19, 1862. Lieutenant Colonel, 24 IA Infantry, Sept. 17, 1862. Colonel, 24 IA Infantry, June 18, 1864. GSW left arm, Cedar Creek, VA, Oct. 19, 1864. Bvt. Colonel, USV, March 13, 1865, for conspicuous gallantry at Cedar Creek, VA, Oct. 19, 1864. Battle honors: Port Gibson, Champion's Hill, Vicksburg Campaign, Jackson Campaign, Operations in the Teche Country (LA), Shenandoah Valley Campaign (Winchester, Fisher's Hill, Cedar Creek).

Born: Oct. 24, 1822, Fort Littleton, PA
Died: Nov. 18, 1864, DOW Winchester, VA
Occupation: Merchant and land speculator
Offices/Honors: Postmaster, Fort Littleton, PA, 1851–53
Miscellaneous: Resided Mount Vernon, Linn Co., IA. His wife and his two children all died in the period, Sept.–Nov. 1864.

William M. Gray Torrence (State Historical Society of Iowa, Des Moines).

John Quincy Wilds (Nicholas P. Picerno Collection).

Buried: Mount Vernon Cemetery, Mount Vernon, IA

References: James P.C. Poulton, "Col. John Q. Wilds," *Annals of Iowa*, 1st Series, Vol. 4, No. 3 (July 1866). Charles R. Tuttle and Daniel S. Durrie. *An Illustrated History of the State of Iowa.* Chicago, IL, 1876. Henry H. Rood, "Sketches of the Thirteenth Iowa," *War Sketches and Incidents Iowa Commandery MOLLUS.* Des Moines, IA, 1893. Bobby Roberts and Carl Moneyhon. *Portraits of Conflict: A Photographic History of Mississippi in the Civil War.* Fayetteville, AR, 1993. Obituary, *Linn County Patriot*, Dec. 1, 1864. Obituary, *Burlington Daily Hawk-Eye*, Dec. 8, 1864. Thaddeus L. Smith, "The Twenty-Fourth Iowa Volunteers," *Annals of Iowa*, 3rd Series, Vol. 1, No. 1–3 (April–Oct. 1893). Charles L. Longley, "The Twenty-Fourth Iowa Volunteers," *Annals of Iowa*, 3rd Series, Vol. 1, No. 7 (Oct. 1894). Military Service File, National Archives. Letters Received, Volunteer Service Branch, Adjutant General's Office, File I569(VS)1864, National Archives.

John Quincy Wilds (Swymmer's Gallery, 147 Canal Street, New Orleans, LA; Roger Davis Collection).

Bartholomew William Wilson

Captain, Co. B, 28 IA Infantry, Oct. 10, 1862. Lieutenant Colonel, 28 IA Infantry, April 7, 1863. Commanded 2 Brigade, 3 Division, 13 Army Corps,

Bartholomew William Wilson (J.A. Sheldon, No. 101 Canal Street, New Orleans, LA).

Department of the Gulf, April 1864. GSW left thigh, Cedar Creek, VA, Oct. 19, 1864. *Colonel*, 28 IA Infantry, June 15, 1865. Honorably mustered out, July 31, 1865. Bvt. Colonel, USV, March 13, 1865, for conspicuous gallantry at Cedar Creek, VA, Oct. 19, 1864. Battle honors: Red River Campaign, Shenandoah Valley Campaign (Winchester, Fisher's Hill, Cedar Creek).

Born: June 17, 1827, near Brownstown, IN

Died: March 4, 1907, Chelsea, IA

Other Wars: Mexican War (Private, Co. G, U.S. Mounted Rifles). Received "Certificate of Merit" from President Polk for "distinguished services" at the battle of Belen Gate, Mexico, Sept. 13, 1847 (War Department, Adjutant General's Office, General Order No. 32, June 26, 1848).

Occupation: Farmer and stock raiser

Miscellaneous: Resided Chelsea, Tama Co., IA; and Jefferson Twp., Poweshiek Co., IA. As a tribute to his bravery, one obituary noted, "No braver little man ever rode on horseback."

Buried: Rector Cemetery, near Chelsea, IA

References: *The History of Poweshiek County, Iowa.* Des Moines, IA, 1880. Pension File and Military Service File, National Archives. Frank W. Blackmar, editor. *Kansas: A Cyclopedia of State History.* Chicago, IL, 1912. Obituary, *Belle Plain Union*, March 6, 1907. Obituary, *Tama Herald*, March 7 and 14, 1907. Obituary, *Cedar Rapids Daily Republican*, March 5, 1907. *History of Tama County, Iowa.* Springfield, IL, 1883.

David Stokely Wilson

Colonel, 6 IA Cavalry, Jan. 9, 1863. Commanded Post of Sioux City (IA), District of Dakota, Department of the Northwest, Oct.–Nov. 1863. Commanded District of Dakota, Department of the Northwest, Nov. 1863. Commanded Post of Sioux City (IA), District of Iowa, Department of the Northwest, Dec. 1863–April 1864. "Incapable of performing the duties of his office in consequence of inguinal hernia and rheumatism," he resigned June 21, 1864. Battle honors: Expedition Against Indians in Dakota (White Stone Hill).
Born: March 18, 1825, Steubenville, OH
Died: April 1, 1881, Dubuque, IA
Other Wars: Mexican War (2 Lieutenant, Morgan's Independent Co., IA Infantry)
Occupation: Lawyer and judge
Offices/Honors: Iowa Territory House of Representatives, 1845–46. Iowa Senate, 1858–62. Circuit Court Judge, 1872. District Court Judge, 1872–78.
Miscellaneous: Resided Dubuque, Dubuque Co., IA
Buried: Linwood Cemetery, Dubuque, IA (Section 1-E, Lot 1249)
References: Edward H. Stiles. *Recollections and Sketches of Notable Lawyers and Public Men of Early Iowa*. Des Moines, IA, 1916. Obituary, *Dubuque Daily Times*, April 2, 1881. *The History of Dubuque County, Iowa*. Chicago, IL, 1880. *The United States Biographical Dictionary and Portrait Gallery of Eminent and Self-Made Men*. Iowa Volume. Chicago and New York, 1878. Charles R. Tuttle and Daniel S. Durrie. *An Illustrated History of the State of Iowa*. Chicago, IL, 1876. Addison A. Stuart. *Iowa Colonels and Regiments*. Des Moines, IA, 1865. Military Service File, National Archives. Franklin T. Oldt and Patrick J. Quigley, editors. *History of Dubuque County, Iowa*. Chicago, IL, 1911. Letters Received, Volunteer Service Branch, Adjutant General's Office, File W1645(VS)1864, National Archives. Benjamin F. Gue. *History of Iowa from the Earliest Times to the Beginning of the Twentieth Century*. New York City, NY, 1903.

David Stokely Wilson (Newberry's Photographs, Camp Hendershott, IA).

David Stokely Wilson (G. G. Johnson's Fine Art Gallery, Cor. Main and Fifth Streets, Dubuque, IA; Roger D. Hunt Collection, USAMHI [RG 98S-CWP207.14]).

Joseph Jackson Woods

Colonel, 12 IA Infantry, Nov. 25, 1861. GSW left leg and right hand, Shiloh, TN, April 6, 1862. Commanded 3 Brigade, 3 Division, 15 Army Corps, Army of the Tennessee, April 3–May 2, 1863 and June 1–Sept. 24, 1863. Commanded 3 Brigade, 1 Division, 16 Army Corps, Right Wing, Army of the Tennessee, June 11–Oct. 19, 1864 and Nov. 3–22, 1864. Commanded 1 Division, 16 Army Corps, Right Wing, Army of the Tennessee, Oct. 19–Nov. 3, 1864. Honorably mustered out, Nov. 22, 1864. Battle honors: Fort Donelson, Shiloh, Vicksburg Campaign, Jackson Campaign, Tupelo, Price's Missouri Expedition.
Born: Jan. 11, 1823, Brown Co., OH
Died: Sept. 27, 1889, Montana, KS
Education: Graduated U.S. Military Academy, West Point, NY, 1847

Above: Joseph Jackson Woods (Walter's Photographic Studio, Manchester, IA). *Below:* Joseph Jackson Woods (courtesy Everitt Bowles).

Other Wars: Mexican War (1 Lieutenant, 1 U.S. Artillery)

Occupation: Farmer, stock raiser, and newspaper editor

Offices/Honors: Kansas House of Representatives, 1872 and 1875

Miscellaneous: Resided Maquoketa, Jackson Co., IA, to 1869; and Montana, Labette Co., KS, after 1869

Buried: Oakwood Cemetery, Parsons, Labette Co., KS

References: David W. Reed, "Life of Col. Joseph J. Woods," *Annals of Jackson County, Iowa.* No. 1. Maquoketa, IA, 1905. James W. Ellis. *History of Jackson County, Iowa.* Chicago, IL, 1910. Addison A. Stuart. *Iowa Colonels and Regiments.* Des Moines, IA, 1865. Alfred T. Andreas. *History of the State of Kansas.* Chicago, IL, 1883. David W. Reed. *Campaigns and Battles of the Twelfth Regiment Iowa Veteran Volunteer Infantry.* Evanston, IL, 1903. *Twenty-First Annual Reunion of the Association of the Graduates of the United States Military Academy at West Point, New York.* Saginaw, MI, 1890. Pension File and Military Service File, National Archives. *Fourth Reunion of the Twelfth Iowa Veteran Volunteer Infantry.* Norfolk, NE, 1892. George W. Cullum. *Biographical Register of the Officers and Graduates of the U.S. Military Academy.* Third Edition. Boston, MA, 1891. Benjamin F. Gue. *History of Iowa from the Earliest Times to the Beginning of the Twentieth Century.* New York City, NY, 1903. Nelson Case. *History of Labette County, Kansas, and Representative Citizens.* Chicago, IL, 1901.

William Hord Worthington

Colonel, 5 IA Infantry, July 15, 1861. Commanded 2 Brigade, 2 Division, Department of the Missouri, Nov.–Dec. 1861. Commanded 2 Brigade,

William Hord Worthington (State Historical Society of Iowa, Des Moines).

2 Division, Army of the Mississippi, Feb. 23–March 4, 1862. Commanded 1 Brigade, 2 Division, Army of the Mississippi, March 4–April 24, 1862. GSW head, near Corinth, MS, May 22, 1862. Battle honors: New Madrid, Island No. 10, Siege of Corinth.

Born: Nov. 2, 1828, Harrodsburg, KY
Died: May 22, 1862, near Corinth, MS (accidentally shot by a Union picket, Mathew Hailey, Co. A, 42 IL Infantry, while acting as general officer of the day)
Education: Attended Bacon College, Harrodsburg, KY
Occupation: Lawyer
Miscellaneous: Resided Keokuk, Lee Co., IA
Buried: Oakland Cemetery, Keokuk, IA (Block 21, Lot 10)
References: Addison A. Stuart. *Iowa Colonels and Regiments*. Des Moines, IA, 1865. Edward H. Stiles. *Recollections and Sketches of Notable Lawyers and Public Men of Early Iowa*. Des Moines, IA, 1916. Obituary, *Burlington Daily Hawk-Eye*, May 26, 1862. Pension File and Military Service File, National Archives. Samuel H.M. Byers. *With Fire and Sword*. New York City, NY, 1911.

John Morris Young

Captain, Co. C, 1 Battalion, NE Cavalry, Oct. 3, 1861. Unit designation changed to Co. C, Curtis Horse, Dec. 20, 1861, and to Co. C, 5 IA Cavalry, June 25, 1862. Major, 5 IA Cavalry, Nov. 1, 1862.

Above: John Morris Young (State Historical Society of Iowa, Des Moines). *Below:* John Morris Young (State Historical Society of Iowa, Des Moines).

John Morris Young (Morse's Gallery of the Cumberland, 25 Cedar Street, Opposite Commercial Hotel, Nashville, TN).

Topographical Engineer, Staff of Colonel William W. Lowe, 3 Division, Cavalry Corps, Army of the Cumberland, May 22–July 23, 1864. Commanded 1 Brigade, 3 Division, Cavalry Corps, Army of the Cumberland, Aug. 26–Sept. 5, 1864. Provost Marshal, Staff of Major Gen. James H. Wilson, Cavalry Corps, Military Division of the Mississippi, Dec. 14, 1864–March 5, 1865. Colonel, 5 IA Cavalry, Jan. 25, 1865. Honorably mustered out Aug. 11, 1865. Battle honors: Atlanta Campaign (Jonesborough), Nashville Campaign (Duck River Crossing), Wilson's Raid.

Born: March 26, 1833, Gosport, IN
Died: Oct. 24, 1906, Salt Lake City, UT
Occupation: Farmer before war. Mining superintendent and lawyer after war.
Offices/Honors: Missouri House of Representatives, 1869–71
Miscellaneous: Resided New York City, NY; Keokuk, Lee Co., IA; and Page Co., IA, before war; Newton Co., MO; Oronogo, Jasper Co., MO; and Salt Lake City, UT, after war
Buried: Mount Olivet Cemetery, Salt Lake City, UT (Section O, Lot 209)
References: Pension File and Military Service File, National Archives. Obituary, *Salt Lake Herald*, Oct. 25, 1906. Marvin L. Van Gilder. *Jasper County: The First Two Hundred Years.* N.p., 1995. Joel T. Livingston. *A History of Jasper County, Missouri, and Its People.* Chicago, IL, 1912. Alfred T. Andreas. *History of the State of Nebraska.* Chicago, IL, 1882. Letters Received, Volunteer Service Branch, Adjutant General's Office, Files Y68(VS)1865 and Y29(VS)1869, National Archives.

Minnesota

Regiments

1st Mounted Rangers

Samuel McPhaill	Dec. 30, 1862	Mustered out Dec. 3, 1863

2nd Cavalry

Robert N. McLaren	Jan. 14, 1864	Mustered out Nov. 17, 1865, **Bvt. Brig. Gen., USV**

1st Heavy Artillery

William Colvill, Jr.	April 26, 1865	Resigned July 13, 1865, **Bvt. Brig. Gen., USV**
Luther L. Baxter	Aug. 12, 1865	Mustered out Sept. 27, 1865

1st Infantry

Willis A. Gorman	April 29, 1861	Promoted **Brig. Gen., USV,** Sept. 7, 1861
Napoleon J.T. Dana	Oct. 2, 1861	Promoted **Brig. Gen., USV,** Feb. 3, 1862
Alfred Sully	March 4, 1862	Promoted **Brig. Gen., USV,** Sept. 26, 1862
George N. Morgan	Nov. 14, 1862	Resigned May 5, 1863, **Bvt. Brig. Gen., USV**
William Colvill, Jr.	June 11, 1863	Mustered out May 5, 1864, **Bvt. Brig. Gen., USV**
Mark W. Downie	April 22, 1865	Mustered out July 14, 1865

2nd Infantry

Horatio P. Van Cleve	July 22, 1861	Promoted **Brig. Gen., USV,** March 21, 1862
James George	March 21, 1862	Mustered out June 29, 1864
Judson W. Bishop	March 26, 1865	Mustered out July 11, 1865, **Bvt. Brig. Gen., USV**

3rd Infantry

Henry C. Lester	Nov. 15, 1861	Dismissed Dec. 1, 1862
Chauncey W. Griggs	Dec. 2, 1862	Resigned July 19, 1863
Christopher C. Andrews	Aug. 9, 1863	Promoted **Brig. Gen., USV,** Jan. 5, 1864
Hans Mattson	April 26, 1864	Mustered out Sept. 2, 1865

4th Infantry

John B. Sanborn	Dec. 23, 1861	Promoted **Brig. Gen., USV,** Aug. 4, 1863
John E. Tourtellotte	Oct. 5, 1864	Resigned June 21, 1865, **Bvt. Brig. Gen., USV**

5th Infantry

Rudolph von Borgersrode	April 30, 1862	Resigned Aug. 31, 1862
Lucius F. Hubbard	Aug. 31, 1862	Mustered out Sept. 6, 1865, **Bvt. Brig. Gen., USV**

6th Infantry

Anderson D. Nelson	Aug. 16, 1862	Resigned Aug. 22, 1862
William Crooks	Aug. 23, 1862	Resigned Oct. 28, 1864
John T. Averill	Nov. 22, 1864	Mustered out Sept. 28, 1865, **Bvt. Brig. Gen., USV**

7th Infantry

Stephen Miller	Aug. 24, 1862	Promoted **Brig. Gen., USV,** Oct. 26, 1863

William R. Marshall	Nov. 6, 1863	Mustered out Aug. 16, 1865, **Bvt. Brig. Gen., USV**

8th Infantry

Minor T. Thomas	Aug. 24, 1862	Mustered out July 11, 1865, **Bvt. Brig. Gen., USV**

9th Infantry

Alexander Wilkin	Aug. 24, 1862	KIA July 14, 1864
Josiah F. Marsh	Aug. 5, 1864	Mustered out Aug. 24, 1865

10th Infantry

James H. Baker	Nov. 17, 1862	Mustered out Oct. 21, 1865, **Bvt. Brig. Gen., USV**

11th Infantry

James Gilfillan	Nov. 3, 1864	Mustered out June 26, 1865

Biographies

Luther Loren Baxter

Captain, Co. A, 4 MN Infantry, Sept. 30, 1861. Commanded Post of Fort Ridgely (MN), Department of the Missouri, Oct. 16, 1861–March 17, 1862. Major, 4 MN Infantry, April 18, 1862. Resigned Sept. 3, 1862, "having been unfit for duty nearly all of the time for the last two months and being now very much debilitated by reason of chronic diarrhea." Major, 1 MN Heavy Artillery, Nov. 25, 1864. Lieutenant Colonel, 1 MN Heavy Artillery, Feb. 22, 1865. Chief of Artillery, Post of Chattanooga (TN), Department of the Cumberland, April 4–Sept. 12, 1865. Colonel, 1 MN Heavy Artillery, Aug. 12, 1865. Honorably mustered out, Sept. 27, 1865. Battle honors: Nashville.

Born: June 8, 1832, Cornwall, VT
Died: May 22, 1915, Fergus Falls, MN

Luther Loren Baxter (Minnesota Historical Society [por 16713 p2]).

Education: Attended Norwich (VT) University
Occupation: Lawyer and judge
Offices/Honors: Minnesota Senate, 1865–68 and 1870–74. Minnesota House of Representatives, 1869, 1875, and 1879–82. District Court Judge, 1885–1911.
Miscellaneous: Resided Geneva, Walworth Co., WI, 1854–57; Chaska, Carver Co., MN, 1857–62 and 1868–82; Shakopee, Scott Co., MN, 1862–68; and Fergus Falls, Otter Tail Co., MN, 1882–1915
Buried: Mount Pleasant Cemetery, Chaska, MN
References: *Illustrated Album of Biography of the Famous Valley of the Red River of the North and the Park Regions.* Chicago,

Luther Loren Baxter (Captain, Co. A, 4 MN Infantry, left, with 1 Lt. Robert B. Young, center, and 2 Lt. Charles Johnson, right) (USAMHI [RG98S-CWP208.49]).

IL, 1889. Cornelius W.G. Hyde and William Stoddard, editors. *History of the Great Northwest and Its Men of Progress.* Minneapolis, MN, 1901. William A. Ellis, editor. *Norwich University, 1819–1911, Her History, Her Graduates, Her Roll of Honor.* Montpelier, VT, 1911. Hiram F. Stevens. *History of the Bench and Bar of Minnesota.* Minneapolis and St, Paul, 1904. Edward D. Neill. *History of the Minnesota Valley, Including the Explorers and Pioneers of Minnesota.* Minneapolis, MN, 1882. Obituary Circular, Whole No. 801, Minnesota MOLLUS. Pension File and Military Service File, National Archives. Letters Received, Volunteer Service Branch, Adjutant General's Office, File B1826(VS)1862, National Archives. Alonzo L. Brown. *History of the Fourth Regiment of Minnesota Infantry Volunteers During the Great Rebellion, 1861–1865.* St. Paul, MN, 1892.

Rudolph von Borgersrode

2 Lieutenant, Co. B, 4 MN Infantry, Sept. 30, 1861. Resigned April 5, 1862, to accept promotion. Colonel, 5 MN Infantry, April 30, 1862. GSW right hand, Camp Clear Creek, MS, June 18, 1862. Arrested on minor charges preferred by his brigade commander, he submitted his resignation, July 22, 1862, citing disability from oblique inguinal hernia and the loss of the thumb of his right hand from gunshot wound. His resignation was accepted to date, Aug. 31, 1862, with Major Gen. Rosecrans' recommendation describing him as an "inefficient officer." Battle honors: Siege of Corinth (Farmington).

Born: May 26, 1810, Torgau, Saxony, Germany
Died: March 19, 1910, Winsted, MN
Education: Graduated Potsdam (Prussia) Military Academy, 1829

Other Wars: Promoted Captain of Hussars in the Prussian army, 1847, he joined the Revolutionary Army during the German Revolution of 1848

Occupation: Coming to America in 1850, he engaged in farming and surveying before war. Civil engineer, surveyor, and farmer after war. Under appointment as military architect, he superintended construction of Fort Shaw, MT Territory, 1866–68.

Miscellaneous: Resided Shakopee, Scott Co., MN, 1854–57; Hutchinson, McLeod Co., MN, 1857–62; Philadelphia, PA, 1862–80; Elizabeth, Otter Tail Co., MN, 1880–87; and Winsted, McLeod Co., MN, 1887–1910

Buried: Winsted Public Cemetery, Winsted, MN

References: Franklyn Curtiss-Wedge, editor. *History of McLeod County, Minnesota.* Chicago, IL, 1917. Obituary, *Hutchinson Leader,* March 25, 1910. Obituary, *Lester Prairie News,* March 24, 1910. Obituary, *Glencoe Enterprise,* March 31, 1910. Pension File and Military Service File, National Archives.

William Crooks

Lieutenant Colonel, 7 MN Infantry, Aug. 22, 1862. Colonel, 6 MN Infantry, Aug. 23, 1862. Commanded District of Minnesota, Department of the Northwest, Feb.–March 1864. Commanded Dis-

Rudolph von Borgersrode (USAMHI [RG98S-CWP188.86]).

William Crooks (Carte de Visite from Martin's Gallery, Third Street, (Upper Town,) Saint Paul, MN; courtesy Ronald S. Coddington).

trict of Eastern Arkansas, Department of Arkansas, Aug. 6–Sept. 28, 1864 and Oct. 7–10, 1864. Resigned Oct. 28, 1864, since "I cannot, in my present physical condition, perform the duties which devolve upon me as Colonel of a regiment." Battle honors: Indian Campaign of 1862 (Birch Coulie, Wood Lake), Dakota Sioux Expedition (Stony Lake).

Born: June 20, 1832, New York City, NY
Died: Dec. 17, 1907, Portland, OR
Education: Attended U.S. Military Academy, West Point, NY (Class of 1854)
Occupation: Railroad construction engineer and railroad executive
Offices/Honors: Minnesota House of Representatives, 1875–77. Minnesota Senate, 1881–82.
Miscellaneous: Resided St. Paul, Ramsey Co., MN; and Portland, Multnomah Co., OR, after 1897. In honor of his railroad services, the first steam locomotive operated in Minnesota was named for him.
Buried: Oakland Cemetery, St. Paul, MN (Section 66, Lot 57)
References: Thomas M. Newson. *Pen Pictures of St. Paul, Minnesota, and Biographical Sketches of Old Settlers*. St. Paul, MN, 1886. Obituary, *St. Paul Daily Pioneer Press*, Dec. 18, 1907. Obituary Circular, Whole No. 201, Oregon MOLLUS. Obituary, *Portland Morning Oregonian*, Dec. 18, 1907. Obituary, *Oregon Daily Journal*, Dec. 17, 1907. J. Fletcher Williams. *A History of the City of Saint Paul, and of the County of Ramsey, Minnesota*. St. Paul, MN, 1876. *Collections of the Minnesota Historical Society*. Vol. 14, (Minnesota Biographies, 1655–1912, compiled by Warren Upham and Rose Barteau Dunlap). St. Paul, MN, 1912. Pension File and Military Service File, National Archives.

Mark William Downie

1 Lieutenant, Co. B, 1 MN Infantry, April 29, 1861. Captain, Co. B, 1 MN Infantry, July 16, 1861. GSW chest, First Bull Run, VA, July 21, 1861. Ordnance Officer, Staff of Major Gen. John Pope, Department of the Northwest, Nov.–Dec. 1862. Major, 1 MN Infantry, May 6, 1863. Two GSW right arm, GSW left foot, and shell wound chest, Gettysburg, PA, July 2, 1863. Lieutenant Colonel, 1 MN Infantry, April 6, 1865. *Colonel*, 1 MN Infantry, April 22, 1865. Honorably mustered out, July 14, 1865. Battle honors: First Bull Run, Peninsular Campaign, Gettysburg, Bristoe Station, Mine Run.

Born: March 15, 1836, Chatham, New Brunswick, Canada
Died: Nov. 12, 1879, Fernandina Beach, FL
Occupation: Bookkeeper and bank cashier before war. Merchant and bookkeeper after war.
Miscellaneous: Resided Stillwater, Washington Co., MN, to 1867; Cedar Key, Levy Co., FL, 1867–71; and Fernandina Beach, Nassau Co., FL, 1871–79
Buried: St. Peter's Episcopal Cemetery, Fernandina Beach, FL (Lot 31)

William Crooks (Whitney's Gallery, St. Paul, MN; Minnesota Historical Society [por 15448 r3]).

Mark William Downie (Massachusetts MOLLUS Collection, USAMHI [Vol. 118, p. 6085L]).

References: Wayne D. Jorgenson. *Every Man Did His Duty: Pictures & Stories of the Men of the First Minnesota.* Minneapolis, MN, 2012. Pension File and Military Service File, National Archives. "Obituary Notice-Colonel Mark Wm. Downie," *The Nassau County Genealogist*, Vol. 5, No. 2 (Spring 1998). Obituary, *Florida Mirror*, Nov. 15, 1879. Letters Received, Volunteer Service Branch, Adjutant General's Office, File D253(VS)1863, National Archives. Return I. Holcombe. *History of the First Regiment Minnesota Volunteer Infantry, 1861–1864.* Stillwater, MN, 1916. Richard Moe. *The Last Full Measure: The Life and Death of the First Minnesota Volunteers.* New York City, NY, 1993. http://www.1stminnesota.net/#/soldier/147.

James George

Captain, Co. C, 2 MN Infantry, June 29, 1861. Lieutenant Colonel, 2 MN Infantry, July 22, 1861. Colonel, 2 MN Infantry, March 21, 1862. Commanded 2 Brigade, 3 Division, 14 Army Corps, Army of the Cumberland, Oct. 10–Nov. 30, 1863. Honorably mustered out, June 29, 1864. Battle honors: Mill Springs, Perryville, Tullahoma Campaign, Chickamauga, Atlanta Campaign.

Born: May 27, 1819, Alexandria, Jefferson Co., NY
Died: March 7, 1882, Rochester, MN

James George (post-war) (The National Archives [BA-189]).

Other Wars: Mexican War (Captain, Co. I, 1 OH Infantry)
Occupation: Lawyer
Miscellaneous: Resided Oronoco, Olmsted Co., MN, 1854–58 and 1864–70; Wasioja, Dodge Co., MN, 1858–64; and Rochester, Olmsted Co., MN, 1870–82
Buried: Oakwood Cemetery, Rochester, MN (Section 3A, Row 4)
References: *The United States Biographical Dictionary and Portrait Gallery of Eminent and Self-Made Men.* Minnesota Volume. New York and Chicago, 1879. *History of Winona and Olmsted Counties.* Chicago, IL, 1883. Obituary, *Rochester Post*, March 10, 1882. Ivan E. Imm, "The Civil War as Seen by Colonel James George," *Olmsted County Historical Society Monthly Bulletin*, Vol. 2, No. 5, (May 1960). Joseph A. Leonard. *History of Olmsted County, Minnesota.* Chicago, IL, 1910. Keith H. George. *George Genealogy.* Kingman, AZ, 1991. Judson W. Bishop. *The Story of a Regiment, Being a Narrative of the Service of the Second Regiment Minnesota Veteran Volunteer Infantry in the Civil War of 1861–1865.* With History of Judson Bishop and Additional Chapters, by Newell L. Chester, editor. St. Cloud, MN, 2000. Pension File and Military Service File, National Archives. Letters Received, Volunteer Service Branch, Adjutant General's Office, File G649(VS) 1864, National Archives.

James George (Judson W. Bishop. *The Story of a Regiment, Being a Narrative of the Service of the Second Regiment Minnesota Veteran Volunteer Infantry in the Civil War of 1861–1865.* St. Paul, MN, 1890).

James Gilfillan

Captain, Co. H, 7 MN Infantry, Sept. 1, 1862. Colonel, 11 MN Infantry, Nov. 3, 1864. Com-

James Gilfillan (second from left, with Lt. Col. John Ball, Surgeon Henry McMahon, and Major Martin Maginnis, left to right) (Minnesota Historical Society [Reserve Album 62 no. 13]).

manded U.S. Forces on Louisville & Nashville Railroad and Post of Gallatin (TN), District of Tennessee, Department of the Cumberland, Nov. 1864–Feb. 1865. Commanded 4 Sub-district, District of Middle Tennessee, Department of the Cumberland, March–June 1865. Honorably mustered out, June 26, 1865. Battle honors: Indian Campaign of 1862 (Wood Lake), Dakota Sioux Expedition (Stony Lake), Tupelo.

Born: March 9, 1829, Bannockburn, Scotland
Died: Dec. 16, 1894, St. Paul, MN
Occupation: Lawyer and judge
Offices/Honors: Chief Justice, Minnesota Supreme Court, 1869–70 and 1875–94
Miscellaneous: Resided St. Paul, Ramsey Co., MN
Buried: Oakland Cemetery, St. Paul, MN (Section 20, Lot 6)
References: Charles E. Flandrau. *Encyclopedia of Biography of Minnesota.* Chicago, IL, 1900. Hiram F. Stevens. *History of the Bench and Bar of Minnesota.* Minneapolis and St. Paul, 1904. Obituary, *St. Paul Daily Globe,* Dec. 17, 1894. Obituary Circular, Whole No. 147, Minnesota MOLLUS. *National Cyclopedia of American Biography. The United States Biographical Dictionary and Portrait Gallery of Eminent and Self-Made Men.* Minnesota Volume. New York and Chicago, 1879. Thomas M. Newson. *Pen Pictures of St. Paul, Minnesota, and Biographical Sketches of Old Settlers.* St. Paul, MN, 1886. Pension File and Military Service File, National Archives.

Chauncey Wright Griggs

Captain, Co. B, 3 MN Infantry, Nov. 7, 1861. Major, 3 MN Infantry, May 1, 1862. Lieutenant Colonel, 3 MN Infantry, May 30, 1862. Taken prisoner, Murfreesboro, TN, July 13, 1862. Confined Madison, GA. Paroled Oct. 12, 1862. Colonel, 3 MN Infantry, Dec. 2, 1862. Commanded Post of Fort Heiman (KY), District of Columbus, Department of the Tennessee, March–May 1863. Citing the reduced strength of the regiment and the availability of highly qualified officers to succeed him, he resigned July 19, 1863, since "my private affairs are such that they require my immediate attention for the protection of my family." Battle honors: Murfreesboro, Vicksburg Campaign.

Born: Dec. 31, 1832, Tolland, CT
Died: Oct. 29, 1910, Tacoma, WA
Education: Attended Monson (MA) Academy
Occupation: Merchant and real estate agent before war. Brick manufacturer, coal and wood dealer, real estate agent, banker, and lumber manufacturer after war.
Offices/Honors: Minnesota House of Representatives, 1866 and 1881–82. Minnesota Senate, 1867–69 and 1883–86.
Miscellaneous: Resided Detroit, MI, 1851–56; St. Paul, Ramsey Co., MN, 1856–64 and 1869–88; Chaska, Carver Co., MN, 1864–69; and Tacoma, Pierce Co., WA, 1888–1910
Buried: Tacoma Cemetery, Tacoma, WA (Section 3, Block D, Lot 39)

References: Henry A. Castle. *Minnesota: Its Story and Biography.* Chicago and New York, 1915. Alonzo Phelps. *Biographical History of the Northwest.* Boston, MA, 1890. Obituary Circular, Whole No. 188, Washington MOLLUS. Obituary, *Tacoma Daily Ledger,* Oct. 30, 1910. *American Lumbermen.* Third Series. Chicago, IL, 1906. William F. Prosser. *A History of the Puget Sound Country: Its Resources, Its Commerce and Its People.* Chicago and New York, 1903. Thomas M. Newson. *Pen Pictures of St. Paul, Minnesota, and Biographical Sketches of Old Settlers.* St. Paul, MN, 1886. Clarence W. Bowen. *History of Woodstock, Connecticut: Genealogies of Woodstock Families.* Vol. 6. Norwood, MA, 1935. Pension File and Military Service File, National Archives. Letters Received, Volunteer Service Branch, Adjutant General's Office, File G349(VS)1869, National Archives. *Minnesota in the Civil and Indian Wars, 1861–1865.* St. Paul, MN, 1890. Myron J. Smith, Jr. *Civil War Biographies from the Western Waters.* Jefferson, NC, 2015.

Chauncey Wright Griggs (Whitney's Gallery, St. Paul, MN; Roger D. Hunt Collection, USAMHI [RG98S-CWP107.36]).

Henry Clay Lester

Captain, Co. K, 1 MN Infantry, April 29, 1861. Acting AAG, Stone's Brigade, Division of the Potomac, Aug. 1861. Colonel, 3 MN Infantry, Nov. 15, 1861. Commanded 23 Independent Brigade,

Henry Clay Lester (Wayne Jorgenson Collection).

District of the Ohio, Department of the Mississippi, May 14–July 10, 1862. Taken prisoner, Murfreesboro, TN, July 13, 1862. Confined Madison, GA. Paroled Oct. 12, 1862. Dismissed (with eight other officers of the 3 MN) Dec. 1, 1862, for "recommending the surrender of their regiment while in the face of the enemy." In rejecting an application for revocation of the dismissal order, Feb. 25, 1867, Judge Advocate Gen. Joseph Holt repeated the words of Major Gen. Buell, "Take it in all its features, few more disgraceful examples of neglect of duty and lack of good conduct can be found in the history of wars." Battle honors: First Bull Run, Murfreesboro.

Born: Nov. 1830, Erie Co., NY
Died: April 5, 1902, Geneseo, NY
Education: Graduated Hamilton College, Clinton, NY, 1850
Occupation: Lawyer, civil engineer, and school teacher
Offices/Honors: District Court Clerk, 1858–61
Miscellaneous: Resided Winona, Winona Co., MN, before war; Fredonia, Chautauqua Co., NY; New York City, NY; Mount Morris, Livingston Co., NY; and Geneseo, Livingston Co., NY, after war
Buried: Temple Hill Cemetery, Geneseo, NY (Section I, Lot 7)
References: Wayne D. Jorgenson. *Every Man Did His Duty: Pictures & Stories of the Men of the First*

Minnesota. Minneapolis, MN, 2012. Walter N. Trenerry, "Lester's Surrender at Murfreesboro," *Minnesota History,* Vol. 39, No. 5 (Spring 1965). *The Hamilton College Bulletin: Necrology/Commencement Announcements.* Vol. 2, No. 3 (April 1919). Obituary, *Livingston Republican,* April 10, 1902. Obituary, *Fredonia Censor,* April 9, 1902. Military Service File, National Archives. Letters Received, Volunteer Service Branch, Adjutant General's Office, Files G893(VS)1862 and L799(VS)1862, National Archives. *Minnesota in the Civil and Indian Wars, 1861–1865.* St. Paul, MN, 1890. Christopher C. Andrews, "The Surrender of the Third Regiment Minnesota Volunteer Infantry," *Glimpses of the Nation's Struggle, Minnesota Commandery, MOLLUS.* Vol. 1. St. Paul, MN, 1887. *History of Winona County.* Chicago, IL, 1883.

Josiah Fay Marsh

Captain, Co. E, 7 MN Infantry, Aug. 22, 1862. Lieutenant Colonel, 9 MN Infantry, Nov. 20, 1862. Commanded Post of Fort Ridgely (MN), District of Minnesota, Department of the Northwest, June–Aug. 1863. Commanded Post of Jefferson City

Josiah Fay Marsh (Tuttle, St. Paul, MN).

(MO), District of Central Missouri, Department of the Missouri, Dec. 1863. Commanded Post of Warrensburg (MO), District of Central Missouri, Department of the Missouri, Feb. 1864. Commanded Post of Kansas City (MO), District of Central Missouri, Department of the Missouri, March 26–April 1, 1864. Colonel, 9 MN Infantry, Aug. 5, 1864. Honorably mustered out, Aug. 24, 1865. Battle honors: Brice's Cross Roads, Tupelo, Nashville, Mobile Campaign (Spanish Fort).

Born: 1825?, Whitby, Ontario, Canada
Died: Nov. 8, 1886, Chicago, IL
Occupation: Lawyer
Offices/Honors: Judge of Probate, Fillmore Co., MN, 1860–62
Miscellaneous: Resided Preston, Fillmore Co., MN; and Waterloo, Black Hawk Co., IA, to 1865; Marion, Perry Co., AL, 1865–68; Dubuque, Dubuque Co., IA, 1868–74; La Porte, La Porte Co., IN, 1874–77; Des Moines, Polk Co., IA, 1877–80; and Chicago, IL, 1880–86
Buried: Rosehill Cemetery, Chicago, IL (Section 114, Lot 86, unmarked)
References: John B. Lundstrom. *One Drop in a Sea of Blue: The Liberators of the Ninth Minnesota*

Josiah Fay Marsh (Whitney's Gallery, St. Paul, MN; Minnesota Historical Society [por 28768 r1]).

St. Paul, MN, 2012. Pension File and Military Service File, National Archives. Obituary, *Chicago Inter Ocean,* Nov. 13, 1886. Franklyn Curtiss-Wedge. *History of Fillmore County, Minnesota.* Chicago, IL, 1912.

Hans Mattson

Captain, Co. D, 3 MN Infantry, Oct. 22, 1861. Major, 3 MN Infantry, May 30, 1862. Lieutenant Colonel, 3 MN Infantry, Aug. 9, 1863. Colonel, 3 MN Infantry, April 26, 1864. Commanded 1 Brigade, 2 Division, District of Little Rock, 7 Army Corps, Department of Arkansas, Oct. 10, 1864–Feb. 6, 1865. Honorably mustered out, Sept. 2, 1865. Battle honors: Vicksburg Campaign.

Born: Dec. 23, 1832, Onnestad, Sweden
Died: March 5, 1893, Minneapolis, MN
Occupation: Lawyer, Swedish emigration agent, newspaper editor, and banker
Offices/Honors: Auditor, Goodhue Co., MN, 1859–61. Minnesota Secretary of State, 1870–72 and 1887–91. U.S. Consul General, Calcutta, India, 1881–83.
Miscellaneous: Resided Vasa, Goodhue Co., MN, 1853–56; Red Wing, Goodhue Co., MN, 1856–68; St. Paul, Ramsey Co., MN; and Minneapolis, Hennepin Co., MN, after 1876
Buried: Lakewood Cemetery, Minneapolis, MN (Section 10, Lot 57)
References: Hans Mattson. *Reminiscences: The Story of an Emigrant.* St. Paul, MN, 1891. Algot E. Strand, editor. *A History of the Swedish-Americans of Minnesota.* Chicago, IL, 1910. *Dictionary of American Biography.* Obituary Circular, Whole No. 122, Minnesota MOLLUS. Obituary, *St. Paul Globe,* March 6, 1893. *History of Goodhue County, Including a Sketch of the Territory and State of Minnesota.* Red Wing, MN, 1878. *The United States Biographical Dictionary and Portrait Gallery of Eminent and Self-Made Men.* Minnesota Volume. New York and Chicago, 1879. W.H.C. Folsom. *Fifty Years in the Northwest.* St. Paul, MN, 1888. Franklyn Curtiss-Wedge, editor. *History of Dakota and Goodhue Counties, Minnesota.* Chicago, IL, 1910. Edward D. Neill. *History of Hennepin County and the City of Minneapolis, Including the Explorers and Pioneers of Minnesota.* Minneapolis, MN, 1881. Pension File and Military Service File, National Archives. Letters Received, Volunteer Service Branch, Adjutant General's Office, File H1462(VS)1865, National Archives.

Hans Mattson (Whitney's Gallery, St. Paul, MN; Wayne Jorgenson Collection).

Hans Mattson (Whitney's Gallery, St. Paul, MN; Minnesota Historical Society [por 15940 r11]).

Samuel McPhaill

Lieutenant Colonel, 1 MN Mounted Rangers, Oct. 17, 1862. Colonel, 1 MN Mounted Rangers, Dec. 30, 1862. Honorably mustered out, Dec. 3,

Above: **Samuel McPhaill (Whitney's Gallery, St. Paul, MN; Minnesota Historical Society [por 29852 r1]).** *Below:* **Samuel McPhaill (Whitney's Gallery, St. Paul, MN; Paul J. Brzozowski Collection).**

Other Wars: Mexican War (Private, Co. C, 3 IL Infantry)
Occupation: Lawyer and farmer
Offices/Honors: County Attorney, Redwood Co., MN, 1865–67. County Attorney, Lincoln Co., MN, 1879–83 and 1885–91.
Miscellaneous: Resided Caledonia, Houston Co., MN, 1853–64; Redwood Falls, Redwood Co., MN, 1864–75; and Alta Vista, Lincoln Co., MN, 1875–1902
Buried: Canby Cemetery, Canby, Yellow Medicine Co., MN
References: *Illustrated Album of Biography of Southwestern Minnesota.* Chicago, IL, 1889. Donald B. Sayner. *The Orders of Col. Samuel McPhail, Minnesota Mounted Rangers, 1863.* Tucson, AZ, 1973. Albert E. Tasker. *Early History of Lincoln County.* Lake Benton, MN, 1936. Franklyn Curtiss-Wedge. *The History of Redwood County, Minnesota.* Chicago, IL, 1916. Obituary, *Minneota Mascot,* March 14, 1902. Edward D. Neill. *History of the Minnesota Valley, Including the Explorers and Pioneers of Minnesota.* Minneapolis, MN, 1882. Obituary, *New York Times,* March 8, 1902. Franklyn Curtiss-Wedge, editor. *History of Houston County, Minnesota.* Winona, MN, 1919. Pension File and Military Service File, National Archives.

Anderson Doniphan Nelson

Captain, 10 U.S. Infantry, March 3, 1855. Superintendent of Volunteer Recruiting Service in Minnesota, Dec. 1861–June 1864. *Colonel,* 6 MN Infantry, Aug. 16, 1862. Sensitive to military etiquette,

1863. Battle honors: Indian Campaign of 1862 (Birch Coulie), Dakota Sioux Expedition (Big Mound, Stony Lake).
   Born: May 2, 1826, Russellville, KY
   Died: March 6, 1902, Alta Vista, MN

Anderson Doniphan Nelson (courtesy Dale Stilwagen Jacobi).

he resigned Aug. 22, 1862, rather than act under the orders of Henry H. Sibley, then a colonel of militia, who was designated by Minnesota Governor Alexander Ramsey to command the expedition to quell the Sioux Indian uprising. Major, 1 U.S. Infantry, March 13, 1863. Provost Marshal, Defenses of New Orleans (LA), June–Sept. 1864. Acting AIG, Staff of Major Gen. Joseph J. Reynolds, 19 Army Corps, Department of the Gulf, Sept.–Dec. 1864. Acting AIG, Staff of Major Gen. Joseph J. Reynolds, Department of Arkansas, Dec. 1864–Aug. 1865. Bvt. Lieutenant Colonel, U.S.A., March 13, 1865, for faithful and efficient services during the war. Bvt. Colonel, U.S.A., March 13, 1865, for faithful and meritorious services during the war.

Born: March 16, 1818, KY
Died: Dec. 30, 1885, Thomasville, GA
Education: Graduated U.S. Military Academy, West Point, NY, 1841
Other Wars: Mexican War (2 Lieutenant, 6 U.S. Infantry)
Occupation: Regular Army (Lieutenant Colonel, 12 U.S. Infantry, retired June 7, 1879)
Miscellaneous: Resided Maysville, Mason Co., KY. Brother of Major Gen. William Nelson.
Buried: Maysville Cemetery, Maysville, KY
References: George W. Cullum. *Biographical Register of the Officers and Graduates of the U.S. Military Academy*. Third Edition. Boston and New York, 1891. *Seventeenth Annual Reunion of the Association of the Graduates of the United States Military Academy at West Point, New York, June 10, 1886*. East Saginaw, MI, 1886. Letters Received, Appointment, Commission, and Personal Branch, Adjutant General's Office, File 7(ACP)1886, National Archives. Letters Received, Adjutant General's Office, File N256(AGO)1862, National Archives. *Minnesota in the Civil and Indian Wars, 1861–1865*. St. Paul, MN, 1890. Frances F. Hamilton. *Ancestral Lines of the Doniphan, Frazee and Hamilton Families*. Greenfield, IN, 1928. Lucius F. Hubbard and Return I. Holcombe. *Minnesota in Three Centuries*. New York City, NY, 1908.

Alexander Wilkin

Captain, Co. A, 1 MN Infantry, April 29, 1861. Captain, 17 U.S. Infantry, Aug. 5, 1861. Major, 2 MN Infantry, Sept. 18, 1861. Lieutenant Colonel, 2 MN Infantry, March 21, 1862. Colonel, 9 MN Infantry, Aug. 24, 1862. Commanded 1 Brigade, Infantry Division, Expedition into Mississippi, June 2–14, 1864. Commanded 2 Brigade, 1 Division, 16 Army Corps, Army of the Tennessee, June 25–July 14, 1864. GSW heart, Tupelo, MS, July 14, 1864. Battle honors: First Bull Run, Mill Springs, Siege of Corinth, Brice's Cross Roads, Tupelo.

Born: Dec. 1, 1819, Goshen, NY

Alexander Wilkin (Whitney's Gallery, St. Paul, MN; Massachusetts MOLLUS Collection, USAMHI [Vol. 118, p. 6057L]).

Died: July 14, 1864, KIA Tupelo, MS
Education: Attended Yale University, New Haven, CT
Other Wars: Mexican War (Captain, 10 U.S. Infantry). Killed Capt. Joshua W. Collett in a duel, Jan. 21, 1848.
Occupation: Lawyer and insurance company executive
Offices/Honors: Secretary, Minnesota Territory, 1851–53
Miscellaneous: Resided St. Paul, Ramsey Co., MN
Buried: Slate Hill Cemetery, Goshen, NY
References: Ronald M. Hubbs, "The Civil War and Alexander Wilkin," *Minnesota History*, Vol. 39, No. 5 (Spring 1965). Christopher C. Andrews, editor. *History of St. Paul, Minnesota*. Syracuse, NY, 1890. Thomas M. Newson. *Pen Pictures of St. Paul, Minnesota, and Biographical Sketches of Old Settlers*. St. Paul, MN, 1886. J. Fletcher Williams. *A History of the City of Saint Paul, and of the County of Ramsey, Minnesota*. St. Paul, MN, 1876. W.H.C. Folsom. *Fifty Years in the Northwest*. St. Paul, MN, 1888. John B. Lundstrom. *One Drop in a Sea of Blue: The Liberators of the Ninth Minnesota*. St. Paul, MN, 2012.

Military Service File, National Archives. Judson W. Bishop. *The Story of a Regiment, Being a Narrative of the Service of the Second Regiment Minnesota Veteran Volunteer Infantry in the Civil War of 1861–1865. With History of Judson Bishop and Additional Chapters*, by Newell L. Chester, editor. St. Cloud, MN, 2000. Return I. Holcombe. *History of the First Regiment Minnesota Volunteer Infantry, 1861–1864*. Stillwater, MN, 1916. http://www.mnopedia.org/person/wilkin-alexander-1819-1864.

WISCONSIN

Regiments

1st Cavalry

Edward Daniels	Dec. 1, 1861	Resigned Feb. 5, 1863
Oscar H. La Grange	Feb. 5, 1863	Mustered out July 19, 1865, **Bvt. Brig. Gen., USV**

2nd Cavalry

Cadwallader C. Washburn	Feb. 6, 1862	Promoted **Brig. Gen., USV,** July 16, 1862
Thomas Stephens	Aug. 1, 1862	Mustered out July 3, 1865
Nicholas H. Dale	Jan. 30, 1865	Mustered out Nov. 15, 1865

3rd Cavalry

William A. Barstow	Jan. 31, 1862	Resigned March 5, 1865
Thomas Derry	June 10, 1865	Mustered out Sept. 8, 1865

4th Cavalry (designation changed from 4th Infantry, Aug. 22, 1863)

Frederick A. Boardman	June 3, 1863	KIA May 3, 1864
Joseph Bailey	June 1, 1864	Promoted **Brig. Gen., USV,** Nov. 10, 1864
Webster P. Moore	Jan. 19, 1865	Resigned July 11, 1865
Nelson F. Craigue	Nov. 9, 1865	Mustered out May 28, 1866

1st Heavy Artillery

Charles C. Meservey	Nov. 12, 1864	Mustered out June 26, 1865

1st Infantry (3 months)

John C. Starkweather	May 17, 1861	Mustered out Aug. 21, 1861, **Brig. Gen., USV**

1st Infantry (3 years)

John C. Starkweather	Oct. 8, 1861	Promoted **Brig. Gen., USV,** July 17, 1863
George B. Bingham	Dec. 18, 1863	Mustered out Oct. 13, 1864

2nd Infantry

S. Park Coon	June 11, 1861	Resigned July 31, 1861
Edgar O'Connor	Aug. 2, 1861	KIA Aug. 28, 1862
Lucius Fairchild	Sept. 1, 1862	Promoted **Brig. Gen., USV,** Oct. 19, 1863
John Mansfield	Feb. 9, 1864	Mustered out Aug. 14, 1864, **Bvt. Brig. Gen., USV**

3rd Infantry

Charles S. Hamilton	May 11, 1861	Promoted **Brig. Gen., USV,** Aug. 10, 1861
Thomas H. Ruger	Sept. 1, 1861	Promoted **Brig. Gen., USV,** Nov. 29, 1862
William Hawley	March 10, 1863	Mustered out July 18, 1865, **Bvt. Brig. Gen., USV**

4th Infantry (designation changed to 4th Cavalry, Aug. 22, 1863)

Halbert E. Paine	July 2, 1861	Promoted **Brig. Gen., USV,** March 13, 1863
Sidney A. Bean	March 17, 1863	KIA May 29, 1863
Frederick A. Boardman	June 3, 1863	KIA May 3, 1864

Wisconsin Regiments

5th Infantry

Amasa Cobb	July 12, 1861	Resigned Dec. 25, 1862, **Bvt. Brig. Gen., USV**
Thomas S. Allen	Jan. 26, 1863	Mustered out June 20, 1865, **Bvt. Brig. Gen., USV**

6th Infantry

Lysander Cutler	July 16, 1861	Promoted **Brig. Gen., USV,** Nov. 29, 1862
Edward S. Bragg	March 24, 1863	Promoted **Brig. Gen., USV,** June 25, 1864
John A. Kellogg	Dec. 18, 1864	Mustered out July 14, 1865, **Bvt. Brig. Gen., USV**

7th Infantry

Joseph Vandor	Aug. 18, 1861	Resigned Jan. 30, 1862
William W. Robinson	Jan. 30, 1862	Resigned July 9, 1864
Mark Finnicum	Aug. 3, 1864	Mustered out Dec. 17, 1864
Hollon Richardson	Dec. 29, 1864	Mustered out July 3, 1865, **Bvt. Brig. Gen., USV**

8th Infantry

Robert C. Murphy	Sept. 4, 1861	Dismissed Jan. 10, 1863
George W. Robbins	Dec. 21, 1862	Resigned Sept. 1, 1863
John W. Jefferson	June 16, 1864	Mustered out Sept. 16, 1864
William B. Britton	March 28, 1865	Mustered out Sept. 5, 1865

9th Infantry

Frederick Salomon	Nov. 26, 1861	Promoted **Brig. Gen., USV,** June 16, 1862
Charles E. Salomon	Sept. 26, 1862	Mustered out Dec. 3, 1864, **Bvt. Brig. Gen., USV**
Arthur Jacobi	Nov. 9, 1865	Mustered out Jan. 30, 1866

10th Infantry

Alfred R. Chapin	Oct. 29, 1861	Resigned Jan. 23, 1863
John G. McMynn	Jan. 24, 1863	Resigned June 16, 1863
Duncan McKercher	Oct. 20, 1864	Mustered out March 11, 1865

11th Infantry

Charles L. Harris	Oct. 21, 1861	Mustered out Sept. 4, 1865, **Bvt. Brig. Gen., USV**

12th Infantry

George E. Bryant	Nov. 7, 1861	Mustered out Nov. 6, 1864
James K. Proudfit	Dec. 17, 1864	Mustered out July 16, 1865, **Bvt. Brig. Gen., USV**

13th Infantry

Maurice Maloney	Oct. 17, 1861	Discharged Aug. 1, 1862
William P. Lyon	Sept. 26, 1862	Mustered out Sept. 11, 1865, **Bvt. Brig. Gen., USV**
Augustus H. Kummel	Oct. 9, 1865	Mustered out Nov. 24, 1865

14th Infantry

David E. Wood	Jan. 30, 1862	Died June 17, 1862
John Hancock	June 17, 1862	Resigned Jan. 23, 1863
Lyman M. Ward	March 13, 1863	Mustered out Oct. 9, 1865, **Bvt. Brig. Gen., USV**

15th Infantry

Hans C. Heg	Feb. 13, 1862	DOW Sept. 20, 1863

16th Infantry

Benjamin Allen	Dec. 23, 1861	Resigned July 17, 1863
Cassius Fairchild	March 17, 1864	Mustered out July 12, 1865, **Bvt. Brig. Gen., USV**

17th Infantry

John L. Doran	March 18, 1862	Resigned Nov. 25, 1862
Adam G. Malloy	Dec. 1, 1862	Mustered out July 14, 1865, **Bvt. Brig. Gen., USV**

18th Infantry

James S. Alban	March 15, 1862	DOW April 7, 1862
Gabriel Bouck	April 22, 1862	Resigned Jan. 4, 1864
Charles H. Jackson	July 1, 1865	Mustered out July 18, 1865

19th Infantry

Horace T. Sanders	April 17, 1862	Mustered out April 29, 1865, **Bvt. Brig. Gen., USV**
Samuel K. Vaughan	Aug. 31, 1865	Mustered out Aug. 9, 1865, **Bvt. Brig. Gen., USV**

20th Infantry

Bertine Pinkney	Aug. 23, 1862	Resigned Dec. 6, 1862
Henry Bertram	Dec. 10, 1862	Mustered out July 14, 1865, **Bvt. Brig. Gen., USV**

21st Infantry

Benjamin J. Sweet	Sept. 5, 1862	Resigned Sept. 8, 1863, **Bvt. Brig. Gen., USV**
Harrison C. Hobart	Nov. 1, 1864	Mustered out June 8, 1865, **Bvt. Brig. Gen., USV**

22nd Infantry

William L. Utley	Sept. 1, 1862	Resigned July 5, 1864
Edward Bloodgood	May 12, 1865	Mustered out June 12, 1865

23rd Infantry

Joshua J. Guppey	Aug. 30, 1862	Mustered out July 4, 1865, **Bvt. Brig. Gen., USV**

24th Infantry

Charles H. Larrabee	Aug. 22, 1862	Resigned Aug. 27, 1863
Theodore S. West	March 4, 1864	Resigned May 12, 1865
Arthur MacArthur, Jr.	June 13, 1865	Mustered out June 10, 1865

25th Infantry

Milton Montgomery	Sept. 14, 1862	Mustered out June 7, 1865, **Bvt. Brig. Gen., USV**

26th Infantry

William H. Jacobs	Sept. 17, 1862	Resigned Jan. 11, 1864
Frederick C. Winkler	Aug. 17, 1864	Mustered out June 13, 1865, **Bvt. Brig. Gen., USV**

27th Infantry

Conrad Krez	March 7, 1863	Mustered out Aug. 29, 1865, **Bvt. Brig. Gen., USV**

28th Infantry

James M. Lewis	Oct. 14, 1862	Discharged Jan. 2, 1864
Edmund B. Gray	March 16, 1864	Mustered out Aug. 23, 1865

29th Infantry

Charles R. Gill	Sept. 27, 1862	Resigned June 27, 1863
William A. Greene	Feb. 9, 1864	Resigned Jan. 26, 1865
Bradford Hancock	April 30, 1865	Mustered out June 22, 1865

30th Infantry

Daniel J. Dill	Oct. 12, 1862	Mustered out Sept. 20, 1865

31st Infantry

Isaac E. Messmore	Dec. 18, 1862	Resigned Oct. 2, 1863
Francis H. West	Feb. 1, 1864	Mustered out June 20, 1865, **Bvt. Brig. Gen., USV**
George D. Rogers	July 8, 1865	Mustered out July 8, 1865

32nd Infantry

James H. Howe	Sept. 25, 1862	Resigned July 6, 1864
Charles H. De Groat	Aug. 2, 1864	Mustered out June 12, 1865, **Bvt. Brig. Gen., USV**

33rd Infantry

Jonathan B. Moore	Oct. 18, 1862	Mustered out Aug. 9, 1865, **Bvt. Brig. Gen., USV**

34th Infantry

Fritz Anneke	Jan. 2, 1863	Dismissed June 20, 1863

35th Infantry

Henry Orff	Feb. 27, 1864	Resigned July 22, 1865
George H. Walther	Oct. 24, 1865	Mustered out March 15, 1866

36th Infantry

Frank A. Haskell	March 23, 1864	KIA June 3, 1864
John A. Savage, Jr.	June 11, 1864	DOW July 4, 1864
Harvey M. Brown	July 15, 1864	Discharged Oct. 27, 1864
Clement E. Warner	May 7, 1865	Mustered out July 12, 1865

37th Infantry

Samuel Harriman	April 26, 1864	Mustered out July 17, 1865, **Bvt. Brig. Gen., USV**
John Green	July 21, 1865	Mustered out July 27, 1865

38th Infantry

James Bintliff	April 27, 1864	Mustered out June 26, 1865, **Bvt. Brig. Gen., USV**
Colwert K. Pier	July 19, 1865	Mustered out July 26, 1865

39th Infantry

Edwin L. Buttrick	June 3, 1864	Mustered out Sept. 22, 1864

40th Infantry

W. Augustus Ray	June 8, 1864	Mustered out Sept. 16, 1864

41st Infantry

George B. Goodwin	May 20, 1864	Mustered out Sept. 24, 1864

42nd Infantry

Ezra T. Sprague	Sept. 14, 1864	Mustered out June 20, 1865, **Bvt. Brig. Gen., USV**

43rd Infantry

Amasa Cobb	Sept. 29, 1864	Mustered out June 24, 1865, **Bvt. Brig. Gen., USV**

44th Infantry

George G. Symes	Feb. 17, 1865	Mustered out Aug. 28, 1865

45th Infantry

Henry F. Belitz	March 2, 1865	Mustered out July 17, 1865

46th Infantry

Frederick S. Lovell	March 2, 1865	Mustered out Sept. 27, 1865, **Bvt. Brig. Gen., USV**

47th Infantry

George C. Ginty	Feb. 23, 1865	Mustered out Sept. 4, 1865, **Bvt. Brig. Gen., USV**

48th Infantry

Uri B. Pearsall	April 12, 1865	Mustered out Dec. 30, 1865, **Bvt. Brig. Gen., USV**
Henry Shears	Jan. 15, 1866	Mustered out March 24, 1866

49th Infantry

Samuel Fallows	Jan. 28, 1865	Mustered out Nov. 1, 1865, **Bvt. Brig. Gen., USV**
Edward Colman	Nov. 14, 1865	Mustered out Nov. 8, 1865

50th Infantry

Charles D. Robinson	Declined	
John G. Clark	Feb. 18, 1865	Mustered out June 14, 1866

51st Infantry

Leonard Martin	April 20, 1865	Mustered out Aug. 26, 1865

52nd Infantry

William C. Webb	Feb. 23, 1865	Not mustered

53rd Infantry

Ole C. Johnson	Feb. 21, 1865	Not mustered

Biographies

James Shane Alban

Colonel, 18 WI Infantry, March 15, 1862. GSW through lungs, Shiloh, TN, April 6, 1862. Battle honors: Shiloh.

Born: Oct. 30, 1809, Jefferson Co., OH
Died: April 7, 1862, DOW Pittsburg Landing, TN
Occupation: Lawyer and judge
Offices/Honors: Portage County (WI) Judge, 1849. Wisconsin Senate, 1852–53.
Miscellaneous: Resided Plover, Portage Co., WI
Buried: Plover Cemetery, Plover, WI
References: Justin Isherwood, "Col. James Alban," *Stevens Point Daily Journal,* May 19, 1992. O.D. Brandenburg, "More About the Alban Family, Pioneer Residents," *Baraboo Daily News,* Nov. 26, 1927. Sarah J. Keifer. *Genealogical and Biographical Sketches of the New Jersey Branch of the Harris Family in the United States.* Madison, WI, 1888. Obituary, *Wisconsin Pinery,* April 23 and 30, 1862. *Report of the Proceedings of the Meetings of the State Bar Association of Wisconsin for the Years 1878, 1881 and 1885.* Madison WI, 1905. Ethel Winifred Albin. *The Virginia Albins: The History of the Albin Family Out of Old Frederick County, 1739–1989.* N.p., 1989. Frederick H. Magdeburg. *Wisconsin at Shiloh: Report of the Commission.* Madison, WI, 1909. Timothy T. Isbell. *Shiloh and Corinth: Sentinels of Stone.* Jackson, MS, 2007. Pension File and Military Service File, National Archives.

Benjamin Allen

Colonel, 16 WI Infantry, Dec. 23, 1861. GSW left forearm, Shiloh, TN, April 6, 1862. Commanded 1 Brigade, 6 Division, Army of the Tennessee, Sept. 21–Oct. 3, 1862 and Oct. 6–Nov. 1, 1862. Suffering from his gunshot wound, right inguinal hernia, and chronic diarrhea, he resigned July 17, 1863, since "I am wholly unfit to do my duty as becomes a soldier." Battle honors: Shiloh, Corinth, Vicksburg Campaign.

Born: Aug. 28, 1807, Woodstock, VT
Died: July 5, 1873, Pepin, WI
Occupation: Lawyer
Offices/Honors: Wisconsin Senate, 1853–54. Postmaster, Pepin, WI, 1857–59.
Buried: Oakwood Cemetery, Pepin, WI
References: George Forrester, editor. *Historical and Biographical Album of the Chippewa Valley, Wisconsin.* Chicago, IL, 1892. Frederick H. Magdeburg.

James Shane Alban (Frederick H. Magdeburg. *Wisconsin at Shiloh: Report of the Commission.* Madison, WI, 1909).

Benjamin Allen (Frederick H. Magdeburg. *Wisconsin at Shiloh: Report of the Commission.* Madison, WI, 1909).

Wisconsin at Shiloh: Report of the Commission. Madison, WI, 1909. Pension File and Military Service File, National Archives. "Col. Ben Allen," *Hudson North Star,* April 30, 1862. Letters Received, Commission Branch, Adjutant General's Office, File A264(CB)1863, National Archives.

Fritz Anneke

Appointed *Colonel,* 1 WI Artillery, Sept. 1861. Not mustered as colonel, however, since the War Department insisted that all Wisconsin light artillery enter U.S. service as independent batteries rather than as a regiment requiring field officers. Appointed *Colonel,* 65 IN Volunteers (2 IN Light Artillery), Nov. 1861. Not mustered as colonel, however, since the War Department insisted that all Indiana light artillery enter U.S. service as independent batteries rather than as a regiment requiring field officers. Volunteer ADC and Chief of Artillery, Staff of Major Gen. John A. McClernand, Reserve Corps, Army of the Tennessee, April–June 1862. Captain, Battery D, 2 IL Light Artillery, May 1, 1862. Acting ADC, Staff of Major Gen. John A. McClernand, District of Jackson (TN), Army of the Tennessee, June–Dec. 1862. Colonel, 34 WI Infantry, Jan. 2, 1863. Tried by court martial on charges of "mutiny, leaving his confinement before being set at liberty, and disobedience of orders," he was found guilty, June 20, 1863, of the last two charges and also guilty of the first charge amended to "behaving himself with contempt and disrespect toward his commanding officer" (Col. Isaac E. Messmore, 31 Wisconsin Infantry, commanding Fort Halleck, Columbus, KY). Still imprisoned, Aug. 22, 1863, and awaiting news of the court's verdict, he sent a thirteen-page letter to Secretary of War Stanton, stating the details of his case and appealing for justice. When news of the verdict, dismissing him from the service, finally reached him, Sept. 13, 1863, after the muster out of the 34 WI Infantry, he renewed his request for justice. The War Department, however, refused to take any action, claiming he "failed to make any satisfactory defense to the charges of which he was convicted." Battle honors: Siege of Corinth.

Born: Jan. 31, 1818, Dortmund, Westphalia, Prussia

Died: Dec. 8, 1872, Chicago, IL (accidental fall)

Other Wars: German Revolution of 1848 (Colonel of Artillery)

Occupation: Journalist and gymnasium operator

Offices/Honors: Wisconsin State Librarian, 1851–52. Secretary of the German Immigration Aid Society of Chicago at his death.

Miscellaneous: Resided Milwaukee, WI; and Chicago, IL, after 1870

Buried: Forest Home Cemetery, Milwaukee, WI (Section 15, Block 3, Lot 2)

References: *Dictionary of Wisconsin Biography.* Madison, WI, 1960. Obituary, *Chicago Daily Tribune,* Dec. 10, 1872. Obituary, *Milwaukee Sentinel,* Dec. 10, 1872. Obituary, *Janesville Daily Gazette,* Dec. 13, 1872. Wilhelm Kaufmann. *The Germans in the American Civil War.* Translated by Steven Rowan and edited by Don Heinrich Tolzmann with Werner D. Mueller and Robert E. Ward. Carlisle, PA, 1999. Adolf E. Zucker, editor. *The Forty-Eighters: Political Refugees of the German Revolution of 1848.* New York City, NY, 1950. Alfred T. Andreas. *History of Milwaukee, Wisconsin.* Chicago, IL, 1881. Military Service File, National Archives. Letters Received, Volunteer Service Branch, Adjutant General's Office, File I3(VS)1862, National Archives. Court-martial Case Files, 1809–1894, File NN-0230, National Archives. John Y. Simon, editor. *The Papers of Ulysses S. Grant.* Volume 9: July 7–Dec. 31, 1863. Carbondale, IL, 1982. Edwin B. Quiner. *The Military History of Wisconsin.* Chicago, IL, 1866. Edwin B. Quiner, *Quiner Scrapbooks: Correspondence of the Wisconsin Volunteers, 1861–1865,* Wisconsin Historical Society. "Indiana Military Matters," *Plymouth (IN) Weekly Democrat,* Dec. 5, 1861. "Col. Anneke," *Indianapolis Daily State Sentinel,* March 13, 1862. "The Case of Col. Anneke," *Milwaukee Semi-Weekly Wisconsin,* Sept. 18, 1863.

Fritz Anneke (Wisconsin Historical Society, WHi-76133).

William Augustus Barstow

Colonel, 3 WI Cavalry, Jan. 31, 1862. Provost

Above: William Augustus Barstow (pre-war, as governor of Wisconsin). *Below:* William Augustus Barstow (Whitehurst Gallery, Washington, DC; Craig T. Johnson Collection).

William Augustus Barstow (*The History of Waukesha County, Wisconsin.* **Chicago, IL, 1880**).

Marshal General, Department of Kansas, May–Sept. 1862. President of General Court Martial and Military Commission at St. Louis, MO, after May 1863. He was described, Sept. 11, 1863, as an "entirely worthless officer" by Major Gen. James G. Blunt, who added, "I would respectfully suggest that he be given a leave of absence until after the termination of the war." Resigned March 5, 1865, "so much impaired [in] my health as to be unfit for field or even other duty."

Born: Sept. 13, 1813, Plainfield, CT
Died: Dec. 13, 1865, Leavenworth, KS
Occupation: Merchant, miller, and banker
Offices/Honors: Secretary of State of Wisconsin, 1850–52. Governor of Wisconsin, 1854–56.
Miscellaneous: Resided Waukesha, Waukesha Co., WI; and Janesville, Rock Co., WI, after 1857
Buried: Brookmere Cemetery, Cleveland, OH (Section F, Lot 248)
References: Edward M. Hunter, "The Civil Life, Services and Character of Gov. Wm. A. Barstow," *Collections of the State Historical Society of Wisconsin.* Vol. 6. Edited by Lyman C. Draper. Madison, WI, 1908. Elias A. Calkins, "William A. Barstow's Military Services," *Collections of the State Historical Society of Wisconsin.* Vol. 6. Edited by Lyman C. Draper. Madison, WI, 1908. *The History of Waukesha County, Wisconsin.* Chicago, IL, 1880. *Dictionary of American Biography.* Arthur H. Radasch. *Barstow-Bestor Genealogy; Descendants of John Barstow and George Barstow.* South Yarmouth, MA, 1964. *Portrait and Biographical Record of Waukesha County, Wisconsin.* Chicago, IL, 1894. *Portrait and Biographical Album of Rock County, Wisconsin.* Chicago,

IL, 1889. Obituary, *Janesville Daily Gazette,* Dec. 19, 1865. Obituary, *Leavenworth Daily Conservative,* Dec. 14, 1865. Obituary, *Cleveland Plain Dealer,* Dec. 19, 1865. *Dictionary of Wisconsin Biography.* Madison, WI, 1960. Pension File and Military Service File, National Archives. *The War of the Rebellion: A Compilation of the Official Records of the Union and Confederate Armies.* (Vol. 22, Part 2, p. 526). Washington, D.C., 1888.

Sidney Alfred Bean

Lieutenant Colonel, 4 WI Infantry, July 2, 1861. Colonel, 4 WI Infantry, March 17, 1863. GSW right lung, Port Hudson, LA, May 29, 1863. Battle honors: Baton Rouge, Fort Bisland, Port Hudson.

Born: Sept. 16, 1833, Chesterfield, Essex Co., NY
Died: May 29, 1863, KIA (sharpshooter bullet) Port Hudson, LA
Education: Graduated University of Michigan, Ann Arbor, MI, 1852
Occupation: Professor of Mathematics (Carroll College, Waukesha, WI) and banker
Miscellaneous: Resided Waukesha, Waukesha Co., WI
Buried: Prairie Home Cemetery, Waukesha, WI (Section M, Block 56, Lot 2)
References: *The History of Waukesha County, Wisconsin.* Chicago, IL, 1880. William DeLoss Love. *Wisconsin in the War of the Rebellion.* Chicago, IL, 1866. Edwin B. Quiner. *The Military History of Wisconsin.* Chicago, IL, 1866. Obituary, *Waukesha Freeman,* June 16, 1863. Obituary, *Chicago Daily Tribune,* June 14, 1863. Obituary, *Waukesha Democrat,*

Sidney Alfred Bean (William DeLoss Love. *Wisconsin in the War of the Rebellion.* Chicago, IL, 1866).

June 16, 1863. Michael J. Martin. *A History of the 4th Wisconsin Infantry and Cavalry in the Civil War.* New York and California, 2006. George W. Carter, "The Fourth Wisconsin at Port Hudson," *War Papers, Wisconsin Commandery, MOLLUS.* Vol. 3. Milwaukee, WI, 1903. Pension File and Military Service File, National Archives.

Henry Frederick Belitz

Captain, Co. K, 9 WI Infantry, Nov. 9, 1861. "Being sick since the month of August and being informed by the surgeon of the regiment that I cannot recover my health if I do not go back to Wisconsin," he resigned Dec. 24, 1862. Colonel, 45 WI Infantry, March 2, 1865. Honorably mustered out, July 17, 1865.

Born: Feb. 16, 1817, Schwedt, Brandenburg, Germany
Died: March 31, 1878, Kiel, WI (carriage accident)
Occupation: Miller and farmer. Also lawyer and justice of the peace after war.
Offices/Honors: Postmaster, Kiel, WI, 1861–64 and 1869–74
Miscellaneous: Resided Kiel, Manitowoc Co., WI. He was known as the "Father of Kiel."
Buried: Kiel Cemetery, Kiel, WI
References: "Kiel Homecoming and July Fourth Program Enjoyed," *Sheboygan Press,* July 5, 1932. Pension File and Military Service File, National Archives. James S. Anderson. *Pioneer Courts and Lawyers of Manitowoc County, Wisconsin.* Manitowoc, WI, 1922. Obituary, *Chilton Times,* April 6, 1878. Ralph G. Plumb. *A History of Manitowoc County.* Manitowoc, WI, 1904. Louis Falge, editor. *History of Manitowoc County, Wisconsin.* Chicago,

Sidney Alfred Bean (Photographed by A.D. Lytle, Main Street, Baton Rouge, LA; U.S. Military Academy Library).

Henry Frederick Belitz (E.R. Curtiss, Photographer, Madison, WI).

IL, 1912. Obituary, *Manitowoc Der Nord-Westen*, April 11, 1878. Letters Received, Volunteer Service Branch, Adjutant General's Office, File W2411(VS) 1864, National Archives. http://www.mccwrt.com/cwveterans/B/Belitz,%20Henry%20F.pdf.

George B. Bingham

Captain, Co. A, 1 WI Infantry (3 months), May 17, 1861. Honorably mustered out, Aug. 21, 1861. Major, 1 WI Infantry (3 years), Oct. 8, 1861. Lieutenant Colonel, 1 WI Infantry, Sept. 4, 1862. *Colonel,* 1 WI Infantry, Dec. 18, 1863. Honorably mustered out, Oct. 13, 1864. Battle honors: Falling Waters, Perryville, Stone's River, Tullahoma Campaign, Chickamauga, Chattanooga-Ringgold Campaign, Dalton, Atlanta Campaign.
  Born: April 29, 1821, Rochester, NY
  Died: Aug. 6, 1893, Westboro, MA
  Occupation: Contractor and builder
  Offices/Honors: U.S. Assessor of Internal Revenue, 1867–69
  Miscellaneous: Resided Milwaukee, WI, to 1878; Coursens Grove, Mitchell Co., KS, 1878–81; and Westboro, Worcester Co., MA, 1881–93
  Buried: Pine Grove Cemetery, Westboro, MA

Above: George B. Bingham (Roger D. Hunt Collection, USAMHI [RG98S-CWP60.35]). *Below:* George B. Bingham (William DeLoss Love. *Wisconsin in the War of the Rebellion.* Chicago, IL, 1866).

References: Herbert C. Damon. *History of the Milwaukee Light Guard.* Milwaukee, WI, 1875. Theodore A. Bingham. *The Bingham Family in the United States, Especially of the State of Connecticut.* Easton, PA, 1927. Donna Bingham Munger. *The Bingham Family in the United States: The Descendants of Thomas Bingham of Connecticut.* New York City, NY, 1996. Pension File and Military Service File, National Archives. William DeLoss Love. *Wis-*

George B. Bingham (left, with Brig. Gen. John C. Starkweather, center, and Brig. Gen. Rufus King, right) (courtesy Perry M. Frohne).

consin in the War of the Rebellion. Chicago, IL, 1866. Obituary, *Milwaukee Sentinel,* Aug. 8, 1893. Obituary, *New York Times,* Aug. 8, 1893. Obituary, *Boston Post,* Aug. 8, 1893.

Edward Bloodgood

Sergeant Major, 1 WI Infantry (3 months), May 17, 1861. Honorably mustered out. Aug. 21, 1861. Captain, Co. G, 1 WI Infantry (3 years), Oct. 8, 1861. Lieutenant Colonel, 22 WI Infantry, Aug. 15, 1862. Taken prisoner, Brentwood, TN, March 25, 1863. Confined Libby Prison, Richmond, VA. Paroled May 5, 1863. As an aftermath of the regiment's disastrous experiences at Thompson's Station and Brentwood, Colonel William L. Utley preferred charges against Bloodgood, accusing him of "misbehavior before the enemy, gross neglect of duty, and insubordination." Found guilty of all charges by a court martial, he was dismissed from the service, Oct. 9, 1863. Upon review of the case, Judge Advocate General Joseph Holt recommended that "the disability under which this officer labors in consequence of his sentence be removed, ... in view of the peculiar circumstances surrounding this case, ... and in the absence of any proof that Lt. Col. Bloodgood manifested ... any want of bravery." Reinstated as Lieutenant Colonel, 22 WI Infantry, Dec. 28, 1863. Commanded 2 Brigade, 3 Division, 20 Army Corps, Army of the Cumberland, Sept. 22–Oct. 30, 1864. Colonel, 22 WI Infantry, May 12,

Edward Bloodgood (Wisconsin Historical Society, WHi-3313).

1865. Honorably mustered out, June 12, 1865. Bvt. Major, USA, March 2, 1867, for gallant and meritorious services in the battle of Resaca, GA. Bvt. Lieutenant Colonel, USA, March 2, 1867, for gallant and meritorious services in the Savannah Campaign. Battle honors: Thompson's Station, Brentwood, Atlanta Campaign (Resaca, New Hope Church, Peach Tree Creek), Savannah Campaign, Campaign of the Carolinas.

Born: June 12, 1831, Fort Houlton, ME
Died: Oct. 22, 1914, near Mukwonago, WI
Occupation: Regular Army (Captain, 38 U.S. Infantry, July 28, 1866; Dismissed Dec. 6, 1869; Reinstated March 28, 1870; Honorably mustered out, Jan. 1, 1871). Postal clerk, U.S. Railway Mail Service, in later life.
Miscellaneous: Resided Delafield, Waukesha Co., WI; Milwaukee, WI; and Waukesha, Waukesha Co., WI, after 1875. Grandson of Colonel William Whistler (4 U.S. Infantry). Nephew of Bvt. Brig. Gen. Joseph N.G. Whistler.
Buried: Nashotah House Cemetery, Delafield, WI
References: Richard H. Groves. *Blooding the Regiment: An Account of the 22nd Wisconsin's Long and Difficult Apprenticeship.* Lanham, MD, 2005. Obituary Circular, Whole No. 545, Wisconsin MOLLUS. Obituary, *Milwaukee Morning Sentinel,* Oct. 23, 1914. Obituary, *Oshkosh Daily Northwest-*

ern, Oct. 23, 1914. George M. Bloodgood, compiler. *Ancestors and Descendants of Captain Frans Janse Bloetgoet, 1462–1966.* N.p., 1980. Pension File and Military Service File, National Archives. Letters Received, Volunteer Service Branch, Adjutant General's Office, File G1003(VS)1863, National Archives. Letters Received, Commission Branch, Adjutant General's Office, File B56(CB)1870, National Archives. Court-martial Case Files, 1809–1894, File NN-0414, National Archives. Edwin L. Buttrick, "The Case of Lt. Col. Bloodgood," *Milwaukee Sentinel,* Nov. 17, 1863. William L. Utley, "Continuation of Bloodgood's Case," *Milwaukee Sentinel,* Dec. 10, 1863. William M. Fliss, "Wisconsin's Abolition Regiment: The Twenty-second Volunteer Infantry in Kentucky, 1862–1863," *Wisconsin Magazine of History,* Vol. 86, No. 2 (Winter 2002–2003). Frank L. Byrne, editor. *The View from Headquarters: Civil War Letters of Harvey Reid.* Madison, WI, 1965.

Frederick Augustus Boardman

Major, 4 WI Infantry, May 28, 1861. Lieutenant Colonel, 4 WI Infantry, May 29, 1863. Colonel, 4 WI Infantry, June 3, 1863. Designation of regiment changed to 4 WI Cavalry, Aug. 22, 1863. GSW head, Olive Branch Creek, LA, May 3, 1864. Battle honors: Baton Rouge, Fort Bisland, Port Hudson, Olive Branch Creek.

Born: March 31, 1832, Fairfield, Herkimer Co., NY

Died: May 3, 1864, KIA Olive Branch Creek, near Baton Rouge, LA

Above: **Frederick Augustus Boardman (William DeLoss Love.** *Wisconsin in the War of the Rebellion.* **Chicago, IL, 1866).** *Below:* **Frederick Augustus Boardman (right, with Colonel Nicholas W. Day, 131 New York Infantry) (B. Moses, No. 1 Camp Street, Corner Canal, New Orleans, LA).**

Frederick Augustus Boardman (Roger D. Hunt Collection, USAMHI [RG98S-CWP64.80]).

Education: Attended U.S. Naval Academy, Annapolis, MD (Class of 1855)
Occupation: Midshipman, USN (Resigned June 19, 1856). Clerk (1860).
Miscellaneous: Resided La Crosse, La Crosse Co., WI; and Milwaukee, WI
Buried: Forest Home Cemetery, Milwaukee, WI (Section 25, Block 15, Lots 15–16)
References: Charlotte Goldthwaite, compiler. *Boardman Genealogy, 1525–1895.* Hartford, CT, 1895. William DeLoss Love. *Wisconsin in the War of the Rebellion.* Chicago, IL, 1866. Edwin B. Quiner. *The Military History of Wisconsin.* Chicago, IL, 1866. Obituary, *Milwaukee Sentinel,* May 13, 1864. Obituary, *Daily Milwaukee News,* May 13, 1864. Michael J. Martin. *A History of the 4th Wisconsin Infantry and Cavalry in the Civil War.* New York City, NY, 2006. Pension File and Military Service File, National Archives.

Gabriel Bouck

Captain, Co. E, 2 WI Infantry, June 11, 1861. Colonel, 18 WI Infantry, April 22, 1862. Commanded 2 Brigade, 6 Division, Left Wing, 13 Army Corps, Army of the Tennessee, Nov. 1–Dec. 18, 1862. Resigned effective Jan. 4, 1864, since "the interests of the service do not demand or require that he

Gabriel Bouck (post-war) (Wisconsin Historical Society, WHi-59453).

should continue in the service, holding a colonel's position with, in fact, less than a major's command." Commanded 1 Brigade, 3 Division, 15 Army Corps, Army of the Tennessee, Feb. 4–March 12, 1864, acceptance of his resignation not being received until March 16, 1864. Battle honors: Corinth, Jackson, Champion's Hill, Vicksburg Campaign, Chattanooga-Ringgold Campaign.
Born: Dec. 16, 1828, Fultonham, Schoharie Co., NY
Died: Feb. 21, 1904, Oshkosh, WI
Education: Graduated Union College, Schenectady, NY, 1847
Occupation: Lawyer
Offices/Honors: Wisconsin Attorney General, 1858–60. Wisconsin State Assembly, 1860 and 1874 (Speaker). U.S. House of Representatives, 1877–81.
Miscellaneous: Resided Oshkosh, Winnebago Co., WI. Son of former New York Governor William C. Bouck. Brother-in-law of Colonel George E. Danforth (134 NY Infantry).
Buried: Riverside Cemetery, Oshkosh, WI (Masonic Section, Block C, Lot 13)
References: *Commemorative Biographical Record of the Fox River Valley Counties of Brown, Outagamie and Winnebago.* Chicago, IL, 1895. Joseph R. Brown, Jr. "Gabriel Bouck, 1828–1904, Son of Governor William C. Bouck," *Schoharie County Historical Review,* Vol. 26, No. 1 (Spring-Summer 1962). "In

Gabriel Bouck (pre-war, as member of 1860 Wisconsin State Assembly) (Wisconsin Historical Society, WHi-119522).

Memoriam: Gabriel Bouck," *Wisconsin Reports: Cases Determined in the Supreme Court of Wisconsin.* Vol. 136. Chicago, IL, 1909. Obituary, *Oshkosh Daily Northwestern,* Feb. 22, 1904. Obituary, *New York Times,* Feb. 22, 1904. William A. Titus, editor. *History of the Fox River Valley, Lake Winnebago and the Green Bay Region.* Chicago, IL, 1930. Publius V. Lawson, editor. *History Winnebago County, Wisconsin, Its Cities, Towns, Resources, People.* Chicago, IL, 1908. *Dictionary of Wisconsin Biography.* Madison, WI, 1960. James L. Harrison, compiler. *Biographical Directory of the American Congress, 1774–1949.* Washington, DC, 1950. Parker McCobb Reed. *The Bench and Bar of Wisconsin: History and Biography.* Milwaukee, WI, 1882. John R. Berryman. *History of the Bench and Bar of Wisconsin.* Chicago, IL, 1898. Military Service File, National Archives. Letters Received, Volunteer Service Branch, Adjutant General's Office, File B467(VS)1862, National Archives. George H. Otis. *The Second Wisconsin Infantry.* Edited by Alan D. Gaff. Dayton, OH, 1984. Alan D. Gaff. *If This is War: A History of the Campaign of Bull's Run by the Wisconsin Regiment Thereafter Known as the Ragged Ass Second.* Dayton, OH, 1991.

William Buckman Britton

Captain, Co. G, 8 WI Infantry, Sept. 4, 1861. Major, 8 WI Infantry, Dec. 21, 1862. Lieutenant Colonel, 8 WI Infantry, Oct. 12, 1864. Colonel, 8 WI Infantry, March 28, 1865. Honorably mustered out,

William Buckman Britton (Porter's Photograph Parlors, Main Street, Opposite McKey's, Janesville, WI; Roger D. Hunt Collection, USAMHI [RG98S-CWP26.90]).

William Buckman Britton (as Colonel, Wisconsin National Guard, 1882) (W.C. Colbron. *The Wisconsin National Guard.* Milwaukee, WI, 1894).

Sept. 5, 1865. Battle honors: Corinth, Vicksburg Campaign, Red River Campaign, Lake Chicot, Nashville, Mobile Campaign (Spanish Fort).

Born: Jan. 8, 1829, Freehold, NJ
Died: Dec. 19, 1910, Janesville, WI
Occupation: Carpenter before war. Furniture maker and undertaker after war.
Miscellaneous: Resided Janesville, Rock Co., WI
Offices/Honors: Wisconsin State Assembly, 1883. Colonel, 1 Wisconsin National Guard, 1882–85.
Buried: Oak Hill Cemetery, Janesville, WI (Block 25, Lot 2, Grave 4)
References: James E. Heg, compiler. *The Blue Book of the State of Wisconsin,* Vol. 22. Milwaukee, WI, 1883. John M. Williams. *"The Eagle Regiment," 8th Wisconsin Infantry Volunteers, A Sketch of Its Marches, Battles and Campaigns, from 1861 to 1865.* Belleville, WI, 1890. Pension File, National Archives. Obituary, *Janesville Daily Gazette,* Dec. 19, 1910. Thomas Walterman. *There Stands "Old Rock," Rock County, Wisconsin, and the War to Preserve the Union.* Friendship, WI, 2001. *The History of Rock County, Wisconsin.* Chicago, IL, 1879. "Arrived in

City Fifty Years Ago: Colonel W.B. Britton Here Half a Century Today," *Janesville Daily Gazette*, May 16, 1905. W.C. Colbron. *The Wisconsin National Guard.* Milwaukee, WI, 1894.

Harvey Maynard Brown

1 Lieutenant, Co. I, 31 WI Infantry, Dec. 28, 1862. Acting Ordnance Officer, District of Columbus (KY), 6 Division, 16 Army Corps, Army of the Tennessee, Sept. 1863–March 1864. Major, 36 WI Infantry, March 24, 1864. Lieutenant Colonel, 36 WI Infantry, June 11, 1864. GSW back and right thigh, Petersburg, VA, June 18, 1864. Colonel, 36 WI Infantry, July 15, 1864. Discharged due to physical disability from wounds, Oct. 27, 1864. Battle honors: North Anna, Cold Harbor, Petersburg.

Born: Dec. 26, 1835, Clinton, NY
Died: Oct. 27, 1893, Columbus, WI
Occupation: Drayman before war. Book, stationery and jewelry dealer after war.
Miscellaneous: Resided Columbus, Columbia Co., WI
Offices/Honors: Postmaster, Columbus, WI, 1886–90
Buried: Hillside Cemetery, Columbus, WI (Addition 1)
References: James M. Aubery. *The Thirty-Sixth Wisconsin Volunteer Infantry, 1st Brigade, 2nd Division, 2nd Army Corps, Army of the Potomac.* Milwaukee, WI, 1900. Obituary, *Columbus Republican*, Nov. 4, 1893. Pension File and Military Service File, National Archives. Letters Received, Volunteer Service Branch, Adjutant General's Office, File W1802(VS)1864, National Archives.

George Edwin Bryant

Captain, Co. E, 1 WI Infantry, May 17, 1861. Honorably mustered out, Aug. 21, 1861. Colonel, 12 WI Infantry, Nov. 7, 1861. Commanded Post of Humboldt (TN), District of Mississippi, Army of the Tennessee, July–Sept. 1862. Commanded 3 Brigade, 4 Division, 16 Army Corps, Army of the Tennessee, Feb. 3–June 9, 1863. Commanded 5 Brigade, 12 Division, 13 Army Corps, Army of the Tennessee, July 1863. Commanded 1 Brigade, 3 Division, 17 Army Corps, Army of the Tennessee, July 22–Oct. 20, 1864. Honorably mustered out, Nov. 6, 1864. Battle honors: Expedition from Memphis, TN, to the Coldwater, MS (Hernando), Vicksburg Campaign, Jackson Campaign, Atlanta Campaign (Kenesaw Mountain, Atlanta, Ezra Church, Jonesborough).

Born: Feb. 11, 1832, Templeton, MA
Died: Feb. 16, 1907, Blooming Grove Twp., Dane Co., WI
Education: Graduated Norwich (VT) University, 1855

Harvey Maynard Brown (James M. Aubery. *The 36th Wisconsin Volunteer Infantry, 1st Brigade, 2nd Division, 2nd Army Corps, Army of the Potomac.* Milwaukee, WI, 1900).

George Edwin Bryant (Massachusetts MOLLUS Collection, USAMHI [Vol. 80, p. 4040]).

George Edwin Bryant (Wisconsin Historical Society, WHi-119512).

Occupation: Lawyer, judge, and farmer
Offices/Honors: Dane County (WI) Judge, 1865–77. Wisconsin Senate, 1875–76. Quartermaster General of Wisconsin, 1876–82. Postmaster, Madison, WI, 1882–86 and 1890–94. Wisconsin State Assembly, 1899.
Miscellaneous: Resided Madison, Dane Co., WI; and Blooming Grove Twp., Dane Co., WI
Buried: Forest Hill Cemetery, Madison, WI (Section 4, Lot 129)
References: William A. Ellis, editor. *Norwich University, 1819–1911: Her History, Her Graduates, Her Roll of Honor.* Montpelier, VT, 1911. David I. Nelke. *The Columbian Biographical Dictionary and Portrait Gallery of the Representative Men of the United States.* Wisconsin Volume. Chicago, IL, 1895. *Soldiers' and Citizens' Album of Biographical Record.* Chicago, IL, 1890. Parker McCobb Reed. *The Bench and Bar of Wisconsin: History and Biography.* Milwaukee, WI, 1882. *The United States Biographical Dictionary and Portrait Gallery of Eminent and Self-Made Men.* Wisconsin Volume. Chicago, Cincinnati and New York, 1877. *Dictionary of Wisconsin Biography.* Madison, WI, 1960. *History of Dane County, Wisconsin.* Chicago, IL, 1880. *Biographical Review of Dane County, Wisconsin.* Chicago, IL, 1893. *George Edwin Bryant: Our Colonel.* Madison, WI, 1907. Obituary, *Wisconsin State Journal,* Feb. 16, 1907. Obituary, *Janesville Daily Gazette,* Feb. 18, 1907. Hosea W. Rood, compiler. *Wisconsin at Vicksburg: Report of the Wisconsin-Vicksburg Monument Commission.* Madison, WI, 1914. Hosea W. Rood. *Story of the Service of Co. E, and of the Twelfth Wisconsin Regiment of Veteran Volunteer Infantry in the War of the Rebellion.* Milwaukee, WI, 1893. Pension File and Military Service File, National Archives.

Edwin Lorenzo Buttrick

Major, Judge Advocate, Staff of Governor Alexander W. Randall, 1861. Lieutenant Colonel, 24 WI Infantry, Aug. 22, 1862. Suffering from "sub-acute laryngitis," he resigned Dec. 24, 1862, since "my constitution, at best delicate, has become impaired by the field service to which I have been subjected, and there is no prospect of regaining my health or of being of any service to the regiment by remaining longer connected with it." Colonel, 39 WI Infantry, June 3, 1864. Commanded 4 Brigade, District of Memphis, Right Wing, 16 Army Corps, Department of the Tennessee, June–Sept. 1864. Honorably mustered out, Sept. 22, 1864. Battle honors: Perryville, Forrest's Attack on Memphis.
Born: Aug. 5, 1824, Boston, MA
Died: Nov. 9, 1908, Allston, MA
Education: Graduated Hamilton College, Clinton, NY, 1842

Edwin Lorenzo Buttrick (W.H. Sherman, Photographic Artist, 16 Wisconsin Street, Milwaukee, WI).

Edwin Lorenzo Buttrick (Wisconsin Historical Society, WHi-70275).

Edwin Lorenzo Buttrick (W.H. Sherman, Photographic Artist, 231 Main Street, Milwaukee, WI; The Wisconsin Veterans Museum, Madison, WI [WVM.1128.I001]).

Occupation: Lawyer
Miscellaneous: Resided Milwaukee, WI; Chicago, IL, 1868–71; Ceredo, Wayne Co., WV, 1871–77; Charleston, Kanawha Co., WV, 1877–1904; and Grafton, Worcester Co., MA. Uncle of U.S. Secretary of State Elihu Root.
Buried: Riverside Cemetery, Grafton, MA
References: *Encyclopedia of Contemporary Biography of West Virginia.* New York City, NY, 1894. Richard P. Butrick. *Butrick, Butterick, Buttrick in the U.S.A., 1635–1978.* N.p., 1979. William J.K. Beaudot. *The 24th Wisconsin Infantry in the Civil War: The Biography of a Regiment.* Mechanicsburg, PA, 2003. Pension File and Military Service File, National Archives. Death notice, *Boston Post,* Nov. 12, 1908. Obituary, *Boston Herald,* Nov. 13, 1908. Obituary Circular, Whole No. 546, District of Columbia MOLLUS. http://www.wssas.org/Research_and_Links.html.

Alfred Rose Chapin

1 Lieutenant, Adjutant, 1 WI Infantry (3 months), May 17, 1861. Acting AAG, Staff of Brig. Gen. John J. Abercrombie, 6 Brigade, 2 Division, Department of Pennsylvania, June–Aug. 1861. Honorably mustered out, Aug. 21, 1861. Colonel, 10 WI Infantry, Oct. 29, 1861. Resigned Jan. 23, 1863, due to disability from chronic diarrhea. Battle honors: Paint Rock Bridge, Perryville, Stone's River.
Born: July 30, 1825, Hartford, CT
Died: Dec. 20, 1866, Rockford, IL
Occupation: Produce commission merchant before war. Hardware merchant after war.
Miscellaneous: Resided Milwaukee, WI; and Rockford, Winnebago Co., IL
Buried: Greenwood Cemetery, Rockford, IL (Block 11, Lot 24)
References: "Short Biographical Sketch of Alfred R. Chapin," *Fourth Annual Reunion of the Tenth Wisconsin Infantry, Held at Tomah, Wis., July 21 and 22, 1898.* Waupun, WI, 1898. Charles A. Church. *Past and Present of the City of Rockford and Winnebago County, Illinois.* Chicago, IL, 1905. Obituary,

Rockford Weekly Gazette, Dec. 27, 1866. Obituary, *Rockford Weekly Register-Gazette*, Dec. 22, 1866. Obituary, *Semi-Weekly Wisconsin*, Dec. 26, 1866. Gilbert W. Chapin, compiler. *The Chapin Book of Genealogical Data*. Hartford, CT, 1924. Pension File and Military Service File, National Archives.

John Garvin Clark

1 Lieutenant, RQM, 5 WI Infantry, July 12, 1861. Resigned May 14, 1863. Captain, Provost Marshal, Board of Enrollment, 3 District of Wisconsin, May 1863–Feb. 1865. Colonel, 50 WI Infantry, Feb. 18, 1865. Commanded 1 Sub-District, District of Central Missouri, Department of the Missouri, May–July 1865. Honorably mustered out, June 14, 1866. Battle honors: Virginia Peninsular Campaign, Antietam, Fredericksburg, Chancellorsville.

Born: July 31, 1825, near Jacksonville, Morgan Co., IL

Died: Nov. 2, 1917, Lancaster, WI

Education: Graduated Illinois College, Jacksonville, IL, 1847

Occupation: Surveyor and lawyer

Offices/Honors: Circuit Court Clerk, 1855–60. Wisconsin State Assembly, 1861. Mayor of Lancaster (WI), 1880–82. Associate Justice, Oklahoma Territory Supreme Court, 1890–93.

Above: Alfred Rose Chapin (W.H. Sherman, Photographic Artist, 16 Wisconsin Street, Milwaukee, WI). *Below:* Alfred Rose Chapin (J.C. Elrod, Louisville, KY; courtesy Stephen and Wendy Osman).

John Garvin Clark (pre-war, as member of 1861 Wisconsin State Assembly) (Wisconsin Historical Society, WHi-101148).

John Garvin Clark (H.N. Roberts, Photographer, Madison, WI; courtesy Henry Deeks).

Miscellaneous: Resided Lancaster, Grant Co., WI

Buried: Hillside Cemetery, Lancaster, WI (unmarked)

References: Ellis Baker Usher. *Wisconsin: Its Story and Biography, 1848–1913.* Chicago and New York, 1914. *Soldiers' and Citizens' Album of Biographical Record.* Chicago, IL, 1890. John R. Berryman. *History of the Bench and Bar of Wisconsin.* Chicago, IL, 1898. Obituary, *Lancaster Teller*, Nov. 8, 1917. Obituary, *Grant County Herald*, Nov. 7, 1917. *History of Grant County, Wisconsin.* Chicago, IL, 1881. Mary McBrien Ziemer, "The Life of Colonel John G. Clark," http://www.prairietree.com/wp/John%20G.%20Clark_ed.pdf. *Catalogue of Phi Alpha Society, Illinois College, 1845–1890.* Jacksonville, IL, 1890. *The Illinois College Alumni Fund Association: Book of Memorial Memberships.* Centennial Edition, 1829–1929. Jacksonville, IL, 1929. Pension File and Military Service File, National Archives. Letters Received, Volunteer Service Branch, Adjutant General's Office, File C1338(VS)1863, National Archives.

Edward Colman

1 Lieutenant, Co. A, 18 WI Infantry, Jan. 13, 1862. GSW face below left eye, Shiloh, TN, April 6, 1862. 1 Lieutenant, Adjutant, 18 WI Infantry, March 28, 1863. GSW right leg, Champion's Hill, MS, May 16, 1863. Resigned April 30, 1864, to accept appointment in the Veteran Reserve Corps. 1 Lieutenant, VRC, May 1, 1864. Captain, Co. E, 14 VRC, Dec. 13, 1864. Resigned March 1, 1865, to accept promotion. Lieutenant Colonel, 49 WI Infantry, March 2, 1865. *Colonel*, 49 WI Infantry, Nov. 14, 1865. Honorably mustered out, Nov. 8, 1865. Battle honors: Shiloh, Jackson, Champion's Hill.

Edward Colman (post-war, as member of 1882 Wisconsin Senate) (Wisconsin Historical Society, WHi-49875).

Born: July 28, 1828, Rochester, NY
Died: Sept. 4, 1898, Sheboygan, WI
Occupation: Civil engineer and farmer before war. Bank clerk, bookkeeper and farmer after war.
Offices/Honors: Wisconsin Superintendent of Public Property, 1866–67. Sheriff of Fond du Lac County, WI, 1878–80. Wisconsin Senate, 1882–83.
Miscellaneous: Resided Fond du Lac, Fond du Lac Co., WI; and Moline, Rock Island Co., IL. Brother-in-law of Brig. Gen. Edward S. Bragg.
Buried: Rienzi Cemetery, Fond du Lac, WI (Section H)
References: Obituary, *Fond du Lac Reporter*, Sept. 5, 1898. Obituary, *Fond du Lac Daily Commonwealth*, Sept. 6, 1898. *The History of Fond du Lac County, Wisconsin.* Chicago, IL, 1880. Obituary Circular, Whole No. 293, Wisconsin MOLLUS. James

E. Heg, compiler. *The Blue Book of the State of Wisconsin*, Vol. 22. Milwaukee, WI, 1883. Obituary, *Sheboygan Times*, Sept. 10, 1898. *Report of the Proceedings of the Society of the Army of the Tennessee at the Thirty-First Meeting*. Cincinnati, OH, 1900. Pension File and Military Service File, National Archives. Letters Received, Volunteer Service Branch, Adjutant General's Office, File C511(VS)1862, National Archives.

Squire Park Coon

Colonel, 2 WI Infantry, June 11, 1861. Volunteer ADC, Staff of Colonel William T. Sherman, 3 Brigade, 1 Division, Army of Northeastern Virginia, July 1861. Lacking the confidence of his line officers, due to his "inordinate use of stimulants," he resigned July 31, 1861. Battle honors: First Bull Run.

Born: March 28, 1820, Covington, Wyoming Co., NY
Died: Oct. 13, 1883, Milwaukee, WI
Education: Attended Norwich (VT) University
Occupation: Lawyer
Offices/Honors: Wisconsin Attorney General, 1850–52
Miscellaneous: Resided Milwaukee, WI; and Chicago, IL
Buried: Forest Home Cemetery, Milwaukee, WI (Section 26, Block 22, Lot 4)
References: Obituary, *Milwaukee Sentinel,* Oct. 16, 1883. John R. Berryman. *History of the Bench and Bar of Wisconsin*. Chicago, IL, 1898. *Report of the Annual Meeting of the Wisconsin State Bar Association, 1900*. Madison, WI, 1901. Obituary, *Janesville Daily Gazette*, Oct. 17, 1883. Jerome A. Watrous, editor. *Memoirs of Milwaukee County*. Madison, WI, 1909. James S. Buck. *Pioneer History of Milwaukee: Milwaukee Under the Charter, from 1847 to 1853, Inclusive*. Milwaukee, WI, 1884. Parker McCobb Reed. *The Bench and Bar of Wisconsin: History and Biography*. Milwaukee, WI, 1882. William A. Ellis, editor. *Norwich University, 1819–1911: Her History, Her Graduates, Her Roll of Honor*. Montpelier, VT, 1911. Military Service File, National Archives. George H. Otis. *The Second Wisconsin Infantry*. Edited by Alan D. Gaff. Dayton, OH, 1984. Alan D. Gaff. *If This is War: A History of the Campaign of Bull's Run by the Wisconsin Regiment Thereafter Known as the Ragged Ass Second*. Dayton, OH, 1991.

Nelson Francis Craigue

Private, Co. F, 4 WI Infantry, July 13, 1861. Corporal, Co. F, 4 WI Infantry, Oct. 30, 1861. Sergeant, Co. F, 4 WI Infantry, Dec. 10, 1861. 2 Lieutenant, Co. F, 4 WI Infantry, Jan. 11, 1862. Captain, Co. F, 4 WI Infantry, Sept. 11, 1862. GSW lower back, Port Hudson, LA, May 27, 1863. Designation of regiment changed to 4 WI Cavalry, Aug. 22, 1863. Commanded Post of Penniston's Cut-Off, District of Baton Rouge, Department of the Gulf, Nov. 1863–Feb. 1864. Major, 4 WI Cavalry, May 24, 1864. Lieutenant Colonel, 4 WI Cavalry, Oct. 7, 1865. *Colonel,* 4 WI Cavalry, Nov. 9, 1865. Honorably mustered out, May 28, 1866. Battle honors: Port Hudson, Expedition to Clinton (LA).

Born: Dec. 24, 1835, Troy, VT

Squire Park Coon (Wisconsin Historical Society, WHi-119439).

Nelson Francis Craigue (Marc and Beth Storch Collection).

Died: Feb. 11, 1916, Weathersfield, VT
Occupation: Grocer, store clerk and farmer
Miscellaneous: Resided Weathersfield, Windsor Co., VT; Racine, Racine Co., WI, 1861–66; Marshalltown, Marshall Co., IA, 1868–73; and Allouez, Keweenaw Co., MI, 1873–87
Buried: Greenbush Cemetery, Weathersfield, VT
References: Pension File and Military Service File, National Archives. Letters Received, Volunteer Service Branch, Adjutant General's Office, File C2046(VS)1864, National Archives. Michael J. Martin. *A History of the 4th Wisconsin Infantry and Cavalry in the Civil War.* New York City, NY, 2006. Jeremiah Spofford. *A Genealogical Record, Including Two Generations in Female Lines of Families Spelling Their Name Spofford, Spafford, Spafard, and Spaford, Descendants of John Spofford and Elizabeth Scott.* Boston, MA, 1888.

Nicholas Harry Dale

Captain, Co. G, 2 WI Cavalry, Jan. 14, 1862. Judge Advocate, Staff of Brig. Gen. Thomas A. Davies, District of Rolla, Department of the Missouri, June–Dec. 1863. Major, 2 WI Cavalry, April 4, 1864. GSW left foot, Concord Church, MS, Dec. 1, 1864. Lieutenant Colonel, 2 WI Cavalry, Jan. 1, 1865. *Colonel,* 2 WI Cavalry, Jan. 30, 1865. Found guilty by court martial, June 10, 1865, of "Using contemptuous and disrespectful language against the President of the United States," he was sentenced to be reprimanded by the General commanding the District of West Tennessee and returned to duty. Honorably mustered out, Nov. 15, 1865. Battle honors: Expedition from Vicksburg to Yazoo City (Concord Church).

Born: April 6, 1827, Mullion, Cornwall, England
Died: July 9, 1878, Neosho, MO
Occupation: Lawyer
Offices/Honors: District Attorney, Racine Co., WI, 1860–62
Miscellaneous: Resided Racine, Racine Co., WI; and Neosho, Newton Co., MO, after 1866
Buried: IOOF Cemetery, Neosho, MO. Cenotaph in Yorkville Cemetery, Yorkville, Racine Co., WI.
References: Obituary, *Neosho Times,* July 11, 1878. Pension File and Military Service File, National Archives. Eugene W. Leach. *Racine County Militant, An Illustrated Narrative of War Times, and a Soldiers' Roster.* Racine, WI, 1915. Fanny S. Stone, editor. *Racine, Belle City of the Lakes, and Racine County, Wisconsin.* Chicago, IL, 1916. Emmet C. West. *History and Reminiscences of the Second Wisconsin Cavalry Regiment.* Portage, WI, 1904. Court-martial Case Files, 1809–1894, File OO-1076, National Archives.

Edward Dwight Daniels

Lieutenant Colonel, 1 WI Cavalry, Sept. 15, 1861. Colonel, 1 WI Cavalry, Dec. 1, 1861. Commanded Post of Cape Girardeau (MO), District of St. Louis, Department of the Mississippi, May–June 1862. Absent on sick leave since Aug. 1862, he finally resigned, Feb. 5, 1863, on account of physical disability due to "hydrothorax, or dropsy of the chest, the right pleural cavity being nearly filled with effused fluid." Battle honors: Chalk Bluff.

Born: Jan. 19, 1828, Cambridge, MA
Died: April 19, 1916, Gunston, VA
Education: Attended Oberlin (OH) College
Occupation: Geologist and mining engineer before war. Agricultural reformer and newspaper editor after war.
Offices/Honors: Wisconsin State Geologist, 1853–54
Miscellaneous: Resided Ripon, Fond du Lac Co., WI; and Waukesha, Waukesha Co., WI, before war; Gunston, Fairfax Co., VA, 1868–91 (owned Gunston Hall, the one-time residence of George Mason, a Revolutionary-era statesman); New York City, NY; and Omaha, NE

Nicholas Harry Dale.

Edward Dwight Daniels (James Harrison Daniels, Jr. *The Daniels-Daniells Family: A Genealogical History of the Descendants of William Daniell of Dorchester and Milton, Massachusetts, 1630–1957.* Baltimore, MD, 1959).

Buried: Arlington National Cemetery, Arlington, VA (Section 2, Lot 3681)

References: Sara B. Bearss, senior editor. *Dictionary of Virginia Biography.* Richmond, VA, 2006. David H. Overy, Jr., "The Wisconsin Carpetbagger: A Group Portrait," *Wisconsin Magazine of History,* Vol. 44, No. 1 (Autumn 1960). *Thirty-second Annual Reunion of the First Wisconsin Cavalry Association.* Oshkosh, WI, 1916. James Harrison Daniels, Jr. *The Daniels-Daniells Family: A Genealogical History of the Descendants of William Daniell of Dorchester and Milton, Massachusetts, 1630–1957.* Baltimore, MD, 1959. *Dictionary of Wisconsin Biography.* Madison, WI, 1960. Obituary, *Alexandria Gazette,* April 29, 1916. Obituary, *Milwaukee Evening Wisconsin,* May 13, 1916. Obituary, *Oshkosh Daily Northwestern,* May 12, 1916. Death notice, *Washington Post,* April 22, 1916. David P. Mapes. *History of the City of Ripon, and of Its Founder, David P. Mapes.* Milwaukee, WI, 1873. *History of Fond du Lac County, Wisconsin.* Chicago, IL, 1880. Pension File and Military Service File, National Archives. Letters Received, Volunteer Service Branch, Adjutant General's Office, File I558(VS)1862, National Archives.

Thomas Derry

Captain, Co. L, 3 WI Cavalry, Dec. 13, 1861. Major, 3 WI Cavalry, Jan. 22, 1864. Colonel, 3 WI Cavalry, June 10, 1865. Commanded District of Southwest Missouri, Department of the Missouri, June–July 1865. Honorably mustered out, Sept. 8, 1865. Battle honors: Expedition from Little Rock to Fort Smith (Clarksville).

Born: Dec. 22, 1832, Lincolnshire, England
Died: Nov. 22, 1913, Pacific Branch, NHDVS, Sawtelle, CA
Occupation: Carpenter and cemetery superintendent
Miscellaneous: Resided Middleton, Dane Co., WI; Vallejo, Solano Co., CA, 1869–73; Napa, Napa Co., CA, 1873–99; and Sawtelle, Los Angeles Co., CA, 1899–1913
Buried: Tulocay Cemetery, Napa, CA (Block 97, Lot 22)
References: Pension File and Military Service File, National Archives. Letters Received, Volunteer Service Branch, Adjutant General's Office, File V210(VS)1865, National Archives. http://freepages.history.rootsweb.ancestry.com/~enderlin/cw/napa/tulocay-cwburials.html. Historical Register of National Homes for Disabled Volunteer Soldiers, 1866–1938, National Archives. Obituary, *Napa Daily Journal,* Nov. 23, 1913.

Thomas Derry (Heald & Stiff, Photographers, Successors to Troxell & Bro., S.W. Corner Fourth & Locust Streets, Entrance on Locust Street, St. Louis, MO; Marc and Beth Storch Collection).

Daniel J. Dill

Captain, Co. B, 6 WI Infantry, June 17, 1861. Colonel, 30 WI Infantry, Oct. 12, 1862. Commanded Fort Rice, Dakota Territory, Department of the Northwest, July–Aug. 1864. Commanded 2 Brigade, 2 Division, Military District of Kentucky, Department of the Ohio, Dec. 20, 1864–Jan. 17, 1865. Commanded Post of Louisville (KY), Military District of Kentucky, Department of Kentucky, Feb. 11–April 17, 1865. Provost Marshal General, Department of Kentucky, April–Sept. 1865. Honorably mustered out, Sept. 20, 1865.

Born: Feb. 24, 1830, Dillsburg, PA
Died: Feb. 7, 1917, Prescott, WI
Occupation: Merchant and farmer
Offices/Honors: Wisconsin State Assembly, 1889 and 1891
Miscellaneous: Resided Dillsburg, York Co., PA; and Prescott, Pierce Co., WI, after 1859
Buried: Pine Glen Cemetery, Prescott, WI
References: Edward D. Neill. *History of Washington County and the St. Croix Valley, Including the Explorers and Pioneers of Minnesota*. Minneapolis, MN, 1881. Obituary, *Pierce County Herald*, Feb. 8, 1917. *Wisconsin Session Laws: Acts, Resolutions and Memorials Passed at the Biennial Session of the Legislature, 1917*. Madison, WI, 1917. Obituary, *River*

Daniel J. Dill (Fuller, Gilman's Block, Madison, WI; Craig T. Johnson Collection).

Falls Journal, Feb. 15, 1917. Ernest G. Timme, compiler. *The Blue Book of the State of Wisconsin*, Vol. 25. Milwaukee, WI, 1889. *History of Cumberland and Adams Counties, Pennsylvania*. Chicago, IL, 1886. Rosalie Jones Dill. *Mathew Dill Genealogy: A Study of the Dill Family of Dillsburg, York County, Pennsylvania, 1698–1934*. Spokane, WA, 1934. Pension File and Military Service File, National Archives. https://thecivilwarandnorthwestwisconsin.wordpress.com/the-soldiers/alphabetical-list-of-all-soldiers-from-northwest-wisconsin/daniel-j-dill-1830-1917/.

John L. Doran

Colonel, 17 WI Infantry, March 18, 1862. Commanded 1 Brigade, 6 Division, Army of the Tennessee, April–May 1862. Facing trial by court martial on charges of "Disobedience of orders" and "Conduct unbecoming an officer and a gentleman," he resigned Nov. 25, 1862, since "my health is poor ... and my usefulness to the service lost with a regiment I spent some four thousand dollars raising." Brig. Gen. Charles S. Hamilton recommended immediate acceptance of the resignation, since "the service and the good of the regiment demands it, as also the services of the General and field officers who are on the court to try him." Brig. Gen. Hamilton further elaborated, "He is a man who maintains no discipline, is at constant fraud with his officers and whose personal and moral character is such as to render him entirely unworthy the position he holds." Battle honors: Corinth.

Born: 1814, County Mayo, Ireland
Died: Jan. 21, 1887, Chicago, IL
Occupation: Lawyer
Offices/Honors: Milwaukee City Attorney,

Daniel J. Dill (R.W. Addis, Photographer, McClees' Gallery, 308 Pennsylvania Avenue, Washington, DC; Craig T. Johnson Collection).

1847. Member of the Wisconsin Constitutional Convention, 1847–48. Wisconsin State Assembly, 1851.

Miscellaneous: Resided Milwaukee, WI; and Chicago, IL, after 1863

Buried: Calvary Cemetery, Evanston, IL (Section S, Block 1, Lot B)

References: Horace A. Tenney and David Atwood. *Memorial Record of the Fathers of Wisconsin.* Madison, WI, 1880. Milo M. Quaife, editor. *The Attainment of Statehood.* Publications of the State Historical Society of Wisconsin, Vol. 29. Madison, WI, 1928. Pension File and Military Service File, National Archives. John Y. Simon, editor. *The Papers of Ulysses S. Grant.* Volume 6: Sept. 1–Dec. 8, 1862. Carbondale, IL, 1977. James S. Buck. *Pioneer History of Milwaukee: Milwaukee Under the Charter, from 1847 to 1853, Inclusive.* Milwaukee, WI, 1884. *Report of the Annual Meeting of the Wisconsin State Bar Association, 1900.* Madison, WI, 1901. Death notice, *Chicago Daily Tribune,* Jan. 23, 1887. Death notice, *Chicago Inter Ocean,* Jan. 23, 1887.

Mark Finnicum

Captain, Co. H, 7 WI Infantry, Aug. 26, 1861. Major, 7 WI Infantry, March 4, 1863. Shell wound right arm, Fitzhugh's Crossing, VA, April 30, 1863. GSW right side of neck, Gettysburg, PA, July 1, 1863. GSW right knee, Gettysburg, PA, July 2, 1863. Lieutenant Colonel, 7 WI Infantry, Jan. 13, 1864. GSW right side of head, Laurel Hill, VA, May 10, 1864. *Colonel,* 7 WI Infantry, Aug. 3, 1864. Honorably mustered out, Dec. 17, 1864. Battle honors: Fitzhugh's Crossing, Gettysburg, Bristoe Station, Mine Run, Wilderness, Spotsylvania Campaign (Laurel Hill), Petersburg Campaign (Weldon Railroad).

Born: Dec. 25, 1823, OH

Died: Nov. 4, 1912, Eubank, KY

Occupation: Merchant before war. Farmer after war.

Offices/Honors: Greenback Party Candidate for U.S. Congress (2nd District of Kansas) in 1882. He withdrew before the election amid speculation of a financial payoff. One reason for his withdrawal may have been his dalliance with a seventeen-year-old girl, with whom he moved back to Indiana, and who eventually became his third wife.

Miscellaneous: Resided Fennimore, Grant Co., WI, to 1867; Dowagiac, Cass Co., MI, 1867–69; Austin, Travis Co., TX, 1869–70; Maysville, Benton Co., AR, 1870–74; Nashville, Brown Co., IN, 1874–75 and 1883–84; Barnesville, Bourbon Co., KS, 1875–83; Washington, Daviess Co., IN, 1884–87; and Pulaski, Pulaski Co., KY, 1887–1912

Buried: Freedom Cemetery, near Pulaski, Pulaski Co., KY

References: Pension File and Military Service File, National Archives. *History of Grant County, Wisconsin.* Chicago, IL, 1881. Lance J. Herdegen. *The Iron Brigade in Civil War and Memory.* El Dorado Hills, CA, 2012. "Col. Mark Finnicum," *Fort Scott Daily Monitor,* Aug. 10, 1882. "Col. M. Finnicum," *Topeka State Journal,* Aug. 14, 1882. "Referring to Finnicum," *Topeka Daily Capital,* Oct. 18, 1882.

Charles Rice Gill

Colonel, 29 WI Infantry, Sept. 27, 1862. Resigned June 27, 1863, due to physical disability from "an attack of hepatitis which has produced a great nervous shock to the system." Battle honors: Port Gibson, Champion's Hill, Vicksburg Campaign.

Born: Aug. 17, 1830, Winfield, Herkimer Co., NY

Died: March 28, 1883, Blooming Grove, WI

Occupation: Lawyer

Offices/Honors: Wisconsin Senate, 1860–61. Wisconsin Attorney General, 1866–70. U.S. Commissioner of Pensions, 1876.

Miscellaneous: Resided Watertown, Jefferson Co., WI; Madison, Dane Co., WI; and Blooming Grove, Dane Co., WI, after 1870

Buried: Forest Hill Cemetery, Madison, WI (Section 28, Lot 50)

References: *History of Dane County, Wisconsin.* Chicago, IL, 1880. Frederic K. Conover, editor. *Wisconsin Supreme Court Reports.* Vol. 57. Chicago, IL, 1883. Obituary, *Wisconsin State Journal,* April 3, 1883. John R. Berryman. *History of the Bench and*

Charles Rice Gill (post-war) (*History of Dane County, Wisconsin.* Chicago, IL, 1880).

Bar of Wisconsin. Chicago, IL, 1898. Edwin B. Quiner. *The Military History of Wisconsin.* Chicago, IL, 1866. Parker McCobb Reed. *The Bench and Bar of Wisconsin: History and Biography.* Milwaukee, WI, 1882. *Dictionary of Wisconsin Biography.* Madison, WI, 1960. Pension File and Military Service File, National Archives. Obituary, *Oshkosh Daily Northwestern,* March 30, 1883. *Report of the Annual Meeting of the Wisconsin State Bar Association, 1900.* Madison, WI, 1901.

George Benjamin Goodwin

Colonel, 41 WI Infantry, May 20, 1864. Lieutenant Colonel, 41 WI Infantry, June 8, 1864. Honorably mustered out, Sept. 24, 1864. Battle honors: Forrest's Attack on Memphis.

Born: Dec. 18, 1834, Mount Morris, Livingston Co., NY

Died: May 1, 1886, Milwaukee, WI

Education: Attended Williams College, Williamstown, MA. Graduated Genesee College, Lima, NY, 1854. Attended Albany (NY) Law School.

Occupation: Lawyer

Offices/Honors: Wisconsin State Assembly, 1860. U.S. Internal Revenue Assessor, 1870–73.

Miscellaneous: Resided Menasha, Winnebago Co., WI; and Milwaukee, WI, after 1865

Buried: Forest Home Cemetery, Milwaukee, WI (Section 47, Block 11, Lot 7)

George Benjamin Goodwin (courtesy Everitt Bowles).

References: Obituary, *Milwaukee Daily Sentinel,* May 2, 1886. Herbert C. Damon. *History of the Milwaukee Light Guard.* Milwaukee, WI, 1875. Jerome A. Watrous, editor. *Memoirs of Milwaukee County.* Madison, WI, 1909. *The United States Biographical Dictionary and Portrait Gallery of Eminent and Self-Made Men.* Wisconsin Volume. Chicago, Cincinnati and New York, 1877. Obituary, *Oshkosh Daily Northwestern,* May 3, 1886. Parker McCobb Reed. *The Bench and Bar of Wisconsin: History and Biography.* Milwaukee, WI, 1882. *Report of the Annual Meeting of the Wisconsin State Bar Association, 1900.* Madison, WI, 1901. Frank Smalley, editor. *Alumni Record and General Catalogue of Syracuse University, 1872–1910, Including Genesee College, 1852–1871, and Geneva Medical College, 1835–1872.* Syracuse, NY, 1911. Pension File and Military Service File, National Archives. Alfred T. Andreas. *History of Milwaukee, Wisconsin.* Chicago, IL, 1881.

Edmund Baldwin Gray

Captain, Co. C, 4 WI Infantry, May 27, 1861. Resigned April 10, 1862, due to "a rapid decline of my health for the past few weeks." Major, 28 WI Infantry, Oct. 14, 1862. Lieutenant Colonel, 28 WI Infantry, May 28, 1863. *Colonel,* 28 WI Infantry, March 16, 1864. Commanded Post of Pine Bluff (AR), Department of Arkansas, March 1864. Honorably mustered out, Aug. 23, 1865. Battle honors: Helena, Camden Expedition, Mobile Campaign.

Born: June 17, 1825, Canton, NY
Died: July 8, 1903, Chicago, IL

George Benjamin Goodwin (pre-war, as a member of 1860 Wisconsin State Assembly) (Wisconsin Historical Society, WHi-119519).

Above: Edmund Baldwin Gray (Craig T. Johnson Collection). *Below:* Edmund Baldwin Gray (post-war) (Wisconsin Historical Society, WHi-119494).

Education: Attended University of Vermont, Burlington, VT

Occupation: School teacher before war. School book agent and insurance agent after war.

Offices/Honors: Postmaster, Whitewater, WI, 1866–68. Adjutant General, National GAR, 1887 and 1893. Assistant Adjutant General, Wisconsin GAR, 1888–91 and 1901. Commander, Wisconsin GAR, 1897.

Miscellaneous: Resided Palmyra, Jefferson Co., WI (1858); Sheboygan, Sheboygan Co., WI (1861); Whitewater, Walworth Co., WI, to 1868; Chicago, IL, 1868–81; Milwaukee, WI; and Madison, Dane Co., WI

Buried: Oakwoods Cemetery, Chicago, IL (Section D, Division 1, Lot 21)

References: *Proceedings of the Twenty-first Annual Reunion of the Society of the 28th Wisconsin Volunteer Infantry.* Milwaukee, WI, 1903. Obituary Circular, Whole No. 370, Wisconsin MOLLUS. Obituary, *Eau Claire Weekly Telegram,* July 9, 1903. Obituary, *Wisconsin Weekly Advocate,* July 9, 1903. Obituary, *Chicago Inter Ocean,* July 9, 1903. Marcus D. Raymond. *Gray Genealogy, Being a Genealogical Record and History of the Descendants of John Gray of Beverly, Mass.* Tarrytown, NY, 1887. Pension File and Military Service File, National Archives. Letters Received, Volunteer Service Branch, Adjutant General's Office, File R873(VS)1863, National Archives.

John Green

Captain, Co. C, 37 WI Infantry, April 13, 1864. Shell wound back, Petersburg, VA, June 17, 1864. Major, 37 WI Infantry, Oct. 18, 1864. Lieutenant Colonel, 37 WI Infantry, Dec. 15, 1864. Commanded 1 Brigade, 1 Division, 9 Army Corps, Department of Washington, July 17–27, 1865. Colonel, 37 WI Infantry, July 21, 1865. Honorably mustered out, July 27, 1865. Battle honors: Petersburg Campaign, Richmond Campaign (Poplar Spring Church), Appomattox Campaign.

Born: 1834, England

Died: July 17, 1877, Middleton, WI

Occupation: Farmer and flour merchant

Offices/Honors: Postmaster, Moscow, WI, 1859–64. Wisconsin State Assembly, 1867.

Miscellaneous: Resided Moscow, Iowa Co., WI; and Middleton, Dane Co., WI

Buried: Forest Hill Cemetery, Madison, WI (Section 16, Lot 23)

References: Obituary, *Wisconsin State Journal,* July 17, 1877. Pension File and Military Service File, National Archives. *Report and Collections of the State Historical Society of Wisconsin, for the Years 1877, 1878 and 1879.* Vol. 8. Madison, WI, 1879. Robert C. Eden. *The Sword and Gun: A History of the 37th Wisconsin Volunteer Infantry.* Madison, WI, 1865. *History of Green County, Wisconsin.* Springfield, IL, 1884. *History of Iowa County, Wisconsin.* Chicago, IL, 1881. Obituary, *Madison Democrat,* July 18, 1877. Letters Received, Volunteer Service Branch, Adjutant General's Office, File G911(VS) 1864, National Archives.

William Augustus Greene

2 Lieutenant, Co. D, 16 WI Infantry, Dec. 30, 1861. 1 Lieutenant, Co. D, 16 WI Infantry, April 12, 1862. *Major*, 22 WI Infantry, July 28, 1862. Major, 29 WI Infantry, Aug. 30, 1862. Lieutenant Colonel, 29 WI Infantry, Feb. 11, 1863. Colonel, 29 WI Infantry, Feb. 9, 1864. Commanded 2 Brigade, 3 Division, 13 Army Corps, District of La Fourche, Department of the Gulf, June 1864. Commanded 2 Brigade, 2 Division, 19 Army Corps, Department of the Gulf, Aug. 1864 and Nov. 2–Dec. 12, 1864. "Considering that my regiment is so much reduced in numbers, the length of time I have been in the service, and the necessity of giving my personal attention to my business," he resigned Jan. 26, 1865. Battle honors: Shiloh, Champion's Hill, Vicksburg Campaign, Jackson Campaign, Operations in the Teche Country.

Born: Sept. 13, 1838, Salisbury, Herkimer Co., NY

Died: July 13, 1880, Milford, Jefferson Co., WI

Education: Attended University of Wisconsin, Madison, WI

Occupation: Merchant before war. Farmer and railroad agent after war.

Offices/Honors: Jefferson County (WI) Treasurer, 1871–73

Miscellaneous: Resided Milford, Jefferson Co., WI

Buried: Evergreen Cemetery, Fort Atkinson, WI

References: Obituary, *Lake Mills Spike*, July 20, 1880. Obituary, *Jefferson Banner*, July 29, 1880. Obituary, *Jefferson County Union*, July 16, 1880. *The History of Jefferson County, Wisconsin*. Chicago, IL, 1879. Pension File and Military Service File, National Archives.

Bradford Hancock

Captain, Co. A, 29 WI Infantry, Aug. 30, 1862. Major, 29 WI Infantry, Feb. 11, 1863. GSW right thigh, Champion's Hill, MS, May 16, 1863. Lieutenant Colonel, 29 WI Infantry, March 15, 1864. Commanded 1 Brigade, 3 Division, 13 Army Corps, Department of the Gulf, April 8–27, 1864. Colonel, 29 WI Infantry, April 30, 1865. Honorably mustered out, June 22, 1865. Battle honors: Port Gibson, Champion's Hill, Red River Campaign (Sabine Cross Roads), Mobile Campaign (Spanish Fort, Fort Blakely).

Born: Jan. 18, 1831, Sackets Harbor, NY

Died: May 15, 1887, Chicago, IL

Occupation: Merchant before war. Assignee in bankruptcy and livestock commission merchant after moving to Chicago.

Offices/Honors: Postmaster, Marshall, WI, 1861–68. Sheriff, Dane Co., WI, 1869–71.

Miscellaneous: Resided Marshall, Dane Co.,

William Augustus Greene (Wisconsin Historical Society, WHi-119510).

Bradford Hancock (J.D. Kellogg, Photographer, Watertown, WI; Craig T. Johnson Collection).

WI; Madison, Dane Co., WI; and Chicago, IL, after 1873

Buried: Graceland Cemetery, Chicago, IL (Section Resub N, Lot 48)

References: Obituary, *Chicago Inter Ocean*, May 16, 1887. Obituary, *Chicago Daily Tribune*, May 16, 1887. Obituary, *Wisconsin State Journal*, May 20, 1887. Pension File and Military Service File, National Archives. Letters Received, Volunteer Service Branch, Adjutant General's Office, File H1278(VS)1864, National Archives. *Report of the Proceedings of the Society of the Army of the Tennessee at the Twenty-Second Meeting.* Cincinnati, OH, 1893. *History of Dane County, Wisconsin.* Chicago, IL, 1880. *Report of Proceedings of the Eighth Annual Reunion of the 29th Wisconsin Regiment Volunteer Infantry, Fox Lake, June 20, 1893.* Milwaukee, WI, 1894. *In Memoriam: Col. Bradford Hancock.* Waterloo, WI, 1887. John E. Hancock. *Hancock Genealogy: Descendants of Isaac Bradford Hancock.* Scotia, NY, 1982.

John Hancock

1 Lieutenant, Co. E, 2 WI Infantry, April 23, 1861. Major, 14 WI Infantry, Jan. 30, 1862. Lieutenant Colonel, 14 WI Infantry, April 7, 1862. Colonel, 14 WI Infantry, June 17, 1862. Resigned Jan. 23, 1863, "the principal reason being the severe illness of my wife, and the urgent and pressing necessity of my being with her." His letter of resignation was accompanied by a certificate of disability citing "general debility produced by chronic diarrhea of nearly one year's duration." Battle honors: First Bull Run, Shiloh, Corinth.

Born: Aug. 12, 1830, Athens, PA

Died: April 9, 1894, City Point, WI

Occupation: Lawyer and cranberry farmer

Offices/Honors: Oshkosh (WI) City Attorney, 1869. U.S. Court Commissioner, 1875–77. Commander, Wisconsin GAR, 1876.

Miscellaneous: Resided Oshkosh, Winnebago Co., WI; and City Point, Jackson Co., WI, after 1884

Buried: Riverside Cemetery, Oshkosh, WI (Old Catholic Section, Block 36, Lot C)

References: Scott Cross, "John Hancock Sees the Civil War," *Voyageur: Northeast Wisconsin's Historical Review*, Vol. 28, No. 1 (Summer/Fall 2011). *The United States Biographical Dictionary and Portrait Gallery of Eminent and Self-Made Men.* Wisconsin Volume. Chicago, Cincinnati and New York, 1877. Obituary, *Oshkosh Daily Northwestern*, April 10, 1894. Pension File and Military Service File, National Archives. "An Old Hero: Reminiscences of the Late Col. John Hancock," *Oshkosh Daily Northwestern*, April 11, 1894. Frederick H. Magdeburg. *Wisconsin at Shiloh: Report of the Commission.* Madison, WI, 1909. John Hancock. *The Fourteenth

John Hancock (Frederick H. Magdeburg. *Wisconsin at Shiloh: Report of the Commission.* Madison, WI, 1909).

Wisconsin, Corinth and Shiloh, 1862–1895. Paper on Battle of Shiloh. Pilgrimage of Engle and Tucker to Battle Fields of Corinth and Shiloh, 1895. Indianapolis, IN, 1895. Alan D. Gaff. *If This is War: A History of the Campaign of Bull's Run by the Wisconsin Regiment Thereafter Known as the Ragged Ass Second.* Dayton, OH, 1991. Obituary, *Marshfield Times*, April 13, 1894. David A. Langkau. *Civil War Veterans of Winnebago County, Wisconsin.* Bowie, MD, 1993.

Frank Aretas Haskell

1 Lieutenant, Co. I, 6 WI Infantry, July 16, 1861. 1 Lieutenant, Adjutant, 6 WI Infantry, Dec. 12, 1861. Acting AAG, Staff of Colonel Lysander Cutler, 3 Brigade, 3 Division, 1 Army Corps, Army of the Potomac, March–April 1862. 1 Lieutenant, Co. D, 6 WI Infantry, April 14, 1862. Acting ADC, Staff of Major Gen. John Gibbon, (1 Army Corps and 2 Army Corps, Army of the Potomac), June 1862–March 1864. Contused GSW right thigh, Gettysburg, PA, July 3, 1863. Colonel, 36 WI Infantry, March 23, 1864. Commanded 1 Brigade, 2 Division, 2 Army Corps, Army of the Potomac, June 3, 1864. GSW head, Cold Harbor, VA, June 3, 1864. Battle honors: Gainesville, Second Bull Run, South

Above: Frank Aretas Haskell (Fuller, Gilman's Block, Madison, WI; Roger D. Hunt Collection, USAMHI [RG98S-CWP60.39]). *Below:* Frank Aretas Haskell (Massachusetts MOLLUS Collection, USAMHI [Vol. 28, p. 1376L]).

Frank Aretas Haskell (James M. Aubery. *The Thirty-Sixth Wisconsin Volunteer Infantry, 1st Brigade, 2nd Division, 2nd Army Corps, Army of the Potomac.* Milwaukee, WI, 1900).

Mountain, Antietam, Fredericksburg, Chancellorsville, Gettysburg, Bristoe Station, Cold Harbor.
Born: July 13, 1828, Tunbridge, Orange Co., VT
Died: June 3, 1864, KIA Cold Harbor, VA
Education: Graduated Dartmouth College, Hanover, NH, 1854
Occupation: Lawyer

Miscellaneous: Resided Columbus, Columbia Co., WI; and Madison, Dane Co., WI
Buried: Silver Lake Cemetery, Portage, WI (Block 18)
References: Frank L. Byrne and Andrew T. Weaver, editors. *Haskell of Gettysburg: His Life and Civil War Papers.* Madison, WI, 1970. Andrew J. Turner, "Col. Frank A. Haskell: His Brilliant Military Record," *Columbus Democrat,* May 29, 1895. James M. Aubery. *The Thirty-Sixth Wisconsin Volunteer Infantry, 1st Brigade, 2nd Division, 2nd Army Corps, Army of the Potomac.* Milwaukee, WI, 1900. Henry A. Hazen and S. Lewis B. Speare, editors. *A History of the Class of 1854 in Dartmouth College, Including Col. Haskell's Narrative of the Battle of Gettysburg.* Boston, MA, 1898. Edwin B. Quiner. *The Military History of Wisconsin.* Chicago, IL, 1866. Lance J. Herdegen. *The Iron Brigade in Civil War and Memory.* El Dorado Hills, CA, 2012. Obituary, *Wisconsin State Journal,* June 4, 1864. Ira J. Haskell. *Chronicles of the Haskell Family.* Lynn, MA, 1943. Military Service File, National Archives.

Hans Christian Heg

Colonel, 15 WI Infantry, Feb. 13, 1862. Commanded 2 Brigade, 1 Division, 20 Army Corps,

Army of the Cumberland, Feb. 15–March 16, 1863. Commanded 3 Brigade, 1 Division, 20 Army Corps, Army of the Cumberland, May 1–Sept. 19, 1863. GSW abdomen, Chickamauga, GA, Sept. 19, 1863. Battle honors: Island No. 10, Perryville, Stone's River, Tullahoma Campaign, Chickamauga.

Born: Dec. 21, 1829, Lier, Norway
Died: Sept. 20, 1863, DOW Chickamauga, GA
Occupation: Farmer and merchant
Offices/Honors: Wisconsin Prison Commissioner, 1860–61
Miscellaneous: Resided Muskego, Waukesha Co., WI; and Waterford, Racine Co., WI
Buried: Norway Hill Churchyard, near Waterford, WI
References: Theodore C. Blegen, editor. *The Civil War Letters of Colonel Hans Christian Heg.* Northfield, MN, 1936. Waldemar Ager. *Colonel Heg and His Boys: A Norwegian Regiment in the American Civil War.* Translated by Della Kittleson Catuna and Clarence A. Clausen. Northfield, MN, 2000. Theodore C. Blegen, "Colonel Hans Christian Heg," *Wisconsin Magazine of History*, Vol. 4, No. 2 (Dec. 1920). Obituary, *Wisconsin State Journal*, Sept. 29, 1863. Obituary, *Racine Weekly Advocate*, Sept. 30, 1863. Albert Skofstad, "Last Moments of Colonel Heg," *Wisconsin State Journal*, Oct. 27, 1863. Ole A. Buslett. *Det Femtende Regiment Wisconsin Frivillige.* Decorah, IA, 1894. Waldemar Ager. *Oberst Heg og hans Gutter.* Eau Claire, WI, 1916. Johan A. Enander.

Hans Christian Heg (Theodore C. Blegen, editor. *The Civil War Letters of Colonel Hans Christian Heg.* Northfield, MN, 1936).

Borgerkrigen i De forenede Stater i Nord Amerika. La Crosse, WI, 1881. Pension File and Military Service File, National Archives. Letters Received, Volunteer Service Branch, Adjutant General's Office, File H1163(VS)1862, National Archives. Ella S. Colbo. *Historic Heg Memorial Park.* Racine, WI, 1940. *Dictionary of Wisconsin Biography.* Madison, WI, 1960. Eugene W. Leach. *Racine County Militant, An Illustrated Narrative of War Times, and a Soldiers' Roster.* Racine, WI, 1915.

James Henry Howe

Colonel, 32 WI Infantry, Sept. 25, 1862. Commanded 2 Brigade, District of Memphis, 5 Division, 16 Army Corps, Army of the Tennessee, July 15–Aug. 15, 1863. Commanded 2 Brigade, 4 Division, 16 Army Corps, Army of the Tennessee, Feb.–April 1864. Commanded 3 Brigade, 4 Division, 16 Army Corps, Army of the Tennessee, April–July 1864. Commanded Post of Decatur (AL), May–June 1864. Resigned July 6, 1864, since "my health is such as to render me unfit for duty during the hot months in this climate." Battle honors: Meridian Expedition, Forrest's Expedition into West Tennessee and Kentucky, Atlanta Campaign.

Born: Dec. 5, 1827, Turner, ME
Died: Jan. 4, 1893, Boston, MA
Occupation: Lawyer and railroad executive
Offices/Honors: Wisconsin Attorney General, 1860–62. U.S. District Judge, 1874–75.

Hans Christian Heg (Craig T. Johnson Collection).

Above: James Henry Howe (pre-war, as Wisconsin Attorney General, 1860) (Wisconsin Historical Society, WHi-119523). *Below:* James Henry Howe (post-war) (Massachusetts MOLLUS Commandery Series, USAMHI [Vol. 30, p. 1358]).

Miscellaneous: Resided Green Bay, Brown Co., WI, before war; and Kenosha, Kenosha Co., WI, after war. Nephew of U.S. Senator Timothy O. Howe.
Buried: Green Ridge Cemetery, Kenosha, WI (Southeast Division, Block 219)

References: Obituary Circular, Whole No. 119, Minnesota MOLLUS. Obituary Circular, Whole No. 226, Wisconsin MOLLUS. Daniel W. Howe. *Howe Genealogies.* Boston, MA, 1929. *Dictionary of Wisconsin Biography.* Madison, WI, 1960. Obituary, *Kenosha Union,* Jan. 12, 1893. John R. Berryman. *History of the Bench and Bar of Wisconsin.* Chicago, IL, 1898. Parker McCobb Reed. *The Bench and Bar of Wisconsin: History and Biography.* Milwaukee, WI, 1882. Military Service File, National Archives. John Stover Arndt. *The Story of the Arndts: The Life, Antecedents and Descendants of Bernhard Arndt who Emigrated to Pennsylvania in the Year 1731.* Philadelphia, PA, 1922.

Charles Henry Jackson

Sergeant, Co. A, 10 IL Infantry (3 months), April 29, 1861. Honorably mustered out, July 29, 1861. Captain, Co. B, 18 WI Infantry, Jan. 26, 1862. Major, 18 WI Infantry, May 13, 1862. Lieutenant Colonel, 18 WI Infantry, March 5, 1864. Commanded Post of Whitesburg (AL), 1 Brigade, 3 Division, 15 Army Corps, Army of the Tennessee, May–June 1864. *Colonel,* 18 WI Infantry, July 1, 1865. Honorably mustered out, July 18, 1865. Battle honors: Shiloh, Corinth, Atlanta Campaign, Allatoona, Campaign of the Carolinas.
Born: Jan. 21, 1831, Uniontown, PA
Died: Nov. 6, 1907, Bentonville, AR
Occupation: Real estate dealer and farmer
Miscellaneous: Resided Brodhead, Green Co., WI; St. Louis, MO, 1866–83; Tracy, Marion Co., IA, 1883–1902; and Bentonville, Benton Co., AR, 1902–07
Buried: Bentonville, AR (according to obituary)
References: Obituary Circular, Whole No. 298, Iowa MOLLUS. Barbara P. Easley, compiler. *Obituaries of Benton County, Arkansas.* Vol. 3 (1905–09). Bowie, MD, 1995. Pension File and Military Service File, National Archives. Letters Received, Volunteer Service Branch, Adjutant General's Office, File W711(VS)1865, National Archives. *Plat Book of Benton County, Arkansas.* Philadelphia, PA, 1903. *History of Green County, Wisconsin.* Springfield, IL, 1884. Horace A. Tenney, compiler. *Genealogy of the Tenney Family.* Madison, WI, 1875.

Arthur Heinrich Hartmann Jacobi

1 Lieutenant, Adjutant, 9 WI Infantry, Oct. 5, 1861. Major, 9 WI Infantry, March 1, 1862. Lieutenant Colonel, 9 WI Infantry, Aug. 15, 1862. Chief of Staff, Staff of Brig. Gen. Frederick Salomon, 1 Brigade, 1 Division, Army of the Frontier, Department of the Missouri, Dec. 1862–Feb. 1863. Commanded Post of Rolla (MO), District of Rolla, Department of the Missouri, June 1863. Com-

Arthur Heinrich Hartmann Jacobi (Manville & Schroeder, Dealers in Photographic Albums, Oval and Square Frames of all descriptions, also Mirror Plates and Frames, Over Sherwood & Holmes' Store, Green Bay, WI; courtesy of the Neville Public Museum of Brown County [6209.245]).

manded 1 Brigade, 1 Division, 7 Army Corps, District of Little Rock, Department of Arkansas, Nov. 25–28, 1864. Provost Marshal General, Department of Arkansas, Aug.–Sept. 1865. *Colonel,* 9 WI Infantry, Nov. 9, 1865. Honorably mustered out, Jan. 30, 1866. Battle honors: Newtonia.

Born: 1825, Simmern, Rhineland-Palatinate, Germany
Died: May 14, 1888, Chicago, IL
Occupation: Lawyer and newspaper editor before war. Civil engineer employed in railroad construction after war.
Miscellaneous: Resided Green Bay, Brown Co., WI; and Chicago, IL, after 1875
Buried: Woodlawn Cemetery, Green Bay, WI (Park B, Lot 30)
References: Obituary, *Green Bay Daily State Gazette,* May 15 and 17, 1888. Pension File and Military Service File, National Archives. Obituary, *Chicago Daily Tribune,* May 16, 1888. Obituary, *Oshkosh Daily Northwestern,* May 16, 1888. Obituary, *Milwaukee Weekly Wisconsin,* May 19, 1888.

William Henry Jacobs

Colonel, 26 WI Infantry, Sept. 17, 1862. Commanded 2 Brigade, 3 Division, 11 Army Corps, Army of the Cumberland, Oct. 1863. Resigned Jan. 11, 1864, since "the health of my wife is such that I feel duty bound to stay at home to save her life." A secondary reason for his resignation was the fact that Colonel Frederick Hecker, 82 IL Infantry, his junior in rank, had been placed in command of a brigade rather than him. His resignation was accepted, upon the recommendation of brigade commander Wladimir Krzyzanowski, "for the good of the service as he has been absent such a large portion of the time since entering the service, and having so often tendered his resignation on frivolous grounds." The order accepting his resignation was, however, amended, July 3, 1866, to omit the derogatory recommendation, upon an appeal to the War Department from Congressman (and former Brig. Gen.) Halbert E. Paine to remove "the lasting stigma on the Colonel's reputation." Battle honors: Chancellorsville.

Born: Nov. 26, 1831, Holzen, Brunswick, Germany
Died: Sept. 11, 1882, Milwaukee, WI
Occupation: Banker
Offices/Honors: Circuit Court Clerk, 1861–62. Wisconsin Senate, 1875–76.

William Henry Jacobs (USAMHI [RG98S-CWP 100.6]).

Miscellaneous: Resided Milwaukee, WI. Gifted with a fine tenor voice, he was a frequent soloist in the concerts of the Milwaukee Musical Society.

Buried: Forest Home Cemetery, Milwaukee, WI (Section 14, Block 3, Lot 7)

References: Ellis Baker Usher. *Wisconsin: Its Story and Biography, 1848–1913*. Chicago and New York, 1914. Jerome A. Watrous, editor. *Memoirs of Milwaukee County*. Madison, WI, 1909. Howard Louis Conard, editor. *History of Milwaukee County from Its First Settlement to the Year 1895*. Chicago and New York, 1895. Obituary, *Milwaukee Republican-Sentinel*, Sept. 12, 1882. Alfred T. Andreas. *History of Milwaukee, Wisconsin*. Chicago, IL, 1881. *Report and Collections of the State Historical Society of Wisconsin for the Years 1883, 1884, and 1885*. Vol. 10. Madison, WI, 1888. James S. Pula. *The Sigel Regiment: A History of the 26th Wisconsin Volunteer Infantry, 1862–1865*. Campbell, CA, 1998. Pension File and Military Service File, National Archives. Letters Received, Volunteer Service Branch, Adjutant General's Office, File P863(VS)1866, National Archives. Obituary, *Oshkosh Daily Northwestern*, Sept. 13, 1882. *Dictionary of Wisconsin Biography*. Madison, WI, 1960. Adolf E. Zucker, editor. *The Forty-Eighters: Political Refugees of the German Revolution of 1848*. New York City, NY, 1950. Wilhelm Kaufmann. *The Germans in the American Civil War*. Translated by Steven Rowan and edited by Don Heinrich Tolzmann with Werner D. Mueller and Robert E. Ward. Carlisle, PA, 1999.

John Wayles Jefferson

Major, 8 WI Infantry, Sept. 28, 1861. GSW shoulder, Corinth, MS, Oct. 3, 1862. Lieutenant Colonel, 8 WI Infantry, Dec. 21, 1862. GSW left hand, Vicksburg, MS, May 22, 1863. Provost Marshal, Post of Young's Point (LA), 2 Brigade, 3 Division, 15 Army Corps, Army of the Tennessee, June 1863. Commanded 2 Brigade, 3 Division, 15 Army Corps, Army of the Tennessee, Sept. 1863. Colonel, 8 WI Infantry, June 16, 1864. His muster as colonel was subsequently revoked since the regiment was below the minimum strength for a colonel. He was held under arrest for several months on charges (later withdrawn) of alleged misrepresentation of the regimental strength. Honorably mustered out Sept. 16, 1864. Battle honors: Farmington, Corinth, Meridian Expedition, Vicksburg Campaign (Vicksburg), Red River Campaign.

Born: May 8, 1835, Charlottesville, VA

Died: June 13, 1892, Memphis, TN

Occupation: Hotelkeeper before war. Cotton commission merchant after war.

Miscellaneous: Resided Madison, Dane Co., WI, before war; and Memphis, Shelby Co., TN, after war. Grandson of President Thomas Jefferson and

Above: **John Wayles Jefferson (Fuller, Gilman's Block, Madison, WI; Roger D. Hunt Collection, USAMHI [RG98S-CWP82.105]).** *Below:* **John Wayles Jefferson (Wisconsin Historical Society, WHi-5104).**

his quadroon slave Sally Hemings. Captain James H. Greene (Co. F, 8 WI Infantry) described him as "a coward and the evil genius of the regiment," alleging that his wound at Vicksburg was self-inflicted. However, Major Gen. Ulysses S. Grant, in a Nov. 15, 1864 testimonial, described him as "an efficient, zealous and faithful officer."

Buried: Forest Hill Cemetery, Madison, WI (Section 3, Lot 18)

References: Fawn M. Brodie, "Thomas Jefferson's Unknown Grand-Children: A Study in Historical Silences," *American Heritage: The Magazine of History*, Vol. 27, No. 6 (Oct. 1976). John M. Williams. *"The Eagle Regiment," 8th Wisconsin Infantry Volunteers, A Sketch of Its Marches, Battles and Campaigns, from 1861 to 1865*. Belleville, WI, 1890. *Biographical Review of Dane County, Wisconsin*. Chicago, IL, 1893. *A Biographical Guide to Forest Hill Cemetery, Madison, Wisconsin*. Revised and Expanded. Madison, WI, 2002. Obituary, *Wisconsin State Journal*, June 13, 1892. Obituary, *Madison Democrat*, June 14, 1892. David H. Overy, Jr., "The Wisconsin Carpetbagger: A Group Portrait," *Wisconsin Magazine of History*, Vol. 44, No. 1 (Autumn 1960). George W. Driggs. *Opening of the Mississippi; or Two Years' Campaigning in the South-West*. Madison, WI, 1864. Military Service File, National Archives. Letters Received, Volunteer Service Branch, Adjutant General's Office, File M2697(VS) 1864, National Archives. J. Harvey Greene. *Letters to My Wife: A Civil War Diary from the Western Front*. Compiled by Sharon L.D. Kraynek. Apollo, PA, 1995.

Ole Carl Johnson (added Shipnes to his name in 1882)

Captain, Co. B, 15 WI Infantry, Dec. 1, 1861. Major, 15 WI Infantry, Nov. 15, 1862. Lieutenant Colonel, 15 WI Infantry, March 15, 1863. Captured Chickamauga, GA, Sept. 20, 1863. Confined Libby Prison, Richmond, VA. Escaped en route to Macon, GA, May 13, 1864, by getting through a hole in the bottom of a box-car and lying between the rails while a long train passed over him. Honorably mustered out, Feb. 10, 1865. *Colonel*, 53 WI Infantry, Feb. 21, 1865. Regiment did not complete organization. Battle honors: Stone's River, Chickamauga, Atlanta Campaign.

Born: Feb. 23, 1838, Skien, Norway
Died: Nov. 4, 1886, Beloit, WI
Education: Attended Beloit (WI) College
Occupation: Farmer before war. Plow manufacturer and banker after war.
Offices/Honors: Wisconsin Commissioner of Immigration, 1871–73
Miscellaneous: Resided Stoughton, Dane Co.,

Above: **Ole Carl Johnson** (Marc and Beth Storch Collection). *Below:* **Ole Carl Johnson** (post-war) (Johan A. Enander. *Borgerkrigen i De forenede Stater i Nord Amerika*. La Crosse, WI, 1881).

WI; Beloit, Rock Co., WI; Madison, Dane Co., WI; and Watertown, Coddington Co., SD. He added Shipnes to his name to restore his Norwegian farm name, which had been dropped when his family migrated to America.

Buried: Oakwood Cemetery, Beloit, WI (1st Addition, Block 18, Lot 15)

References: Obituary, *Beloit Weekly Free Press*, Nov. 11, 1886. Obituary, *Wisconsin State Journal*,

Nov. 12, 1886. Obituary, *Janesville Daily Gazette*, Nov. 6, 1886. Waldemar Ager. *Colonel Heg and His Boys: A Norwegian Regiment in the American Civil War*. Translated by Della Kittleson Catuna and Clarence A. Clausen. Northfield, MN, 2000. Ole A. Buslett. *Det Femtende Regiment Wisconsin Frivillige*. Decorah, IA, 1894. Waldemar Ager. *Oberst Heg og hans Gutter*. Eau Claire, WI, 1916. Johan A. Enander. *Borgerkrigen i De forenede Stater i Nord Amerika*. La Crosse, WI, 1881. Pension File and Military Service File, National Archives. Letters Received, Volunteer Service Branch, Adjutant General's Office, File J798(VS)1864, National Archives. http://vesterheim.org/collections/civil-war-database/j/joh/004926.html.

Augustus Henry Kummel

Captain, Co. C, 13 WI Infantry, Oct. 17, 1861. Acting Assistant Ordnance Officer, Post of Chattanooga (TN), Department of the Cumberland, May 1864–Feb. 1865. Lieutenant Colonel, 13 WI Infantry, Jan. 6, 1865. *Colonel*, 13 WI Infantry, Oct. 9, 1865. Honorably mustered out, Nov. 24, 1865.

Born: April 13, 1820, Hesse-Cassel, Germany
Died: Nov. 23, 1872, Lawrence, KS (found in a dying condition at the grave of his wife)
Other Wars: Mexican War (2 Lieutenant, Co. I, 4 LA Infantry)
Occupation: Farmer and toy merchant
Miscellaneous: Resided Sharon, Walworth Co., WI; and Lawrence, Douglas Co., KS, after 1866
Buried: Oak Hill Cemetery, Lawrence, KS (Section 2, Lot 146)
References: Obituary, *Daily Kansas Tribune*, Nov. 24, 1872. Obituary, *Lawrence Western Home Journal*, Nov. 28, 1872. R. Burnham Moffat. *Moffat Genealogies: Descent from Rev. John Moffat of Ulster County, New York*. New York City, NY, 1909. Military Service File, National Archives. Letters Received, Volunteer Service Branch, Adjutant General's Office, File K18(VS)1864, National Archives. William P. Lyon. *Reminiscences of the Civil War*. San Jose, CA, 1907.

Charles Hathaway Larrabee

Major, 5 WI Infantry, June 11, 1861. Resigned July 25, 1862, due to physical disability from "dysentery with a tendency to typhoid fever." Colonel, 24 WI Infantry, Aug. 22, 1862. Commanded 1 Brigade, 3 Division, 20 Army Corps, Army of the Cumberland, May 1863. Facing charges of "Disloyalty to the Government of the United States" and "Drunkenness on Duty" preferred by officers of his regiment, he resigned Aug. 27, 1863, since "there is a belief prevailing among a portion of my officers and men that I am disloyal to the Government. ... The fact that it exists impairs my influence to such an extent that I think my duty to the regiment and to myself demands that I give way to someone else." Battle honors: Virginia Peninsular Campaign (Lee's Mill, Williamsburg), Perryville, Tullahoma Campaign.

Born: Nov. 9, 1820, Rome, NY

Augustus Henry Kummel (Marc and Beth Storch Collection).

Charles Hathaway Larrabee (Brady's National Photographic Portrait Gallery, 352 Pennsylvania Avenue, Washington, DC; Library of Congress [LC-DIG-cwpb-06395]).

Died: Jan. 20, 1883, Tehachapi, CA (killed in railroad accident)
Education: Attended Woodward High School, Cincinnati, OH. Attended Granville (OH) College.
Occupation: Lawyer and judge
Offices/Honors: Member of the Wisconsin Constitutional Convention, 1847–48. Associate Justice, Wisconsin Supreme Court, 1848–53. Circuit Court Judge, 1853–58. U.S. House of Representatives, 1859–61.
Miscellaneous: Resided Horicon, Dodge Co., WI, before war; Los Angeles, CA (1870); San Francisco, CA; Seattle, WA (1880); and San Bernardino, San Bernardino Co., CA
Buried: San Francisco National Cemetery, San Francisco, CA (Section OS, Plot 67, Grave 3)
References: Lyman C. Draper, "Sketch of Hon. Charles H. Larrabee," *Report and Collections of the State Historical Society of Wisconsin, for the Years 1880, 1881, and 1882.* Vol. 9. Madison, WI, 1882. *Dictionary of American Biography.* James S. Anderson. *Pioneer Courts and Lawyers of Manitowoc County, Wisconsin.* Manitowoc, WI, 1921. John B. Winslow. *The Story of a Great Court.* Chicago, IL, 1912. Homer B. Hubbell. *Dodge County, Wisconsin, Past and Present.* Chicago, IL, 1913. Parker McCobb Reed. *The Bench and Bar of Wisconsin: History and Biography.* Milwaukee, WI, 1882. John R. Berryman. *History of the Bench and Bar of Wisconsin.* Chicago, IL, 1898. *Report of the Annual Meeting of the Wisconsin State Bar Association, 1900.* Madison, WI, 1901. Horace A. Tenney and David Atwood. *Memorial Record of the Fathers of Wisconsin.* Madison, WI, 1880. Obituary, *Los Angeles Herald,* Jan. 26, 1883. Obituary, *Janesville Daily Gazette,* Jan. 23, 1883. James L. Harrison, compiler. *Biographical Directory of the American Congress, 1774–1949.* Washington, D.C., 1950. *Dictionary of Wisconsin Biography.* Madison, WI, 1960. William J.K. Beaudot. *The 24th Wisconsin Infantry in the Civil War: The Biography of a Regiment.* Mechanicsburg, PA, 2003. Pension File and Military Service File, National Archives. Letters Received, Volunteer Service Branch, Adjutant General's Office, File L76(VS)1863, National Archives. Gideon T. Ridlon. *Saco Valley Settlements and Families.* Portland, ME, 1895.

James Milton Lewis

Surgeon, 2 WI Infantry, April 29, 1861. Taken prisoner, First Bull Run, VA, July 21, 1861. Confined Richmond, VA. Paroled Aug. 18, 1861. Lieutenant Colonel, 1 WI Cavalry, Jan. 6, 1862. Exchanged May 27, 1862. Colonel, 28 WI Infantry, Oct. 14, 1862. Commanded 2 Brigade, 13 Division, 13 Army Corps, District of Eastern Arkansas, Army of the Tennessee, Jan. 22–Feb. 8, 1863. Provost Marshal, Post of Helena (AR), District of Eastern Arkansas, July 1863. Commanded 2 Brigade, 3 Division,

Charles Hathaway Larrabee (post-war) (Massachusetts MOLLUS Collection, USAMHI [Vol. 112, p. 5793]).

James Milton Lewis (H. S. Brown, Photographer, 201 E. Water St., Milwaukee, WI; courtesy Henry Deeks).

Arkansas Expedition, Aug. 6–25, 1863. Commanded 2 Brigade, 3 Division, Army of Arkansas, Department of the Missouri, Nov. 16, 1863–Jan. 6, 1864. Commanded 2 Brigade, 3 Division, 7 Army Corps, Department of Arkansas, Jan. 6–Feb. 1, 1864. Discharged for disability, to date Jan. 2, 1864, due to "extreme nervous debility resulting from remittent fever of typhoid character." Battle honors: First Bull Run, Yazoo Pass Expedition.

Born: Feb. 24, 1827, Falmouth, MA
Died: May 17, 1907, St. Petersburg, FL
Education: Attended Bowdoin College, Brunswick, ME. Graduated Jefferson Medical College, Philadelphia, PA, 1850.
Occupation: Physician before war. Physician, railroad executive, and farmer after war.
Offices/Honors: Arkansas Commissioner of Immigration and State Lands, 1868–72
Miscellaneous: Resided Oconomowoc, Waukesha Co., WI, before war; Little Rock, Pulaski Co., AR, 1865–73; Gunston, Fairfax Co., VA, 1873–81; Kinsley, Edwards Co., KS, 1881–90; Grove City, Charlotte Co., FL; and St. Petersburg, Pinellas Co., FL
Buried: Oak Grove Cemetery, Falmouth, MA
References: Obituary Circular, Whole No. 293, Kansas MOLLUS. *Proceedings of the Twenty-fifth Annual Reunion of the 28th Regiment Wisconsin Volunteer Infantry.* Milwaukee, WI, 1907. Obituary, *Kinsley Graphic*, May 24, 1907. David H. Overy, Jr., "The Wisconsin Carpetbagger: A Group Portrait," *Wisconsin Magazine of History*, Vol. 44, No. 1 (Autumn 1960). Pension File and Military Service File, National Archives. Letters Received, Volunteer Service Branch, Adjutant General's Office, File L825(VS)1863, National Archives. Alan D. Gaff. *If This is War: A History of the Campaign of Bull's Run by the Wisconsin Regiment Thereafter Known as the Ragged Ass Second.* Dayton, OH, 1991. Powell Clayton. *The Aftermath of the Civil War, in Arkansas.* New York City, NY, 1915. "Colonel J.M. Lewis," *Chicago Daily Tribune*, March 15, 1864.

Arthur MacArthur, Jr.

1 Lieutenant, Adjutant, 24 WI Infantry, Aug. 4, 1862. Major, 24 WI Infantry, Jan. 25, 1864. GSW chest and right wrist, Kenesaw Mountain, GA, June 22, 1864. GSW left shoulder and left leg, Franklin, TN, Nov. 30, 1864. Lieutenant Colonel, 24 WI Infantry, May 3, 1865. *Colonel*, 24 WI Infantry, June 13, 1865. Honorably mustered out, June 10, 1865. Bvt. Lieutenant Colonel, USV, March 13, 1865, for gallant and meritorious services in the battles of Perryville (KY), Stone's River, Missionary Ridge and Dandridge (TN). Bvt. Colonel, USV, March 13, 1865, for gallant and meritorious services in the battle of Franklin (TN) and in the Atlanta Campaign.

James Milton Lewis (post-war) (Obituary Circular, Whole No. 293, Kansas MOLLUS).

Arthur MacArthur, Jr. (W.H. Sherman, Photographic Artist, 16 Wisconsin Street, Milwaukee, WI; Wisconsin Historical Society, WHi-4502).

Battle honors: Perryville, Stone's River, Missionary Ridge, Dandridge, Atlanta Campaign (Resaca, Kenesaw Mountain, Peach Tree Creek), Franklin.
  Born: June 2, 1845, Springfield, MA
  Died: Sept. 5, 1912, Milwaukee, WI
  Other Wars: Spanish American War and Philippine Insurrection (Major Gen., USV)
  Occupation: Regular Army (Lieutenant General, USA, retired June 2, 1909)
  Offices/Honors: Medal of Honor, Missionary Ridge, TN, Nov. 25, 1863. "Seized the colors of his regiment at a critical moment and planted them on the captured works on the crest of Missionary Ridge."
  Miscellaneous: Resided Milwaukee, WI. Father of General Douglas MacArthur.
  Buried: Arlington National Cemetery, Arlington, VA (Section 2, Lot 845-A)
  References: Kenneth R. Young. *The General's General: The Life and Times of Arthur MacArthur.* Boulder, CO, 1994. Harris E. Starr, editor. *Dictionary of American Biography.* Supplement 1. New York City, NY, 1944. *National Cyclopedia of American Biography.* Ellis Baker Usher. *Wisconsin: Its Story and Biography, 1848–1913.* Chicago and New York, 1914. William J.K. Beaudot. *The 24th Wisconsin Infantry in the Civil War: The Biography of a Regiment.* Mechanicsburg, PA, 2003. *Biographical Sketches of Distinguished Officers of the Army and Navy.* New York City, NY, 1905. William DeLoss Love. *Wisconsin in the War of the Rebellion.* Chicago, IL, 1866. Obituary Circular, Whole No. 506, Wisconsin MOLLUS. *Dictionary of Wisconsin Biography.* Madison, WI, 1960. Jerome A. Watrous, editor. *Memoirs of Milwaukee County.* Madison, WI, 1909. Pension File and Military Service File, National Archives.

Maurice Maloney

Captain, 4 U.S. Infantry, Nov. 22, 1854. Colonel, 13 WI Infantry, Oct. 17, 1861. Commanded Post of Columbus (KY), District of Mississippi, Army of the Tennessee, June–July 1862. Honorably discharged from Volunteer Service, Aug. 1, 1862, upon the request of Wisconsin Governor Edward Salomon, acting upon a petition from twenty-six officers of the regiment, documenting "the deliberate opinion that Col. Maloney is utterly destitute of that executive ability and that humane character so necessary to the health, discipline, and efficiency of a regiment of volunteer soldiers." Major, 1 U.S. Infantry, Sept. 16, 1862. Commissary of musters, Staff of Major Gen. John A. McClernand, 13 Army Corps, Department of the Gulf, March 1864. Bvt. Lieutenant Colonel, USA, July 4, 1863, for gallant and meritorious services during the siege of Vicksburg, MS. Bvt. Colonel, USA, March 13, 1865, for gallant and meritorious services during the war. Battle honors: Vicksburg Campaign.
  Born: 1812?, County Limerick, Ireland
  Died: Jan. 8, 1872, Green Bay, WI
  Other Wars: Florida Seminole War (Sergeant, 4 U.S. Infantry). Mexican War (1 Lieutenant, 4 U.S. Infantry. Bvt. Captain, USA, Sept. 13, 1847, for gallant and meritorious conduct at the battle of Chapultepec, Mexico)
  Occupation: Regular Army (Lieutenant Colonel, 16 U.S. Infantry, retired Dec. 15, 1870)
  Miscellaneous: Resided Green Bay, Brown Co., WI

Arthur MacArthur, Jr. (William DeLoss Love. *Wisconsin in the War of the Rebellion.* Chicago, IL, 1866).

Maurice Maloney (A. Pattiani, Photographer, No. 75 Lake Street, Chicago, IL).

Buried: Woodlawn Cemetery, Green Bay, WI (Park G, Lot 272)

References: Obituary, *Green Bay Daily State Gazette,* Jan. 8, 1872. Letters Received, Appointment, Commission and Personal Branch, Adjutant General's Office, File 100(ACP)1872, National Archives. Pension File and Military Service File, National Archives. Letters Received, Volunteer Service Branch, Adjutant General's Office, File W404(VS)1862, National Archives. Thomas Walterman. *There Stands "Old Rock," Rock County, Wisconsin, and the War to Preserve the Union.* Friendship, WI, 2001. William M. Sweeny, "Colonel Maurice Maloney, U.S. Army," *Journal of the American Irish Historical Society,* Vol. 25 (1926). James Grant Wilson and John Fiske, editors. *Appletons' Cyclopedia of American Biography.* New York City, NY, 1888. Guy V. Henry. *Military Record of Civilian Appointments in the United States Army.* New York City, NY, 1869.

Maurice Maloney (Courtesy of the Neville Public Museum of Brown County [3558/2349]).

Leonard Martin

2 Lieutenant, 4 U.S. Artillery, May 6, 1861. 1 Lieutenant, Battery F, 5 U.S. Artillery, May 14, 1861. Colonel, 51 WI Infantry, April 20, 1865. Commanded 3 Sub-District, District of Central Missouri, Department of the Missouri, May–June 1865. Commanded 2 Sub-District, District of Central Missouri, Department of the Missouri, July–Aug. 1865. Honorably mustered out of Volunteer Service, Aug. 26, 1865. "The return of peace depriving me of excitement and opportunity for early promotion together with a feeling that not entire justice had been done me in the conferring of brevet rank," he overstayed a leave of absence and was dropped from the rolls of the Regular Army, April 3, 1866. His appeal for permission to resign was approved by Lieutenant General Grant, resulting in the acceptance of his resignation, to date April 3, 1866. Battle honors: Virginia Peninsular Campaign (Malvern Hill), Maryland Campaign (Crampton's Gap, Antietam), Fredericksburg, Gettysburg, Bristoe Station, Rappahannock Station, Mine Run, Petersburg Campaign.

Born: Aug. 26, 1838, Green Bay, WI
Died: April 14, 1890, Winnebago, WI
Education: Attended Lawrence University, Appleton, WI. Graduated U.S. Military Academy, West Point, NY, May 1861.
Occupation: Civil engineer, post trader, and U.S. Pension examiner
Miscellaneous: Resided Green Bay, Brown Co., WI; Chicago, IL; and Washington, D.C.
Buried: Woodlawn Cemetery, Green Bay, WI (Park B, Lot 17)
References: *Twenty-First Annual Reunion of the Association of the Graduates of the United States Military Academy at West Point, New York.* Saginaw, MI,

Leonard Martin (pre-war, as West Point cadet) (USAMHI [RG25S-West Point Album 1861. 18]).

1890. Obituary, *Green Bay Daily State Gazette,* April 28, 1890. George W. Cullum. *Biographical Register of the Officers and Graduates of the U.S. Military Academy.* 3rd Edition. Boston, MA, 1891. Mary Elizabeth Sergent. *They Lie Forgotten: The United States Military Academy, 1856–1861, Together with a Class Album for the Class of May 1861.* Middletown, NY, 1986. Pension File and Military Service File, National Archives. Letters Received, Volunteer Service Branch, Adjutant General's Office, File M335(VS)1865, National Archives. Letters Received, Commission Branch, Adjutant General's Office, File M1034(CB)1866, National Archives.

Leonard Martin (Hoelke & Benecke, S.E. Corner 4th and Market Streets, St. Louis, MO; courtesy Steve Meadow).

Duncan McKercher

Captain, Co. H, 10 WI Infantry, Oct. 5, 1861. Major, 10 WI Infantry, June 17, 1863. Taken prisoner, Chickamauga, GA, Sept. 20, 1863. Confined Libby Prison, Richmond, VA; Macon, GA; Charleston, SC; and Camp Asylum, Columbia, SC. Paroled March 1, 1865. *Colonel,* 10 WI Infantry, Oct. 20, 1864. Honorably mustered out, March 11, 1865. Battle honors: Perryville, Stone's River, Chickamauga.

Born: Jan. 14, 1819, York, Livingston Co., NY
Died: March 9, 1900, Newton, KS
Education: Attended Temple Hill Academy, Geneseo, NY
Occupation: Farmer, real estate agent, and insurance agent

Duncan McKercher (*Fifth Annual Reunion of the Tenth Wisconsin Infantry, Held at Black River Falls, Wis., July 25 and 26, 1899.* Waupun, WI, 1900).

Offices/Honors: Postmaster, Ripon, WI, 1866–70
Miscellaneous: Resided New Lisbon, Juneau Co., WI; Ripon, Fond du Lac Co., WI, 1865–71; and Peabody, Marion Co., KS, after 1871
Buried: Prairie Lawn Cemetery, Peabody, KS (Section 4)
References: Obituary Circular, Whole No. 216, Kansas MOLLUS. Alfred T. Andreas. *History of the State of Kansas.* Chicago, IL, 1883. Obituary, *Peabody Gazette,* March 15, 1900. *Fifth Annual Reunion of the Tenth Wisconsin Infantry, Held at Black River Falls, Wis., July 25 and 26, 1899.* Waupun, WI, 1900. Pension File and Military Service File, National Archives. Letters Received, Volunteer Service Branch, Adjutant General's Office, File M831(VS)1865, National Archives. Henry M. Benedict. *The Genealogy of the Benedicts in America.* Albany, NY, 1870.

John Gibson McMynn

Major, 10 WI Infantry, Oct. 5, 1861. Lieutenant Colonel, 10 WI Infantry, July 26, 1862. Colonel, 10 WI Infantry, Jan. 24, 1863. Resigned June 16, 1863, since "the serious illness of my wife demands that I should leave the service." Battle honors: Perryville, Stone's River.

Born: July 9, 1824, Palatine Bridge, Montgomery Co., NY

Died: June 5, 1900, Madison, WI
Education: Graduated Williams College, Williamstown, MA, 1848
Occupation: School teacher and educator
Offices/Honors: Wisconsin State Superintendent of Public Instruction, 1864–68
Miscellaneous: Resided Racine, Racine Co., WI; and Madison, Dane Co., WI, after 1886
Buried: Mound Cemetery, Racine, WI (Block 6, Lot 2)
References: Howard Greene. *McMynn Genealogy.* N.p., 1926. Obituary Circular, Whole No. 324, Wisconsin MOLLUS. *The United States Biographical Dictionary and Portrait Gallery of Eminent and Self-Made Men.* Wisconsin Volume. Chicago, Cincinnati and New York, 1877. Obituary, *Racine Daily Journal,* June 5, 1900. *The History of Racine and Kenosha Counties, Wisconsin.* Chicago, IL, 1879. Obituary, *Wisconsin State Journal,* June 6, 1900. Fanny S. Stone, editor. *Racine, Belle City of the Lakes, and Racine County, Wisconsin.* Chicago, IL, 1916. *Dictionary of Wisconsin Biography.* Madison, WI, 1960. Eugene W. Leach. *Racine County Militant, An Illustrated Narrative of War Times, and a Soldiers' Roster.* Racine, WI, 1915. Pension File and Military Service File, National Archives. *Fifth Annual Reunion of the Tenth Wisconsin Infantry, Held at Black River Falls, Wis., July 25 and 26, 1899.* Waupun, WI, 1900. Joseph Schafer, "Genesis of Wisconsin's Free High School System," *Wisconsin Magazine of History,* Vol. 10, No. 2 (December 1926).

Charles Clement Meservey

1 Sergeant, Co. B, 2 WI Infantry, June 11, 1861. 2 Lieutenant, Co. A, 1 WI Heavy Artillery, Aug. 17, 1861. 1 Lieutenant, Co. A, 1 WI Heavy Artillery, Jan. 1, 1862. Captain, Co. A, 1 WI Heavy Artillery, Feb. 12, 1863. Major, 1 WI Heavy Artillery, Nov. 11, 1863. Commanded 4 Brigade, De Russy's Division, 22 Army Corps, Department of Washington, July 1–Aug. 6, 1864. Commanded 4 Brigade, De Russy's Division, 22 Army Corps, Department of Washington, Middle Military Division, Oct. 6, 1864–June 26, 1865. Colonel, 1 WI Heavy Artillery, Nov. 12, 1864. Honorably mustered out, June 26, 1865. Battle honors: First Bull Run.
Born: Sept. 23, 1831, Hallowell, ME
Died: Oct. 18, 1888, Nyack, NY
Occupation: Newspaper editor and printing company executive

John Gibson McMynn (Eugene W. Leach. *Racine County Militant, an Illustrated Narrative of War Times, and a Soldiers' Roster.* Racine, WI, 1915).

Charles Clement Meservey (Marc and Beth Storch Collection).

Miscellaneous: Resided La Crosse, La Crosse Co., WI; Winona, Winona Co., MN; Milwaukee, WI, to 1870; New York City, NY, 1870–85; and Nyack, Rockland Co., NY, 1885–88

Buried: LeRaysville Borough Cemetery, LeRaysville, PA

References: Obituary, *Nyack City and Country*, Oct. 20, 1888. Obituary, *New York Tribune*, Oct. 19, 1888. Obituary, *New York Times*, Oct. 19, 1888. Pension File and Military Service File, National Archives. Letters Received, Volunteer Service Branch, Adjutant General's Office, File L1061(VS) 1865, National Archives. Alan D. Gaff. *If This is War: A History of the Campaign of Bull's Run by the Wisconsin Regiment Thereafter Known as the Ragged Ass Second*. Dayton, OH, 1991.

Isaac Elijah Messmore

Lieutenant Colonel, 14 WI Infantry, Nov. 16, 1861. Resigned April 7, 1862, since "my health will not allow me to participate in the active duties of the field, on account of an affection of the spinal column occasioned by an injury received some two years since." Colonel, 31 WI Infantry, Dec. 18, 1862. Commanded Fort Halleck, District of Columbus (KY), Department of the Tennessee, March–July 1863. "Suffering from fistula in ano, which has rendered him entirely unfit for duty for the past two months, and which must render him entirely unfit for field service for a long time to come," he resigned Oct. 2, 1863. Battle honors: Shiloh.

Born: Aug. 21, 1821, MI
Died: Jan. 8, 1902, Los Angeles, CA
Education: Attended Oberlin (OH) College
Occupation: Lawyer and newspaper editor
Offices/Honors: Wisconsin State Assembly, 1861. Circuit Court Judge, 1861. Deputy Commissioner of U.S. Internal Revenue, 1866–67 (removed from office amid unsubstantiated allegations of corruption).

Miscellaneous: Resided Montreal, Canada, 1852–59; La Crosse, La Crosse Co., WI, 1859–65; Washington, D.C., 1865–68; Grand Rapids, Kent Co., MI, 1868–86; Los Angeles, CA, 1886–1902

Buried: Rosedale Cemetery, Los Angeles, CA (Section M, Lot 147)

References: Obituary, *Los Angeles Times*, Jan. 9, 1902. Obituary, *Grand Rapids Herald*, Jan. 10, 1902. *History of Kent County, Michigan*. Chicago, IL, 1881. Obituary, *Eau Claire Weekly Telegram*, Jan. 16, 1902. *History of La Crosse County, Wisconsin*. Chicago, IL, 1881. *Report of the Annual Meeting of the Wisconsin State Bar Association, 1903*. Madison, WI, 1903. Pension File and Military Service File, National Archives. Letters Received, Volunteer Service Branch, Adjutant General's Office, Files J198(VS) 1863 and M1365(VS)1863, National Archives. Frederick H. Magdeburg. *Wisconsin at Shiloh: Report of the Commission*. Madison, WI, 1909. "A Radical's Opinion of Messmore," *Daily Milwaukee News*, Oct. 2, 1867. "Deputy Commissioner of Internal Revenue Isaac E. Messmore," *New York Daily Tribune*, Oct. 12, 1867. Abel C. Stelle. *1861 to 1865, Memoirs of the Civil War, the 31st Regiment Wisconsin Volunteer Infantry*. New Albany, IN, 1904.

Webster Porter Moore

Captain, Co. E, 4 WI Infantry, June 8, 1861. Major, 4 WI Infantry, June 3, 1863. Designation of regiment changed to 4 WI Cavalry, Aug. 22, 1863. Lieutenant Colonel, 4 WI Cavalry, May 24, 1864. Colonel, 4 WI Cavalry, Jan. 19, 1865. Commanded 2 Brigade, Cavalry Division, Department of the Gulf, Military Division of West Mississippi, Jan.–Feb. 1865. Commanded Cavalry Brigade, District of Baton Rouge (LA), Department of the Gulf, Military Division of West Mississippi, Feb. 27–March 18, 1865. Muster as colonel revoked, June 1865, due to reduced strength of the regiment at the time of muster. Resigned July 11, 1865, since "my personal interests now call me into civil life again." Battle honors: Fort Bisland, Port Hudson, Mobile Campaign.

Isaac Elijah Messmore (Frederick H. Magdeburg. *Wisconsin at Shiloh: Report of the Commission*. Madison, WI, 1909).

Born: July 4, 1836, Lunenburg, VT
Died: Oct. 23, 1917, Chicago, IL
Education: Graduated Beloit (WI) College, 1858
Occupation: Lawyer, railway superintendent, and farmer
Miscellaneous: Resided Beloit, Rock Co., WI, before war; Chicago, IL (1870); Council Bluffs, Pottawattamie Co., IA; Quincy, Adams Co., IL (1880); and Bassett, Kenosha Co., WI
Buried: Oakwood Cemetery, Beloit, WI (Original Part, Block A, Lot 13, Grave 10)
References: *Commemorative Biographical Record of Prominent and Representative Men of Racine and Kenosha Counties, Wisconsin.* Chicago, IL, 1906. Frank H. Lyman. *The City of Kenosha and Kenosha County, Wisconsin.* Chicago, IL, 1916. Obituary circular, Whole No. 585, Wisconsin MOLLUS. Obituary, *Beloit Daily Free Press,* Oct. 23, 1917. Obituary, *Chicago Daily Tribune,* Oct. 24, 1917. Obituary, *Racine Journal-News,* Oct. 24, 1917. Michael J. Martin. *A History of the 4th Wisconsin Infantry and Cavalry in the Civil War.* New York City, NY, 2006. Pension File and Military Service File, National Archives. Letters Received, Volunteer Service Branch, Adjutant General's Office, File M2844(VS) 1864, National Archives.

Robert Creighton Murphy

Colonel, 8 WI Infantry, Sept. 4, 1861. Commanded 2 Brigade. 2 Division, Army of the Mississippi, May–Aug. 1862. Charged with "Misbehaving himself in the face of the enemy" and "Shamefully abandoning a Post which he had been commanded to defend," while in command of the Post of Iuka, MS, he was acquitted by court martial, Oct. 23, 1862, and returned to duty, despite the disapproval of Major Gen. William S. Rosecrans, who commented, "The evidence shows fully the abandonment of the Post and public stores without pressure from the enemy." Commanded Post of Holly Springs (MS), District of the Tallahatchie, Department of the Tennessee, Dec. 1862. Taken prisoner and paroled, Holly Springs, MS, Dec. 20, 1862. Dismissed Jan. 10, 1863, for "allowing his command to be surprised at Holly Springs, MS, without having taken proper steps to protect his post or repulse the enemy, and his troops having been found in bed at the time of attack." Upon review of the case, Judge Advocate General Joseph Holt decided that no clear neglect of duty had occurred, since Murphy's force was inadequate and his instructions confusing. On May 30, 1863, he recommended that the dismissal order be revoked and that Murphy be tried by court

Webster Porter Moore.

Robert Creighton Murphy (Massachusetts MOLLUS Collection, USAMHI [Vol. 80, p. 4042]).

martial. This course of action was, however, determined to be "impracticable," since George W. Robbins had already been mustered as colonel to replace Murphy. Battle honors: Fredericktown, Siege of Corinth, Iuka, Holly Springs.

Born: Feb. 18, 1827, Chillicothe, OH
Died: April 8, 1888, Washington, D.C.
Education: Graduated Miami University, Oxford, OH, 1845. Attended Cincinnati (OH) Law School.
Occupation: Lawyer and U.S. Government clerk
Offices/Honors: U.S. Consul, Shanghai, China, 1854–57
Miscellaneous: Resided St. Croix Falls, Polk Co., WI; and Washington, D.C.
Buried: Congressional Cemetery, Washington, D.C. (Range 48, Site 106, unmarked)
References: Eric Politzer, "Robert Creighton Murphy: U.S. Consul at Shanghai, Brigade Commander, National Scapegoat," *Newsletter of the Association for the Preservation of Historic Congressional Cemetery*, Fall 2002. W.H.C. Folsom. *Fifty Years in the Northwest.* St. Paul, MN, 1888. *General Catalogue of the Graduates and Former Students of Miami University During Its First Century, 1809–1909.* Oxford, OH, 1909. "Sketch of the Field Officers of the 8th Regiment, W.V.," *Wisconsin State Journal*, Oct. 10, 1861. Letters Received, Volunteer Service Branch, Adjutant General's Office, File T684(VS)1862, National Archives. Court-martial Case Files, 1809–1894, File KK-303, National Archives. John Y. Simon, editor. *The Papers of Ulysses S. Grant.* Volume 7: Dec. 9, 1862–March 31, 1863. Carbondale, IL, 1979. John M. Williams. *"The Eagle Regiment," 8th Wisconsin Infantry Volunteers, A Sketch of Its Marches, Battles and Campaigns, from 1861 to 1865.* Belleville, WI, 1890. George W. Driggs. *Opening of the Mississippi; or Two Years' Campaigning in the South-West.* Madison, WI, 1864. Thomas E. Parson, "Van Dorn's Holly Springs Raid," *Blue & Gray Magazine*, Vol. 27, Issue 3 (2010). Military Service File, National Archives. Thomas P. Lowry. *Tarnished Eagles: The Courts-Martial of Fifty Union Colonels and Lieutenant Colonels.* Mechanicsburg, PA, 1997. Death Notice, *Washington Evening Star*, April 10, 1888. https://thecivilwarandnorthwestwisconsin.wordpress.com/the-soldiers/alphabetical-list-of-all-soldiers-from-northwest-wisconsin/robert-c-murphy/.

Edgar O'Connor

Colonel, 2 WI Infantry, Aug. 2, 1861. GSW groin and arm, Gainesville, VA, Aug. 28, 1862. Battle honors: Gainesville.

Born: Aug. 29, 1833, Cleveland, OH
Died: Aug. 28, 1862, KIA Gainesville, VA

Above: Edgar O'Connor (Massachusetts MOLLUS Collection, USAMHI [Vol. 73, p. 3611]).
Below: Edgar O'Connor (courtesy Steve Meadow).

Education: Graduated U.S. Military Academy, West Point, NY, 1854
Occupation: Lawyer, after resigning, Oct. 22, 1858, as 2 Lieutenant, RQM, 7 U.S. Infantry
Miscellaneous: Resided Shopiere, Rock Co., WI

Buried: Arlington National Cemetery, Arlington, VA (Section 1, Lot 45-A)

References: Obituary, *Janesville Daily Gazette*, Sept. 5, 1862. Obituary, *Daily Milwaukee News*, Sept. 7, 1862. George W. Cullum. *Biographical Register of the Officers and Graduates of the U.S. Military Academy*. 3rd Edition. Boston, MA, 1891. George H. Otis. *The Second Wisconsin Infantry*. Edited by Alan D. Gaff. Dayton, OH, 1984. Alan D. Gaff. *If This is War: A History of the Campaign of Bull's Run by the Wisconsin Regiment Thereafter Known as the Ragged Ass Second*. Dayton, OH, 1991. Thomas Walterman. *There Stands "Old Rock," Rock County, Wisconsin, and the War to Preserve the Union*. Friendship, WI, 2001. Alan T. Nolan. *The Iron Brigade: A Military History*. Ann Arbor, MI, 1983. Lance J. Herdegen. *The Iron Brigade in Civil War and Memory*. El Dorado Hills, CA, 2012. "Letter from Col. Fairchild Upon the Death of Col. O'Connor," *Daily Milwaukee News*, Sept. 20, 1862. "Wisconsin Hero Highly Honored: Monument Over the Grave of the Late Colonel Edgar O'Connor Unveiled at Washington," *Janesville Daily Gazette*, May 31, 1902. Pension File and Military Service File, National Archives.

Henry Orff

Major, 9 WI Infantry, Oct. 5, 1861. Lieutenant Colonel, 9 WI Infantry, Feb. 13, 1862. Resigned Aug, 14, 1862, due to physical disability from "a derangement in his circulatory system, which on several occasions ... have threatened to destroy his life." Lieutenant Colonel, 34 WI Infantry, Dec. 24, 1862. Honorably mustered out, Sept. 8, 1863. Colonel, 35 WI Infantry, Feb. 27, 1864. Commanded 1 Brigade, 3 Division, 13 Army Corps, Military Division of West Mississippi, May 28–June 3, 1865. Resigned July 22, 1865, due to physical disability. Battle honors: Mobile Campaign (Spanish Fort).

Born: March 29, 1822, Bavaria
Died: Nov. 10, 1894, Milwaukee, WI
Occupation: Newspaper editor and bookkeeper
Offices/Honors: Deputy Inspector, Milwaukee County House of Correction, 1866–73
Miscellaneous: Resided Milwaukee, WI
Buried: Forest Home Cemetery, Milwaukee, WI (Section 9, Lot 3)
References: Obituary, *Milwaukee Daily News*, Nov. 12, 1894. Pension File and Military Service

Henry Orff (with Field and Staff Officers of the 9 Wisconsin Infantry, left to right, Surgeon Herman Naumann, Lt. Col. Alfred G. Wrisberg, Adjutant Arthur Jacobi, Colonel Frederick Salomon, Major Henry Orff, and Quartermaster William Finkler) (The Wisconsin Veterans Museum, Madison, WI [WVM.1119.I001]).

File, National Archives. Letters Received, Volunteer Service Branch, Adjutant General's Office, File G80(VS)1867, National Archives.

Colwert Kendall Pier

Private, Co. I, 1 WI Infantry (3 months), April 20, 1861. Honorably mustered out, Aug. 21, 1861. Lieutenant Colonel, 38 WI Infantry, April 4, 1864. Shell wound left ankle, Petersburg, VA, June 18, 1864. Commanded 109 NY Infantry, March–April 1865. *Colonel,* 38 WI Infantry, July 19, 1865. Honorably mustered out, July 26, 1865. Battle honors: Petersburg Campaign (Mine Explosion, Weldon Railroad, Poplar Spring Church, Hatcher's Run, Fort Stedman), Appomattox Campaign (Fort Mahone).

Born: June 7, 1841, Fond du Lac, WI
Died: April 14, 1895, Milwaukee, WI
Education: Attended Lombard University, Galesburg, IL. Attended Albany (NY) Law School.
Occupation: Lawyer and banker
Miscellaneous: Resided Fond du Lac, Fond du Lac Co., WI; and Milwaukee, WI, after 1889
Buried: Pier Cemetery, Fond du Lac, WI
References: *The History of Fond du Lac County, Wisconsin.* Chicago, IL, 1880. *Soldiers' and Citizens' Album of Biographical Record.* Chicago, IL, 1890. Obituary, *Milwaukee Sentinel,* April 15, 1895. Parker

Colwert Kendall Pier (*The History of Fond du Lac County, Wisconsin.* Chicago, IL, 1880).

McCobb Reed. *The Bench and Bar of Wisconsin: History and Biography.* Milwaukee, WI, 1882. John R. Berryman. *History of the Bench and Bar of Wisconsin.* Chicago, IL, 1898. Obituary, *Oshkosh Daily Northwestern,* April 15, 1895. Solon W. Pierce. *Battle Fields and Camp Fires of the Thirty-Eighth.* Milwaukee, WI, 1866. Pension File and Military Service File, National Archives. Letters Received, Volunteer Service Branch, Adjutant General's Office, File P453(VS)1865, National Archives. "An Historic Cemetery: The Resting Place of Pioneers," *Fond du Lac Commonwealth,* Nov. 29, 1895.

Bertine Pinkney

Major, 3 WI Infantry, June 7, 1861. Lieutenant Colonel, 3 WI Infantry, Sept. 1, 1861. Resigned May 30, 1862, to accept promotion. Colonel, 20 WI Infantry, Aug. 23, 1862. Commanded 1 Brigade, 3 Division, Army of the Frontier, Department of the Missouri, Oct. 12–Dec. 6, 1862. Resigned Dec. 6, 1862, due to "continued ill health" from "miasmatic influences."

Born: April 26, 1824, New York City, NY
Died: Dec. 26, 1909, Peabody, KS
Occupation: Civil engineer and farmer
Offices/Honors: Wisconsin State Assembly, 1850. Wisconsin Senate, 1852–53. Mayor of Ripon, WI, 1864. Kansas House of Representatives, 1874. Postmaster, Peabody, KS, 1877–85.
Miscellaneous: Resided Rosendale, Fond du Lac Co., WI; Ripon, Fond du Lac Co., WI; and Peabody, Marion Co., KS, after 1871
Buried: Prairie Lawn Cemetery, Peabody, KS

Colwert Kendall Pier (Fuller, Gilman's Block, Madison, WI; Roger D. Hunt Collection, USA MHI [RG98S-CWP21.72]).

Above: Bertine Pinkney (Charles D. Fredricks & Co., "Specialite," 587 Broadway, New York). *Below:* Bertine Pinkney (Wisconsin Historical Society, WHi-119503).

References: *Portrait and Biographical Record of Dickinson, Saline, McPherson, and Marion Counties, Kansas.* Chicago, IL, 1893. Obituary, *Peabody Gazette,* Dec. 30, 1909. Alfred T. Andreas. *History of the State of Kansas.* Chicago, IL, 1883. Pension File and Military Service File, National Archives. Letters Received, Volunteer Service Branch, Adjutant General's Office, File W368(VS) 1862, National Archives. "Colonel of the 20th Regiment," *Wisconsin Daily State Journal,* May 29, 1862. Edwin E. Bryant. *History of the Third Regiment of Wisconsin Veteran Volunteer Infantry, 1861–1865.* Madison, WI, 1891. *The History of Fond du Lac County, Wisconsin.* Chicago, IL, 1880.

William Augustus Ray

Colonel, 40 WI Infantry, June 8, 1864. Honorably mustered out, Sept. 16, 1864. Battle honors: Forrest's Attack on Memphis.

Born: May 21, 1829, Kingston, NY
Died: April 8, 1897, Blue Island, IL
Occupation: Banker and grain commission merchant
Miscellaneous: Resided Delavan, Walworth Co., WI; Chicago, IL; Pasadena, Los Angeles Co., CA, 1887–90; and Blue Island, Cook Co., IL, after 1890. An unnamed veteran of his regiment described him as "a man having neither the accent of soldier nor the gait of soldier—who strutted and bellowed, and imitated a soldier abominably."

William Augustus Ray (Wisconsin Historical Society, WHi-119517).

Buried: Rosehill Cemetery, Chicago, IL (Section J, Lot 4)

References: *Album of Genealogy and Biography Cook County, Illinois.* Chicago, IL, 1895. Obituary, *Chicago Inter Ocean*, April 9, 1897. Obituary, *Chicago Daily Tribune*, April 9, 1897. *Annals of the Fortieth. Sundry Proceedings, Sayings, Doings and "Undoings" of the 40th Reg. Wis. Vol. Inf.,* Wisconsin Historical Society. Pension File and Military Service File, National Archives. "Colonel Ray Is Ill: Sketch of His Career," *Chicago Inter Ocean*, April 7, 1897.

George Washington Robbins

Lieutenant Colonel, 8 WI Infantry, Sept. 27, 1861. GSW abdomen, Corinth, MS, Oct. 3, 1862. Colonel, 8 WI Infantry, Dec. 21, 1862. Resigned Sept. 1, 1863, due to physical disability from injuries received when his horse fell on him. Battle honors: New Madrid, Island No. 10, Iuka, Corinth, Vicksburg Campaign.

Born: Feb. 2, 1839, Avon, MA
Died: Jan. 18, 1906, Avon, MA
Education: Attended New Haven Collegiate and Commercial Institute (also known as Russell's Military Academy), New Haven, CT
Occupation: Livery stable operator and expressman, after a few years of mining and keeping a hotel in Nevada
Miscellaneous: Resided Madison, Dane Co., WI, 1858–64; Austin and Pinto Creek, Lander Co., NV, 1864–70; and Avon, Norfolk Co., MA, after 1870
Buried: Avon Cemetery, Avon, MA
References: *Biographical Review, Volume XXV, Containing Life Sketches of Leading Citizens of Norfolk County, Massachusetts.* Boston, MA, 1898. John M. Williams. *"The Eagle Regiment," 8th Wisconsin Infantry Volunteers, A Sketch of Its Marches, Battles and Campaigns, from 1861 to 1865.* Belleville, WI, 1890. George W. Driggs. *Opening of the Mississippi; or Two Years' Campaigning in the South-West.* Madison, WI, 1864. Pension File and Military Service File, National Archives. Letters Received, Volunteer Service Branch, Adjutant General's Office, File J281(VS)1864, National Archives. Obituary, *Boston Post,* Jan. 19, 1906.

Charles Dayon Robinson

Captain, AQM, USV, Sept. 4, 1861. Quartermaster, Staff of Brig. Gen. Rufus King, Department of the Rappahannock, and later 1 Division, 3 Army Corps, Army of Virginia, March–Sept. 1862. Suffering from "internal hemorrhoids," he resigned, April 21, 1864, due to "severe and continued disability rendering me entirely unfit for service." Colonel, 50 WI Infantry (declined).

George Washington Robbins (John M. Williams. *"The Eagle Regiment," 8th Wisconsin Infantry Volunteers, A Sketch of Its Marches, Battles and Campaigns, from 1861 to 1865.* Belleville, WI, 1890).

Charles Dayon Robinson (USAMHI [RG98S-CWP13.15]).

Born: Oct. 29, 1822, Marcellus, NY
Died: Sept. 25, 1886, Green Bay, WI
Occupation: Newspaper editor
Offices/Honors: Wisconsin State Assembly, 1850. Wisconsin Secretary of State, 1852–54.
Miscellaneous: Resided Green Bay, Brown Co., WI
Buried: Woodlawn Cemetery, Green Bay, WI (Park C)
References: *The United States Biographical Dictionary and Portrait Gallery of Eminent and Self-Made Men.* Wisconsin Volume. Chicago, Cincinnati and New York, 1877. Alfred T. Andreas. *History of Northern Wisconsin.* Chicago, IL, 1881. "Sketch of Charles D. Robinson," *Green Bay Advocate,* March 15, 1888. Bella French, editor. *The American Sketch Book: A Collection of Historical Incidents with Descriptions of Corresponding Localities.* Vol. 3. Green Bay, WI, 1876. Obituary, *Oshkosh Daily Northwestern,* Sept. 27, 1886. Obituary Circular, Whole No. 150, Wisconsin MOLLUS. Pension File, National Archives. *Dictionary of Wisconsin Biography.* Madison, WI, 1960. Jerome A. Watrous, "The Eagles and Stars," *War Papers, Wisconsin MOLLUS.* Vol. 1. Milwaukee, WI, 1891.

Charles Dayon Robinson (post-war) (Wisconsin Historical Society, WHi-119518).

William Wallace Robinson

Lieutenant Colonel, 7 WI Infantry, Aug. 18, 1861. Colonel, 7 WI Infantry, Jan. 30, 1862. GSW left leg, Gainesville, VA, Aug. 28, 1862. Commanded 4 Brigade, 1 Division, 1 Army Corps, Army of the Potomac, Feb.–March 1863. Commanded 1 Brigade, 1 Division, 1 Army Corps, Army of the Potomac, July 1, 1863–Jan. 3, 1864 and Feb. 28–March 24, 1864. Commanded 1 Brigade, 4 Division, 5 Army Corps, Army of the Potomac, May 6–June 7, 1864. Relieved from brigade command upon the recommendation of Brig. Gen. Lysander Cutler for alleged inefficiency, he submitted a twenty-page defense of his actions to a Board of Inquiry, which found "nothing adverse to the officer in so much as relates to his conduct and efficiency." Feeling that "my services are unnecessary with the regiment" since it is "reduced to less than 150 muskets in the field" with "a full complement of field officers," he resigned July 9, 1864. Battle honors: Gainesville, Fredericksburg, Chancellorsville, Gettysburg, Mine Run, Wilderness, Spotsylvania Court House, North Anna, Cold Harbor.

Born: Dec. 14, 1819, Fairhaven, VT
Died: April 27, 1903, Seattle, WA
Education: Attended Norwich (VT) University (not confirmed by attendance records)
Other Wars: Mexican War (Captain, Co. G, 3 OH Infantry)
Occupation: Farmer and coal merchant in later years
Offices/Honors: U.S. Consul to Madagascar, 1875–86
Miscellaneous: Resided Wilton, Waseca Co., MN, and Sparta, Monroe Co., WI, before war; Cataract, Monroe Co., WI, to 1873; Chippewa Falls, Chippewa Co., WI, 1873–95; and Seattle, King Co.,

William Wallace Robinson (Wisconsin Historical Society, WHi-1795).

WA, after 1895. Father-in-law of Bvt. Brig. Gen. Hollon Richardson.
Buried: Fort Lawton Cemetery, Seattle, WA
References: *Soldiers' and Citizens' Album of Biographical Record.* Chicago, IL, 1890. Paul Johnson, "William Wallace Robinson," *Loyal Legion Historical Journal,* Vol. 68, No. 4 (Winter 2011). Frederick Clifton Pierce. *Fiske and Fisk Family.* Chicago, IL, 1896. Pension File and Military Service File, National Archives. Obituary, *Seattle Daily Times,* April 28, 1903. Obituary, *Seattle Star,* April 28, 1903. Alan T. Nolan. *The Iron Brigade: A Military History.* Ann Arbor, MI, 1983. Lance J. Herdegen. *The Iron Brigade in Civil War and Memory.* El Dorado Hills, CA, 2012. Obituary Circular, Whole No. 101, Washington MOLLUS.

George Dickerson Rogers

Captain, Co. G, 31 WI Infantry, Dec. 24, 1862. Major, 31 WI Infantry, Oct. 7, 1863. Lieutenant Colonel, 31 WI Infantry, Oct. 31, 1863. *Colonel,* 31 WI Infantry, July 8, 1865. Honorably mustered out, July 8, 1865. Battle honors: Savannah Campaign, Campaign of the Carolinas (Bentonville).
Born: Sept. 30, 1830, Warren, Bradford Co., PA
Died: Feb. 11, 1918, Minneapolis, MN
Occupation: Farmer and miller before war. Grain merchant after war.

Offices/Honors: Founder and long-time Secretary of Minneapolis Chamber of Commerce
Miscellaneous: Resided York, Green Co., WI, to 1865; Conover and Calmar, Winneshiek Co., IA, 1865–73; and Minneapolis, Hennepin Co., MN, after 1873
Buried: Lakewood Cemetery, Minneapolis, MN (Section 11, Lot 890)
References: Marion D. Shutter. *History of Minneapolis: Gateway to the Northwest.* Chicago and Minneapolis, 1923. Obituary Circular, Whole No. 849, Minnesota MOLLUS. Obituary, *Minneapolis Morning Tribune,* Feb. 12, 1918. Edward D. Neill. *History of Hennepin County and the City of Minneapolis, Including the Explorers and Pioneers of Minnesota.* Minneapolis, MN, 1881. Pension File and Military Service File, National Archives.

John Adams Savage, Jr.

1 Lieutenant, Adjutant, 28 WI Infantry, Sept. 5, 1862. Suffering from "malarial fever complicated by chronic inflammation of the liver," he resigned Aug. 5, 1863, since "a year's trial has satisfied me that a constitution much shattered at the commencement of my term of service will not much longer bear the exposure and fatigue of military life." Lieutenant Colonel, 36 WI Infantry, March 18, 1864. Colonel, 36 WI Infantry, June 11, 1864. GSW right shoulder and left arm, Petersburg, VA, June 18, 1864. Battle honors: Cold Harbor, Petersburg.

George Dickerson Rogers.

John Adams Savage, Jr. (James M. Aubery. *The 36th Wisconsin Volunteer Infantry, 1st Brigade, 2nd Division, 2nd Army Corps, Army of the Potomac.* **Milwaukee, WI, 1900).**

Born: July 24, 1832, Ogdensburg, NY
Died: July 4, 1864, DOW Washington, D.C.
Education: Attended Ogdensburg (NY) Academy
Occupation: Lawyer
Miscellaneous: Resided Waukesha, Waukesha Co., WI; and Milwaukee, WI
Buried: Forest Home Cemetery, Milwaukee, WI (Section 32, Block 3, Lot 6, unmarked)
References: James M. Aubery. *The Thirty-Sixth Wisconsin Volunteer Infantry, 1st Brigade, 2nd Division, 2nd Army Corps, Army of the Potomac.* Milwaukee, WI, 1900. *Proceedings of the Eighteenth Annual Reunion of the Society of the 28th Wisconsin Volunteer Infantry.* Milwaukee, WI, 1901. Pension File and Military Service File, National Archives. Obituary, *Daily Milwaukee News,* July 6, 8, and 10, 1864. Obituary, *Waukesha Freeman,* July 5 and 12, 1864. William DeLoss Love. *Wisconsin in the War of the Rebellion.* Chicago, IL, 1866. Letters Received, Commission Branch, Adjutant General's Office, File S1331(CB)1863, National Archives.

Henry Shears

Captain, Co. B, 39 WI Infantry, June 3, 1864. Honorably mustered out, Sept. 22, 1864. Lieutenant Colonel, 48 WI Infantry, Feb. 25, 1865. *Colonel,* 48 WI Infantry, Jan. 15, 1866. Honorably mustered out, March 24, 1866.
Born: Aug. 9, 1816, Sheffield, MA
Died: March 5, 1882, Jacksonville, FL
Occupation: Miller and U.S. Internal Revenue official
Offices/Honors: Wisconsin State Assembly,

Henry Shears (Mrs. Ten Eyck, 89 Wisconsin Street, Milwaukee, WI; Vernon County Historical Society, Viroqua, WI).

Henry Shears (post-war) (*The History of Waukesha County, Wisconsin.* Chicago, IL, 1880).

1850. Postmaster, North Lake, WI, 1866–70. U.S. Internal Revenue Storekeeper, 1873–77.
Miscellaneous: Resided Merton, Waukesha Co., WI; and North Lake, Waukesha Co., WI
Buried: St. Peters Episcopal Churchyard, North Lake, WI
References: *The History of Waukesha County, Wisconsin.* Chicago, IL, 1880. Obituary, *Waukesha Freeman,* March 16, 1882. Pension File and Military Service File, National Archives.

Thomas Stephens

Lieutenant Colonel, 2 WI Cavalry, Jan. 14, 1862. Colonel, 2 WI Cavalry, Aug. 1, 1862. Commanded 3 Brigade, 5 Division, 16 Army Corps, Army of the Tennessee, March 31–May 1, 1863. Commanded Cavalry Brigade, 15 Army Corps, Army of the Tennessee, July–Aug. 1863. Commanded Cavalry Brigade, District of Vicksburg, Department of the Tennessee, May–June 1864. On Oct. 26, 1864, he submitted his resignation, since "for the last eighteen months my health has been exceedingly poor, and I now feel myself unequal to the proper discharge of my duties in the field." However, before his resignation could be accepted, he was, by direction of the President, dishonorably dismissed, Nov. 17, 1864, "for general worthlessness and for the good of the service," apparently due to a longstanding feud with Lt. Col. Harry E. Eastman and suspected fraud in the handling of contraband cotton. Meanwhile, his resignation was accepted at the Headquarters of the Military Division of West Mississippi, to date Dec. 1, 1864. On Jan. 23, 1865 the order dismissing him was suspended "with a view to his trial by court martial upon any charges you may have to make against him." Since existing charges against him could no longer be found, he was restored, Feb. 18, 1865, to command of his regiment. Honorably mustered out, July 3, 1865. The order accepting his resignation was finally revoked, July 2, 1867. Battle honors: Vicksburg Campaign, Jackson Campaign.

Born: May 3, 1815, Tavistock, Devonshire, England
Died: July 22, 1871, Dodgeville, WI
Education: Military education and service in Queen's Life Guards in England
Occupation: Hotelkeeper and land speculator after early career as instructor of swordsmanship
Miscellaneous: Resided Dodgeville, Iowa Co., WI
Buried: East Side Cemetery, Dodgeville, WI
References: *Commemorative Biographical Record of the Counties of Rock, Green, Grant, Iowa and Lafayette, Wisconsin.* Chicago, IL, 1901. *History of Iowa County, Wisconsin.* Chicago, IL, 1881. Obituary, *Dodgeville Chronicle,* July 28, 1871. Pension File and Military Service File, National Archives. Letters Received, Volunteer Service Branch, Adjutant General's Office, File C2404(VS)1864, National Archives. Emmet C. West. *History and Reminiscences of the Second Wisconsin Cavalry Regiment.* Portage, WI, 1904.

George Gifford Symes

Private, Co. B, 2 WI Infantry, June 11, 1861. GSW right hand, 1st Bull Run, VA, July 21, 1861. Discharged for disability, Nov. 30, 1861, due to phthisis pulmonalis. 1 Lieutenant, Adjutant, 25 WI Infantry, Aug. 16, 1862. Captain, Co. F, 25 WI Infantry, Nov. 1, 1863. GSW left side, Decatur, GA, July 22, 1864. Colonel, 44 WI Infantry, Feb. 17, 1865. Commanded Post of Paducah (KY), District of Western Kentucky, Department of Kentucky, June–Aug. 1865. Honorably mustered out, Aug. 28, 1865. Battle honors: 1st Bull Run, Vicksburg Campaign, Atlanta Campaign (Decatur).

Born: April 28, 1840, Ashtabula Co., OH
Died: Nov. 3, 1893, Denver, CO (committed suicide by gunshot)
Occupation: Lawyer and judge
Offices/Honors: Associate Justice, Montana Territory Supreme Court, 1869–71. U.S. House of Representatives, 1885–89.
Miscellaneous: Resided La Crosse, La Crosse Co., WI, to 1866; Paducah, McCracken Co., KY, 1866–69; Helena, Lewis and Clark Co., MT, 1869–74; and Denver, Arapahoe Co., CO, 1874–93
Buried: Fairmount Cemetery, Denver, CO (Block 5, Lot 105)
References: *History of the City of Denver, Arapahoe County, and Colorado.* Chicago, IL, 1880. Obituary Circular, Whole No. 71, Colorado MOLLUS. Obituary, *Rocky Mountain News,* Nov. 5, 1893. William C. Ferril. *Sketches of Colorado: Being an Analytical Summary and Biographical History of the State of Colorado.* Denver, CO, 1911. Society of the

Thomas Stephens (*Commemorative Biographical Record of the Counties of Rock, Green, Grant, Iowa and Lafayette, Wisconsin.* Chicago, IL, 1901).

George Gifford Symes (post-war) (*History of the City of Denver, Arapahoe County, and Colorado.* Chicago, IL, 1880).

Army of the Cumberland. Twenty-Fifth Reunion, Chattanooga, TN, 1895. Cincinnati, OH, 1896. Pension File and Military Service File, National Archives. Letters Received, Volunteer Service Branch, Adjutant General's Office, File W3422(VS) 1864, National Archives. *Representative Men of Colorado in the Nineteenth Century.* Denver, CO, 1902. *Reunion of the Twenty-Fifth Regiment of Wisconsin Volunteer Infantry.* Sparta, WI, 1887. James L. Harrison, compiler. *Biographical Directory of the American Congress, 1774–1949.* Washington, D.C., 1950.

George Gifford Symes (post-war) (C.M. Bell, 463, 465 Pennsylvania Avenue, Washington, DC).

William Lawrence Utley

Colonel, 22 WI Infantry, Sept. 1, 1862. Taken prisoner Thompson's Station, TN, March 5, 1863. Confined Libby Prison, Richmond, VA. Paroled May 5, 1863. Commanded 3 Brigade, 1 Division, Reserve Corps, Army of the Cumberland, June 8–24, 1863. Commanded Post of Murfreesboro (TN), Department of the Cumberland, Oct.–Nov. 1863. Commanded 2 Brigade, 3 Division, 20 Army Corps, Army of the Cumberland, April 1864. Anticipating charges of incompetency and suffering from "chronic affection of the spine, disease of the lungs, and an affection of the urinary organs," he resigned July 5, 1864, "in consideration of my health, which has been failing me for the past six months and, at present, renders me totally unfit for active field duty." Battle honors: Thompson's Station, Atlanta Campaign (Resaca, New Hope Church).

William Lawrence Utley (Eugene W. Leach. *Racine County Militant, An Illustrated Narrative of War Times, and a Soldiers' Roster.* Racine, WI, 1915).

Born: July 10, 1814, Monson, MA
Died: March 4, 1887, Racine, WI
Occupation: Portrait painter and hotelkeeper before war. Newspaper editor and postmaster after war.
Offices/Honors: Wisconsin State Assembly, 1851–52. Wisconsin Adjutant General, 1852–54 and 1861–62. Wisconsin Senate, 1861–62. Postmaster, Racine, WI, 1869–77.
Miscellaneous: Resided Racine, Racine Co., WI. Gained nation-wide attention in November 1862 while stationed near Louisville, KY, for refusing to deliver a fugitive slave to his master, in spite of a Kentucky circuit court order.
Buried: Mound Cemetery, Racine, WI (Block 6, Lot 87)
References: *Portrait and Biographical Album of Racine and Kenosha Counties, Wisconsin.* Chicago, IL, 1892. Obituary, *Racine Daily Journal*, March 5, 1887. Obituary, *Racine Advocate*, March 5, 1887. Obituary, *Wisconsin State Journal*, March 5, 1887. *History of Geauga and Lake Counties, Ohio.* Philadelphia, PA, 1878. *The History of Racine and Kenosha*

Counties, Wisconsin. Chicago, IL, 1879. *The United States Biographical Dictionary and Portrait Gallery of Eminent and Self-Made Men.* Wisconsin Volume. Chicago, Cincinnati and New York, 1877. *Dictionary of Wisconsin Biography.* Madison, WI, 1960. Richard H. Groves. *Blooding the Regiment: An Account of the 22nd Wisconsin's Long and Difficult Apprenticeship.* Lanham, MD, 2005. Pension File and Military Service File, National Archives. Fanny S. Stone, editor. *Racine, Belle City of the Lakes, and Racine County, Wisconsin.* Chicago, IL, 1916. Eugene W. Leach. *Racine County Militant, An Illustrated Narrative of War Times, and a Soldiers' Roster.* Racine, WI, 1915. William M. Fliss, "Wisconsin's Abolition Regiment: The Twenty-second Volunteer Infantry in Kentucky, 1862–1863," *Wisconsin Magazine of History,* Vol. 86, No. 2 (Winter 2002–2003). Frank L. Byrne, editor. *The View from Headquarters: Civil War Letters of Harvey Reid.* Madison, WI, 1965.

Joseph Vandor

Colonel, 7 WI Infantry, Aug. 18, 1861. Resigned Jan. 30, 1862, "for the benefit of the service, there being an ill feeling on the part of the commissioned officers of the regiment," ... who "by written petition directed to him requested him to resign his post," ... making his position "painful and disagreeable to him and inconsistent with his honor as a soldier and a gentleman."

Born: Nov. 23, 1823, Hungary
Died: May 7, 1873, San Francisco, CA
Education: Graduated Imperial Military Academy, Vienna, Austria, 1839. Graduated Harvard University Law School, Cambridge, MA, 1857.
Other Wars: An officer of infantry in the Austrian Army to 1845, and subsequently a major in the Hungarian Army (1848–49)
Occupation: Lawyer
Offices/Honors: U.S. Consul, Tahiti, 1862–68
Miscellaneous: Resided Milwaukee, WI; and San Francisco, CA. Brother-in-law of Colonel Charles Knobelsdorff (44 IL Infantry).
Buried: San Francisco National Cemetery, San Francisco, CA (Section OSA, Plot 69, Grave 8)
References: Paul E. Vandor. *History of Fresno County, California, with Biographical Sketches.* Los Angeles, CA, 1919. Istvan Kornel Vida. *Hungarian Emigres in the American Civil War.* Jefferson, NC, 2012. Obituary, *San Francisco Evening Bulletin,* May 10, 1873. Pension File and Military Service File, National Archives. Alan T. Nolan. *The Iron Brigade: A Military History.* Ann Arbor, MI, 1983. Lance J. Herdegen. *The Iron Brigade in Civil War and Memory.* El Dorado Hills, CA, 2012. Letters Received, Volunteer Service Branch, Adjutant General's Office, File M51(VS)1861, National Archives. *The War of the Rebellion: A Compilation of the Official Records of the Union and Confederate Armies.* (Series 3, Vol. 1, p. 763). Washington, D.C., 1899. *Quinquennial Catalogue of the Law School of Harvard University, 1817–1924.* Cambridge, MA, 1925. Marriage Certificate, Milwaukee County, State of Wisconsin, Aug. 22, 1857. "Justice in Early Days," *Milwaukee Daily Journal,* Oct. 24, 1891.

George Henry Walther

Captain, Co. I, 7 WI Infantry, Aug. 20, 1861. GSW right shoulder, Gainesville, VA, Aug. 28, 1862. Major, 34 WI Infantry, Jan. 30, 1863. Honorably mustered out, Sept. 8, 1863. Major, 35 WI Infantry, Feb. 15, 1864. Lieutenant Colonel, 35 WI Infantry, Aug. 24, 1865. Colonel, 35 WI Infantry, Oct. 24, 1865. Honorably mustered out, March 15, 1866. Battle honors: Gainesville, Mobile Campaign (Spanish Fort).

Born: Nov. 23, 1828, Betzigerode, Hesse-Cassel, Germany
Died: Aug. 6, 1895, Milwaukee, WI
Occupation: Surveyor, civil engineer, and justice of the peace
Offices/Honors: Wisconsin State Assembly, 1876
Miscellaneous: Resided Theresa, Dodge Co., WI, to 1866; and Milwaukee, WI, after 1866
Buried: Forest Home Cemetery, Milwaukee, WI (Section 4, Block 43, Lot 10)

George Henry Walther (Marc and Beth Storch Collection).

References: Robert M. Bashford, compiler. *The Legislative Manual of the State of Wisconsin.* Fifteenth Annual Edition. Madison, WI, 1876. Obituary, *Milwaukee Daily News,* Aug. 6, 1895. Obituary, *Milwaukee Weekly Wisconsin,* Aug. 10, 1895. Alfred T. Andreas. *History of Milwaukee, Wisconsin.* Chicago, IL, 1881. Pension File and Military Service File, National Archives.

Clement Edson Warner

Captain, Co. B, 36 WI Infantry, March 4, 1864. Major, 36 WI Infantry, June 11, 1864. Lieutenant Colonel, 36 WI Infantry, July 15, 1864. GSW left arm (amputated), Deep Bottom, VA, Aug. 14, 1864. *Colonel,* 36 WI Infantry, May 7, 1865. Honorably mustered out, July 12, 1865. Battle honors: Spotsylvania, North Anna, Cold Harbor, Petersburg Cam-

Clement Edson Warner (E.R. Curtiss, Photographer, Klauber's New Block, Madison, WI; Wisconsin Historical Society, WHi-40694).

Left, top: George Henry Walther (Brady's National Photographic Portrait Gallery, Broadway & Tenth Street, New York; Marc and Beth Storch Collection). *Bottom:* George Henry Walther (Hugo Broich, Photographic Artist, No. 365 West Water Street, Corner of Chestnut, Milwaukee, WI; The Wisconsin Veterans Museum, Madison, WI [WVM.1922.I001]).

paign (Deep Bottom), Hatcher's Run, Appomattox Campaign.

Born: Feb. 23, 1836, Batavia, NY
Died: May 22, 1916, Windsor, WI
Education: Attended University of Wisconsin, Madison, WI
Occupation: Farmer
Offices/Honors: Wisconsin Senate, 1867–68. Wisconsin State Assembly, 1883.
Miscellaneous: Resided Windsor, Dane Co., WI
Buried: Windsor Cemetery, Windsor, WI
References: Fanny Warner and Lathrop Ezra Smith, editors. *In Memoriam: Clement Edson Warner.* Madison, WI, 1917. Lucien C. Warner and Mrs. Josephine Genung Nichols, compilers. *The Descendants of Andrew Warner.* New Haven, CT, 1919. Obituary Circular, Whole No. 573, Wisconsin MOLLUS. Obituary, *De Forest Times,* May 26, 1916. *History of Dane County, Wisconsin.* Chicago, IL, 1880. *History of Dane County: Biographical and Genealogical.* Madison, WI, 1906. James M. Aubery. *The Thirty-Sixth Wisconsin Volunteer Infantry, 1st Brigade, 2nd Division, 2nd Army Corps, Army of the Potomac.* Milwaukee, WI, 1900. Pension File and Military Service File, National Archives. Letters Received, Volunteer Service Branch, Adjutant General's Office, File W1481(VS)1865, National Archives. James E. Heg, compiler. *The Blue Book of the State of Wisconsin,* Vol. 22. Milwaukee, WI, 1883.

William Craw Webb

1 Lieutenant, RQM, 37 WI Infantry, March 12, 1864. *Colonel,* 52 WI Infantry, Feb. 23, 1865. Resigned as 1 Lieutenant, RQM, 37 WI Infantry, March 16, 1865, to accept promotion. The 52 WI Infantry, however, failed to complete organization, so his discharge from the 37 WI Infantry was revoked, June 6, 1865, and he was restored to his position in that regiment. Since he never rejoined the regiment, the date of his discharge reverted to the date of his resignation, March 16, 1865. Battle honors: Petersburg Campaign.

Born: April 21, 1824, Ridgebury, Bradford Co., PA
Died: April 19, 1898, Topeka, KS
Occupation: Lawyer and judge
Offices/Honors: Wisconsin State Assembly, 1858 and 1862–64. District Judge, 1870. Kansas House of Representatives, 1870–71 and 1891. Kansas State Superintendent of Insurance, 1871–73.
Miscellaneous: Resided Wautoma, Waushara Co., WI, to 1866; Girard, Crawford Co., KS; Fort Scott, Bourbon Co., KS; and Topeka, Shawnee Co., KS, after 1875
Buried: Topeka Cemetery, Topeka, KS (Section 55, Lot 24)
References: James L. King, editor. *History of*

William Craw Webb (Wisconsin Historical Society, WHi-119507).

Shawnee County, Kansas, and Representative Citizens. Chicago, IL, 1905. Obituary, *Topeka Daily Capital,* April 20, 1898. Obituary Circular, Whole No. 194, Kansas MOLLUS. Obituary, *Topeka State Journal,* April 19, 1898. *Report of the Annual Meeting of the Wisconsin State Bar Association, 1900.* Madison, WI, 1901. John R. Berryman. *History of the Bench and Bar of Wisconsin.* Chicago, IL, 1898. Pension File and Military Service File, National Archives. Letters Received, Volunteer Service Branch, Adjutant General's Office, File W744(VS)1865, National Archives. Reynold Webb Wilcox, compiler. *The Descendants of William Wilcoxson, Vincent Meigs, and Richard Webb.* New York City, NY, 1893. Robert C. Eden. *The Sword and Gun: A History of the 37th Wisconsin Volunteer Infantry.* Madison, WI, 1865.

Theodore Sterling West

2 Lieutenant, Co. K, 5 WI Infantry, July 12, 1861. 1 Lieutenant, Adjutant, 5 WI Infantry, July 13, 1861. GSW Williamsburg, VA, May 5, 1862. Resigned Sept. 3, 1862, to accept promotion. Lieutenant Colonel, 24 WI Infantry, March 31, 1863. Shell wound left hip and taken prisoner, Chickamauga, GA, Sept. 20, 1863. Confined Libby Prison, Richmond, VA. Escaped Feb. 9, 1864. *Colonel,* 24 WI Infantry, March 4, 1864. GSW left foot, Resaca, GA, May 14, 1864. Still suffering from the effects of his wounds, he resigned May 12, 1865. Battle honors: Williamsburg, Chickamauga, Atlanta Campaign (Resaca).

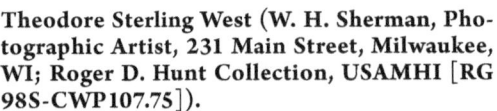

Theodore Sterling West (W. H. Sherman, Photographic Artist, 231 Main Street, Milwaukee, WI; Roger D. Hunt Collection, USAMHI [RG 98S-CWP107.75]).

Above: Theodore Sterling West (W.H. Sherman, Photographic Artist, 16 Wisconsin Street, Milwaukee, WI). *Below:* Theodore Sterling West (post-war) (Photographed by B.F. Reimer, No. 624 Arch Street, Philadelphia, PA).

Born: 1835?, Philadelphia, PA
Died: Aug. 15, 1889, Asbury Park, NJ
Occupation: Engaged in railroading before war. Merchant, manufacturer, U.S. Customs official, and hotelkeeper after war.
Offices/Honors: While Special Agent of the U.S. Treasury Department, 1886–87, he was prosecuted in San Francisco for "violating the secrecy of the United States mails." Although he was widely-known as "General West," he never attained that rank, General Grant rejecting his 1868 recommendation for brevet brigadier general with the words, "Not approved."
Miscellaneous: Resided Waukesha, Waukesha Co., WI; Milwaukee, WI; Philadelphia, PA; San Francisco, CA; and Washington, D.C. At first it was thought that he died from injuries received in a previous altercation with a disgruntled hotel patron, but an autopsy confirmed that he died from chronic Bright's disease. His widow was a daughter of Brig. Gen. Marcellus M. Crocker.
Buried: Arlington National Cemetery, Arlington, VA (Section 1, Lot 10-D)
References: Obituary, *Washington Post,* Aug. 16, 1889. Obituary, *Washington Evening Star,* Aug. 15, 1889. Obituary, *New York Times,* Aug. 16, 1889. Obituary, *Waukesha Journal,* Aug. 17, 1889. Obituary, *Milwaukee Weekly Wisconsin,* Aug. 24, 1889. William J.K. Beaudot. *The 24th Wisconsin Infantry in the Civil War: The Biography of a Regiment.* Mechanicsburg, PA, 2003. Pension File and Military Service File, National Archives. Letters Received, Volunteer Service Branch, Adjutant General's Office, File W717(VS)1862, National Archives. Letters Received, Commission Branch, Adjutant General's Office, File W124(CB)1868, National Archives. "It Was Not a Homicide," *Washington Evening Star,* Aug. 19, 1889. "Gen. West Arrested," *San Francisco Chronicle,* Oct. 17, 1886. George A. Robertson, "Out of Libby Prison," *Washington National Tribune,* Sept. 23, 1886.

David Evans Wood

Colonel, 14 WI Infantry, Jan. 30, 1862. Battle honors: Shiloh.

Born: Dec. 10, 1823, New Bedford, Lawrence Co., PA

Died: June 17, 1862, Fond du Lac, WI (typhoid fever)

Education: Graduated Washington (PA) College, 1846

Occupation: Lawyer and judge

Offices/Honors: Wisconsin State Assembly, 1850. Fond du Lac County Judge, 1854–57.

Miscellaneous: Resided Manchester, Calumet Co., WI; and Fond du Lac, Fond du Lac Co., WI

Buried: Rienzi Cemetery, Fond du Lac, WI (Old Grounds, Mountain Side, Lot 159)

References: Obituary, *Fond du Lac Commonwealth*, June 18, 1862. *Report of the Proceedings of the*

David Evans Wood (Frederick H. Magdeburg. *Wisconsin at Shiloh: Report of the Commission.* Madison, WI, 1909).

Meetings of the State Bar Association of Wisconsin for the Years 1878, 1881, and 1885. Madison, WI, 1905. John R. Berryman. *History of the Bench and Bar of Wisconsin.* Chicago, IL, 1898. *Biographical and Historical Catalogue of Washington and Jefferson College.* Cincinnati, OH, 1889. Military Service File, National Archives. Frederick H. Magdeburg. *Wisconsin at Shiloh: Report of the Commission.* Madison, WI, 1909. John Hancock. *The Fourteenth Wisconsin, Corinth and Shiloh, 1862–1895.* Paper on Battle of Shiloh. *Pilgrimage of Engle and Tucker to Battle Fields of Corinth and Shiloh, 1895.* Indianapolis, IN, 1895.

David Evans Wood (Chicago History Museum [ICHi-68792]).

BIBLIOGRAPHY

Books

Abbot, Henry L. *United States Military Academy: Half Century of a West Point Class, 1850 to 1854.* Boston: Thomas Todd, Printer, 1904.

Adair, John M. *Historical Sketch of the 45th Illinois Regiment.* Lanark, IL: Carroll County Gazette Print, 1869.

Address of Col. W. Bowen Moore, Late Adjutant of the 2nd Regiment Illinois Cavalry, Delivered Before the Reunion of the Survivors of the Regiment, at Urbana, Champaign Co., Illinois, Oct. 15, 1879. N.p., 1879.

Ager, Waldemar. *Colonel Heg and His Boys: A Norwegian Regiment in the American Civil War.* Translated by Della Kittleson Catuna and Clarence A. Clausen. Northfield, MN: Norwegian-American Historical Association, 2000.

_____. *Oberst Heg og hans Gutter.* Eau Claire, WI: Fremad Publishing Co., 1916.

Albin, Ethel Winifred. *The Virginia Albins: The History of the Albin Family Out of Old Frederick County, 1739–1989.* N.p.: E.W. Albin, 1989.

Album of Genealogy and Biography Cook County, Illinois. Chicago: Calumet Book & Engraving Co., 1897.

Aldrich, C. Knight, ed. *Quest for a Star: The Civil War Letters and Diaries of Colonel Francis T. Sherman of the 88th Illinois.* Knoxville, TN: University of Tennessee Press, 1999.

Alexander, W.E. *History of Winneshiek and Allamakee Counties, Iowa.* Sioux City, IA: Western Publishing Co., 1882.

Altshuler, Constance Wynn. *Cavalry Yellow & Infantry Blue: Army Officers in Arizona Between 1851 and 1886.* Tucson, AZ: Arizona Historical Society, 1991.

Ambrose, D. Leib. *History of the 7th Regiment Illinois Volunteer Infantry.* Springfield, IL: Illinois Journal Co., 1868.

American Lumbermen. Third Series. Chicago: The American Lumberman, 1906.

Anderson, James S. *Pioneer Courts and Lawyers of Manitowoc County, Wisconsin.* Manitowoc, WI: Manitowoc Pilot, 1922.

Andreas, Alfred T. *Atlas Map of Peoria County, Illinois.* Chicago: Alfred T. Andreas, 1873.

_____. *Atlas Map of Pike County, Illinois.* Davenport, IA: Alfred T. Andreas, 1872.

_____. *History of Chicago from the Earliest Period to the Present Time.* Chicago: Alfred T. Andreas, 1885.

_____. *History of Milwaukee, Wisconsin.* Chicago: Western Historical Co., 1881.

_____. *History of Northern Wisconsin.* Chicago: Western Historical Co., 1881.

_____. *History of the State of Kansas.* Chicago: Alfred T. Andreas, 1883.

_____. *History of the State of Nebraska.* Chicago: Western Historical Co., 1882.

Andrews, Christopher C., ed. *History of St. Paul, Minnesota.* Syracuse, NY: D. Mason & Co., 1890.

_____. "The Surrender of the Third Regiment Minnesota Volunteer Infantry," *Glimpses of the Nation's Struggle, Minnesota Commandery, MOLLUS.* Vol. 1. St. Paul, MN: St. Paul Book & Stationery Co., 1887.

Angle, Paul M., ed. *Three Years in the Army of the Cumberland: The Letters and Diary of Major James A. Connolly.* Bloomington, IN: Indiana University Press, 1959.

Annals of Jackson County, Iowa. No. 5 (May 1907-Aug. 1908). Maquoketa, IA: Jackson County Historical Society, 1908.

Annual Catalogue of the Ohio University, 1875. Athens, OH: Ohio University, 1876.

Arndt, John Stover. *The Story of the Arndts: The Life, Antecedents and Descendants of Bernhard Arndt who Emigrated to Pennsylvania in the Year 1731.* Philadelphia: Christopher Sower Co., 1922.

Aten, Henry J. *History of the Eighty-Fifth Regiment Illinois Volunteer Infantry.* Hiawatha, KS: Regimental Association, 1901.

Atlas of Kankakee County, Illinois. Chicago: J.H. Beers & Co., 1883.

Aubery, James M. *The Thirty-Sixth Wisconsin Volunteer Infantry, 1st Brigade, 2nd Division, 2nd Army Corps, Army of the Potomac.* Milwaukee, WI: Evening Wisconsin Co., 1900.

Avery, Lillian D. *A Genealogy of the Ingersoll Family in America, 1629–1925.* New York City: The Grafton Press, 1926.

Avery, Phineas O. *History of the 4th Illinois Cavalry Regiment.* Humboldt, NE: The Enterprise, 1903.

Babcock, Stephen. *The Babcock Genealogy.* New York City: Eaton & Mains, 1903.

Bibliography

Bailey, Dana R. *History of Minnehaha County, South Dakota*. Sioux Falls, SD: Brown & Saenger, Printers, 1899.

Bailey, Edwin C. *Past and Present of Winneshiek County, Iowa*. Chicago: S.J. Clarke Publishing Co., 1913.

Baldwin, Charles C. *The Baldwin Genealogy from 1500 to 1881*. Cleveland, OH: Leader Printing Co., 1881.

Banasik, Michael E., ed. *Duty, Honor and Country: The Civil War Experiences of Captain William P. Black, Thirty-Seventh Illinois Infantry*. Iowa City, IA: Camp Pope Bookshop, 2006.

Barber, Lucius W. *Army Memoirs of Lucius W. Barber, Co. D, 15th Illinois Volunteer Infantry*. Chicago: J.M.W. Jones Stationery & Printing Co., 1894.

Barker, Lorenzo A. *Military History (Michigan Boys) Company D, 66th Illinois, Birge's Western Sharpshooters in the Civil War, 1861–1865*. Huntington, WV: Blue Acorn Press, 1994.

Barnet, James, ed. *The Martyrs and Heroes of Illinois in the Great Rebellion*. Second Edition. Chicago: James Barnet, 1866.

Bashford, Robert M., comp. *The Legislative Manual of the State of Wisconsin*. Fifteenth Annual Edition. Madison, WI: E.B. Bolens, 1876.

Basler, Roy P., ed. *The Collected Works of Abraham Lincoln*. New Brunswick, NJ: Rutgers University Press, 1953.

Bateman, Newton, and Paul Selby. *Biographical and Memorial Edition of the Historical Encyclopedia of Illinois*. Chicago: Munsell Publishing Co., 1915.

_____, and _____, eds. *Historical Encyclopedia of Illinois*. Chicago and New York: Munsell Publishing Co., 1900.

_____, and _____, eds. *Historical Encyclopedia of Illinois and History of Sangamon County*. Chicago: Munsell Publishing Co., 1912.

_____, _____, and Joseph O. Cunningham, eds. *Historical Encyclopedia of Illinois and History of Champaign County*. Chicago: Munsell Publishing Co., 1905.

_____, _____, and Charles Edward Wilson, eds. *Historical Encyclopedia of Illinois and History of Coles County*. Chicago: Munsell Publishing Co., 1906.

_____, _____, and Henry Van Sellar, editors. *Historical Encyclopedia of Illinois and History of Edgar County*. Chicago: Munsell Publishing Co., 1905.

_____, _____, and Jesse Heylin, eds. *Historical Encyclopedia of Illinois and History of Fulton County*. Chicago: Munsell Publishing Co., 1908.

_____, _____, and John S. Wilcox, eds. *Historical Encyclopedia of Illinois and History of Kane County*. Chicago: Munsell Publishing Co., 1904.

_____, _____, and A.C. Bardwell, eds. *Historical Encyclopedia of Illinois and History of Lee County*. Chicago: Munsell Publishing Co., 1904.

_____, _____, and David McCulloch, eds. *Historical Encyclopedia of Illinois and History of Peoria County*. Chicago and Peoria, IL: Munsell Publishing Co., 1902.

_____, _____, and Ben C. Allensworth, eds. *Historical Encyclopedia of Illinois and History of Tazewell County*. Chicago: Munsell Publishing Co., 1905.

_____, _____, and Charles A. Church, eds. *Historical Encyclopedia of Illinois and History of Winnebago County*. Chicago: Munsell Publishing Co., 1916.

_____, _____, Harvey B. Hurd, and Robert D. Sheppard, eds. *Historical Encyclopedia of Illinois and History of Evanston*. Chicago: Munsell Publishing Co., 1906.

_____, _____, William F. Kenaga, and George R. Letourneau, eds. *Historical Encyclopedia of Illinois and History of Kankakee County*. Chicago: Middle-West Publishing Co., 1906.

_____, _____, W. Selden Gale, and George C. Gale, eds. *Historical Encyclopedia of Illinois and Knox County*. Chicago and New York: Munsell Publishing Co., 1899.

_____, _____, Ezra M. Prince, and John H. Burnham, eds. *Historical Encyclopedia of Illinois and History of McLean County*. Chicago: Munsell Publishing Co., 1908.

_____, _____, A.S. Wilderman, and A.A. Wilderman, eds. *Historical Encyclopedia of Illinois and History of St. Clair County*. Chicago: Munsell Publishing Co., 1907.

Battey, Herbert V., comp. *Samson Battey of Rhode Island*. Council Bluffs, IA: H.V. Battey, 1932.

Baumgartner, Richard A. *Blue Lightning: Wilder's Mounted Infantry Brigade in the Battle of Chickamauga*. Huntington, WV: Blue Acorn Press, 1997.

Bearss, Sara B., senior ed. *Dictionary of Virginia Biography*. Richmond, VA: Library of Virginia, 2006.

Beaudot, William J.K. *The 24th Wisconsin Infantry in the Civil War: The Biography of a Regiment*. Mechanicsburg, PA: Stackpole Books, 2003.

Beckwith, Hiram W. *History of Iroquois County, Together With Historic Notes on the Northwest*. Chicago: H.H. Hill & Co., 1880.

_____. *History of Vermilion County, Together With Historic Notes on the Northwest*. Chicago: H.H. Hill & Co., 1879.

Behrens, Robert H. *From Salt Fork to Chickamauga: Champaign County Soldiers in the Civil War*. Urbana, IL: Urbana Free Library, 1988.

Belknap, William W. *History of the Fifteenth Regiment Iowa Veteran Volunteer Infantry, from October 1861 to August 1865*. Keokuk, IA: R.B. Ogden & Son, 1887.

Bell, John T. *Tramps and Triumphs of the Second Iowa Infantry, Briefly Sketched*. Des Moines, IA: Kieffer Associates, 1961.

The Bench and Bar of Chicago: Biographical Sketches. Chicago: American Biographical Publishing Co., 1883.

Benedict, Henry M. *The Genealogy of the Benedicts in America*. Albany, NY: Joel Munsell, 1870.

Bennett, Lyman G., and William M. Haigh. *History of the 36th Regiment Illinois Volunteers During the War of the Rebellion*. Aurora, IL: Knickerbocker & Hodder, Printers, 1876.

Bent, Charles, ed. *History of Whiteside County, Illinois,*

from Its First Settlement to the Present Time. Morrison, IL: L.P. Allen, Printer and Binder, 1877.

Bentley, William H. *History of the 77th Illinois Volunteer Infantry.* Peoria, IL: Edward Hine, Printer, 1883.

Berger, Catherine M. *Op den Graeff, Updegraff, Updegrove: Indices and Pedigrees of Known Descendants of Herman Op den Graeff.* Sacramento, CA: Links Genealogy Publications, 1991.

Berryman, John R. *History of the Bench and Bar of Wisconsin.* Chicago: H.C. Cooper, Jr., & Co., 1898.

Beyer, W.F., and O.F. Keydel, eds. *Deeds of Valor.* Detroit, MI: Perrien-Keydel Co., 1906.

Bingham, Theodore A. *The Bingham Family in the United States, Especially of the State of Connecticut.* Easton, PA: Bingham Association, 1927.

Biographical and Genealogical Record of La Salle County, Illinois. Chicago: Lewis Publishing Co., 1900.

Biographical and Historical Catalogue of Washington and Jefferson College. Cincinnati: Elm Street Printing Co., 1889.

Biographical and Reminiscent History of Richland, Clay and Marion Counties, Illinois. Indianapolis, IN: B.F. Bowen & Co., 1909.

Biographical Catalog of the Matriculates of Haverford College, 1833–1922. Philadelphia: Alumni Association, 1922.

Biographical Dictionary and Portrait Gallery of Representative Men of Chicago, Minnesota Cities and the World's Columbian Exposition. Chicago and New York: American Biographical Publishing Co., 1892.

Biographical Dictionary and Portrait Gallery of Representative Men of Chicago and the World's Columbian Exposition. Chicago and New York: American Biographical Publishing Co., 1892.

Biographical Encyclopedia of Illinois of the Nineteenth Century. Philadelphia: Galaxy Publishing Co., 1875.

A Biographical Guide to Forest Hill Cemetery, Madison, Wisconsin. Revised and Expanded. Madison, WI: Historic Madison, 2002.

Biographical History of Cherokee County, Iowa. Chicago: W.S. Dunbar & Co., 1889.

A Biographical History with Portraits of Prominent Men of the Great West. Chicago: Manhattan Publishing Co., 1894.

Biographical Record of the Class of 1850 of Yale College. New Haven, CT: Tuttle, Morehouse & Taylor, Printers, 1877.

The Biographical Record of Clinton County, Iowa. Chicago: S.J. Clarke Publishing Co., 1901.

The Biographical Record of DeWitt County, Illinois. Chicago: S.J. Clarke Publishing Co., 1901.

Biographical Review of Dane County, Wisconsin. Chicago: Biographical Review Publishing Co., 1893.

Biographical Review of Des Moines County, Iowa. Chicago: Hobart Publishing Co., 1905.

Biographical Review of Hancock County, Illinois. Chicago: Hobart Publishing Co., 1907.

The Biographical Review of Johnson, Massac, Pope, and Hardin Counties, Illinois. Chicago: Biographical Publishing Co., 1893.

Biographical Review, Volume XXV, Containing Life Sketches of Leading Citizens of Norfolk County, Massachusetts. Boston: Biographical Review Publishing Co., 1898.

Biographical Sketches of Distinguished Officers of the Army and Navy. New York City: L.R. Hamersly, 1905.

Bishop, Judson W. *The Story of a Regiment, Being a Narrative of the Service of the Second Regiment Minnesota Veteran Volunteer Infantry in the Civil War of 1861–1865. With History of Judson Bishop and Additional Chapters,* by Newell L. Chester, editor. St. Cloud, MN: North Star Press of St. Cloud, 2000.

Blackmar, Frank W., ed. *Kansas: A Cyclopedia of State History.* Chicago: Standard Publishing Co., 1912.

Blegen, Theodore C., ed. *The Civil War Letters of Colonel Hans Christian Heg.* Northfield, MN: Norwegian-American Historical Association, 1936.

Bloodgood, George M., comp. *Ancestors and Descendants of Captain Frans Janse Bloetgoet, 1462–1966.* N.p.: G.M. Bloodgood, 1980.

Boltwood, Lucius M., comp. *History and Genealogy of the Family of Thomas Noble of Westfield, Massachusetts.* Hartford, CT: Case, Lockwood & Brainard Co., 1878.

Bowen, Clarence W. *History of Woodstock, Connecticut: Genealogies of Woodstock Families.* Vol. 6. Norwood, MA: Plimpton Press, 1935.

Brackett, Herbert I. *Brackett Genealogy: Descendants of Anthony Brackett of Portsmouth and Captain Richard Brackett of Braintree.* Portland, ME: H.I. Brackett, 1907.

Bradsby, H.C., ed. *History of Bureau County, Illinois.* Chicago: World Publishing Co., 1885.

Brewer, Luther A., and Barthinius L. Wick. *History of Linn County, Iowa, from Its Earliest Settlement to the Present Time.* Cedar Rapids, IA: The Torch Press, 1911.

Briggs, Ralph Tallmadge. *Our Family Heritage and History, Comprising McColgin Clan and Some Allied Families.* Las Vegas, NV: R.T. Briggs, 1986.

Brigham, Johnson. *Des Moines Together with the History of Polk County, Iowa.* Chicago: S.J. Clarke Publishing Co., 1911.

Brinkerhoff, J.H.G. *Brinkerhoff's History of Marion County, Illinois.* Indianapolis: B.F. Bowen & Co., 1909.

Brown, Alonzo L. *History of the Fourth Regiment of Minnesota Infantry Volunteers During the Great Rebellion, 1861–1865.* St. Paul, MN: Pioneer Press Co., 1892.

Brown, Leonard. *American Patriotism; or, Memoirs of "Common Men."* Des Moines, IA: Redhead and Wellslager, 1869.

Brush, Stuart C., comp. *The Descendants of Thomas and Richard Brush of Huntington, Long Island.* Baltimore, MD: Gateway Press, 1982.

Bryant, Edwin E. *History of the Third Regiment of Wisconsin Veteran Volunteer Infantry, 1861–1865.* Madison, WI: Veteran Association of the Regiment, 1891.

Bibliography

Bryner, Byron Cloyd. *Bugle Echoes: The Story of Illinois 47th.* Springfield, IL: Phillips Bros., Printers, 1905.

Buck, James S. *Pioneer History of Milwaukee: Milwaukee Under the Charter, from 1847 to 1853, Inclusive.* Milwaukee, WI: Symes, Swain & Co., 1884.

Burdette, Robert J. *The Drums of the 47th.* Indianapolis, IN: Bobbs-Merrill Co., 1914.

Burhop, Ray. *The Twenty-Fourth Illinois Infantry Regiment: 1861–1864.* Lexington, KY: Ray Burhop, 2013.

Burnette, Patricia B. *James F. Jaquess; Scholar, Soldier and Private Agent for President Lincoln.* Jefferson, NC: McFarland & Co., 2013.

Burton, William L. *Melting Pot Soldiers: The Union's Ethnic Regiments.* Ames, IA: Iowa State University Press, 1988.

Buslett, Ole A. *Det Femtende Regiment Wisconsin Frivillige.* Decorah, IA: B. Amundsen, 1894.

Butrick, Richard P. *Butrick, Butterick, Buttrick in the U.S.A., 1635–1978.* N.p.: R.P. Butrick, 1979.

Byam, Edwin C. *Descendants of George Byam (?–1680).* Suffield, CT: Rich Lithographing Co., 1975.

Byers, Samuel H.M. *With Fire and Sword.* New York City: Neale Publishing Co., 1911.

Byrne, Frank L., ed. *The View from Headquarters: Civil War Letters of Harvey Reid.* Madison, WI: State Historical Society of Wisconsin, 1965.

_____, and Andrew T. Weaver, eds. *Haskell of Gettysburg: His Life and Civil War Papers.* Madison, WI: State Historical Society of Wisconsin, 1970.

Calkins, Elias A., "William A. Barstow's Military Services," *Collections of the State Historical Society of Wisconsin.* Vol. 6. Edited by Lyman C. Draper. Madison, WI: Wisconsin Historical Society, 1908.

Calkins, William W. *The History of the 104th Regiment of Illinois Volunteer Infantry. War of the Great Rebellion, 1862–1865.* Chicago: Donohue & Henneberry, 1895.

Carlock, Marion P. *History and Genealogy of the Judy-Judah-Tschudy-Tschudin-Tschudi-Schudi Family.* Los Angeles: The Bookman Press, 1954.

Carter, George W., "The Fourth Wisconsin at Port Hudson," *War Papers, Wisconsin Commandery, MOLLUS.* Vol. 3. Milwaukee, WI: Burdick & Allen, 1903.

Case, Nelson. *History of Labette County, Kansas, and Representative Citizens.* Chicago: Biographical Publishing Co., 1901.

Case, Theodore S., ed. *History of Kansas City, Missouri.* Syracuse, NY: D. Mason & Co., 1888.

Castle, Henry A. *Minnesota, Its Story and Biography.* Chicago and New York: Lewis Publishing Co., 1915.

Catalogue of Phi Alpha Society, Illinois College, 1845–1890. Jacksonville, IL: Phi Alpha Society, 1890.

A Centennial Biographical History of the City of Columbus and Franklin County, Ohio. Chicago: Lewis Publishing Co., 1901.

Chandler, George. *The Chandler Family. The Descendants of William and Annis Chandler Who Settled in Roxbury, Mass., 1637.* Worcester, MA: Press of Charles Hamilton, 1883.

Chapin, Gilbert W., comp. *The Chapin Book of Genealogical Data.* Hartford, CT: Chapin Family Association, 1924.

Chapman. Charles C. *History of Knox County, Illinois.* Chicago: Blakely, Brown & Marsh, Printers, 1878.

Chappell, Harry Church, and Katharyn Joella Chappell. *History of Buchanan County, Iowa, and Its People.* Chicago: S.J. Clarke Publishing Co., 1914.

Cherrington, Dean C., and Henrietta C. Evans. *The Cherrington Family History and Genealogy.* Scotch Plains, NJ: D.C. Cherrington, 1999.

Church, Charles A. *History of Rockford and Winnebago County, Illinois, from the First Settlement in 1834 to the Civil War.* Rockford, IL: W.P. Lamb, Book and Job Printer, 1900.

_____. *Past and Present of the City of Rockford and Winnebago County, Illinois.* Chicago: S.J. Clarke Publishing Co., 1905.

Clark, Charles B., and Roger D. Bowen. *University Recruits; Company C, 12th Iowa Infantry Regiment, U.S.A., 1861–1866.* Elverson, PA: Mennonite Family History, 1991.

Clark, Charles M. *The History of the 39th Regiment Illinois Volunteer Veteran Infantry (Yates Phalanx) in the War of the Rebellion, 1861–1865.* Chicago: Veteran Association of the Regiment, 1889.

Clayton, Powell. *The Aftermath of the Civil War, in Arkansas.* New York City: Neale Publishing Co., 1915.

Cluett, William W. *History of the 57th Regiment Illinois Volunteer Infantry.* Princeton, IL: T.P. Streeter, 1886.

Cochrane, Joseph. *Centennial History of Mason County.* Springfield, IL: Rokker's Steam Printing House, 1876.

Coffin, Selden J. *Record of the Men of Lafayette: Brief Biographical Sketches of the Alumni of Lafayette College.* Easton, PA: Skinner & Finch, Printers, 1879.

Colbo, Ella S. *Historic Heg Memorial Park.* Racine, WI: E.S. Colbo, 1940.

Colbron, W.C. *The Wisconsin National Guard.* Milwaukee, WI: King-Fowle-McGee Co., 1894.

Collections of the Minnesota Historical Society. Vol. 14 (Minnesota Biographies, 1655–1912, compiled by Warren Upham and Rose Barteau Dunlap). St. Paul, MN: Minnesota Historical Society, 1912.

Collins, Lewis, and Richard H. Collins. *Collins' Historical Sketches of Kentucky: History of Kentucky.* Frankfort, KY: Kentucky Historical Society, 1966.

Collins, William H., and Cicero F. Perry. *Past and Present of the City of Quincy and Adams County, Illinois.* Chicago: S.J. Clarke Publishing Co., 1905.

Combined History of Randolph, Monroe and Perry Counties, Illinois. Philadelphia: J.L. McDonough & Co., 1883.

Combined History of Shelby and Moultrie Counties, Illinois. Philadelphia: Brink, McDonough & Co., 1881.

Commemorative Biographical and Historical Record of Kane County, Illinois. Chicago: Beers, Leggett & Co., 1888.

Commemorative Biographical Record of the Counties of Rock, Green, Grant, Iowa and Lafayette, Wisconsin. Chicago: J.H. Beers & Co., 1901.

Commemorative Biographical Record of the Fox River Valley Counties of Brown, Outagamie and Winnebago. Chicago: J.H. Beers & Co., 1895.

Commemorative Biographical Record of Prominent and Representative Men of Racine and Kenosha Counties, Wisconsin. Chicago: J.H. Beers & Co., 1906.

Companions of the Military Order of the Loyal Legion of the United States. New York City: L.R. Hamersly Co., 1901.

Conard, Howard Louis, ed. *History of Milwaukee County from Its First Settlement to the Year 1895.* Chicago and New York: American Biographical Publishing Co., 1895.

Connelley, William E. *A Standard History of Kansas and Kansans.* Chicago and New York: Lewis Publishing Co., 1918.

Conover, Frederic K., ed. *Wisconsin Supreme Court Reports.* Vol. 57. Chicago: Callaghan & Co., 1883.

Corbit, Robert M., ed. *History of Jones County, Iowa, Past and Present.* Chicago: S.J. Clarke Publishing Co., 1910.

County of Douglas, Illinois: Historical and Biographical. Chicago: F.A. Battey & Co., 1884.

Cowles, Calvin D., comp. *The Genealogy of the Cowles Families in America.* New Haven, CT: Tuttle, Morehouse & Taylor Co., 1929.

Cowtan, Charles W. *Services of the 10th New York Volunteers (National Zouaves) in the War of the Rebellion.* New York City: Charles H. Ludwig, 1882.

Craft, Alice, comp. *Tolar, Toler, Toller, Towler: A One Name Study.* Cambridge, England: Midsummer Books, 1996.

Creel, George, and John Slavens, comps. *Men Who Are Making Kansas City: A Biographical Directory.* Kansas City, MO: Hudson-Kimberly Publishing Co., 1902.

Crisp, Carol A., comp. *Pope County, Illinois, Cemeteries: Results of a Graveyard Obsession.* Vol. 3. N.p.: C.A. Crisp, 2010.

Crooke, George, comp. *The Twenty-first Regiment of Iowa Volunteer Infantry: A Narrative of Its Experience in Active Service.* Milwaukee, WI: King, Fowle & Co., 1891.

Crossley, Frederic B. *Courts and Lawyers of Illinois.* Chicago: American Historical Society, 1916.

Cullum, George W. *Biographical Register of the Officers and Graduates of the U.S. Military Academy.* 3rd Edition. Boston: Houghton, Mifflin, 1891.

Curtiss-Wedge, Franklyn, ed. *History of Dakota and Goodhue Counties, Minnesota.* Chicago: H.C. Cooper, Jr., & Co., 1910.

_____. *History of Fillmore County, Minnesota.* Chicago: H.C. Cooper, Jr., & Co., 1912.

_____, ed. *History of Houston County, Minnesota.* Winona, MN: H.C. Cooper, Jr., & Co., 1919.

_____, ed. *History of McLeod County, Minnesota.* Chicago and Winona, MN: H.C. Cooper, Jr., & Co., 1917.

_____. *The History of Redwood County, Minnesota.* Chicago: H.C. Cooper, Jr., & Co., 1916.

Cushman, Henry W. *A Historical and Biographical Genealogy of the Cushmans: The Descendants of Robert Cushman, the Puritan, from the Year 1617 to 1855.* Boston: Little, Brown, and Co., 1855.

Damon, Herbert C. *History of the Milwaukee Light Guard.* Milwaukee, WI: Sentinel Co., 1875.

Daniels, James Harrison, Jr. *The Daniels-Daniells Family: A Genealogical History of the Descendants of William Daniell of Dorchester and Milton, Massachusetts, 1630–1957.* Baltimore, MD: N.A. Gossmann Publishing Co., 1959.

Davenport, Edward A., ed. *History of the Ninth Regiment Illinois Cavalry Volunteers.* Chicago: Donohue & Henneberry, 1888.

Davis, J. Merle. *Davis: Soldier, Missionary. A Biography of Rev. Jerome D. Davis.* Boston and Chicago: The Pilgrim Press, 1916.

Davis, William W. *History of Whiteside County, Illinois, from Its Earliest Settlement to 1908.* Chicago: Pioneer Publishing Co., 1908.

Dawson, Joseph G., III, ed. *The Louisiana Governors: From Iberville to Edwards.* Baton Rouge, LA: Louisiana State University Press, 1990.

Dawson, Mark R. *Ho! for the War! The Eleventh Illinois Cavalry: A Regimental History.* N.p.: M.R. Dawson, 2010.

Dexter, Darrel. *A House Divided: Union County, Illinois, 1818–1865.* Anna, IL: Reppert Publications, 1994.

_____, comp. *Union County, Illinois, Soldiers.* Carterville, IL: Genealogy Society of Southern Illinois, 1997.

Dickerman, Edward D., and George S. Dickerman. *Dickerman Genealogy: Descendants of Thomas Dickerman, An Early Settler of Dorchester, Massachusetts.* New Haven, CT: Tuttle, Morehouse & Taylor Press, 1922.

Dictionary of American Biography.

Dictionary of Wisconsin Biography. Madison, WI: State Historical Society of Wisconsin, 1960.

Dill, Rosalie Jones. *Mathew Dill Genealogy: A Study of the Dill Family of Dillsburg, York County, Pennsylvania, 1698–1934.* Spokane, WA: R.J. Dill, 1934.

Dodge, William Sumner. *History of the Old Second Division, Army of the Cumberland.* Chicago: Church & Goodman, 1864.

_____. *A Waif of the War; or, The History of the 75th Illinois Infantry, Embracing the Entire Campaigns of the Army of the Cumberland.* Chicago: Church & Goodman, 1866.

Downing, Alexander G. *Downing's Civil War Diary.* Edited by Olynthus B. Clark. Des Moines, IA: Historical Department of Iowa, 1916.

Draper, Lyman C., "Sketch of Hon. Charles H. Larrabee," *Report and Collections of the State Historical Society of Wisconsin, for the Years 1880, 1881, and 1882.* Vol. 9. Madison, WI: David Atwood, 1882.

Driggs, George W. *Opening of the Mississippi; or Two Years' Campaigning in the South-West.* Madison, WI: William J. Park & Co., 1864.

Dukett, Drew D. *Glimpses of Glory: The Regimental History of the 61st Illinois Volunteers.* Bowie, MD: Heritage Books, 1999.

Bibliography

Duncan, L. Wallace, comp. *History of Montgomery County, Kansas.* Iola, KS: Press of Iola Register, 1903.

_____, and Charles F. Scott, eds. *History of Allen and Woodson Counties, Kansas.* Iola, KS: Iola Register, Printers and Binders, 1901.

Dungan, J. Irvine. *History of the Nineteenth Regiment Iowa Volunteer Infantry.* Davenport, IA: Luse & Griggs, 1865.

Dyer, Frederick H. *A Compendium of the War of the Rebellion.* 3 Vol. Des Moines, IA: F.H. Dyer, 1908.

Eames, Charles M., comp. *Historic Morgan and Classic Jacksonville.* Jacksonville, IL: Daily Journal Steam Job Printing Office, 1885.

Easley, Barbara P., comp. *Obituaries of Benton County, Arkansas.* Vol. 3 (1905–09). Bowie, MD: Heritage Books, 1995.

Eberhart, Uriah. *History of the Eberharts in Germany and the United States.* Chicago: Donohue & Henneberry, 1891.

Eddy, Thomas M. *The Patriotism of Illinois.* Chicago: Clarke & Co., 1865.

Eden, Robert C. *The Sword and Gun: A History of the 37th Wisconsin Volunteer Infantry.* Madison, WI: Atwood & Rublee, 1865.

Edmunds, A.C. *Pen Sketches of Nebraskans.* Lincoln, NE: R. & J. Wilbur, Stationers, 1871.

Ege, Thompson P. *History and Genealogy of the Ege Family in the United States, 1738–1911.* Harrisburg, PA: Star Printing Co., 1911.

Ellis, James W. *History of Jackson County, Iowa.* Chicago: S.J. Clarke Publishing Co., 1910.

Ellis, William A., ed. *History of Norwich University, 1819–1911, Her History, Her Graduates, Her Roll of Honor.* Montpelier, VT: Capital City Press, 1911.

Emery, Tom. *The Other John Logan: Col. John Logan and the 32nd Illinois.* Carlinville, IL: History in Print, 1998.

Enander, Johan A. *Borgerkrigen i De forenede Stater i Nord Amerika.* La Crosse, WI: Trykt i Fædrelandet og emigrantens officin, 1881.

Encyclopedia of Contemporary Biography of West Virginia. New York City: Atlantic Publishing & Engraving Co., 1894.

Erwin, Milo. *The History of Williamson County, Illinois. from the Earliest Times, Down to the Present.* Marion, IL, 1876.

Evans, David. *Sherman's Horsemen: Union Cavalry Operations in the Atlanta Campaign.* Bloomington, IN: Indiana University Press, 1996.

Falge, Louis, ed. *History of Manitowoc County, Wisconsin.* Chicago: Goodspeed Historical Association, 1912.

Farthing, Paul and Chester, eds. *Philo History: Chronicles and Biographies of the Philosophian Literary Society of McKendree College.* Lebanon, IL: Philosophian Literary Society, 1911.

Feldhake, Hilda Engbring, ed. *Effingham County Illinois—Past and Present.* Effingham, IL: Effingham Regional Historical Society, 1968.

Fellows, Paul E., ed. *Massac County Memories, Volume 1, 1849–67.* Metropolis, IL: Massac Printing, 1992.

Ferrell, Ed. *Biographies and Genealogical Abstracts from Hardin County, Illinois, Newspapers, 1872–1938.* Bowie, MD: Heritage Books, 1999.

Ferril, William C. *Sketches of Colorado: Being an Analytical Summary and Biographical History of the State of Colorado.* Denver, CO: Western Press Bureau Co., 1911.

Fifth Annual Reunion of the Tenth Wisconsin Infantry, Held at Black River Falls, Wis., July 25 and 26, 1899. Waupun, WI: Oliver Bros., 1900.

Fisher, George E., ed. *Catalogue of the Delta Kappa Epsilon Fraternity: Biographical and Statistical.* New York City: Council Publishing Co., 1890.

Fisher, Kathy. *In the Beginning There Was Land: A History of Washington County, Iowa.* Washington, IA: Washington County Historical Society, 1978.

Fitch, John. *Annals of the Army of the Cumberland.* Philadelphia: J.B. Lippincott & Co., 1864.

Flandrau, Charles E. *Encyclopedia of Biography of Minnesota.* Chicago: Century Publishing & Engraving Co., 1900.

Fleharty, Stephen F. *Our Regiment: A History of the 102nd Illinois Infantry Volunteers.* Chicago: Brewster & Hanscom, Printers, 1865.

Fletcher, Samuel H. *The History of Company A, 2nd Illinois Cavalry.* Chicago, 1912.

Folsom, W.H.C. *Fifty Years in the Northwest.* St. Paul, MN: Pioneer Press Co., 1888.

Forrester, George, ed. *Historical and Biographical Album of the Chippewa Valley, Wisconsin.* Chicago: A. Warner, 1892.

Fourth Reunion of the Twelfth Iowa Veteran Volunteer Infantry. Norfolk, NE: Press of the Daily News, 1892.

Fowler, James A., and Miles M. Miller. *History of the 30th Iowa Infantry Volunteers.* Mediapolis, IA: T.A. Merrill, Printer, 1908.

Franklin College Register: Biographical and Historical. Wheeling, WV: West Virginia Printing Co., 1908.

Frazee, George. *Our Judges: Brief Sketches of the Judges Who Have Occupied the Bench in the First Judicial District of Iowa.* Burlington, IA: Acres, Blackmar & Co., 1895.

Freitag, Sabine. *Friedrich Hecker: Two Lives for Liberty.* Translated from the German and edited by Steven Rowan. St. Louis: St. Louis Mercantile Library, 2006.

French, Bella, ed. *The American Sketch Book: A Collection of Historical Incidents with Descriptions of Corresponding Localities.* Vol. 3. Green Bay, WI: American Sketch Book Co., 1876.

Fulwider, Addison L. *History of Stephenson County, Illinois: A Record of Its Settlement, Organization and Three-Quarters of a Century of Progress.* Chicago: S.J. Clarke Publishing Co., 1910.

Futhey, J. Smith, and Gilbert Cope. *History of Chester County, Pennsylvania, With Genealogical and Biographical Sketches.* Philadelphia: Louis H. Everts, 1881.

Gaff, Alan D. *If This is War: A History of the Campaign of Bull's Run by the Wisconsin Regiment Thereafter Known as the Ragged Ass Second.* Dayton, OH: Morningside House, 1991.

General Catalogue of the Graduates and Former Students of Miami University During Its First Century, 1809–1909. Oxford, OH: Miami University, 1909.

General Catalogue of Kimball Union Academy, Meriden, NH, 1813–1930. Hanover, NH: Dartmouth Press, 1930.

Genoways, Ted, and Hugh H. Genoways, eds. *A Perfect Picture of Hell: Eyewitness Accounts by Civil War Prisoners from the 12th Iowa.* Iowa City, IA: University of Iowa Press, 2001.

George Edwin Bryant: Our Colonel. Madison, WI, 1907.

George, Keith H. *George Genealogy.* Kingman, AZ: H & H Printers, 1991.

Gerling, Edwin G. *The One Hundred Seventeenth Illinois Infantry Volunteers (The McKendree Regiment) 1862–1865.* Highland, IL: E.G. Gerling, 1992.

Gilmore, James R. *Personal Recollections of Abraham Lincoln and the Civil War.* Boston: L.C. Page & Co., 1898.

Godwin, David W. *A Biographical History of Western Star Lodge No. 240 A.F. & A.M.* Champaign, IL: D.W. Godwin, 1998.

Goldthwaite, Charlotte, comp. *Boardman Genealogy, 1525–1895.* Hartford, CT: Case, Lockwood & Brainard Co., 1895.

Gordon, Charles Ulysses. *Chicago Postmasters from Jonathan Nash Bailey to Ernest J. Kruetgen, 1831 to 1945.* Chicago: C.U. Gordon, 1953.

Gove, Gertrude B. *A History of St. Cloud in the Civil War, 1858–1865.* St. Cloud, MN: Stearns County Historical Society, 1976.

Greene, Howard. *McMynn Genealogy.* N.p.: Howard Greene, 1926.

Greene, J. Harvey. *Letters to My Wife: A Civil War Diary from the Western Front.* Compiled by Sharon L.D. Kraynek. Apollo, PA: Closson Press, 1995.

Greene, William W. *Semi-Centennial History of the Alpha Zeta Society of Shurtleff College.* Alton, IL: Melling & Gaskins, 1898.

Gresham, John. *Historical and Biographical Record of Douglas County, Illinois.* Logansport, IN: Press of Wilson, Humphreys & Co., 1900.

Groves, Richard H. *Blooding the Regiment: An Account of the 22nd Wisconsin's Long and Difficult Apprenticeship.* Lanham, MD: Scarecrow Press, 2005.

Guandolo, Joseph, ed. *Centennial McKendree College, With St. Clair County History.* Lebanon, IL: McKendree College, 1928.

Gue, Benjamin F. *Biographies and Portraits of the Progressive Men of Iowa: Leaders in Business, Politics and the Professions.* Des Moines, IA: Conaway & Shaw, 1899.

_____. *History of Iowa from the Earliest Times to the Beginning of the Twentieth Century.* New York City, NY: Century History Co., 1903.

Guinn, James M. *Historical and Biographical Record of Los Angeles and Vicinity.* Chicago: Chapman Publishing Co., 1901.

Hallum, John. *Biographical and Pictorial History of Arkansas.* Albany, NY: Weed, Parsons & Co., 1887.

Hamilton, Frances F. *Ancestral Lines of the Doniphan, Frazee and Hamilton Families.* Greenfield, IN: William Mitchell Printing Co., 1928.

Hammond, Frederick S. *History and Genealogies of the Hammond Families in America.* Oneida, NY: Ryan & Burkhart, Printers, 1902.

Hancock, John. *The Fourteenth Wisconsin, Corinth and Shiloh, 1862–1895. Paper on Battle of Shiloh. Pilgrimage of Engle and Tucker to Battle Fields of Corinth and Shiloh, 1895.* Indianapolis, IN: F.E. Engle & Son, 1895.

Hancock, John E. *Hancock Genealogy: Descendants of Isaac Bradford Hancock.* Scotia, NY: J.E. Hancock, 1982.

Hannum, Curtis H., comp. *Genealogy of the Hannum Family Descended from John and Margery Hannum.* West Chester, PA: Horace F. Temple, 1911.

Hard, Abner. *History of the Eighth Cavalry Regiment, Illinois Volunteers, During the Great Rebellion.* Aurora, IL: Abner Hard, 1868.

Hare, Linda Alstrom. *Seven Hares in the Civil War.* Atlanta, KS: HHR Consulting and Publishing, 2005.

Harper, Douglas R. *"If Thee Must Fight," A Civil War History of Chester County, Pennsylvania.* West Chester, PA: Chester County Historical Society, 1990.

Harrington, George B. *Past and Present of Bureau County, Illinois.* Chicago: Pioneer Publishing Co., 1906.

Harris, Shirley D. *The Chenoweth Family in America: Some Descendants of John Chenoweth, Born ca 1682.* Tucson, AZ: Post Litho Printing, 1994.

Harrison, James L., comp. *Biographical Directory of the American Congress, 1774–1949.* Washington, D.C.: Government Printing Office, 1950.

Hart, Ephraim J. *History of the Fortieth Illinois Infantry (Volunteers).* Cincinnati: H.S. Bosworth, 1864.

Hart, Jessie W. *The Callaway Family of Virginia and Some Kentucky Descendants.* Los Angeles: J.W. Hart, 1928.

Hasbrouck, Jacob L. *History of McLean County, Illinois.* Topeka and Indianapolis: Historical Publishing Co., 1924.

Haskell, Ira J. *Chronicles of the Haskell Family.* Lynn, MA: Ellis Printing Co., 1943.

Haynie, J. Henry, ed. *The Nineteenth Illinois: A Memoir of a Regiment of Volunteer Infantry Famous in the Civil War of Fifty Years Ago for Its Drill, Bravery, and Distinguished Services.* Chicago: M.A. Donohue & Co., 1912.

Hazen, Henry A., and S. Lewis B. Speare, eds. *A History of the Class of 1854 in Dartmouth College, Including Col. Haskell's Narrative of the Battle of Gettysburg.* Boston: Alfred Mudge & Son, 1898.

Heg, James E., comp. *The Blue Book of the State of Wisconsin,* Vol. 22. Milwaukee, WI: Milwaukee Lithographing & Engraving Co., 1883.

Bibliography

Heitman, Francis B. *Historical Register and Dictionary of the United States Army.* Washington, D.C.: Government Printing Office, 1903.

Henry, Guy V. *Military Record of Civilian Appointments in the United States Army.* New York City: Carleton, 1869.

Herdegen, Lance J. *The Iron Brigade in Civil War and Memory.* El Dorado Hills, CA: Savas Beatie, 2012.

Herringshaw, Thomas W., ed. *Herringshaw's Encyclopedia of American Biography of the Nineteenth Century.* Chicago: American Publishers Association, 1906.

Hickenlooper, Frank. *An Illustrated History of Monroe County, Iowa.* Kansas City, MO: Hudson-Kimberly Publishing Co., 1896.

Historic Rock Island County. Rock Island, IL: Kramer & Co., 1908.

Historical Memoranda of the 52nd Regiment Illinois Infantry Volunteers, from Its Organization, Nov. 19th, 1861, to Its Muster Out, on the 6th Day of July, 1865. Elgin, IL: Gilbert & Post, 1868.

An Historical Sketch of the State Normal College at Albany, N.Y., and a History of Its Graduates for Fifty Years. Albany, NY: Brandow Printing Co., 1894.

The History of Adams County, Illinois. Chicago: Murray, Williamson & Phelps, 1879.

The History of Benton County, Iowa. Chicago: Western Historical Co., 1878.

History of Buchanan County, Iowa. Cleveland, OH: Williams Bros., 1881.

History of Caldwell and Livingston Counties, Missouri. St. Louis: National Historical Co., 1886.

History of Champaign County, Illinois. Philadelphia: Brink, McDonough & Co., 1878.

History of the City of Denver, Arapahoe County, and Colorado. Chicago: O.L. Baskin & Co., 1880.

History of Clear Creek and Boulder Valleys, Colorado. Chicago: O.L. Baskin & Co., 1880.

The History of Clinton County, Iowa. Chicago: Western Historical Co., 1879.

The History of Coles County, Illinois. Chicago: William Le Baron, Jr., & Co., 1879.

History of Cumberland and Adams Counties, Pennsylvania. Chicago: Warner, Beers & Co., 1886.

History of Dane County: Biographical and Genealogical. Madison, WI: Western Historical Association, 1906.

History of Dane County, Wisconsin. Chicago: Western Historical Co., 1880.

History of Davis County, Iowa. Des Moines, IA: State Historical Co., 1882.

The History of Des Moines County, Iowa. Chicago: Western Historical Co., 1879.

History of DeWitt County, Illinois. Philadelphia: W.R. Brink & Co., 1882.

History of DeWitt County, Illinois. Chicago: Pioneer Publishing Co., 1910.

The History of Dubuque County, Iowa. Chicago: Western Historical Co., 1880.

The History of Edgar County, Illinois. Chicago: William Le Baron, Jr., & Co., 1879.

History of Fayette County, Illinois. Philadelphia: Brink, McDonough & Co., 1878.

The History of Fond du Lac County, Wisconsin. Chicago: Western Historical Co., 1880.

History of Fremont County, Iowa. Des Moines, IA: Iowa Historical Co., 1881.

History of Gallatin, Saline, Hamilton, Franklin and Williamson Counties, Illinois. Chicago: Goodspeed Publishing Co., 1887.

History of Geauga and Lake Counties, Ohio. Philadelphia: Williams Brothers, 1878.

History of Goodhue County, Including a Sketch of the Territory and State of Minnesota. Red Wing, MN: Wood, Alley & Co., 1878.

History of Grant County, Wisconsin. Chicago: Western Historical Co., 1881.

History of Green County, Wisconsin. Springfield, IL: Union Publishing Co., 1884.

History of Greene and Jersey Counties, Illinois. Springfield, IL: Continental Historical Co., 1885.

History of Greene County, Illinois: Its Past and Present. Chicago: Donnelley, Gassette & Loyd, 1879.

History of Guthrie and Adair Counties, Iowa. Springfield, IL: Continental Historical Co., 1884.

The History of Henry County, Iowa. Chicago: Western Historical Co., 1879.

The History of Iowa County, Iowa. Des Moines, IA: Union Historical Co., 1881.

History of Iowa County, Wisconsin. Chicago: Western Historical Co., 1881.

History of Jackson County, Illinois. Philadelphia: Brink, McDonough & Co., 1878.

The History of Jasper County, Iowa. Chicago, IL: Western Historical Co., 1878.

The History of Jefferson County, Wisconsin. Chicago: Western Historical Co., 1879.

History of Johnson County, Missouri. Kansas City, MO: Kansas City Historical Co., 1881.

The History of Jones County, Iowa. Chicago: Western Historical Co., 1879.

History of Kent County, Michigan. Chicago: Chas. C. Chapman & Co., 1881.

The History of Keokuk County, Iowa. Des Moines, IA: Union Historical Co., 1880.

History of La Crosse County, Wisconsin. Chicago: Western Historical Co., 1881.

History of La Salle County, Illinois. Chicago: Inter-State Publishing Co., 1886.

The History of Lee County, Iowa. Chicago: Western Historical Co., 1879.

The History of Linn County, Iowa. Chicago: Western Historical Co., 1878.

History of Logan County, Illinois. Chicago: Inter-State Publishing Co., 1886.

History of Logan County, Illinois: Its Past and Present. Chicago: Donnelley, Loyd & Co., 1878.

History of Macon County, Illinois. Philadelphia: Brink, McDonough & Co., 1880.

History of Macoupin County, Illinois. Philadelphia: Brink, McDonough & Co., 1879.

History of Madison County, Illinois. Edwardsville, IL: W.R. Brink & Co., 1882.

The History of Marshall County, Iowa. Chicago: Western Historical Co., 1878.

History of McDonough County, Illinois. Springfield, IL: Continental Historical Co., 1885.

History of McHenry County, Illinois. Chicago: Inter-State Publishing Co., 1885.

The History of McLean County, Illinois. Chicago: William Le Baron, Jr., & Co., 1879.

The History of Menard and Mason Counties, Illinois. Chicago: O.L. Baskin & Co., 1879.

History of Monroe County, Iowa. Chicago: Western Historical Co., 1878.

History of Morgan County, Illinois: Its Past and Present. Chicago: Donnelley, Loyd & Co., 1878.

The History of Muscatine County, Iowa. Chicago: Western Historical Co., 1879.

History of Muscatine County, Iowa, from the Earliest Settlements to the Present Time. Chicago: S.J. Clarke Publishing Co., 1911.

The History of Peoria County, Illinois. Chicago: Johnson & Co., 1880.

The History of Pettis County, Missouri. N.p., 1882.

History of Pike County, Illinois. Chicago: Charles C. Chapman & Co., 1880.

The History of Polk County, Iowa. Des Moines, IA: Union Historical Co., 1880.

History of Pottawattamie County, Iowa. Chicago: O.L. Baskin & Co., 1883.

The History of Poweshiek County, Iowa. Des Moines, IA: Union Historical Co., 1880.

The History of Racine and Kenosha Counties, Wisconsin. Chicago: Western Historical Co., 1879.

The History of Rock County, Wisconsin. Chicago: Western Historical Co., 1879.

History of Sangamon County, Illinois. Chicago: Inter-State Publishing Co., 1881.

The History of Stephenson County, Illinois. Chicago: Western Historical Co., 1880.

History of Tama County, Iowa. Springfield, IL: Union Publishing Co., 1883.

History of the Upper Ohio Valley. Madison, WI: Brant & Fuller, 1891.

The History of Wapello County, Iowa. Chicago: Western Historical Co., 1878.

The History of Warren County, Iowa. Des Moines, IA: Union Historical Co., 1879.

The History of Waukesha County, Wisconsin. Chicago: Western Historical Co., 1880.

History of Wayne and Clay Counties, Illinois. Chicago: Globe Publishing Co., 1884.

History of White County, Illinois. Chicago: Inter-State Publishing Co., 1883.

History of Winnebago County, Illinois, Its Past and Present. Chicago: H.F. Kett & Co., 1877.

History of Winona County. Chicago: H.H. Hill & Co., 1883.

History of Winona and Olmsted Counties. Chicago: H.H. Hill & Co., 1883.

Hoar, Jay S. *Callow Brave and True: A Gospel of Civil War Youth.* Gettysburg, PA: Thomas Publications, 1999.

Hobart, Edwin L. *Semi-History of a Boy-Veteran of the Twenty-Eighth Regiment Illinois Infantry Volunteers, in a Black Regiment.* Denver, CO: E.L. Hobart, 1905.

Hoffman, Urias J. *History of La Salle County, Illinois.* Chicago: S.J. Clarke Publishing Co., 1906.

Hogan, Sally Coplen, ed. *General Reub Williams' Memories of Civil War Times.* Westminster, MD: Heritage Books, 2006.

Hokanson, Nels. *Swedish Immigrants in Lincoln's Time.* New York and London: Harper & Brothers, 1942.

Holcombe, Return I. *History of the First Regiment Minnesota Volunteer Infantry, 1861–1864.* Stillwater, MN: Easton & Masterman, Printers, 1916.

Honeyman, A. Van Doren. *Joannes Nevius and His Descendants, 1627–1900.* Plainfield, NJ: Honeyman & Co., 1900.

Hopkins, Timothy. *The Kelloggs in the Old World and the New.* San Francisco: Sunset Press and Photo Engraving Co., 1903.

Howard, Richard L. *History of the 124th Regiment Illinois Infantry Volunteers, Otherwise Known as the "Hundred and Two Dozen," from August 1862 to August 1865.* Springfield, IL: H.W. Rokker, 1880.

Howard, Timothy E. *A History of St. Joseph County, Indiana.* Chicago and New York: Lewis Publishing Co., 1907.

Howe, Daniel W. *Howe Genealogies.* Boston: New England Historic Genealogical Society, 1929.

Hubbard, Lucius F., and Return I. Holcombe. *Minnesota in Three Centuries.* New York City: Publishing Society of Minnesota, 1908.

Hubbell, Homer B. *Dodge County, Wisconsin, Past and Present.* Chicago: S.J. Clarke Publishing Co., 1913.

Hubert, Charles F. *History of the 50th Regiment Illinois Volunteer Infantry in the War of the Union.* Kansas City, MO: Western Veteran Publishing Co., 1894.

Huffstodt, Jim. *Hard Dying Men: The Story of General W. H. L. Wallace, General T. E. G. Ransom, and Their "Old Eleventh" Illinois Infantry in the American Civil War (1861–1865).* Bowie, MD: Heritage Books, 1991.

Hughes, Nathaniel C., Jr. *The Battle of Belmont: Grant Strikes South.* Chapel Hill, NC: University of North Carolina Press, 1991.

Hunter, Edward M., "The Civil Life, Services and Character of Gov. Wm. A. Barstow," *Collections of the State Historical Society of Wisconsin.* Vol. 6. Edited by Lyman C. Draper. Madison, WI: Wisconsin Historical Society, 1908.

Huntington, Elijah B. *A Genealogical Memoir of the Lo-Lathrop Family in This Country.* Ridgefield, CT: Julia M. Huntington, 1884.

Huntley, Virgil W. *John Huntley of Boston and Roxbury, MA, and Lyme, CT, 1647–1996.* Raleigh, NC: V.W. Huntley, 1996.

Hurlbut, Henry H. *The Hurlbut Genealogy, or Record of the Descendants of Thomas Hurlbut.* Albany, NY: Joel Munsell's Sons, 1888.

Hyde, Cornelius W.G., and William Stoddard, eds. *History of the Great Northwest and Its Men of Progress*. Minneapolis: Minneapolis Journal, 1901.

Illinois at Vicksburg. Chicago: Illinois-Vicksburg Military Park Commission, 1907.

The Illinois College Alumni Fund Association: Book of Memorial Memberships. Centennial Edition, 1829–1929. Jacksonville, IL: Alumni Fund Association, 1929.

Illustrated Album of Biography of the Famous Valley of the Red River of the North and the Park Regions. Chicago: Alden, Ogle & Co., 1889.

Illustrated Album of Biography of Southwestern Minnesota. Chicago: Occidental Publishing Co., 1889.

In the Foot-Prints of the Pioneers of Stephenson County, Illinois: A Genealogical Record. Freeport, IL: Pioneer Publishing Co., 1900.

Ingersoll, Lurton D. *Iowa and the Rebellion*. Philadelphia: J.B. Lippincott & Co., 1866.

In Memoriam: Amos C. Babcock, Born Jan. 20, 1828, Died Feb. 25, 1899. N.p., 1899.

In Memoriam, Charles Wilder Davis, Born October 11, 1833, Died December 15, 1898. Chicago: Chicago Literary Club, 1899.

In Memoriam: Col. Bradford Hancock. Waterloo, WI, 1887.

"In Memoriam: Gabriel Bouck," *Wisconsin Reports: Cases Determined in the Supreme Court of Wisconsin*. Vol. 136. Chicago: Callaghan & Co., 1909.

In Memoriam: William Tuckerman Shaw, 1822–1909. Anamosa, IA: Anamosa National Bank, 1910.

Isbell, Timothy T. *Shiloh and Corinth: Sentinels of Stone*. Jackson, MS: University Press of Mississippi, 2007.

Ives, Sarah Noble. *Altadena*. Pasadena, CA: Star-News Publishing Co., 1938.

Jacoby, Susan. *The Great Agnostic: Robert Ingersoll and American Freethought*. New Haven, CT: Yale University Press, 2013.

Johnson, Kathy. *Colonel Frederick Bartleson*. Lockport, IL: Will County Historical Society, 1983.

Johnston, Carrie P., and W. H. S. McGlumphy. *History of Clinton and Caldwell Counties, Missouri*. Topeka, KS: Historical Publishing Co., 1923.

Johnston, Jean. *Mattoon: A Pictorial History*. St. Louis: G. Bradley Publishing Co., 1988.

Jones, Lottie E. *History of Vermilion County, Illinois*. Chicago: Pioneer Publishing Co., 1911.

Jones, P. Michael, Robert R. Morefield, and Clifton Swafford, comps. *Murphysboro Illinois 150 Years: A Pictorial History, 1843–1993*. Murphysboro, IL: Jackson County Historical Society, 1994.

Jones, Thomas B. *Complete History of the 46th Regiment Illinois Volunteer Infantry*. Freeport, IL: William H. Wagner & Sons, 1907.

Jorgenson, Wayne D. *Every Man Did His Duty: Pictures & Stories of the Men of the First Minnesota*. Minneapolis: Tasora Books, 2012.

Kaufmann, Wilhelm. *The Germans in the American Civil War*. Translated by Steven Rowan and edited by Don Heinrich Tolzmann with Werner D. Mueller and Robert E. Ward. Carlisle, PA: John Kallmann, 1999.

Keifer, Sarah J. *Genealogical and Biographical Sketches of the New Jersey Branch of the Harris Family in the United States*. Madison, WI: S.J. Keifer, 1888.

Keleher, William A. *The Fabulous Frontier: Twelve New Mexico Items*. Santa Fe, NM: The Rydal Press, 1945.

Kellogg, D.O., ed. *A Young Scholar's Letters: Being a Memoir of Byron Caldwell Smith*. New York and London: G.P. Putnam's Sons, 1897.

Kern, James W. *Past and Present of Iroquois County, Illinois*. Chicago: S.J. Clarke Publishing Co., 1907.

Kilborn, Lawson S. *Dedication of the Wilder Brigade Monument on Chickamauga Battlefield*. Marshall, IL: The Herald Press, 1900.

King, James L., ed. *History of Shawnee County, Kansas, and Representative Citizens*. Chicago: Richmond & Arnold, 1905.

Kingman Brothers, comp. *Combination Atlas Map of Kosciusko County, IN*. Chicago: Kingman Brothers, 1879.

Kingsbury, George W. *History of Dakota Territory*. Chicago: S.J. Clarke Publishing Co., 1915.

Kinnear, John R. *History of the 86th Regiment Illinois Volunteer Infantry, During Its Term of Service*. Chicago: Tribune Company's Book and Job Printing Office, 1866.

Kirkland, Frazar. *The Pictorial Book of Anecdotes and Incidents of the War of the Rebellion*. Hartford, CT: Hartford Publishing Co., 1867.

Kittredge, Mabel T. *The Kittredge Family in America*. Rutland, VT: Tuttle Publishing Co., 1936.

Klement, Frank L. *The Copperheads in the Middle West*. Chicago: University of Chicago Press, 1960.

Kohl, Rhonda M. *The Prairie Boys Go To War: The Fifth Illinois Cavalry, 1861–1865*. Carbondale, IL: Southern Illinois University Press, 2013.

Lang, George, Raymond L. Collins, and Gerard F. White, comp. *Medal of Honor Recipients, 1863–1994*. 2 Vol. New York City: Facts on File, 1995.

Langkau, David A. *Civil War Veterans of Winnebago County, Wisconsin*. Bowie, MD: Heritage Books, 1993.

Larke, Julian K., ed. *Strong's Pictorial and Biographical Record of the Great Rebellion*. New York City: T.W. Strong, 1866.

Lawson, Publius V., ed. *History Winnebago County, Wisconsin, Its Cities, Towns, Resources, People*. Chicago: C.F. Cooper & Co., 1908.

Leach, Eugene W. *Racine County Militant, An Illustrated Narrative of War Times, and a Soldiers' Roster*. Racine, WI: E.W. Leach, 1915.

Leeson, Michael A. *Documents and Biography Pertaining to the Settlement and Progress of Stark County, Illinois*. Chicago: M.A. Leeson & Co., 1887.

_____. *History of Montana, 1739–1885*. Chicago: Warner, Beers & Co., 1885.

Leonard, Joseph A. *History of Olmsted County, Minnesota*. Chicago: Goodspeed Historical Association, 1910.

Levy, George. *To Die in Chicago: Confederate Prisoners at Camp Douglas, 1862–65*. Gretna, LA: Pelican Publishing Co., 1999.

Lindsley, Philip, and Luther B. Hill, eds. *A History of Greater Dallas and Vicinity*. Chicago: Lewis Publishing Co., 1909.

Littlefield, Barbara Jeanne Grim. *Descendants of Herman (Harmon) Hitt and Mary Weaver*. Decorah, IA: Anundsen Publishing Co., 1999.

Livingston, Joel T. *A History of Jasper County, Missouri, and Its People*. Chicago: Lewis Publishing Co., 1912.

Loomis, Elisha S. *Descendants of Joseph Loomis in America and His Antecedents in the Old World*. Berea, OH: E.S. Loomis, 1909.

Lothrop, Charles H. *A History of the First Regiment Iowa Cavalry Veteran Volunteers*. Lyons, IA: Beers & Eaton, Printers, 1890.

Love, William DeLoss. *Wisconsin in the War of the Rebellion*. Chicago: Church and Goodman, 1866.

Lowry, Thomas P. *Tarnished Eagles: The Courts-Martial of Fifty Union Colonels and Lieutenant Colonels*. Mechanicsburg, PA: Stackpole Books, 1997.

Lundstrom, John B. *One Drop in a Sea of Blue: The Liberators of the Ninth Minnesota*. St. Paul, MN: Minnesota Historical Society Press, 2012.

Lutz, June (Shaull). *History of the Op Den Graef/Updegraff Family*. Grand Rapids, MI: J.S. Lutz, 1988.

Lyman, Frank H. *The City of Kenosha and Kenosha County, Wisconsin*. Chicago: S.J. Clarke Publishing Co., 1916.

Lyon, William P. *Reminiscences of the Civil War*. San Jose, CA: Press of Muirson & Wright, 1907.

Magdeburg, Frederick H. *Wisconsin at Shiloh: Report of the Commission*. Madison, WI: Democrat Printing Co., 1909.

Mann, Clair V. *An Account of the Life and Career of Col. John B. Wyman, Intrepid Leader of the Thirteenth Regiment of Illinois Volunteer Infantry*. Rolla, MO: C.V. Mann, 1962.

Mansfield, Dolorus Briggs. *History of the Briggs-Bridge Family: Since Its Settlement in America (Virginia) in 1752*. Edmonds, WA: R.A. Mansfield, 1960.

Mapes, David P. *History of the City of Ripon, and of Its Founder, David P. Mapes*. Milwaukee, WI: Cramer, Aikens & Cramer, 1873.

Marsh, Dwight W. *Marsh Genealogy: Giving Several Thousand Descendants of John Marsh of Hartford, CT, 1636–1895*. Amherst, MA: Press of Carpenter & Morehouse, 1895.

Martin, Charles A., ed. *DePauw University: Alumnal Register of Officers, Faculties and Graduates, 1837–1900*. Greencastle, IN: DePauw University, 1901.

Martin County Historical and Genealogical Society. *Martin County, Kentucky Veterans*. Morley, MO: Acclaim Press, 2011.

Martin, Michael J. *A History of the 4th Wisconsin Infantry and Cavalry in the Civil War*. New York and California: Savas Beatie, 2006.

Martin, W.C. *History of Warren County, Iowa, from Its Earliest Settlement Until 1908*. Chicago: S.J. Clarke Publishing Co., 1908.

Massie, Melville D. *Past and Present of Pike County, Illinois*. Chicago: S.J. Clarke Publishing Co., 1906.

Mathews, Milton W., and Lewis A. McLean. *Early History and Pioneers of Champaign County*. Urbana, IL: Champaign County Herald, 1886.

Mattson, Hans. *Reminiscences: The Story of an Emigrant*. St. Paul, MN: D.D. Merrill Co., 1891.

McAlexander, Ulysses G. *History of the Thirteenth Regiment United States Infantry*. Fort McDowell, CA: Regimental Press, Thirteenth Infantry, F.D. Gunn, 1905.

McDonald, Granville B. *A History of the 30th Illinois Veteran Volunteer Regiment of Infantry*. Sparta, IL: Sparta News, 1916.

McIntosh, Charles, ed. *Past and Present of Piatt County, Illinois*. Chicago: S.J. Clarke Publishing Co., 1903.

McLain, David E. *Descendants of James and Lettice Carskaddon of Chillisquaque Township, Northumberland County, Pennsylvania*. Moorhead, MN: D. E. McLain, 1970.

McPherson, Lucy Harmon. *Life and Letters of Oscar Fitzalan Harmon*. Trenton, NJ: MacCrellish & Quigley Co., 1914.

Mead, Homer. *The 8th Iowa Cavalry in the Civil War*. Carthage, IL: S.C. Davidson, 1927.

A Memorial and Biographical Record of Iowa. Chicago: Lewis Publishing Co., 1896.

Memorials, Addresses, and Poems, on the Life and Character of Hon. Chas. F. Springer of Illinois. Davenport, IA: Egbert, Fidlar & Chambers, Printers, 1877.

Memorials of Deceased Companions of the Commandery of the State of Illinois MOLLUS, from May 8, 1879 to July 1, 1901. Chicago: Illinois Commandery MOLLUS, 1901.

Memorials of Deceased Companions of the Commandery of the State of Illinois MOLLUS, from July 1, 1901 to Dec. 31, 1911. Chicago: Illinois Commandery MOLLUS, 1912.

Memorials of Deceased Companions of the Commandery of the State of Illinois MOLLUS, from Jan. 1, 1912 to Dec. 31, 1922. Chicago: Illinois Commandery MOLLUS, 1923.

Military History and Reminiscences of the 13th Regiment of Illinois Volunteer Infantry in the Civil War in the United States, 1861–1865. Chicago: Woman's Temperance Publishing Association, 1892.

Mills, Frank Moody. *Early Days in a College Town and Wabash College in Early Days and Now*. Sioux Falls, SD: Sessions Printing Co., 1924.

_____. *Something About the Mills Family and Its Collateral Branches with Autobiographical Reminiscences*. Sioux Falls, SD: F.M. Mills, 1911.

Miner, Edward. *Past and Present of Greene County, Illinois*. Chicago: S.J. Clarke Publishing Co., 1905.

Minnesota in the Civil and Indian Wars, 1861–1865. 2 Vol. St. Paul, MN: Pioneer Press Co., 1890–1893.

Moe, Richard. *The Last Full Measure: The Life and*

Death of the First Minnesota Volunteers. New York City: Henry Holt & Co., 1993.

Moffat, R. Burnham. *Moffat Genealogies: Descent from Rev. John Moffat of Ulster County, New York.* New York City: Press of L. Middleditch Co., 1909.

Morgan, Perl W., ed. *History of Wyandotte County, Kansas, and Its People.* Chicago: Lewis Publishing Co., 1911.

Morris, John E., comp. *The Felt Genealogy, A Record of the Descendants of George Felt of Casco Bay.* Hartford, CT: Case, Lockwood & Brainard Co., 1893.

Morris, William S. *History 31st Illinois Volunteers, Organized by John A. Logan.* Evansville, IN: Keller Printing & Publishing Co., 1902.

Morrison, Marion. *A History of the Ninth Regiment Illinois Volunteer Infantry, With the Regimental Roster.* Carbondale, IL: Southern Illinois University Press, 1997.

Moses, John, ed. *Biographical Dictionary and Portrait Gallery of the Representative Men of the United States.* Illinois Volume. Chicago: Lewis Publishing Co., 1896.

Mueller, Herman A., ed. *History of Madison County, Iowa, and Its People.* Chicago: S.J. Clarke Publishing Co., 1915.

Mullins, Michael A. *The Fremont Rifles: A History of the 37th Illinois Veteran Volunteer Infantry.* Wilmington, NC: Broadfoot Publishing Co., 1990.

Munger, Donna Bingham. *The Bingham Family in the United States: The Descendants of Thomas Bingham of Connecticut.* New York City: Bingham Association, 1996.

Murray, Janette Stevenson. *They Came to North Tama: Old Buckingham Tranquillity Folk.* Traer, IA: Traer Star-Clipper, 1953.

National Cyclopedia of American Biography. New York: James T. White, 1898–1926.

Neill, Edward D. *History of Hennepin County and the City of Minneapolis, Including the Explorers and Pioneers of Minnesota.* Minneapolis: North Star Publishing Co., 1881.

_____. *History of the Minnesota Valley, Including the Explorers and Pioneers of Minnesota.* Minneapolis: North Star Publishing Co., 1882.

_____. *History of Washington County and the St. Croix Valley, Including the Explorers and Pioneers of Minnesota.* Minneapolis: North Star Publishing Co., 1881.

Nelke, David I. *The Columbian Biographical Dictionary and Portrait Gallery of the Representative Men of the United States.* Wisconsin Volume. Chicago: Lewis Publishing Co., 1895.

Nelson, William E., ed. *City of Decatur and Macon County, Illinois: A Record of Settlement, Organization, Progress and Achievement.* Chicago: Pioneer Publishing Co., 1910.

Newlin, William H. *A History of the 73rd Regiment of Illinois Infantry Volunteers.* Springfield, IL: Regimental Reunion Association, 1890.

Newsome, Edmund. *Experience in the War of the Great Rebellion, by a Soldier of the 81st Regiment Illinois Volunteer Infantry, from August 1862 to August 1865.* Second Edition. Carbondale, IL: Edmund Newsome, 1880.

Newson, Thomas M. *Pen Pictures of St. Paul, Minnesota, and Biographical Sketches of Old Settlers.* St. Paul, MN: T.M. Newson, 1886.

Nichols, John D., "A Splendid Example: A Sketch of Judge Shane by an Old Time Contemporary," *Proceedings Crocker's Iowa Brigade at the Tenth Biennial Reunion.* Cedar Rapids, IA: Record Printing Co., 1902.

Nolan, Alan T. *The Iron Brigade: A Military History.* Ann Arbor, MI: Historical Society of Michigan, 1983.

Norton, W.T., ed. *Centennial History of Madison County, Illinois, and Its People, 1812–1912.* Chicago and New York: Lewis Publishing Co., 1912.

Obituary Record of Graduates of Yale University Deceased from June 1890 to June 1900. New Haven, CT: Tuttle, Morehouse & Taylor Co., 1900.

O'Byrne, Michael C. *History of La Salle County, Illinois.* Chicago and New York: Lewis Publishing Co., 1924.

Official Army Register of the Volunteer Force of the United States Army for the Years 1861, '62, '63, '64, '65. 8 Vol. Washington, D.C.: Government Printing Office, 1865–1867.

Oldt, Franklin T., and Patrick J. Quigley, eds. *History of Dubuque County, Iowa.* Chicago: Goodspeed Historical Association, 1911.

Olson, Ernst W., ed. *History of the Swedes of Illinois.* Chicago: Engberg-Holmberg Publishing Co., 1908.

O'Meara, William J. *Colonel Timothy O'Meara "An Unknown Hero of the War."* Brooklyn, NY: W.J. O'Meara, 1914.

Otis, George H. *The Second Wisconsin Infantry.* Edited by Alan D. Gaff. Dayton, OH: Press of Morningside Bookshop, 1984.

Page, Oliver J. *History of Massac County, Illinois.* Metropolis, IL, 1900.

Palmer, John M., ed. *The Bench and Bar of Illinois: Historical and Reminiscent.* Chicago: Lewis Publishing Co., 1899.

Palmer, Walter B. *The History of the Phi Delta Theta Fraternity.* Menasha, WI: George Banta Publishing Co., 1906.

Parker, Harvey M. *Proceedings of the First Reunion of the 11th Regiment Illinois Volunteer Infantry.* Ottawa, IL: Osman & Hapeman, Printers, 1875.

Past and Present of the City of Decatur and Macon County, Illinois. Chicago: S.J. Clarke Publishing Co., 1903.

Past and Present of Fayette County, Iowa. Indianapolis, IN: B.F. Bowen & Co., 1910.

Paxton, William M. *The Marshall Family.* Cincinnati: Robert Clarke, 1885.

Payne, Edwin W. *History of the 34th Regiment of Illinois Volunteer Infantry.* Clinton, IA: Allen Printing Co., 1902.

Peelle, Margaret W., ed. *Letters from Libby Prison.* New York City: Greenwich Book Publishers, 1956.

Perrin, William H., ed. *History of Alexander, Union and*

Pulaski Counties, Illinois. Chicago: O.L. Baskin & Co., 1883.

_____, ed. *History of Bond and Montgomery Counties, Illinois.* Chicago: O.L. Baskin & Co., 1882.

_____, ed. *History of Effingham County, Illinois.* Chicago: O.L. Baskin & Co., 1883.

_____, ed. *History of Jefferson County, Illinois.* Chicago: Globe Publishing Co., 1883.

Perry, Albert J. *History of Knox County, Illinois: Its Cities, Towns and People.* Chicago: S.J. Clarke Publishing Co., 1912.

Phelps, Alonzo. *Biographical History of the Northwest.* Boston: Ticknor & Co., 1890.

Phillips, Donna P. *Gilbert Gallery: Family Quest.* Vol. 1 (Jan. 1986). Spokane, WA: D.P. Phillips, 1986.

Piatt, Emma C. *History of Piatt County Together With a Brief History of Illinois from the Discovery of the Upper Mississippi to the Present Time.* Chicago: Shepard & Johnston, Printers, 1883.

Pierce, Frederick Clifton. *Fiske and Fisk Family.* Chicago: F.C. Pierce, 1896.

_____. *Whitney: The Descendants of John Whitney, Who Came from London, England, to Watertown, Massachusetts, in 1635.* Chicago: W.B. Conkey Co., 1895.

Pierce, Solon W. *Battle Fields and Camp Fires of the Thirty-Eighth.* Milwaukee, WI: Daily Wisconsin Printing House, 1866.

Pitman, H. Minot. *Fahnestock Genealogy: Descendants of Johann Diedrich Fahnestock.* Concord, NH: Rumford Press, 1945.

Pivany, Eugene. *Hungarians in the American Civil War.* Cleveland, OH: E. Pivany, 1913.

Plat Book of Benton County, Arkansas. Philadelphia: Imperial Publishing Co., 1903.

Plumb, Ralph G. *A History of Manitowoc County.* Manitowoc, WI: Brandt Printing & Binding Co., 1904.

Pope County, Illinois: History and Families, 1816–1989. Paducah, KY: Turner Publishing Co., 1989.

Portrait and Biographical Album of Champaign County, Illinois. Chicago: Chapman Brothers, 1887.

Portrait and Biographical Album of Coles County, Illinois. Chicago: Chapman Brothers, 1887.

Portrait and Biographical Album of Des Moines County, Iowa. Chicago: Acme Publishing Co., 1888.

Portrait and Biographical Album of DeWitt and Piatt Counties, Illinois. Chicago: Chapman Bros., 1891.

Portrait and Biographical Album of Fayette County, Iowa. Chicago: Lake City Publishing Co., 1891.

Portrait and Biographical Album of Henry County, Iowa. Chicago: Acme Publishing Co., 1888.

Portrait and Biographical Album of Knox County, Illinois. Chicago: Biographical Publishing Co., 1886.

Portrait and Biographical Album of McLean County, Illinois. Chicago: Chapman Brothers, 1887.

Portrait and Biographical Album of Muscatine County, Iowa. Chicago: Acme Publishing Co., 1889.

Portrait and Biographical Album of Peoria County, Illinois. Chicago: Biographical Publishing Co., 1890.

Portrait and Biographical Album of Pike and Calhoun Counties, Illinois. Chicago: Biographical Publishing Co., 1891.

Portrait and Biographical Album of Polk County, Iowa. Chicago: Lake City Publishing Co., 1890.

Portrait and Biographical Album of Racine and Kenosha Counties, Wisconsin. Chicago: Lake City Publishing Co., 1892.

Portrait and Biographical Album of Rock County, Wisconsin. Chicago: Acme Publishing Co., 1889.

Portrait and Biographical Album of Rock Island County, Illinois. Chicago: Biographical Publishing Co., 1885.

Portrait and Biographical Album of Sangamon County, Illinois. Chicago: Chapman Bros., 1891.

Portrait and Biographical Album of Stephenson County, Illinois. Chicago: Chapman Brothers, 1888.

Portrait and Biographical Album of Vermilion and Edgar Counties, Illinois. Chicago: Chapman Bros., 1889.

Portrait and Biographical Record of Adams County, Illinois. Chicago: Chapman Bros., 1892.

Portrait and Biographical Record of Dickinson, Saline, McPherson, and Marion Counties, Kansas. Chicago: Chapman Bros., 1893.

Portrait and Biographical Record of Dubuque, Jones and Clayton Counties, Iowa. Chicago: Chapman Publishing Co., 1894.

Portrait and Biographical Record of DuPage and Cook Counties, Illinois. Chicago: Lake City Publishing Co., 1894.

Portrait and Biographical Record of Johnson and Pettis Counties, Missouri. Chicago: Chapman Publishing Co., 1895.

Portrait and Biographical Record of Lee County, Illinois. Chicago: Biographical Publishing Co., 1892.

Portrait and Biographical Record of Macoupin County, Illinois. Chicago: Biographical Publishing Co., 1891.

Portrait and Biographical Record of Madison County, Illinois. Chicago: Biographical Publishing Co., 1894.

Portrait and Biographical Record of Randolph, Jackson, Perry, and Monroe Counties, Illinois. Chicago: Biographical Publishing Co., 1894.

Portrait and Biographical Record of Waukesha County, Wisconsin. Chicago: Excelsior Publishing Co., 1894.

Powell, William H., ed. *Officers of the Army and Navy (Volunteer) Who Served in the Civil War.* Philadelphia: L.R. Hamersly & Co., 1893.

_____, and Edward Shippen, eds. *Officers of the Army and Navy (Regular) Who Served in the Civil War.* Philadelphia: L.R. Hamersly & Co., 1892.

Price, George F. *Across the Continent with the Fifth Cavalry.* New York City: D. Van Nostrand, 1883.

Prindle, Paul W., and Katherine E. Schultz. *The McChesney Family of Rensselaer County, NY.* Annville, PA: Katherine E. Schultz, 1969.

Proceedings Crocker's Iowa Brigade at the Eleventh Biennial Reunion and Twelfth Biennial Reunion. Cedar Rapids, IA: Press of the Record Printing Co., 1905.

Proceedings Crocker's Iowa Brigade at the Thirteenth Biennial Reunion and Fourteenth Biennial Reunion. Mount Vernon, IA: McCutcheon, Printer, 1910.

Proceedings of the Reunion Held in 1906 by the Associa-

Bibliography

tion of Survivors 2nd Regiment Illinois Veteran Cavalry Volunteers at Springfield, Illinois. Pana, IL: Kerr's Printing House, 1907.

Proceedings of the Reunion Held in 1910 by the Association of Survivors 7th Regiment Illinois Veteran Infantry Volunteers. Springfield, IL: State Register Printing House, 1911.

Proceedings of the Eighteenth Annual Reunion of the Society of the 28th Wisconsin Volunteer Infantry. Milwaukee, WI: Houtkamp & Cannon, 1901.

Proceedings of the Twenty-first Annual Reunion of the Society of the 28th Wisconsin Volunteer Infantry. Milwaukee, WI: Houtkamp Printing Co., 1903.

Proceedings of the Twenty-fifth Annual Reunion of the 28th Regiment Wisconsin Volunteer Infantry. Milwaukee, WI: Houtkamp Printing Co., 1907.

Progressive Men of the State of Montana. Chicago: A.W. Bowen & Co., 1902.

Prosser, William F. *A History of the Puget Sound Country: Its Resources, Its Commerce and Its People.* Chicago and New York: Lewis Publishing Co., 1903.

Pula, James S. *The Sigel Regiment: A History of the 26th Wisconsin Volunteer Infantry, 1862–1865.* Campbell, CA: Savas Publishing Co., 1998.

Pulliam, Carla. *Obits and Tidbits, Franklin County, Illinois, 1885–1899.* West Frankfort, IL: Carla Pulliam, 1996.

Quaife, Milo M., ed. *The Attainment of Statehood.* Publications of the State Historical Society of Wisconsin, Vol. 29. Madison, WI: State Historical Society of Wisconsin, 1928.

Quiner, Edwin B. *The Military History of Wisconsin.* Chicago: Clarke & Co., 1866.

Quinquennial Catalogue of the Law School of Harvard University, 1817–1924. Cambridge, MA: Harvard University Law School, 1925.

Radasch, Arthur H. *Barstow-Bestor Genealogy; Descendants of John Barstow and George Barstow.* South Yarmouth, MA: A.H. Radasch, 1964.

Ransom, Wyllys C. *Historical Outline of the Ransom Family of America and Genealogical Record of the Colchester, Conn., Branch.* Ann Arbor, MI: Richmond & Backus Co., 1903.

Raymond, Marcus D. *Gray Genealogy, Being a Genealogical Record and History of the Descendants of John Gray of Beverly, Mass.* Tarrytown, NY: M.D. Raymond, 1887.

Raymond, Steve. *In the Very Thickest of the Fight: The Civil War Service of the 78th Illinois Volunteer Infantry Regiment.* Guilford, CT: Globe Pequot Press, 2012.

Redmond, Patrick H. *History of Quincy and Its Men of Mark.* Quincy, IL: Heirs & Russell, 1869.

Reed, David W. *Campaigns and Battles of the Twelfth Regiment Iowa Veteran Volunteer Infantry.* Evanston, IL: D.W. Reed, 1903.

Reed, Jacob W. *History of the Reed Family in Europe and America.* Boston: John Wilson & Son, 1861.

Reed, Parker McCobb. *The Bench and Bar of Wisconsin: History and Biography.* Milwaukee, WI: P.M. Reed, 1882.

Reid, Franklin Thomas. *History and Reminiscences of Col. John B. Reid and Family.* Springfield, IL: F.T. Reid, 1903.

Reid, John B. *Civil War Letters of John B. Reid.* Greenville, IL: Bond County Genealogical Society, 1991.

Reminiscences of the Civil War from Diaries of Members of the 103rd Illinois Volunteer Infantry. Chicago: J.F. Leaming & Co., 1904.

Report and Collections of the State Historical Society of Wisconsin, for the Years 1877, 1878 and 1879. Vol. 8. Madison, WI: David Atwood, 1879.

Report and Collections of the State Historical Society of Wisconsin for the Years 1883, 1884, and 1885. Vol. 10. Madison, WI: Democrat Printing Co., 1888.

Report of the Adjutant General of the State of Illinois. Containing Reports for the Years 1861–66. Revised by Brig. Gen. J. N. Reece. 8 Vol. Springfield, IL: Phillips Bros., 1900–1902.

Report of the Annual Meeting of the Wisconsin State Bar Association, 1900. Madison, WI: Taylor & Gleason, Book & Job Printers, 1901.

Report of the Annual Meeting of the Wisconsin State Bar Association, 1903. Madison, WI: Taylor & Gleason, Book & Job Printers, 1903.

Report of Proceedings of the Eighth Annual Reunion of the 29th Wisconsin Regiment Volunteer Infantry, Fox Lake, June 20, 1893. Milwaukee, WI: Survivors Association, 1894.

Report of the Proceedings of the Meetings of the State Bar Association of Wisconsin for the Years 1878, 1881 and 1885. Madison WI: Taylor & Gleason, Book & Job Printers, 1905.

Report of the Proceedings of the Society of the Army of the Tennessee at the Eighth Annual Meeting. Cincinnati: Society of the Army of the Tennessee, 1877.

Report of the Proceedings of the Society of the Army of the Tennessee at the Ninth Annual Meeting. Cincinnati: Society of the Army of the Tennessee, 1877.

Report of the Proceedings of the Society of the Army of the Tennessee at the Twenty-Second Meeting. Cincinnati: Society of the Army of the Tennessee, 1893.

Report of the Proceedings of the Society of the Army of the Tennessee at the Twenty-Third Meeting. Cincinnati: Society of the Army of the Tennessee, 1893.

Report of the Proceedings of the Society of the Army of the Tennessee at the Twenty-Ninth Meeting. Cincinnati: Press of F.W. Freeman, 1898.

Report of the Proceedings of the Society of the Army of the Tennessee at the Thirty-First Meeting. Cincinnati: Press of F.W. Freeman, 1900.

Report of the Proceedings of the Society of the Army of the Tennessee at the Thirty-Second Meeting. Cincinnati: Press of F.W. Freeman, 1901.

Representative Men of Colorado in the Nineteenth Century. Denver, CO: Rowell Art Publishing Co., 1902.

Reunion of the Twenty-Fifth Regiment of Wisconsin Volunteer Infantry. Sparta, WI, 1887.

Reyburn, Philip J. *Clear the Track: A History of the 89th Illinois Volunteer Infantry, The Railroad Regiment.* Bloomington, IN: AuthorHouse, 2012.

_____, and Terry L. Wilson, eds. *"Jottings from Dixie": The Civil War Dispatches of Sergeant Major Stephen F. Fleharty, U.S.A.* Baton Rouge, LA: Louisiana State University Press, 1999.

Rice, James M. *Peoria City and County, Illinois.* Chicago: S.J. Clarke Publishing Co., 1912.

Richman, Irving B., ed. *History of Muscatine County, Iowa, from the Earliest Settlements to the Present Time.* Chicago: S.J. Clarke Publishing Co., 1911.

Richter, Donald G. *Vermilion County and the Civil War ... We are Coming, Father Abraham, Three Hundred Thousand More!* Danville, IL: Versa Press, 2011.

Ridlon, Gideon T. *Saco Valley Settlements and Families.* Portland, ME: G.T. Ridlon, 1895.

Ritter, Charles F., and Jon L. Wakelyn. *American Legislative Leaders, 1850–1910.* Westport, CT: Greenwood Press, 1989.

Roberts, Bobby, and Carl Moneyhon. *Portraits of Conflict: A Photographic History of Mississippi in the Civil War.* Fayetteville, AR: University of Arkansas Press, 1993.

Roberts, Nelson C., and S.W. Moorhead, eds. *Story of Lee County, Iowa.* Chicago: S.J. Clarke Publishing Co., 1914.

Robinson, Doane. *Doane Robinson's Encyclopedia of South Dakota.* Pierre, SD: Doane Robinson, 1925.

Rogers, Cameron. *Colonel Bob Ingersoll: A Biographical Narrative of the Great American Orator and Agnostic.* Garden City, NY: Doubleday, Page & Co., 1927.

Rogers, Robert M. *The 125th Regiment Illinois Volunteer Infantry. Attention Batallion!* Champaign, IL: Gazette Steam Print, 1882.

Rogers, Sophie Selden, Elizabeth Selden Lane, and Edwin Van Deusen Selden. *Selden Ancestry: A Family History Giving the Ancestors and Descendants of George Shattuck Selden and His Wife Elizabeth Wright Clark.* Oil City, PA: E.V.D. Selden, 1931.

Rood, Henry H., "Sketches of the Thirteenth Iowa," *War Sketches and Incidents Iowa Commandery MOLLUS.* Des Moines, IA: Press of P.C. Kenyon, 1893.

Rood, Hosea W. *Story of the Service of Co. E, and of the Twelfth Wisconsin Regiment of Veteran Volunteer Infantry in the War of the Rebellion.* Milwaukee, WI: Swain & Tate Co., Printers, 1893.

_____, comp. *Wisconsin at Vicksburg: Report of the Wisconsin-Vicksburg Monument Commission.* Madison, WI: Wisconsin-Vicksburg Monument Commission, 1914.

Rosengarten, Joseph G. *The German Soldier in the Wars of the United States.* Second edition, revised and enlarged. Philadelphia: J.B. Lippincott Co., 1890.

Roster and Record of Iowa Soldiers in the War of the Rebellion, Together with Historical Sketches of Volunteer Organizations, 1861–1866. 6 Vol. Des Moines, IA: E.H. English, State Printer, 1908–1911.

Roster of Wisconsin Volunteers, War of the Rebellion, 1861–1865. 2 Vol. Madison, WI: Democrat Printing Co., 1886.

Sanders, Helen Fitzgerald. *A History of Montana.* Chicago and New York: Lewis Publishing Co., 1913.

Sanford, Mrs. Nettie. *History of Marshall County, Iowa.* Clinton, IA: Leslie, McAllaster & Co., 1867.

Sanford, Washington L., compiler. *History of 14th Illinois Cavalry and the Brigades to Which It Belonged.* Chicago: R.R. Donnelley & Sons, 1898.

Satterlee, John L. *The Journal & the 114th, 1861 to 1865.* Springfield, IL: Phillips Brothers, 1979.

Sayner, Donald B. *The Orders of Col. Samuel McPhail, Minnesota Mounted Rangers, 1863.* Tucson, AZ: D.B. Sayner, 1973.

Scharf, John Thomas. *History of Western Maryland, Being a History of Frederick, Montgomery, Carroll, Washington, Allegany, and Garrett Counties from the Earliest Period to the Present Day.* Philadelphia: L.H. Everts, 1882.

Schmitt, William A. *History of the Twenty-Seventh Illinois Volunteers, With a Roster of the Surviving Members.* Winchester, IL: Standard Printing House, 1892.

Scott, Franklin W., ed. *The Semi-Centennial Alumni Record of the University of Illinois.* Chicago: R.R. Donnelley & Sons, 1918.

Scott, John. *Story of the Thirty Second Iowa Infantry Volunteers.* Nevada, IA: John Scott, 1896.

Scott, William Forse. *The Story of a Cavalry Regiment: The Career of the Fourth Iowa Veteran Volunteers.* New York and London: G.P. Putnam's Sons, 1893.

Sedgwick, T.E., ed. *York County, Nebraska, and Its People.* Chicago: S.J. Clarke Publishing Co., 1921.

Sergent, Mary Elizabeth. *They Lie Forgotten: The United States Military Academy, 1856–1861, Together with a Class Album for the Class of May 1861.* Middletown, NY: Prior King Press, 1986.

Seventeenth Annual Reunion of the Association of the Graduates of the United States Military Academy at West Point, New York, June 10, 1886. East Saginaw, MI: Evening News Printers and Binders, 1886.

Shaw, William C., comp. *Illustrated Roster of the Department of Illinois Grand Army of the Republic.* Chicago: Department of Illinois GAR, 1914.

Sherard, Gerald E., comp. *Civil War Veterans York County, Nebraska.* Knoxville, TN: G.E. Sherard, 1985.

"Short Biographical Sketch of Alfred R. Chapin," *Fourth Annual Reunion of the Tenth Wisconsin Infantry, Held at Tomah, Wis., July 21 and 22, 1898.* Waupun, WI: Oliver Bros., Printers, 1898.

Shutter, Marion D. *History of Minneapolis: Gateway to the Northwest.* Chicago and Minneapolis: S.J. Clarke Publishing Co., 1923.

Simon, John Y., ed. *The Papers of Ulysses S. Grant.* Volume 4: January 8-March 31, 1862. Carbondale, IL: Southern Illinois University Press, 1972.

_____, ed. *The Papers of Ulysses S. Grant.* Volume 6: September 1, 1862-December 8, 1862. Carbondale, IL: Southern Illinois University Press, 1977.

_____, ed. *The Papers of Ulysses S. Grant.* Volume 7: December 9, 1862-March 31, 1863. Carbondale, IL: Southern Illinois University Press, 1979.

_____, ed. *The Papers of Ulysses S. Grant.* Volume 8: April 1-July 6, 1863. Carbondale, IL: Southern Illinois University Press, 1979.

_____, ed. *The Papers of Ulysses S. Grant.* Volume 9: July 7-Dec. 31, 1863. Carbondale, IL: Southern Illinois University Press, 1982.

_____, ed. *The Papers of Ulysses S. Grant.* Volume 19: July 1, 1868-October 31, 1869. Carbondale, IL: Southern Illinois University Press, 1995.

Sketch of Gen. Hugh J. Campbell. N.p., N.d.

Sketches of Men of Mark. New York City: New York and Hartford Publishing Co., 1871.

Smalley, Frank, ed. *Alumni Record and General Catalogue of Syracuse University, 1872–1910, Including Genesee College, 1852–1871, and Geneva Medical College, 1835–1872.* Syracuse, NY: Alumni Association of Syracuse University, 1911.

Smith, Clifford Neal. *Early Nineteenth-Century German Settlers in Ohio, Kentucky, and Other States.* McNeal, AZ: Westland Publications, 1988.

Smith, Edward Garstin. *The Life and Reminiscences of Robert G. Ingersoll.* New York City: National Weekly Publishing Co., 1904.

Smith, George Washington. *A History of Southern Illinois.* Chicago and New York: Lewis Publishing Co., 1912.

Smith, Henry I. *History of the Seventh Iowa Veteran Volunteer Infantry During the Civil War.* Mason City, IA: E. Hitchcock, Printer, 1903.

Smith, Myron J., Jr. *Civil War Biographies from the Western Waters.* Jefferson, NC: McFarland & Co., 2015.

Society of the Army of the Cumberland. Fourth Reunion, Cleveland, OH, 1870. Cincinnati: Robert Clarke & Co., 1870.

Society of the Army of the Cumberland. Twenty-Fourth Reunion, Cleveland, OH, 1893. Cincinnati: Robert Clarke & Co., 1894.

Society of the Army of the Cumberland. Twenty-Fifth Reunion, Chattanooga, TN, 1895. Cincinnati: Robert Clarke & Co., 1896.

Society of the Army of the Cumberland. Thirty-First Reunion, Washington, D.C., Oct. 14, 15, 16, 1903. Cincinnati: Robert Clarke & Co., 1904.

Society of the Army of the Cumberland. Thirty-Third Reunion, Chattanooga, TN, Sept. 18, 19, 20, 1905. Cincinnati: Robert Clarke & Co., 1906.

Society of the 74th Illinois Volunteer Infantry: Reunion Proceedings and History of the Regiment. Rockford, IL: W.P. Lamb, Book and Job Printer, 1903.

Soldiers' and Citizens' Album of Biographical Record. Chicago: Grand Army Publishing Co., 1890.

Soldiers' and Patriots' Biographical Album. Chicago: Union Veteran Publishing Co., 1892.

Sorley, Merrow E. *Lewis of Warner Hall: The History of a Family.* Columbia, MO: E.W. Stephens Co., 1937.

South, Fred S. *It Never Recoiled: A History of the 75th Illinois Volunteer Infantry.* Prophetstown, IL: F.S. South, 2003.

Sparks, Charles H. *History of Winneshiek County, with Biographical Sketches of Its Eminent Men.* Decorah, IA: James Alexander Leonard, 1877.

Speed, John G. *The Gilmers in America.* New York City: J.G. Speed, 1897.

Sperry, Andrew F. *History of the 33d Iowa Infantry Volunteer Regiment, 1863–6.* Edited by Gregory J.W. Urwin and Cathy Kunzinger Urwin. Fayetteville, AR: University of Arkansas Press, 1999.

Spofford, Jeremiah. *A Genealogical Record, Including Two Generations in Female Lines of Families Spelling Their Name Spofford, Spafford, Spafard, and Spaford, Descendants of John Spofford and Elizabeth Scott.* Boston: Alfred Mudge & Son, 1888.

Starr, Harris E., ed. *Dictionary of American Biography.* Supplement 1. New York City: Charles Scribner's Sons, 1944.

Stelle, Abel C. *1861 to 1865, Memoirs of the Civil War, the 31st Regiment Wisconsin Volunteer Infantry.* New Albany, IN: A.C. Stelle, 1904.

Stephens, James D. *Reflections: A Portrait-Biography of the Kentucky Military Institute (1845–1971).* Georgetown, KY: Kentucky Military Institute, 1991.

Stevens, Frank E. *History of Lee County, Illinois.* Chicago: S.J. Clarke Publishing Co., 1914.

Stevens, Harriet, ed. *The Graybeards: The Letters of Major Lyman Allen, of the 37th Regiment Iowa Volunteer Infantry.* Iowa City, IA: Camp Pope Bookshop, 1998.

Stevens, Hiram F. *History of the Bench and Bar of Minnesota.* Minneapolis and St. Paul: Legal Publishing and Engraving Co., 1904.

Stevens, William W. *Past and Present of Will County, Illinois.* Chicago: S.J. Clarke Publishing Co., 1907.

Stickney, Lucy W. *The Kinsman Family: Genealogical Record of the Descendants of Robert Kinsman of Ipswich, Mass.* Boston: Alfred Mudge & Son, 1876.

Stiles, Edward H. *Recollections and Sketches of Notable Lawyers and Public Men of Early Iowa.* Des Moines, IA: Homestead Publishing Co., 1916.

Stillwell, Leander. *The Story of a Common Soldier of Army Life in the Civil War, 1861–1865.* Second Edition. Erie, KS: Franklin Hudson Publishing Co., 1920.

Stone, Fanny S., ed. *Racine, Belle City of the Lakes, and Racine County, Wisconsin.* Chicago: S.J. Clarke Publishing Co., 1916.

The Story of the Fifty-Fifth Regiment Illinois Volunteer Infantry in the Civil War, 1861–1865. Huntington, WV: Blue Acorn Press, 1993.

Strand, Algot E., ed. *A History of the Swedish-Americans of Minnesota.* Chicago: Lewis Publishing Co., 1910.

Strayer, Larry M., and Richard A. Baumgartner, eds. *Echoes of Battle: The Atlanta Campaign.* Huntington, WV: Blue Acorn Press, 1991.

Stuart, Addison A. *Iowa Colonels and Regiments.* Des Moines, IA: Mills & Co., 1865.

Summers, Alexander. *Gone to Glory at Farmington: A Profile of Col. James Monroe of Mattoon, Hero of Two Regiments in the Civil War.* Mattoon, IL: Mattoon Historical Society, 1963.

Sunderland, Glenn W. *Lightning at Hoover's Gap: Wilder's Brigade in the Civil War.* New York City: Thomas Yoseloff, 1969.

Surby, Richard W. *Grierson Raids, and Hatch's Sixty-*

Four Days March, with Biographical Sketches, Also the Life and Adventures of Chickasaw, the Scout. Chicago: Rounds & James, Steam Book and Job Printers, 1865.

Swan, James B. *Chicago's Irish Legion: The 90th Illinois Volunteers in the Civil War.* Carbondale, IL: Southern Illinois University Press, 2009.

Talkington, N. Dale, and Deone K. Pearcy. *Tributes of Blue: Obituaries of Civil War Union Soldiers and Sailors Buried in Oklahoma.* Tehachapi, CA: T.P. Productions, 1996.

Tasker, Albert E. *Early History of Lincoln County.* Lake Benton, MN: Lake Benton News Print, 1936.

Tenney, Horace A., comp. *Genealogy of the Tenney Family.* Madison, WI: M.J. Cantwell, 1875.

_____, and David Atwood. *Memorial Record of the Fathers of Wisconsin.* Madison, WI: David Atwood, 1880.

Thirty-second Annual Reunion of the First Wisconsin Cavalry Association. Oshkosh, WI: Castle Pierce Printing Co., 1916.

Thompson, Seymour D. *Recollections with the Third Iowa Regiment.* Cincinnati: S.D. Thompson, 1864.

Timme, Ernest G., comp. *The Blue Book of the State of Wisconsin,* Vol. 25. Milwaukee, WI: Milwaukee Lithographing & Engraving Co., 1889.

Tischler, Allan L. *The History of the Harpers Ferry Cavalry Expedition, September 14 & 15, 1862.* Winchester, VA: Five Cedars Press, 1993.

Titus, William A., ed. *History of the Fox River Valley, Lake Winnebago and the Green Bay Region.* Chicago: S.J. Clarke Publishing Co., 1930.

Torrence, Robert M. *Torrence and Allied Families.* Philadelphia: Wickersham Press, 1938.

Transactions of the McLean County Historical Society, Volume 1, War Record of McLean County with Other Papers. Bloomington, IL: Pantagraph Printing & Stationery Co., 1899.

Treman, Ebenezer Mack, and Murray E. Poole. *History of the Treman, Tremaine, Truman Family in America; With the Related Families of Mack, Dey, Board and Ayers.* Ithaca, NY: Press of the Ithaca Democrat, 1901.

Trimble, Harvey M., ed. *History of the 93rd Regiment Illinois Volunteer Infantry.* Chicago: Blakely Printing Co., 1898.

Tupper, Eleanor. *Tupper Genealogy, 1578–1971.* Beverly, MA: Eleanor Tupper, 1972.

Tuttle, Charles R., and Daniel S. Durrie. *An Illustrated History of the State of Iowa.* Chicago: Richard S. Peale & Co., 1876.

Twenty-First Annual Reunion of the Association of the Graduates of the United States Military Academy at West Point, New York. Saginaw, MI: Evening News Printing and Binding House, 1890.

The Union Army. 8 Vol. Madison, WI: Federal Publishing Co., 1908.

The United States Biographical Dictionary. Kansas Volume. Chicago and Kansas City: S. Lewis & Co., 1879.

The United States Biographical Dictionary and Portrait Gallery of Eminent and Self-Made Men. Illinois Volume. Chicago, Cincinnati, and New York: American Biographical Publishing Co., 1876.

The United States Biographical Dictionary and Portrait Gallery of Eminent and Self-Made Men. Illinois Volume. Chicago and New York: American Biographical Publishing Co., 1883.

The United States Biographical Dictionary and Portrait Gallery of Eminent and Self-Made Men. Iowa Volume. Chicago and New York: American Biographical Publishing Co., 1878.

The United States Biographical Dictionary and Portrait Gallery of Eminent and Self-Made Men. Minnesota Volume. New York and Chicago: American Biographical Publishing Co., 1879.

The United States Biographical Dictionary and Portrait Gallery of Eminent and Self-Made Men. Missouri Volume. New York, Chicago, St. Louis, and Kansas City: United States Biographical Publishing Co., 1878.

The United States Biographical Dictionary and Portrait Gallery of Eminent and Self-Made Men. Wisconsin Volume. Chicago, Cincinnati and New York: American Biographical Publishing Co., 1877.

Usher, Ellis Baker. *Wisconsin: Its Story and Biography, 1848–1913.* Chicago and New York: Lewis Publishing Co., 1914.

Vandor, Paul E. *History of Fresno County, California, with Biographical Sketches.* Los Angeles: Historic Record Co., 1919.

Van Gilder, Marvin L. *Jasper County: The First Two Hundred Years.* N.p.: M.L. Van Gilder, 1995.

Van Metre, Isaiah, ed. *History of Black Hawk County, Iowa, and Representative Citizens.* Chicago: Biographical Publishing Co., 1904.

Van Vleck, Carter. *Emerging Leader: The Letters of Carter Van Vleck to His Wife, Patty, 1862–1864.* Transcribed and edited by Teresa K. Lehr and Philip L. Gerber. Bloomington, IN: iUniverse, 2012.

Van Vleck, Jane. *Ancestry and Descendants of Tielman Van Vleeck of New Amsterdam.* New York City: Jane Van Vleck, 1955.

Vasvary, Edmund. *Lincoln's Hungarian Heroes: The Participation of Hungarians in the Civil War, 1861–1865.* Washington, D.C.: Hungarian Reformed Federation of America, 1939.

Vaught, Harriet B., ed. *Letters Written by Dr. Daniel Berry to Marry Berry Crebs Berry During the Civil War.* Carmi, IL: H. B. Vaught, 1976.

Vida, Istvan Kornel. *Hungarian Emigres in the American Civil War.* Jefferson, NC: McFarland & Co., 2012.

Walker, Charles A., ed. *History of Macoupin County, Illinois: Biographical and Pictorial.* Chicago: S.J. Clarke Publishing Co., 1911.

Wallace, Joseph. *Past and Present of the City of Springfield and Sangamon County, Illinois.* Chicago: S.J. Clarke Publishing Co., 1904.

Walterman, Thomas. *There Stands "Old Rock," Rock County, Wisconsin, and the War to Preserve the Union.* Friendship, WI: New Past Press, 2001.

Bibliography

Walworth, Clarence A. *The Walworths of America*. Albany, NY: Weed-Parsons Printing Co., 1897.

Walworth, Reginald W. *Walworth-Walsworth Genealogy, 1689–1962*. Centreville, MD: Queen Anne's Publishing Co., 1962.

The War of the Rebellion: A Compilation of the Official Records of the Union and Confederate Armies. 128 Vol. Washington, D.C.: Government Printing Office, 1880–1901.

Ward, William H., ed. *Records of Members of the Grand Army of the Republic*. San Francisco: H.S. Crocker & Co., 1886.

Ware, Eugene F. *The Indian War of 1864*. New York City: St. Martin's Press, 1960.

_____. *The Lyon Campaign in Missouri, Being a History of the First Iowa Infantry*. Topeka, KS: Crane & Co., 1907.

Warner, Fanny, and Lathrop Ezra Smith, eds. *In Memoriam: Clement Edson Warner*. Madison, WI: Times Publishing Co., 1917.

Warner, Lucien C., and Mrs. Josephine Genung Nichols, comps. *The Descendants of Andrew Warner*. New Haven, CT: Tuttle, Morehouse & Taylor Co., 1919.

Warvelle, George W., ed. *A Compendium of Freemasonry in Illinois*. Chicago: Lewis Publishing Co., 1897.

Waterman, Arba N., ed. *Historical Review of Chicago and Cook County and Selected Biography*. Chicago and New York: Lewis Publishing Co., 1908.

Watrous, Jerome A., "The Eagles and Stars," *War Papers, Wisconsin MOLLUS*. Vol. 1. Milwaukee, WI: Burdick, Armitage & Allen, 1891.

_____, ed. *Memoirs of Milwaukee County*. Madison, WI: Western Historical Association, 1909.

West, Emmet C. *History and Reminiscences of the Second Wisconsin Cavalry Regiment*. Portage, WI: State Register Print, 1904.

Whitney, Loren Harper. *A Question of Miracles: Parallels in the Lives of Buddha and Jesus*. Chicago: The Library Shelf, 1908.

Whittelsey, Charles B. *Genealogy of the Whittlesey-Whittelsey Family*. Second Edition. New York and London: Whittlesey House, 1941.

Who Was Who in America. Vol. 1, 1897–1942. Chicago: A.N. Marquis Co., 1942.

Wilcox, David F., ed. *Quincy and Adams County History and Representative Men*. Chicago and New York: Lewis Publishing Co., 1919.

Wilcox, Reynold Webb, comp. *The Descendants of William Wilcoxson, Vincent Meigs, and Richard Webb*. New York City: T.A. Wright, 1893.

Wildman, David. *Iowa's Martyr Regiment: The Story of the Thirty-eighth Iowa Infantry*. Iowa City, IA: Camp Pope Publishing, 2010.

Wilkie, Franc B. *Sketches and Notices of the Chicago Bar*. Chicago: Henry A. Sumner, 1871.

Williams, Claire A. *The Silent Park: The Old Cemetery of Carmi, Illinois, 1817–1966*. Carmi, IL: C.A. Williams, 1985.

Williams, J. Fletcher. *A History of the City of Saint Paul, and of the County of Ramsey, Minnesota*. St. Paul, MN: Minnesota Historical Society, 1876.

Williams, John M. *"The Eagle Regiment," 8th Wisconsin Infantry Volunteers, A Sketch of Its Marches, Battles and Campaigns, from 1861 to 1865*. Belleville, WI: Recorder Print, 1890.

Williams, Miles C. *The Descendants of Richard Dollins of Albemarle County, VA*. Logan, UT: M.C. Williams, 1973.

Williams, Mrs. Sarah J. *The Coler Family History and Genealogy*. Warrensburg, MO: S.J. Williams, 1900.

Wilson, Ephraim A. *Memoirs of the War*. Cleveland, OH: W.M. Bayne Printing Co., 1893.

Wilson, James Grant, and John Fiske, eds. *Appletons' Cyclopedia of American Biography*. New York City: D. Appleton & Co., 1888.

_____, ed. *Appletons' Cyclopedia of American Biography*. Vol. 7. New York City: D. Appleton & Co., 1900.

_____. *Biographical Sketches of Illinois Officers Engaged in the War Against the Rebellion of 1861*. Chicago: James Barnet, 1862.

_____. *Biographical Sketches of Illinois Officers Engaged in the War Against the Rebellion of 1861*. Third Edition. Chicago: James Barnet, 1863.

Winship, Amy Davis. *My Life Story*. Boston: The Gorham Press, 1920.

Winslow, John B. *The Story of a Great Court*. Chicago: T.H. Flood & Co., 1912.

Wisconsin Session Laws: Acts, Resolutions and Memorials Passed at the Biennial Session of the Legislature, 1917. Madison, WI: Democrat Printing Co., 1917.

Wolfe, Patrick B., ed. *Wolfe's History of Clinton County, Iowa*. Indianapolis, IN: B.F. Bowen & Co., 1911.

Wood, Wales W. *A History of the 95th Regiment Illinois Infantry Volunteers*. Belvidere, IL: Boone County Historical Society, 1993.

Woodruff, George H. *Fifteen Years Ago: or The Patriotism of Will County*. Joliet, IL: Joliet Republican Book and Job Steam Printing House, 1876.

Wright, Anne Mims. *A Record of the Descendants of Isaac Ross and Jean Brown*. Jackson, MS: Consumers Stationery & Print Co., 1911.

Wright, Henry H. *A History of the Sixth Iowa Infantry*. Iowa City, IA: State Historical Society of Iowa, 1923.

Wright, John W.D. *A History of Early Carbondale, Illinois, 1852–1905*. Carbondale, IL: Southern Illinois University Press, 1977.

Wyandotte County and Kansas City, Kansas, Historical and Biographical. Chicago: Goodspeed Publishing Co., 1890.

Wylie, Theophilus A. *Indiana University, Its History from 1820 to 1890*. Indianapolis: William B. Burford, 1890.

Young, Kenneth R. *The General's General: The Life and Times of Arthur MacArthur*. Boulder, CO: Westview Press, 1994.

Young, Sarah S. *Genealogical Narrative of the Hart Family in the United States*. Memphis, TN: S.C. Toof & Co., 1882.

Zillier, Carl, ed. *History of Sheboygan County, Wisconsin, Past and Present.* Chicago: S.J. Clarke Publishing Co., 1912.

Zucker, Adolf E., editor. *The Forty-Eighters: Political Refugees of the German Revolution of 1848.* New York City: Columbia University Press, 1950.

Articles in Periodicals and Newspapers

"Aaron Brown," *Annals of Iowa,* 3rd Series, Vol. 6, No. 8 (Jan. 1905).

Adolphson, Steven J., "'Our Little Colonel': Douglas Hapeman," *Lincoln Herald,* Vol. 75, No. 1 (Spring 1973).

Anderson, William M., "The Fulton County War at Home and in the Field," *Illinois Historical Journal,* Vol. 85, No. 1 (Spring, 1992).

"Arrived in City Fifty Years Ago: Colonel W.B. Britton Here Half a Century Today," *Janesville Daily Gazette,* May 16, 1905.

Barton, Dick, "Charge at Big Black River," *America's Civil War,* Vol. 12, No. 4 (Sept. 1999).

"Benjamin Beach," *Annals of Iowa,* 3rd Series, Vol. 11, No. 2–3 (July-Oct. 1913).

Blackham, George E., "Memoir of Thad S. Up de Graff, M.D., F.R.M.S.," *Proceedings of the American Society of Microscopists,* Vol. 7, Eighth Annual Meeting (1885).

Blegen, Theodore C., "Colonel Hans Christian Heg," *Wisconsin Magazine of History,* Vol. 4, No. 2 (Dec. 1920).

Brandenburg, O.D., "More About the Alban Family, Pioneer Residents," *Baraboo Daily News,* Nov. 26, 1927.

"Breaks Col. Snell's Will: Illinois Supreme Court Decides Aged Millionaire Was of Unsound Mind," *New York Times,* Feb. 17, 1910.

Brodie, Fawn M., "Thomas Jefferson's Unknown Grand-Children: A Study in Historical Silences," *American Heritage: The Magazine of History,* Vol. 27, No. 6 (Oct. 1976).

Brown, D. Alexander, "A Civil War Love Story," *Civil War Times Illustrated,* Vol. 5, No. 9 (Jan. 1967).

Brown, Joseph R., Jr. "Gabriel Bouck, 1828–1904, Son of Governor William C. Bouck," *Schoharie County Historical Review,* Vol. 26, No. 1 (Spring-Summer 1962).

Burr, Barbara, "Letters from Two Wars," *Journal of the Illinois State Historical Society,* Vol. 30, No. 1 (April 1937).

Buttrick, Edwin L., "The Case of Lt. Col. Bloodgood," *Milwaukee Sentinel,* Nov. 17, 1863.

Campbell, A.K., "Col. John A. Garrett," *Annals of Iowa,* 1st Series, Vol. 9, No. 1 (January 1871).

Campbell, J., "Regarding the History of the Dental Profession in the West and South," *Missouri Dental Journal,* Vol. 7, No. 9 (Sept. 1875).

Campbell, Robert W., "Brief History of the 17th Regiment Illinois Volunteer Infantry, 1861–1864," *Transactions of the Illinois State Historical Society for the Year 1914.* Springfield, IL, 1915.

"The Case of Col. Anneke," *Milwaukee Semi-Weekly Wisconsin,* Sept. 18, 1863.

"The Case of Col. Thomas Snell," *Chicago Daily Tribune.* Dec. 13, 1862.

"The Case of Col. Updegraff," *Illinois State Journal,* Oct. 25 and Dec. 5, 1861.

Castle, Henry A., "A Perilous Trip to Richmond," *The National Tribune,* March 5, 1903.

Chafee, George D., "Dudley Chase Smith, 1833–1920," *Journal of the Illinois State Historical Society,* Vol. 13, No. 2 (July 1920).

"Chief Justice Miller," *Annals of Iowa,* 1st Series, Vol. 12, No. 4 (Oct. 1874).

"Col. Amos C. Babcock, Who Died Saturday," *Chicago Daily Tribune,* Feb. 27, 1899.

"Col. Anneke," *Indianapolis Daily State Sentinel,* March 13, 1862.

"Col. Ben Allen," *Hudson North Star,* April 30, 1862.

"Col. James Stuart," *Illinois State Register,* May 13, 16 and 17, 1871.

"Col. J.W. Rankin," *Iowa State Register,* Oct. 22, 1862.

"Col. M. Finnicum," *Topeka State Journal,* Aug. 14, 1882.

"Col. Mark Finnicum," *Fort Scott Daily Monitor,* Aug. 10, 1882.

"Col. Risdon M. Moore," *Journal of the Illinois State Historical Society,* Vol. 2, No. 1 (April 1909).

"Col. Silas Noble, Cavalry Officer," *Dixon Evening Telegraph,* Centennial Edition, May 1, 1951.

"Col. Thomas A. Marshall—Response to the Charges Against Him," *Illinois State Register,* Oct. 4, 1861.

"Colonel of the 20th Regiment," *Wisconsin Daily State Journal,* May 29, 1862.

"Colonel Dougherty of the Twenty-Second Illinois Regiment," *Harper's Weekly,* Vol. 5, No. 256 (Nov. 23, 1861).

"Colonel J.M. Lewis," *Chicago Daily Tribune,* March 15, 1864.

"Colonel Ray is Ill: Sketch of His Career," *Chicago Inter Ocean,* April 7, 1897.

"Colonel Silas C. Toler," *Jonesboro Weekly Gazette,* April 11, 1863.

Coyle, John G., "An Unknown Hero of the Great Civil War," *The Journal of the American Irish Historical Society,* Vol. 15, No. 3 (Oct. 1916).

Cross, Scott, "John Hancock Sees the Civil War," *Voyageur: Northeast Wisconsin's Historical Review,* Vol. 28, No. 1 (Summer/Fall 2011).

"Daniel Anderson," *Annals of Iowa,* 3rd Series, Vol. 5, No. 1 (April 1901).

"The Death of Col. Stewart Below Vicksburgh," *New York Times,* Feb. 8, 1863.

"Death of Lieut. Col. Stuart," *Chicago Daily Tribune,* Dec. 4, 1863.

"Deputy Commissioner of Internal Revenue Isaac E. Messmore," *New York Daily Tribune,* Oct. 12, 1867.

Dexter, Richard P., "Colonel Silas D. Baldwin: Guilty

or Not Guilty? A Case of Command Influence?," *Journal of the Illinois State Historical Society*, Vol. 107, Nos. 3–4 (Fall/Winter 2014).

Dodge, Grenville M., "Colonel William H. Kinsman," *Annals of Iowa*, 3rd Series, Vol. 5, No. 4 (Jan. 1902).

"Dr. Edgar Denman Swain," *The Dental Cosmos*, Vol. 46, No. 6 (June 1904).

"Dr. Updegraff's Idea: A Perpetual Motion Machine That Ran for Eight Years," *Philadelphia Inquirer*, July 17, 1876.

Eisenschiml, Otto, "The 55th Illinois at Shiloh," *Journal of the Illinois State Historical Society*, Vol. 56, No. 2 (Summer 1963).

"First Illinois Cavalry Disbanded," *Illinois State Register*, July 10, 1862.

"First Mayor Was Soldier," *Decatur Daily Review*, Feb. 23, 1957.

Fischer, LeRoy H., "Lincoln's 1858 Visit to Pittsfield, Illinois," *Journal of the Illinois State Historical Society*, Vol. 61, No. 3 (Autumn 1968).

Fleming, William H., "Governor Samuel Merrill," *Annals of Iowa*, 3rd Series, Vol. 5, No.5 (April 1902).

Fliss, William M., "Wisconsin's Abolition Regiment: The Twenty-second Volunteer Infantry in Kentucky, 1862–1863," *Wisconsin Magazine of History*, Vol. 86, No. 2 (Winter 2002–2003).

"Funeral of Col. M. F. Wood," *Illinois State Journal*, Aug. 16, 1865.

"Funeral of Col. Raith," *Daily Missouri Republican*, April 28, 1862.

"The Funeral of Col. W.A. Webb," *Chicago Daily Tribune*, Dec. 29, 1861.

Gaul, Alma, "Walls CAN Talk: Home's Builder Fled Hungary, Became Civil War General," *Quad-City Times*, Nov. 3, 2013.

"Gen. West Arrested," *San Francisco Chronicle*, Oct. 17, 1886.

George, Tom M., "Mechem or Mack: How a One-Word Correction in the *Collected Works of Abraham Lincoln* Reveals the Truth About an 1856 Political Event," *Journal of the Abraham Lincoln Association*, Vol. 33, Issue 2 (Summer 2012).

"Grandfather of Ozburn Slain in Carbondale," *Carbondale Daily Free Press*, July 5, 1930.

The Hamilton College Bulletin: Necrology/Commencement Announcements. Vol. 2, No. 3 (April 1919).

"Henry J.B. Cummings," *Annals of Iowa*, 3rd Series, Vol. 9, No. 1 (April 1909).

"He Scotched the Vipers: Sketch of the Career of Colonel Lyman Guinnip in Dealing with Copperheads," *Chicago Inter Ocean*, Sept. 25, 1888.

"An Historic Cemetery: The Resting Place of Pioneers," *Fond du Lac Commonwealth*, Nov. 29, 1895.

Hoing, Willard L., "David B. Henderson: Speaker of the House," *Iowa Journal of History*, Vol. 55, No. 1 (Jan. 1957).

Hubbs, Ronald M., "The Civil War and Alexander Wilkin," *Minnesota History*, Vol. 39, No. 5 (Spring 1965).

Huelskamp, John W., "Never Forsake the Colors! Colonel Holden Putnam and the 93rd Illinois Volunteer Infantry," *Civil War Regiments: A Journal of the American Civil War*, Vol. 3, No. 3 (1993).

_____, "We are Coming, Father Abraham ... Colonel Putnam Answers Lincoln's Call," *The Gun Report*, Vol. 39, No. 3 (August 1993).

Huffstodt, James T., "One Who Didn't Come Back: The Story of Colonel Garrett Nevius," *Lincoln Herald*, Vol. 82, No. 1 (Spring 1980).

Imm, Ivan E., "The Civil War as Seen by Colonel James George," *Olmsted County Historical Society Monthly Bulletin*, Vol. 2, No. 5 (May 1960).

"Important Invention," *Harrisburg Telegraph*, Aug. 25, 1868.

"Indiana Military Matters," *Plymouth (IN) Weekly Democrat*, Dec. 5, 1861.

"The Irish Ninetieth," *Chicago Inter Ocean*, Nov. 26, 1890.

Isherwood, Justin, "Col. James Alban," *Stevens Point Daily Journal*, May 19, 1992.

"An Item That Will Interest the Old Members of Twentieth Illinois Regiment," *Clinton (IL) Public*, Nov. 2, 1883.

"It Was Not a Homicide," *Washington Evening Star*, Aug. 19, 1889.

"Jabez Banbury," *Annals of Iowa*, 3rd Series, Vol. 4, No. 8 (January 1901).

"Jed Lake," *Annals of Iowa*, 3rd Series, Vol. 11, No. 6 (July 1914).

"John Shane," *Annals of Iowa*, 3rd Series, Vol. 4, No. 3 (Oct. 1899).

Johnson, Paul, "William Wallace Robinson," *Loyal Legion Historical Journal*, Vol. 68, No. 4 (Winter 2011).

"Justice in Early Days," *Milwaukee Daily Journal*, Oct. 24, 1891.

"J.W. Jenkins," *Annals of Iowa*, 3rd Series, Vol. 6, No. 3 (Oct. 1903).

Kerner, Robert J., ed., "The Diary of Edward W. Crippin, Private 27th Illinois Volunteers, War of the Rebellion, August 7, 1861 to September 19, 1863," *Transactions of the Illinois State Historical Society for the Year 1909*. Springfield, IL, 1910.

"Kiel Homecoming and July Fourth Program Enjoyed," *Sheboygan Press*, July 5, 1932.

Knudsen, Dean, "Southern-born Union Colonel," *Civil War Times Illustrated*, Vol. 33, No. 2 (May/June 1994).

Kohl, Rhonda M., "On Grant's Front Line: The Fifth Illinois Cavalry in Mississippi," *Illinois Historical Journal*, Vol. 91, No. 1 (Spring, 1998).

"The Last of the Mechanic Fusileers," *Chicago Daily Tribune*, Feb. 6, 1862.

"Late Colonel Bush First Editor to Support Lincoln," *Portland Sunday Oregonian*, July 27, 1913.

"The Late General J.B. Wyman," *Chicago Daily Tribune*, Feb. 4, 1864.

"Letter from Col. Fairchild Upon the Death of Col. O'Connor," *Daily Milwaukee News*, Sept. 20, 1862.

"Letter from J.E. Maddux," *Decatur Daily Republican*, Sept. 17, 1889.

Lloyd, Frederick, "War Memories," *Iowa Historical Record*, Vol. 5, No. 1 (Jan. 1889).

Longley, Charles L., "The Twenty-Fourth Iowa Volunteers," *Annals of Iowa*, 3rd Series, Vol. 1, No. 7 (Oct. 1894).

"Lyman Guinnip," *Louisville Daily Democrat*, Nov. 12, 1862.

"Major General Hugh J. Campbell," *Louisiana Democrat (Alexandria, LA)*, May 11, 1870.

Mann, Curtis, "Historian Tracks Fate of Faded Family That Helped Shape Area," *Historico: Sangamon County Historical Society Newsletter*, Dec. 2009-Jan. 2010.

McAdams, Benton, "Greybeards in Blue," *Civil War Times Illustrated*, Vol. 36, No. 7 (Feb. 1998).

"Memoir of Col. N.W. Mills," *Annals of Iowa*, 1st Series, Vol. 8, No. 3 (July 1870).

"Milestones in *The Clinton Public* for the Year 1881," *DeWitt County Genealogical Quarterly*, Vol. 18, No. 1 (Spring 1992).

"Milo Smith," *Annals of Iowa*, 3rd Series, Vol. 6, No. 5 (April 1904).

"Mourn Death of Col. Starr," *Jacksonville Journal Courier*, Oct. 11, 1964.

"The Murder of Col. Cromwell of the 47th Illinois Vols.," *Peoria Transcript*, June 11, 1863.

"Obituary Notice-Colonel Mark Wm. Downie," *The Nassau County Genealogist*, Vol. 5, No. 2 (Spring 1998).

"Obsequies of Col. W.A. Thrush," *Peoria Transcript*, Oct. 20, 1862.

"An Old Hero: Reminiscences of the Late Col. John Hancock," *Oshkosh Daily Northwestern*, April 11, 1894.

"The Old 63rd Illinois Infantry," *Decatur Weekly Republican*, Aug. 29, 1889.

"The Osage Iron Works Co.," *Sedalia Daily Democrat*, June 14, 1873.

Overy, David H., Jr., "The Wisconsin Carpetbagger: A Group Portrait," *Wisconsin Magazine of History*, Vol. 44, No. 1 (Autumn 1960).

Parker, Sylvester E., "The Death of Colonel Torrence," *Washington National Tribune*, April 10, 1884.

Parks, George E., "One Story of the 109th Illinois Volunteer Infantry Regiment," *Journal of the Illinois State Historical Society*, Vol. 56, No. 2 (Summer 1963).

Parson, Thomas E., "Van Dorn's Holly Springs Raid," *Blue & Gray Magazine*, Vol. 27, Issue 3 (2010).

Pickett, Thomas J., "Reminiscences of Abraham Lincoln," Introduction by Ernest E. East, *Lincoln Herald*, Vol. 45, No. 4 (Dec. 1943).

Piston, William Garrett, "The 1st Iowa Volunteers: Honor and Community in a Ninety-Day Regiment," *Civil War History*, Vol. 44, No. 1 (March 1998).

Pitstick, Jerry W., "A Presentation Colt M1851 Navy," *Man at Arms*, Vol. 20, No. 3 (June 1998).

Politzer, Eric, "Robert Creighton Murphy: U.S. Consul at Shanghai, Brigade Commander, National Scapegoat," *Newsletter of the Association for the Preservation of Historic Congressional Cemetery*, Fall 2002.

"Portraits of Chicago's Postmasters in a Giant Frame," *Chicago Sunday Times-Herald*, July 30, 1899.

Poulton, James P.C., "Col. John Q. Wilds," *Annals of Iowa*, 1st Series, Vol. 4, No. 3 (July 1866).

Quinlivan, Bridget, "Once Upon a Time: Moses Bane: Doctor, Lawyer, Soldier ... Tax Guy?," *Quincy Herald-Whig*, Sept. 16, 2012.

"A Radical's Opinion of Messmore," *Daily Milwaukee News*, Oct. 2, 1867.

Ranstead, William H., "The Case of Col. Austin Light," *Chicago Daily Tribune*, Dec. 7, 1861.

Reed, David W., "Life of Col. Joseph J. Woods," *Annals of Jackson County, Iowa*. No. 1. Maquoketa, IA, 1905.

"Referring to Finnicum," *Topeka Daily Capital*, Oct. 18, 1882.

"Regimental Election," *Joliet Signal*, May 21, 1861.

Reid, Harvey, "Col. J. W. Jenkins, a Soldier and Pioneer," *Annals of Jackson County, Iowa*. No. 2. Maquoketa, IA, 1906.

"Re-Interment of Col. Chas. F. Springer," *Anamosa Eureka*, May 6, 1875.

"Resignation of Col. Babcock," *Peoria Transcript*, Oct. 20, 1862.

Robertson, George A., "Out of Libby Prison," *Washington National Tribune*, Sept. 23, 1886.

"Samuel Merrill," *Annals of Iowa*, 3rd Series, Vol. 4, No. 3 (Oct. 1899).

"Scandalous Conduct of a Radical State Senator," *Ouachita Telegraph (Monroe, LA)*, Oct. 2, 1869.

Schafer, Joseph, "Genesis of Wisconsin's Free High School System," *Wisconsin Magazine of History*, Vol. 10, No. 2 (December 1926).

Semmes, Ryan P., "From Pea Ridge to the Potomac: Lemon G. Hine and the 44th Illinois Regiment, 1861-1862," *Journal of the Illinois State Historical Society*, Vol. 104, No. 1-2 (Spring-Summer 2011).

Shaw, William T., "The Battle of Pleasant Hill," *Annals of Iowa*, 3rd Series, Vol. 3, Nos. 5-6 (April-July 1898).

"Sketch of Charles D. Robinson," *Green Bay Advocate*, March 15, 1888.

"Sketch of the Field Officers of the 8th Regiment, W.V.," *Wisconsin State Journal*, Oct. 10, 1861.

Skofstad, Albert, "Last Moments of Colonel Heg," *Wisconsin State Journal*, Oct. 27, 1863.

Smith, Thaddeus L., "The Twenty-Fourth Iowa Volunteers," *Annals of Iowa*, 3rd Series, Vol. 1, No. 1-3 (April-Oct. 1893).

"Sponsor of the German Theater in Cincinnati Dies: Colonel Christian Thielemann," *Der Deutsche Pionier*, Vol. 7, No. 8 (Oct. 1875).

"Statement Concerning the Remains of Col. Stewart," *Illinois State Journal*, Feb. 10, 1863.

Sweeny, William M., "Colonel Maurice Maloney, U.S. Army," *Journal of the American Irish Historical Society*, Vol. 25 (1926).

Swift, Lester L., "Tribulations of the Rev. Col. Jaquess and the Preacher Regiment: A New Lincoln Note Discovered," *Lincoln Herald*, Vol. 69, No. 4 (Winter 1967).

Temple, Wayne C., "Lincoln and W. H. W. Cushman," *Lincoln Herald*, Vol. 68, No. 2 (Summer 1966).

Bibliography

Tendick, Cecil, "Forrest Cavalry Raids Memphis: Col. Starr a Victim of Raid," *Jacksonville Journal Courier*, Aug. 23, 1964.

Thomas, David L., "Danville's Forgotten Hero of the Civil War," *The Heritage of Vermilion County*, Vol. 22, No. 3 (Summer 1986).

Trenerry, Walter N., "Lester's Surrender at Murfreesboro," *Minnesota History*, Vol. 39, No. 5 (Spring 1965).

"The Trouble in Col. Wilson's Mechanic Fusileer Regiment," *Chicago Daily Tribune*, Dec. 18, 1861.

Turner, Andrew J., "Col. Frank A. Haskell: His Brilliant Military Record," *Columbus Democrat*, May 29, 1895.

Utley, William L., "Continuation of Bloodgood's Case," *Milwaukee Sentinel*, Dec. 10, 1863.

"William P. Chandler," *The Kimball Family News*, Vol. 1, No. 1 (January 1898).

Wilson, Charles L., "Representative Men: Colonel Thomas Johnson Pickett, of Nebraska, the Man Who First Proposed the Nomination of Abraham Lincoln." *The Midland Monthly*, Vol. 5, No. 6 (June 1896).

"Wisconsin Hero Highly Honored: Monument Over the Grave of the Late Colonel Edgar O'Connor Unveiled at Washington," *Janesville Daily Gazette*, May 31, 1902.

Internet Sources

Col. David D. Irons (1816–1863)-Find A Grave Memorial.

Beszedits, "The Life and Times of Nicholas Perczel," http://www.sk-szeged.hu/statikus_html/vasvary/newsletter/06jun/perczel.html.

Field, Anne Healy, "Descendants of Elmira Peirce and William Rearden of White County, Illinois," www.annefield.net/elmira_peirce_rearden_desc_04.pdf.

https://thecivilwarandnorthwestwisconsin.wordpress.com/the-soldiers/alphabetical-list-of-all-soldiers-from-northwest-wisconsin/daniel-j-dill-1830-1917/.

https://thecivilwarandnorthwestwisconsin.wordpress.com/the-soldiers/alphabetical-list-of-all-soldiers-from-northwest-wisconsin/robert-c-murphy/.

http://civilwar.illinoisgenweb.org/photos/moorewmpcolonel.html.

http://freepages.history.rootsweb.ancestry.com/~enderlin/cw/napa/tulocay-cwburials.html.

http://marvel.hoosierroots.com/getperson.php?pid=117.

http://ozarkscivilwar.org/photographs/dewey-william/.

http://vesterheim.org/collections/civil-war-database/j/joh/004926.html.

http://www.colfab.org/BartlesonFrederickA.html.

http://www.findagrave.com.

http://www.greathouse.us/library/biographies/greathouse-lucien.htm.

http://www.jackwhitesfrontporch.com/17971.html.

http://www.mccwrt.com/cwveterans/B/Belitz,%20Henry%20F.pdf.

http://www.1stminnesota.net/#/soldier/147.

http://www.mihp.org/2012/12/hundley-robert-m/.

http://www.mnopedia.org/person/wilkin-alexander-1819–1864.

http://www.wssas.org/Research_and_Links.html.

"Rich Hanson's Civil War Stories: Colonel Horace H. Willsie," http://monmouthrlhcw.blogspot.com/2013/08/colonel-horace-h-willsie_31.html.

Ziemer, Mary McBrien, "The Life of Colonel John G. Clark," http://www.prairietree.com/wp/John%20G.%20Clark_ed.pdf.

Manuscript Sources

Abraham Lincoln Presidential Library, Springfield, IL

Allen Buckner Papers (SC 1855).

Brumgardt, John R., "A Scottish Printer at 'Johnston's Heels': The Civil War Letters of Colonel Owen Stuart (90th Illinois)," Owen Stuart Papers (SC 2405).

John Nelson Cromwell Papers (SC 357).

Taylor, James E., *Portrait Gallery Officers of the Union & Confederate Armies. 1861-65*.

Chicago History Museum

Taylor, James E., *Portrait Gallery of Union Generals & Colonels That Fell by the Bullet and Disease in the Civil War* (1986.0480 PPL).

The Filson Historical Society, Special Collections, Louisville, KY

Marshall Family Papers, 1815–1897, A\M367.

House of Representatives, 50th Congress, 1st Session, Report No. 3485, Sept. 19, 1888.

Interment Records, Graceland Cemetery, Chicago, IL.

Military Order of the Loyal Legion of the United States (MOLLUS)

Obituary Circulars of Various State Commanderies

National Archives

Card Records of Headstones Provided for Deceased Union Civil War Veterans, 1879–1903 (Record Group 92).

Court-martial Case Files, 1809–1894 (Record Group 153).

Historical Register of National Homes for Disabled Volunteer Soldiers, 1866–1938 (Record Group 15).

Letters Received, Adjutant General's Office (Record Group 94).

Letters Received, Appointment, Commission, and Personal Branch, Adjutant General's Office (Record Group 94).

Letters Received, Commission Branch, Adjutant General's Office (Record Group 94).

Letters Received by the Secretary of War, Irregular Series, 1861–1866 (Record Group 107).

Letters Received, Volunteer Service Branch, Adjutant General's Office (Record Group 94).
Military Service Files (Record Group 94).
Pension Files (Record Group 15).
Register of Enlistments in the United States Army, 1798–1914 (Record Group 94).
Regular Army Enlistment Papers, 1798–1912 (Record Group 94).
U.S. Census Records (Record Group 29).
U.S. Military Academy Cadet Application Papers, 1805–1866 (Record Group 94).

U.S. Military Academy Library, West Point, NY Cullum File.

Vermont Vital Records Through 1870.

Wisconsin Historical Society

Annals of the Fortieth. Sundry Proceedings, Sayings, Doings and "Undoings" of the 40th Reg. Wis. Vol. Inf.
Quiner, Edwin B., *Quiner Scrapbooks: Correspondence of the Wisconsin Volunteers, 1861–1865.*
William A. Greene Papers (M2009-042).

Newspapers

Albany (IL) Review
Albia (IA) Republican
Alexandria (VA) Gazette
Alton (IL) Evening Telegraph
Alton (IL) Telegraph
Alton (IL) Weekly Telegraph
Amboy (IL) News
Anamosa (IA) Eureka
Aurora (IL) Beacon
Baldwin (KS) Ledger
Baton Rouge (LA) Daily Advocate
Belle Plain (IA) Union
Beloit (KS) Courier
Beloit (WI) Daily Free Press
Beloit (WI) Weekly Free Press
Bloomington (IL) Daily Pantagraph
Bloomington (IL) Pantagraph
Boston (MA) Evening Transcript
Boston (MA) Herald
Boston (MA) Post
Brooklyn (NY) Daily Eagle
Buffalo (NY) Morning Express
Bureau County (IL) Republican
Burlington (IA) Daily Hawk-Eye
Burlington (IA) Weekly Hawk-Eye
Cairo (IL) Evening Citizen
Cairo (IL) Weekly Citizen
Canton (IL) Daily Register
Carlinville (IL) Democrat
Carlyle (IL) Banner
Carlyle (IL) Union Banner
Carmi (IL) Courier
Carrollton (IL) Gazette
Cedar Rapids (IA) Daily Republican
Cedar Rapids (IA) Evening Gazette
Cedar Rapids (IA) Republican
Champaign County (IL) Gazette
Champaign (IL) Daily Gazette
Cherokee (IA) Times-Herald
Chetopa (KS) Advance
Chicago (IL) Daily Tribune
Chicago (IL) Inter Ocean
Chilton (WI) Times
Cincinnati (OH) Commercial
Cleveland (OH) Plain Dealer
Clinton (IA) Age
Clinton (IL) Public
Clinton (IL) Register
Columbus (WI) Republican
Council Bluffs (IA) Daily Nonpareil
Daily Alta California (San Francisco)
Daily Illinois State Register (Springfield)
Daily Iowa Capital (Des Moines)
Daily Kansas Tribune (Lawrence)
Daily Milwaukee (WI) News
Daily Missouri Republican (St. Louis)
Daily Nebraska State Journal (Lincoln)
Dallas (TX) Morning News
Danville (IL) Daily Commercial
Danville (IL) Evening Commercial
Danville (IL) Times
Davenport (IA) Daily Gazette
Davenport (IA) Daily Republican
Davenport (IA) Morning Tribune
Decatur (IL) Daily Herald
De Forest (WI) Times
Des Moines (IA) Daily News
Des Moines (IA) News
Detroit (MI) Sunday News-Tribune
Dixon (IL) Evening Telegraph
Dixon (IL) Telegraph
Dodgeville (WI) Chronicle
Dubuque (IA) Daily Times
Dubuque (IA) Democratic Herald
Eau Claire (WI) Weekly Telegram
Edwardsville (IL) Intelligencer
Effingham (IL) Democrat
Eureka (KS) Democratic Messenger
Florida Mirror (Fernandina)
Fond du Lac (WI) Commonwealth
Fond du Lac (WI) Daily Commonwealth
Fond du Lac (WI) Reporter
Fredonia (NY) Censor
Freeport (IL) Bulletin
Fremont (OH) Journal
Fulton County (IL) Ledger
Galesburg (IL) Republican-Register
Galveston (TX) Daily News
Glencoe (MN) Enterprise
Grand Rapids (MI) Herald
Grant County (WI) Herald
Green Bay (WI) Daily State Gazette
Greenville (IL) Advocate
Hamilton (MO) Advocate-Hamiltonian
Hickman (KY) Courier
Howard (KS) Courant

Bibliography

Humboldt (KS) Union
Hutchinson (MN) Leader
Illinois State Journal (Springfield)
Illinois State Register (Springfield)
Independence (IA) Bulletin-Journal
Independence (KS) Star and Kansan
Indianola (IA) Herald
Iowa City (IA) Daily Press
Iowa Postal Card (Fayette, IA)
Iowa State Register (Des Moines)
Irish American (New York City)
Iron County (MO) Register
Jacksonville (IL) Daily Courier
Jacksonville (IL) Journal
Jacksonville (IL) Sentinel
Janesville (WI) Daily Gazette
Jefferson (WI) Banner
Jefferson County (WI) Union
Jonesboro (IL) Gazette
Jonesboro (IL) Weekly Gazette
Kankakee (IL) Gazette
Kansas City (MO) Star
Kenosha (WI) Union
Keokuk County (IA) News
Keokuk (IA) Daily Gate City
Kinsley (KS) Graphic
Kirwin (KS) Chief
Labette County (KS) Democrat
Lake Mills (WI) Spike
LaMoille (IL) Gazette
Lancaster (WI) Teller
Lawrence (KS) Western Home Journal
Leavenworth (KS) Daily Conservative
Le Meschacebe (English edition), Edgard, LA
Lester Prairie (MN) News
Lincoln (IL) Daily Courier
Linn County (IA) Patriot
Livingston (NY) Republican
Los Angeles (CA) Herald
Los Angeles (CA) Times
Madison (WI) Democrat
Manhattan (KS) Nationalist
Marion (IL) Egyptian Press
Marion (IL) Monitor
Marion (IA) Register
Marion (IA) Weekly Register
Marshalltown (IA) Evening Times-Republican
Marshfield (WI) Times
Mattoon (IL) Daily Journal-Gazette
Mattoon (IL) Weekly Gazette
Medford (OR) Mail
Metropolis (IL) Promulgator
Milwaukee (WI) Daily News
Milwaukee (WI) Daily Sentinel
Milwaukee (WI) Evening Wisconsin
Milwaukee (WI) Morning Sentinel
Milwaukee (WI) Republican-Sentinel
Milwaukee (WI) Sentinel
Milwaukee (WI) Weekly Wisconsin
Minneapolis (MN) Morning Tribune

Minneota (MN) Mascot
Monroe County (IA) News and Albia Democrat
Monticello (IA) Express
Muscatine (IA) Journal
Muscatine (IA) News-Tribune
Napa (CA) Daily Journal
Nashville (TN) Daily Union
Nebraska State Journal (Lincoln)
Neosho (MO) Times
New Orleans (LA) Daily Picayune
New York (NY) Herald
New York (NY) Times
New York (NY) Tribune
Nyack (NY) City and Country
Oakland (CA) Tribune
Oberlin (OH) News
Ohio State Journal (Columbus)
Olney (IL) Advocate
Olney (IL) Times
Oregon Daily Journal (Portland)
Orleans (NY) Republican
Oshkosh (WI) Daily Northwestern
Oskaloosa (IA) Daily Herald
Oswego (KS) Independent
Ottawa (IL) Free Trader
Ottawa (IL) Republican
Ottawa (IL) Republican-Times
Paris (IL) Daily Beacon
Pasadena (CA) Evening Star
Peabody (KS) Gazette
Peoria (IL) Daily Transcript
Peoria (IL) Herald-Transcript
Peoria (IL) Journal-Transcript
Peoria (IL) Transcript
Petersburg (IL) Observer
Petroleum Centre (PA) Daily Record
Philadelphia (PA) Inquirer
Philadelphia (PA) Public Ledger
Piatt County (IL) Herald
Pierce County (WI) Herald
Pike County (IL) Democrat
Portland (OR) Morning Oregonian
Quincy (IL) Daily Herald
Quincy (IL) Daily Journal
Quincy (IL) Daily Whig
Racine (WI) Advocate
Racine (WI) Daily Journal
Racine (WI) Journal-News
Racine (WI) Weekly Advocate
River Falls (WI) Journal
Riverside (CA) Daily Press
Rochester (NY) Democrat and Chronicle
Rochester (MN) Post
Rockford (IL) Daily Gazette
Rockford (IL) Daily Register
Rockford (IL) Register-Gazette
Rockford (IL) Weekly Gazette
Rockford (IL) Weekly Register-Gazette
Rocky Mountain News (Denver, CO)
St. Joseph County (IN) Forum

St. Joseph Valley (IN) Register
St. Louis (MO) Globe-Democrat
St. Louis (MO) Post-Dispatch
St. Paul (MN) Daily Globe
St. Paul (MN) Globe
St. Paul (MN) Daily Pioneer Press
St. Paul (MN) Pioneer Press
Saline County (KS) Journal
Salt Lake (UT) Herald
Salt Lake (UT) Tribune
San Antonio (TX) Daily Express
San Diego (CA) Union
San Francisco (CA) Chronicle
San Francisco (CA) Evening Bulletin
Seattle (WA) Daily Times
Seattle (WA) Post-Intelligencer
Seattle (WA) Star
Sedalia (MO) Daily Capital
Semi-Weekly Wisconsin (Milwaukee)
Shawnee (IL) Herald
Sheboygan (WI) Times
Sioux Falls (SD) Daily Argus-Leader
Steubenville (OH) Daily Herald
Summit County (CO) Journal
Sumner (IL) Press
Tacoma (WA) Daily Ledger
Tama (IA) Herald
Toledo (IA) Chronicle

Topeka (KS) Daily Capital
Topeka (KS) Daily Commonwealth
Topeka (KS) State Journal
Troy (NY) Daily Whig
Tulsa (OK) Democrat
Ventura (CA) Daily Free Press
Virginia City (MT) Madisonian
Warsaw (IL) Bulletin
Warsaw (IN) Daily Times
Washington (DC) Evening Star
Washington (DC) National Republican
Washington (DC) National Tribune
Washington (DC) Post
Waterloo (IA) Daily Courier
Waterloo (IA) Evening Courier and Reporter
Waterloo (IL) Republican
Waukesha (WI) Democrat
Waukesha (WI) Freeman
Waukesha (WI) Journal
Wayne County (IL) Press
Wheaton (IL) Illinoisan
Wichita (KS) Daily Beacon
Winterset (IA) Madisonian
Wisconsin Pinery (Stevens Point)
Wisconsin State Journal (Madison)
Wisconsin Weekly Advocate (Milwaukee)
Woodstock (IL) Sentinel

INDEX

Page numbers in ***bold italics*** indicate pages with photographs.

Abbott, Charles Henry 157, ***158***
Abercrombie, John Cree 155, ***158***
Abercrombie, John J. 232
Alban, James Shane 218, ***221***
Alden, Andrew Jackson 15
Alden, George Marcus 4, ***15***
Alexander, John Washington Shields 6, ***15***
Allen, Benjamin 218, ***221***
Allen, Thomas G. 10, 16
Allen, Thomas S. 218
Anderson, Daniel 154, ***159***
Anderson, Jabez Jarvis 5, 16
Anderson, William B. 9, 51
Andrews, Christopher C. 205
Andrews, Timothy P. 148
Ankeny, Rollin V. 14
Anneke, Fritz 219, ***222***
Apperson, Thomas A. 138
Archer, Sampson Mathew 156, ***159, 160***
Atkins, Smith D. 11
Averill, John T. 205

Babcock, Amos Charles 12, ***16***
Babcock, Andrew Jackson 4, ***17***
Bacon, George Albert 4, 17, ***18***
Bailey, George Washington Kelly 11, ***18***
Bailey, Joseph 217
Baker, James 155, ***160***, 196
Baker, James H. 206
Baldwin, Silas Delos 9, 18, ***19***
Ball, John ***210***
Ballance, Charles 10, ***20***
Banbury, Jabez 155, ***161***
Bane, Moses Milton 8, ***20, 21***
Barner, Horatio Gates 154, ***161***
Barnes, Myron S. 7, 21, ***22***
Barret, James Allen 3, 22
Barret, Joseph A. 22

Barrett, Wallace W. 7
Barstow, William Augustus 217, 222, ***223***
Bartleson, Frederick A. 11, 22, ***23***
Bates, Edward P. ***35***
Bates, Erastus N. 10
Bates, John Francis 154, ***162***
Battey, Frederick Adolphus 9, 23, ***24***
Baxter, Luther Loren 205, ***206***
Beach, Benjamin 155, 162, ***163***
Beal, Lucius Wells 13, ***24***
Bean, Sidney Alfred 217, ***224***
Belitz, Henry Frederick 220, 224, ***225***
Belknap, William W. 156, 174
Bell, Joseph W. 4
Benneson, William H. 10, 24, ***25***
Bennett, John E. 10
Benton, Thomas H., Jr. 156
Benton, William P. 93
Bereman, Alvah Hamilton 157, ***163***
Bertram, Henry 219
Beveridge, John L. 4
Biggs, Jonathan 13
Bingham, George B. 217, ***225, 226***
Bintliff, James 220
Bishop, Judson W. 205
Black, John C. 7
Blanden, Leander 11
Bloodgood, Edward 219, ***226***
Bloomfield, Ira J. 6
Blunt, James G. 223
Boardman, Frederick Augustus 217, ***227***
Bond, Shadrach 134
Borgersrode, Rudolph von 205, ***207***
Bouck, Gabriel 218, ***228***
Bouck, William C. 228

Bowen, Edwin Anson 8, ***25***
Boyd, James S. 8, 25, ***26***
Brackett, Albert Gallatin 3, ***26, 27***
Bradley, Daniel 6, ***27***
Bradley, Luther P. 8
Bragg, Edward S. 218, 234
Brayman, Mason 6, 118
Bristol, Hiram Warren 7, 28
Britton, William Buckman 218, ***229***
Bronson, Stephen 14
Brown, Aaron 155, 163, ***164***
Brown, Harvey Maynard 220, ***230***
Brown, William Robert 9, ***28***
Bruce, John 156
Brush, Daniel H. 5
Brush, William 157, ***164***
Bryan, Thomas James 10, 28, ***29***, 35
Bryant, George Edwin 218, ***230, 231***
Bryner, John 8, ***29***
Buckner, Allen 10, 29, ***30***
Buell, Don Carlos 211
Buford, Napoleon B. 6
Burke, Patrick Edmund 9, ***30, 31***
Burroughs, Wilson 35
Busey, John S. 38
Busey, Samuel T. 10
Bush, Daniel Brown, Jr. 3, ***31***
Bussey, Cyrus 154
Buswell, Nicholas Colby 11, ***32***
Buttrick, Edwin Lorenzo 220, ***231, 232***
Byam, Commodore Perry 165
Byam, Eber Cole 156, ***165***

Caldwell, Henry Clay 154, ***165***
Callaway, James Edmund 6, 32, ***33***

301

Index

Cameron, Daniel 9, 132
Campbell, Andrew K. 9, 33, **34**
Campbell, Benjamin Franklin 7, **34, 35**
Campbell, Franklin 10, 35
Campbell, Hugh James 156, **166**
Capron, Horace 4
Carlin, William P. 7, 16, 99
Carnahan, Robert H. 3
Carr, Eugene A. 3
Carskaddon, David 155, 166, **167**
Case, Henry 13
Casey, Thomas Sloo 12, 35, **36**
Cavanaugh, Thomas Horne 3, 36
Chambers, Alexander 156
Champion, Thomas E. 11
Chandler, William Palmer 7, **36**
Chapin, Alfred Rose 218, 232, **233**
Chetlain, Augustus L. 5
Christopher, John 11, 37
Church, Lawrence Smith 11, **37**
Clark, George W. 157
Clark, John Garvin 220, **233, 234**
Clune, William Henry 155, **167**
Coates, James H. 5
Cobb, Amasa 218, 220
Coler, William Nichols 6, **38**
Collett, Joshua W. 215
Colman, Edward 220, **234**
Colvill, William, Jr. 205
Colyer, Edward 7, 38, **39**
Connell, John 156, 167, **168**
Conrad, Joseph 25
Cook, John 4
Coon, Datus E. 154
Coon, Squire Park 217, **235**
Cooper, Douglas H. 93
Corse, John M. 155, 167
Crabb, Benjamin 156, **168, 169**
Craigue, Nelson Francis 217, **235**
Crebs, John Montgomery 11, **39**
Crocker, Marcellus M. 155, 272
Cromwell, John Nelson 8, 39, **40**
Crooks, William 205, **207, 208**
Crosley, George W. **164**
Cumming, Gilbert W. 8
Cummings, Henry Johnson Brodhead 157, **169, 170**
Curtis, Samuel R. 26, 154
Cushman, William Hercules Washburn 8, **40, 41**
Cutler, Lysander 218, 243, 264

Dale, Nicholas Harry 217, **236**
Dana, Napoleon J.T. 93, 192, 205
Danforth, George E. 228

Daniels, Edward Dwight 217, 236, **237**
Davidson, Francis Marion 4, 41, 135
Davidson, John W. 32, 165, 182
Davidson, Peter 14, 41
Davies, Thomas A. 236
Davis, Charles Wilder 8, **42**
Davis, Hasbrouck 4
Davis, Jefferson 72
Davis, Jefferson C. 78
Davis, Jerome Dean 8, **42, 43**
Davis, John A. 8, **43**
Day, Henry M. 11
Dean, Henry Hobart 14, **44**
De Groat, Charles H. 219
Dengler, Adolf 7, **45**
Dennis, Elias S. 6
Derry, Thomas 217, **237**
Dewey, William 156, **170**
Dickerman, Willard Arms 12, 45, **46**
Dickey, Theophilus Lyle 3, **46**
Dill, Daniel J. 219, **238**
Dilworth, Caleb J. 10
Dodge, Grenville M. 19, 155, 178
Dollins, James Jackson 10, **47**
Doran, John L. 218, 238
Dornblaser, Benjamin 8
Dorr, Joseph Bartlett 154, 170, **171**
Dougherty, Henry 6, **48**
Downie, Mark William 205, **208**
Dox, Hamilton B. 4
Drake, Francis M. **183**, 184
Duer, John O. 8
Dustin, Daniel 12
Dwight, William 193
Dye, William McE. 156
Dysart, Alexander P. 7, 48, **49**

Earl, Seth Clark 8, **49**
Eastman, Harry E. 266
Eberhart, Gustavus Adolphus 157, **171**
Edwards, John 156
Ege, Joseph A. 50
Ege, Peter 7, **49, 50**
Eldridge, Hamilton N. 13
Elliott, Isaac H. 7
Elliott, Washington L. 154
Ellsworth, Elmer 124
Engelmann, Adolph 7
English, George Harrison 7, **50**
Erskine, Albert 4
Evans, George W. 9, **51**
Ewing, Hugh 167

Fahnestock, Allen Lewis 11, 51, **52**

Fairchild, Cassius 218
Fairchild, Lucius 217
Fallows, Samuel 220
Farnsworth, John F. 3
Ferrell, Charles M. 6, 52
Finkler, William **260**
Finnicum, Mark 218, 239
Floyd, Spencer Beebe 13, 52, **53**
Fonda, John G. 12
Ford, Caswell Pierce 6, **53**
Fouke, Philip Bond 6, 53, **54**
Fox, Charles H. 11, **54**
Fremont, John C. 65
Fry, Jacob 9, **55**
Fry, James B. 55
Funke, Otto 4
Funkhouser, John Jackson 11, **55**

Gaines, Thomas W. **21**
Galbraith, Ashley T. 8, **56**
Gale, James M. **74**
Gamble, William 3
Garrett, John Alexander 157, **172**
Geddes, James L. 155
George, James 205, **209**
Gibbon, John 243
Gilbert, Charles C. 24
Gilbert, James I. 103, 156, 184
Gilbert, Othniel 10, 56
Gilfillan, James 206, 209, **210**
Gill, Charles Rice 219, **239**
Gillmore, Robert Addison 6, 57
Gilmer, Daniel Harvie 7, **57**
Gilmore, James R. 72
Ginty, George C. 220
Glasgow, Samuel L. 156
Goodwin, George Benjamin 220, **240**
Goodwin, John W. 14, 57
Gorgas, Adam Bassler 5, 57
Gorman, Willis A. 205
Gower, James Otis 154, 172, **173**
Graham, Harvey 156
Graham, John M. 3, 58
Granger, Gordon 34, 80
Grant, Ulysses S. 6, 46, 90, 104, 108, 116, 118, 249, 254, 272
Grass, Daniel 9, **58**
Gray, Edmund Baldwin 219, 240, **241**
Greathouse, Lucien 8, **59**
Green, John 220, 241
Greene, James H. 249
Greene, William Augustus 219, **242**
Greusel, Nicholas 7, **59, 60**
Grier, David P. 10
Grierson, Benjamin H. 3, 129
Griffiths, Joseph Murray 157, **173**

Index

Griggs, Chauncey Wright 205, 210, **211**
Guinnip, Lyman 10, 60
Guppey, Joshua J. 219

Hackleman, Pleasant A. 189
Hailey, Mathew 203
Hall, Cyrus 5, 14
Hall, John P. 9, 60, **61**
Hall, William 155, **174**
Halleck, Henry W. 90, 108
Hamilton, Augustus H. **183**
Hamilton, Charles S. 217, 238
Hammond, Charles Morrel 11, **61**
Hancock, Bradford 219, **242**
Hancock, John 218, **243**
Hanna, William 8, **21**
Hapeman, Douglas 12, **62**
Harding, Abner C. 10
Hare, Abraham M. 155, 174, **175**
Hare, Michael H. **183**
Harmon, Oscar Fitzalan 13, **62, 63**
Harper, Joseph Wilson 3, **63**
Harriman, Samuel 220
Harrington, Fazilo A. 6, **64**
Harris, Charles L. 218
Harris, Thomas Woolen 8, **64, 65**
Harrow, William 151
Haskell, Frank Aretas 220, 243, **244**
Hatch, Edward 154
Hatch, Ozias M. 32
Hawley, William 217
Haynie, Isham N. 8
Healy, Robert W. 9
Heath, Herman H. 154
Hecker, Friedrich Karl Franz 6, 10, **65**, 247
Heckman, Charles A. 93
Hedrick, John M. 156
Heg, Hans Christian 218, 244, **245**
Hemings, Sally 249
Henderson, David Bremner 157, **175, 176**
Henderson, Paris Perrin 155, 176, **177**
Henderson, Stephen Howard 157, **177**
Henderson, Thomas J. 12, 177
Herbert, Josiah Thompson 156, **178**
Hicks, Stephen G. 7, **66**
Hill, Sylvester G. 157
Hillis, David B. 156
Hitt, Daniel Fletcher 8, **66, 67**
Hobart, Harrison C. 219

Hoffman, William 37
Hoge, George B. 12
Holt, Joseph 126, 132, 184, 194, 211, 226, 258
Hotchkiss, Charles T. 11
Hough, Rosell Marion 9, **67, 68**
Houghtaling, Charles 4
Hovey, Charles E. 7
Howard, Noel Byron 155, **178, 179**
Howe, James Henry 219, 245, **246**
Howe, John H. 13, 126
Hubbard, Lucius F. 205
Hughes, Daniel Henry 157, 179, **180**
Hughes, Samuel T. 5, **68**
Humphrey, Thomas W. 11
Hundley, Robert M. 13, 68, **69**
Hunter, David 67
Huntley, Judson John 7, 69
Hurlbut, Frederick Judson 9, **69**
Hurlbut, Stephen A. 19
Ingersoll, Robert Green 4, **70**

Irons, David D. 11, **71**
Isaminger, James 9, **71**

Jackson, Charles Henry 218, 246
Jacobi, Arthur Heinrich Hartmann 218, 246, **247**, 260
Jacobs, William Henry 219, **247**
Jamison, William H. 6, **72**
Jaquess, James Frazier 10, 72, **73**
Jefferson, John Wayles 218, **248**
Jefferson, Thomas 248
Jenkins, Jeremiah Williams 157, **180**
Johns, Frederick A. 13, 73
Johnson, Amory Kinney 6, 73, **74**
Johnson, Andrew 184
Johnson, Charles **206**
Johnson, Ole Carl 220, **249**
Juarez, Benito 111
Judy, James William 12, **75**

Keener, George U. 14, 76
Kellogg, John A. 218
Kellogg, William Pitt 3, **76**
Kelly, John H. 77
Kelly, Joseph James 12, 76, **77**
Kelton, John C. 9
Kennicott, Ransom 7, 77, **78**
Kent, Loren 6
Kerr, Charles Deal 5, **78, 79**
Kerr, Lucien H. 4, **79**
Kincaid, George Washington 157, 180, **181**
King, Henry 6, 80

King, John F. 12
King, Rufus **226**, 263
Kinney, Thomas J. 13
Kinsman, William Henry 156, 181, **182**
Kirk, Edward N. 7
Kirkham, Robert 9, 80
Kitchell, Edward 11
Kittredge, Charles Woodman 157, **183, 184**
Knobelsdorff, Charles 7, 80, 269
Krez, Conrad 219
Krzyzanowski, Wladimir 247
Kueffner, William C. 14
Kuhn, John Henry 14, 81
Kummel, Augustus Henry 218, **250**

Lackey, George W. 14, **81**
La Grange, Oscar H. 217
Lake, Jed 156, **184, 185**
Langley, James Weston 13, 81, **82**
Larrabee, Charles Hathaway 219, **250, 251**
Latham, Robert Briggs 12, 82, **83**
Lauman, Jacob G. 155
Lawler, Michael K. 5, 69, 118
Leggett, Mortimer D. 27
Le Sage, John B. 11, 54, **83**
Lester, Henry Clay 205, **211**
Lewis, James Milton 219, **251, 252**
Light, Austin 7, 83
Lincoln, Abraham 19, 21, 60, 72, 75, 80, 82, 87, 103, 113, 122, 126, 128, 132, 194
Lippincott, Charles E. 7
Lipscomb, Henry S. 76
Logan, John 7, **84**
Logan, John A. 6, 47, 59, 143, 151, 189
Logan, Thomas M. **112**
Longworth, Abel **100**
Loomis, John Mason 6, **85**
Lovell, Frederick S. 220
Lowe, William W. 154, 204
Lowry, Francis Hubert 12, **86**
Lubbers, John 156, **185**
Lynch, John 3, **86**
Lynch, William F. 9
Lyon, William P. 218

MacArthur, Arthur, Jr. **35**, 219, **252, 253**
MacArthur, Douglas 253
Mack, Alonzo W. 10, 87
Mackey, Cyrus H. 157, **186**
Maddux, John Edward 12, **87**

Index

Magee, David W. 8
Maginnis, Martin **210**
Mahon, Stephen K. **183**
Malloy, Adam G. 218
Malmborg, Oscar 8, **88**
Maloney, Maurice 218, **253, 254**
Maltby, Jasper A. 8
Mann, Orrin L. 7
Mansfield, John 217
Marsh, Benjamin Franklin, Jr. 3, 32, **89**
Marsh, Charles Carroll 6, 27, 57, **90**, 148
Marsh, Jason 10, **91**
Marsh, Josiah Fay 206, **212**
Marshall, Thomas Alexander 3, **91**
Marshall, William R. 206
Martin, James S. 12
Martin, Leonard 220, **254, 255**
Martin, Lewis Drake 11, **92**
Marvel, George Rogers 4, 92
Mather, Thomas S. 4
Matthews, Asa Carrington 11, **93**
Matthews, Stanley 122
Matthies, Charles L. 155, 195
Mattson, Hans 205, **213**
McArthur, John 5
McChesney, Waters W. 13, 93, **94**
McClanahan, John W. 8, **94**
McClelland, James S. 53
McClernand, John A. 105, 106, 108, 109, 130, 131, 222, 253
McClure, John Dickson 8, **95**
McConnell, John 3
McCook, Alexander McD. 108
McCook, Edwin S. 6, **112**
McCown, Joseph B. 9, 95, **96**
McCrillis, Lafayette 3
McDowell, Irvin 187
McDowell, John Adair 155, 186, **187**
McFadden, Robert Hugh 8, **96**
McKeaig, George Williamson 13, 96
McKercher, Duncan 218, **255**
McLaren, Robert N. 205
McMahon, Henry **210**
McMurtry, William 12, **97**
McMynn, John Gibson 218, 255, **256**
McNulta, John 11
McPhaill, Samuel 205, 213, **214**
McPherson, James B. 88
Merrill, Samuel 156, 187, **188**
Merrill, Stevens W. **183**
Mersy, August 5

Meservey, Charles Clement 217, **256**
Messmore, Isaac Elijah 219, 222, **257**
Mihalotzy, Geza 6, **97**
Miles, Jonathan Rice 6, **98**
Milholland, Thomas J. 12, 99
Miller, Charles Henry 12, **99**
Miller, Samuel F. 191
Miller, Silas 7, 99, **100**
Miller, Stephen 205
Miller, William Edward 156, **188**
Mills, James K. 22
Mills, Noah Webster 155, **189**
Mitchell, Greenville M. 8
Monroe, James 13, 100, **101**
Montgomery, Milton 219
Moore, Absalom B. 12, 101
Moore, Jesse H. 12
Moore, Jonathan B. 219
Moore, Risdon Marshall 12, 101, **102**
Moore, Robert Steele 10, **102**
Moore, Webster Porter 217, 257, **258**
Moore, William Pinckard 8, **103**
Morgan, George N. 205
Morgan, James D. 5
Moro, Francis 9, 103, **104**
Morrill, John 9
Morris, Thomas A. 127
Morrison, William Ralls 8, **104, 105**
Moses, Albert J. 74
Mower, Joseph A. 69
Mudd, John January 3, **105**
Mulligan, James A. 6
Murphy, Robert Creighton 218, **258**

Naumann, Herman **260**
Neely, George Washington 13, **106**
Nelson, Anderson Doniphan 205, **214**
Nelson, William 215
Nevius, Garrett Voorhees 5, 106, **107**
Nichols, Samuel D. 155, 189, **190**
Niles, Nathaniel 13
Nimmo, Alexander Jackson 12, 107
Noble, Henry T. 108
Noble, John W. 154
Noble, Silas 3, 108
Nodine, Richard Howard 6, 53, **108**
Norton, Addison S. 5, 108, **109**
Nulton, Jerome Bonaparte 9, **109**

O'Connor, Edgar 217, **259**
Oglesby, Richard J. 4, 113
Ohr, Simon P. 9, **110**
O'Meara, Timothy J. 11, **110, 111**
Opdycke, Emerson **35**
Orff, Henry 219, **260**
Orme, William W. 11, 127
Osborn, Thomas O. 7
Osterhaus, Peter J. 189
Ozburn, Lindorf 6, **111, 112**

Paine, Eleazer A. 4, 5, 143
Paine, Halbert E. 217, 247
Palmer, John M. 5
Parkhurst, Irving **100**
Parrott, James C. 155
Pearsall, Uri B. 220
Pearson, Robert N. 6
Pease, Phineas 8
Peirce, William P. **35**
Perczel, Nicholas 155, **190**
Phillips, Thaddeus 13, 112
Pickett, Thomas Johnson 13, **112**
Pier, Colwert Kendall 220, **261**
Pinkney, Bertine 219, 261, **262**
Pleasanton, Alfred 140
Polk, James K. 200
Pollock, Samuel M. 154
Pope, John 208
Porter, Asbury Bateman 154, **191**
Post, John Pratt 4, 113
Post, Philip S. 9
Prentiss, Benjamin M. 5
Prince, Edward 3, **113, 114**
Proudfit, James K. 218
Pugh, Isaac C. 7
Putnam, Holden 11, **114**

Quinby, Isaac F. 64, 108

Raith, Julius 7, **115**
Ralston, Thomas A. **74**
Ramsey, Alexander 215
Randall, Alexander W. 231
Rankin, John Walker 156, 191, **192**
Ransom, Thomas E.G. 5
Raum, Green B. 9
Ray, William Augustus 220, **262**
Read, Daniel 116
Read, Sheridan Pitt 10, **115**, 127
Read, Theodore 116
Rearden, James Siddall 6, 116
Rees, John D. **112**
Reeves, Owen Thornton 10, **116**
Reid, Hugh T. 156
Reid, John Barclay 13, **117**
Reynolds, Joseph J. 184, 215

Rhoads, Franklin Lawrence 4, *118*
Rhodes, Eugene Manlove 119
Rhodes, Hinman 6, *118, 119*
Rice, Elliott W. 155
Rice, Samuel A. 157
Richardson, Hollon 218, 265
Richmond, Jonathan 13, *119, 120*
Rinaker, John I. 13
Ritter, Richard 6, 120
Robbins, George Washington 218, 259, *263*
Roberts, George Williamson 7, *120, 121*
Robinson, Charles Dayon 220, *263, 264*
Robinson, William Wallace 218, *264*
Rodgers, Andrew Fuller 10, *121*
Rogers, Andrew Watts 10, *122*
Rogers, George C. 5
Rogers, George Dickerson 219, *265*
Root, Elihu 232
Rosecrans, William S. 80, 81, 127, 191, 207, 258
Ross, Leonard F. 5
Rowett, Richard 4
Ruger, Thomas H. 217
Russell, John *35*
Rutherford, Friend Smith 11, 122, *123*
Rutherford, George V. 122
Rutherford, Reuben C. 122
Ryan, Abraham H. 39
Ryon, George 10, 123

Salomon, Charles E. 218
Salomon, Edward 253
Salomon, Edward S. 10
Salomon, Frederick 218, 246, *260*
Sanborn, John B. 205
Sanders, Horace T. 219
Sanford, James Pomeroy 157, *192*
Sanford, William Wilson 8, 123, *124*
Savage, John Adams, Jr. 220, *265*
Schmitt, William A. 6
Schofield, John M. 26
Scott, John 157
Scott, Joseph R. 5, *124*
Sealy, Robert P. 8, *125*
Shane, John 155, *193*
Shaw, Robert Gould 194
Shaw, William Tuckerman 155, 193, *194*
Shears, Henry 220, *266*

Shedd, Warren 6
Sheetz, Josiah A. 4
Sherman, Francis T. 11
Sherman, William T. 59, 75, 235
Shoup, Samuel N. 12
Sibley, Henry H. 215
Sickles, Hiram F. 14
Sill, Joshua W. 60
Silsby, William Hayes 155, 194, *195*
Simison, Samuel Andrew 6, *125*
Sloan, Thomas J. 13, 125, *126*
Small, William Edward 155, *195, 196*
Smith, Alfred Theophilus 14, *126*
Smith, Andrew J. 194
Smith, Arthur A. 10
Smith, Dudley Chase 14, 116, 127
Smith, Franklin C. 12
Smith, George Price 13, 127
Smith, George W. *35*
Smith, Giles A. 178
Smith, Gustavus A. 7, 14
Smith, John E. 8, 126, 127, 160
Smith, Milo 156, *196*
Smith, Morgan L. 87
Smith, Robert F. 5
Smith, Robert W. 4, 134
Smith, William Sooy 167
Smyth, William 157, *197*
Snell, Thomas 12, 127, *128*
Speed, Joshua 60
Sprague, Ezra T. 220
Springer, Charles Franklin 14, *128*
Stanton, Edwin M. 19, 128, 222
Starkweather, John C. 217, *226*
Starr, Matthew Henry 3, *129*
Starring, Frederick A. 10
Steedman, James B. 32
Steele, Frederick 155
Stephens, Thomas 217, 266, *267*
Stephenson, Ferdinand D. 14, 129, *130*
Stewart, Warren 4, *130, 131*
Stewart, William S. 9
Stibbs, John H. 155
Stone, George A. 156
Stone, William M. 156
Strong, Colin G. *183*
Stuart, David 8
Stuart, Elias 9, 131
Stuart, James 4, 131
Stuart, Owen 11, 132
Stubbs, William 155, 197, *198*
Sullivan, Jeremiah C. 70
Sully, Alfred 205

Summers, Samuel William 154, *198*
Swain, Edgar Denman 7, *132, 133*
Swanwick, Francis 14, *133, 134*
Sweeny, Thomas W. 8
Sweet, Benjamin J. 219
Swift, Richard K. 124
Symes, George Gifford 220, *267, 268*

Taylor, Ezra 4
Thielemann, Christian 4, *134*
Thomas, Minor T. 206
Thompson, M. Jeff 42
Thompson, William 154
Thrush, William A. 8, *135*
Tillson, John 5, 149
Toler, Silas Cox 9, 41, *135*
Torrence, William M. Gray 157, *199*
Totten, James 166
Tourtellotte, John E. 205
True, James M. 9, 136
True, Lewis Corbin 9, 135, *136*
Trumbull, Matthew M. 154
Tucker, Joseph H. 9, 136
Tullis, James *164*
Tupper, Nathan Willis 12, *137*
Turchin, John B. 5, 124
Turner, Charles 12
Turner, Thomas Johnston 5, *137, 138*
Tuttle, James M. 95, 155

Updegraff, John Jacob 3, 138
Updegraff, Joseph M. 138
Updegraff, Thaddeus S. 138
Utley, William Lawrence 219, 226, *268*

Van Arman, John 13, 138, *139*
Van Cleve, Horatio P. 205
Vandever, William 155
Vandor, Joseph 80, 218, 269
Van Sellar, Henry 5, *139*
Van Vleck, Carter 10, *140*
Vaughan, Samuel K. 219
Vernon, Maris Ralph 10, 140
Vifquain, Victor 11
Voss, Arno 4, 140

Walker, James R. *74*
Wallace, Martin R.M. 3
Wallace, William H.L. 5, 47
Walther, George Henry 219, *269, 270*
Walworth, Nathan Halbert 7, *141*
Ward, Lyman M. 218

Index

Warner, Clement Edson 220, *270*
Warner, John Baptist 12, 141, *142*
Warren, Fitz Henry 154
Washburn, Cadwallader C. 217
Waters, Louis H. 10
Watie, Stand 93
Weaver, James B. 155
Weaver, William 111
Webb, William Appleton 7, *142*
Webb, William Craw 220, *271*
Webber, Jules C. 5
Webster, Joseph D. 4
Weems, Thomas Leroy Braxton 8, 142, *143*
West, Francis H. 219
West, Theodore Sterling 219, 271, *272*
Wever, Clark R. 156
Wheaton, Loyd 4, *143*
Whistler, Joseph N.G. 226
Whistler, William 226
White, Julius 7, 79
Whiting, John E. 11, 144

Whitney, Lorenzo Harper 14, *144*
Wickersham, Dudley 4, *145*
Wilcox, John S. 8
Wilds, John Quincy 156, *199, 200*
Wiley, Benjamin L. 138
Wilkin, Alexander 206, *215*
Williams, Nelson G. 155
Williams, Thomas Dean 6, 145, *146*
Williamson, James A. 155
Willsie, Horace Hudson 14, *146*
Wilson, Bartholomew William 156, *200*
Wilson, David Stokely 154, *201*
Wilson, Hall 3, 147
Wilson, Isaac Grant 8, *147*
Wilson, James 155
Wilson, James H. 204
Wilson, James M. 148
Wilson, James W. 9, 147, *148*
Winkler, Frederick C. 219
Winslow, Edward F. 154
Wofford, William T. 150

Wolfe, John Simms 13, 82, 148, *149*
Wood, David Evans 218, *273*
Wood, John 13, *149*
Wood, McLean F. 14, 149, *150*
Woodall, French Battelle 14, *150, 151*
Woodruff, William E. 53
Woods, Joseph Jackson 155, 201, *202*
Worthington, William Hord 155, *202*
Wright, Ed 156
Wright, George Washington 12, *151*
Wrisberg, Alfred G. *260*
Wyman, John Baker 5, *152*

Yates, Henry, Jr. 12
Yates, Richard 19, *74*, 80, 131, 136
Young, John Morris 154, *203*
Young, Robert B. *206*

www.ingramcontent.com/pod-product-compliance
Lightning Source LLC
Chambersburg PA
CBHW081540300426
44116CB00015B/2695